SOCIAL PATHOLOGY

A SYSTEMATIC APPROACH TO THE THEORY OF SOCIOPATHIC BEHAVIOR

EDWIN M. LEMERT
University of California at Los Angeles

New York • Toronto • London
McGRAW-HILL BOOK COMPANY, INC.
1951

SOCIAL PATHOLOGY

10 11 12 13 14 - M P - 9 8 7

37185

To My Family

Nulle chose n'est bonne ni mauvaise;
seule la conception que l'on a d'elle
et la réaction publique la rend telle

From *Monologues Sociales*
by Jacques Lorot, Paris, 1882

PREFACE

Perhaps this book is best described as the outcome of an effort to write, in a context of discovery and exploration, within a rigorously delimited area of human behavior. This delimitation of the field of study, together with the conceptual orientation of the work, will be found in Part One. In Part Two an attempt is made to test the sufficiency of the theory with data drawn from what, with the possible exception of radicalism, are conventionally regarded as social "pathologies." The theoretical portion of the work presumes a minimum familiarity on the part of the reader with the elemental sociological concepts, and no effort has been made to direct the discussions to any particular student level. If students experience difficulties in understanding the content of the first four chapters, these difficulties should be considerably mitigated by the explicit and implicit reiteration of the theory in the substantive chapters which follow. Case-history studies of deviants by the students are suggested as a teaching aid to permit a better mastery of the theoretical ideas in the book. An outline for such case-history studies will be found in the Appendix.

Some of the author's associates have kindly given of their time to read and criticize portions of the book while it was still in manuscript form. Leonard Broom read the theoretical material and the chapter on prostitution. Phillip Selznick and Scott Greer offered critical suggestions on the chapter on radicalism. Ralph Turner gave his critical attention to the chapter on mental disorders, and Don Cressey went over the discussion of crime. Charles Van Riper must be credited with inspiring the writer's early interest in speech defects. The writer freely acknowledges his indebtedness to these persons for the opportunities they provided to exchange ideas on the subjects in the book. Final responsibility for the contents of the chapters remains, of course, with the author alone.

In preparing the manuscript for publication, Betty Omohundro relieved the writer of many burdensome chores, and Frances Ishida did some important last-minute stints on the typewriter, for which thanks are hereby tendered. A respectful salute is also due the author's many students who entered into the spirit of exploratory analysis and raised lively debates over the "concepts."

EDWIN M. LEMERT

WEST LOS ANGELES, CALIF.
January, 1951

CONTENTS

PART ONE

THEORY

CHAPTER 1

INTRODUCTION

Early Viewpoints on Social Problems

In the earlier history of sociology the basis for judging what constituted society's ills was candidly and uncritically moralistic. By this we mean that sociologists bothered little or not at all about the method by which they placed their ethical tags of "good" or "bad" on various social conditions or behaviors. They simply drew upon their own sense of the rightness of things or took their cue from social reformers of the time – usually the social workers (from whom they were not always distinguishable)– and condemned poverty, crime, prostitution, alcoholism, and related behavior as evils to be stamped out. Like General Custer's, their tactics were simple; they "rode to the sound of the guns."

Generally speaking, these late nineteenth- and early twentieth-century sociologists grouped together under the heading of "social pathology" those human actions which ran contrary to ideals of residential stability, property ownership, sobriety, thrift, habituation to work, small business enterprise, sexual discretion, family solidarity, neighborliness, and discipline of the will. In effect, social problems were considered to be any forms of behavior violating the mores from which these ideals were projected. The mores behind the ideals, for the most part, were those of rural, small-town, and middle-class America, translated into public policy through the rural domination of county boards of supervisors and state legislatures and through the reform activities of humanitarian social workers and Protestant religious federations. In this connection we note with special interest that many of the early writers on social pathology lived their more formative years in rural communities and small towns; often, too, they had had theological training and experience, so that it was only natural that they should look upon many forms of behavior associated with urban life and industrial society as destructive of moral values they cherished as universally good and true.[1]

Although some few sociologists still adhere to this point of view in one form or another, there has grown up among many of them a scientific

[1] Mills, C. W., "The Professional Ideology of Social Pathologists," *American Journal of Sociology*, 49, September, 1943, pp. 165–180

sophistication – even cynicism – about the reform movements which flourished around the turn of the present century. Many sociologists would now agree that reform movements often create more problems than they solve and that in such cases the "problem" turns out to be the reform action itself. It is likewise beginning to be plain to some of these sociologists that the sanctioned values of the culture have an important function in producing the behaviors which reform groups disapprove of and seek to eliminate. From the recognition of such facts has come the newer emphasis in the field of social pathology – the tendency to look upon problem-defining behavior as an integral part of the data to be studied as well as the objective conditions which strike reformers as being "problems."

In studying the problem-defining reactions of a community, it can be shown that public consciousness of "problems" and aggregate moral reactions frequently center around forms of behavior which on closer analysis often prove to be of minor importance in the social system. Conversely, community members not infrequently ignore behavior which is a major disruptive influence in their lives. We are all familiar with the way in which populations in various cities and states have been aroused to frenzied punitive action against sex offenders. Nevertheless, in these same areas the people as a whole often are indifferent toward crimes committed by businessmen or corporations – crimes which affect far more people and which may be far more serious over a period of time. It is well known that collective efforts to eradicate juvenile delinquency nearly always strike a chord of immediate response from the public, whereas "problems" of the conservation of soil, water, and natural resources remain the concern of only a few specialized groups which often struggle in vain to stir up support for their programs.

The Definition of Problems by "Experts"

The generally unreliable nature of moral indignation and public dissatisfaction as guides to the definition of social problems led a few of the early social pathologists to the belief that responsibility for guiding a community's thinking about its problems should rest with its leaders. Thus, specific indication of the conditions or behavior in need of remediable action should come from a consensus of competent authorities, presumably intelligent lay leaders and professional people, such as social workers, physicians, attorneys, and churchmen. Unfortunately for this point of view, deciding just who are the "competent" authorities of a society or a community is no easy task. Furthermore, competent authorities or experts at times have a way of being embarrassingly wrong in their analysis and prediction of social phenomena. In the final count the consensus of such leaders may prove to be a projection of moral beliefs or special interests of certain power groups in the community, with little to distinguish them from the moral judgments of the uninformed laity save, perhaps, a more convincing top-dressing of rationalizations.

The Role of the Sociologist with Reference to Social Problems

Here and there we encounter the belief that social scientists, being the best informed persons we have on such matters, should assume a dominant role in pointing out those aspects of our social life which should be modified or ameliorated. Among sociologists this question appears in the controversy over whether students of society and culture should make value-judgments about the data they examine. One group has strongly insisted that it is impossible not to make value-judgments; merely by the selection of the particular social phenomena he studies and by publishing the results of his investigations the sociologist makes value-laden decisions. On the other side of this argument are sociologists who maintain that the making of value-judgments is incompatible with science as we know it and that if sociology is to be a science then it must forego ethical generalizations.

In providing a working answer to this controversy let us freely grant several things. First of all, let us admit that certain values do inhere in science itself, there is behind science the idea that, generally speaking, free (even irresponsible) and systematic inquiry into natural phenomena is a valuable technique of aiding mankind individually and collectively in the achievement of goals, *whatever they may be*. Beyond this lies the more generalized ethical conviction that through reliance upon science modern societies will become more conducive to the satisfactions of the people who live in them. With further candor we can say that sociologists do indeed select data for study which is of topical interest to large numbers of people or which is of practical concern to persons in positions of power.

But do these admissions mean that the sociologist must break out his colors and show whose side he is on in public controversies? We think not, within the generalized value-context of science there is nothing which demands that the scientist advocate or condemn the discoveries he makes. Furthermore, there is nothing in science as it has been defined which can prove that anything is good or bad. The function of sociology as a science is to study and describe the uniformities of human behavior, the relatively repetitive sequences of human events. Those who argue that sociologists in their research on human cultures and societies must push beyond this function to evaluate the uniformities or sequences of sociocultural events which they discover are saying in effect that sociology is not a science, that it is a philosophy. Yet we cannot, in the light of the recent history of sociology, give any serious consideration to this claim.[2]

Up to this point we seem to be saying that there is no way of objectively determining what social problems are in the sense of what is "bad" or undesirable about a society or culture. If this seems to be an uncomfortable agnostic position to the reader, then he must be reminded that it is not incompatible with the dominant democratic philosophy of our society, which carries the assumption that groups and individuals will formulate their own values, objectives, and goals within fairly broad limits of freedom. In a democratic society (as well as in other types of society) the social scientist can best function to inform policymakers what the consequences of certain lines of social action are likely to be, and also to enlighten them, if possible, as to the most economical means of reaching their goals.[3] By delimiting his function the sociologist not only increases his value to society, but he also makes his social status more secure and more effectively integrates his occupational personality.[4]

Conclusions about the Social-problems Point of View

While the social-problems approach remains in favor with many sociologists and probably will continue to be the orientation of academic

[2] We see no objection to establishing a set of goals for a culture or society and then trying to decide how they may be reached. We simply insist that this function be kept separate from the scientific function of the sociologist. Such courses in a curriculum would be most appropriately labeled as "social ethics" or something comparable. C C. North followed a procedure something like this in one of his early books, see his *Social Problems and Social Planning, 1934.*

[3] George Lundberg, who is sometimes referred to as a leading representative of the neopositivists in sociology, apparently believes that science is authoritarian and that there can and should be a "scientific morality" or moral law in conformity with natural law as discovered by science. See his "Sociologists and the Peace," *American Sociological Review,* 9, February, 1944, p. 5; also his "Human Social Problems as a Type of Disequilibrium in a Biological Integration," *ibid.*, 13, December, 1948, p 695, and *Can Science Save Us?*, 1947. Lundberg gives a much more positive and specific valuation to science than we have given. There is good reason to believe, from present-day knowledge of community organization, social planning, and industrial relations, that modern science and technology are more congenial to nonauthoritarian leadership and control than they are to specific directives from authority. We can probably all agree that the findings of social science *ought* to be used more in social planning and public administration, however, there is little consensus on *how* this should be accomplished. See the author's "Social Participation and Totalitarian War," *American Sociological Review,* 8, October, 1943, pp. 531–536

[4] In some respects the situation of the sociologist is similar to that of the social worker. In recent years social workers have strived to delimit more sharply and clearly their function in society on the grounds that by so doing it relieves them of the job of "playing God" to clients and makes them more efficient within the areas where they do provide service to the client. See Witmer, H., *Social Work,* 1942, Chap. 1.

courses in sociology for some time to come, nonetheless it is not clear that this approach corresponds to any precisely delimited field or to any system of well-defined concepts. In so far as the approach can be said to be distinctive, its main features have been as follows: (1) a low level of abstraction or conceptualization; (2) a stress upon the immediate, practical, "everyday" difficulties of human beings; (3) the discussion of "problems" as discrete and unrelated phenomena; (4) the injection of moral judgments into many of these discussions.[5]

The recognition of the methodological weaknesses of the traditional social-problems orientation has led those who still pay it allegiance to employ the concept of social problems in a purely descriptive or classificatory way. The term "social problems" is taken by them to mean a social situation about which a large number of people feel disturbed and unhappy – this and nothing more. Defined in this way, without any implications that the situation is dangerous or undesirable, the term "social problems" achieves a maximum clarity and acceptance by sociologists. Questions as to whether social problems thus defined are unanticipated consequences, secondary stabilizing derivatives, or necessary preconditions of the sociocultural system in which they develop are left open for inquiry and further research. Whatever the answers to such questions may be, there is a mounting awareness among sociologists that social problems are functions of the structure of a total social system, not congeries of disunited parts operating through unique processes of their own.[6]

Social Disorganization

An alternative formulation of the field of our interest, which to some extent overlaps and in some ways supplements the social-problems viewpoint, is phrased in terms of "social disorganization." This general theoretical position can be traced back to the ideas and writings of Hegel, Marx, Darwin, Auguste Comte, and Herbert Spencer, and has numerous contemporary representatives. Practically all variants of this view associate such things as social change, uneven development of culture, maladaptiveness, disharmony, conflict, and lack of consensus, together with social disorganization and personal disorganization, as aspects of a separate field of sociological inquiry. While nearly all the social-disorganization (sometimes disintegration) theorists start their analyses with the ideas of change and organic process, nevertheless extremely divergent conclusions have been reached as to what organized and disorganized societies are. On one hand we have the "cultural-lag" theory which postulates as an

[5] Mills, *op. cit.*

[6] See the discussion by A. Cohen of F. E. Merill's "The Study of Social Problems," *American Sociological Review*, 13, June, 1948, pp. 259–260.

organized society one in which the various parts of its culture change evenly and in conformity with scientific and technological developments. Conversely, an unevenly changing culture, particularly one in which other changes are not geared to technology and invention, suffers from cultural lag, a condition equatable with social disorganization.[7]

Standing in what would seem to be almost a direct contradiction of the cultural-lag conception is the viewpoint of those writers on social disorganization who find the prototype of the organized society in the prescientific, preindustrial society. In this version. an organized society is identified by its qualities of stability; intimate, personal interaction; continuity of social relationships; and high degree of consensus among its members. Contrariwise, the disorganized society becomes synonymous with a rapidly changing society which is unstable, has little continuity of experience from one group to the next, and which lacks agreements among its members on the common concerns of everyday life. The disappearance of organic intimacy of social relationships which is taken as the mark of a disorganized society makes way for a highly individuated, self-seeking behavior. The fractured, atomistic social contacts of the disorganized society are assumed to leave its participants frustrated and thwarted in fulfilling their deeper personal needs and desires. Because science, industry, and urbanism have initiated the changes leading to such conditions, we are left with the fairly definite impression that they give birth to societies which not only cannot be integrated but which can never be humanly satisfying.[8]

[7] See Ogburn, W F., *Social Change*, 1922, Barnes, H. E., *Society in Transition*, 1939, Elliott, M. A., and F. E Merill, *Social Disorganization*, 1941, Queen, S, W. Bodenhafer, and E Harper, *Social Organization and Disorganization*, 1935, for criticisms of the concept see Mills, *op. cit.;* also, Woodward, J., "Critical Notes on the Cultural Lag Concept," *Social Forces*, March, 1934.

[8] A parallel theoretical development in anthropology reinforcing this particular notion of social disorganization comes from the dichotomous distinctions which have been made between "folk" and "urban" societies. The folk society as conceived in anthropology is essentially a nonindustrial society which is spatially isolated, resistant to change and integrated through tradition and sacred institutions. The implication to be drawn from the discussion of the folk society is that a science-orientated urban society cannot be integrated. This idea is made quite clear in still another anthropological distinction between "genuine" and "spurious" societies. The genuine society is simply another term for the folk society. The folk versus urban distinction is that of R. Redfield, *Folk Culture of Yucatan*, 1941; the genuine versus spurious distinction comes from E. Sapir, "Culture, Genuine and Spurious," *American Journal of Sociology*, 29, January, 1924, pp. 410–412; the fundamental similarity between the two classifications, together with criticisms, has been pointed out by M. Tumin, "Culture, Genuine and Spurious: A Re-evaluation," *American Sociological Review*, 10, April, 1945, pp 199–207; for an example of the use of folk society as the equivalent of an organized or "successful" society see R E L Faris, *Social Disorganization*, 1948

The nostalgic ideal of an organized society which is advanced in the above statement of social disorganization has a long history in sociology. As we made clear previously, it was implicit in most of the early treatments of social problems. It was made explicit in the writings of such pioneer sociologists as W. I. Thomas and Charles H. Cooley and has appeared as variations on a common theme in the thought of many sociologists up to the present day. Of all the sociologists who have laid heavy emphasis upon the normality of the small, intimate, primary community and the abnormality of the large, formally organized community, none has stated the view more cogently or been more influential than Cooley. For this reason let us scrutinize his ideas more closely.

THE DEAD HAND OF COOLEY

Central to the Cooley formulation is the notion of social life as an organic process involving the mutual interaction of society and the individual. Social disorganization is to be found in the nature of the dynamic relationships between individuals and the institutions of their society. Institutions are looked upon as devices for fulfilling human needs which at the same time function to limit or control the responses of individuals. However, when institutions are no longer responsive to these needs, a condition exists in which the institutional symbols no longer exercise this control. Such a condition or process is known as "formalism," which was Cooley's term for social disorganization.

A further summary of Cooley's ideas is at hand in the following excerpt in which the writer of a text on social disorganization gratefully acknowledges his indebtedness and that of others for their theoretical premises. Thus he says:[9]

> However, none of the various approaches to the study of social disorganization come potentially to grips with the fundamental problem of the relationship between individual and social disorganization. This was left to the philosophically organic viewpoint of Charles H. Cooley and his followers. In fact, in the solution to the question of the interrelationships between personal and social disorganization lies the distinctive characteristics of the philosophically organic approach.
>
> Basic to Cooley's point of view is his microscopic-macroscopic conception of the relation between society and the individual. In the Cooley formulation both are but different aspects of one and the same thing, social life. When one views social life from the point of view of the discrete units of which it is made up, he sees the individual. When, on the other hand, his view is that of

[9] Mowrer, E., *Disorganization, Personal and Social*, 1942, pp. 23*ff*. Quoted by permission of the J. B. Lippincott Company, Philadelphia. Others seeming more or less to follow Cooley are Elliott and Merrill, *op. cit.;* Queen, Bodenhafer, and Harper, *op. cit.;* Faris, *op. cit.;* Brown, L. Guy, *Social Pathology*, 1942.

the collectivity, he sees society. Society and the individual are thus complimentary aspects of a larger reality which incorporates both.... Social disorganization is both cause and effect, but the same can be said for personal disorganization. Social disorganization leads to breakdown in institutional controls and allows man's elemental nature to function again, unrestrained by social patterns. It is the formalism of institutional controls which function externally upon the individual leaving him internally without guidance that develops into social disorganization in which institutional patterns lose their effectiveness....

Not all of Cooley's conceptions have survived the decades since he wrote them; for example, few sociologists today make use of the idea of formalism, and they have grown skeptical of the belief that intimate personal social relationships are indispensable to an organized society.[10] However, his concept of personal and social disorganization as interactional phases of the same process, is still the foundation for most thinking on the subject, as can be seen from the above excerpt. Unfortunately, analysis still rests pretty much at the level of large generalization and reiteration where Cooley left it; there has been a poverty of subsidiary hypotheses deduced from his general theory and subjected to empirical testing. In textbooks on social disorganization where the theory has been adopted there is an unsatisfying gap and discontinuity between the introductory chapters where the theory is presented and the succeeding chapters where specific data are introduced and treated. In many instances there is little difference between these latter substantive chapters and those found in books on social problems. The promise of Cooley's theory, then, has remained largely unfulfilled.

In no small degree the source of the difficulties can be discovered in Cooley's writing itself, which draws heavily upon analogies and literary allusions for its effectiveness and which at times grows mystical. His literary and philosophical predilections present salient difficulties when it comes to finding empirical referents for his ideas, a fact which probably accounts for the failure of his writings to inspire any considerable body of research. Even his apologists have perceived this defect, one comments as follows: "... As an organic thinker who thought in terms of wholes and larger entities he was bound to find the task of studying the many intricate parts which make up the whole not only irksome but also a hindrance to larger thoughts." [11]

[10] See Mills, *op. cit.;* also Smith, T V., *Beyond Conscience,* p 111. In fairness to Cooley it should be said that he did present an alternative ideal to the integration of urban society through extension of the primary group values. This alternative was the extension of the institution of the market so that all human needs might be represented in pecuniary exchanges See his "The Institutional Nature of Pecuniary Valuation," in *Social Process,* 1918

[11] Jandy, E. C., *Charles Horton Cooley,* 1942, p. 231.

The Inadequacy of Multiple-factor Interaction as a Theory

Cooley was averse to assigning to any particular factors a fixed causative value in so far as social phenomena were concerned. Thus, in his scheme of thinking, economic factors held no more importance than political, religious, or any other factors. Rather, it was the way in which various factors worked together, mutually influencing one another, which impressed Cooley. Around this, his idea of interaction, there has grown up a whole school of "interactional theorists." As sometimes happens, the followers of Cooley's provocative thought have tended to push his concept of interaction beyond what can be its proper use – perhaps beyond the use he intended for it. In any event we find in some cases that interaction has been accentuated by writers to the point of invoking it as an explanatory or determining factor, much like instincts or genes were once employed.[12]

The concept that the factors of human behavior have no fixed value but instead derive their value solely from dynamic interplay is an extreme of thinking which creates serious methodological problems. It sets us off on what amounts to a directionless inquiry into sociocultural phenomena, ending in a morass of dog-in-the-manger variables, none of which have priority. By postulating society and culture as being in a state of continuous flux we make the extraction of repetitive sequences and uniformities of human behavior a most difficult or impossible task. The weakness of interaction as a theory comes to the fore most disturbingly where the formulating of programs of active social control is concerned. If interaction is more important than the factors of a social situation, how can it be decided where and when and to what extent social control shall be intruded? If changes must be made simultaneously in many phases of a culture or social situation, how can decisions be made as to the specific nature of these changes if it is not their substantive character but their interaction which is the determiner?

More careful analysis tells us that interaction is not a theory or explanation at all, but rather it is a condition of inquiry which amounts to a confession of open-minded ignorance about how factors work together. The interactional orientation was valuable as a necessary methodological step away from reified and particularistic theories of the causation of human behavior held by nineteenth-century writers (*e.g.*, the instinct theory). Properly used, it corrects and supplements purely static or structural analysis, but it does not abolish the significance of social forms and structures as limiting factors in human behavior.

[12] For instance, L. Guy Brown goes so far as to say: "Everything plays its role and gets its meaning in interaction, hence, interaction becomes a chief concept in every explanation." Brown, *op cit.*, p. 9

Interaction Takes Place within Limits

Our position here is that there are limits to the variable meanings which interaction can give to geographic, biological, and sociocultural facts. For example, while there is undoubtedly a great range of attitudinal reactions or "meanings" to such things as blindness, feeble-mindedness, or selling sexual favors, there is also a common core of meaning or an average impact of sociocultural facts upon a person or persons differentiated from others in these ways. Blind persons are incapable of reacting to the visual-esthetic aspects of our culture; there are no feeble-minded mathematicians, and most prostitutes dissociate sentiment and emotion from the occupational sex act. It is perhaps for the reason that sociologists have not had a systematic description of these, the more negative and limiting aspects of social pathology, that one textbook has approached the subject almost exclusively from the standpoint of obstacles to social participation.[13]

Social and Personal Disorganization — How Are They Related?

Apart from the general shortcomings of interaction as a theory per se it will be noted that it has not paid many dividends in clarifying the relationship between social disorganization and personal disorganization. This holds true despite the fact that here is precisely the area where the greatest contribution of the interactional "theory" is supposed to have been made. Supporters of the theory have failed to work out in usable detail the mechanisms of social interaction and the precise manner in which culture impinges upon the individual as he develops.[14] While it is all well and good to say that there is an "organic" or close interdependence between social disorganization and personal disorganization, this does not give us any more than analogical insight into how a given cultural environment works to produce a sociopathic person. Above all, it does not take us very far in understanding the differential responses which two individuals make to the same sociopathic influences. The deteriorated areas of certain of our larger cities perennially produce large numbers of juvenile delinquents; this is a predictable and usable fact for community planning and organization. But it is also true that within the heart of such areas a sibling or a boy living next door to the leader of a delinquent gang, ostensibly exposed to the same cultural influences, may become a scout leader or an outstanding school athlete. Seen in the context of social control, this same problem is manifested by the residual persons or groups who do not respond to the symbols and techniques which suffice to manipulate the behavior of the average or modal group. For example, a program to

[13] Queen, S., and J. Gruener, *Social Pathology*, 1940

[14] Young, K., *Personality and Problems of Adjustment*, 1940, p. 296.

decrease traffic fatalities in a community may succeed in reducing automobile accidents by 90 per cent but still leave a seemingly irreducible 10 per cent of "repeaters" despite all sorts of ingenuity employed by agencies at work on the situation. Knowing that social interaction is involved in the situation is small help in getting at the reasons for the differential reactions of the repeaters group.

An Unsolved Methodological Problem

The solution to the problem of how social and personal disorganization are related to one another has not yet been provided. There have been efforts, not wholly successful, both by psychologists and sociologists, to supplement purely sociological analysis by the study of personality traits, by efforts to isolate personality types and patterns, and more recently by "field theory." In this last conceptual scheme the individual is thought of as a point in fields of forces mutually affecting one another; one field is the "person field" and the other is the "social field." Along with these formulations there has been an attempt by some students to establish the existence of natural histories or repetitive sequences in the development of deviant personalities. In spite of all this endeavor we remain limited in our understanding of the focus of social interaction in the person.

The lacunae in our knowledge about the human personality are well expressed in the following statement:[15]

> The phrase psychological states and processes is admittedly vague, and it seems wiser to leave it so. We probably know less about the actual content and structure of personality than about any other aspect of the individual. Personalities are configurations of a unique sort, one which has no close parallel at the level of physical phenomena. . . .
>
> It is not surprising, therefore, that many of the current chartings of personality are reminiscent of seventeenth-century maps. The coast lines are clear enough, but the blankness of the interior is masked by sketches of the hairy, ithyphallic id, the haloed superego, and the inscription: "*Hereabouts there be complexes.*"

Candid recognition that our methods of studying personality at best are crude and primitive should not be a basis for discarding them or for discouraging further research in such directions as they suggest. Whatever the ultimate success or failure of such research may be it is well to bear in mind that in the meantime the sociologist will have performed a task of tremendous worth if he can systematically conceptualize and demonstrate the various ways in which social and cultural stimuli impinge upon the deviant individual. With such knowledge it may become possible to elim-

[15] Linton, R., *The Cultural Background of Personality*, 1945, pp 85*ff*. Quoted by permission of Appleton-Century-Crofts, Inc., New York

inate or change certain phases of culture and social organization in terms of an average effect which is socially disruptive. Perhaps, as Cooley once said, dependency and poverty can never be completely prevented, but the institutionalization of these and related behaviors can be anticipated and averted.

Exhaustive Knowledge of the Person Not Needed for Our Purposes

In summing up our objectives with reference to the study of the deviant personality we may parenthetically comment upon the writings of Otto Rank, which seem to have a growing influence on American social welfare workers and to some extent on clinical psychologists. Rank has made a point of formally repudiating the idea that the finer workings of the human personality can or need be reduced to scientific laws and generalizations. According to his line of thought, which has grown out of his concern with psychotherapy, preoccupation with the more complex, especially the developmental, aspects of individual maladjustment — as is done in Freudian psychoanalysis — is futile for the purpose of understanding the individual and even detrimental when it is employed as a clinical procedure.[16] In Rank's estimation the clinical subject would much better be treated as a striving, aggressive phenomenon by both himself and the clinical agents of society, with therapeutic emphasis upon the empirically controlled social expression of what are essentially irrational inner drives and impulses.

While we need not proceed to the extremes explicit and implicit in Rank's assumptions, nevertheless it is well to consider how much of an invasion of the inner life or "private worlds" of the individual is required in order to clarify the societal-individual interactional process. There seems to be a very definite trend away from the compelling notion that complete and detailed knowledge of the person is the prerequisite to effective educational, rehabilitative, therapeutic, or general control processes. The trend is most clearly captioned in the writings of John Dewey and those of the "progressive educators"; it is further exemplified in newer social work and clinical procedures embodying highly permissive social relationships between client and practitioner, and especially does the trend stand out in present-day clinical group work.[17]

In conceptualizing the person or the individual as a factor in the study

[16] Rank, Otto, *Beyond Psychology*, 1941, Chap 1 Rank's main criticism of the Freudian psychoanalysis was that it creates a sense of guilt over aggressive acts. By seeking to reeducate the client to "adjust to" or "accept" reality the Freudians deny the obviously aggressive, emergent, and creative nature of human activity. From this point of view Freudianism is a disguised variety of ancient Hebraic conservatism.

[17] Clinard, Marshall, "The Group Approach to Social Reintegration," *American Sociological Review*, 14, April, 1949, pp 257–262.

of human behavior a large area of response must be left more or less open and unpredictable, probably because of the impossibility of defining it This means that in scientific descriptions of the person we may have to be content to specify the nature and form of variable limits of response which he or she makes to certain social stimuli – in this case to the social stimuli which are sociopathic. From this theoretical vantage point one person is seen as having a set of limits or existing claims upon him which makes him relatively accessible to sociopathic stimuli in a given area, whereas another person is seen responding within a more constricted matrix of limits which curtail the sociopathic stimuli which he may incorporate from his social setting. This type of analysis, which we have only just touched upon here and which will be treated in some detail in a following chapter, has value in that it does take into account the substantive or structured aspects of personality without falling into the error of making them determining factors. At the same time the dynamic analysis which must supplement structural analysis of personality does not, at one extreme, become one of mechanical sequence or, at the other extreme, become one of vague process and continuous flux.

Conclusions about the Social Disorganization Point of View

The social-disorganization point of view represents an advance over the concept of social problems to the degree that it seeks to place social situations within the larger context of whole societies and cultures. Its supporters have been somewhat less open advocates of a particular type of moral order, but nevertheless value-judgments inhere in the varying definitions and usages of the term. Reliance upon concepts of "process," "interaction," and "cultural lag" without giving detailed meaning to the terms has left the larger term "social disorganization" vague and difficult to demonstrate.[18] In this connection it is especially important to note down the blurring and lack of sharp distinction between social disorganization and personal disorganization. Even where a fairly clear distinction is maintained between these two phenomena, little is offered to clarify their interrelationship save "organic interaction," which appears not to be a

[18] The cultural-lag concept is theoretically much more defensible than the other two. Unfortunately the concept tells us nothing of the degree of interdependence between unevenly changing parts of a culture Obviously, uneven rates of change in two different culture complexes can scarcely be a lag if no dependent relationship exists between them. Establishing the correlation between the culture complexes must either be done by arbitrarily assuming it to be true of all culture segments or it must be done by informal analysis. This strikes the writer as being the chief weakness of an otherwise challenging method for quantitatively determining the degree of integration in a given culture suggested by Read Bain See his "Culture Conflict and Social Integration," *American Journal of Sociology*, 44, January, 1939, pp. 499–509.

theory at all In short, the writers on social disorganization have marked out in a very rough way a field of common interest and they have established several philosophical points of view toward the phenomena falling within it. However, it cannot be said that in a strict sense they have created a body of concepts which can be called "systematic theory."

Toward a Systematic Theory of Sociopathic Behavior

It is our intention in this work to set up a systematic theory of sociopathic behavior. If this seems to be an ambitious project, we may say that it is done with an awareness that it is somewhat tangential to the strong empirical interests of many American sociologists and also that it is being done with an awareness of the difficulties to be met. The problem at hand is a special phase of the larger problem of conceptual integration which has occupied sociologists for many years. The latent danger of zealous pursuit of conceptual integration is that such industry will degenerate into system building alone, or into an exercise in abstraction with but indifferent attention to the possibilities of empirical demonstration of the theoretical system. It is perhaps for this reason that the word "system" has collected barnaclelike many unfavorable connotations since the days when Comte, Spencer, Ward and Ross created their systematic sociologies.

In reacting against the grandiose system building of early sociologists later critics undoubtedly were correct in claiming that architectonic integration of all sociological knowledge is likely to lose in value because of its world-girdling inclusiveness. However, we should be careful not to follow the lead of those who would throw the baby out with the bath water by discarding theory in all forms in favor of pure empiricism. It is hard to see any valid objections to the creation of abbreviated conceptual systems which are data orientations within delimited fields of human behavior. Indeed, this seems to be the direction of much sociological development today.[19] Thought of in this way, theory is no less important than the gathering of facts and information. It can be urged strongly that empirical research is as much dependent upon sound theoretical work as theory is obviously dependent upon sound empirical research.

The Requirements for a Systematic Theory

A systematic theory, as might be expected, is not constructed in a random or purely intuitive fashion. There are certain rules which serve as guides in taking up the task. Thus, while sociologists, in building a system of concepts, will keep one eye on the evidence behind them, they will have

[19] Merton, R., "Sociological Theory," *American Journal of Sociology*, 50, May, 1945, pp. 462–473; also Merton's discussion of T. Parson's paper in the *American Sociological Review*, 13, April, 1948, pp 165*f*.

a strong preliminary interest in the epistemological qualities of their theory. They will ask certain questions having usefulness for research purposes. These questions are a way of setting up requirements or criteria for the critical evaluation of the theory and other theories from a methodological standpoint. Armed with these criteria, sociologists are able to make explicit the bases upon which their theoretical criticisms rest. Communication between them becomes more precise, and their comparison of different theories in an objective manner is facilitated.[20]

Among the criteria of a systematic theory some may be thought of as absolute requirements, while others are merely desirable or recommended. We choose to list here only those criteria which are minimum requirements and to express them in terms of the particular study area with which we are concerned, *i.e.*, sociopathic behavior:[21]

1. The field of study, sociopathic behavior, must be strictly delimited.
2. The systematic conceptualization of the field should be derived from a limited number of postulates.
3. The conceptual system should be not only internally consistent but should also be consistent with and an integral part of a general theory of human behavior.
4. The concepts should be necessary and sufficient, *i.e.*, they should explain the bulk of the facts classified as "sociopathic."
5. The hypotheses must be logically compatible with the postulates.
6. Concepts should be sufficiently detailed to explain the phenomena studied without the use of analogies. Processual analysis must be explicit.

Making Use of the Criteria

The criteria which we have enumerated can be drawn into our discussion in a number of different ways. However, we plan to use them primarily to raise a priori questions as to whether several nonsociological approaches, about which we have said nothing up to the present time, can be sanctioned as systematic theory for the study of sociopathic behavior. Following this, we shall state in contrast what we deem to be the indispensable features of a sociological approach to the study of this field. As an immediate sequel to this it will be our job to set forth the propositions or postulates which have been evolved by us in the effort to meet the requirements for a systematic theory. Let us now turn to the first application of the criteria.

[20] Levine, S., and A. Dornblum, "The Implications of Science as a Logical System," *American Sociological Review*, 4, June, 1939, pp. 381–387, Stafford, A B, and H. Phelps, "Criteria of a Systematic Sociology," *ibid.*, p 388, Bain, Read, discussion of Leonard Cottrell's paper, "Situational Fields in Social Psychology," *ibid.*, 7, June, 1942, pp. 383–387.

[21] The criteria are adapted from Bain, *op. cit.*

The Biological Approach to the Study of Sociopathic Behavior

While biologists have shown a lively interest in social pathology, we may question whether their conceptualizations can be dignified with the classification of "systematic theory." Mostly, the generalizations in the field of biology which pertain to pathological deviants, or to the "defective classes" as they tend to be called, are parenthetical observations found usually in chapters appended to treatises on human genetics, with only the odd book completely devoted to social biology. Biologists interested in social pathology, and those who defer to their opinions, believe that certain forms of socially disapproved behavior, like homosexuality, chronic alcoholism, or mental disorder, arise in one of the following ways: (1) through the inheritance of a gene or a gene combination (or its absence) which directly causes the behavior, (2) through the inheritance of an unspecified type of tendency to behave in these ways, or (3) through the inheritance of an unspecified type of constitutional weakness which produces the sociopathic behavior.

Apart from the general criticism that they are not presented in the form of systematic theory, biological concepts of social pathology fail to satisfy the first of our criteria in that the field of study is not strictly delimited. Thus such widely divergent anatomical and physiological facts as brachydactylism and diabetes insipidus are included along with socially and culturally defined phenomena such as crime and mental disease to be understood as expressions of genetic factors. Furthermore, the biological position on social pathology is compromised by such explicit admissions that "Some forms of mental disease are inherited but others are not," or that "while some epileptics become psychotic others become geniuses." Consequently, the biological attempts at explanations of sociopathic behavior also fail to satisfy criterion number four, *i.e.*, that they should explain the bulk of the phenomena classified as "social pathology." It may be that a small percentage of cases of certain forms of sociopathic behavior is caused by the fact that the structural and physiological foundations of behavior have been congenitally destroyed, and for these select cases biological explanations become directly relevant. However, beyond these, biological factors are only indirectly important in explaining deviant behavior. To press direct explanations of sociopathic behavior within a biological frame of reference also violates criterion number six: the necessity of making clear the details of the process of effective causation. Thus, for example, where writers claim that mental disorder is hereditary, they provide no description of how the hereditary factors become elaborated into a demonstrable structure or function which produces the mental symptoms. The application of biological theories to the collective aspects of social pathology, such as organized or professional crime, results in an even grosser disregard for the details of causation.

Psychological and Psychiatric Approaches to the Study of Sociopathic Behavior

Psychological and psychiatric viewpoints on social pathology more commonly take the form of systematic theory than is true of biological conceptions. They also go much farther in explaining the facts at hand, undeniably shedding much light upon the subjective dynamics of pathological human behavior. Consequently, they often supply us with necessary, although not always sufficient, concepts to account for many aspects of social pathology. In their search for the key to why people transgress social norms, psychologists have variously stressed such things as general or abstract intelligence, personality traits, thought processes, motives, attitudes, and "vectors" of the mind. Psychiatrists have been somewhat less versatile in their explanations, mainly looking for emotional conflicts or "psychopathology" behind the misconduct of deviants.

The points at which many psychological and psychiatric theories reveal their inadequacies are in respect to criteria numbers four and six. The concepts they advance are seldom if ever sufficient to give us useful explanations of pathological behavior in its collective aspects and often they fail to make sense out of many actions of the individual deviant. To follow those psychologists who have conceived of such things as crime, prostitution, and drug addiction as cumulative or summated expressions of discrete, individual intelligence capacities, personality traits, thought processes, or motives leaves us with too many significant questions about the pathologies unanswered. Likewise, to follow the lead of traditional psychiatric thought in these matters shunts us into intellectual by-passes. For example, imputing psychopathic mental processes to individuals in order to account for their criminal behavior is illuminating only in some few of the more unusual cases of crime. Such a procedure obviously ignores the commission of crime by persons who are in no way pathological mentally. Rare, indeed, is the person who at one time or another has not committed a felony. To ascribe this to mental pathology is to make the term lose its meaning, for most of us would have to be called "episodic psychopaths."

The designation of crime as a psychopathic symptom obscures rather than clarifies how criminal activity becomes integrated into forms of social organization which are participated in by persons with a wide variety of personal motives and psychological orientations. Criminals may operate illegal gambling establishments, but their patrons include the respectable citizens of the community. Bankers operate banks for noncriminal use, but many such bankers in the past have knowingly accepted deposits of money gained dishonestly by criminals. Lawyers, labor unions, insurance companies, and newspapers have been known to enter into collusion with criminals. Even presidents of the United States have appointed members of criminally corrupt political machines to high offices. Unless we wish to diagnose all their patrons or customers and those who cooperate economically or politically with criminals as psychopathic, we are driven to the conclusions that "reductionist" psychiatric theories of organized crime in terms of abnormal mental processes are insufficient. The same criticism is applicable to psychiatric theories applying to other forms of sociopathic deviation.

The failure of psychological and psychiatric schema to satisfy the sixth criterion for systematic theory can be traced back to the failure to meet our fourth requirement. The general tendency of men in these fields to think of cultural phenomena as aggregate manifestations of individual psychic factors leaves them with no detailed explanation of the collective or organized aspects of social pathology. Hence, they have often fallen back upon implicit or explicit analogies. Oddly enough, if logically pursued, these analogies take us back to a variety of group-mind concepts, which have been the object of vigorous criticism among the psychologists themselves. Society and social organization become like individuals in that what happens socially is taken as epiphenomena of the mind. The details of the process by which psychological factors lead to social pathology are ignored or they are assumed to be unnecessary. Even in the more dynamic psychological formulations where the concepts of "person field" and "social field" have been brought in to make room for collective factors, the relationship between the two is left unclear.

A Sociological Approach to the Study of Sociopathic Behavior

The early tendency to regard sociology as a synthetic discipline which combines items of biological, psychological, psychiatric, geographic, and demographic knowledge in order to explain human behavior has pretty well disappeared. Sociologists now hold to the notion that theirs is a separate field of study requiring concepts and generalizations which are unique to this field. Sociologists now generalize at "their own level" rather than trying to reduce their generalizations to the level of other fields. The only remnants of the synthetic tradition, if it can be called that, lie in a certain amount of confusion over how to reckon theoretically with nonsociological factors which have a marginal or indirect bearing upon human behavior.

Our own position on this matter is that the direct or significant factors of sociopathic behavior are sociological or sociopsychological in nature, expressible by such concepts as social structure, group, role, status, and symbolic interaction. To the extent that factors falling outside of those which are strictly sociological must be taken into consideration in analyzing pathological human behavior they must be related in a verifiable way to the sociological variables. Such factors as physical size and strength, biological anomalies, aggressiveness, hallucinations, monetary income, age, sex, and position in space can be applied in only a limited way to explain variation in social and cultural factors, which in turn are the chief interacting determiners of human behavior. Where variables such as the former must be taken into account, it must be shown how they affect social organization, role, status, social participation, self-definitions, and the other variables which we define as "sociological." The actual details of effective causation can be given at this last, a sociological or sociopsychological level. Starting with these assumptions as to the nature of the sociological approach and guided by the criteria of a systematic theory, we can now proceed to the series of propositions or postulates which are the elements of our theory of sociopathic behavior.

A General Statement of Our Theory

Stated in the most general way, our theory is one of social differentiation, deviation, and individuation. For a summary description we may turn to an excerpt from a paper by the present writer:[22]

> We may pertinently ask at this juncture whether the time has not come to break abruptly with the traditions of older social pathologists and abandon once and for all the archaic and medicinal idea that human beings can be divided into normal and pathological, or, at least, if such a division must be made, to divest the term "pathological" of its moralistic unscientific overtones. As a step in this direction, the writer suggests that the concepts of social differentiation and individuation be rescued from the limbo of older textbooks on sociology, dusted off, and given scientific airing, perhaps being supplemented and given statistical meaning with the perfectly usable concept of deviation. There seems to be no cogent reason why the bulk of the data discussed in textbooks and courses on social pathology cannot be treated as a special phase of social and cultural differentiation and thus conveniently integrated with general sociological theory as taught in courses in introductory sociology. . . .
>
> Because some method must be found to distinguish that portion of differentiation which can be designated as appropriately falling within the field of social pathology, the second necessary postulate is that there is a space-time limited societal awareness and reaction to deviation, ranging from strong ap-

[22] Lemert, Edwin M., "Some Aspects of a General Theory of Sociopathic Behavior," *Proceedings of the Pacific Sociological Society*, 1948, Research Studies, State College of Washington, 16, No 1, pp. 24f

proval through indifference to strong disapproval. Thus, by further definition, sociopathic phenomena simply become differentiated behavior which at a given time and place is socially disapproved even though the same behavior may be socially approved at other times and in other places.

To recapitulate, then, we start with the idea that persons and groups are differentiated in various ways, some of which result in social penalties, rejection, and segregation. These penalties and segregative reactions of society or the community are dynamic factors which increase, decrease, and condition the form which the initial differentiation or deviation takes. This process of deviation and societal reaction, together with its structural or substantive products, can be studied both from its collective and its distributive aspects. In the first instance, we are concerned with sociopathic differentiation; and, in the second, our concern is with sociopathic individuation.

The Postulates With Which We Start

In order to give further precision to the above statement, it can be resolved into a series of postulates. These postulates are simple statements of fact for which the writer feels no obligation to supply proof. They differ from axioms, upon which mathematical and symbolic systems are constructed, in that they contain empirical elements. They are the building blocks for the theory of this treatise and *ipso facto* they must be accepted as points of departure for the analysis which follows. The question as to whether these postulates are the relevant ones or whether they are too few must await answer until after the theory has been tested. The postulates are as follows:[23]

1. There are modalities in human behavior and clusters of deviations from these modalities which can be identified and described for situations specified in time and space.

[23] While in general we found the social problems and the social disorganization viewpoints lacking in theoretical fulfillment, it is not our intention here to insist that all recent treatments of social pathology are without value and that "ours is the only theory." Several books on social pathology have presented fairly defensible theoretical positions. L. Guy Brown's *Social Pathology* is distinguished in the main for its internal consistency and interrelated framework of ideas, and for the integrity with which its central scheme is made the basis for each successive discussion of problem behavior *Social Pathology*, by Stuart Queen and Jeannette Gruener, merits favorable comment for the simplicity and economy of its conceptual presentation, features which, as we have shown, are desirable in all theory. Whether their attempt to study social pathology exclusively in terms of social participation is an oversimplification remains to be seen. Certainly it is a necessary concept, as we shall try to show, but alone, at least as it has been used by others, it remains an incomplete formulation. Another position which deserves comment here because of its obvious bearing upon certain phases of our theory is the value-conflict conception of social problems. In this conception,

2. Behavioral deviations are a function of culture conflict which is expressed through social organization.

3. There are societal reactions to deviations ranging from strong approval through indifference to strong disapproval.

4. Sociopathic behavior is deviation which is *effectively* disapproved.

5. The deviant person is one whose role, status, function, and self-definition are importantly shaped by how much deviation he engages in, by the degree of its social visibility, by the *particular* exposure he has to the societal reaction, and by the nature and strength of the societal reaction.

6. There are patterns of restriction and freedom in the social participation of deviants which are related directly to their status, role, and self-definitions. The biological strictures upon social participation of deviants are directly significant in comparatively few cases.

7. Deviants are individuated with respect to their vulnerability to the societal reaction because: *(a)* the person is a dynamic agent, *(b)* there is a structuring to each personality which acts as a set of limits within which the societal reaction operates.

The Place of This Theory in General Sociological Theory

In keeping with our high scientific resolve the various terms employed in stating our postulates are intended to be amoral and nonevaluational, having obvious statistical implications and derivations. There is no intimation that concepts like "restricted participation," "sociopathic behavior," or "deviation" connote either goodness or badness. The objective of this work is to study a limited part of deviation in human behavior and a certain range of societal reactions, together with their interactional products, and by the methods of science to arrive at generalizations about the uniformities in these events. The aim is to study sociopathic behavior in the same light as normal behavior and, by implication, with extensions or derivations of general sociological theory. By the same token, we hold

chief emphasis is placed upon the clash of ideals, opinions, judgments, and meanings as the source of social problems. In our estimation this is a special variety of culture-conflict theory, and we freely recognize its importance in studying deviation. However, the value-conflict theory remains a highly generalized statement which fails to make a sharp delimitation of the field. For example, it does not tell us how much or what kind of conflict is necessary in order to have a social problem No distinction is struck between effective value-conflicts and those which are purely spurious and have little or no effect upon the organization and interaction of groups and participating individuals. Furthermore, it makes no allowance for cultural inconsistencies or contradictory value systems within the same culture which are reciprocals or necessary derivatives of each other. For statements of the value-conflict view see Waller, W., "Social Problems and the Mores," *American Sociological Review*, 1, December, 1936, pp. 922–933, Fuller, R., and R. Myers, "Some Aspects of a Theory of Social Problems," *ibid.*, 6, February, 1941, pp. 24–32; Cuber, J., and R. Harper, *Problems of American Society*, 1948.

that, with certain modifications in our frame of reference, variations from social norms in desirable and enviable directions should be explored as profitably as the more frequently studied sociopathic variations. The behavior of the genius, the motion-picture star, the exceptionally beautiful woman, and the renowned athlete [24] should lend itself to the same systematic analysis as that which is applied to the criminal, the pauper, or the sex delinquent.[25]

A question for parenthetical consideration is whether or not it is possible to apply our theory with logical extensions to the analysis of behavior systems and persons which are differentiated but which do not excite polarized reactions of social approbation or disapproval. In data like these the chief conditioning factors appear to be the special qualities of the societal reaction. Thus, for example, the primary influences in forming the occupational personality of a locomotive engineer are such things as time, mobility, and income. The small amount of dislike for the railroad man sometimes found in small towns has little to do with the formation of his role and self-conception.[26] Whatever may be the answer to our question, we can readily recognize the gains to be made by integrating the growing body of research on behavior systems of occupational and functional groups and the sort of trend in sociological analysis this book represents. Such an integration would broaden the possible scope of this kind of research and generalization to encompass such monographic studies as those of the railroader, the waitress, and the musician, as well as those of the professional thief, the hobo, or the beggar.[27]

THE FINAL TEST OF A THEORY

Comparing various theories of social pathology in the light of the degree to which they fulfill the logical requirements for a satisfactory theory can

[24] We lack a good concept to designate this kind of deviation. We think of such terms as "honorific behavior" or "emulative behavior" without being very satisfied with them.

[25] We have raised the question in graduate seminars as to whether our theory is applicable to the study of minority or ethnic groups. Generally this question has to be left unanswered. While ethnic groups are often comparable to the type of deviant groups in which we are interested, it is also true that in some cases their large size and occasional positions of considerable power in local areas mean that they differ significantly from the deviant groups we shall be studying.

[26] See Cottrell, W. F., *The Railroader*, 1940.

[27] It is only fitting to acknowledge the contribution which has been made by E H Sutherland in his criminological research by bringing before American sociologists the importance of behavior systems as research areas See also Hollingshead, A. B., "Behavior Systems as a Field of Research," *American Sociological Review*, 4, December, 1939, pp. 816–822.

give us only a partial measure of their value. The final gauge of all theory is the extent to which it meets the empirical test, *i.e.*, how well it is borne out by the evidence, or how well it explains the phenomena we are interested in. Beyond this, there is the ultimate objective of all theory to avoid *ad hoc* explanations. This means that if the theory achieves a true generality it will permit generalizations and predictions covering any of the data falling into the field of behavior which has been marked off by the theory.

It is unfortunate that in our field of interest much of the research data do not exist in such a form that they can be employed in a flexible manner to test hypotheses deduced or deducible from different theoretical constructs. The data seldom are set up or tabulated so that they can be remanipulated by those occupied in verifying or disproving hypotheses other than the ones submitted by persons originally collecting the data. For this reason a textbook writer is driven to testing his intuitions with case-history excerpts and with impressionistic, quasi-journalistic accounts of social life. The present writer makes no claim that these deficiencies can be remedied easily. The available data have to be utilized chiefly because no one person can collect enough materials of his own to test a theory as he would like. However, this can be done with a conscious awareness by the person who uses them of the gaps and shortcomings in the data, pointing up in the process of analysis various areas where research is needed. We hope to do this and do it in such a way as to stimulate others to test some of the propositions deduced or deducible from this theory.

Conclusion

In this chapter we have briefly described and criticized the general points of view of sociologists toward social pathology. We have enumerated criteria for a systematic theory of sociopathic behavior. Following these discussions we delimited the field of study and put down the postulates of our theory. In the next three chapters we shall attempt to develop this theory in greater detail. We shall take up in order, deviation, the societal reaction to deviation, and the process by which the deviant becomes individuated.

Selected Readings

Brown, L. Guy *Social Pathology*, 1942, Part 1, pp 3–77

Frank, L. K.. "Society as the Patient," *American Journal of Sociology*, 42, 1936, pp. 335–344

Fuller, R. G., and R. Myers "Some Aspects of a Theory of Social Problems," *American Sociological Review*, 6, February, 1941, pp 24–32.

LEMERT, EDWIN M.. "Some Aspects of a General Theory of Sociopathic Behavior," *Proceedings of the Pacific Sociological Society*, 1948, Research Studies, State College of Washington, 16, No. 1, pp. 23–29.

MILLS, C. W.: "The Professional Ideology of Social Pathologists," *American Journal of Sociology*, 49, September, 1943, pp. 165–180

WALLER, W.: "Social Problems and the Mores," *American Sociological Review*, 1, December, 1936, pp. 922–933

WARREN, R · "Social Disorganization and the Interrelationship of Cultural Roles," *American Sociological Review*, 14, February, 1949, pp. 83–87.

CHAPTER 2

DEVIATION AND DIFFERENTIATION

In this chapter we are interested in bringing out how human beings differ and deviate from the central tendencies or average characteristics of populations in which they are found and in which they interact. We are not concerned with differentiation per se so much as we are with differentiation which can be related to modal structures and values. This kind of differentiation can be expressed either schematically or literally by the statistical term "deviation."

The Need for Homogeneous Classifications of Sociopathic Deviation

When we turn to the classifications which sociologists have habitually employed to designate different forms of sociopathic deviation, we run into all sorts of expedients. Legal, medical, economic and psychiatric concepts have been borrowed and incorporated into sociological terminology with but little thought for their relevance to sociologically significant facts about the deviation involved. The concept of crime is a case in point; it has been borrowed with almost no modification from the legal profession. As this term has been applied. it covers a tremendously heterogenous range of behaviors which have but one characteristic in common, *i.e.*, they are all violations of a law. The fact that they are violations of a legal rule is of very limited meaning in so far as giving any hint as to the many ways in which crimes differ – as to situations in which they occur, as to the techniques employed to commit the crimes, and above all, as to the context of symbols within which they take place. Much the same can be said about many sociological definitions of juvenile delinquency, prostitution, homosexuality, vagrancy, and other forms of deviant behavior.[1]

It is clear that we must describe deviation in more ways than those set

[1] Sutherland, E. H., *Principles of Criminology*, 1947, rev ed. One way of demonstrating the consequences of the lack of meaningful sociological categories of pathological behavior is simply to add together all the estimates of the numbers of different types of pathological deviants as set down in representative textbooks on social problems, social disorganization, and social pathology This exercise was carried out by the author, with the result that he got a figure of 104,000,000 pathological deviants out of a total United States population of 127,250,000 for the year 1935 This staggering total

down in the legal or medical records of public control agencies with whom deviants have contacts. Otherwise, our theory of sociopathic behavior will remain too generalized to be of any great use or else it will be narrowly adapted to a single, practical community purpose. One method of avoiding this is to break down deviation into various aspects (overt and covert) and then to put deviant behavior into several types of personal and social contexts. In doing this we must not miss the point here that our regard is primarily centered upon the behavioral aspects of deviation together with their interrelationships and contexts. Beyond these lie two nonbehavioral aspects of deviation which we shall deal with but which can be assigned only a marginal significance in our theory. We refer here to the biological and demographic differentiation of deviants. We include these in our aspectual description of deviation for purposes of rounding out our analysis as much as possible. Their bearing upon deviant behavior will be brought out in the paragraphs immediately following.

Biological Differentiation

One of the immediate and most obvious ways in which human beings are differentiated from one another is with respect to their biological characteristics. However, not all such differentiation, as we previously stated, can be thought of as deviation. Among the biological differentiations which have a deviational meaning are the various racial stigmas which serve to set off many ethnic populations in our society and involve them in nexi of segregative social relationships. Within the broad, racial divisions of our population biological deviation appears as extremes of height, weight, facial contours and profiles, bodily shape and proportions, and unusual pigmentation. Somewhat apart from these, but falling into the same deviational class, are biological anomalies such as scars, crossed eyes, birthmarks, and perhaps close physical similarity to some other persons, as seen in twins and multiple births. Finally, within this category we include those who are distinguished biologically from the great majority of the population by physical handicaps in which injury or disease has destroyed or damaged the mechanisms underlying behavior.

Some of the more common physical handicaps, in which damage to biological structures or their anomalous biological development is involved, are orthopedic disabilities coming from the loss or immobilization

---

was quite obviously a consequence of not having mutually exclusive definitions for the grouping of pathological deviants. The figure means that overlapping deviations caused persons to be counted once, twice, thrice, or many times. Thus the alcoholic may be chronically ill, a relief client, and a petty criminal all at the same time See Lemert, Edwin M, "Some Aspects of a General Theory of Sociopathic Behavior," *Proceedings of The Pacific Sociological Society*, 1948, Research Studies, State College of Washington, 16, No. 1, p 23

of body members, such as arms or legs. Other common physical handicaps are the sensory defects, chiefly deafness and blindness. Close to these, in that they interfere with the physical mechanics of communication, are speech defects, including lisping, cleft-palate speech, stuttering, aphasias, and aphonias. Other physical disabilities do not immobilize parts of the body or disrupt the mechanics of communication so much as they produce grotesque and uncontrollable malfunctioning of the body. Here we refer to such things as tics, tremors, spastic or choreiform movements, and epileptic seizures. Not all of these, nor indeed all of the other handicaps (such as stuttering) that we have mentioned, are associated with discernible defects or lesions of biological structure. Some of them are simply a matter of pathological functioning of otherwise normal bodily parts. Much of the disability caused by disease falls into this category.

As far as we know, little of the specific form of deviant behavior can be attributed to biological structures or processes per se, except in a negative or limiting way. Physical handicaps, as the term clearly signifies, make certain types of perception and behavioral responses impossible, depending upon the nature and the extent of the structural defects. Persons so differentiated from others are defective in that they are unable to perform actions which are necessary to implement certain social roles. Such limitations tend to be transcultural in the sense that they are found all over the world. However, the *extent* to which the handicaps physically limit the playing of social roles is culturally variable, being modifiable by technological devices such as hearing aids, reading aids, and prosthetic attachments.

Biological variations which do not impede bodily functions become a basis for deviation only through interaction with cultural definitions and social perceptions. The biological differential in such instances is relatively nondynamic, being little more than a cue for the invocation of discriminatory societal responses. There is nothing intrinsic in a disfiguring scar or in extreme hairiness on the body of a woman which interferes in any way with physiological activity or with the potential fulfillment of social roles. Nevertheless, a culture may *impute* a set of mythical physiological limits to such differentiae and thus cause them to become criteria for social exclusion and penalty.

It is likewise true that those biological differentiae which have a demonstrable handicapping effect upon behavior are overlaid with culturally conceived ideas as to how far the handicaps go. In fact, it is these cultural stereotypes which give the larger part of the social meaning to physical handicaps. We see this very clearly in the discrepancies between judgments made by experimental groups of the physical weight and height of human subjects and the objective measurements of these same subjects.

People often seem taller or shorter than they really are. Another illustration of this point is the failure of friends and associates to note facial improvements which a person may obtain through expensive plastic surgery. The biological transfiguration often has to be called to their attention in order to be noted. Often it does not directly intrude itself into the process of social communication.

Demographic Differentiation of Deviants

Along with biological and other aspects of deviation it is necessary for our purposes to consider the demographic differences of whole classes of deviants. Here we must turn to such features of deviant populations as their age and sex composition, nativity, national origin, economic class, educational and religious status. Marital status, birth and death rates, plus geographic distribution of deviant aggregates need to be further specified as part of the demographic analysis. It is by no means clear that description of deviant populations in these terms is sociological in the strictest sense, despite the large number of sociologists who have shown preferences for these more readily quantified data in their study of human behavior. Nevertheless, the value of demographic description of deviant populations as a preliminary step in locating them in the larger social organization or in "social space" is undeniable. From population data often come the cues to conflict situations which generate deviation. They also give us leads to the patterns of organization among deviants and provide suggestive data on the nature of the symbolic environments in which various types of deviation take on meaning.

Normal and Deviant Behavior

The main emphasis of our treatise, as we have said, is upon deviant behavior, for it is largely what people do or fail to do which brings them into public focus as deviants. Although sociologists freely employ the term "deviant" as well as "abnormal" and "maladjusted," it is by no means clear in many sociological discussions, just what constitute the referents of "normal" behavior. Hence, in order to clarify the concept of deviant behavior, we must jointly consider normal behavior. It is obvious that the concept of deviation can only have value if there are adequate means of describing and delimiting social norms. But this is no easy task. In small, isolated, and relatively well-integrated societies the task of ascertaining what are the norms against which deviant behavior can be defined and the deviant person distinguished is comparatively simple, although careful study is needed even here. In large, complex, urban-industrial societies whose cultures have been continually fractured by rapid change the difficulties in the way of depicting the modalities and variations in behavior are vastly greater. In fact, one writer has contended that the concept of deviation can have little meaning in a "multi-norm" society such as our own.[2]

There is no need, however, to go to such extremes in recognizing the presence of a wide diversity of norms in modern society. All societies, even if they function on low levels of effectiveness, must have mass conformities to some sort of rules. The real problem here is to avoid reifying the concepts (such as mores) which are used to describe the mass conformities and regularities in human behavior. Such concepts should be taken for what they are – convenient ways of summarizing the tendencies of human beings in their various roles to respond in a similar fashion in social situations. Our existing sociological concepts used for this purpose are crude at best; and to employ them to the best advantage, they must be amended to show the many ways norms are qualified in space and time and with reference to such status indicators as age, sex, and economic class. Care must be taken not to artificially abstract norms from the social situations in which they function and of which they are merely points of reference.

Norms Defined

In the context of our theory norms refer to limits of variation in behavior explicitly or implicitly held and recognized in retrospect by members of a group, community, or society. The assertion that norms are seen in retrospect is another way of saying that few people, unless they are professional social scientists, are conscious of the standards of behavior in their culture. On the whole, people tend to be aware of norms only when they are breached, and only projectively, that is, people discuss the action of others after it takes place, from the standpoint of its specific appropriateness and what "ought to have been done" in the situation. Few persons in a situation ever conform exactly with the norms of their group; the more likely occurrence in some sort of statistical distribution around verbally or otherwise projected norms.[3] For some forms of behavior, such as punctuality of college students in attending classes, the characteristics of conformity distributions, when shown graphically, take on the appearance of the so-called "normal" or Gaussian frequency curve. On the other hand,

[2] See review of Brown, L. Guy, *Social Pathology*, by Fuller, R., *American Journal of Sociology*, 49, July, 1943, pp. 104–105.

[3] Ford, C. S, "Society, Culture and the Organism," *Journal of General Psychology*, 20, January, 1939, pp. 135–179, Linton, R, "Society, Culture and the Individual," *Journal of Abnormal and Social Psychology*, June, 1938, pp.. 221–227, Opler, M. E, "Rule and Practise in Behavior between Jicarilla Apache Affinal Relatives," *American Anthropologist*, 49, September, 1947, pp. 453–462, Lee, A. M., "Levels of Culture as Levels of Generalization," *American Sociological Review*, 10, August, 1945, pp. 485–495.

according to a substantial body of research in social psychology, there are other forms of normative behavior in which the distributions approximate a J-shaped curve instead of a bell-shaped one. In these latter studies, the conformity reactions, instead of clustering around a central value, tend to fall into one main class interval, with variation in one direction only. The accompanying figure illustrates such a distribution in a situation involving promptness in registering to ensure continued employment on a work relief project.[4]

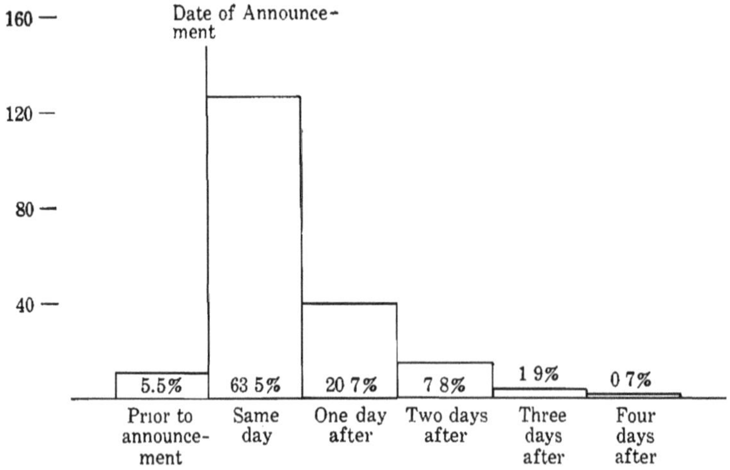

FIG. 1. Distribution of 271 registrations by city welfare-department employees for employment with the civilian works administration by one-day class intervals

Other studies which have brought to light a J-curve type of conformity concern such things as the belief of Catholic men in a personal deity, observance of stop signs at intersections by motorists, motorists overparking, and observance of various religious rituals.[5]

THE COMPULSIVENESS OF NORMS

The characteristics of the J-curve distributions have led its students to insist that they apply only in cases of conformity to institutional norms. This may be expanded to mean that they materialize where the norms are symbols of ideological loyalties and in group affiliations. From this it follows that all norms might be divided into two large classes: institutional

[4] Allport, Floyd, "The J-curve Hypothesis of Conforming Behavior," *Journal of Social Psychology*, 5, May, 1934, pp. 141–183.

[5] A good review of these studies can be found in D. Katz and R Schanck, *Social Psychology*, 1938. There are a number of criticisms of this research, but they need not concern us here

and noninstitutional. However, other research[6] indicates that a wide variety of patterns of conformity and deviation in human behavior is possible, with a broad gamut of conformity curves, from symmetrical, bell-shaped to J- or even I-shaped figures. Consequently, it seems wiser not to insist that a simple dual classification of norms into institutional and noninstitutional will serve for all situations. The relative skewing of the conformity curves probably can be taken just as well as a measure of the *degree* of the institutionalization of the norms involved, or perhaps even better, as a measure of the degree of their compulsiveness as shown upon a hypothetical continuum of permissiveness-compulsiveness. Such a continuum would show at one end those norms whose violations provoke a strong societal reaction and symbolic complications in the deviant. At the other end of the scale would be permissive norms whose disregard excites few or no sanctions from the community and hardly ruffle the consciousness of the individual who chooses to ignore them.

Negative and Positive Norms

If such a serial classification as we have suggested is feasible, then further subclassification of norms in terms of their positive and negative emphasis can be undertaken. It can be shown that norms distribute themselves continuously from highly compulsive, must-do, positive norms through mild or minimum compulsion and permissiveness to urgently forbidden behavior, taboos, or negative norms. In other words, our scale takes on another dimension. This positive-negative dimension has an especially important bearing upon the norms of our culture. Generally speaking, in American culture, in contrast to, say, feudal English culture, there is a preponderance of negatively phrased norms over those with a positive emphasis, a reflection of our individualistic, private-rights type of law and political philosophy. This fact probably has implications in the strong punitive and segregative features of social control applied to sociopathic deviants in our society.

Sociopathic Deviation More Likely to Be Culturally Recognized Than Conformity or Behavior Surpassing the Norm

It was stated before that norms of behavior are implicit in the attitudes and reactions of members of the group who are confronted with a breach of the rule. Conformities to societal requirements generally pass without notice or comment, but not so with deviations, which intrude upon the

[6] Bernard, J., *American Family Behavior*, 1941, Chaps. V–VI, Fearing, F., and E. Kruse, "Conforming Behavior and the J-curve Hypothesis," *Journal of Social Psychology*, 14, August, 1941, pp. 109–118.

consciousness of those who are witness to them. Deviations are eventful, provocative, and sometimes menacing to the rights and privileges of others. Consequently, they are more likely to be made explicit in oral or written form than are the norms of the society. This is plain to be seen in the myths of many primitive cultures, in which deviations often are described in lurid, salacious detail, or personified in accounts of culture heroes both bad and good. While deviations in socially enviable directions may be specified as guides for conduct, it is much more common to find sociopathic deviation precisely conceptualized in written laws or in tribal lore. The reason for this is that people can more easily agree upon minimum conformities and intolerable deviations than they can upon what constitutes ideal behavior. An additional reason for this difference is that societies and groups more often can afford to ignore behavior which surpasses its norms, whereas they can seldom disregard sociopathic behavior.

The Aspects of Deviant Behavior

Any complete description of deviant behavior will necessarily be from points of reference such as space, time, and the special demands of social roles based upon age, sex, and other differentiae of the persons who deviate. In other words, it must be shown that the behavior is deviant for a given locality at a certain time and for persons of one or both sexes, above or below a given age and having a specified socioeconomic status. Relevant description will also permit singling out the aspects of the person's behavior within which the deviation can and does occur. These aspects are factored out of the total response of the person, for we make no assumptions that deviation is an all-inclusive thing. Separation of these aspects becomes a crude classification of deviations in terms of their possible associations with differing societal reactions and cultural definitions.

The main distinction to be observed between the aspects of deviant behavior falling in our purview is that between (1) overt aspects and (2) covert symbolic aspects. Subclassification of these permits us to break down the former into (*a*) overt verbal deviation (*b*) overt nonverbal deviation.[7] When we speak of deviation in overt verbal behavior, we have in mind unusual or nontypical content and apparent meaning of the verbal responses made by a person. Among the deviations of this class we may cite such behavior as slang, profanity, obscenity, dialects, argots, ungrammatical expressions, and advocacy of unconventional or radical ideas about economic, religious, or political institutions or about the whole social structure.

Overt, nonverbal deviation, by exclusion, refers to deviation in all gross

[7] For discussions of overt and covert behavior see LaPiere, R, *Social Psychology*, 1949, rev. ed, Part II, Young, K, *Personality and Problems of Adjustment*, 1940, Chap. 6.

bodily behavior except vocal responses. Any or all of the conventionally delimited "problems" behaviors or social pathologies qualify under this heading; chronic alcoholism, addictions to narcotic drugs, prostitution, and crime are illustrations in point. Ideally, we would have some further principle of subclassification of these behaviors; however, it is probably too soon to attempt such a scheme until after we have had more conceptually guided research along these lines.

Covert Symbolic Deviation

Covert symbolic deviation is a term we have chosen to apply in general to aberrant attitudes and emotions, especially with reference to the meaning which they have for the person who experiences them. Certain difficulties stand in the way of adequately describing this aspect of deviation, but there can be no doubt that in their interactions human beings do make distinctions between covert behavior and behavior which is more readily observed. We find testimony to this in the importance which was once attached in medieval court procedure to the establishing of the *mens rea*, or the criminal intent, behind criminal actions. For many classes of offenses in our laws today this cultural recognized distinction is still importantly maintained. Consider the time and money which were expended by the United States government during the Second World War to determine whether objectors to military duty were "conscientious" or not.

Although we have introduced the idea of covert deviation because people act as if it exists and because in their collective capacities they predicate programs of social control upon the assumption that it does exist, this does not mean that we believe human behavior to be a dual order of phenomenon. Neither do we believe that the study of covert symbolic behavior necessitates a subjective methodology. We hold that deviation in covert symbolic processes can be studied empirically through language which is conceived of as behavior. This means that we pay heed not so much to what people say or to the formal meaning of their words as we do to the function of their language in a total configuration of personal and social behavior. Taken in this way, their language symbolizes many things which are never said. The specific referents of the words, like the exposed portion of an iceberg, often reveal only a small part of the total symbolic process.

The special phase or expression of this symbolic process which is of greatest interest to students of deviation has to do with the way in which the "self" is symbolized in relation to symbolic environments or to the environments of "others." The self is thought of here as the reflective part of the symbolic process, or the awareness of how the person differs from others plus evaluations of these differences. The more exact formulation of deviation in this self-symbolizing process will be left for Chap. 4. Parenthetically we may state that the temptation to employ the term "psychopathic deviation" here in the interests of conceptual consistency was a strong one. However, the vagueness of the term as generally applied together with its moral connotations made such a choice unwise.

Interrelationships of the Aspects of Deviation

The interrelationships of the various aspects of deviation which have been described are a problem for research rather than a subject for a priori statement. We must avoid the preconception that deviation in one aspect of behavior begets deviation in other aspects. Deviation can and does occur in single aspects of behavior as well as in combinations within the same individual, social situation, or group. Thus people may be obscene in their speech without necessarily deviating in their overt sexual behavior; they may make their living by systematic stealing, yet be at complete ease with their selves; furthermore, the private symbolic reactions of an individual may be considerably variant (*i.e.*, with respect to the self attitudes) without disposing him to break the rules of his society; in fact, these symbolic peculiarities may be the very means by which he keeps from immoral or criminal behavior, or, in some cases, may be the means by which he deviates in honorific as opposed to sociopathic directions.

While our procedure of factoring deviation into several aspects may seem somewhat pedantic, nevertheless we believe that in so doing we are measurably aided in keeping apart cases of deviation which hitherto have been mixed up and confused in sociological treatments of social pathology. We now should be able to distinguish (1) persons whose behavior is a "problem" to others but not to themselves, (2) persons whose behavior is a "problem" to themselves but not to others, (3) persons whose behavior is a "problem" both to others and to themselves.

The Personal and Social Contexts within Which Deviation Takes Place

In the above discussion we developed a plan for classifying deviation from the standpoint of the features of the behavior itself. We also raised the question as to how these features or aspects are interrelated. In order to be theoretically prepared to give satisfactory answers to these questions and to profitably exploit the larger notion of sociopathic deviation, we must have some good way of conceiving of it in personal and sociocultural contexts. In other words, we must turn to the configurational aspects of deviation. Deviant behavior, in common with all human behavior, does not arise *sui generis* in isolation nor does it get communicated or transmitted as atomistic segments in a void. Deviations which are quite similar in form in two different individuals often take on entirely different qualities when viewed in the context of their respective personal and social configurations. A crime like forgery becomes several orders of social phenomena when it is committed by the person who in so doing expresses hatred of his employer, when it is committed by a chronic alcoholic at a bar as a desperate measure to obtain liquor, and when committed by the cool professional forger who makes his living by "laying paper." In consideration of these facts we have seen fit to introduce a threefold functional classification of deviation: (1) individual, (2) situational, and (3) systematic.

Individual Deviation

Some deviation seems to be a relatively personal phenomenon in that it occurs in close association with the unique and unshared attributes of persons. It emanates from "within the skin" of the person, so to speak. It is related to biological variations and anomalies which are due to heredity, disease, or accident. More commonly, where no biological differentiation is present, the deviation results from the special way in which social and cultural influences impinge upon and interact with normal hereditary qualities of the person. Often this kind of deviation is symptomatic of deep-lying, intrapsychic conflicts or of conflicts over major role identifications. Conflicts of this order have their *origins* in other contexts but subsequently they assume an integrity and momentum of their own. Some of the behavior which can be classed as individual deviation is that of the inventor, the exceptional child, the musical genius, the religious fanatic, and the psychotic person. This is not to insist that individual deviation is nonsocial in nature, or that it occurs entirely apart from groups and social situations, but rather it is to say that, for a complete understanding of certain deviant actions, it is necessary to study human behavior in its distributive and personally delimited context rather than as the *direct* and *immediate* reciprocal of social and cultural stimuli.[8]

Situational Deviation

In other forms of deviation there is comparatively little need to consider the individual as such as an interactive factor in the total picture of deviation. The deviation can be defined pretty much as a function of the impact of forces in the situation external to the person or in the situation of which the individual is an integral part. Situations have a compelling force and may cause persons to transgress rules of conduct to which they

[8] Our concept of individual deviation also may be thought of as arising out of what K. Young has called "personal social conditioning." See his *Social Psychology*, 1945, pp. 9f

have rigidly adhered in the past and which presumably have been incorporated as part of their personality structures. If a man's family is starving and there is no other way to obtain food for them, the man may steal it. Likewise a girl may prostitute herself because of a dissatisfaction with her job, the wages of which deny her the type of clothes she desires. Groups as well as isolated persons may deviate from prescribed norms as a result of psychological transformations wrought by the situations. The riotous behavior of mobs or the demoralization of armies are illustrations of such phenomena.

Making the Concept of Situational Deviation More Precise

While it is easy enough to perceive that the social situation is a necessary factor in pathological human behavior and while so-called "situational analysis" seems to be well established in sociology, it is by no means clear just what is meant by the "social situation"; the term is often employed in a very broad and vague way to cover such things as social institutions, social relationships, and momentary, adventitious phenomena.[9] Consequently, it is important to delimit its meaning in a more precise fashion. In brief, the social situation may be taken as a referent of behavior in which pressures, limits, or stimuli coming from persons and groups external to the individual are relatively more dynamic than internal factors in evoking his responses. Space and time are always dimensions of the social situation. An operational test to determine whether deviant behavior is situational or not would be simply to measure the extent to which it recurs without significant change in dissimilar situations, or the extent to which it disappears when the situation changes.

Some situational deviation, like some individual deviation, is a generalized rather than a specific response, taking shape in random or unstable deviant reactions. In other cases the situation is so structured as to reduce the limits of possible responses, with the result that the form of the deviation is much more of an implicit manifestation of the situation. Again, some situational deviation is almost purely adventitious, that is, it springs from chance combinations of environmental factors. A great deal of artistic creation comes under this head. However, deviation arising from this sort of situation is probably of small importance in relation to the vast amount of variant behavior that derives from repetitive or persistent situations within a given society or culture, in which deviant reactions are both generalized and specific. This latter deviation assumes aggregate and cumulative form, and it is much more directly associated with what many writers have in mind when they talk of "social disorganization." Let us consider it in more detail.

[9] See a critical discussion by A. Green, "The Social Situation in Personality Theory," *American Sociological Review,* 7, June, 1942, pp.. 388–393.

Cumulative Situational Deviation – Culture Conflict

Societal, cultural, and environmental conditions often interact to create a number of similar and recurring situations confronting discrete individuals, so that the resultant deviation, while taking place as separate actions, uniformly involves a large segment of the population. This we call "cumulative deviation." Most, if not all, of the cumulative situational deviation in our society is an outgrowth of culture conflict. At least, this is the postulate upon which we are proceeding – that most deviation comes out of situations of culture conflict.

The concept of culture conflict, like that of the social situation, has suffered from loose usage and by different writers has been taken to mean (1) conflict between the individual and society, (2) conflict between the values or practices of two or more groups, (3) the introjected conflicts within a person who participates in groups with contradictory values.[10] As used in this discussion, the concept combines the second and third meanings in this list, which in reality describe the same phenomenon, but from two different vantage points. In other words, culture conflict refers to situations which bring incompatible social or group pressures to bear upon persons in such a way as to generate unintegrated tensions or anxieties which are expressed in aberrant or novel behavior. In demonstrating the rise of deviation out of culture conflict it is not enough to show merely in a general way that a person or persons engage in inconsistent overt behavior or that they live in an area where there are warring values and ideologies. Instead, it must be shown how the culture conflict affects their overt behavior in other contexts and how it complicates their immediate social participation. The son of an immigrant from rural Italy may remain relatively unbothered by his father's generalized criticism of the bad habits he has supposedly acquired from associating with children of American parents. However, when the father demands that he come in the house an hour earlier at night than the other boys on the corner, or when he insists that any money earned by the boy be turned over to him instead of going for a football or a baseball bat, then the concept of culture conflict begins to take on useful meaning in terms of social organization and social participation.

Many illustrations of cumulative situational deviation can be drawn from our culture. Every year, for example, hotels lose countless articles such as towels, lamps, pictures, and rugs, stolen or damaged by people who as often as not turn out to be respected members of their local communities. The lowering of morale and the shift to verbal radicalism among a certain percentage of unemployed industrial workers and professional

[10] Sellin, T., "Culture Conflict and Crime," *American Journal of Sociology*, 44, July, 1938, pp. 97–103.

people during periods of depression are quite obviously responses to a situation. So-called "adolescent revolt" and menopausic distress among middle-aged women in our culture appear to be widespread situational, rather than personalized, forms of deviation. Much of our present-day sexual deviation springs from a common conflict associated with the postponement of marriage beyond biological maturity, and from the intensive erotic stimulation in the absence of opportunities for sexual gratification in our society. Homosexuality apparently develops rather easily in our numerous isolated one-sex groups and probably out of the predatory, competitive nature of heterosexual relationships and disorganized family life in our culture. Prison homosexuality appears to be largely a response to deprivation of contacts with members of the opposite sex. That this fairly common sexual aberrancy is situational seems emphasized by the facts that it is more frequent among the most heterosexual prisoners and that upon release the majority of such deviants revert to heterosexual behavior.[11]

American Culture Conducive to Deviation

There have been some rather good, generalized historical culture-conflict explanations for the great amount of sociopathic deviation, especially criminal, in our society. Attention has been directed to the following factors: (1) the breakdown in feudalism and attendant shift from an ideology of positive duties and obligations to one of negative rights and individualism in England at the time when America was colonized, (2) the breakdown of local social controls caused by urbanization; (3) intensification of competition for status; (4) rising levels of aspiration to material affluence. Sociologists have given special weight to the last two of these factors in their discussions of how crime and general sociopathic behavior grow up in our culture.[12]

American culture generally, due to its individualistic, competitive ethos, is a high-tension-inducing culture in contrast to many other world cultures. Competitive struggle has been formalized in the "Protestant ethic," the code of the middle class which bestows moral worth upon those who succeed and leaves the stigma of worthlessness upon those who fail. Conflict in the individual precipitates from the discrepancy between aspiration and achievement, and from the anticipations of social failure. Through advertising and agencies of mass impression, and formal and informal education, our culture has progressively elevated its standards of achievement

[11] Nelson, Victor, *Prison Days and Prison Nights*, 1933, Chap. V.

[12] Anderson, H. W, Introduction to *Report on the Causes of Crime*, National Committee on Law Observance and Enforcement, 1, No. 13, Bain, Read, "Culture Conflict and Social Integration," *American Journal of Sociology*, 44, January, 1939, pp 499–509, Sutherland, E. H., *op. cit.*, Chap. V.

and created highly specialized, often exotic, material life goals. These, in the absence of opportunities for mass fulfillments, have generated all manner of individual anxieties, insecurities, and inferiority feelings. These situationally induced disorders of the symbolic life of innumerable persons find overt expression in a wide variety of socially depreciated deviant behaviors, including crime, rebellion, addictive medications, sexual immorality, and radicalism. We also see their results in accidents, sabotage, and slowdowns in industry and in vandalism.[13]

Anomie as a Source of Deviation

One treatment of the sociocultural sources of deviant behavior has sought to rise above the level of purely historical and cross-sectional description by setting up a typology of social structures which exert differential pressures upon members of society to engage in nonconformist conduct. The implementation of this conceptual scheme rests upon a distinction between the goals of a culture and the institutional means prescribed for attaining them. Polarized types of social structures are postulated; in one type there is disproportionate, at times virtually exclusive, emphasis upon the value of specific goals, involving only slight concern for the appropriate ways of achieving these goals. Opposed to this type is the social structure found in a ritualized culture, where institutional means tend to become transformed into ends, where means become ends in themselves. The integrated culture is assumed to lie in between these two polarized types of social structure. The identification of our culture with the first polar type is easy and obvious. Ours is a culture in which "nothing succeeds like success," wherein the intensity of aspirations to material-success symbols generates endemic deviations, or, as the author of this theory calls it, "anomie." [14]

This conceptualization in terms of "anomie" represents a definite advance in sociological thinking by permitting us to account for deviation in the light of the general features of a type of culture or an institutional nexus rather than entirely by reference to the inconsistencies of the specific patterns it has acquired in the process of growth and change. However, in common with historical explanations of nonconformist behavior, it does not supply us with a method as detailed as we would like for revealing the differential impact of these cultural types upon various groups, classes, and institutional complexes of a society. Referents, or the things which correspond to "goals" and "means," which can be used in demonstrating such differential impacts are not easy to find. We are left

[13] Prescott, A., *Emotion and the Educative Process*, 1938.

[14] Merton, R., "Social Structure and Anomie," *American Sociological Review*, 3, October, 1938, pp 672–682. The concept originally comes from Durkheim.

without refined techniques for isolating the critical social and spatial areas within the culture where tensions or "anomie" rise to greater proportions than in others.

Cultural Discontinuities as Critical Points Where Deviation Arises

In a very general way sociologists have taken heed of critical deviation-inducing areas within our culture in their discussions of such things as "mass" society, the "marginal man," the adolescent, the aged person, the professional woman, and the "neurotic housewife." However, at best these have been an oblique or indirect recognition of tension areas in the culture. The stress has been primarily upon the personal concomitants rather than upon the limits, choices, and demands of the objective situation. One important exception to this has been the attempt to conceptualize objective social situations on the basis of discontinuity of cultural conditioning. In this particular treatment of cultural stress a scheme is presented which allows the comparing of different cultures as to the degree of discontinuity in the life cycles of participating members as they mature and pass from one major role to another. Discontinuity is a function of the amount of contrast in the demands of responsible action, dominance-submission, and sexual participation made by major social roles juxtaposed in the life history of the person. Thus, if a person in a given culture (like ours) must move from the role of an adolescent, in which he is irresponsible, submissive to parental authority, and sexually naive, to the role of an adult, in which without preparation responsibility suddenly falls upon him along with prerogatives of authority and sexual indulgence, presumably we have a highly discontinuous type of cultural conditioning.[15] We may append the obvious conclusion that the unbridged gap between the roles is a cultural crisis point and potentially one in which deviation may appear.

A Possible Method for Studying the Extent to Which Deviation Is Implicit in a Social Situation

There is a need to further supplement and go beyond the conceptualizations we have touched on here in order to more accurately assess the special role of tension in bringing about deviation and also to determine just how far the form of deviation is implicit in the situation. One such analysis of embezzlement has been made through reference to a factoral scheme which embraces organismic (physiological), psychic, interpersonal, and cultural conditions of the individual's adjustment. Embezzlement, according to the author's derived hypothesis, is preceded by the

[15] Benedict, Ruth, "Continuities and Discontinuities of Cultural Conditioning," *Psychiatry*, May, 1939, pp. 161–167.

accumulation of tension which cannot be reduced through internal alternatives, or through any external alternative save this particular form of criminal action.[16] While this formulation makes allowance for the situational factor in the shape of external alternatives, nevertheless its application to specific cases of embezzlement is handicapped by the author's excessive preoccupation with the internal dynamics of the embezzler's behavior. The interpersonal and cultural parts of his scheme are slighted in so far as showing how they restrict the external alternatives.

It occurs to us that research of this sort into the tension-inducing and choice-limiting impact of the social situation as they relate to embezzlement might be facilitated by examining different kinds of business situations in which the person is included rather than treating the embezzler as an abstracted case. For example, various banking offices might be studied with reference to (1) the differential aspirational levels of the employees, (2) the differential opportunities for advancement among those who have the opportunity to embezzle, (3) the differential probability of apprehension if money is taken. These variables then might be correlated with rates of embezzlement to see whether the situation thus defined becomes a significant factor in this form of deviation.

Tension Alone Does Not Explain Deviation

It should be made plain at this point that tensions and anxieties and other sociopsychological manifestations are not in themselves responsible for deviation in socially undesired directions. As a matter of fact, tension and tension reduction are features of all human activity. Relatively well-integrated cultures may impinge upon persons in such a way as to generate all sorts of situationally oriented hostilities, aggressions, anxieties, ambivalences, and generally high-tensional states, as may be noted in connection with Northwest Pacific Coast Indian tribes where the imperative to ego aggrandizement is central to the integration of many of the local cultures. While the degree and peculiar qualities of this psychic stuff are of some incidental importance, it is increasingly apparent that the special social and cultural forms through which tension and other psychological reactions are expressed act as the most significant determiners of deviation.

Thus, in our own culture, even "normal" conformity to sex and family mores may build up considerable frustration, aggression, or withdrawal reactions within men and women. Whether these reactions or those springing more directly from culture conflict lead to sociopathic aberrations hinges upon the accessory resources set up within the culture to channelize

[16] Lottier, S., "A Tension Theory of Criminal Behavior," *American Sociological Review*, 7, December, 1942, pp. 840–848, there are several other conceptions of criminal behavior quite similar to this. See Tappan, P, *Juvenile Delinquency*, 1949, pp 65–71, also, Reckless, Walter, *The Crime Problem*, 1950, p 29.

them, and upon the symbolizing process within its institutions assigning values to them.

If it is publicly recognized or if it is publicly imputed that these derivative culture patterns or individual behaviors impede or prevent the efficient functioning of other institutions and groups within the society, and, more particularly, if cultural and private definitions of these behaviors by their invidious connotations and denotations engender further tensions in their effect upon participating persons, then situational deviation tends to be compounded rather than reduced. Thus adjustive behavior, because of its social reception or because of the person's symbolic reception of his own behavior, may reduce one set of tensions only to create another set. This second set of tensions will beget further deviation. In general summary then, cumulative situational deviation springs from cultural situations which generate high tensions without socially acceptable opportunities for their reduction.[17]

Systematic Deviation

There is little deviation, even psychotic behavior, that does not involve some communication of the particular pattern of activity involved. Situational, especially cumulative situational, deviation, is often facilitated by the knowledge that others have met the conflict situation in an atypical, socially disapproved way. When such communication carries specific content, when rapport develops between deviants and common rationalizations make their appearance, the unique and situational forms of deviation are converted to organized or systematic deviation.

Systematic deviation appears as a subculture or as a behavior system, accompanied by a special social organization and formalized status, roles, morals, and morale distinct from the larger culture. A definite professionalization of conduct by deviant group members develops, along with craft pride similar to that found among integrated occupational groups. Informal and formal social controls function to induce conformity by the "deviant deviants" within the group. In other words, all the characteristics of any social group are present, the chief conditioning factors of the behavior system being the degree of deviation in the core behavior, the amount of differentiation of the deviants, and the extent and nature of the disapproving societal reaction to them.

How Deviant Groups Arise

While each deviant organization will have its own unique history, certain common backgrounds in culture conflict seem to be present in all

[17] Gillin, J., "Acquired Drives in Culture Contact," *American Anthropologist*, 44, October–December, 1942, pp. 454–465.

cases. Groups of this sort originally appear and proliferate out of the process of cultural change and usually among persons situated at the points of greatest conflict and discontinuity in the culture. The spatial reflection of this can be seen in the rapid growth of religious sects on the American frontier in the nineteenth century, in their great multiplication in areas of high-migration and mobility, such as Southern California, and also in the growth of criminal gangs among adolescent children in the interstitial areas of large urban communities. The fact that second-generation immigrants in certain areas have more frequently than first-generation immigrants entered into criminal activities bears further testimony on this point. Many persons who later become leaders of radical political groups have been nurtured in conflicting cultural settings, they have been so-called "marginal" personalities: Adolf Hitler, Joseph Stalin, Kemal Atatürk, Napoleon, and many others can be cited as examples.

Deviant social organization within a given culture may appear quite spontaneously, deriving from cumulative situational deviation, in which many deviants come to communicate with one another and to perceive their common interests plus the necessity for defensive or aggressive organization. Examples of this have been such things as the formation of labor unions in early days when they were regarded as conspiratorial agencies, or in recent years the rapid and widespread growth of Alcoholics Anonymous organizations throughout our country. Such group developments frequently appear to have a character of inevitability; they are "in the air" so to speak, needing only an activating factor to bring them into existence. In other instances, deviant groupings emanate from deliberate cultural innovators and inventors, who may for a long time remain more or less socially isolated pending the acquisition of a sympathetic audience or following. Gradually, by a combined use of persuasion, propaganda, rewards, and other means of social control, they contrive to attract a personal following which becomes the spearhead of a new organization and the surrogate of a novel culture complex. Many religious sects, Mormonism, Christian Science, and the exotic religion of Father Divine, as well as many radical, political, and economic organizations, have such a history.

While many deviant groupings are unique in their patterns of organization, ritual, and codes, others closely resemble groups with established status in their society. These latter are the product of a splintering process through which they break away from a parental organization, being deviant and disapproved of by virtue of the fact that they are competing for power with the older organization. This process is not only perceived in connection with sectarian groups but also may operate to split entire societies. American Indian bands at times were rent with factional conflicts which subsequently lead to cultural fissions and to the establishment of variant offshoot cultures. The origin of some of our early colonial communities lay in a process such as this.

In large, complex, and dynamic "mass" societies the proliferation of cults, sects, and social movements spontaneously and around deviant personalities is a manifold, and probably accelerating, occurrence. No attempt at counting these groups has ever been made, but a census might well run the total figure into hundreds of thousands. Their appearance and growth is a response to the drive of individuals to achieve tension reductions in a chaotic and conflicting culture. However, this is not to say that the same motivation or psychological homogeneity is present among all persons who join a sect of a deviant group; a wide variety of individual deviation as well as socially accepted behaviors may be integrated within deviant groups. On the whole, because deviant organizations cater to needs of persons under extreme tension, they tend to become social microcosms, tightly knit little social worlds which become a common denominator for the other social experiences of its members. Integration, at least in the early history of such deviant groups, is largely through conflict with other groups and external threat; if differences between the group and the rest of society are not great enough to generate conflict, then they may be deliberately increased by its leaders in order to achieve the integration. This can be done through such techniques as nonintercourse with outsiders, secrecy, and the use of a separate vocabulary.[18]

The mortality rate for deviant groups of the sort just described undoubtedly is very high, and few of them achieve stability and integration into the larger social system on the basis of acceptance, or upon any basis, for that matter. Social change itself frequently undercuts the ideologies upon which the sects are founded, or they disintegrate because of discredited leadership, lack of resources, or mounting societal hostility. Those few which do become integrated formally into the larger social system tend to lose their deviant characteristics and undergo a change of personnel and leadership.

The Diffusion of Systematic Sociopathic Behavior

A great deal of the behavior and organization ordinarily classed as "pathological" or as "problem" behavior has ensued from the process of culture diffusion. In other words, sociopathic behavior and organization which originated in other societies was brought to this country by migrants, travelers, entrepreneurs, and adventurers. Begging, prostitution, gambling, and many kinds of crime are historically old forms of sociopathic behavior which were brought to this country by its settlers. There

[18] Faris, E., "The Sect and Sectarian," in *Personality and the Social Group*, 1929, p 134.

is reason to believe that certain techniques of committing crime, known vaguely as "gangsterism" arose from the old-world criminal traits of Sicilians in Chicago, taken over and adapted to the needs of American-born criminals. Socialism appears to have been transported to this country by German immigrants of the worker class. While it is easy to exaggerate the alien influences involved, on account of their political implications, there is sufficient evidence to believe that many, if not most, of the specific patterns of American communism were an importation. It is well known that the early strength of the Communist party in the United States lay in Russian, Lettish, Finnish, and Jewish immigrant membership. More important, apart from the incidentally criminal and radical aspects of immigrant culture, there is the whole heritage of transplanted cultural groups which differentiates them from the peoples among whom they settle. Crime and radicalism may be disapproved of within the immigrant group as well as by native groups, but in other instances the modal practices of the immigrant groups become a form of disapproved deviation in a different cultural context. The Molokans, a sect of Russian origin which settled in Los Angeles prior to the First World War, became a target for public hostility because of their refusal to bear arms and make the appropriate patriotic obeisances to the American flag and other national symbols. Certain of the Dukhobor sects in Canada became outcast groups as a consequence of their refusal to send their children to public schools and their nude parades of protest when sect members were jailed for noncompliances with local laws.

Why Deviants Organize or Do Not Organize

A pertinent inquiry can be raised as to why some types of deviants organize themselves into groups and others do not, and also why similar deviants vary in the degree to which they participate in or become members of such organizations once they are created. Only partial answers to such questions exist. In some cases, the peculiar qualities of the deviation preclude organization of those so differentiated. Stutterers, for example, do not organize into groups apparently because of the difficulties of sufficiently communicating to carry on the duties of such organization, and also probably because of the increased visibility and intensification of social penalties that the fact of aggregation brings about. On the other hand, we know that crime of certain kinds and prostitution are highly organized deviant phenomena in our society, as well as in other societies.

One of the variables generally operating as a conditioner of organization among deviant persons is the extent to which society makes survival for the deviant possible without organization. Stutterers can usually work out some sort of adjustment to society, albeit associated with an unpleasant and penalized status. On the other hand, considering the difficulties of obtaining narcotics in our society, recourse to organization becomes an indispensable implement to the adjustment of the drug addict. Another generally operating variable influencing the organization of deviants has to do with their organizability as affected by age-sex composition, economic, occupational, and educational status, homogeneity, physical contiguity of the deviant persons, and the presence or absence of adequate leadership. In one community, a number of disabled war veterans may remain unorganized owing to lack of leadership on account of some age cleavage or because of the fact that there is excessive cultural heterogeneity among them. In another community, in the face of such obstacles, a competent organization may result because of the presence among them of a few highly gifted leaders.

The Forms Which Deviant Social Organization May Take

The organization of a deviant group may range all the way from the informal, loose ties of a Bohemian colony to a highly integrated, rigidly disciplined, radical or revolutionary actionist group. There is an ambivalent tendency among the uninformed to look upon some of our outcast groups as either incapable of organization or as so well organized over vast areas that they insidiously infiltrate our entire social structure. There has been, for example, considerable loose writing about criminal "syndicates" and criminal "business" organization on a nationwide or even international scale. In the light of the illegal status, mobility, and heterogeneity of criminals, a much more defensible hypothesis is that the social relationships of criminals are quite tenuous and much more likely to take the form of transient combinations and reciprocity than that of tightly knit groups with fixed personnel. Subversive political groups which are the object of police persecution often have been organized in a similar way, tending to have small units of highly dependable workers with peripheries of adherents whose use to the group depends upon the significance of the task at hand.

The nature of the organization as well as the culture of the deviant group is closely dependent upon the central function of the group. Included in the culture there is often a well-defined technology associated directly with the deviation. Among many handicapped persons, such as the blind, the deaf, or the crippled, culture and social organization centers around a core problem of locomotion, communication, avoiding ubiquitous hazards in the environment, and earning a living. Drug addicts, as we have seen, are continually preoccupied with obtaining and building up a reserve supply of narcotics. In the case of prostitutes the basic function is pleasing the polymorphous sexual desires of men, and sexual technique in a broad sense becomes a basis for organization affiliation, status, and ranking of the women who follow this profession. Political radicals find their personal and group life dominated by the constant need to influence public opinion, communication, and legislative processes.

The Mores of Deviant Groups

In common with normal groups, deviant groups have morals and a morale of their own. The morals of deviant groups tend to be segmental and specialized rather than generally differentiated from those of other

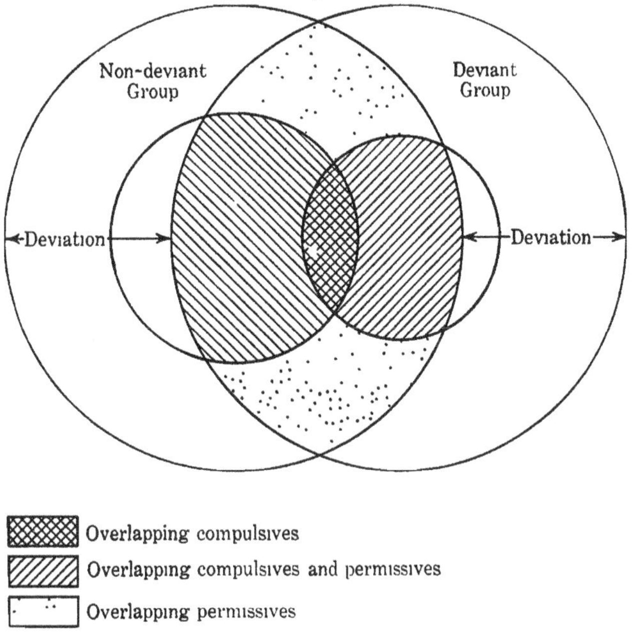

Fig. 2. Graphic representation of the moralities of two groups, deviant and non-deviant.

groups. As in normal groups it is possible to mark out a range of norms, embracing positive cultural compulsives, a spread or area of permissive behaviors, and at the other end of the hypothetical continuum a cluster of increasingly strong taboos. It is important to note that the mores of the deviant group overlap and coincide at many points with the mores of groups having more acceptable general status in the community. For example, professional shoplifters apparently have taboos against the use of narcotics which are at least as strong, if not stronger, than those found among law-abiding groups. The rationalizations for this common morality, of course, differ in the former case, the argument against using drugs is that a member of the organization when he is arrested can be forced too easily to divulge information if he is deprived of his narcotics by the police. Prostitutes or their managers may be just as insistent upon medical examinations and prophylaxis as military authorities but for the reason that it is "good business" to observe such safeguards. In other cases, differentiation simply amounts to a discrepancy between compulsives and permissives; what is tabooed behavior in one group is held to be permissible in another. Criminal groups tend to be indifferent to nonmarital sex indulgence rather than compel it, although there may be some disapproval of strong sexual attachments on the grounds that they are likely to impede the mobility or efficiency of the organization.

The accompanying figure attempts to give a graphic portrayal of the relationship of the moralities of two groups; it can be seen that there is a small area where the compulsive norms of the two groups are the same, represented by the double cross-hatched space. A much larger area of the compulsive behavior for the nondeviant group falls into the permissive zone of the deviant group. Below the double-cross hatched center of overlapping compulsives there is a third area of overlap in which the deviant compulsives are the less strongly sanctioned permissives of the conformist group. On either side of the center the speckled areas show congruity between the permissive norms of both groups. The unshaded areas represent pure deviation in two different directions. It should be stressed that the inner circle containing compulsive norms is not necessarily constant; it may be larger or smaller for both classes of groups. Likewise, the amount of total overlapping of the circles may be much greater or much smaller.

Morality of Deviant Groups Sometimes More Stringent Than That of Nondeviant Groups

The figure here indicates that a fairly wide area of compulsive behavior for the deviant group is only permissive for the nondeviant group. Oddly enough, this relationship holds true for many of the laws of the community. A deviant group with precarious status, such as a criminal group or a radical sect, continuously threatened by police action, apart from the crime they specialize in may actually conform more carefully than other groups to the general laws of the community. This is to avoid the ever-present possibility of being picked up and given a long sentence or a "bum rap" for the violation of some minor law. Indirect evidence of this is the fact that in recent years authorities have had to use income-tax violations as a means of imprisoning notorious criminals. Many political radicals and religious deviants, such as conscientious objectors, are very much conformist in areas of behavior outside the fields of their radicalism.[19] This is most likely due to the oblique way in which the community brings pressure to bear upon such persons. Because of the emphasis on freedom of

[19] Harper, R., "Is Conformity a General or a Specific Behavior Trait?" *American Sociological Review*, 12, February, 1947, pp. 81–86.

speech, a radical in our culture is often an awkward problem for those seeking to penalize him, hence is often attacked because of alleged sexual immorality or for technical violations of legal regulations rather than for his beliefs.

The Relationship of Deviation and the Societal Reaction

The degree of deviation shown by an individual or a group can be taken as a partial gauge of the probable societal reaction. Other things being equal or ignored, a particularly heinous crime will arouse more public action than a mild one, or an increase in the number of traffic offenses will cause more vigorous policing of the community. In order to predict societal reactions, techniques for estimating deviation are necessary. However, few efforts have been made to measure deviational behavior. Hypothetically, the sum total of deviation in a given situation will consist of the variance of the actions from prescribed social norms multiplied by the number of persons who engage in such actions. Measured or informally estimated in this way, the deviation in disapproved categories should be reciprocated by a comparatively intense reaction from the aggregates and groups whose sanctions have been violated. However, there are at least two other factors which interact with the gross deviation to condition the extent and nature of the societal reaction. One of these is the social visibility of the deviation.

Social Visibility

In order for deviation to provoke a community reaction, it must have a minimum degree of visibility, that is, it must be apparent to others and be identified as deviation, A vast amount of sexual deviation in our society is clandestine and consequently escapes the public eye, which is to say that it has a low visibility, a fact probably related to the puritanical background of our culture. This is not to say that no social influence is present, since the deviant in such cases may still, through the action of covert symbolic processes, imagine the reaction of "others" to his behavior and acquire feelings of guilt or anxiety. However, he or she does avoid the traumatic impact of public identification as an immoral person and also evades the sequence of differential reactions and penalty which follow such an identification.

Criminal statistics are generally held to be unreliable for the very reason that such a vast amount of crime escapes the notice and records of the law-enforcement agencies. Low-visibility crimes include hundreds of thousands of abortions, many sexual crimes, passing of counterfeit money, shortchanging of business patrons, confidence games, pocket picking, shoplifting, gambling, and many others.[20]

[20] Von Hentig, H., *Crime, Cause and Conditions*, 1947, p 21.

While many forms of criminal deviation remain concealed in our society, in other forms of deviation a high degree of visibility is present because of the intrinsic qualities of the behavior involved, because of the nature of the situation, or because of the physical and social characteristics of the persons involved. It is ordinarily believed that the misconduct of members of racial minorities receives more publicity than similar violations by majority-group persons. It has been the habit of many newspapers to call attention to the fact that a person committing a crime is a Negro or a Mexican, or an Indian, or an alien. This operates strongly to build up a stereotype of the group in question as being a criminally inclined "race" and thus heightens the societal reaction to their future violations. The low economic and unpropertied status of minority-group members means that they seldom appear as plaintiffs in civil and criminal proceedings and nearly always as defendants. This, too, heightens their visibility as deviants.

The member of an immigrant group living in an area not predominantly inhabited by persons of his own nationality is also likely to be more conspicuous when he transgresses the rules of society. The member of an upper social class is apt to have his behavior more carefully scrutinized for shortcomings when he is interacting with persons of low status than when he is with his compeers, although this probably varies a good deal.

A factor which has considerable effect in magnifying the visibility of any given deviation emerges from the adjustment which the deviants make to such a deviation. The adjustment consists of secondary, often habitual or unverbalized, responses which may be either compensatory in nature, or an integral part of a formalized deviant role. Reference intended here is to such things as the grimaces the stutterer makes in trying to speak, the bizarre posturings of crippled or blind persons, the mannerisms which the professional criminal elects to symbolize his difference from other members of society or from other criminals, or, finally, the flamboyant dress of the traditional prostitute.

Subtle Nature of Visibility in Certain Forms of Deviation

The exact way in which some deviation is perceived and just how it sets off a chain of social reactions are sometimes hard to explain. This is especially true of physical handicaps and, to a lesser extent, it seems to be true of deviants like homosexuals. The visible cues of physical defects enter into and complicate the empathic responses of normal persons in ways not entirely clear to us. Undoubtedly many of the symbols operating in the interaction between the physically handicapped and normal persons are implicit in gesture and posture. Evidence for this has been provided by an experiment in which action pictures of healthy and crippled children were shown to two hundred physically normal subjects. No reference was made to the fact that the pictures were of both crippled and normal children. Many of the handicapped children were not recognized as being crippled. The results of this test revealed that 60 per cent of the judgments of crippled children not identified as crippled were unfavorable, whereas the unfavorable judgments for the normal youngsters came to only 46 per cent.[21]

Apparently in the perception of certain types of deviation some sort of subliminal stimulation functions to disrupt or innervate the empathic responses and give meaning to the more formal societal reaction. Clearly this is an area needing much more research if our analysis is to be carried beyond the study of the formal, verbal phases of the societal reaction

Conclusion

In this chapter we have described deviation in its different aspects and in the different contexts in which it occurs. Careful attention was given to situational deviation, systematic deviation, and to the distinction between deviant and nondeviant moralities. Deviation was shown to be one of the factors, but not a direct determiner, of the societal reaction; the degree to which deviation is socially visible, for example, is an important intervening variable. An additional mediating factor between deviation and the societal reaction is patterned or institutionalized conflict between groups and their combinations. For a consideration of this and the societal reaction we now turn to the following chapter.

Selected Readings

Bain, R. "Culture Integration and Social Conflict," *American Journal of Sociology*, 44, January, 1939, pp. 499–509

Benedict, R. "Continuities and Discontinuities in Cultural Conditioning," *Psychiatry*, May, 1939, pp. 161–167.

Bernard, J. *American Family Behavior*, 1941, Chaps V–VI

Ford, C. S "Society, Culture and the Organism," *Journal of General Psychology*, 20, January, 1939, pp. 135–137

Gillin, J "Acquired Drives in Culture Contact," *American Anthropologist*, 44, October–December, 1942, pp. 454–465

LaPiere, R T, and P Farnsworth *Social Psychology*, 1949, rev 3rd ed, Chaps 19, 25.

Merton, R. K.. "Social Structure and Anomie," *American Sociological Review*, 3, October, 1938, pp 672–682

Mowrer, E. A : *Disorganization, Personal and Social*, 1942, Chaps I–III

[21] Winkler, H., *Psychische Entwicklung und Kruppeltum*, summarized in R G Barker *et al*, "Adjustment to Physical Handicap and Illness," Social Science Research Council *Bulletin* 55, 1946, p. 83.

CHAPTER 3

THE SOCIETAL REACTION

The socially visible deviations within a group, community, or society stir its members to a wide variety of expressive reactions and attitudes, depending upon the nature of the deviations and the expectancies of the conforming majority. Admiration, awe, envy, sympathy, fear, repulsion, disgust, hate, and anger are felt and manifested by those confronted by departures from their sanctioned ways of behaving. These are the elemental stuff from which the societal reaction is compounded.

The Pristine Form of the Societal Reaction

In informally organized groups and communities there is a direct and spontaneous quality in the societal reaction which tends to be immediately relevant to the deviation. This continues to be the case, even in more formally organized groups and communities, so long as there is a close correspondence between the informal and formal organizations. Under these conditions the societal reaction tends to be a pure function of the interaction of deviation and the norms of the group which are transgressed. Other things being equal, the societal reaction will reciprocate in intensity the degree, amount, and visibility of the deviation. Beyond these, the compulsiveness of the norms violated or deviated from interacts to limit the severity of the societal reaction. Given constants and similarity of deviation, the public reaction in two different communities will vary with the respective importance attached to norms covering the deviations.

To illustrate what has been said in the preceding paragraph, we may take drunkenness for our example. Ordinarily, when a man is brought into court on a charge of "drunk and disorderly," he is warned or lectured and his case is dismissed. However, subsequent offenses are apt to result in fines and jail sentences. Ultimately, if his alcoholic disturbances persist over a long period of time, he may be placed in an institution.

This is a common pattern of reaction to drunken misdemeanants in many American communities. But from one community to another there may be variations in the policy for dealing with drunken persons. Drunkenness is handled with differing amounts of leniency because of the varying conceptions of the importance of sobriety. Some communities do not arrest drunks at all, but hold them in protective custody until they are sober again. In communities with heavy contingents of foreign-born in the population, the public reactions to drunkenness may be mitigated by the receptive attitudes of these groups toward this behavior. On the other hand in many Methodist communities in Kansas and Mormon communities in Utah, we see much greater public disapproval of drunkenness than in most other American communities.

In pursuing the more complex aspects of the societal reaction, some distinction must be observed between "innovating" and "recurrent" deviations. A sociopathic deviation which is entirely new and for which there is no historical antecedent often leaves a group or society at a loss for effective means of coping with it. This has often been the case where alcoholic liquors have been introduced by white men into primitive societies, leading to drunkenness which heretofore had been outside the experience of the group. Under conditions such as these the members of the group must rely or fall back upon informal expressions of their disapproval. These reactions may make the deviants uncomfortable and distressed but they do not necessarily impair their formal status.

Recurrent deviations and the growth of a deviant population bring alterations in the culture and social organization of the community within which they occur. Mythologies, stigma, stereotypes, patterns of exploitation, accommodation, segregation, and methods of control spring up and crystallize in the interaction between the deviants and the rest of society. The informal societal reaction is extended and formalized in the routinized procedures of agents and agencies delegated with direct responsibility for penalizing and restraining or reforming the deviants. The status of the deviants is redefined, and special pariah roles may be assigned to them.

Spurious Qualities of the Societal Reaction

The simple factoring of the societal reaction which we have done thus far is not sufficient to explain its complexities in groups or societies where the close organic relation between the deviation and attitudinal responses to it is mediated by a chain of formal relationships. Out of these a greatly attenuated societal reaction may appear, even in cases where there has been extensive, visible deviation from highly compulsive norms. It is fairly easy to think of situations in which serious offenses against laws commanding public respect have brought only a mild penalty or have gone entirely unpunished. Conversely, cases are easily discovered in which a somewhat minor violation of legal rules has provoked surprisingly stringent penalties. The societal reaction, especially under the second condition, has a spurious quality out of proportion to the deviation which engendered it. This spurious surplus of the societal reaction results in an exaggeration and distortion of the facts of deviation, so that a large measure of the deviation becomes "putative." The putative deviation is that portion of the societal definition of the deviant which has no foundation in his objective behavior. Frequently these fallacious imputations are incorporated into myth and stereotype and mediate much of the formal treatment of the deviant. We shall find many examples of this in the folklore about various specific forms of deviation which are to be treated in later chapters. One quick illustration is the common belief in our culture that the taking of narcotic drugs disposes people to sexual depravity and criminality—beliefs for which there is little or no proof.

To take into our reckoning all the factors which produce disproportions in the reciprocal relationship between deviation and the societal reaction would carry us too far afield into the subjects of public opinion and social control. Let it suffice to mention a few of the factors involved and then dwell upon one of the more important of these. Such things as purely technical demands of formal procedure, lack of resources and personnel of control agencies, personal idiosyncrasies of the persons in power, the nature and jurisdiction of the authority held by formal community agencies and the bureaucratic encystment of such agencies, isolating them from public opinion, should all be counted as significant variables in the formal societal reaction.

A factor of supervening importance which very often introduces a spurious element in the societal reaction is the rivalry or conflict of groups in the situation as they aspire to power or struggle to maintain their position in a hegemony of power relations. In other words, the situation in which deviation is present becomes structured in conflict terms and values. This is not an uncommon occurrence in our culture. The institutionalization of conflict and factionalism as a means of intergroup adjustment frequently leads to an amplification of the societal reaction in the presence of minutiae of deviation. Trivial or insignificant departures from social norms are stimuli for hair-trigger public reactions, "storms of protest" and "controversies." Closer inspection of these reactions often reveals that a political alignment within the community is seeking to embarrass the party in power and has seized upon some otherwise unimportant deviant event — a crime or a license violation — for this purpose.

The phenomenon we have been describing here is repeatedly observed in the various "reform" movements which have swept urban politics in the United States. In such vice and crime cleanup drives it has often been the practice of police to arrest only amateur, "small-fry" offenders, or even to arrest members of minority ethnic groups and unemployed migratory workers at random, herding them into jails and holding them on meaningless charges. Older illustration of an almost purely spurious societal reaction in a different context is recorded in the history of New

Orleans after its occupation by Union troops during the Civil War. It seems that the commanding general of the Northern troops was much offended by what he regarded as the "insulting" treatment accorded Union officers by women in the town. Consequently he issued an order that any woman insulting a Yankee officer was to be liable to treatment as a common prostitute.[1]

The Tolerance Quotient

The complex of variables of which the societal reaction is a function can be summed up and expressed in the concept of the tolerance quotient. As formally stated, the concept appears to be a quantitative expression of deviation and the willingness of the community to accept or reject it.[2]

> It is . . . maintained that the sociologically important aspects of behavior along the various vectors of deviation from normal or approved conduct may be expressed as a tolerance quotient which is a ratio between the behavior in objective terms and the community's willingness to tolerate it, with a critical point for each case where the community in its corporate capacity goes into action.

This concept suggests to us the possibility of handling sociopathic deviation and the reaction to it in the community as a mathematical ratio or a fraction. The top of our fraction, the numerator, will be a measure of the amount of some disapproved conduct in a stated locality, the denominator will measure the degree of tolerance which the people in this locality have for the behavior in question. It is assumed that both numerator and denominator in this ratio may change, either by increasing or decreasing, or that one may change in either of these ways while the other remains unchanged. When, as a result of such changes, this ratio reaches a certain point, let us say 1 to 1, the people in the locality will begin to do something about the deviant behavior. They will hold public meetings, urge authorities to take action, or perhaps organize themselves into an action group to eradicate the undesirable behavior. This is the critical point in the tolerance quotient.

[1] The denouement of this action is also of some interest to students of deviation. The story goes that the actual prostitutes in New Orleans were more incensed by the order than the other female citizenry. According to the account they tore down pictures of the commanding general which had been posted in public places and pasted his portrait in the inside bottom of their "tinkle pots." Whereupon troops were dispatched to the houses of prostitution with orders to smash with hammers all tinkle pots having this unseemly decoration. See Asbury, Herbert, *The French Quarter*, 1938, pp. 225–228

[2] Van Vechten, C., "The Tolerance Quotient as a Device for Defining Certain Social Concepts," *American Journal of Sociology*, 46, July, 1940, pp. 35–42

The tolerance ratio can be the same for two communities even though the absolute (or rates of) deviation may differ widely from one another. The amount of drunkenness in one city may be quite high, while in another city of comparable size it may be quite low. Yet these two cities might have identical tolerance quotients because the tolerance would be high in the first community and low in the second. Crises over the "drunkenness problem" might arise in both cities, in the first caused by a lowering of tolerance, in the second, caused by an increase in cases of drunken behavior.

It would, of course, be pretentious to claim that we are in a position to apply this concept to our data in a rigorous quantitative fashion. Nevertheless, by schematically converting our thinking into this form, we achieve a great deal of insight into the relationship of the societal reaction to deviation. The comparison of community reactions to deviations is facilitated, as is also the analysis of linear or cyclical trends in the history of sociopathic behaviors. Perhaps in time this can be done in the strict quantitative manner suggested by the concept. However, we shall be content to employ the concept of the tolerance quotient as a schematic device in our subsequent discussions.

Sequence in the Societal Reaction

Despite the fact that when it first appears deviation can theoretically provoke approval, indifference, or disapproval, there is reason to believe that all innovations in behavior arouse some initial disapproval. The reason for this lies in the difficulty of immediately demonstrating the utility of the new behavior. Utility, is a function of understanding the deviation and is not always at once apparent to the great majority of people.[3] Thus in the past many inventions, such as anesthesia and vaccination, were resisted by the public and even by members of the medical profession itself. Another reason why early departures from customary ways of behaving are unfavorably received by society or groups is that they upset a system of reciprocity between groups, extending to groups and persons who receive no direct value from the innovation. Moreover, the normative or value-systems of individuals may be so strongly reified that variations from expected behavior automatically awaken hostile reactions.

Once an innovation in behavior occurs and takes hold of a sizable number of persons, a dynamic interplay is observable between it and the social situation in which it takes place. Presumably there is a patterning in the sequence of events associated with the societal reaction. At least in such things as reform movements in urban politics there seems to be a similarity sufficiently recognizable to justify the terms "sequence" or "cycle." One

[3] Mowrer, E., *Disorganization, Personal and Social*, 1942, p. 28.

attempt at analysis of the sequential aspects of communal reactions to disapproved behavior has been undertaken under the heading of "the natural history of a social problem." The deviation under consideration in this study was the appearance in Detroit, Michigan, of the pattern of family living in trailers and the growth of trailer camps in places where these families congregated and set up subcommunity organizations among themselves. The societal reaction to this new development was found to fall into three phases: (1) awareness, (2) policy determination, and (3) reform.

The time span between the first trailer-camp establishments and the peak of the community agitation and reaction to the "problem" was from ten to fifteen years. Visibility of the behavior was very low at first, then it tended to spread through geographic and social space until newspapers began to reflect the strong concern of many community groups at different social levels. As the hostility toward the inhabitants of these camps mounted, other groups were drawn into the situation, on the side of the trailer people as well as among their opponents. The chief advocates of the new behavior and defenders of the trailer dwellers were the companies manufacturing trailers and trailer equipment. Conflicts over policy gave rise to alignments of groups for and against various proposals to control the situation or to do away with the behavior. Finally, after a period of public controversy, the reaction to the "problem" tended to shift to an administrative level, with new ordinances and regulations put into effect by city and county officials. We are left to believe that the behavior which in its original form was disapproved of was finally integrated into the community culture.[4]

No One Sequence or Pattern in the Societal Reaction

While the analysis has much to commend it, there is some doubt as to whether it is a sufficient one. It is questionable whether the community reaction to variant behavior always follows the course and eventuates in the manner indicated by this research. The sequence described seems entirely too unilinear and mechanical. At least three possible end products of the community reaction are indicated: (1) ultimate acceptance of the variant behavior and its integration into the general, local, or special culture; (2) an unstable equilibrium or symbiotic relationship between the aberrant social organization and the normal; and (3) complete and unqualified rejection of the sociocultural novelty. The first alternative, which impressed the students of the Detroit situation, simply means that the deviation and societal reaction become a phase of social and cultural

[4] Fuller, R., and R Myers, "The Natural History of a Social Problem," *American Sociological Review*, 6, June, 1941, pp. 320–329.

change. History records many similar instances of this sort. Trailer housing is not only well established in given localities but is pretty well accepted throughout our entire society. The use of lipstick, rouge, silk stockings, and smoking and drinking were all once confined to women with low social status or to prostitutes, yet today they are universally sanctioned as normal behavior for women of all classes. The Republican and Democratic parties in the United States have promoted and passed legislation in recent years which was once condemned as being socialistic and communistic. The proposals for graduated income taxes and the income tax generally were held to be radical and subversive in principle when first proposed; nevertheless, today these taxes are regarded as necessary parts of our whole financial structure.

Unstable Equilibrium in the Societal Reaction

The second large alternative, societal reaction, seems to be present in conjunction with many of our historically old "social problems," such as pauperism and many kinds of crime and prostitution, the forms of which have their roots in our European cultural antecedents. The societal reaction to these sociopathic behaviors in many areas is a compound of acceptance and rejection, frequently manifesting itself as the tacit tolerance of variant social patterns coupled with a nominal or formal disapproval and rejection. In this case the waxing deviation seems to have been halted at a certain point, giving rise to a tenuous integration between it and the older, accepted social organization. A situation obtains in which community tolerance is precariously stabilized just short of a critical point in the tolerance quotient at which collective action is taken.

The impasse which is reached in the societal reaction is partly explained by generalized culture conflict which affects such a large majority of the population that little consistent action is possible. This can be seen in ambivalent attitudes toward such things as begging and gambling. In the latter case most people realize that it is a costly and meaningless form of behavior, but the attitude is complicated by the fact that most people have gambled at some time or another. Even our churches have utilized gambling to raise money. In other words, gambling is both situational and systematic deviation. Consequently, fears are easily awakened that controls set up to eliminate the systematic gambling will be applied to gambling in other contexts. Drawing up legislation which will penalize the unwanted deviation without jeopardizing the status of the numerous casual participants is exceedingly difficult.

Other forms of sociopathic behavior are strictly systematic, and a sharp distinction can be made between the minority of persons who participate in it and the majority who do not. Here the explanation of the truncated societal reaction must be sought in the structuring of group relationships and the distribution of power within the community. The socially disapproved behavior in question may stir up a fairly strong and constant desire in the community for change and reform, but its importance in a reciprocal economy of group relations makes it impossible to root it out and destroy it.

The Consequences of the Ties between Political, Economic, and Deviant Social Organization

A number of writers have made it clear that graft, corruption, vice, and the crime that goes with them in many American cities are fairly natural outgrowths of our social organization; that there is a necessary interdependence between economic, political, and criminal organization. The political party in our society is an extralegal development but obviously a very indispensable one. This can be explained by the fact that constitutional provisions originally localized and split up power into units and fractions in such a way as to make government unworkable without it. The party supplies the important unity and dynamic which make government move past dead-center equilibrium and function in a positive manner. In many areas the political party has come to depend for financial support upon campaign contributions made by criminal as well as by reputable business agencies. Businessmen usually make donations to the politicians because they are dependent upon them for licenses to operate, for fair or favorable tax assessments, and more directly for lucrative contracts let by the government for materials and services. The collective efforts of the community through civic reform groups to stamp out crime and vice are resisted by politicians and by businessmen who are beholden to them. Moreover, business establishments often profit directly or indirectly from illegal activities and consequently are not anxious to see their sources of revenue disturbed. Telephone and telegraph companies have been known to make large profits through leasing special wires to gamblers, and in many cities owners of real estate in vice areas have received handsome rents for their properties from proprietors of houses of prostitution.[5]

Figure 3 is a graphic representation in hypothetical form of the nexus of social relationships which directly or indirectly ties criminal and vice organization in with the other groups in a community. In such a social integration aggressive attacks by any one group upon another are bound to have repercussions upon all, the strength of these repercussions depending upon the number and importance of the patterns of reciprocity be-

[5] For a good discussion of political corruption, see Elliott, M., and F. Merill, *Social Disorganization*, 1941, Chaps 22–23; also White, C., *Street Corner Society*, 1943, Part IV

tween the different groups. A strong community reaction against deviant groups tends to become blurred and distorted as a result of the resistances that progressively build up against it. A chain of compromises is struck, and the societal reaction in effect simmers down to a regulation of the deviation. This means that the worst features of the deviation are eliminated in response to public dissatisfaction and its visibility is reduced.

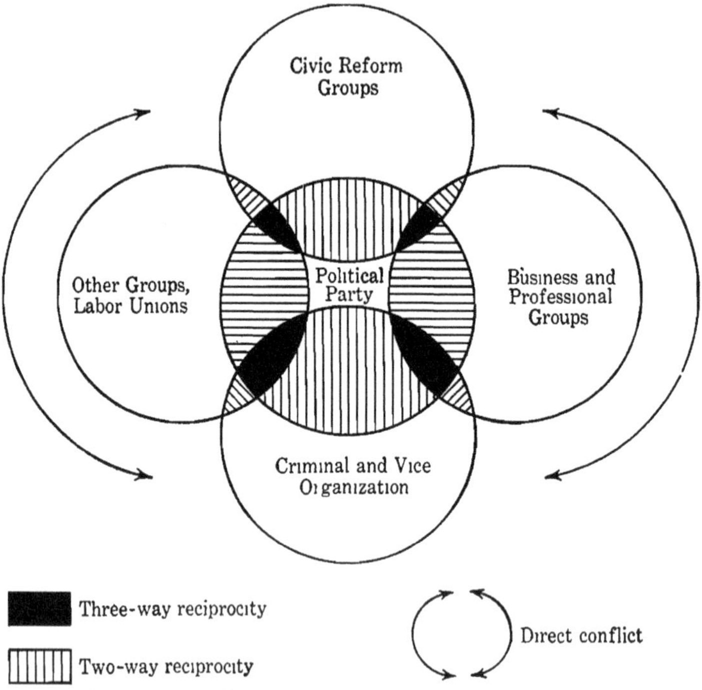

FIG. 3. Interrelationships of sociopathic and nonsociopathic groups within a community setting.

Informal status and responsibility are conferred upon the deviants along with their spatial segregation within the community. The practice of sealing off areas of sociopathic culture within urban communities in the past created such notorious districts as the Barbary Coast in San Francisco, the French Quarter in New Orleans, the Bowery in New York, and Over the Rhine in Cincinnati. It is much more difficult to find spatial reflections of pathological deviations in present-day cities, at least in the picturesque forms in which they once existed. Generally, in recent years trends toward the decentralization of vice and crime have taken place in response to the regionalization of urban populations. Vice resorts and criminal activities have moved out to the peripheries and hinterlands of the large cities. Along with such developments the social visibility of these forms of behavior has been considerably diminished so that they can diffuse into respectable residential zones without undue fear of detection.

"Reform" Movements

The instability of the accommodations worked out between outcast organizations and the rest of the community can easily be exploited by political or other groups seeking to better their status within the local social system. Newspapers have been known to heighten the social visibility of pathological activities for the purpose of increasing circulation and advertising revenue. These facts inject a large measure of inconsistency and oscillation into the societal reaction in the guise of "clean-up" drives by police against vice and crime or in the shape of "reform" movements to eradicate political graft and corruption. More often than not the police drives prove to be abortive; they are only nominal gestures and disappear with the subsidence in the public clamor for better law enforcement. With few exceptions political and social reform movements in urban communities have done little to alter the fundamental patterns of reciprocity between legal and illegal groups. Men who have come into office on a program of reform have in turn been ousted on charges similar to those which led to the downfall of their predecessors. The oscillation in the societal reaction is one of the factors which condition deviant personalities and organization. For example, racketeers and other criminals learn to anticipate the ups and downs of law enforcement and adjust themselves and their group function accordingly. Techniques for meeting the "crises" are perfected and incorporated into the deviant culture.

Complete Repression of Deviation

The third and final outcome of the societal reaction leads to complete rejection and actual or attempted repression of deviant conduct. When the norms violated are highly compulsive and universal in the culture, then efforts converging from many directions will be made to eliminate the variant behavior and to smash any organization which may be associated with it. The reaction to incest in many preliterate societies is to put the offenders to death. The contemporary reaction to murder, drug addiction, and to many sex crimes comes close to being one of unmitigated repression. The reaction to horse stealing on our Western frontier was one of unqualified hostility and stern repression. Underground radical and revolutionary or resistance groups in European countries have at times been ruthlessly hunted down and destroyed. Polygyny, at least in most areas where it existed, was stamped out in the United States. Being the target for harsh persecution undoubtedly modifies the role and status of deviants and their social organization in many ways. One of the important research needs in this connection is to discover, if possible, crucial points of human beings and organizations under severe stress at which they break and undergo demoralization and disintegration.

Isolating and Segregating Reactions

Certain corollary processes are common to the last two of the above-mentioned societal reactions; first of all, if the deviant behavior persists for any length of time, stereotyped stigmas tend to be attached to the deviant along with societal definitions of the deviant and his or her putative role. Often it is possible to distinguish a definite folklore and mythology built up around the deviant in the oral tradition and literature of the society which rejects him. An integral part of this is the body of rationalizations which are employed to justify the rejections and penalties inflicted upon the deviant as a result of the societal reaction. The societal definitions may not exist in all cases, or they may be only vaguely formulated or even contradictory and ambivalent. In any event it is assumed that where societal definitions do appear they become deeply laden with emotions and meanings. These serve to define the deviant's expected behavior in social interaction, and they become the reciprocal of the individual deviant's own self-definition.

Social Distance between Deviants and Others

Closely connected with the societal definition and a phase of the societal reactions of nonacceptance and isolation is the growth of social distance. This concept has been used in two ways by sociologists: one meaning has to do with the degree of *felt* intimacy between groups or between individuals, the other has signified the degree of intimacy between groups or individuals as measured by objective indexes of exclusiveness, such as actual rates of intermarriage or exclusion from membership in various groups. Generally, the testing of the social-distance concept has been done in the field of race relations and in the study of interpersonal interaction, employing the methods of sociometry. Application of these techniques to the measurement of social distance between deviants and society has been rather scant, with the exception of studies of the physically handicapped. Even here it is questionable whether the research studies can rightly be called "social-distance" studies; more often they are "social-attitude" surveys phrased in terms of attitudes of liking and disliking toward the handicapped. One such study is reproduced in the following table.

Table 1 Percentage Distribution of Attitudes of 3,000 Men toward Persons with Certain Types of Distinguishing Physical Characteristics*

Distinguishing traits	Liking	Disliking	Indifferent
Very old people	45	11	44
Cripples ..	29	13	58
Foreigners	25	14	61
Blind people	25	16	59
Sick people	22	28	50
Deaf mutes	16	25	59
Negroes	13	32	55
People with protruding jaws	6	42	52
People with hooked noses	4	38	58
People with gold teeth	4	46	50
Side-show freaks	4	77	19

* Cited in Barker, R. G., *et al.*, "Adjustments to Physical Handicap and Illness," Social Science Research Council *Bulletin* 55, 1946, p. 186.

The difficulty in using attitudes of liking and disliking as indexes of social distance is that persons may like differentiated classes but still feel no intimacy with them in so far as mutual social participation is concerned. Liking and disliking are patently attitudinal correlates of social distance, but we may question whether they are its determiners. Strong liking for a class of persons may nevertheless be associated with a wide variety of isolating reactions by persons who profess the attitude, and it is also true that hostilities may be covered up with sentimental overtures of acceptance toward handicapped persons. Blind persons are a case in point. Another complicating fact is that close interpersonal relationships flourish between sociopathic deviants and nondeviants, with the social distance appearing only in certain types of situations. So, for example, social workers often have a warm personal regard, even a maternalistic affection, for their clients, but for professional reasons would not risk inviting them into their homes. For these reasons it is probably best to reserve the term "social distance" to designate the degree of intimacy between persons and groups in formal or public situations; otherwise, a distinction must be maintained between "public" and "personal" social distance.

The Exploitative Culture

The sociopathic deviant, because of his or her extralegal, ambiguous, or weakly delimited status, or because of aspirations to "normal" status, often becomes the object of exploitation. Historically, hunchbacks, crippled persons, mentally deficient people, and stutterers in many places were made court jesters, entertainers, or became tools of beggars. The rise of

Protestantism and the "Protestant ethic" appears to have opened the way for the harsh exploitation of dependent children under the pretext of apprenticeship training and education in middle-class virtues, a tradition that has retained a remarkable vitality in Anglo-Saxon cultures. At different periods in American history, following wars, discharged soldiers have been shamelessly duped and relieved of their money by gamblers, prostitutes, amusement proprietors, lawyers, and "business" promoters. A lengthy volume could be devoted exclusively to the sharp practices used to deprive American Indians of their land, furs, minerals, and any other wealth they managed to accumulate. During periods of heavy immigration many foreigners were first introduced to this country by dishonest operators who sold them worthless articles and services, profited exorbitantly from their labor and investments, and in some cases inducted their women into prostitution.

In our present-day, highly competitive, commercialized society a special exploitative culture surrounds a wide variety of deviants. Physically ill persons as well as the crippled, obese, and ugly, the aged and widowed, ex-convicts and aliens are all preyed upon by fraudulent persons and organizations. Patent-medicine and appliance manufacturers, quack doctors, faith healers, cultists, various "schools" and "hospitals" and "charities" through sales, fees, solicitations, and "tuition" garner a rich pecuniary harvest from their activities. An estimate places the number of persons treating illness apart from the medical profession at 36,000 and the costs of the "treatment" administered by this group at $125,000,000.[6] Exploitation perhaps reaches its height in our society in the activities of various "psychological consultants" who profess to cure the ailments of neurotic and psychotic persons. One radio program devoted to the emotional travails of unsophisticated participants is supposed to have earned, directly or indirectly, for the person responsible over a million dollars, besides helping to sell the commerial product of the sponsor.[7]

Tentative Generalizations about Exploitation

There has been little that could be called systematic sociological research touching upon the exploitation of sociopathic deviants. Generalizations on the subject perforce have to be impressionistic and informal in nature, with the need for better conceptualization and careful testing being obvious. In many instances the persons or groups doing the exploiting are themselves in a socially questionable or disapproved category, *i.e.*, they are themselves sociopathic deviants. It is a fair conclusion that the precariousness of the status of this class of exploiters has an immediate

[6] Reed, L. S., *The Healing Cults*, 1932

[7] Steiner, L., *Where Do People Take Their Troubles?* 1945, p. 59.

bearing upon the avariciousness and ruthlessness with which they exploit those persons who must depend upon them. The abortionist who performs an illegal operation upon a prostitute generally has a less acceptable status than his patient. Under such circumstances, assuming both deviants are not part of the same vice organization, there will be few if any bounds to the exploitation, and the person who is the victim has few recourses to law or public opinion. In contrast to this, a vast amount of exploitation is carried on by persons with approved status, either under the cover of business enterprise or as an integral part of it. Some doctors are not above treating people for nonexistent diseases or recommending unnecessary operations. Realtors in some cases have few compunctions about charging exorbitant rents to persons using their properties for immoral or illegal purposes.

Some exploitative techniques make much use of propaganda and publicity which is contrived, often in a most subtle manner, to play upon the fears and unrealistic hopes of handicapped and socially declassed persons. The objective in the majority of these cases is to "hook the sucker," sell him or her worthless, unneeded, or harmful goods and services for as much as the traffic will bear, or to use crude coercive devices such as extortion or blackmail. In the operation of exploitative "schools," hospitals, and "institutes," the common element seems to be working to achieve the largest possible volume of business and quick turnover of clientele. Complaints are likely to be few, and it is easy to handle them by arguing that the person treated "didn't follow the method" or "didn't use the contrivance correctly." Rationalizations of the exploitation of the deviant are easy to formulate, because of the inconsistencies within our culture. It is interesting to note that many of the quacks and charlatans in our society believe their own rationalizations – a reflection of the tendency for them to become increasingly isolated and differentiated.

From the standpoint of this volume, it is of special interest to know the circumstances under which the deviant is subjected to exploitation and also the number of exploitative experiences he has had. What is the average impact of exploitation upon deviant persons and deviant organizations? What happens to the human personality after a long series of exploitative episodes? For example, what range of reaction patterns develop in orphan children as the result of being overworked in a series of farm-home placements? What possible distortion, if any, occurs in the illegitimate girl from the presumptive sexual advances of men when she reaches adolescence? How does a feeble-minded boy feel when he comes to realize that he is being paid less for the same work than other workers, or when he realizes he is being made the dupe for a gang of petty criminals? What of the deaf person who begins to suspect that his "operation" never had a chance for success from the very first? Is exploitation demoralizing or does it strengthen and confirm variant behavior tendencies? How much does it contribute to the isolation of the deviant?

THE SOCIETAL CONTROL CULTURE

Another set of impacts upon the pathological social variant springs from the various agencies, both private and public, which society or the community has organized to aid, repress, rehabilitate, or otherwise deal with its "problems." These agencies are more or less formally organized and collectively sanctioned as bearing immediate responsibility for the manipulation of outcast and handicapped persons and groups. Ostensibly, these agencies have devised programs which serve the needs of both society and persons falling within their province of treatment or jurisdiction. Presumably their programs are based upon rational knowledge and competent administration. In reality, the publicized functions of many such organizations are a far cry from their real functions; accomplishments proclaimed in their annual reports are hard to prove or disprove. Such reports sometimes are far more like "window dressing" to obtain public support than genuinely self-critical analyses of agency activities. What is behind the reports is left to our imagination. Agencies and institutions have a private as well as a public history, but the former, thanks to careful attention to public relations and publicity, seldom becomes common knowledge.

Not only do many reform and rehabilitative institutions in our society fail to demonstrate scientifically that their work actually accomplishes what is claimed for it, but their staffs would be hard put to prove that their efforts did not have effects opposite from what was intended. Many of the social-welfare policies of post-Elizabethan England and nineteenth-century United States created as many pauperized individuals as they eliminated. Public policies governing venereal disease in the United States may have had the partial effect of increasing the number of cases of infection and may produce interruptions of treatment and procrastination. Some observers are inclined to the belief that treatment in our mental hospitals precipitates psychoses in many patients and fixes or aggravates the emotional disturbances of others. Certainly it is not hard to show that our penology and administrative policies toward criminals are important factors in recidivism.

THE OBJECTIVES OF CONTROL AGENCIES DEALING WITH DEVIANTS

The objectives of social control instituted by agencies dealing with pathological persons and groups may be clearly and systematically formulated, or on the other hand they may be vague or contradictory. The degree to which clarity is achieved in agency policy and function will show up in the effectiveness of the control it exercises over persons with whom it has dealings. The fraud and cynicism among the clients of nineteenth- and early twentieth-century charity organizations were pretty much a response to the vacillatory sentimental indulgence and smug superarrogance of the middle-class persons who sponsored them. A strong counteraction to vagueness in the rationale for social work has arisen in the modern philosophy of "functionalism," which seeks the sharp demarcation of the general and special fields of social work from society's other institutions.

The crystallized thinking of control agencies includes theories of causation of human behavior which inevitably enter into and condition their functions or their interaction with their special "problem" clientele. Many agencies in our society are strongly biased in favor of theories of individual causation and not infrequently make the error of treating situational and systematic deviation as if it were all a manifestation of isolated individual behavior. In other instances institutional policies are conceived with no allowance whatever for individual variation. We see this most frequently in law-enforcement agencies and tax-supported agencies.

The Relationship of the Control Agency to the Larger Social Structure a Factor in Its Activities and Policies

The peculiar way in which a control agency is tied into the general social structure of the community or society sets a pattern for its activity and does much to shape its over-all policy. It is generally believed, for example, that private welfare agencies are able to organize along less rigid lines than public welfare agencies. The argument runs that they are also able to administer their policies in a more flexible way and that they are freer to experiment with new ideas and methods. It is well known that community pressures may compel control agencies to stress protective and security functions over and above, and perhaps to the exclusion of, treatment and rehabilitation of their clientele. Likewise, public niggardliness on the part of legislatures may result in such low appropriations that agency functions degenerate into purely custodial care or mere dole. Furthermore, statutes may regulate the degree to which an agency may intrude itself into the aberrant person's life and also specify the duration of an agency's jurisdiction over clients. Thus the exposure of the deviant person to a special socializing process can vary greatly from one agency to another. Contacts and control may range from the all-inclusive, totalitarian control within an institution, such as a foster home, reformatory, or mental hospital, to the transitory, limited services provided by a traveler's aid society.

It should be emphasized that the relationship between agencies of social control and the over-all society are not uniformly stable and enduring.

Agencies, especially in the public domain, have their ups and downs where public support is concerned. Many are, or have been, laid open to attacks from this group and that. Some have become political "footballs" or public "whipping boys." The effects of these public aggressions and abortive attempts at administrative reform and reorganization can be seen in the condition of agency morale and in the organizational characteristics of the agencies. These, in turn, have significant effects upon the socialization of the deviants who come under their authority.

Sociological Analysis of "Therapy" Needed

Much is needed in the way of scientific analysis of clinical or therapeutic situations and processes within the setting of clinics, hospitals, special schools, and other control agencies. Until this whole field of therapy has been explored systematically and some sociological light shed upon it, efforts at the control and rehabilitation of pathological deviants will necessarily remain at a primitive level. Studies of this sort will have to be formulated in such a manner as to facilitate objective comparisons between various therapeutic procedures in the light of the social and cultural demands being made upon the client in the situation. Thus, instead of partisan controversies over the universal merits of various applied psychological theories and instead of the cultlike division of field workers into "schools" of thought, there should materialize an easy ability of these workers to adopt methods relevant to the nature and extent of the sociopathic deviation with which they are working.

The Symbolic Consequences of Control

Among the unanticipated consequences of therapy, treatment, or administrative manipulations, none are more important than those which are symbolic in nature. More and more we are coming to realize that the actual symbolic impact of a control or therapeutic experience often is a far cry from what has been intended. The way in which a social worker, a psychiatrist, or a judge conceives of his own role and the meaning of the administrative or clinical situation for the deviant may or may not coincide with the average or modal perception of the latter. If we are to understand in a worth-while way the reactions of deviants brought under societal control we must get at the effective rather than the formal or intended symbols in control situations. They are not the whole of the symbolic environment in which deviation develops, but they make up a very significant part of it. Frequently they are instrumental in giving unintended but critical meanings to deviant conduct. Court hearings, home investigations by social workers, arrests, clinical visits, segregation within the school system and other formal dispositions of deviants under the aegis of public welfare or public protection in many instances are cause for dramatic redefinitions of the self and role of deviants which may or may not be desired.

Sociological Questions about Control Agencies

A start in the scientific study of the social control of sociopathic deviants can be made through employing a series of exploratory sociological questions. It is assumed that these will aid us to bring out factors relevant to the collective and individual reactions of deviants. These questions are not intended as norms for an ethical critique of society's welfare and protective agencies but rather as guides for research. We intend to use them for depicting and analyzing the administrative impact of the societal reaction upon those who are the subjects of control. The questions are as follows:

1. How many areas of social participation of the deviant or deviants are controlled?
2. What is the intensity of the withdrawal symptoms occasioned by entrance of deviants into the area of control exercised by the agency?
3. What is the degree of physical and social isolation produced by control over the deviants? Is the isolation symbolized? If so, how?
a. How does this apply to the agents of control involved: prison guards, ward attendants, police, psychiatrists, social workers, clinicians, physicians, and teachers? Are they likewise isolated? How do their roles color and give specific meaning to the more general societal reaction?
b. How does the relation of the agency to the larger society and its own internal structure affect the amount of isolation?
4. To what extent is a social microcosm created in the control experience?
5. To what extent are control contacts and interaction an integrated set of experiences? Is conflict kept at a minimum or is it allowed to function roughly in proportion to its functioning outside the control area?
6. Where clinical therapy is used, what effects does it have in terms of self-definitions, self-help, and dependence? Is communication established? How well are therapeutic facilities correlated with the client's needs in time?
7. How much instability and inconsistency are there in the agency functioning which are caused by internal disruptive and external intrusive factors?
8. What opportunity exists for the development of deviant social organization within the framework of the agency organization? What use, if any, is made of it where it exists?
9. Are patterns of control (*a*) Authoritative? (*b*) Democratic?
10. After contacts and interaction with societal-control agencies what opportunities exist for the entrance of deviants into groups from which they were formerly excluded? What groups now exclude the deviants as a result of contacts with the control agency?

Conclusion

In this chapter we have dealt with the ways in which groups, communities, and whole societies react to forms of disapproved behavior and to persons who engage in it. The hypothesis of a "natural history" of social problems (*i.e.*, a natural history of the deviation-reaction process) was examined and rejected in favor of several possibilities in so far as the course of the societal reaction goes. Exploitation of deviants was briefly discussed, and a theoretical prospectus for sociological study of society's control agencies was presented. We are thus to some degree equipped theoretically to go on to Chap. 4 to see how the societal reaction impinges upon the deviant person and sets the limits for his individuation along sociopathic lines.

Selected Readings

ELLIOTT, M., and F. MERILL *Social Disorganization*, 1941, Chap 32

FULLER, R. G., and R. MYERS "The Natural History of a Social Problem," *American Sociological Review*, 6, June, 1941, pp. 320–329.

GOSNELL, H F. *Machine Politics, Chicago Model*, 1937

STEINER, L *Where Do People Take Their Troubles?*, 1945.

VAN RIPER, C. *Principles of Speech Correction*, 1947, rev, Chap. 1, "The Handicapped in Society"

VAN VECHTEN, C. "The Tolerance Quotient As a Device for Defining Certain Social Concepts," *American Journal of Sociology*, 46, July, 1940, pp 35–42

WHYTE, W F *Street Corner Society*, 1943, Part II, Chaps 4, 5, 6, and pp 98–104

CHAPTER 4

SOCIOPATHIC INDIVIDUATION

The deviant person is a product of differentiating and isolating processes. Some persons are individually differentiated from others from the time of birth onward, as in the case of a child born with a congenital physical defect or repulsive appearance, and as in the case of a child born into a minority racial or cultural group. Other persons grow to maturity in a family or in a social class where pauperism, begging, or crime are more or less institutionalized ways of life for the entire group. In these latter instances the person's sociopsychological growth may be normal in every way, his status as a deviant being entirely caused by his maturation within the framework of social organization and culture designated as "pathological" by the larger society. This is true of many delinquent children in our society.[1]

> It is a matter of great significance that the delinquent child, growing up in the delinquency areas of the city, has very little access to the cultural heritages of the larger conventional society. His infrequent contacts with this larger society are for the most part formal and external. Quite naturally his conception of moral values is shaped and molded by the moral code prevailing in his play groups and the local community in which he lives ... the young delinquent has very little appreciation of the meaning of the traditions and formal laws of society. ... Hence the conflict between the delinquent and the agencies of society is, in its broader aspects, a conflict of divergent cultures.

The same sort of gradual, unconscious process which operates in the socialization of the deviant child may also be recognized in the acquisition of socially unacceptable behavior by persons after having reached adulthood. However, with more verbal and sophisticated adults, step-by-step violations of societal norms tend to be progressively rationalized in the light of what is socially acceptable. Changes of this nature can take place at the level of either overt or covert behavior, but with a greater likelihood that adults will preface overt behavior changes with projective symbolic departures from society's norms. When the latter occur, the subsequent overt changes may appear to be "sudden" personality modifications. However, whether these changes are completely radical ones is to some extent a moot point. One writer holds strongly to the opinion that sudden and

[1] Shaw, C, *The Natural History of a Delinquent Career*, Chicago, 1941, pp. 75–76 Quoted by permission of the University of Chicago Press, Chicago.

dramatic shifts in behavior from normal to abnormal are seldom the case, that a sequence of small preparatory transformations must be the prelude to such apparently sudden behavior changes. This writer is impressed by the day-by-day growth of "reserve potentialities" within personalities of all individuals, and he contends that many normal persons carry potentialities for abnormal behavior, which, given proper conditions, can easily be called into play.[2]

Personality Changes Not Always Gradual

This argument is admittedly sound for most cases, but it must be taken into consideration that traumatic experiences often speed up changes in personality.[3] Nor can the "trauma" in these experiences universally be attributed to the unique way in which the person conceives of the experience subjectively. Cases exist to show that personality modifications can be telescoped or that there can be an acceleration of such changes caused largely by the intensity and variety of the social stimulation. Most soldiers undoubtedly have entirely different conceptions of their roles after intensive combat experience. Many admit to having "lived a lifetime" in a relatively short period of time after they have been under heavy fire in battle for the first time. Many generals have remarked that their men have to be a little "shooted" or "blooded" in order to become good soldiers. In the process of group formation, crises and interactional amplification are vital requisites to forging true, role-oriented group behavior out of individuated behavior.[4]

The importance of the person's conscious symbolic reactions to his or her own behavior cannot be overstressed in explaining the shift from normal to abnormal behavior or from one type of pathological behavior to another, particularly where behavior variations become systematized or structured into pathological roles. This is not to say that conscious choice is a determining factor in the differentiating process. Nor does it mean that the awareness of the self is a purely conscious perception. Much of the process of self-perception is doubtless marginal from the point of view of consciousness.[5] But however it may be perceived, the individual's self-definition is closely connected with such things as self-acceptance, the subordination of minor to major roles, and with the motivation involved in learning the skills, techniques, and values of a new role. *Self-definitions or self-realizations are likely to be the result of sudden perceptions and they are especially significant when they are followed imme-*

[2] Brown, L. Guy, *Social Pathology*, 1942, pp 44–45
[3] Allport, G., *Personality, A Psychological Interpretation*, 1947, p 57
[4] Slavson, S. R., *An Introduction to Group Psychotherapy*, 1943, pp. 10, 229*ff*.
[5] Murphy, G , *Personality*, 1947, p 482

diately by overt demonstrations of the new role they symbolize. The self-defining junctures are critical points of personality genesis and in the special case of the atypical person they mark a division between two different types of deviation.

Primary and Secondary Deviation

There has been an embarrassingly large number of theories, often without any relationship to a general theory, advanced to account for various specific pathologies in human behavior. For certain types of pathology, such as alcoholism, crime, or stuttering, there are almost as many theories as there are writers on these subjects. This has been occasioned in no small way by the preoccupation with the origins of pathological behavior and by the fallacy of confusing *original* causes with *effective* causes. All such theories have elements of truth, and the divergent viewpoints they contain can be reconciled with the general theory here if it is granted that original causes or antecedents of deviant behaviors are many and diversified. This holds especially for the psychological processes leading to similar pathological behavior, but it also holds for the situational concomitants of the initial aberrant conduct. A person may come to use excessive alcohol not only for a wide variety of subjective reasons but also because of diversified situational influences, such as the death of a loved one, business failure, or participating in some sort of organized group activity calling for heavy drinking of liquor. Whatever the original reasons for violating the norms of the community, they are important only for certain research purposes, such as assessing the extent of the "social problem" at a given time or determining the requirements for a rational program of social control. From a narrower sociological viewpoint the deviations are not significant until they are organized subjectively and transformed into active roles and become the social criteria for assigning status. The deviant individuals must react symbolically to their own behavior aberrations and fix them in their sociopsychological patterns. The deviations remain primary deviations or symptomatic and situational as long as they are rationalized or otherwise dealt with as functions of a socially acceptable role. Under such conditions normal and pathological behaviors remain strange and somewhat tensional bedfellows in the same person. Undeniably a vast amount of such segmental and partially integrated pathological behavior exists in our society and has impressed many writers in the field of social pathology.

Just how far and for how long a person may go in dissociating his sociopathic tendencies so that they are merely troublesome adjuncts of normally conceived roles is not known. Perhaps it depends upon the number of alternative definitions of the same overt behavior that he can develop, perhaps certain physiological factors (limits) are also involved. However, if the deviant acts are repetitive and have a high visibility, and if there is a severe societal reaction, which, through a process of identification is incorporated as part of the "me" of the individual, the probability is greatly increased that the integration of existing roles will be disrupted and that reorganization based upon a new role or roles will occur. (The "me" in this context is simply the subjective aspect of the societal reaction.) Reorganization may be the adoption of another normal role in which the tendencies previously defined as "pathological" are given a more acceptable social expression. The other general possibility is the assumption of a deviant role, if such exists; or, more rarely, the person may organize an aberrant sect or group in which he creates a special role of his own. *When a person begins to employ his deviant behavior or a role based upon it as a means of defense, attack, or adjustment to the overt and covert problems created by the consequent societal reaction to him, his deviation is secondary.* Objective evidences of this change will be found in the symbolic appurtenances of the new role, in clothes, speech, posture, and mannerisms, which in some cases heighten social visibility, and which in some cases serve as symbolic cues to professionalization.

Role Conceptions of the Individual Must Be Reinforced by Reactions of Others

It is seldom that one deviant act will provoke a sufficiently strong societal reaction to bring about secondary deviation, unless in the process of introjection the individual imputes or projects meanings into the social situation which are not present. In this case anticipatory fears are involved. For example, in a culture where a child is taught sharp distinctions between "good" women and "bad" women, a single act of questionable morality might conceivably have a profound meaning for the girl so indulging. However, in the absence of reactions by the person's family, neighbors, or the larger community, reinforcing the tentative "bad-girl" self-definition, it is questionable whether a transition to secondary deviation would take place. It is also doubtful whether a temporary exposure to a severe punitive reaction by the community will lead a person to identify himself with a pathological role, unless, as we have said, the experience is highly traumatic. Most frequently there is a progressive reciprocal relationship between the deviation of the individual and the societal reaction, with a compounding of the societal reaction out of the minute accretions in the deviant behavior, until a point is reached where ingrouping and outgrouping between society and the deviant is manifest.[6] At this

[6] Mead, G., "The Psychology of Punitive Justice," *American Journal of Sociology*, 23, March, 1918, pp. 577–602

point a stigmatizing of the deviant occurs in the form of name calling, labeling, or stereotyping.

The sequence of interaction leading to secondary deviation is roughly as follows: (1) primary deviation; (2) social penalties; (3) further primary deviation; (4) stronger penalties and rejections; (5) further deviation, perhaps with hostilities and resentment beginning to focus upon those doing the penalizing; (6) crisis reached in the tolerance quotient, expressed in formal action by the community stigmatizing of the deviant; (7) strengthening of the deviant conduct as a reaction to the stigmatizing and penalties; (8) ultimate acceptance of deviant social status and efforts at adjustment on the basis of the associated role.

As an illustration of this sequence the behavior of an errant schoolboy can be cited. For one reason or another, let us say excessive energy, the schoolboy engages in a classroom prank. He is penalized for it by the teacher. Later, due to clumsiness, he creates another disturbance and again he is reprimanded. Then, as sometimes happens, the boy is blamed for something he did not do. When the teacher uses the tag "bad boy" or "mischief maker" or other invidious terms, hostility and resentment are excited in the boy, and he may feel that he is blocked in playing the role expected of him. Thereafter, there may be a strong temptation to assume his role in the class as defined by the teacher, particularly when he discovers that there are rewards as well as penalties deriving from such a role. There is, of course, no implication here that such boys go on to become delinquents or criminals, for the mischief-maker role may later become integrated with or retrospectively rationalized as part of a role more acceptable to school authorities.[7] If such a boy continues this unacceptable role and becomes delinquent, the process must be accounted for in the light of the general theory of this volume. There must be a spreading corroboration of a sociopathic self-conception and societal reinforcement at each step in the process.

The most significant personality changes are manifest when societal definitions and their subjective counterpart become generalized. When this happens, the range of major role choices becomes narrowed to one general class.[8] This was very obvious in the case of a young girl who was the daughter of a paroled convict and who was attending a small Middle Western college. She continually argued with herself and with the author, in whom she had confided, that in reality she belonged on the "other side of the railroad tracks" and that her life could be enormously simplified by acquiescing in this verdict and living accordingly. While in her case

[7] Evidence for fixed or inevitable sequences from predelinquency to crime is absent. Sutherland, E. H., *Principles of Criminology*, 1939, 4th ed , p 202.

[8] Sutherland seems to say something of this sort in connection with the development of criminal behavior *Ibid.*, p. 86.

there was a tendency to dramatize her conflicts, nevertheless there was enough societal reinforcement of her self-conception by the treatment she received in her relationship with her father and on dates with college boys to lend it a painful reality. Once these boys took her home to the shoddy dwelling in a slum area where she lived with her father, who was often in a drunken condition, they abruptly stopped seeing her again or else became sexually presumptive.

Social Participation – Alternatives and Choices

Given a person who has identified with a general class of people held undesirable by society at large, what explains his or her selection of a specific role within the broader range of pathological behavior patterns? Again, what factors operate in the selection of approved or disapproved roles subsidiary to the major role? In dealing with these rhetorical questions it is well to dispense with the deterministic logic explicit and implicit in much statistical analysis, or at least restate it in another form. The human personality, whether it is normal or abnormal, has to be understood as a dynamic, creative, choice-making organism. Human behavior is always in the form of urgent thrusting and seeking in terms of positive satisfactions as well as avoidances, powered by animal energies and rhythms. Recognition of this dynamic cast of human behavior has led some theorists to search for direct relationships between physiological processes and the strictly human aspects of behavior. The sociologist's position is distinctive in that these physiological mainsprings of action are looked upon as always or "90 per cent of the time" asserting themselves as social and cultural transmutations. In other words, the goals of human action are inevitably social and cultural goals. Man does not desire glucose or carbohydrates, he desires French pastry or certain varieties of candies. He does not want to release gonadal secretions but rather wants a date with a "cute blonde girl" or whatever his particular socially derived tastes in femininity happen to dictate. For these reasons the satisfactions sought by the person cannot be defined by any narrow physiological, implicit, pain-pleasure calculus, or by any principle of "least effort." Furthermore, it is the specific differentiation of the goals from one person to another rather than the fact that there are generalized goals, wishes, desires, and drives which becomes the factor of transcending importance in human motivation. Finally, it must be noted that means tend to become ends and that their separation is a methodological convenience. Many of the aspects of social roles are originally means of reaching goals, but in time these techniques become satisfactions or ends in themselves. Hence, factoring a role into ends and means is not always necessary; in the analysis here the social role will be taken as embracing the goals as well as the means of behavior.

The search for reasons why the individual settles upon one form of pathological behavior in place of another is made difficult by some of the same methodological problems which are met in accounting for the growth of sociocultural systems. The part played by fortuitous and accidental factors is a very great one. The operation of hereditary processes which give one person a brown or yellow skin cannot be explained directly in sociological terms. Disfigurement, maiming, or blindness, deafness, and invalidism ensuing from accident or disease arbitrarily impose role definitions and status upon the persons so differentiated. The geographic presence of persons in social situations conducive to deviation is often a happenstance. Explaining why a particular individual chances to be in a situation where a given set of role choices confront him lies beyond the scope of this volume. Certain facts must be taken as "given" with analysis proceeding from that point.

The Hypothesis That Sociopathic Deviation Is Inconsistent and Unstable

There is a theory among some of the writers on social and personality disorganization that there is no demonstrable stability in the choice of sociopathic roles, that, given personal disorganization, it finds random and inconsistent expression in many varieties of social disorganization. One such writer has discovered fairly high correlations between a number of selected indexes of social disorganization: bastardy, divorce, suicide, non-support, juvenile delinquency, boys' court cases, contributing to delinquency, insanity, and general arrest rates. These data together with his investigations of case histories lead him to the rather strongly couched conclusion that:[9]

> Case analysis . . . supports the conclusion arrived at through correlation analysis. That is, case studies often reveal that the individual has expressed his basic personal disorganization in various ways at various times. The traditional notion that each form of personal disorganization constitutes a separate entity is nowhere borne out. Thus the delinquent may also be a homosexual or may manifest some other form of segmental behavior, the radical may show psychotic trends; and the alcoholic may eventually turn to suicide. In fact there is no form of social disorganization of which the personally disorganized individual is not potentially capable.

In criticism of this extreme viewpoint it can be seen that many of the correlations found by Mowrer are precisely those which would be

[9] Mowrer, E., *Disorganization, Personal and Social*, 1942, p. 571. Quoted by permission of the J B Lippincott Company, Philadelphia.

expected, *i.e.*, those between bastardy, nonsupport, and contributing to delinquency, or those between boys' court cases, juvenile delinquency, and general arrest rates. In other words, the correlations are between different statistical definitions of the same deviant behavior. The conclusion overlooks or ignores the fact that on numerous occasions otherwise normal persons engage in sociopathic behavior. It confuses situational deviation and systematic deviation with what has herein been called "individual" deviation. The assumption behind such reasoning, that relatively stable and integrated lives upon the basis of pathological social roles cannot be achieved, has been seriously challenged by careful scientific studies.[10] Admittedly, a deviant role may encompass a variety of socially disapproved behavior, but this does not prove that there is no structuring, no limits to the deviation. The criminal, as has already been shown, may have areas of compulsive and permissive behavior in conflict with society's codes, but there is also overlapping. The man who conceives of himself as a "hood" (hoodlum) may perform many criminal and immoral acts, but he will normally stop short of others—rape, for example.[11]

Tabulation of persons who at any given time and place engaging in what is held to be socially deleterious behavior admittedly will embrace those who are "personally disorganized" or demoralized and who are participating on a hedonistic level of choice. However, it will contain others who are preserving a socially tolerable albeit neurotic equilibrium through the occasional use of aberrant behavior. In addition there will be those who have pursued the particular behavior in question for years at a time and who for practical purposes can be called well adjusted—even rigidly set—in their roles. There are fraudulent pitchmen who have conducted borderline and outright criminal operations for years and who would have as much difficulty in adjusting to the status of a beggar as a businessman might have in becoming a dock-walloper.

Instead of employing stability of overt behavior as the criterion for discrete classifications of normal and pathological, it is far preferable to conceive of it as a general feature of all human behavior. Unstable persons are just as capable of shifting more or less capriciously to various normal roles as they are likely to fluctuate between a large number of sociopathic behaviors. Consequently, stability is best handled as a quantitative variable, defined best on a continuum. At one end of such a continuum will be located the unstable "psychopathic" person, while at the other terminal will be found the relatively stable behavior of the professional prostitute

[10] Sutherland, E. H., *The Professional Thief*, 1937, Whyte, W. F, *Street Corner Society*, 1943, Chap. V, "The Racketeer in Cornerville"; Gilmore, H, *The Beggar*, 1940, Anderson, N, *The Hobo*, 1933.

[11] See incident in Shaw, *op. cit.*, Chap. X

or professional thief.[12] The research problem in reality is to describe stability in relation to specific situations, in relation to behavior systems of deviants, and with reference to sociopsychological variables or the symbolic process.

Proceeding upon the assumption or hypothesis that deviant roles are capable of integration and stabilization, it follows that the choice of deviant roles, while obviously conditioned by dynamic goal seeking, is not a random or capricious process. These dynamic explorations of the human being function in a structured context in all cases; they operate within sets of external and internal limits.

The External Limits

The most immediate external limits imposed upon the person identified and stigmatized as pathological or as socially disadvantaged are those erected by the community or society in the form of barriers to social participation. These barriers not only exclude the deviant from many general and special social and economic roles in the socially respectable community but also isolate the deviant from opportunities to participate in sociopathic roles. The ex-convict finds most occupations closed to him in the normal segment of society, except the low-paying, low-status, menial positions, with only the odd chance at better jobs in dubious, tension-generating roles, such as that of a strikebreaker or a marginal criminal role. The criteria for membership in organized sociopathic groups may be just as rigid and exclusive. If the ex-convict is a Negro, he may be denied entrance into certain criminal gangs in the same way that he is barred from other groups, simply because he has a black skin. A person who has been a beggar may have difficulty in entering the more "aristocratic" criminal trades. A college boy running away from a scandal in his home community may aspire to the fellowship of a group of fast-traveling hobos, only to be ignored because of his faulty skills or because of his obvious class affiliations. Patriotic considerations may lead prostitutes to shun the girl who has willingly submitted to the sexual advances of enemy troops or civilians.

All these illustrations make it plain that any person aspiring to a given role, whether it is organized around approved or disapproved behavior, will be restricted by the social definition of his preexisting social status. This status will be indicated by such things as age, sex, physical characteristics, nativity, kinship, religious affiliation, economic position, and social class. Not all of these dimensions of one's social status are of equal impor-

[12] Lindesmith, A., and H. Dunham, "Some Principles of Criminal Typology," *Social Forces*, 19, March, 1941, pp. 307–314.

tance, hence we shall consider here only those which seem to have a more direct effect upon the life choices of the deviant.

Limits Based upon Age, Sex, and Physical Characteristics

Rules, regulations, prejudices, and stereotypes associated with age, sex, size, degree of beauty, physical stigmas, and physical defects all have the effect of facilitating or ruling out a person's potential enactment of various social roles, abnormal as well as normal. We know considerably more about the effects of such limits upon the choices of nondeviant persons than upon those of sociopathic individuals. A little-known and little-explored area is the effect of sociological aging upon the status of deviants. Much knowledge is needed about the occupational life spans of such deviants as prostitutes, criminals, homosexuals, hobos, and radicals. We need to know how much cultural discontinuity and crisis is created by the aging of persons of this class and what alternatives and choices remain open to them as they move into their older years. In the case of prostitutes the general consequences of aging are fairly obvious, but not so for the others we have mentioned. In the case of homosexuals there is reason to believe that the crisis of middle age may be as great as it is for women in general in our society. With the loss of his physical attractiveness, other homosexuals apparently come to reject the older sex pervert in a heartless fashion, referring to him as an "old aunty." Yet while these things come out in occasional case histories, we still do not know in much detail what necessary modifications are made in the role of the homosexual as a result of such rejections.

The areas of social participation which are closed or opened to the deviant person because of his or her sex are much less obscure than is true of age factors. Fairly reliable data tell us that there are fewer female criminals, hobos, radicals, and gamblers. While this can be explained partly as being due to internal limits which make certain roles unattractive to women, it is also a partial measure of the unwillingness of others to accept women in certain sociopathic roles. A young woman without a physical handicap is seldom a professional beggar chiefly because most men who encountered her in such a role would treat her as a prostitute, as would the police. For much the same reason there are few women hobos. Even though prostitution is a fairly easy choice for women, sexually promiscuous girls often are declared feeble-minded by the courts and institutionalized on that basis in preference to handling them as prostitutes. The nature of many criminal activities is such that women are "out of place" trying to participate in them. Thus they are more likely to be found in auxiliary roles in those few cases where they do participate in crime. This, we believe, is reflected in the lenient attitudes of our courts, where women are less likely to be held to strict criminal accountability than are men. This has been exemplified in a number of cases where women guilty of murder have been able with small difficulty to have themselves declared insane as a means of escaping legal penalties.

Limits of Strength, Agility, and Endurance Are Socially Ascribed to Age, Sex, and Physical Handicaps

At first thought such things as strength, agility, and energy seem to be largely internal limits growing out of age, sex differences, and damage to the organism. However, closer inspection reveals that they are originally external limits in the sense that the real debilities are overlaid or obscured by the putative limitations which the culture ascribes to age, sex, and physical defect. This is most easily seen in the isolating reactions toward physically handicapped persons – the deaf, epileptic, crippled, physically ill, and speech defectives. The spastic child, for example, is commonly thought to be feeble-minded – sometimes even by its parents. Consequently it is often treated on such an assumption, and little effort is made to teach it to talk or to educate it up to the physical limits of its handicap. Many of the blind are surprised and irritated to find others reacting to them as if they were deaf as well as visually disabled.

The sociocultural limits which tend to exclude the physically handicapped from full economic participation in our society have been rationalized largely in terms of biological incapacities. Thus many employers have the idea that handicapped workers are more likely to have accidents in the plant and to have higher absenteeism rates than other workers and that consequently they will be less productive. The fallacy of such employer attitudes was brought out during the Second World War when personnel managers, following empirical procedures in hiring and firing, were surprised to discover that many of the physically handicapped persons could effectively perform jobs of which they were previously thought incapable.

The frustrations which many of the physically handicapped meet with in their efforts to interact with the opposite sex seem to be connected with tenuous ideas held by others about the sexual potentialities of these deviants. Feelings of revulsion and unpleasant empathic responses toward physically defective persons may be associated with notions of their innate hypersexuality or their supposed sexual impotency. Here we recall older folk tales about the great sexual prowess of hunchbacks and dwarfs.

We have little information as to whether physically handicapped persons are discriminated against by other sociopathic deviants and if so, in what ways. We may safely guess, of course, that the madam of a house of prostitution is not apt to take in a physically deformed girl as an inmate.

Furthermore, there is a popular belief that people who are deformed in some way are more inclined to turn to crime. Data to show that physical defects are somewhat more prevalent in prison populations than they are in the general population [13] might be cited in support of this belief. However, we are on very unfirm ground here. In the case of organized criminal groups it may well be that the physically handicapped person is less acceptable because his higher visibility might make the whole group more conspicuous.

Economic Limits

The economic status of the deviant does much to determine what groups he may enter and those which are closed to him. This works in two ways: (1) The possession of adequate money permits deviants to move more freely in their environments and is means for formal entree into many groups. (2) The conspicuous expenditure of money becomes a prestige or "success" symbol for the deviant, which has a "halo" or whitewashing effect upon the less enviable aspects of his role. Thus we see how wealthy criminals or gamblers are able to stay at the best hotels and live in upper class residential areas in our larger communities. They have been known to consort informally with socially elite persons at fashionable summer and winter resorts. The part played by the possession of adequate income in differentiating the role and status of criminals can also be observed very clearly within prisons.

A deviant whose role and status varies quite closely with his financial resources is the drug addict. If he is poor he is practically forced into criminal pursuits, but if he has a substantial income he avoids this necessity. The status of any of the physically handicapped deviants who are unable to find gainful employment can be greatly modified and improved by the possession of an ample income. We recall here the case of a blind woman who inherited considerable money from her husband. With this the whole problem of movement in her environment was solved, for she simply hired taxicab drivers who took her through city traffic and escorted her on shopping tours.

Limits Based upon Geographic and Demographic Factors

The location, size, technological specialization, and demographic composition of the community in which the deviant happens to be located are other sources of externally imposed limits upon his life choices. In a small, geographically isolated town the deviant person may have no opportunity to engage in homosexual behavior or to make habitual use of narcotic drugs. On the other hand, in a rural community a feeble-minded person

[13] Sutherland, *Principles of Criminology*, p. 92*f*.

may be tolerated in certain roles by the conforming members of the community and also by nonconforming groups. We know of one such community in which a feeble-minded man enjoys a virtual monopoly of cesspool digging. Interestingly enough, this same man prior to settling down to these labors had run with a gang of rowdies in the township, who put up with him largely in order to use him as a scapegoat for their petty crimes. In contrast to this, it is very unlikely that there will be any place for a person of defective intelligence in more highly organized crime found in urban areas. However, the large, complex urban community is ordinarily thought of as being more congenial to the deviant person. The diversity of social roles and the range of sociopathic behavior systems in existence there maximizes the opportunities the deviant has to gravitate into a role or roles most compatible with his particular deviant tendencies.

Mobility as a Limit

Mobility of the deviant person or deviant group member is another important external limit upon social participation. Persons with low spatial and vertical mobility must live within a closely circumscribed participational area determined by their immediate locality or social class. On the other hand, if persons who are culturally disenfranchised in one area are in a position to migrate, they may gain status in a different social organization or they may move back and forth between different communities and by this means widen their range of choices. In rural Italian communities of the past the girl who engaged in sex relations before marriage was likely to be ostracized by her family, the church, and the rest of the community. If she was not in a position to migrate, she often was left the unenviable alternative of becoming the village prostitute. If she could migrate, then she might travel to an urban community where she could become a shopgirl or a professional prostitute.

While high mobility increases the potential range of social participation in many respects, nevertheless it may have the opposite effect. Continuously mobile persons are likely to be isolated in ways which could not affect the person dwelling regularly in one community. For example, the highly mobile criminal must renounce the family as a means of affectional and sexual gratification. His friendships are likely to be few, and he will be regarded with suspicion by local criminals as well as by the police until he has demonstrated to them that he is safe to associate with.

The Internal Limits

In addition to the external limits precluding the choice of roles and blocking avenues of social participation, the reacting individual is bound and hedged by the internal structuring of his personality. It is pretty well agreed that there is a selective economy in personality which sorts and picks among the social stimuli coming to it from the external world. At any given point in the personality development of the individual there is a definable set of alternative roles which are subjectively congenial to him, in terms of his covert symbolic processes and perhaps in terms of his unverbalized responses. This subjectively delimited area of choice may lie within the range of the external limits or it may fall outside, and while the external limits may be comparable for different persons, these internal limits tend to be much more variable. Aspirations to status and roles arise within the scope of the internal limits; likewise, social pressures upon the individual to accept certain roles and status which fall beyond the internal limits will be resisted, circumvented, selected out, and rejected.

Internal Limits Are the Structural Aspect of Personality

The subjective component which has here been called "internal limits" and which reacts upon social stimuli has been described in various ways and from different points of view. Some writers have spoken of the "apperceptive mass"; others choose to think in terms of "sets in human nature," personality traits, or personality patterns, or "regions" and "barriers" with differing communicability between the regions, or, finally "status personality." It matters little what we call these factors so long as we admit that there is a structural and delimiting aspect of personality.

The case of a delinquent boy who had organized his life around the role of a "jack-roller" (one who makes a living by robbing drunken men) reveals how internal limits function to demarcate congeries of congenial roles. The boy in the case was characterized as being egocentric, aggressive, and rebellious toward authority, which characteristics became the basis for his selection of delinquent roles and later nondelinquent roles. In the boy's ultimate "reformation" he attempted a number of different occupational roles, all involving direct supervision by his employers, before he fell into a job compatible with his personality structure; as a high-pressure salesman he found a role in which his "traits" were put to a definite advantage.[14] Although the case history does not dwell upon the point, it can be inferred from the data that certain forms of crime were as unattractive to him as certain legitimate jobs. A criminal role making imperative close cooperation with others and providing no outlets for aggressiveness presumably would have little appeal for such a person. Not only because of the compulsives of the criminal code to which he adheres but also because of his hostilities toward the police, the role of a stool pigeon would be unthinkable to such a person. Similarly, a man disposed to painful stomach disorders and who is penurious may find the role of the alcoholic beyond

[14] Shaw, *op. cit.*

his tolerance simply because of the inroads excessive drinking would make upon his health and his pocketbook. A girl with a strong fear of venereal disease or hatred of bodily contacts will be fortified to that extent against situational pressures to enter prostitution. Some few people apparently are incapable of securing any sensations at all from morphine injections, which means that addiction to the drug in their cases becomes an impossibility.

Attitudinal Limits

Many persons whose status is well secured within the community have a fairly wide knowledge of deviant roles, including the language, mannerisms, and skills involved. Social caseworkers become adept at imitating the mannerisms of their pauperized and sexually casual clients; professors of criminology occasionally can delectate their students with exhibitions of pocket picking and the reproduction of criminal argot. The internal limits which presumably make such roles undesirable to the persons concerned consist in the verbalized and unverbalized fears and antipathies to playing them in any other than specious social contexts. In some cases such as these, normal persons go as far as to make a subjective identification with a sociopathic role, but some strongly encysted deterrent facts prevent them from making the transition to overt participation in the role.

Knowledge and Skill as Limits

In other instances the internal limits are simply the lack of acquaintance with the skills and values of the role and an inability to conceptualize it. Children and mentally deficient adults are internally limited in this respect more than others. It can be supposed that limits of this sort, unless they are reacted to symbolically and become an emotional blocking or a sense of inferiority, more easily give way in the face of situational pressures to play a given sociopathic role than is true of the other limits we have classed as internal.

Interrelationships of the Limits

The interrelationships between the various external limits and between the external and the internal limits on social participation can be described only in a very general fashion. It is both deducible and demonstrable that these limits tend to cluster together and to reinforce one another in various ways. The study of these tendencies with reference to the external limits unfortunately has been rather narrowly centered upon the relationship between socioeconomic status and degree of social participation. From empirical research into this matter it has been established that there is a positive correlation between these two factors; persons with low socioeconomic status have been found to participate in fewer organized activities and to know fewer people. A related finding is that persons of low socioeconomic status are less mobile than those above them in status; the former are not only less interactive socially but they also interact in more restricted spatial areas.[15] While ethnic factors and perhaps kinship in some instances may have been confused with economic status in some of the studies on this subject, there is no reason to question the general conclusions which have been reached.

In expanding the scope of research into the relationship between the external limits it will be meaningful to try to discover to what extent patterns of discrimination against deviants are generalized. We know, for instance, that the ex-convict meets with multiple rejections in our society, he has difficulty getting employment, he is politically disenfranchised, the armed services do not want him, and the more respectable females of the community will have little to do with him. Furthermore, our society is so organized that the carry-over of the ex-convict identity is more or less formally and automatically determined. On the other hand, this is not so true of the ex-prostitute.

In small, geographically isolated communities the individual who becomes a *persona non grata* by reason of disapproved behavior may be excluded from practically all social participation. Apparently the informal student-status systems of some small, isolated colleges and universities operate in a similar way against those "who don't belong."[16] Data such as these suggest to us that it may be possible ultimately to classify the environments of deviants in terms of the degree to which they become closed participational circles or perhaps in terms of the degree to which they are held together by centripetal social pressures. This classification will undoubtedly cut across rural-urban community differences, for closed participational systems do seem to operate within large urban communities. We have indicated that our society tends to function in this way toward the ex-convict. There is also reason to believe that the limits surrounding certain sectarian radicals are of this kind. The social participation of these particular radicals comes to be an "all-or-none" variety, because of pressures from outside the radical organization and also from within the group. They must carefully live with a prescribed circle of groups and acquaintances.

The Interplay of External and Internal Limits

It is, of course, almost axiomatic in sociology that the inner mental life of the person will be shaped by his various group activities. To put it into

[15] Knupfer, G., "Portrait of the Underdog," *Public Opinion Quarterly*, 11, Spring, 1947, pp. 103–114 See also Queen, S, and J Gruener, *Social Pathology*, Chap 12.

[16] Loomis, S., and A. Green, "The Pattern of Mental Conflict in a Typical State University," *Journal of Abnormal and Social Psychology*, 42, July, 1947, pp 342–355

the language we have been using, there is a continuous interplay between the external and internal limits. Narrowing of the range of the internal limits of choice goes along with the constrictions externally imposed upon social participation. Here, again, the empirical research upon this subject has been pretty much into the effects of economic limitations upon such things as interest, attention, and responses to new experiences. The research reveals that persons in the low socioeconomic strata of our society usually have more limited knowledge of roles and that they apparently entertain more limited aspirations to roles which are outside of their general status categories. Credulity, naívetė, and suspiciousness or dread of unknown things also have been assigned as qualities of the thought life which spring out of and also restrict the social participation of "lower class" persons.[17]

It should be noted that statistical comparisons between groups or categories with varying socioeconomic status do not always give large and consistent differences with reference to their social participation and their sociopsychological horizons. If persons of low status are socially isolated, it can be shown that extreme wealth or "old-family" prestige also cuts persons off from the main stream of social life and pinches their intellectual outlook. Thus, to express these realities we have the folk concept of the "poor little rich boy" and the literary stereotype of the "Late George Apley." From the standpoint of understanding sociopathic choices it is of equal importance to comprehend the mental rigidities of the middle- and high-ranking person as well as those of the "lower class" person.

Employing a single facet of status to study the restriction of social participation at best can give us clues for further research. More detailed knowledge of life choices must come from the analysis of the way in which constellations of limits are formed through the identification of persons with roles. Role is the configurating aspect of status which denotes the specific claims upon the time, interest, attention, energy, and loyalties of the sociopathic as well as the non-sociopathic person. How the various limits converge and merge and mutually condition one another can be perceived in the process of integration of roles.

The Integration of Roles

After a person achieves, accepts, or is compelled to adopt an aberrant role, an integrational process comes into play wherein the other roles played by the individual are segregated out or subordinated to the major role. Subjectively a status personality[18] materializes out of the unorganized or disorganized behavior which prevails during the transition from one

[17] Knupfer, *op. cit.*, pp. 160*ff*.

[18] The concept is R. Linton's, see his *Study of Man*, 1936, p. 477.

role to another. In other words, the role becomes a new set of external and internal limits which is now superimposed upon the previous pattern of limits. Implicit in the role at first, these limits gradually become explicit demands upon the time, interest, attention, loyalties, and energies of the person. Claims are made upon the person by the central function of his role and by loyalties to new groups in which he participates. In order to integrate his roles, the deviant must come to deal with the external and internal limits in such a way as to minimize tensions or to sufficiently contain them so that they do not disrupt the new configuration. This calls for an active seeking out of areas of social participation or subsidiary roles in which the visibility of the deviation is reduced, penalties lessened, and rewards increased.

A special phase of the process of integration of roles has to do with the societal definition associated with the major sociopathic role assumed by a deviant. This societal definition (as distinct from the self-definition) is implicit and inferable from the barriers set up by the surrogates of society on the social participation of the deviant. At the same time it may be made explicit in categorical terms which currently describe and caption the characteristics of the deviant. The reciprocal of the societal definition is found in the self-definition which emerges from the symbolic process. This conception which the deviant has of himself undoubtedly influences his aspirations to other roles and also tends to select out those subsidiary roles he regards as compatible with his status.

An illustration of the point we have just made comes from events in eighteenth- and nineteenth-century England, at which time the stigma of "pauper" grew up, carrying with it well-defined ideas of improvidence, laziness, sexual immorality, and proneness to fraud in obtaining relief and charity. There can be little doubt, as histories of the period amply testify, that this generalized societal definition was taken over by large numbers of the poor, who saw their impoverished lot as inevitable and irremediable. For these people the ways of life of the burgeoning middle class were not only closed to them by economic barriers but, even more importantly, by the inconceivability of and probably the distaste for privileges and responsibilities such social roles would thrust upon them.

The Primacy of Roles

It is possible that our insight into the integration of sociopathic roles can be furthered by the classification of social roles in terms of their *primacy*, or the degree to which a given role takes precedence over other roles. We can see this rather easily in the narrowed choices of the blind person, whose urgent necessity to continually orient himself in space not only excludes him from many roles but ultimately colors and acts as a common denominator for all roles he is potentially able to play. Likewise, we see this same phenomenon in the drug addict's life, which is everywhere dominated by the ubiquitous fear that his supply of drugs will be exhausted and that the horrible "shakes" or withdrawal pains will overtake him. In employing the concept of primacy we are assuming that some roles are potentially capable of being integrated with a large variety of subsidiary roles, while other roles are compatible only with a much narrower range of roles.

Adjustment – Maladjustment

There is a stubborn folk idea that persons leading lives condemned by society perforce must be unhappy, demoralized, and emotionally maladjusted. The idea is expressed in notions that "crime never pays," that prostitutes lead a "life of shame," or that the drug addict is destined to end his life hopelessly insane. A deduction from the general theory of this treatise is that neither adjustment nor maladjustment are the inevitable consequences of departing from society's approved rules and regulations. It follows that maladjustment and adjustment must be accounted for in the same general terms which explain their relation to normal roles and normal status in society.

Our method for defining maladjustment is quantitative and is based upon attitudes toward the self. The degree to which a deviant is adjusted will be expressed by the amount of congruence between the societal definition and the individual's definition of the self. A person is well adjusted in the covert symbolic sense to the extent that there is a consistent societal definition of what he is and which he accepts, taking it over and introjecting it as his self-definition and playing the associated role. This might be called a Popeye philosophy of "I yam what I yam." Of course, there is never a perfect congruence between these societal definitions and self-definitions, largely because there never can be perfect communication between society and the individual. Besides this, a complete and candid reception of society's evaluations would be too painful for most people. Hence, there is always a certain amount of misinterpretation of the societal self-defining stimuli and corresponding psychological subterfuge in even well-adjusted persons. It is here that the so-called dynamisms or mechanisms of the mind – dissociation, rationalization, projection, and substitution – come into play to strike a working balance between the societal definitions and self-definitions, or, to put it in completely subjective terms, between the "I" and the "me."

The Maladjusted Deviant

A person is badly adjusted when a wide gulf appears between society's version of him and his role and his own version. The process by which this comes to pass must be seen as an interaction of objective and subjective factors. Objectively, roles may be forced upon individuals for which they have neither the associated aspirations nor the capacity to carry out. The role makes demands upon these individuals incompatible with the internal limits of their personalities, bearing with them self-definitions that are unsatisfying or intolerable. As a consequence, the person under these circumstances rejects the self-definition and struggles inwardly to conceive the self otherwise. The red-haired girl is often confronted with this in the public stereotype of herself as one who is easily angered and, more disturbingly, one whose sexual passions are easily aroused. If the girl comes from a puritanical family background, she may become sensitive about her hair or develop a set of defensive reactions to the wholly normal sexual interests of men. The climacteric is a critical point in the lives of many women because of the intolerable implications of the physiological changes for the self, tokening the change to the status of "old woman"

In all probability the greatest conflicts over role and self-definitions arise where previously there has existed a crystallized pattern of adjustment far removed from the deviant role, and there is but a very short time in which to take over the new sociopathic role. People who have reached adulthood and then are suddenly blinded or crippled often undergo deep conflicts and indulge in all sorts of symbolic attacks upon themselves and upon others. There is some evidence that persons who eventually turn to begging after a business or professional career never achieve the integration of persons who have begged all their lives.[19]

Discrepancies between societal definition and self-definition can also arise where a person moves from a less desirable to a more desirable status. The phenomenon can be seen in the movement of the *nouveau riche* up the social scale. The wealth of this group entitles its members to play a number of enviable roles, yet their status is attenuated by rejections from the "inner elite." Insecurities grow from the real or fancied inability to acquire the more refined skills and nuances of meaning in their roles. Combat soldiers on leave who are treated as returning heroes by their families and the community are often restless and guilt-ridden because of their inability to define their war behavior in hero-coward categories. The same general problem makes its appearance in other deviant groups; a man whose religious affiliations and background entitle, and perhaps compel, him to register as a conscientious objector in wartime may be tortured with self-doubts and self-attacks, despite the societal acceptance of him in such a role.

In extreme cases of personal maladjustment there is a complete breakdown of the process of social communication so that no correspondence whatsoever remains between the societal definition and self-definition, at

[19] Gilmore, *op. cit.*, p 165

least no correspondence understandable to society. When this happens, massive conflicts over roles shatter the personality, the self may disintegrate, breaking down into several or many selves, or it may become rigidly integrated upon a delusional basis, producing bizarre or dangerous overt behavior.

One or two cautions should be injected at this point. One is the necessity to avoid confusing the societal definition with scientific reality. A community may be entirely wrong in its estimation of a young woman's behavior, mistaking unconventionality for immorality. But yet the fact remains that however much its reaction is founded upon false premises, it is still the immediate social reality to which the woman must respond. This is qualified by the aforementioned fact that the person reacts selectively to such contacts and by the fact that the social valuations of some persons and groups carry far more weight with the individual than others. The adolescent in our society seems to react almost exclusively to a narrow facet of the societal reaction composed of the valuations of his peer group.[20] Often a person who by all indications should be psychotic manages to preserve a temporary working equilibrium with the community simply by maintaining a clear channel of communication with one or two groups in the community, or even at times with one person.

Social Isolation — Progressive Narrowing of Choices — Total Blockage

In certain categories of deviation and in the case of certain persons, the external and internal limits upon the choice of roles converge in space and time in such a manner that few or no alternatives are open to the individual. The full impact of this attenuated status may not be felt or perceived until the deviant has suffered a long series of penalties and rejections, deepening and fixing self- and "other"-attack reactions. The phenomenon comes to attention in connection with persons who are maladjusted because of their inability to gain external social acceptance in roles they covet and who simultaneously reject on subjective grounds the majority of the roles open to them. So-called "marginal men" exemplify conflicts of this order. The chief difference between a general narrowing of role choices and that which is synonymous with marginality is that in the latter case the choices tend to be organized into dramatic dichotomies each with a high degree of primacy. The marginal person is one who is presented with dual role choices but because of internal or external limits

20 Demerath, N. J., "Adolescent Status Demands and Student Experiences of Twenty Schizophrenics," *American Sociological Review*, 8, October, 1943, pp 513–518

or their combinations is unable to integrate his life on the basis of either role.

The discussion of marginality by sociologists has been largely confined to the anomalous positions of certain members of minority racial and cultural groups. Examples are given of the racial hybrid, the second-generation immigrant, and the intellectual or "emancipated" Jew. In the last case the concept has reference to the Jew who repudiates his status in the orthodox, conservative, reformed, or other Jewish groups in the community, yet who cannot secure entree into gentile groups on terms which he desires. The kinds of alternative roles which provide opportunities for satisfactory adjustment to these persons may be limited to those found in radical political organizations which condemn all anti-Semitism and adhere to revolutionary programs promising an end to all race prejudice and minority-group discrimination. Such membership and social participation may enable the person to acquire a sense of identification and status in groups which are compatible with his internal personality structure.[21] Needless to say, such membership and status creates its own peculiar problems of social participation and self-acceptance.

It is unfortunate that sociologists have been so preoccupied with the subjective manifestations of marginality – the confusions and conflicts associated with the status. The concept most properly needs demonstration in the light of what is done to the social participation of the person. Modified in this way there seems to be no reason why the concept of marginality should not be applied to a wide variety of maladjustments, including such things as marginal age status, sex, marital status, and the various sociopathic statuses. We believe it can be applied to the partially blind person who has been very independent and self-reliant prior to his loss of sight. Such partly handicapped persons often rebel strongly against the conventional occupational roles open to persons with their defect, yet they have few alternative vocational chances save the odd opportunity to serve on the staff of welfare agencies or teaching staffs of agencies providing services for the blind. A similar type of life impasse may confront the ex mental patient or the ex-convict.

Total Blockage of Choices

Some forms of sociopathic behavior seem more likely than others to lead to complete blockage, so that each new effort to work out an adjustment on either a normal or deviant basis generates continuing disruptive tensions within the person. In these cases the sociopathic activity assumes a compulsive quality and the role and self-definitions are undesired by-

[21] One writer argues that in New York City there is a "marginal culture" in which marginal Jewish persons may find satisfactory roles and status. Goldberg, M., "A Qualification of the Marginal Man Theory," *American Sociological Review,* 6, February, 1941, pp. 52–58.

products of the activity rather than the result of aspiration or choice. Alcoholism is of this sort; not only is the chronic alcoholic progressively excluded from more and more groups, but pervasive anxieties and guilt feelings instilled by the societal reaction to his drinking eventually carry over into every role he seeks to play, becoming a system of all-exclusive internal limits. All rational control tends to give way in such persons, and in the common parlance he becomes "a slave of his habit." Other pathologies which seem to share these general attributes are drug addiction, stuttering, autoeroticism, gambling, and many compulsive neurotic and psychotic behaviors.[22]

Counterfeit Roles

A few persons among certain classes of greatly isolated deviants contrive to mitigate the penalties associated with their status and role by assuming spurious or counterfeit pathological roles. Members of minority groups or criminals may change their names and have plastic surgery done in order to escape many of the penalties of their status. In some cases this means that they can take over a normal role. Every year an unknown but probably considerable number of Negroes who are sufficiently light in color "pass" over into the white group. In some Southern states Negroes have found relatively satisfactory status as Indians. Feigning lameness, blindness, and madness are historically old shrifts resorted to by paupers or professional beggars both to mitigate penalties and enhance rewards of their roles. It is possible to discover instances where psychotic persons and epileptics conceal their real status by passing themselves off as alcoholics. Moreover, there are cases where lepers have preferred to be publicly known as insane. The writer has recorded a number of cases in which economically unsuccessful persons have counterfeited the symptoms of insanity in order to retreat to the relative security of a mental hospital. The number of cases in which alternatives of this sort are a partial resolution of conflict and buffers to complete social isolation is undeniably small, and they serve to accentuate the intense isolation and poverty of choices of the deviants who are driven to such solutions of their dilemmas.

Flexibility, Rigidity, and Marginality

In the accompanying Fig. 4 a graphic summary is given to show a number of the possible variations in the structure of internal and external limits as they would be seen in cross section at given points in space and time in the life history of the person. The arc of circles stands for the different roles within the immediate social plane of the individual, with disapproved deviant roles starting on the left and ranging over to non-

[22] The process described here seems very similar to the "vicious circles" discussed by Read Bain; see Becker, H., and R. Hill, *Marriage and the Family*, 1942, p. 147.

sociopathic roles on the right. The broken lines mark off the internal limits, while the unbroken lines indicate the external limits. In the first illustration, the internal limits are wide enough to make the person potentially adaptable to a fairly large number of deviant as well as normal roles. However, it will be noted that the choices allowable in his social setting is much smaller. Should he aspire to roles outside of the external limits, presumably he would experience a complication of his social participation. In the second case, the structure of limits tends to be reversed. We may speak of

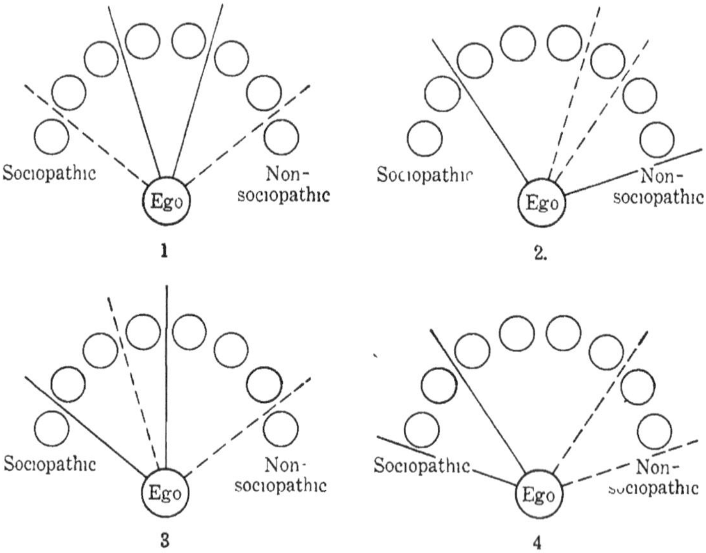

Fig. 4. Graphic representation of internal and external limits of role choice.

such an individual as "rigid" because of his specialized internal demands which cause him to be highly discriminative in so far as the assumption of any large number of roles available to him is concerned. Should circumstances compel him to step into any of these roles, we assume that he will be maladjusted in the sense in which we use the concept.

The third illustration is that of a marginal person for whom there is one alternative role externally possible and subjectively congenial. A completely marginal person will have no point of contact whatsoever between the external and internal limits. The representation of this condition is seen in the fourth illustration.

The Adjusted Pathological Deviant

The adjusted sociopathic person is simply one who accepts his status, role, and self-definition. There are two reasons why acceptance of society's general and specific designations of the sociopathic deviant's character aids him in achieving a satisfactory personal adjustment. First of all, it frees a fund of energy which hitherto has been consumed in a continuous struggle to repudiate the societal definition, or in fruitless battles between the "I" and the "me." The energy thus freed can now be applied to adjustment on a deviant basis. If society has institutionalized some sort of role for the particular deviant, he can now avail himself of the special skills and habits of the role and enjoy the rewards pertaining to it. If a person in feudal European society could reconcile himself to his physical handicap, he could make a reasonably satisfactory adjustment as a beggar. Even today in our society if a blind person can accept the unrealistic and sentimental attitudes of the public toward his handicap, he can exploit them very profitably and live very comfortably in the community. He becomes a professional blind man.

Where no traditional or well-defined role has been set up for the deviant and there is no deviant social organization and special culture, the problem of adjustment is much more complex. Further complications are created by the ambiguity and inconsistency of societal definitions in such cases. Not only is such a deviant an isolant, but his difficulties are multiplied by the absence of any adjustment techniques and skills which he may learn from others. This throws him completely upon his own resources and makes tremendous demands upon his energies, even where he has no conflicts over his self-definition. However, if he is sufficiently resourceful, the deviant who is isolated in this way can nevertheless build up a set of informal social acceptances and devise methods of increasing his social participation. Needless to say, the little social worlds created in this fashion have a very tenuous footing in the social structure and are very often a source of continual anxiety to their propagators.

A considerably different situation is present when a deviant has entree into a well-structured deviant social organization. Here he has the opportunity to become part of a group or group system, to identify with a set of values, to enjoy a social solidarity with others of his kind, and to defend his personal integrity from societal aggressions through the media of rationalizations and ideologies of the specialized culture. Of course, deviant social organizations vary in their value to the participating deviants. From one such organization to another, significant differences will appear in such things as the degree of solidarity within the group, its size, resources, its social power, and the availability of the power in time and space. It should be remembered, too, that the deviant must make a personal adjustment within this group, as well as rely upon the group in his struggle with society.

Predictions as to whether a deviant is apt to become maladjusted demand a fairly broad catalogue of facts, which may be expressed here as a series of rhetorical questions. How far and in how many ways does the person deviate from the norms of society? What is the nature of the societal reaction in his particular family, school, social class, and locality? To what extent is the deviant behavior capable of integration in nonsociopathic roles for which the deviant can qualify? Is there a role based upon the deviant behavior? How well defined is the role within the culture? Is there a social organization of like deviants with which he can affiliate? If he is a member of a deviant social organization, what is his status within this group? How do members of the deviant group react to him and define his individuality in terms of the subculture? Does the deviant accept his role and self-definition within this group? Is marginality present? What areas of social participation are closed to the person as a consequence of his affiliation? What new areas are opened? How do these relate to the internal limits of his personality?

Conclusion

In this chapter we have described the individuation of the sociopathic deviant as a process which at a critical point produces a qualitative change in the context of the deviation. The concepts of primary and secondary deviation were applied to the two general phases of this process. The deviant person was viewed as a dynamic agent acting in a choice-making capacity within sets of external and internal limits. These limits vary with each person and may be broad or may be narrowly constricted. Adjustment of deviants was defined as a relationship between societal definitions and self-definitions.

With this chapter we have terminated our theoretical discussion and stand ready to give systematic consideration to various kinds of sociopathic behaviors, which are the subject matter of Part Two.

Selected Readings

KNUPFER, G "Portrait of the Underdog," *Public Opinion Quarterly*, 11, Spring, 1947, pp. 103–114

LINTON, R.: *The Cultural Backgrounds of Personality*, 1945

MEAD, M.· *From the South Seas*, 1939, Book III, Chap. 18, "The Deviant"

MURPHY, G *Personality*, 1947, Chaps 20–22, 38–39

QUEEN, S, and J. GRUENER *Social Pathology*, 1940, Part 1, Chaps. 1–3

YOUNG, KIMBALL *Social Psychology*, 1945, Chap 7, "The Rise of the Self."

PART TWO

DEVIATION AND DEVIANTS

CHAPTER 5

BLINDNESS AND THE BLIND

Blindness is at once a dramatic and engaging handicap that is found among all peoples of the world. It holds a salient position among the biological defects because of the gross curtailment which it brings in the symbolic contacts and visual-mediated social participation of the persons so differentiated. The fanciful notions woven into our culture about this group of deviants have interacted with these considerable biological limits to produce an economic disenfranchisement with few parallels in other deviant groups. The anomalous persistence of age-old dependent roles for the blind in a culture such as ours which apotheosizes the self-reliant individual is a challenge to the irresponsibly inquisitive social scientist as well as to the welfare agencies seeking effective means of their rehabilitation.

The Nature of the Deviation

Although initial impressions lead us to regard blindness as a simple matter of not seeing, in actuality blindness exists in many different forms and degrees, and results from many different biological conditions. Medically, blindness is defined in terms of "visual acuity," "field of vision," and "muscular control." The degree of vision is expressed as a ratio between the distance at which a "blind" person sees letters on a chart and the distance at which a sighted person can see them. Thus 20/20 vision is normal, whereas 20/200 vision with 20 degrees of peripheral vision or less after correction for most purposes constitutes blindness. The 20/200 figure means that what a normally sighted person sees at 200 feet can be seen by the blind person only if he is within 20 feet of the object or a hypothetical letter on a chart. Some persons have normal visual acuity, but their field of vision is restricted; for example, often it is tubular in nature. According to one estimate, one-half to two-thirds of the blind have no vision whatsoever beyond the occasional perception of light and darkness.[1] The partially sighted group making up the remainder of the blind are marginal cases not only in a biological sense but very often in a sociological sense. In many ways they furnish the most intriguing variations of the behavior complex growing out of this pathology.

The commonest condition of the eyes which destroys or impairs vision is cataracts. These are growths over the lens which may either be con-

[1] Best, Harry, *Blindness and the Blind in the United States*, 1934, p 167

genital or else result from disease and accidents. Ophthalmia neonatorum or "babies' sore eyes" brought about by infection of the eyes at birth, especially by gonorrhea, was once a leading source of blindness. However, since the passage of laws in most states requiring prophylactic medication of all infants' eyes at birth this form of blindness has receded dramatically in its importance. Trachoma, an infectious eye disease, likewise was once a common cause of blindness, but recently due to treatment with new drugs its incidence has dropped greatly. Various chronic illnesses, such as syphilis, tuberculosis, and diabetes also contribute a sizable number of cases of blindness. About 15 per cent of the cases of blindness follow from accidential injuries. All in all, about one-half of the cases of blindness are the consequences of exogenous factors, the rest being congenital and hereditary in nature.[2]

It is important for our purposes to keep in mind that the social and cultural definitions of blindness do not necessarily coincide with the medical facts. Legal and administrative definitions of blindness for purposes of providing financial aid and other services vary considerably. Some countries have no official definition of blindness, simply relying upon empirical rules to distinguish the condition, while other countries carefully define a general category of blindness and several subcategories. Some distinguish blindness in adults from that in children. The American Academy of Ophthalmology and Otolaryngology has distinguished and defined four grades of visual handicap: (1) economic blindness, (2) vocational blindness, (3) educational blindness, and (4) total blindness.[3]

Another fact of considerable importance which should be noted here is that the individual's conception of his own role and status is not rigidly determined by the degree of impairment of his vision. Persons with serious defects in their vision have been known to spend their lives without ever thinking of themselves as being handicapped. A fair number of older persons who are on relief and become blind have refused to apply for blind status, even though it means an accretion in the size of their monthly allotment in many states. Conversely, there have been persons with questionable borderline vision who prefer the role and status of the blind. Once in awhile an instance of feigned blindness is recorded, although presumably this is far less common than it was in the medieval past.

Demographic Differentiation of the Blind

The total number of blind in the United States is not known with any exactness. The 1930 United States Census gave a figure of 63,489 blind, but this was probably a gross undercount. Reasons for believing this figure to be an undercount lie in the discrepancies between independent

[2] Lende, Helga (ed.), *What of the Blind?* 1938, Vol I, pp. 23–31.

[3] Proceedings, House of Delegates, American Medical Association, *Journal of the American Medical Association*, 102, June, 1934, p. 2205.

local enumerations and those of the United States Census. For example, the 1930 census listed 2,597 blind for the state of California, while the records of the state included names of 3,216 persons receiving blind aid in 1935.[4] When it is recalled that less than 50 per cent of the blind are recipients of such aid, it becomes obvious that the census figure is far too low, even when allowance is made for annual increment of the state blind population. A recent estimate places the rate of blindness at 1.7 per 1,000 population, with a total for the nation of 230,354.[5]

The blind are differentiated in the aggregate by having a very high sex ratio: 135.7 as compared with 102.5 for the general population. In so far as estimates and the figures from the last census taken of the blind are reliable, they show that 57.5 per cent of the blind are males and 42.5 per cent are females. It is ordinarily believed that the greater incidence of congenital defects among male infants plus the greater exposure of adult males to accident and disease account for this variation in sex rates.

The older census data on the age composition of the blind revealed that the majority, 52.7 per cent, were sixty years of age or over. According to these same 1930 data the percentage of the blind under twenty years was 8.6. However, as the following table shows, while the figure for the percentage of those sixty years of age and over may have been fairly accurate, that for the age group below twenty years probably was an underenumeration (see Table 2).

TABLE 2 PERCENTAGE DISTRIBUTION OF THE BLIND BY AGE, THREE ENUMERATIONS AT SPECIFIED YEARS

Age group	U.S Census, 1930	California census, 1935*	Washington survey, 1937†
Under 20	8.6	12.1	10.9
20–59	38 9	33 3	35.9
60 and over	52.5	54 6	53 2

* "A Census and Economic Survey of the Blind in California," California State Department of Education, *Bulletin* 7, Apr. 1, 1935.

† *Survey of the Blind in the State of Washington*, State Department of Social Security, May, 1937.

[4] "A Census and Economic Survey of the Blind in California," California State Department of Education, *Bulletin* 7, Apr. 1, 1935.

[5] Hurlin, R. G., *et al.*, *Causes of Blindness among Recipients of Aid to the Blind*, Federal Security Agency, 1947, Table 3, p. 13. Another estimate is somewhat lower, 1.38 per 1,000 being the rate and 192,677 being the calculated total for the United States. *Report of the Interdepartment Committee on Study of Problems of and Services for the Blind*, California State Departments of Education, Mental Hygiene, Public Health, and Social Welfare, 1946, p. 11 See also Britten, R. H., "Blindness as Recorded in the National Health Survey," *Public Health Reports*, 56, No. 46, November, 1941; Hurlin, R. G., "Estimates of Blindness in the United States," *Social Security Bulletin*, 8, No. 3, March, 1945; and Sanders, B. S., "The Blind—Their Number and Characteristics," *ibid.*, 6, No. 10, October, 1943.

There is good reason to believe that the age composition of the blind population has been changing rapidly in recent years, with a substantial increase in the proportions of the aged blind and a proportionate decrease of extremely young blind persons. Two California studies, shown in Table 3, seem to bear this out.

TABLE 3. PERCENTAGE AGE DISTRIBUTION FOR THE CALIFORNIA BLIND POPULATION, 1935 AND 1945

Age group	1935*	1945†
Under 16	8.	5.4
16–50	22.7	20.3
Over 50	69.3	74.3

* "A Census and Economic Survey of the Blind in California," California State Department of Education, *Bulletin* 7, Apr. 1, 1935, computed from Table III, p. 5.

† *Report of the Interdepartment Committee on Study of Problems of and Services for the Blind*, California State Departments of Education, Mental Hygiene, Public Health, and Social Welfare, 1946, p. 11

The reasons for this shift are found in the improvement of public health and other measures taken to safeguard the sight of newly born infants. It is also caused by the general aging of our population, which means that more persons are now alive at ages when blindness is likely to occur as the result of degenerative diseases.

Ethnic status has a differentiating influence upon rates of blindness, as can be seen in Table 4.

TABLE 4 PERCENTAGE DISTRIBUTION OF RECIPIENTS OF AID TO BLIND* IN 20 STATES BY ETHNIC STATUS†

Ethnic status	Per cent of blind recipients	Per cent of total U.S. population
White	77.8	89.3
Negro	20.3	10.3
Indian	1.6	0.3

* Hurlin, R. G., *et al.*, *Causes of Blindness among Recipients of Aid to the Blind*, Federal Security Agency, 1947, adapted from Table 6, p. 22.

† Although this is taken from what might be deemed a biased sample, other studies tend to verify the differences in the table. See *Blind and Deaf Mutes in The United States, United States Census, 1930,* Britten, R. H.,"Blindness as Recorded in the National Health Survey," *Public Health Reports*, 56, No 46, November, 1941

Indians, particularly in the past, have surpassed all other racial groups in the incidence of blindness among them, caused no doubt by their widespread infection with trachoma and venereal disease. The Mexican minority in the United States also has very high rates for this handicap, as well as the foreign-born population in contrast with the native-born. Higher incidence of chronic disease, deficiency diseases, specific eye infections, and lack of adequate medical care associated with low economic status all conspire to raise the blindness rates of these ethnic groups above those of the native white population.

There is some regional concentration of the blind in the Southern and Eastern states; evidence also points to heavier concentrations of the blind population in smaller cities and rural areas.[6] This probably reflects both a higher incidence of the pathology in these areas and a lower mobility of blind deviants so far as rural-urban migration is concerned. It may be that the blind fit into a rural environment with greater ease than in the large city with its many hazards. From what little we know about it, no significant ecological concentration of the blind exists within the community. Within urban areas the blind show no great tendency to mass in any one section. For example, a study of the blind population in Hennepin County, Minnesota, found the visually handicapped distributed in all but 5 of the 121 census tracts of Minneapolis. The largest numbers were found located in two adjacent census tracts near the center of the city, but they were all dwelling in two charitable boarding homes.[7]

THE CONTEXTS OF BLINDNESS

Viewed by the sociologist, the blind are a very heterogeneous population group, so much so that generalizations made for the aggregate become thin and meaningless. For example, among the blind we find that many (15 to 20 per cent) lose their sight after the age of fifty years. In these cases old age rather than blindness is the prime role determiner, the blindness being merely an added handicap in that "last scene of all," when, as Shakespeare phrased it, many are "sans eyes . . . sans everything." In all likelihood, for blindness to be a primary influence upon the role and status of the person, it must occur before the age of fifty. In the same vein it is deducible that the most direct impact of blindness upon role and status will be seen in those who have been blinded before the age of twenty.

Occasionally clinicians are faced with a case of hysterical blindness in which the deviation has no organic basis, where the defective vision is symptomatic of some intricate conflicts over other roles, which have never been successfully met and solved. The concomitants and symbolic aspects of this blindness are clearly atypical. In some such cases the hysteria may relate closely to a temporary life impasse and may rightly be thought of as situational deviation, although both of these types of cases are admittedly rare.

Some difficulty is experienced in trying to place the blind in the context of a subculture within our contemporary society. It is true that there exist

[6] Britten, *op. cit*, pp 12–13, 19.

[7] "The Blind of Hennepin County," *Final Report of the Blind Study Committee*, Central Planning and Research Department, Minneapolis Council of Social Agencies, 1946, p. 8.

special skills and knowledge, such as the use of Braille and special techniques for travel and housekeeping, which have been acquired by many of the blind, but these tend to be the products of other groups which have more or less superimposed them upon the blind. The special culture is communicated under the sponsorship of sighted groups rather than being an indigenous cultural growth among those without vision. The blind are occupationally specialized to some degree, but again this is largely the result of training, teaching, and placement by sighted persons. An exception to this is found in those cases where blind persons have taken over the behavior system of begging. This represents diffusion and transmission of culture from beggars in general, with some supplementing of the behavior system by interlearning between blind beggars themselves. How much of the latter there is cannot be determined.

The blind in our culture have no special argot of their own beyond some slang terms such as "blinks" – a word some few humorously apply to themselves. According to one informant, some of the blind have a habit of giving names to their canes. Beyond such things as these, a differentiating ingroup language seems to be entirely absent. All in all, in our society the need to develop a special culture is missing among the blind, for, as will be shown, the nature of the societal reaction removes this necessity. In contrast to the lack of a blind subculture in our society, apparently the blind of Japan at one time, beginning in the ninth century A.D., monopolized traditional skills of chanting, massage, shampooing, and carried on the treatment of illness by means of counterirritants. These skills were associated with a guild organization which governed their transmission from blind masters to apprentices.[8] At one time in medieval European countries it was the custom of the blind to be organized into guilds, presumably with powers and functions comparable to other craft guilds.

The most highly organized expression of a blind subculture in Europe grew up in Russia in the medieval era, where special beggars' orders of the blind were founded for purposes of self-help. The members of these orders were called the "earnest or never-laughing pilgrims." Government of the orders was carried out by an elected master who mediated disputes between the blind and imposed a species of discipline and justice. Apparently a special language called "Gegawatsche" was used, which had meaning only for the mendicants. However, its vocabulary was extremely limited.[9]

Organizations of the Blind

The number of organizations exclusively composed of blind members in our society today is rather limited. Among the more durable ones are the

[8] Dixon, J. M., "The Habits of the Blind in Japan," *Transactions of the Asiatic Society of Japan*, 28, 1890–1891

[9] Wilber, L., *Vocations for the Visually Handicapped*, 1937, p 15

associations consisting of the alumni of the special schools for the blind. The strength of these groupings rests in the informal ties and loyalties which were built up from the intimate interaction of blind students during their boarding-school days. In addition to these there are various local organizations set up for purposes of fellowship and recreation. These are not always too well supported, particularly in large cities where a great deal of travel is required for attendance. In quite a few areas there are special associations of "street workers," or of vendors and news dealers to which the blind belong. In some respects organizations like the former resemble the old beggars' guilds. A few of the more aggressive blind workers have joined unions, and in a few of the sheltered workshops throughout the country small unions of blind workers have been organized and become affiliated with the labor movement.

The blind themselves are rarely organized in a strictly political capacity. Generally, the organizations which work in the special interests of the visually handicapped are "of and for the blind." Groupings of this type, which enlist charitable, service, and philanthropic agencies, have grown into state-wide, national, and even international federations. The political leverage of these organizations is amply attested to by workers with the blind. One social worker to whom the writer talked called the blind and their allies the "best organized minority group in the world." These groups maintain a careful watch on legislatures and administrators, and through their publications and mailing lists keep the blind well informed on matters directly affecting their interests. However, the organizational efficiency of these groups has been exaggerated. They are probably no better organized than other pressure groups, but their power is greater because of the susceptibility of the public to the sentimental appeals addressed to it in support of concessions to the blind. This is best demonstrated by the fact that the blind have long relied upon personal appearances before legislative bodies for effectiveness in their lobbying activities.[10]

Some of the more militant groups of the blind have evolved in a sectarian direction. In Minneapolis one of the local societies of the blind in its early history excluded all sighted persons from membership. Later it retreated from this strong stand far enough to permit sighted persons to become nonvoting members. Another group in the same community still stands dead against the admission of any sighted persons. Furthermore, in its bylaws it has specifically prohibited entree to blind social workers. The chief complaints of the two groups have been directed toward what they regard as the patronizing attitudes of other community welfare groups. They have insisted that their suggestions for various measures to improve the services for the blind are persistently disregarded. This seems to have

[10] Best, *op cit.*, p 314, footnote 5

isolated these two groups from public support as administered through the established welfare agencies. An interesting sidelight on the local power structure comes from the fact that in its feud with the welfare agencies one of the groups has been able to secure some financial aid from organized labor in the community.[11]

All these facts create interesting speculation. While the actions of the two groups may be regarded as the group equivalent of tantrum behavior,

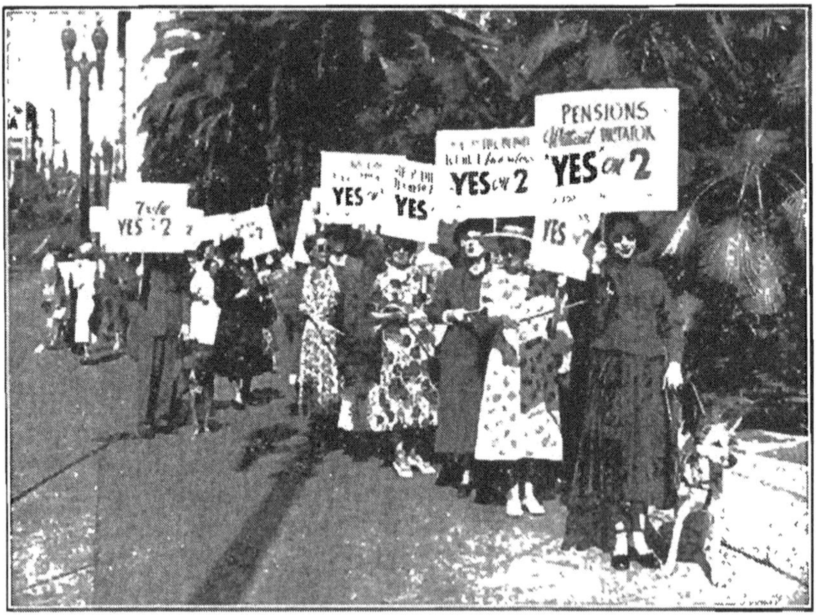

FIG 5. The political techniques of the blind – a parade

they also raise a question as to what happens when the blind in a collective capacity desert their traditional roles of humility and agitate in an independent way like any other pressure group. As we shall see from later discussion, something more than a mere "problem in community organization" is involved here.

THE SOCIAL VISIBILITY OF THE BLIND

The blind have always held the most conspicuous and dramatic position of the handicapped groups, clearly indicated by the frequency of allusions to their affliction in prose, drama, and poetry. The lay person as well as the poet is struck by the "sad, wan faces" of the blind, their fumbling and groping and bizarre posturings. Because much blindness results from accident and disease, it is to be expected that physical disfigurements would

11 "The Blind of Hennepin County," pp. 100–133.

be more prevalent in this group,[12] which serve to accentuate their major handicap. The fact that the eyes are involved in this handicap has a special effect in so far as visibility is concerned. Much of human expressive behavior centers in the eyes, so that when they are continually closed or unfocused or functioning independently of the voice they are distractions which increase the interactional visibility of the blind person.

Another major source of the visibility of the blind is found in the secondary behavior manifestations of blindness, unconscious in nature, which are known to students and workers with the blind as "blindisms." These are probably most common in persons blinded at birth or at early ages. In many of these cases the absence of sight complicates the process of speech acquisition so that many blind children have speech defects, delayed speech, infantile speech, or they stutter. Even though speech is normal, in many other respects it may have conspicuous qualities such as a peculiar flatness or lack of expression. Some of the blind have a "broadcasting voice" caused by their lack of space perception, in a public restaurant, for example, they may boom forth words in a manner more fitting to a congressional speech than to table conversation.[13]

Other blindisms include odd postures, rocking, moving the head rhythmically, poking and rubbing the eyes, exploring bodily appendages and orifices, feeling and snapping objects, groping and fluttering the hands in front of the eyes. Dark glasses and thick lenses which magnify the eyes, canes, seeing-eye and guide dogs, and other mechanical aids also make the blind more noticeable in public places. In cultures where the blind have been highly professionalized, certain symbolic devices have been chosen deliberately in order to identify the blind man and announce his role to others. In ancient Japan a shaved head was traditionally the badge of blindness, a custom which apparently persists there even today. The most commonly accepted symbol of blindness in our present-day society is the red-and-white cane. One survey of a sample of one hundred blind in a Middle Western community revealed that 60 per cent made use of white canes.[14]

Not all blind persons are visible as such, even where total blindness exists. In other words, blindisms or stigmas are not the inevitable accompaniments of blindness by any means. However, blind persons with low visibility may elect to symbolize their handicap simply for safety reasons and for convenience. One totally blind boy who had a very normal appearance suffered so many unfortunate experiences from being taken for

[12] In the Minneapolis area 19 per cent of the blind had other physical handicaps, 43 per cent had chronic illnesses, 37 per cent were in average to good health. *Ibid.*, p. 19

[13] Cutsforth, T D , *The Blind in School and Society*, 1933, Chap. 1, Fladeland, S V , "Speech Defects of Blind Children," *Teacher's Forum* (Blind), 3, 1930, pp. 6–8

[14] "The Blind of Hennepin County," p. 47.

sighted that he began to carry a cane even though he made not the slightest use of it in getting about in his environment. Cases of this sort emphasize the extreme importance of visible symbols of the defect in setting the pattern of interaction between the sighted and the blind.

The case history excerpt we present below is almost a classical illustration of how the secondary manifestations of blindness give it special social meaning:[15]

At the age of twenty-four, when he entered the institution, Bert presented a cadaverous, apelike appearance. He was of average height, but 40 pounds underweight. His physical emaciation was due to several food aversions he had been permitted to acquire and to a severely pointed dental arch which interfered with the mastication of food. He had acquired a double curvature of the spine which not only exaggerated the slovenly stoop in his shoulders, but also threw his head back until his face was turned skyward. The eccentricity of his posture was increased by the attempt to employ to its maximum advantage the small visual field of one eye that the operation had provided. For near objects Bert supplemented this slight amount of vision with a small tubular eyepiece taken from a microscope, which he held and adjusted with his hand. For distant vision he employed an 8-inch section of a brass telescope. He kept his mouth wide open, and, due to the position of his head, he developed a ticlike cough or bark, originally caused by saliva draining into the trachea. This ticlike bark occurred in a rhythm of about one each minute and a half. When either walking or passively sitting he continually fluttered his hands before his face or between his knees. His manual activity would vary to include manipulation of some erogenous area of his body.

Bert's customary social behavior was to take a standing position on the remote periphery of a group where he could hear the conversation. While listening he would fixate some spot upon the ceiling, a street light, or the moon and make responses in a muttered soliloquy. Intermittently, about every minute and a half, he would emit his ticlike bark. This bark would increase in frequency and intensity upon emotional changes aroused by the subject of conversation or by the danger of being approached. He desired no form of communication with anyone and, if approached, would either hurry away or cover his face with both hands and bend double until his head was below his waistline.

The aggregate visibility of the blind is affected by such things as their spatial concentration, if any, within the community, the frequency with which they appear on the streets, and the space given to them in newspapers and in other media of mass communication. While most of the blind are immobilized because of illnesses or because of extreme dependency, some blind mendicants are able to move fairly well through their environments. A few of the latter working in a community may give the impression of large numbers. The visibility of the blind individual will

[15] Cutsforth, *op. cit.*, pp 27*f*. By permission of Appleton-Century-Crofts, Inc, New York.

importantly influence his immediate role and status; on the other hand, the aggregate visibility of the blind interacts with the over-all societal reaction to condition such things as social-welfare legislation and the administration of the agencies dealing with the visually handicapped.

The Societal Reaction – Folklore about Blindness

An ancient and remarkably vital folklore surrounds the subject of blindness and the blind. This takes the form of imputing mystical abilities to the blind which are not possessed by sighted persons and grossly fallacious estimates of what the blind can do and cannot do, all overlaid with vague notions about the origins of blindness in sin. Common among the fixed notions of the abilities of the blind is the idea that they possess supernormal powers of hearing, touch, taste, smell, and memory, or some sort of "sixth sense" permitting miracles of perception. Fantastic stories are told of blind persons who can "feel colors," or of the blind schoolteacher who can pick out of her class the child who is chewing gum. Much has been written about "facial vision," sometimes as if it, too, were an ability not present or capable of development in ordinary persons. Little in the way of scientific evidence can be adduced to give truth to these ideas. No proof of a special psychology or special physiology of the blind exists. Careful study of blind children has demonstrated that as a class they are not distinguishable from other children in so far as the distribution of nonvisual sensory acuity is concerned.[16] Many blind people do make better use of their remaining senses than sighted persons, largely through a process of learning and adjustment; but when an unaccustomed demand is made upon them, no superiority in sense perception is apparent. Not all persons without vision even possess tactile sensitivity sufficiently keen for the mastery of Braille. When a sound, such as the clicking of a key, is divorced from its environment and associations, a group of blind persons has the same curve of auditory perception of the stimulus as sighted persons.[17]

Despite the falsity of these notions about the blind they are viable elements of the myth symbolizing and maintaining social distance between the blind and the sighted worlds. Additional symbols of this dichotomy come from the folk stereotype that the blind live in a "world of darkness." There is no support for this belief in the testimony of the blind themselves. Many, never having known light, are incapable of conceiving its opposite, and those blinded after a sighted period soon lose the idea of light. Some of the blind "see" colors which are something like fireworks, but if blindness is total, nothing else can be perceived visually. Some of

[16] Hayes, Samuel, "The Psychology of Blindness," in Lende, *op. cit.*, Chap. V.
[17] *Ibid.*

the blind who once have had vision retain visual memories, presumably such a fund of memories is of some aid in physical adjustments of the blind, but the subject has not been carefully studied.

Perhaps the most significant aspect of the societal definition of the blind, reinforced by certain emphatic responses, consists of the beliefs about the intense difficulties under which the blind labor and about the deep sorrow

FIG. 6. Attitudes toward the blind. The photograph was taken from a newspaper and carried the caption "Clown's Comic Features Bring Smiles to Blind Youngsters Happy smiles light up the faces of these blind children as they 'see' circus clown Emmett Kelly for the first time, tenderly outlining his comic features with their fingertips The dramatic moment came at the climax of a free show put on by the circus in Madison Square Garden for New York City's crippled, blind, and underprivileged children." *(By permission of Acme Photo, New York City)*

and unhappiness the blind feel over being deprived of vision. Associated with these beliefs are the excessive sympathy, compulsive assistance, and widespread, often injudicious, charity which characterize the general reaction to the blind. Stereotyped beliefs of this class function in the economic separation of the blind, increasing the salient barrier to their occupational integration into our society. They have further important implications for the general self-definitions of the blind. Casual, matter-of-fact adjustments of blind persons to their handicaps are made difficult by the convictions of others that these persons are showing great courage or that they have assumed a "mantle of cheerfulness" to hide their grief, playing a Pagliacci role in the face of tragic handicap.

Changing Reactions to the Blind

The societal definitions and fixed public responses to the blind are best understood as cultural accretions of great age which in the past century have been undercut by modern science, changing technology, and urbanization. A historical review of the changing patterns of reaction to blindness and the blind carries us clear back into pre-Christian cultures of the Mediterranean area. Fragments of historical data tell of several kinds of attitudes toward the blind in ancient civilizations of the Near East, in Greece, and in Rome. These range from quasi reverence to open hostility and distrust. The expression of the attitudes in culturally established roles for the blind has varied from their tolerance as slaves, beggars, and prostitutes, to their more equitable acceptance as employed workers, seers, tutors, musicians, and poets. Among the early Hebrews begging was customarily dictated as the blind man's role, although his reception in this role was far from gracious. Christianity was generally associated with an improvement in the status of the blind in those countries to which it was diffused, for ministering to penniless wanderers, the sick, and the handicapped came to be the sanctioned means of gaining religious merit. Begging was closely integrated with the medieval-feudal Christian ethic; beggars became sacred personages, the necessary recipients of ritual charity, for which they repaid donors by prayers murmured at the church door. Feudal society also made room for the blind as troubadours, poets, and minstrels, who were held in no small esteem.

The decline of European feudalism saw a waning of the golden era of begging, and with this the status of the blind declined measurably. Post-feudal cultural change witnessed a tremendous increment of beggars in many European countries. Impostors, fakers, rogues, rascals, among whom were many real or feigned cases of physical handicap, appeared in variants of the beggar's role and preyed industriously upon the settled population. This parasitic class was especially numerous in England following the wars of Henry VII and during the reigns of Henry VIII and of Elizabeth. It was at this time that the aura of evil and rascality settled upon the beggar, a connotation which persists somewhat even today. Restrictive legislation against begging appeared as early as the twelfth century in European towns. Later in England under Queen Elizabeth the first attempts were made at systematizing poor relief and organized repression of begging. Under the poor laws the blind were grouped with paupers, mentally disordered persons, and displaced children in an omnibus dependent class. There they remained until the specialization of welfare services for different kinds of dependent groups arose in the eighteenth and nineteenth centuries.

Nineteenth- and Twentieth-century Attitudes toward the Blind

Nineteenth-century industrialization and urbanization had several consequences for the status of the blind. The humanitarianism and organized philanthropy of the second half of the century in England and the United States introduced the conception of character defect as a middle-class explanation of pauperism, which had the concomitant result of associating physical defect with personality weakness and lack of self-resolution. This became the contemporary variant of the ancient idea of the origins of blindness in sin. At the same time the humanitarian movement was responsible for the special regard for the blind which gave them a more secure relief status than other dependent groups. It was also middle-class interest and concern with methods of restoring the self-reliance of the individual which led to the creation of special schools for the blind and to the generalized convictions of their educability and employability.

Much of the culture conflict as to what should be the role and status of the blind came to a focus in the thinking of early educators of the blind. At first a romantic optimism colored educational philosophy in the blind schools, which is best interpreted as a reflection of the ebullient convictions of the American middle class that, given initiative and knowledge, anything could be accomplished by the individual entrepreneur. In a way, at this time the blind became culture heroes personifying the American "success story." Many nineteenth- and early twentieth-century books about the blind and by the blind were analogues of the Horatio Alger stories, having such titles as *Heroes of Darkness*, *Beauties and Achievements of the Blind*, *True Stories of the Heroic Blind* and *Fighting with His Eyes Shut.*

In time there came a disillusionment with the philosophy that through education the blind could compete successfully in the socioeconomic system. Graduates of blind schools simply did not fulfill the high hopes cherished by their sponsors. It became plain that something besides education was needed, for despite their qualifications, the educated blind found employers skeptical and reluctant to hire them. Idleness, charity, and public dole continued to be the choices of the blind, with a newly added expedient of "sheltered employment."

Two world wars in the twentieth century have stimulated programs of vocational rehabilitation, with a new emphasis upon propaganda and education directed at transforming employer attitudes toward the physically handicapped. But the process of change is a glacial one, and the mass of archaic and medieval attitudes toward the blind has yielded but slowly to the efforts at reform. The discrepancy between the rehabilitative ideal and cultural actuality has inspired widespread conservatism among many groups of the blind which causes them to resist all efforts to change legislation affecting their status. It is significant that the baiting of rehabilitation training with higher allowances than those granted on relief has been necessary to recruit candidates to these programs. The burden of proof falls heavily upon those who claim that a real break in continuity of the traditions of blind dependency has come with rehabilitation programs.

Area Variations in Reactions to the Blind

Thus far we have abstracted some of the elements common to the fixed notions and customary reactions to the blind for the whole culture. The space-time configurations of the societal reaction vary considerably in a diversified culture and decentralized society such as ours. At the level of region and community the societal reaction is a product of several interactive factors besides the generalized public stereotypes of the blind. These interactive factors embrace the special reactions of welfare agencies, policies of the local police department, the personnel practices of industry, and the programs and activities of pressure groups seeking to better the lot of the blind. Ideally, these would be expressed in a tolerance quotient, but lacking methods for doing this we must fall back upon informal estimates and indirect measures of differential deviation and differential tolerances for the blind from one area to another.

A very superficial kind of comparison can be made between the situation of the blind in the area of Detroit, Michigan, and that in Southern California. On the whole in the recent past, there seems to have been much more of a blind "problem" in the former community than in the latter. Mendicancy among the blind seems to have been not only common but also of a more flagrant sort in Detroit, especially during the Second World War. At that time concern with begging ran high, as was shown by the amount of newspaper space taken up by stories of the blind who sought to eke out their incomes in this way. Controversies were aired over the issuance of vendors' licenses, and police were much more aggressive in enforcing ordinances on this matter. In this they were no doubt encouraged and aided by the presence of a blind judge in the courts who actively combated begging by others with his handicap. Welfare workers in Detroit agencies took a rather positive stand during the war period with respect to soliciting alms, holding firmly to the requirement that the blind observe their no-begging pledges in order to retain eligibility for relief.

In the Los Angeles area, in the past several years at least, little public agitation over begging by the blind has reached the newspapers. Police interviewed by the author have not thought of begging by the blind as any special problem, although they readily admit of a limited number of cases in which it is carried on. It may well be true that the higher relief standards for the blind in California may have lessened somewhat the need of the blind to engage in charity soliciting.

In striving to assess the part of political factors in the treatment of the blind by welfare agencies in an area, it must be remembered that the blind are one of several groups competing for access to relief support. These include the aged, dependent children, and the poor receiving general assistance. Each group has a historical basis for its appeals and each group has its organized partisans. Table 5 contains certain comparisons of the relief status of dependent groups in California and in Michigan for 1943.

TABLE 5. CASE RATES AND AVERAGE PUBLIC-ASSISTANCE GRANT PER CASE FOR FOUR DEPENDENT GROUPS IN CALIFORNIA AND MICHIGAN, 1943*

State	Blind		Aged		Dependent children		General assistance	
	Cases per 100,000 population	Average grant	Cases per 100,000 population	Average grant	Cases per 100,000 population	Average grant	Cases per 100,000 population	Average grant
California	93	$47.17	254	$47.28	12	$67 69	308	$29 66
Michigan	24	32 21	246	27.95	22	57.25	536	26 54

* Compiled from "Report on Public Assistance," *Social Security Bulletin*, No. 10, October, 1943, pp 27–37.

From this comparison it can be seen that Michigan at the time was carrying proportionately much heavier general-assistance and aid-to-dependent-children case loads than California. The case load for the aged was about the same, but in relative terms almost four times as many blind were being aided in California as in Michigan. While California averaged higher grants to all these dependent groups than did Michigan, the greatest differences appear in the case of the aged and the blind.

Undeniably this table reflects differing incidences of dependency in these various groups in the two states. Thus the proportionately larger numbers of general-assistance cases may have meant that less money remained for the aid of the blind in Michigan. The rural nature of much of Michigan outside of the Detroit area may have meant a greater degree of support of the blind in Michigan by their families. Furthermore, more of the blind there may have been carried as general-assistance cases.

Outside of factors such as these, which are difficult to analyze, it must be said that the differences seen in the table conform to what we know of welfare emphasis in the two states. Michigan would appear to be more alert to child-welfare "problems" than California, if comparative data on child-guidance clinics, delinquency-control programs, and the like can be taken as indications. In California on the other hand, especially in the southern area, the aged and the blind for some years have been the main object of considerable special welfare legislation. California was one of the early leaders in organizing special schools for the blind as well as a separate state-assistance program.

The political power of the blind in California, which enters in to differentiate the situations in the two states, is tokened by the great responsiveness on the part of social workers to demands of the blind. For example, there have been instances in which decisions by social workers in public agencies have been directly countermanded by county and state officials. The blind, at least in Los Angeles County, have the right to read their own case records, something denied to other recipient groups. Their right of administrative appeal is far greater than for other groups receiving aid and is much more formalized. During periods of rising living costs their aid has been increased before others on public assistance. Finally, the blind, in contrast to other dependent groups, have obtained substantial state tax exemptions. Changes favorable to the blind have been enacted by every legislature meeting since passage of the original blind-assistance law in 1929.[18]

While the special advantages gained by the blind apply to all the visually handicapped in the state, there is good indication that the political weight of the large blind group in the southern area has been behind the legislative and administrative concessions. In 1945, 61.7 per cent of the blind were in Southern California counties and 45 per cent lived in Los Angeles County alone.[19] Additional evidence of the political power of the blind in this area is found in the fact that in a referendum election of 1949 the blind groups felt sufficiently strong to dissociate themselves from the aged groups to work for the defeat of legislation affecting both groups.

Although we have no direct proof of it, we are disposed to the idea that the agitation for improved public provision for the blind may be related to absence of opportunities for employment in the southern part of the state. An older study has shown employers in the Los Angeles area to be a great deal less favorable to the employment of handicapped persons than other California communities. The comparisons are presented in Table 6. It is clear from these data that Los Angeles stands low in its economic hospitality to the blind, at least as manifested by employer attitudes. While these attitudes may reflect some general ideological variation, apparently they may also stem from the nature of the economic specialization of the community. It is known, for example, that a community with

18 *Report of the Interdepartment Committee on Study of Problems of and Services for the Blind*, p. 46.

19 *Ibid.*, p. 11

many canning factories or metal-working industries tends to absorb more handicapped workers than a town given over to retail trade or a railroad shop town.[20] However, we would hesitate at this time to attempt to explain how the industrial and business specialization of the Los Angeles area lowers employer receptivity to handicapped labor, if this is the case. Much research is needed upon relationships of this sort, perhaps under the head of "handicapped-labor market analysis." With findings from such studies we may be in a position to answer questions of this kind for specific communities and for selected handicaps and also be prepared to give the general concept of differential tolerances for the blind a more accurate meaning.

TABLE 6. PERCENTAGE OF EMPLOYERS IN SPECIFIED CALIFORNIA COMMUNITIES FAVORABLE TO THE EMPLOYMENT OF PHYSICALLY HANDICAPPED PERSONS*

City	Per Cent
Oakland....	74 4
Eureka	74.4
Fresno	63 3
Santa Rosa	57.7
Monterey	56 8
Los Angeles	42.7
Richmond	29.2

* "Census and Industrial Survey of the Physically Handicapped in California," California State Department of Education *Bulletin* 9, 1935, p 28.

It is entirely possible that some sort of counterbalance exists in various communities between the economic tolerance of the blind and the tolerances manifested by public and private welfare functions. Thus we might reason that a community which rejects the blind economically feels greater pressure on its relief resources than some other community which makes economic opportunities available to this class of deviants. This hypothetical second community may give harsher treatment to blind mendicants and be less receptive in general to dependency on the part of the blind. Of course, the interplay of political factors must be taken into consideration in a relationship of this kind, more so in the present day than in the past. Reliance upon political techniques by handicapped groups to improve and secure their status seems to be a trend in many of our states today.

It might be tentatively held here that to the extent that handicapped groups exert political pressure upon the state the Christian humanitarian justification for special concessions to them will be weakened. There is a possibility that mounting tax costs of relief to handicapped groups resulting from these pressures ultimately will produce a critical awareness of

20 "Census and Industrial Survey of the Physically Handicapped in California," California State Department of Education *Bulletin* 9, 1935, p. 28.

the alternatives to relief on the part of those groups which are primarily responsible for economic exclusion of the handicapped. Business and industrial power alignments then may take really effective steps to render the blind along with other handicapped persons an economically more productive class.

Special Aspects of the Societal Reaction – Family Attitudes and Responses

Thus far our interest has been in the more general nature of the societal reaction to which all or most of the blind are exposed, or by which most of them have their lives directly or indirectly affected. Other reactions to the blind are much more variable; whether or not they are operative factors depends upon the particular status of the blind persons and upon the character of persons and groups with which the blind have social contacts and interaction. Among the special reactions which may vary considerably are those of the family group in which the blind person develops. These reactions, of course, are pertinent only in cases where blindness has been congenital or where it has occurred in the early years of life.

The reaction of the family to the birth and presence of a blind child in its midst runs a broad gamut of response from rejection, through non-emotional acceptance, to overprotection and indulgence. Overprotection and indulgence seem to be the more common reactions to handicapped children.[21] The number of families able to accept a blind child with equanimity and aid it to grow in an independent way within the limits of its handicap is in the minority. The reasons for this are closely related to the nature of our culture. The highly competitive nature of our ethos, working in conjunction with close identifications between parents and children, typically leads to anxieties about the birth and growth of physically normal children. The real or imagined blight cast upon the social status of parents bearing an imperfect child magnifies these anxieties enormously, and the consequent sense of inferiority may be intolerable. An all-too-common reaction to the birth of a blind child is to interpret it as a symbol of divine punishment. The old Biblical doctrine that "sins of the fathers shall be visited upon the children even unto the third and fourth generations" gets entangled with garbled modern knowledge of heredity, so that strong feelings of guilt arise and are expressed in rejection of the child.

Rejection of the blind child is often closely related to beliefs that blindness is caused by venereal disease in the parents, traceable in part to the

[21] Barker, R. G., *et al.*, "Adjustment to Physical Handicap and Illness," Social Science Research Council *Bulletin* 55, 1946, pp. 74–76.

fact that it is generally known that a number of cases of congenital blindness do result from syphilis and gonorrhea. A sense of guilt over a blind offspring may similarly spring from actual or fancied violations of the middle-class, Puritan sex mores. Latent guilt over permarital sexual intercourse, perversions, or use of abortifacients may be activiated by the birth of a blind child, leading to rejection of the child as the living symbol of the parental sins.[22] The question may be raised as to whether decisions to send blind children to special preschools and institutions for the blind are not in many instances caused primarily by rejection of the children and secondarily rationalized in terms of their welfare.

Most parents lack the knowledge and skills to effect a full growth of the blind child's personality. The result tends to be either neglect or indulgence and a one-sided adjustment of the family life to the needs of the blind child. Teaching the blind child to use language in a meaningful way is a task often beyond the scope of parental abilities. In attempts to remedy the sensory deficiency of the child, parents often overwhelm it with a flood of auditory stimulation, which is responsible to a high degree for the verbal unreality that characterizes the speech and writing of so many of the blind.[23] A family may rear a child successfully up through the lower age levels but fail to prepare it realistically for the crisis of adolescence. This may be particularly true for middle-class families, where occupational and marital hazards facing the child are often ignored or unduly minimized.

Control Agencies — Educational

The most important of the social control agencies set up by society to deal with the blind, apart from relief and rehabilitative agencies, are its special educational facilities and institutions. The regular public schools have varied considerably in their willingness and ability to take in blind students. Many have not been equipped to handle blind students, while others — probably the majority — have arrangements whereby the blind may go to school along with sighted students. Under such arrangements the blind students are differentiated in such ways as having special home rooms and privileges of leaving class at certain times.

The educational facilities instituted exclusively for the blind include home teaching services, day schools, and residential schools. Most of the blind acquire what education they have through home instruction or through the above-mentioned kind of instruction provided in the public schools or through combinations of both. A much smaller proportion of the blind receive their training in residential schools or in some kind of

22 Sommers, Vita Stein, *The Influence of Parental Attitudes and Social Environment on the Personality Development of the Adolescent Blind*, 1944, Chap V

23 Cutsforth, *op. cit.*, Chap. 3.

workshop. While recent figures are not available, nevertheless some idea of these proportions can be had from old census statistics. According to the 1910 data about 43 per cent of the blind had attended some kind of school. About 23 per cent had been in a residential school or workshop for training, and about two-thirds of the latter had no other educational experience outside of these two types of institutions. The younger the age at which blindness occurred, the greater was the likelihood of training in a special school. So, for example, slightly over 60 per cent of the persons blinded below the age of twenty had gone to a special school. Furthermore at the time, four-fifths of all blind children were in special educational institutions, although there were extremely wide variations in this ratio from state to state.[24] The absolute percentages given here are no longer applicable today. However, the ratio of those going to special schools to those receiving other forms of training may not have changed much. The central fact that those who are born blind or blinded early in life tend to go to special schools is even less likely to have changed.

There is a dearth of research on the sociological position of the blind children in the public-school system; the patterns of interaction and segregation, especially of an informal nature, remain an unknown area. However, it would be generally held that the ability of blind children to compete with sighted children in the school situation is limited by their lower educability in terms of a sighted culture. To the extent that the formal arrangements for their education with the sighted children become a compromise with standards, informal distinctions of an invidious kind easily appear. We suspect that the sensing of their inability to compete under such arrangements may account for dropping out of school by many blind students or for decisions by their parents to remove them or to place them in special schools. It is at this point that aspirational levels of parents become important in the further differentiation of the blind child which comes from placing it in an institutional school.

While fewer of the blind attend residential schools, nevertheless these schools are of special sociological interest primarily because it is those born blind or blinded early in life who receive their education there. These schools further engage our interest because of the cloistered environment they represent. Whereas blind children are least isolated socially when they are integrated into a regular school system, and somewhat more so in day schools, they are most isolated in a residential school. In these institutions the child is under twenty-four-hour control, usually for nine months out of the year. Furthermore, the average amount of time spent in these schools is quite high, at one time running to seven years per

[24] Best, Harry, *The Blind – Their Condition and What Is Being Done for Them*, 1919, pp 359–361.

child.[25] There is small doubt that the differential association of blind with blind and with the seeing staff in these schools does much to shape the role and status of a significant portion of the visually handicapped population.

While efforts may be made in a residential school to duplicate the outside social environment, essential elements are missing, and the external culture is always mediated by the structure and personnel of the on-going institution. The teaching and administrative staffs of schools for the blind have special qualities, being the products of a selective process influenced by lower salaries, less keen competition for positions, and the promise of security the positions offer. A certain percentage of the teaching staff usually consists of blind persons, themselves the graduates of such schools. All these facts underscore the refuge or "asylum" features of the school. Close personal bonds often grow up between blind children and their teachers, which tend to magnify the impact of isolant-type personalities upon the child. When these identifications are with blind teachers, the scene is often set for communication to the students of implicit cynicism or ancient informal precepts of dependence.

The institutional environment tends to be rigid and tends to reward conformity at the price of individuality and growth. This is an inescapable characteristic shared with all public institutions and is enhanced by the political vulnerability of tax-supported agencies in our social system.[26] Institutional loyalties become of ascending importance in a situation such as this and they, in turn, become a basis for isolating the agency staff and residents.

Institutional policy in the residential school tends to be adapted to meet the least possible criticism from any and all groups and even from single individuals. The result of this conservatism, we believe, is to sharpen the traditional stereotype of what the blind are expected to be like and to incorporate it into educational policy. Great efforts are thus made to reduce the publicly objectionable features of the blind, lower their visibility, and make them into "cheerful," even-tempered, well-behaved products of the school. The subjective aspect of this can sometimes be seen in the great sensitivity of the graduates of such schools to public opinion about their appearance and mannerisms.

The organizational identity of institutions for the blind, nominally educational but in reality often charitable in nature, carries a powerful symbolic impact for those under their control. In many states the administration of schools for the blind is in the hands of the department of education,

[25] Best, *Blindness and the Blind in the United States.*

[26] Wells, F. L., "The State School as a Social System," *Journal of Psychology*, 5, January, 1938, pp 119–124

but as late as 1943 schools for the blind were under the direct supervision of departments of social welfare in at least nine states and possibly in more. In 13 other states home teaching was administered by divisions of the department of social welfare. In still other states there were organizational ties between the relief agencies of the state and those educating and rehabilitating the blind.[27]

The knowledge that their education is somehow associated with the care of the deaf, mentally deficient, insane, diseased, and dependent classes must ultimately be communicated to the blind students in many ways. Despite efforts at redefinition of the blind school and the attempts to dissociate it from relief and welfare institutions, the societal conception of the blind as "defective" is often implicit in its organizational status, in its traditions, and in its unrationalized procedures. The stamp of inferiority cannot be easily escaped by the blind child under its control.

Discontinuity in the Education of the Blind

The influence of Samuel Gridley Howe, who was largely responsible for the system of blind education set up at the Perkins Institute in Massachusetts in 1832, has been pervasive and enduring in determining the curriculum and techniques of the schools for the blind. The emphasis has been upon a classical education, heavily weighted with literary training, based upon the militant assumption that the blind should be educated just like any other children. The modal impact of this is dually manifested: First of all, it perpetuates and aggrandizes the verbal unreality already noted as a common result of parental ineptitude in training the blind preschool child. This is strikingly obvious in the writing of many blind persons, which has a strangely stilted and trite character. A vast amount of the education in the schools for the blind is thus in the nature of encumbrance with words having visual associations and little meaning for the blind child beyond speciously identifying him with the visual, esthetic phases of our culture. A second result of this orientation is that, in their efforts to treat blind children as similar to those without handicaps and simply requiring "special methods," educators of the blind are frequently ignoring the real differentiation and social meaning of the handicaps of blindness. While it is probably true that most of our schools generally fail to prepare children for adult roles in our culture, this omission is more grossly true of the schools for the blind. Presumably the teachers of the blind, particularly those without vision themselves, are cognizant of the gulf between the curriculum and the socioeconomic realities which will

[27] Lende, Helga (ed), *Directory of Activities for the Blind in the United States and Canada,* American Foundation for the Blind, 1943

confront their students after graduation. If this is true, then to that extent it must be a demoralizing factor to the more sincere and insightful members of the teaching staff. This can scarcely fail to affect the students in turn. Many of the blind persons interviewed by the writer have shown strong ambivalent attitudes toward their schooling in special institutions.

In recent years many changes have been brought about in the administration and educational philosophy of the schools for the blind. The deliberate striving to treat the blind as special educational problems rather than as welfare problems is tokened in the growing movement to emancipate the schools from their welfare stigma and to place them under departments of education. Closer integration of the blind school with the surrounding community is a partial reality as well as a goal in many areas. Ancient institutional precepts have been liberalized, for example, in such things as greater comingling of the sexes. However, until more adequate opportunities for fuller social participation are opened up, educational privileges of the blind child are likely to remain as a recompense rather than become a means of continuous individual growth and placement in society.

Welfare Agencies

Since the passage of the Federal Social Security laws practically all our states have state-subsidized programs of aid and assistance for the blind. In some of the states administration of these programs has been through special state agencies, but in most states it is shared with a local agency, usually the county welfare department. Financial help to the blind in nearly all cases is on the basis of need, which places the blind strictly in a relief or dependent category along with the poor, the aged, and dependent children. In some states, providing that eligibility for this relief is established, the blind may "go on the county" and retain this status for the rest of their lives. Partial efforts to control begging by the blind have been made in about one-half of the states, by making mendicancy a disqualification for assistance. Fewer than half of the states make willingness to undergo remedial surgery a condition of aid. In 1939, 22 states had neither of these qualifications for blind assistance, being states which in their laws gave little or no heed to the possibilities of rehabilitating the visually handicapped.[28]

A small number of our states have had rehabilitative programs for the blind for several decades, but most such programs have originated since the passage of Federal laws in 1936 and 1943 aimed at training the blind to fill useful economic functions in society. However, rehabilitation of the blind under either state or joint state-Federal auspices has not been too successful. For example, in California from 1921 to 1946 altogether only

[28] White, R. C., *Administration of Public Welfare*, 1940, pp 175–178

662 blind persons were rehabilitated, an average of about 26 per year.[29] Blind persons on the whole make poor risks for vocational training because of their ingrained attitudes toward work. They are unaccustomed to factory and other work environments and often feel ill at ease in the presence of sighted workers with whom they know they cannot compete. Again placement of blind persons after a course of training is not easy, as we have already noted. Often placements of the blind do not correspond with the vocational training they have received. Such facts as these have been important considerations in the organization of sheltered workshops for the blind.

The immediate interaction between visually defective clients and the social workers who administer assistance and rehabilitation is not always carried on at a high level of rapport. A sample of the Minneapolis blind group indicated that 27 per cent were hostile toward social workers.[30] Social workers in public agencies which serve the blind are not always well trained to do casework. Like many lay persons, they are apt to follow the easy assumption of the unemployability of the blind. The ambivalance of the blind toward the type of training they wish to follow and their often impractical ideas of business enterprise are frustrating to the social worker. Under the best conditions the blind are complicated casework problems; more commonly their behavior reflects culture conflicts beyond the power of the social caseworker to solve.

Individuation of the Blind

While there are many different factors interacting to create a broad diversity of individual reactions to blindness, the more dynamic interactors are the degree of blindness, the age at which the blindness came on, and the quality of the special societal reactions at certain critical points in the history of the blind individual. The child who has been blind since birth will differ from the person blinded in young adulthood or middle age, as well as from the aged who lose their vision toward the end of their lives. The maximum social impact of blindness is seen in the congenital blind. For this reason most of the following discussion is devoted to this class of blind persons.

The blind child begins life and spends his infancy in a symbolic environment which varies from that of the sighted child chiefly because of the differential responses made to it by its parents. The early insight and

29 *Report of the Interdepartment Committee on Study of Problems of and Services for the Blind*, p 101. Rehabilitations have increased in recent years, for all the states together about 13,000 of the blind have been placed through rehabilitation services in the past twelve years Yahres, H., "Don't Pity the Blind," *Collier's*, Apr 8, 1950.

30 "The Blind of Hennepin County," p. 38.

motivations of the visually handicapped child are influenced with little outside mediation at every point of social contact with the parents. Some blind children remain apathetic or overgrown infants simply because they receive insufficient stimulation to become socialized in accordance with their ages. Significantly, we find a higher percentage of mentally deficient cases among the blind as a deviant class. While many of these cases have organic complications, many others are purely the consequences of isolation within the family. Where blind children are overtly rejected and subjected to a flood of invidious comparisons made between them and other siblings, they frequently react by withdrawal or strong aggressions against their surroundings. The commonest pattern of behavior observable in blind children is a pronounced egocentrism, no doubt built up by the overprotective attitudes of many parents. Quite early, then, in many families, the blind child learns of the possibility of manipulating others through trading upon his handicap. Here the foundation is laid for the insistent, demanding behavior of many of the adult blind, which is clearly perceptible in their interaction with those who work with them in public capacities.

Primary Deviation

The blind remain primary deviants so long as they do not symbolize themselves as invidiously different from those around them. This can be seen most easily in persons blinded at birth or in their very early years. For the most part, primary deviation coincides with infancy in these cases; the awareness of differences and their social significance is but vaguely developed in the blind preschool child or entirely absent. Inadequacies and differences are quite often ignored or they are crudely rationalized by the child in terms of a normal, sighted role. Thus in one case which came before the writer, involving very limited vision, the person as a child was continually falling down but she explained it to herself as being occasioned by natural clumsiness rather than to poor vision on her part. The time at which the study of Braille is undertaken generally serves as a critical self-defining period for most blind children, the point at which secondary deviation occurs. This suggests the tremendous symbolic importance of the social contacts at this time in conveying the societal conception of the blind as defective and inferior. The context in which Braille must be learned nearly always carries these traditional connotations. One writer has commented upon the fact in New York City that one automatically becomes a "case" in a social-service agency when one learns Braille, and that there is no place in the United States where one may pay to acquire this skill.[31]

[31] Chevigny, H., *My Eyes Have a Cold Nose*, 1946, p. 99.

The self-symbolizing process of the growing blind child is progressively invaded from many sources by the fixed notions of defectiveness. Infantilisms are strengthened and converted into habits of dependency by the cumulative restriction of choices which might lead in other directions. The child's role in the family and school remains one of dependence rather than changing in the direction of greater self-determination. A critical juncture is reached at adolescence, when the child's sense of inadequacy is crystallized by the realization of the difficulty of fulfilling adult economic and sexual roles. Cultural discontinuity in adolescent transition is extreme for normal children in our culture, but it is doubly so for the blind child.

A partial measure of the gulf which comes to separate the blind child and his parents around the time of adolescence is furnished in a study of the respective appraisals by both the child and its parents of the child's life outlook in 72 cases of blind children of ages fourteen to twenty-one, all of whom were blind since birth or early infancy. The blind child and his parents made appraisals of the child on a five-step scale ranging from "discouraged, disappointed, a failure" up to "cheerful, optimistic, light-hearted." The results are tabulated in Table 7.

TABLE 7. COMPARISON BETWEEN PARENT'S APPRAISAL AND CHILD'S SELF-APPRAISAL FOR 72 BLIND CHILDREN AGES FOURTEEN TO TWENTY-ONE*

Item	No. of parents and children	Per cent
Parents and children agree	22	30
Parents rate child two steps better than child himself	24	33
Parents rate child one step better than child himself	20	28
Parents rate child one step lower than child himself	6	9
Total.	72	100

* Sommers, Vita Stein, *The Influence of Parental Attitudes and Social Environment on the Personality Development of the Adolescent Blind*, 1944, Table VI, p. 94.

It will be seen that the tendency is for parents in more than 60 per cent of the cases to overrate their blind offspring. This tendency is also brought out in interview data. Not a few blind students have communicated to the writer a substantial bitterness over the lack of realism about their abilities and over the undue optimism shown by their parents with regard to the difficulties of the adjustments to be faced in adulthood.

In our culture the inability to find and hold an occupation on the part of any adult, particularly male, nearly always imparts a social stigma. The puritanical values which associate unemployment with immorality and improvidence are almost impossible to escape by the blind as well as others who are occupationally unplaced. The nature of the jobs open to the more aggressive blind seeking work generally possess low status value, such occupations as piano tuning, basket and reed working, door-to-door selling, poultry raising, mattress making, chiropractice and massage, weaving, and the operation of stands are far from prestigeful. A few isolated cases of blind persons are known in which a comparatively high income has been earned at jobs of this sort, but usually only by those willing to exploit their handicap within the roles. The professions, of course, are an exception to our generalizations about the low prestige value of occupations for the blind, but only a small number of the blind gain entree into them; of one group of 265 trained for the professions, for example, only 65 were placed.[32]

The sponsorship of many of the enterprises making jobs available to the blind gives them a special symbolic value. In sheltered workshops there is much paternalism and maternalism on the part of supervisors, and all sorts of compromises are made with industrial efficiency which reflect upon the status of the jobs there. The knowledge that one is weaving a rug by hand which could be woven in a fraction of the time required if it were done by machine gives the job a "make-work" quality which cannot avoid posing a problem of its acceptance by the more independent blind person

The blind who go into business for themselves with public help in order to become partially self-supporting find that they must continually report to welfare agencies, so that a real severance of the umbilical cord of dependence never comes. The placement of blind stand operators in public buildings has been hailed as a step toward their vocational rehabilitation on a competitive basis. Yet the sponsorship of these stands leaves something to be desired from the standpoint of a blind person really striving for self-reliance. A blinded war veteran comments upon them as follows:[33]

> We also found out several things about this kind of business that we did not like. The concession selects the people who are to run these stands, and the stand is controlled through the State Commission for the Blind. While the person is the sole owner of all the equipment and stock in his business, the commission retains control over the business to the extent that the proprietor has to make a regular report of his business to the commission. The commission, also, has the right to restrict the sales of any item on any of these stands. This stand we visited gave the owner a very nice income, but somehow it rankled my independent spirit to imagine myself in such a position. I can't understand why the man, once he has been set up and is doing a good business, couldn't be allowed complete independence, as were his sighted competitors

From what has been said thus far, it is clear that the role choices open to the blind at adulthood contain many ambiguities and conflicts between

[32] *A Census and Economic Survey of the Blind in California*, pp. 16, 18.

[33] Fox, Monroe, *Blind Adventure*, 1946, p 173 By permission of J B Lippincott Company, Philadelphia

the values of the larger culture stressing full independence and those of a special protective control culture sanctioning what can only be thinly disguised dependency. A great many of the blind slip into these roles by dissociating the sense of nonfulfillment of the larger cultural values. These mostly are persons who were blinded early in life and who have been so situated as to escape urgent social pressure to become emancipated adults.

The Person Blinded in Adult Life

The person who has been blinded as a young adult or in middle age presents a different picture from the class discussed above. The critical point in his or her personal history occurs immediately following the blindness itself. Blindness of this kind, when it comes suddenly, is usually very traumatic in its effects, as is to be expected in the light of the tragic cultural stereotype we have of blindness. If at this point some sort of new role definition based upon blindness can be accepted and some positive incorporation of the conception in overt behavior – such as learning Braille – is achieved, chances are good that social rehabilitation can occur. Evidence for this comes from the empirical emphasis which caseworkers place upon contacting the newly blinded person and getting training started immediately.[34] The employed adult who loses his vision has more personal resources; in place of dependent attitudes he is likely to possess well-established or long-held habits of self-reliance and initiative. The crisis of adolescence is past, and the person may have a family of his own to mediate his isolation and be of tangible assistance. If no great shift of occupation is necessary and the problem of movement can be solved, the crisis of blindness may be passed and a satisfactory measure of social participation worked out.

We are lacking in careful studies of economic rehabilitation in relation to the differentiation and individuation of the blind. Such data as we have, however, tend to confirm the above conclusions which we have arrived at more or less deductively. Thus, of the blind rehabilitated over a twenty-four-year period in California, 68 per cent were under forty years of age, and less than 30 per cent were cases of congenital blindness (who make up around 50 per cent of all the blind). It has also been the empirical finding of workers with the blind that the blind who have been shielded by their families (the congenitally blind?) are more difficult to rehabilitate.[35]

A slowly developing blindness or long hospitalization coupled with medical uncertainty as to whether the blindness will be permanent or not

[34] Holtzer, B., "The Adjustment of the Newly Blind," in Lende, *What of the Blind?* pp. 109*ff*

[35] *Report of the Interdepartment Committee for Study of Problems of the Blind*, pp. 104, 107 On rehabilitation, also see *Comeback*, Administrative Service Series 43, 1947, Federal Security Agency, Office of Vocational Rehabilitation.

are also important factors in the individuation of the visually handicapped person. In these cases the uncertainty as to what will be the ultimate role of the person may cause him to cling desperately to his sighted role and produce habitual procrastination in so far as learning the techniques of the blind is concerned. The ambivalences of the critical period of transition may create endogenous conflicts and symbolic disturbances of an enduring sort. Conflicts of this order are very similar to or identical with those in marginal blindness. We shall have occasion to return to this subject in our discussion of the symbolic adjustment of the blind.

Social Participation of the Blind

The first thing to notice about the social participation of the blind is the very heavy demand which the handicap makes upon their energies in order to solve what are for most people simple habitual adjustments—locomotion through space, manual manipulations necessary for washing, eating, dressing, and reading. Some idea of the energy output of the blind is told in the experience of a newly blinded war veteran who on his first trip alone required two hours to travel 300 yards from one building to another on the hospital grounds. He was covered with perspiration and collapsed with fatigue at the end of his journey. Of course, it should be said that a great measure of his fatigue was the result of anticipatory fears and insecurity, the bulk of which he eventually lost. However, even in the spatially well-oriented blind person, there is always a high level of tension underlying physical adjustments. In learning to move around without sight, the blind usually have taken painful falls, so that anticipatory fears are associated with movement in all but the foolhardy. Barked shins and skinned noses are the inevitable marks of the highly mobile blind man. In stabilized environments the tensions are naturally reduced somewhat, but in complex, technologically mediated urban environments stability can only be relative. A street without parked cars for two months may overnight become lined with sharp-edged automobile hazards, or previously covered cellars on the sidewalks may suddenly become dangerous pitfalls. Such contingencies are never far from the consciousness of the blind person.

Moving into new areas calls for much careful planning, memorizing, and inquiries on the part of the blind. This suggests the tendency for the blind to become routinized in their movements through space and to develop participational patterns which necessitate a minimum of travel, particularly where changes from one form of transportation to another are required. It is interesting to note the modification of time patterns in the behavior of blind workers in a protected workshop in one large city. Most of them, on days when it was permissible, came to work before

7:30 A.M. and left before 4 P.M. chiefly to avoid the difficult hazards of rush-hour traffic. Activities requiring movement of the blind will be chosen with extreme care, the criteria for selection being their direct bearing upon the adjustment needs of the blind individual and the proven satisfactions they bring to him.

Recently much publicity has been given to "seeing-eye" dogs as the solution to the problem of movement by the blind. Yet only a very small percentage of blind persons use the dogs. Many of the blind dislike the dogs for various reasons or they are temperamentally unsuited to use them. The dogs can be trained to aid their blind masters to avoid most obstacles in the environment, but the possibility of their becoming confused in traffic is always present, especially by the friendly but sometimes dangerous overtures of sighted pedestrians. It might be said that the interaction of archaic reactions of overhelpfulness by the public with modern traffic conditions in urban communities actually decreases the social participation of the blind in activities requiring mobility, despite the development of new techniques for facilitating their travel.

Economic Participation

There is good reason to believe, as the result of experimental placements and wartime industrial experiences, that blind persons can within limits adequately fill a wide variety of jobs.[36] They are not capable of doing everything, as some fanciful and romantic propaganda would have us believe. However, a sufficient occupational versatility is present to warrant the contention that as a group they can be economically productive to society. Be that as it may, the fact remains that only an insignificant number of the blind are employed. The 1920 census showed 25.4 per cent of the blind employed in contrast to 78.2 per cent for the general population.[37] However, this is most probably an overstatement of the proportions employed even at that time. A 1935 survey in California showed only 5 per cent of 3,512 blind contacted holding jobs, giving a proportion of 1 out of every 20 blind persons with any kind of employment at all, including sheltered and protected workshops.[38] Since this was still a Depression year, the extent of unemployment among the blind was probably greater than would normally be the case. The economic status of the blind population in California during an economically prosperous year (1945) is presented in Table 8.

[36] One source lists 113 occupations in which blind workers have functioned successfully Lende, Helga (ed.), *Directory of Activities for the Blind in the United States and Canada*, pp. 134*ff*.

[37] *The Blind Population*, U. S. Bureau of the Census, 1920.

[38] *A Census and Economic Survey of the Blind in California*, p. 13

Table 8 indicates that about a thousand blind persons, or less than 10 per cent of the group, were actually or nominally independent in the economic sense. The percentage of the blind from birth who have made themselves economically self-sustaining may run very close to this figure, as indicated in Table 9.

TABLE 8. CURRENT STATUS OF 12,800 BLIND RESIDENTS OF CALIFORNIA*

Status	Number
In school ...	340
In state workshops	315
Receiving home instruction	600
Employed or self-employed	700
Recipients of state aid	6,000
In mental institutions	258
On direct relief or old-age assistance	4,587
Total	12,800

* *Report of Interdepartment Committee on Study of Problems of and Services for the Blind*, California State Departments of Education, Mental Hygiene, Public Health, and Social Welfare, 1946, p. 12.

TABLE 9 MEANS OF SUPPORT OF PERSONS BLIND SINCE BIRTH IN WASHINGTON, 1937*

Means of support	Number	Per cent
By earnings	10	8 3
By relatives	41	33.8
Blind relief	62	51.2
Old-age assistance	1	0 8
Other relief	3	2.4
Savings	0	0
Industrial compensation	0	0
No report .	4	3 3
Total	121	99 01

* *Survey of the Blind in the State of Washington*, State Department of Social Security May, 1937, adapted from Table IX appendixes.

Those blind who have established themselves in jobs tend to concentrate in manufacturing and mechanical industries, trade, and the professions. As shown above, a large number of those engaged in industrial work are employed in protected or sheltered workshops. The figures for those in trade or business include a goodly number who are little more than mendicants formally classified as employed. These facts should be kept in mind in reading Table 10.

The earnings of the blind are seldom sufficient for self-support save in a fractional percentage of cases. In California in 1937, only 88 persons of 3,512 surveyed reported that they were making even a bare living.[39] While

[39] *Ibid*, p 14.

the blind, like many others at the time, were adversely affected by economic conditions, this figure is still fantastically low. Even under more favorable economic conditions blind workers are likely to receive the lower paid jobs in the factory, and there is some evidence that upgrading is much slower for them. A study of a group of 1,815 handicapped persons in the aviation industry including 345 visually handicapped, concluded that for the handicapped in general advancement in lower grade jobs was more rapid than for a control group but slower from grade jobs to managerial ones.[40] Even in sheltered workshops wage rates for the blind are often below prevailing rates. It is significant that in 25 states special licenses

TABLE 10 NUMBER AND PERCENTAGE OF 176 BLIND PERSONS EMPLOYED BY CLASS OF OCCUPATION, CALIFORNIA, 1937*

Occupational class	Number	Per cent
Manufacturing and mechanical	21	11 9
Trade	57	32.9
Farming	6	3.5
Domestic service	7	3 9
Professional	65	36.5
Miscellaneous	20	11.3
Total	176	100 0

* *A Census and Economic Survey of the Blind in California*, California State Department of Education, No 7, Apr. 1, 1935, adapted from Table XIX, pp 17–18

may be obtained by employers to permit them to pay substandard wages to the handicapped, including the blind.

During the Second World War the blind, along with many other handicapped and marginal workers, were absorbed into industry in greater numbers. The war was a stimulant to vocational rehabilitation, both from the standpoint of increasing man power in defense industry and of reintegrating the handicapped veteran into society. However, more recently, resistance to the employment of the blind and handicapped has grown. Productivity has become of greater concern to employers, who as a consequence have insisted that the difficulty of shifting blind workers from one type of work to another in slack periods makes hiring them more costly. This plus the reticence of employers to reprimand or discharge blind workers who are inefficient perpetuates the formidable barriers against economic integration of the blind into our society. The influence of these barriers does not stop here, however; it extends to many other areas of social participation, decreasing opportunities for marriage, parenthood, recreation, and often compelling their acceptance of relief status.

[40] Brighouse, G., *The Physically Handicapped Worker in Industry*, California Institute of Technology, Industrial Relations Section, 1946

Sex and Marital Participation

Statistics on the marriage of the blind are often valueless in showing how blindness affects the chances for marriage because they group together those blinded at early ages with those who have become blind in advanced ages after marriage already has taken place. Taken as a heterogeneous group the blind are not significantly different from the general population in so far as marital status is concerned. However, among males and females alike marriage has taken place in direct ratio to the age at loss of vision. About one-fourth (25.2 per cent) of males and one-fifth (21.8 per cent) of females whose sight was lost in childhood or youth (under twenty years) have been married, while four-fifths (80.2 per cent) of males and nine-tenths (93.8 per cent) of females who lost their sight after twenty years have been married. [41] There are more widowed blind, possibly due to the smaller likelihood of their remarriage. Marriage of blind to the blind is comparatively rare for reasons which are obvious. In addition to the economic handicaps of the blind lending hazards to the idea of marriage in general, the great social isolation of the blind leaves them with fewer opportunities to meet members of the opposite sex in such a way as to lead to courtship and marriage. The fear or dislike of connubial responsibility and of parenthood also deter the blind from marrying.

Little is known of the sex life of the single blind person. Many sighted persons shun the idea of close physical contact with any type of handicapped persons, so that heterosexual indulgence of the blind with sighted persons presumably is less likely to occur. On the other hand, maternalistic women, or women who are insecure in sexual competition, may be drawn to the blind man as well as to other handicapped men. Some few case histories of blind students reveal promiscuous sex behavior, with a long series of love affairs with sighted girls. The greater isolation of the blind girl, suggested by her much lower marriage rate,[42] may make her more sexually accessible than other women under certain circumstances. Several blind male informants argued that this was true because the blind woman often had no other hold upon a man than her sex attraction. However, these comments should be accepted with a great deal of caution on account of their inferential quality.

Writers have commented upon the prevalence of autoerotic practices among the blind, but there are no studies of its extent. Some cases of homosexuality among the blind have been encountered by the writer, but again there is no way of ascertaining its incidence in the group. One survey of

[41] Best, *Blindness and the Blind in the United States*, p. 207. These data are old, but there is no reason to suspect any significant changes in them, unless the percentages for the young blind who marry has been reduced.

[42] *Ibid.*

studies on the differential sexuality of handicapped persons in general is rather inconclusive.[43]

Our knowledge of the family life of the adult blind is very scanty. Brief surveys have been made of the "living arrangements" of the blind,[44] but the results have not been tabulated by age and by age of the onset of blindness. However, certain facts, such as the low marriage rate of persons blind since birth or infancy, suggest that a high percentage of those blinded early in life remain with their parental family group. While many such blind play minor but important domestic roles, others are relegated to the status of almost complete uselessness. In the parlance of some of the blind themselves, they become "rocking-chair Annies."

Almost nothing has been written upon the interaction of the married blind with their own families. However, certain tentative generalizations can be made. The marriage choices of the blind man obviously will be limited by his typically low economic status. He probably seldom marries above his class unless he stands to inherit some money. Furthermore, his appeal will be to women with strong needs for mothering others and for security. Once married, the blind man's family becomes his chief media of social participation, which probably imparts a greater intimacy to his family life than found in other marriages. In most ways his isolation will become his wife's isolation. It would be interesting to know whether the egocentrisms of blind childhood carry over into the married life of the blind person. Several case histories obtained by the author include divorces of blind men whose wives have been unable to tolerate their domineering dispositions. A further enlightened guess about blindness and marriage might be that the frustrations of the blind, which they must often conceal in other social contacts, tend to become projected into their marital lives and create instability there.

Religious Participation

There are no studies to tell us how important religious activities are in the life of the blind. Impressions of those who work with the blind are that as a group the blind have little interest in church and that often they are hostile toward religion as a result of their bitterness toward a deity who has deprived them of their vision. Resentment is also believed to arise out of the religious imputations of inferiority and sin to blindness and the blind. However, such reasoning tends to "psychologize" the rather complex and variable behavior of the blind. A very limited survey, conducted

[43] Barker *et al.*, *op. cit.*, p 66.

[44] See *Survey of the Blind in the State of Washington*, State Department of Social Security, May, 1937, Table VIII, p. 22, "The Blind in Hennepin County," p. 10.

by the author, of a group of employees of a blind workshop showed that 13 out of 21 were church members, which is at least as great a proportion of church members as in the general population. However, only 5 of the 21 attended church with any regularity. The rest attended occasionally, seldom, or not at all. The reasons for not attending were quite varied; many said they simply had drifted away from church like sighted people, while others found it more convenient to listen to religious programs over the radio. Others had to spend Sundays in tending to domestic duties or were too tired to go to the church, were too far away, or had no one to take them.

It is probably true that a certain undetermined proportion of the blind avoid church because of unpleasant experiences there. Their awkwardness may have made them painfully conspicuous during rituals; this in turn may lead members of the church to overwhelm them with attentions, "literally carrying them around," as one blind informant put it. A reverse tendency, discomfiting as well, is one of ignoring or even shunning the blind person in the church situation. It is also true that clergymen who have strong Biblical leanings may at times single out the blind in a peculiar light. They may mention them in sermons or prayers or hold them up as examples to sighted members of the congregation. Evangelistic clergymen may pray over the blind and seek to perform miraculous cures. All the blind in the workshop survey agreed that clergymen had no special insight into problems of the blind.

Manifestations of the traditional religious attitudes toward the blind probably are more repellent to the highly educated, sensitive, and aggressive blind striving for a measure of independence than to others of the group. The fact that a number of autobiographies of blind persons touch on this and the fact that the workers with the blind attribute to the blind attitudes of hostility toward religion would seem to substantiate in some part the idea that these reactions are limited to a selected group. On the other hand, a certain portion of the blind, the professional blind, may actually be attracted to the church for the very reasons that the above group is alienated by it. For example, two of the blind surveyed in the workshop group were devoutly religious, to the extent that they tithed their meager incomes.

Political Participation

The vigorous organization of groups working in behalf of the blind has already been commented upon. While support comes from many sighted persons and groups, the participation of the blind themselves is importantly responsible for the power of the "blind lobby." Generally speaking, a high majority of the blind who have ever received public aid of any sort are familiar with the legislation which directly affects their status, which is to say that they "know their rights." The survey of the blind workshop employees showed that 8 out of 21 received and read literature circulated by lobbying groups in support of or opposed to new and projected legislation affecting the blind. A somewhat smaller number, 6 out of 21, had at one time or another engaged in what might be called "pressure" or lobbying activities for the benefit of their group. It must be remembered that this was a somewhat select group, consisting of employed blind who traveled with some facility in their environment. Also, the workshop itself served to bring the workers more in contact with political activities. However, there has also been a general trend toward political organization of several recipient groups in welfare agencies, including the blind. It may well be that a narrow, self-interested political participation of a passive sort uniformly characterizes the adult blind population.

It probably is not necessary for large numbers of the blind to be actively participant in lobbying, chiefly because a few blind lobbyists "go a long way." In many areas there are a few energetic blind leaders, usually drawn from the professions, who carry the main burden of guarding the special interests of the blind.[45] The ease with which they can enlist the support of community groups and gain a favorable press means that mass inundation of legislators with letters and telegrams does not have to be resorted to as is the case with other pressure groups.

Some social workers dealing with the blind have stated that there is little general political participation by the blind in such things as national, state, and local elections. The workshop survey, however, revealed that 13 out of 21 workers were registered with political parties and the same number voted in the last national election. No generalizations are warranted by this scanty data; the figure may or may not be representative.

Recreation

It is clear that the social lives of the blind, for the most part, are narrowly circumscribed, a fact which is apparent in their recreational as well as in other aspects of their participation. In the past the blind have been noted for their physical inactivity and their lack of outdoor life and exercise. Only 6 per cent of the former pupils of a Pennsylvania institution were found to avail themselves of means of recreation.[46] The advent of the radio undoubtedly has opened up a whole new area of participation for the blind, but it is still a passive form of recreation. The blind nowadays

[45] According to an estimate of an informed participant, there were about five thousand blind persons in the California Council of the Blind in 1949. This would be about one-third of the state's total blind population However, attendance at Los Angeles meetings of this group seldom exceeds 250.

[46] *Publication of Pennsylvania Institution for the Blind*, No. 3, 1924, p. 21

also find attending motion pictures an enjoyable pastime. There are a number of other forms of recreation in which the blind can indulge with satisfaction, including chess, checkers, even a variety of baseball. More recently, quite a number of the blind have taken to bowling with more than casual success. However, to the extent that recreation has become an organized phenomenon it raises the common problem of travel for the blind person. There are organized recreational groups for and of the blind in many communities, but their success as measured by attendance is often questionable.

Adjustment and Maladjustment

Role acceptance by the blind is fraught with complications, even under ideal conditions of socioeconomic adjustment. One blind welfare worker, self-supporting and independent in all respects, told the author of difficulties she met in casual public contacts. Unsolicited, people often put coins in her lap as she rode on street cars; in other instances, when she entered public restaurants, she was told politely but firmly that no solicitors were allowed. In addition, there was always the unsought assistance from pedestrians and others on the streets. Such things mean that in the mental process of self-enhancement the blind must continually dissociate many feelings and impulses toward sighted persons. A sense of humor or wisecracks do not always relieve the irritation at the interference of "benefactors," for they are apt to be misunderstood as lack of gratitude which is traditionally supposed to be standard equipment of the blind. Nor can tensions be discharged through normal overt anger, as this is contrary to the idea that the blind are eternally cheerful in the face of adversity. It is perhaps for this reason that many of the blind rely extensively upon fantasies as balancing mechanisms; in some recorded instances the fantasies of the blind have been found to betray fierce aggressions toward the surrogates of society.[47] The more independent blind persons who achieve integrations between their private conceptions of their roles and the public conception are probably a very limited group. As a well-known blind writer puts it:[48] "It is the rare blind individual who emotionally treads the middle ground by conforming outwardly, when it is discreet to do so, to the evaluation of the seeing and at the same time preserves his self-respect by emotionally thumbing his nose at those who would love to aid him by unwittingly achieving his complete destruction."

A considerable, albeit unknown, number of the blind reject their social roles, as we have already noted in connection with those receiving old-age assistance. Even in cases where blind relief is received, some clients strug-

[47] Cutsforth, *op. cit.*, pp 77*ff*

[48] *Ibid.*, pp. 124*ff*

gle to conceal the facts of their blindness, urging welfare workers not to visit them at their residence. Of course, the high visibility of blindness makes concealment extremely difficult; usually this can be done with success only among those with partial vision. Except among the aged where such denials of reality can be accepted amusedly as "cantankerousness," role subterfuges like this suggest psychotic discrepancy between individual and societal definitions of the self. Of the extreme sociopsychological maladjustment of the blind, however, we know little. The relation of blindness to mental disorders is relatively unexplored. In 1945 in California there were 258 blind and 302 partially blind in mental hospitals out of a blind population of 12,800.[49] To what extent blindness was interactional and to what extent incidental to the mental disorders in these cases cannot be stated.

Marginal Blindness

Anywhere from 50 to 60 per cent of those classed as blind possess partial vision, a significantly large proportion of the total in this handicapped group.[50] These persons are socially qualified neither for the role of the blind nor for that of the sighted, hence conflicts over their roles in these cases are common. As one partially sighted person phrased it, "It's a lot harder to be in between." Driven by economic rejections, the marginal blind person may qualify for blind relief or placement in a sheltered workshop. Yet the picture of the abject and apathetic totally blind with whom they must identify in such places must, in a great many such cases, be a source of conflict and discomfort. The social acceptance of the marginal cases is usually a tempered one, and the pressure for their rehabilitation is greater from social-service agencies. The following case illustrates some of the features of blind marginality:

Miss S . . . is thirty-four years old, and her appearance in no way suggests her limited vision. She has 4/200 vision in one eye and 10/200 in the other. Bright light tires her eyes, and she prefers to keep the shades of her home, where she lives with her parents, drawn most of the time. She has a fear of complete blindness, somehow associated with a fear of snakes. As a child she never thought of herself as visually handicapped, until she found she couldn't keep up with other students in school. She dropped out of school after four years, but managed to teach herself to read and write. Her efforts at obtaining work all ended in rejections, so she contented herself with doing housework for her parents and working sporadically in her father's truck garden. She is physically attractive and has had three offers of marriage but has refused because of the responsibility marriage would involve. Having children around her makes her very nervous, for she continually fears something will happen to them. She

[49] *Report of Interdepartment Committee*, p. 12.
[50] Best, *Blindness and the Blind in the United States*, p. 167.

conceals the extent of her handicap, so that even her parents have no realistic appreciation of its extent. This often leads her to undertake tasks which are beyond her ability – as when she painted the living room, or when she goes on errands through traffic which frightens her. Also she cannot bring herself to ask for help that might simplify her adjustments. Although receiving blind aid, she does not want to be associated with the blind or known as blind, for which reason she refuses to consider a rehabilitation program or an operation to improve her vision. She is very withdrawn and has few friends and prefers to stay home most of the time. She now realizes that the extreme age of her parents makes some sort of change in her status imminent. However, it is questionable if she will of her own volition make any new adjustments until necessity compels them.

It will be noted in this case that the adjustment of the girl combines economic dependence with a rather strong independence in other respects. Perhaps the most characteristic trait here, as well as in other marginal cases, was the inability of the girl to define her role and her consequent inability to keep her aspirations within the limits of her handicap. In another similar case presented in autobiographical form, the person was even less able to mark out areas of effective social competition. Her life, as a result of a lack of clear-cut role defintion, turned out to be a continuous struggle to play a sighted role, with a mental breakdown eventuating from her drive to attain higher educational degrees.[51]

The Professional Blind

It is paradoxical that the better adjusted blind, in terms of role acceptance, are those who live by values contrary to our individualistic, competitive culture. We refer to the professional blind man, who lives by and exploits the traditional stereotype of what the blind are supposed to be like. Professionalization is seen in the autobiographies of the blind who write with a sighted vocabulary, recounting their life stories as courageous struggles and as dramatic entrees into a world of light from that of darkness. Helen Keller's writings fall into this class, along with many others.

More typically professionalized are the blind who have accepted the status of public charges and those who become beggars. Perhaps the latter group is the best exemplification of this type of role. The number of blind mendicants remains a matter for guess and estimate, for begging is often disguised by various forms of peddling and selling. The blind beggar often makes a far better economic adjustment than the blind on relief or in workshops. When blind beggars in Detroit were asked why they solicited money on the streets, they frankly told social workers it was because that was the way in which they could earn the most money. The blind mendicant who vends pencils or shoestrings or plays a musical instrument

[51] Dahl, Borghild, *I Wanted to See*, 1945.

in public displays traditional attiudes of obeisance, humility, and gratitude, harking back to medieval times when giving alms conferred religious merit upon the giver and when the beggar was regarded as a sacred personage. But the blind beggar is not necessarily demoralized, for working the street calls for skills, audacity, persistence – even defiance and rebellion under certain conditions – traits which are all too rare in the blind supported by organized charity. The blind beggar must be mobile and must endure all sorts of inclement weather to further his trade. He is consistently motivated and can, through rationalizations drawn from a culture having no few major contradictions, rather easily integrate his personality upon the basis of the begging role.

The following newspaper clipping [52] illustrates the relative ease with which the public may be manipulated by the blind:

Blind man Robert S . . . , 67, of 106 W. . . . th St., didn't have much faith in people – not after Thursday, that is, when a thief posing as a room hunter stole S . . .'s small table-model radio.

But yesterday that faith was restored to overflowing when Samuel A. T . . . , 10035 . . . th St., presented him with a console radio to replace the stolen set.

T . . . had read of S . . .'s plight in the paper and said he'd be glad to donate a radio to the blind man.

When T . . . called on S . . . in his modest quarters, the old Spanish War veteran could hardly believe his good fortune

"Boys, I don't know . . . ," his voice trailed off.

"When some dirty skunk steals something," he went on, "it's unusual for somebody to replace it."

Music poured from the instrument, and with it tears came to unseeing eyes as the outside world once more came into the blind man's dark world.

Then he began to worry.

"My wife's out to the store," he said, "trying to buy another one for me. She works awfully hard, she can't afford it, don't let her do it" A sympathetic neighbor caught her just in time.

He blew his nose loudly. Even T . . . , who owns a radio and appliance shop at 134 W . . Blvd. was visibly affected.

"I can't think of anyone who deserves it more," he said. "After all," he said, "my wife Jeanne should get the credit because she believes that what you do with dollars is what counts."

This news story has value for us not only to illustrate the pathetic attitudes of the reading public toward blindness but also to bring out how the drive of the newspaper for human-interest materials and the pecuniary interests of the businessman converge in this instance to revive and help perpetuate the medieval stereotype of the blind.

[52] Los Angeles, June, 1949

As long as the societal reaction toward the blind remains as it is, there will continue to be a sizable number of the blind who make a profession of dependency.

Selected Readings

BEST, HARRY: *Blindness and the Blind in the United States*, 1934

CHEVIGNY, HECTOR *My Eyes Have a Cold Nose*, 1946, Chap 7 especially.

CUTSFORTH, T. D. *The Blind in School and Society*, 1933

LENDE, HELGA (ed) *What of the Blind?* 1938, 2 vols.

QUEEN, S., and J. GRUENER: *Social Pathology*, 1940, Chap 6

SANDERS, B. S. "The Blind—Their Number and Characteristics," *Social Security Bulletin* 3, March, 1945, pp 17-26.

CHAPTER 6

SPEECH DEFECTS AND THE SPEECH DEFECTIVE

In this chapter we shall be concerned with deviation in the overt verbal aspects of behavior, in particular with disturbances in the mechanics of speech itself. Generally speaking, sociologists have given little or no heed to this phase of deviation in human behavior, which is surprising in view of the extent to which it exists in our society and in view of the stress which sociologists have placed upon language and speech as factors in socialization. For this reason the bulk of the data upon speech disorders has to be taken from other fields and more or less recast in our frame of reference.

The Nature of the Deviation

Speech disorders are conventionally divided into those of articulation, rhythm, phonation, and symbolization. More specifically these include such things as lisping, baby talk, lalling, stuttering, stammering, cleft-palate speech, atypical pitch, aphonia, and various forms of dysphasia. Most of these are familiar enough, with the possible exception of the last two. Aphonia has reference to conditions in which persons are unable to make any sounds whatsoever, sometimes apparent as hysterical or temporary muteness among persons whose occupations call for constant reliance upon their voices. Dysphasia, on the other hand, refers to all disorders in which the process of symbol formation itself becomes disorganized. Persons showing symptoms of dysphasia grope futilely to name objects or they substitute one word for another, in some cases being further distinguished by weirdly confused hearing. While these are all designed as mutually exclusive classifications, it is not always true that speech deviant is accurately classifiable in any one of them, for some such deviants fall into two or more categories. A stutterer, for instance, not infrequently combines peculiar pitch patterns and other voice disorders with his broken speech rhythms.

Most of our discussion here will revolve around stuttering, mainly because of the large numbers in our population showing this behavior and because of its direct effect upon social participation. Viewed in a strictly physiological way, stuttering is any disruption of speech rhythm following or associated with blocking of the lips, contraction of the tongue, spasms in the vocal chords, and tension of the diaphragm which disturbs the breathing process. The spasms may be of continuous or *tonic* variety, or they may be *clonic*, which means alternating contractions and relaxations, rapid or otherwise, of the muscles producing speech. Spasms or blocks appear on an average of 10 per cent of the words used by the stutterer and have an average duration of one or two seconds, although the range of variability is quite wide.[1] Changes in blood pressure, cardiac changes, and modifications of brain volume also accompany stuttering.

There is a division of opinion as to whether stuttering is a unitary defect, sharply setting off stutterers from all other speakers, or whether it is a normal variation in speech. Support for the latter view lies in research indicating that hesitations, prolongations, repetitions, and other breaks in rhythm are common in the speech of many children who are considered "normal" or who subsequently grow into "normal" speakers.[2] This position is further bolstered by the fact that many adults obviously have arhythmic speech in various forms: blocks, pauses, "ers" and "ahs," and transpositions of syllables and sounds. When it is recalled that there are 72 pairs of muscles activated in speaking, it seems not unusual that children should err in all sorts of ways in mastering speech and that adults should normally fluctuate widely in their fluency and have epochs when they are far more articulate than at other times.

Those who hold to an opposing view have made a distinction between normal speech awkwardness of children, which they call "filibustering," and sharp, staccato repetitions which come on the syllables of words rather than on whole words.[3] These latter, it is claimed, are the essential stuttering symptoms. It is further contended that special tremor patterns and rates can be detected in generic stuttering responses

More research is probably needed upon this subject, especially by persons not so strongly identified in the field of speech pathology with special theoretical positions. The burden of the proof in this research must be left with those who adhere to the qualitative definition of stuttering Physiological and constitutional correlates of unique stuttering behavior must be demonstrated to our greater satisfaction before the concept can have validity.

[1] Johnson, W., *et al*, *Speech Handicapped School Children*, 1948, p. 186

[2] Davis, D. M., "The Relation of Repetitions in the Speech of Young Children to Certain Measures of Language Maturity and Situational Factors," *Journal of Speech Disorders*, 5, September, 1940, pp 235-246

[3] Van Riper, C, *Speech Correction*, 1947, rev ed, p 277

Do Stutterers Have an Abnormal Genetic Constitution?

Those who have favored the conception of stuttering as a special, qualitative syndrome of abnormal behavior have also, in many cases, looked upon it as part of, or an expression of, a kind of hereditary entity. In other words, these writers believe that constitutional differentiae mark off stutterers from the rest of our population. The evidence which has been marshaled to support this view is found in studies, not entirely in agreement, showing that there are more stutterers among left-handed and ambidextrous persons and among those who have had their handedness changed as children. One older conclusion from these data is that stutterers are genetically distinguished from others by having a narrow margin of cerebral dominance, that is, a condition in which neither cerebral hemisphere consistently leads or controls the paired muscles of the body. This explanation is invoked to account for the contradictory and competing neural impulses in the speech block. Other studies of a similar kind purport to show that stutterers have a characteristic body build, a special body chemistry, and inferior bodily coordination.[4]

Unfortunately for those who would have us believe that stutterers are constitutionally different from others, there is an accretion of research with completely contrary indications. In fact, the most comprehensive critical reviews of the literature on the relationships of constitutional and biochemical factors to stuttering have discovered little proof that such constitutional differences exist.[5] However, we are not prepared to dismiss entirely the notion that in a certain percentage of cases biological differentiae interact to bring on stuttering. It is quite possible that stutterers are drawn from both biologically normal and biologically abnormal segments of the population. We must recognize that the neuromuscular basis for speech can be weakened both congenitally and environmentally, even though we suspect that the number of cases in the former category will be comparatively few.

Other evidence for the existence of genetic differences among stutterers comes from genealogical (as opposed to constitutional) studies. These reveal that stutterers are indeed more likely to have stuttering relatives than nonstutterers. One investigation found that 33 per cent of stuttering children had relatives similarly affected, whereas only 9 per cent of a control sample of nonstuttering children had relatives with the defect. It

[4] Bender, J., "Personality Traits of College Stutterers," *Proceedings of the American Speech Correction Association*, 9, 1939, pp. 48ff.

[5] Hill, H., "Stuttering I. A Critical Review and Evaluation of Biochemical Investigation," *Journal of Speech Disorders*, 9, December, 1944, pp. 245-261, "Stuttering II A Review and Integration of Physiological Data," *ibid.*, pp. 289-324.

was also discovered that over three times as many of the stuttering children had speech-handicapped parents as did nonstuttering children.[6] Yet despite the surface indications these data give, it must be said that they provide only inferential evidence of a special heredity for stutterers, and that they readily admit of alternative explanations. As one writer has commented, several generations of Republicans or Democrats in a family need not be regarded as a *hereditary* handicap, so why should we look upon stuttering as being such? A highly defensible alternative explanation is that the differential family incidence of stuttering is a measure of variable patterns of definition and symbolic evaluation which are transmitted as a part of family heritages.[7]

Demographic Characteristics and Differences of Stutterers

While there have been many surveys to determine the number of speech defectives in our population, great variation is to be noted in the results, chiefly because of the lack of agreement as to what a speech defect is. It is believed that most studies err on the side of conservatism rather than overstating the facts. A figure of 10 to 12 per cent of young children with speech handicaps is not too large.[8] The great majority of these are youngsters who have articulatory defects. Generally these are less penalized than other speech defects, and they are disposed to disappear with passing time. According to estimate, about 1 per cent of the population are stutterers and about 4 out of every 100 persons stutter at some time during their lives.[9] The total number of stutterers in the population has been put at the extremely high figure of 1,400,000.[10]

A very high sex ratio characterizes stutterers in the aggregate. Anywhere from 2 to 10 male stutterers for every female stutterer have been found in various studies on the subject. The ratio varies with the age group studied. Along with this greater incidence of stuttering among males, it has been observed that their symptoms are typically more severe and that they are less likely to outgrow them. Stuttering is primarily a deviation of childhood, although it occurs and persists for some persons throughout all of the age periods. The largest number of stutterers will be found at the ages of six to seven years.[11]

[6] Johnson, W., *et al.*, "The Onset and Development of Stuttering," *Journal of Speech Disorders*, 7, September, 1942, pp. 251-257.

[7] Johnson, *et al.*, *Speech Handicapped School Children*, p. 190.

[8] *White House Conference on Child Health and Protection, Special Education*, 1931, Francis, J, *A Survey of Speech Defectives in Iowa City, Iowa*, master's thesis, University of Iowa, 1930, unpublished.

[9] Blanton, Smiley, and Margaret Blanton, *For Stutterers*, 1939, p. 70.

[10] Van Riper, *op. cit.*, p. 266

[11] Blanton and Blanton, *op. cit*, p 71.

Beyond the fairly reliable investigations into the age and sex composition of the population of speech defectives, there are scant data to describe such things as their ethnic composition, distribution by community type and region, or the educational and socioeconomic status of their parents. There are a few indications that speech defects are more common among Negroes than among whites,[12] but these differences may well be caused by differing economic status of the two ethnic classes. One study has shown stuttering to be more frequent in bilingual families, suggesting that there may be more stutterers among second-generation immigrants. However, the conclusion of the study is hedged by the statement that the bilingualism is not necessarily the cause of the speech difficulty.[13] Other research reports completely negative findings in so far as the relationship of nativity and amount of foreign language spoken in the home to stuttering is concerned.[14]

Somewhat inconclusive data have raised the possibility that speech defects in general may be more common in rural areas than in urban communities.[15] Otherwise there is little to inform us on the spatial distribution of speech-handicapped persons. Several research items contain evidence that speech defects occur with greater-than-normal frequency in families with lower occupational and educational status. These defects generally take the form of retardation rather than stuttering. Results consistent with this idea come out of other inquiries which show that speech development in general appears to be slower among children of laboring-class parents than among those whose fathers are professional and clerical workers or businessmen.[16] However, there is nothing in these studies which can tell us whether stuttering is relatively more frequent in any given socioeconomic strata. If it is assumed that the different rates of speech development reflect varying standards of what constitutes normal speech develop-

[12] Boome, E J., *et al*, *Abnormal Speech*, 1939, p. 117, Cahart, R, "Some Notes on Official Statistics of Speech Disorders Encountered during World War II," *Journal of Speech Disorders*, 8, June, 1943, p 100.

[13] Travis, L, *et al.*, "The Relation of Bilingualism to Stuttering," *Journal of Speech Disorders*, 2, March, 1937, pp. 185-189

[14] Morris, D W, "A Survey of Speech Defects in Central High School, Kansas City, Missouri," *Quarterly Journal of Speech*, 25, April, 1939, pp. 262-269

[15] Louttit, C M, "Survey of Speech Defects among Public School Children of Indiana," *Journal of Speech Disorders*, 1, September, 1936, pp 73-80.

[16] Becky, R, "A Study of Certain Factors Related to Retardation of Speech," *Journal of Speech Disorders*, 7, September, 1942, pp. 223-249, Irvin, O. C., "Infant Speech. The Effect of Occupational Status and of Age on the Use of Sound Types," *Journal of Speech and Hearing Disorders*, 13, September, 1948, pp. 224-226, "Infant Speech· The Effect of Family Occupational Status and of Age on Sound Frequency," *ibid.*, pp 320-323; Read, A., "Speech Defects and Mannerisms among Slaves and Servants of Colonial America," *Quarterly Journal of Speech*, 24, October, 1938, pp 397-401.

ment held by laboring-class parents in contrast with those of the so-called "middle-class" professional, clerical, and businessmen, parents then it is possible that stuttering may be more of a middle-class phenomenon. The inference would be that those parents with higher standards of speech excellence exert more pressure on their maturing children and thus create a situation potential for stuttering. Yet after this hypothesis is checked, we may discover that variations between families of the same economic status may be more significant than the class variation in the matter of rigorous speech training.

The Contexts of Stuttering

Any person who has had even a brief clinical contact with stutterers will agree that the defect can appear in conjunction with numerous types of conflicts and situations. It is not difficult to single out persons in whom speech defects and stuttering are symptomatic of unintegrated elements of social roles other than that of a socially defined stutterer. For such persons stuttering may have a therapeutic effect or it may be the mechanism by which a precarious personal equilibrium is preserved.[17] An example of this general context of speech disorders would be an adult woman who used baby talk because of regressive impulses to become a child again. A case in which stuttering was the symptom rather than the fulcrum of a role came to light in a socially inept girl who steadfastly resisted all efforts to relieve her stuttering. Free speech for her would have meant facing a whole series of social and sexual adjustments which she feared more than anything else. Hence, she clung to her symptoms as a means of avoiding these demands. Speech defects and stuttering of the blind, the deaf, and of the mentally deficient all come under a symptomatic classification.

A vast amount of generalized nonfluency as well as definitely recognizable stuttering is situational, being a response to exogenous stresses and strains. For large numbers of children stuttering is a transitional condition which they leave behind on entering school. Many persons stutter during certain periods in their lives and possess free speech at others. In fact, situational variability is one of the outstanding features of stuttering. Some people stutter when they are excited, and others have trouble when they are calm; some stutter in the presence of the opposite sex, some with the same sex. Some children have speech trouble at school, others at home. Some soldiers have been known to have their speech blocks at the front lines, while others stutter only in the rear lines. Apparently combat fatigue precipitated a fair number of stuttering cases during the late war, cases

[17] Travis, L., "The Need for Stuttering," *Journal of Speech Disorders*, 5, September, 1940, pp. 193-202.

which later cleared up with rest and care. The fluctuations in the stuttering frequency and pattern of the individual often prove mystifying and baffling to him as well as to others (including clinicians). Undoubtedly what is involved in this apparent complexity of stuttering is an interaction of certain internal limits, such as word fears and personal morale, with tension-inducing factors in the situation. Some situations, for example,—telephone conversations, seem to be bugaboos for a very high percentage of stutterers. Other situations are much more variable in their effects with respect to the inducing of stuttering.

Disregarding cases with demonstrable organic complications, we are inclined to believe that all initial stuttering or extreme nonfluency as it develops in small children is situational. Furthermore, there is reason to think that the large number of stutterers are products of similar situations in our culture. It would be difficult at this stage of our knowledge to describe in an exact fashion just what elements in our culture are conducive to stuttering. However, it is clear that competitive stress and conflict generally characteristic of our culture are somehow, in some way, operative.

Limited data upon certain preliterate societies – the Navaho, Australian groups, New Guinea tribes, Polar Eskimo, Bannock, Shoshoni, and Northern Kalabash – show stuttering to be extremely rare or nonexistent.[18] In explanation of the apparent lack of stuttering among American Indian tribes, it has been pointed out that in many of these cultures no pressure is placed upon the child to talk, that long deliberation prior to speaking is culturally sanctioned, and that monosyllabic expressions of opinion are often customary. The absence of cultural symbols for the deviation has also been commented upon.[19]

First, these Indians had no word for stuttering in their language. In fact, when he asked whether there were any stutterers in the tribes, he had to demonstrate stuttering to the chiefs and council members before they could understand what he was talking about. They were intensely amused by his demonstrations. Second, their standards of child care and training appeared to be extraordinarily lax in comparison with our own. With respect to speech in particular, it seemed to be the case that every Indian child was regarded as a satisfactory or normal speaker regardless of the manner in which the child spoke. Speech defects simply were not recognized. Indian children were not criticized or evaluated on the basis of their speech, no comments were made about it, no

[18] Bullen, A. K., "A Cross Cultural Approach to the Study of Stuttering," *Child Development*, 16, March-June, 1945, pp 1-88, Johnson, W., "The Indians Have No Word for It, Stuttering in Children," *Quarterly Journal of Speech*, 30, October, 1944, pp. 330-337; Snidecor, J C, "Why the Indian Does Not Stutter," *ibid.*, 33, December, 1947, pp. 493-495, Van Riper, C., "Speech Defects among the Kalabash," *Marquette County Historical Society*, Centennial, 8, December, 1946, pp 333-337

[19] Johnson, "The Indians Have No Word for It," p. 332.

issue was made of it. In their semantic environments there appeared to be no speech anxieties or tensions to interiorize, to adopt as their own. This, together with the absence of a word for stuttering in the Indian's language, constitutes the only basis on which the writer can, at this time, suggest an explanation for the fact that there were no stutterers among these Indians.

Of course, all this is not to conclude that primitive peoples as a class do not have speech defects or suffer the handicap of stuttering. It has already been discovered that some of the aborigines of Argentina have speech deviants within their population who are invidiously differentiated by their use of baby talk and by functional muteness. Furthermore, these deviations seem clearly related to tensions and anxieties which are culturally induced.[20] While no stuttering was observed in this group, nevertheless it is logical and probable that further research will bring to light examples of preliterate peoples whose children do become differentiated in this way.

What is important about the cursory research which has been done thus far on stuttering among primitive peoples is that it provides comparative data to show that in *some* cultures stuttering, as we know it, does not occur. This measurably strengthens the hypothesis that cultural settings are dynamic factors in the growth of stuttering. However, we must avoid crude cultural determinism in our analysis by recognizing the importance of the intervening variable of social organization. The process by which cultural values are sieved through family organization before they impinge upon the child is an important variable in any explanation of stuttering. It is conceivable that, even though a culture is highly competitive and highly productive of invidious distinctions between persons and groups, its social organization might be such that children in the modal family would not be subjected to competitive stresses. In our culture, however, it can be safely said that this is not the case.

In American culture the presence of culture conflicts which disrupt general family relationships and parent-child relations is a well-recognized fact. That many parents project their thwarted ambitions and anxieties over social status onto their children is likewise well known. A wide variety of childhood maladjustments or deviations can be traced to this funneling of conflicts into the child's life. Both gross speech difficulties and abnormal reactions of parents to average nonfluency in their children are derived from conflict situations centering about speech behavior.[21]

The following sequence of events taken from the case history of a boy who began to stutter at thirty-six months of age is a very revealing picture of culture conflict as it bears upon the child through the family. It not

[20] Henry, J., and M. Henry, "Speech Disturbances among the Pialagi Indians," *American Journal of Orthopsychiatry*, 10, April, 1940, pp. 362-69.

[21] Wood, K. S., "Parental Maladjustment and Functional Articulatory Defects in Children," *Journal of Speech Disorders*, 11, December, 1946, pp. 255-275.

only depicts the general feeling of tension in the family but also the specific parts played by an overanxious mother and certain trauma in localizing the boy's anxieties in the vocal tract·

1. Severe beating by mother at twenty-one months for soiling his pants.
2. Continuous pressure from mother on toilet training.
3. First baby sister born.
4. Signs of competition with baby sister.
5. Large household of visiting relatives for six months.
6. Mother cares for bedridden aunt in home for six months.
7. Three changes of residence.
8. Alcoholic grandfather moves in, causing constant conflict between father and mother.
9. Father undertakes new business, works late at night.
10. Financial difficulties occur.
11. Boy begins to sense and fear peculiarities of grandfather.
12. Boy's stomach pumped three times within one month due to poisoning from ant paste.
13. Severe poisoning from lead in water pipes.
14. Tonsils removed, continued recall of the operation.
15. Age thirty-four months: mother takes child to uncredited psychoanalyst. On her recommendation mother tries to break thumb-sucking habit of the boy by compulsory methods.
16. Three weeks later: signs of primary stuttering or nonfluencies appear, especially repetitions of first syllables of words.
17. Death of grandfather. During week of burial the boy was scarcely able to talk, having many blocks lasting as long as a minute.

It is interesting for us to know that a year later, when the family routine became more normal, the stuttering in this case disappeared completely.

Systematic deviation does not occur with stuttering, according to all available records. Although several persons in the same family and members of different generations of the same family often show stuttering symptoms, there is no proof that this behavior is ever learned. There may be some communication of learning of techniques for covering up or handling blocks between stutterers in clinical situations, but beyond this it would be in error to claim any special culture for stutterers. Nor is there any indication of social organization among stutterers. As far as is known, stutterers outside of clinics do not seek out one another's company, nor do they form groups among themselves. In fact, the effort of one speech correctionist, known to the author, to organize a community group of stutterers failed conspicuously. It is not surprising that stutterers have no special group life when it is remembered that communication is the medium of culture and the requisite for social organization. The social situation is the nemesis of the stutterer, hence he tends to avoid it whenever he can, unless he can enter into it as a nonverbal participant. A further important reason for the absence of a behavior system of stuttering inheres in the nature of the societal reaction to this deviation.

Social Visibility of the Stutterer

The early stuttering of small children and that of the occasional adult has very low social visibility. For the most part their blocks are easy and effortless, and, while imparting a somewhat peculiar quality to speech, in no way interfere with the process of communication. Other stuttering is amplified by the anticipatory reactions which the stutterers make to their oncoming speech. In some instances they substitute other words for those on which they fear a block, giving their speech a high-flown, bombastic quality. Instead of saying "farmer" the stutterer may substitute something like "bucolic person." Others develop strange inflections or accents to help them talk. Some talk extremely fast, as if to race over the fearsome words before they have a chance to stumble on them. One man with whose case the author was acquainted talked with a jerky, constantly rising pitch, so that within a minute or two of speech he was hooting very much like an angry owl. "Starter" words or movements as well as long, patience-wearing pauses stand high in the list of devices which serve as crutches to enable stutterers to speak. The most conspicuous stutterers are those whose speech is blocked or forced out with the accompaniment of tics, tremors, facial grimaces, gross bodily contortions, writhings, flushing, grunting, straining, and stamping the feet. For example, one man jerked his head and screwed up his mouth in such a manner that when he struggled to speak he resembled a pig rooting in a trough. An incident starkly portraying the social visibility of a stutterer's handicap was that which took place during the review of some troops by an important high-ranking officer during the Second World War. The officer happened to stop in front of a stuttering soldier and asked his name. Unable to speak, the man blushed and strained to force out the words. Finally, with a great effort he spit directly into the general's face!

In contrast to these more painfully conspicuous stutterers there are some who successfully manage to hide their handicap and pass themselves off as normal speakers. However, these are few in number, and the success they achieve is at great psychological cost to themselves. Such persons often are known publicly not as stutterers but as "shy," timid," or "taciturn" individuals.

The Societal Reaction

While there is not such a definite and venerable folklore about stuttering as that which clusters around blindness, nevertheless a number of fallacious beliefs about this handicap have gained currency with the public. These largely concern the causes of the defect. Some of the commonly encountered folk explanations of stuttering are phrased in terms of injury, illness, bad heredity, shock, nervousness, imitating other stutterers, thinking too fast, talking too fast, and, perhaps most significantly, lack of will power. Some parents express the belief that stuttering is a phase through which all children must pass. The diffusion of scientific knowledge about stuttering seems to be at a minimum among members of the general public.[22]

Stuttering more often provokes laughter and amusement among those who hear it than it does hostility or deep sympathy. Added to these is a degree of embarrassment and irritation, prevalent among those who empathize the reactions of the stutterer. This is perceived overtly in the impulsive tendency of a stutterer's auditors to supply words and finish sentences for him, or in other cases in the looking away and breaking eye contact with the person as he speaks. Some persons, often complete strangers, feel a responsibility to instruct the stuttering individual as to how he should overcome his handicap. From such persons come all the timeworn remedies which he has heard so many times before and which he knows will do him no whit of good. He is told to watch his breathing or to talk slowly, all with an unconscious arrogance that is humiliating and infuriating to the stutterer, who often is his unsought mentor's intellectual superior. Occasionally the stutterer becomes the butt of crude practical jokes.

Unlike the blind, the speech defective is not sought out and made the object of charitable activity. If the stutterer keeps his mouth shut and remains on the periphery of social groups, as he usually does, he will be ignored by others. Perhaps for this reason so few persons have interested themselves in speech deviants that they have become the object of a great deal of little-publicized exploitation. The bulk of this takes place in speech "schools" and "institutes" in various parts of the country and at the hands of unqualified psychological "consultants." These organizations, operated by quack speech correctionists, ply their trade through advertisements in newspapers and magazines, often the slick-paper variety, following up inquiries with form letters designed to frighten the prospective client into contracting for their services. These letters paint a dismal future for the stutterer, with an unmarried existence, divorce, job failure, and even insanity promised as his fate unless he obtains a cure.[23]

Such schools usually charge all the traffic will bear, so that if the person

[22] Johnson, W , *Influence of Stuttering on Personality*, University of Iowa Studies in Child Welfare, 5, No 5, 1932, p. 56.

[23] See Blumel, C S., *Stammering and Cognate Defects of Speech*, 1913, Vol. II, Chap. VIII, "Stammering Schools,"

has $600 then the fee is set at that figure. For this the person receives lessons by mail, a series of office interviews, or the dubious privilege of living for a month to six weeks a barrackslike existence with a number of others having his handicap. He may be ordered into complete silence for a month period, at the end of which time he must learn certain exercises and master rules for his speech. Techniques used at such places vary; most of them, however, utilize a conscious rhythm-inducing exercise, with counting or tapping out of the words the person wishes to say. The "figure eight" or imaginary telephone dialing of the first letters of words with the fingers is taught in some of these schools. These tricks are actually successful in so far as freeing the stutterer's speech is concerned, which explains some of the difficulties of controlling fraud in this field. What makes these devices worthless is the fact that the slow, measured, or drawled speech they effect is as conspicuous and abnormal as the stuttering. Furthermore, such devices work at all only so long as the stutterer is consciously mastering their use. Once they have been reduced to the level of habit, and the consciousness is again filled with anticipatory fears, the old blocks are back – sometimes worse than before. The tapping or dialing movements in the fingers may then be added to the speech spasm.

There is no way of determining how extensive are the operations of exploitative speech schools and institutes in the United States, but some indication can be drawn from the fact that the newspapers of nearly every large urban community run ads for such agencies. One such institute in the Middle West has carried on its business for years and is reported to have earned its proprietor over a million dollars.

An indirect type of exploitation of stutterers is their caricature by entertainers and comedians on the stage, in the motion pictures, and over the radio. One popular song based upon the mockery of stuttering is still being sung many years after its publication.[24]

Differential Tolerance for Stuttering

The tolerance quotient with reference to stuttering, to be a functioning research tool, would have to be arrived at by consideration of the severity of stuttering symptoms and such things as the occupational structure, size, and social organization of the community. Studies clearly show that there is far less rejection of mild stutterers than of those who are close to being inarticulate because of their spasms.[25] Rejections also vary with the type of group the stutterer seeks to enter. For example, occupations vary considerably in the amount of speech required in order to carry them on with

[24] For a good description of the general reaction to the speech defective, see Van Riper, *Speech Correction*, Chap. I, "The Handicapped Individual in Society."

[25] Johnson, *Influence of Stuttering on Personality*, Chap. V.

success. Farm labor, factory labor, office work, and a number of the construction trades call for relatively little talking, so that even severe stutterers may be able to obtain and hold such employment. On the other hand, a severe or even mild stutterer has difficulty getting placed in a job in an exclusive shopping community where most of the openings are for salesclerks.

The small rural community and small town may be more receptive to the stutterer than the urban community. Employment as a farm worker or in food-processing plants is a greater possibility. Furthermore, the rural community often has to accept the more marginal worker, especially in the professions, simply because it can do no better. Thus, a stutterer may be placed as a teacher in a county-school system where he would be unable to compete for better positions in urban schools.

The more formalized employment procedures in urban communities complicate the stutterer's search for employment. Most employers, save for certain types of work, usually require an oral interview as a precondition of hiring. The prospective worker frequently is judged almost entirely upon the basis of this limited segmental contact, largely verbal in nature. The tensions implicit in the situation for the stutterer often exaggerate his symptoms, with the corresponding increase in the probability of a rejection. On the other hand, the occupational diversity of the urban community plus the impersonality of social relations offer more opportunity for concealment of the handicap and lowering its visibility. In so far as the rural community retains its characteristics of intimacy of social relations, the stutterer's handicap will have a higher visibility there and will excite more laughter and crude humor.

So far as can be discovered, speech defectives have never been so numerous or so concentrated in any one community as to become an aggregate problem. Deviants of this kind are never a menace to persons or property nor do they stir public sympathies the way some of the other handicapped groups do. Such awareness of the "problem" as there is comes from specialized welfare groups which take in large areas. Working through child-welfare organizations, these groups in recent years have generated a growing regional and state-wide consciousness of the extent and seriousness of speech defects among school children. This has been reflected in the increase of speech surveys in schools, the growth of local and traveling speech clinics in some areas, and in a demand for speech-training programs for public-school teachers and speech correctionists.[26] Behind these trends can be seen a whole complex of changing standards and norms of child development.

[26] Strother, C., "Trends in Speech Pathology," *Quarterly Journal of Speech*, 29 February, 1943, pp. 76–80

The Family Reaction

The reactions of parents to the stuttering child are in close accord with the particular conception they have as to what causes the disorder. Where parents have the idea that stuttering is caused by nervousness, they are apt to keep the child from exciting experiences, carefully supervise his eating and sleeping habits, and even give him medication in hopes of correcting the condition. If parents believe that the stuttering consists of bad habits and that it tokens a loss of will power, then their efforts will take the form of inspirational advice about "taking it slow" or "think it out first," all with the implicit attitude that a character defect underlies the difficulty.

More drastic parental remedies run to severe criticism, commands to speak right, and even harsh punishment. Some parents have been known to whip their stuttering offspring. In odd instances the shock of severe discipline has actually effected a cessation of symptoms, as in a case known to the author, whose father hit him over the head with a newspaper and harshly ordered him to stop stuttering, miraculously enough producing the desired result. Obviously in many situations the punishment of a stuttering child does no more than symbolize its rejection by the parents. However, as was true of parental reactions to the blind child, the most frequent reaction of parents is overprotection of the stutterer. The child is shielded from traumatic situations by the parents' making purchases for him, talking for him over the telephone, ordering his meals in public restaurants, and otherwise functioning for him in situations where speech is required.

As the stuttering child grows older and devises ways and means of masking his speech spasms, the parents are inclined to assume that the defect has disappeared or that their folk treatment has worked successfully. This may lead them to ignore the speech symptoms or to believe they no longer exist, which is responsible for the growth of social distance between them and the child, who sorely appreciates the real meaning of his struggle for fluency. The parents thus urge the child to undertake activities or they uphold vocational aims for which he feels unprepared. It is the secondary manifestations of the stuttering, the timidity, shyness, and refusal to take part in social activities or go through with educational plans, which are the greatest source of frustration to parents and which lead to the strongest parental rejections of the child. The bitterness of the parental disappointment at the stuttering son's failures may be very great where they have a local reputation to uphold or where there is a traditional family occupational role calling for speaking skills. Illustrative cases include that of an outstanding attorney in a small town who came to despise his speechless offspring because of the pall he cast upon the family reputation for leadership and ability, and of a minister who continually berated his stuttering son for his unwillingness to assume a leadership role in the youth groups of his church.

Other Group Reactions

The experiences of the stuttering child in his peer age group are much more likely to be traumatic ones, in contrast to the sheltering he receives in the family. Small children at best are only partially socialized. Their reactions to deviants in their group are simple, direct, and uninhibited, and they are capable of great cruelty to handicapped playmates – especially in the absence of supervision. In play situations they mock and mimic the child with a speech handicap and use him as the object of their aggressions in many other ways. It is in the play group that nicknames and trait labels are invented and applied to its members, and it is there that sharply invidious distinctions are drawn between the deviant and the rest of the group. The impact of these experiences is intensified where the child with a speech defect has had no preparation for them. Often his parents are unable to offer anything better than mere sympathy and indulgence to counteract their effects.

The outstanding features of the reaction of schoolteachers to the stuttering child are neglect and inconsistency of classroom treatment. A measure of this neglect is seen in the scholastic progress of the speech-handicapped child. Although tests do not show that stutterers are low in general intelligence, nevertheless as a group they are retarded in school on an average of from one to two years.[27] Teachers follow a conglomeration of policies with respect to the stutterers in their classes. One study revealed that 32 different methods had been used by 50 teachers in handling 72 stutterers in their classrooms.[28] Some teachers excuse stutterers completely from class recitation, requiring that the deficiency be remedied by extra written work of some sort. Others only partially relieve the stuttering child of responsibility for recitation, while some follow a "sink-or-swim" policy, according to which the child must attempt to recite upon a basis of equality with other students. On the whole, however, more teachers are moved to give special consideration to the child with a stuttering handicap, for they usually have a deep sympathy for the plight of the child. Despite their sympathetic attitudes, teachers do not mitigate much, if any, the frustrating impact of the school situation. For the greater part, they have as yet no special training to equip them to handle the speech-defective child in the classroom group. They themselves are hampered in efforts to be of tangible assistance by virtue of their having to work within the

[27] Pinstner, Rudolph, Jon Eisenson, and Mildred Stanton, *The Psychology of the Physically Handicapped,* 1941, p 323

[28] Knudson, Thelma A , "Oral Recitation Problems of Stutterers," *Proceedings of the American Speech Correction Association,* 9, 1939, pp 9ff.

framework of the individualistic, competitive educational process, highly conducive to invidious differentiation of the children.

Control Agencies

The public control agencies established to deal with speech deviants per se are very few in number. Speech clinics are operated in conjunction with departments of speech and psychology in a number of our colleges and universities, in which diagnostic and consultative services as well as treatment are offered. Speech correctionists are also retained by some public-school systems to conduct group treatment of speech disorders through special classes organized for this purpose. Outside of the schools some supplementary services to speech defectives are provided by child-guidance clinics and other child-welfare agencies. Rural areas are notoriously deficient in services and agencies for aiding children and adults with speech handicaps. This has prompted the initiation of traveling speech clinics in some areas, Iowa and Michigan, for example. Such expedients as the latter are undoubtedly of some value in surveying the extent of speech problems among school children in an area, but it must be admitted that the amount of therapy which can be made available by these means is minimal. All in all, the speech deviant is grossly neglected in comparison with the public concern for the blind and the crippled. Table 11 gives figures amply attesting to this discrepancy:

Table 11 Average per Capita Expenditures for Special Education in New York City Schools*

Type of Handicap	Average Expenditures per Handicapped Pupil
Blind	$515.26
Deaf	570.67
Crippled	267.86
Speech defective	5.65

* *Physically Handicapped Children in New York City*, 1941, Board of Education of New York City.

Generalizations about the impact of clinical experiences upon the stutterer are difficult to make. The nature of the therapeutic experience is variably colored and influenced, if not determined, by the theoretical premises of the clinician in charge. These range widely, so much so that there are almost as many theories as there are speech correctionists.[29] Some clinicians prefer to see stuttering as a symptom of personal maladjustment, others are impressed by the alaterality of the nervous system as a cause, while others regard this disorder as a habit-formation problem, and still

[29] For the various theories, see Eugene Holm, *Stuttering, Significant Theories and Therapies*, 1943.

others look upon it as a function of the "semantic environment." Probably there is a selective process which operates to bring different types of cases to the various clinics, thus, for example, one clinician will accept cases for treatment only if they are capable of absolute subordination to his authority. This selectivity of cases may account, in part, for the diversity of theories on the "cause" of stuttering in the literature on the subject.

Psychiatrists who treat stuttering frequently favor medical conceptions of the disorder and in the process of treatment they may implant rather firmly the notion of physical disease or bad heredity in the mind of the person being treated. The search for a "cure" in the case may strengthen the sense of dichotomy between the speech of the stutterer and other speakers. If the psychoanalytic view has been adopted by the clinician, then the stutterer is apt to have his difficulties defined in terms of sex conflicts which may or may not exist, or which have only an indirect bearing upon the speech if they do exist. Beneath its scientific guise the bias in favor of the priority of personality disorder as a "cause" may have the middle-class symbolic effect of imputing a character defect to the person under treatment. The therapists who define the stuttering by minimizing it as a "bad habit," or as purely and simply the function of subjective attitudes toward the speech, may have quasi-psychotic effects upon the case in the sense that the very real social differentiation of the stuttering individual as perceived by others is being ignored or dismissed.

Symbolic Impacts of Speech Therapy

Aside from these more speculative comments we may safely say that going to a speech clinic in all cases confronts the individual with a clear-cut societal definition of the stuttering self. The association with other stutterers and with speech cases in the clinic situation has a clear implication for self and role, as well as the knowledge that other students or members of the community know the function of the clinic. One well-known clinic, at a Middle Western college, makes it more or less of a prerequisite for treatment of adult stutterers that they make frank avowals in speech and behavior that they are stutterers. This is done by having the stutterers practice blocks in front of mirrors, exaggerate them, copy one another's blocks, and have or fake blocks in public social situations. While there are several objectives behind this procedure, one of its chief consequences is to instill an unequivocal self-definition in the stutterer as one who is different from others, although not necessarily as one whose speech difference must always be so bad as to be severely penalized. Ultimately, if the therapy is successful, the person is left with a self-conception of one whose physiology differs from normal persons and who, even though speaking with a minimum of blocks, must always be prepared for periods of bad speech. The person continues to think of himself as a stutterer, but as one who stutters easily and fluently. Presumably this kind of role definition makes the integration of fluctuations in speech fluency easier than would be the case if a "cure" were claimed and the person thought of himself as a completely "normal" speaker.

Not all stutterers benefit from this clinical treatment. How many fail to improve and how many have serious relapses after leaving the clinic can only be a matter for guess, since speech clinics do not keep, or at least do not publish, such data. Failures of this sort at the hands of scientifically trained speech correctionists can deepen the sense of hopelessness in the stutterer, perhaps even more than when they are the result of exploitative "treatment" by a fraudulent speech correctionist. We are in the dark as to what effect diagnosing speech defects and their treatment by partially trained correctionists in public-school systems has upon young primary stutterers. However, there is a possibility that symbolizing the variations as defects may play a part in producing secondary stuttering. Findings in one survey revealed that three-fifths of children "with defects" were unaware of them.[30] Assumptions made by correctionists that primary stuttering must be treated may themselves be part of the symbolic complex leading to sociopathic differentiation of the child. Some idea of the unanticipated symbolic consequences of a child's being placed in a speech-correction class in a public school can be gathered from the following autobiographical document:

At the age of eight I was placed in a speech-correction class. At that time I was attending a grade school in Michigan. I was placed in this class not by the wishes of my parents but by the wishes of my teachers. My teachers felt that my lisping was so bad that it was difficult for me to be understood by others.

When I was placed in this class I hated it, and I didn't look forward to Thursday which was the day I was required to attend. While I was attending the class, the other children were allowed to go out and play. The result was that I felt I was being punished for something I couldn't help. I believed at that time my difficulty was not due to any speech defect but was due to an accident when I was four years old which caused me to lose my two front teeth.

The class itself was made up of students who had many different speech difficulties. Some of the students were stutterers, others got their words mixed up, and there were others who were simply too afraid to speak. The teacher of the class would visit each school one day a week. If one were to ask me what I learned from this class, I am afraid I would have to say that the only thing I can remember is the vowels. Our class lesson was usually to keep repeating vowels until we were able to pronounce them correctly. The reac-

[30] Morris, *op. cit.*, p 269

tions of the other students were mixed so far as their attitude toward me went Most of them wanted to know why I couldn't go out and play with them. On the other hand some of them would make fun of those of us in the class, saying that "So-and-so can't talk."

When I came out to California I was glad because at that time I thought I wouldn't have to go to another speech-correction class. But lo and behold, in junior high school they caught up with me. This may sound as if I were a criminal. At least I felt like one. Class was held every week, and I would be excused from my home-room period. I felt again that I was being punished, because every time the class would meet, something important seemed to happen which I would miss out on. I couldn't wait until I got out of junior high school because I was told that there were no speech-correction classes in high school.

INDIVIDUATION OF THE STUTTERER

There is little direct proof that stuttering sufficiently pronounced to be thought of as a speech defect is hereditary. It is possible that congenital weaknesses in the speech-coordinating structures may occur in a small percentage of children, but it is more likely that in such cases there will be damage to the whole organism. Such "weaknesses," interacting with a family environment in which the child feels insecure or in which he is subjected to inordinate ridicule, punishment, or excessive stimulation at a time when he is mastering speech, may produce disrhythmic speech. However it must be accepted as an equal possibility that children with ordinary powers of neuromuscular integration, when confronted with environmental pressures beyond their maturational capacities to cope with, may likewise develop broken speech in varying degrees. A third possibility is interaction of normal childish speech with hypersensitive, hypercritical, foreboding attitudes of parents, which eventuates in speech disorders. Whatever relevance physiological factors may have to the initiation of speech difficulties in the child, they have little to do with the fully developed patterns of stuttering which change the status and self-conceptions of the child. Stuttering in this sense must be defined and analysed as a "sociopsychological phenomenon." [31] The best evidence we can cite in behalf of this contention is that cases exist in which persons who have no demonstrable speech blocks nevertheless have stutterers' fears, think of themselves as stutterers, and must be treated as such clinically.[32]

Practically all stuttering (85 per cent of the cases) makes its appearance in children by the time they are eight years of age. In the remainder of the cases the children have begun to stutter by the time they reach adoles-

[31] Johnson, W, "The Role of Evaluation in Stuttering Behavior," *Journal of Speech Disorders*, 3, June, 1938, pp 85–89.

[32] Blanton and Blanton, *op. cit.*, p 74

cence.[33] Critical points in the history of the stutterer's personality occur at six years, ten years, and at adolescence, at which times the defect either disappears or tends to become more deeply fixed in the individual's behavior.[34] The crisis at six years coincides with the child's entry into school, the implications of which have already been touched upon. Just why ten years of age should be crucial for the stutterer is not clear, unless this be the period around which identifications with peer age groups begin The crisis set up by adolescence, with its imminent sexual and vocational demands of an adult role, is to be expected normally in our culture. That it should be a making or breaking point for the stutterer is understandable. Just how the crisis of old age affects the stutterer is unknown, although it may be that the release from more stringent responsibilities brought on by age may ease his lot somewhat.

The early or primary speech deviation in the child, as has been shown, is not severe enough to be greatly visible or to seriously interfere with communication. When the child first begins to stutter, the only apparent reactions are either rapid, easy repetitions or short, effortless prolongations, called the primary symptoms of stuttering.[35] At this stage the child is usually completely unaware of these features of his speech. If nothing happens to call these minor speech differences into the child's consciousness during the period when he is establishing his speech habits, they may disappear. They may even, under such circumstances, persist into adulthood and become integrated into a socially accepted role without ever leading to the sociopsychological differentiation of the person as a "stutterer."

Secondary Stuttering

In the case of those children who become self-defined stutterers, the stage of nonreacting acceptance eventually gives way to one of awareness brought about by the reactions of parents, siblings, playmates, or teachers to the speech differences. In the symbolic process of self and "other" role playing, the child somehow senses or feels that the differences in his speech are "bad" or undesirable. It is at this point that labeling as a "stutterer" takes place, *i.e.*, secondary deviation occurs. However, the mere act of calling a child a stutterer, even when stuttering speech is present, does not necessarily make the child a self-conscious stutterer. One investigation into the symbolic concomitants of stuttering makes this very clear. This study of a group of college students whose speech was normal or slightly

33 Reid, L. D., "Some Facts about Stuttering," *Journal of Speech Disorders*, 11, March, 1946, pp. 3–12.

34 Blanton and Blanton, *op. cit*, pp. 71f

35 Blumel, C. S., "Primary and Secondary Stuttering," *Proceedings of the American Speech Correction Association*, 1932, pp 91–102.

above average brought out the fact that while somewhat more than 19 per cent had actually had a stuttering defect of speech, nevertheless 30 per cent of the group had been said to have been stuttering as children. Only 4.2 per cent of these students had been called "stutterers," but 6.3 per cent had applied this term to themselves. More detailed figures are included in Table 12·

TABLE 12. NUMBER AND PERCENTAGE OF POSITIVE REPLIES TO QUESTIONS ABOUT STUTTERING AND ITS SYMBOLIZATION BY 96 NORMAL COLLEGE SPEAKERS BY SEX*

Questions	Male		Female		Total	
	No.	Per cent	No	Per cent	No.	Per cent
Have had a stuttering defect of speech	10	10.4	9	9 4	19	19.8
Had been called a stutterer	4	4 2	0	0	4	4 2
Had been said to have been stuttering	20	20 8	9	9 4	29	30 2
Thought they had spoken stutteringly	38	39 6	32	33.3	70	72.9
Thought they still had the habit	1	1 0	0	0	1	1 0
Had called themselves a stutterer	4	4.2	2	2.1	6	6.3

*Voelker, C. H., "On the Semantic Aspects of Stuttering in Non-stutterers," *Quarterly Journal of Speech*, 28, February, 1942, pp 78–80. Percentages do not total 100 because each person gave replies to more than one question

The "pencil-and-paper," quiz, and recording methods employed in this research admittedly detract from its value. Nevertheless it reemphasizes the fact that the symbolic determinants of stuttering comprehend something beyond mere linguistic reactions of others. It also suggests that the juxtaposition of stuttering and symbolic responses in a social context must be understood more fully in the analysis of stuttering Just why these persons did not become self-conscious stutterers in these cases where they were called "stutterers" remains a problem for more intensive research into the symbolic impact of early childhood environments of stutterers. While there are no data to corroborate the contention, we believe that the answer to the problem lies in the hypothesis advanced in the theoretical section of the book, namely, that in order to develop secondary stuttering symptoms, not only must an identification with the role of stutterer be made symbolically but it must be immediately followed by a series of penalized speech spasms which integrate the symbol in behavioral reactions.

The secondary symptoms of stuttering associated with the stutterer's role at first may be no more than attempts to force out the words. Tantrum behavior often follows, with the child shouting, crying, laughing, spitting, or hitting at playmates when he experiences the now undesirable interferences with his speaking. Subsequent to this, finding these infantile reactions do not give relief, the child begins to fear stuttering. These fears are attached to certain words, persons, and situations. In time the fears spread to invest other words and situations. Finally the fears become generalized in the sense that the stutterer symbolically visualizes situations in which the stuttering appears, together with the anticipated social penalties. This is the cause of rather complex anticipatory behavior in which the stutterer plans his speech far in advance in order to avoid spasms on feared words. Other more immediate anticipatory behavior takes shape in postponement of words, avoidance, substitution, release devices, pitch and attitudinal disguises, all of which function to increase or decrease the previously mentioned social visibility of the stuttering. Generally this is found only in older stutterers, but tricks of the sort described have been observed in children as young as four years.[36]

Social Participation

In order to understand the interaction between stuttering and social participation of the adult stutterer, something of the tensional impact of the handicap must be known. When the stutterer is younger, he may enjoy free speech in certain situations; but as he grows older and nothing intervenes to alleviate his symptoms, the primacy of his stuttering role increases. There is a progressive involvement of his roles in many social situations. With each stuttering experience there are social failures and a corresponding sense of unpleasantness, inferiority, and anticipatory fear. The anticipatory fears create tensions and the greater likelihood of stuttering in each new situation he enters. Furthermore, the self-consciousness associated with normal learning errors and the tensions of extraneous social failures are likely to set off the stuttering response. The predominant self of which he is conscious at these times is that of a "stutterer," and more and more his social failures are subjectively taken as validation of the role. When this point is reached, the speech deviation has become secondary, and it may correctly be said that the person now stutters because he stutters.

The common denominator of fear underlying the stutterer's social participation is insightfully depicted in the following autobiographical excerpt:[37]

> . . . the external world becomes little more than a shadowy domain whose chief importance is as a source from whence comes the occasion for nervous tension

[36] Van Riper, C., "The Growth of the Stuttering Spasm," *Quarterly Journal of Speech*, 23, September, 1937, pp 70–73.

[37] Gustavson, Carl, "A Talisman and a Convalescence," *Quarterly Journal of Speech*, 30, December, 1944, p 467.

and the precipitation of blockage. The real world in which one's whole endeavor is immersed is the inner world of the self. Or rather, one's attention is concentrated on that limited portion of the inner self which reflects the struggle associated with the stuttering. His being is wracked by the tension which has been built up through years of nervousness when in the presence of the stuttering situation. This condition carries with it a hyperesthetic perception of certain words or letters of the alphabet, of certain situations, of certain persons whose presence may lead to stuttering. One wanders perpetually on the edge of the vortex of stuttering and at intervals is drawn into it. In the mode of introversion there is a rigid fixation on the procession of spoken words and upon it plays an inflamed suggestibility, in turn fed from acute memories of unpleasant experiences with this word or situation before. The details of the experience may have dropped from conscious memory but the tension instantaneously appears when suggested by the hair-trigger reaction of the memory of an intense unpleasantness.

It is clear that the stutterer's role has a high degree of primacy in the sense that subjectively it pervades practically all of his other roles. Although speech pathologists have emphasized the societal rejection of the stutterer, it is the internal rather than external limits which seem the more significant in explaining his social participation. A Negro or a drunken hobo would never be permitted to enter a fashionable restaurant, but the stutterer, assuming he is properly dressed, may freely do so, and if he can endure the laughter or smirking of the waitress, can order and eat a meal. It is important to note that stutterers *try* and *fail* at a wide variety of occupations, in contrast with the blind who seldom have the opportunity to fail at most types of work. Choice becomes subjectively delimited in the stutterer. and he withdraws from social activity to minimize his tensions.

Economic Participation

Generalizations about the economic participation of stutterers is made difficult by the paucity and selected character of the sample data which are at hand. One study of 47 stutterers, mostly college trained, none over thirty-four years of age, which was based upon reports of all the various jobs they had held, pointed to a concentration of job experiences in the unskilled, professional, and clerical occupations. Another study of handicapped workers in industry disclosed that persons with speech defects in general tended to be found in greater-than-expected frequencies in the unskilled, skilled, and clerical groups. While the data are not the most satisfactory to prove the point, they nevertheless suggest that stuttering and speech defects do serve as a barrier keeping many persons so handicapped at lower occupational levels. The data are presented in Table 13:

TABLE 13. NUMBER AND PERCENTAGE DISTRIBUTION OF A GROUP OF STUTTERERS AND A GROUP OF INDUSTRIAL EMPLOYEES WITH SPEECH DEFECTS BY OCCUPATIONAL CLASS

Occupational class	College-trained group*		California industrial employees†		U.S Census occupational distribution 1940§
	No.	Per cent	No.	Per cent	Per cent
Professional	38	25.4	2	4.7	6.5
Proprietors and managers	1	0 6	2	4.7	17 7
Clerical	32	21 7	11	26.1	17 1
Skilled	13	8.8	7	16 6	11 7
Semiskilled	11	7.4	5	11.9	20.9
Unskilled	52	35.3	15	35.7	25.8
Total	147	99 2	42	99.7	99 7

* Johnson, W., *Influence of Stuttering on Personality*, University of Iowa Studies in Child Welfare, 5, No. 5, 1932, Chap. V.

† *Census and Industrial Survey of Physically Handicapped in California*, 1945, Table 14

§ *Comparative Occupational Statistics in the United States, 1870–1940*, U.S. Bureau of the Census, 1943.

Additional corroboration of this conclusion comes from information gathered from one hundred stutterers admitted as patients to a New England hospital. The average earnings of this group were discovered to be 35 per cent below the average income of other workers.[38]

Perhaps more significant than the occupational concentration of stutterers according to status level of occupations is their apparent tendency to gravitate into occupations requiring little or no speech. Table 14 makes this very clear. It would seem from this that, depending upon the severity of his symptoms, the stutterer actively seeks out jobs which fix and con-

TABLE 14. DISTRIBUTION OF OCCUPATIONAL EXPERIENCES OF MILD, AVERAGE, AND SEVERE STUTTERERS BY AMOUNT OF SPEAKING REQUIRED IN OCCUPATIONS*

Occupational speech requirements	Degree of stuttering			
	Mild	Average	Severe	Total
Great deal of speech	13	3	3	19
Average amount of speech	6	12	7	25
Relatively little speech	9	16	12	37
Total	28	31	22	81

* Johnson, W , "The Role of Evaluation in Stuttering Behavior," *Journal of Speech Disorders*, 3, June, 1938.

[38] Green, J , and E Wells, *The Cause and Cure of Stuttering*, 1927, p 181.

firm his isolation from others. This in turn strengthens or increases his subjectively felt isolation.

Sex and Marital Participation

Presumably the economic disability of stutterers, together with their preference for isolant occupations and their general withdrawal reactions, affect their opportunities and inclinations for sexual indulgence and marriage. The avoidance by many stutterers of all but necessary social contacts undoubtedly retards and to some extent distorts their psychosexual development. Some partial idea of this can be gathered from the results of an inquiry into the adjustments of a group of stutterers consisting of 25 males and 5 females, all unmarried, averaging twenty-four years of age:

Table 15. Sexual Activities and Characteristics of 30 Stutterers*

	Fear of opposite sex	Has sweetheart	Suspected homosexuality	Heterosexual experience
Yes	22	10	3	11
No	5	18	25	13
No information	3	2	2	6

* Case, H., *Stuttering and Speech Blocking, A Comparative Study of Maladjustment*, Ph.D. dissertation, University of California at Los Angeles, 1940, Table 9, p. 65a.

The size of this sample is obviously small, and its representativeness can be questioned. However, in the light of our other knowledge about the social participation of stutterers, the high percentage, 73.3, of those who had definite fears of the opposite sex seems meaningful. The number of those without a sweetheart strikes us as being overly large for this age group, but then there are no control studies to confirm the impression. The 10.7 per cent suspected of homosexuality is higher than the estimated 3 to 5 per cent of the general population with this form of sexual behavior. The 45 per cent of those who had had heterosexual experience may be somewhat low for a predominantly male group. Three out of four of the female cases, where information was available, had indulged in heterosexual relationships. This hints at sexual precocity for a portion of female stutterers. However, contrary to this, many female cases encountered in clinics display a sexual naiveté of a sort one might expect in older spinsters. Beneath this behavior and the sexually promiscuous ways of the occasional female stutterer can be seen a more generalized psychosexual immaturity.

The male who stutters is likewise slow to grow up sexually. However, his situation, in so far as sexual opportunities are concerned, is distinguished by the presence of a certain percentage of strongly maternalistic or perhaps insecure members of the opposite sex who are attracted to handicapped men. Nevertheless, even though he associates with women, the speech-handicapped male frequently finds his heterosexual activities unsatisfying, so that his dating or love affairs are often irregular and unstable. The behavior of one rather handsome stutterer is illustrative; getting dates was easy for him, and many girls succumbed to his attractions. Nevertheless, nearly all of his relations with girls ended after a few dates mainly because he compulsively insulted them and quarreled with them in order to hurt them as much as possible. In intimate courtship and dating relationships involving dominance and submission, the possibility is a strong one that the speech-defective man's aggressions toward others or toward himself will be focused upon his female companion who becomes their surrogate. Be this as it may, nevertheless informal dating in small groups where they are intimately known remains one of the more common forms of social participation for young adult stutterers.[39]

Up to the present time little interest has been evinced in the relationship of stuttering to marriage and family life. As a consequence, data on stutterers' marriage rates are not at hand. However, it is highly probable that a severe stuttering defect lessens the likelihood of marriage, perhaps more for women than for men. Delayed marriage for stutterers may be even more common, at least some data gathered through the writers' students give this impression. There are several reasons for believing that stuttering has these consequences in so far as marital status goes. The problems of establishing themselves economically make the support of a wife and family a somewhat more hazardous undertaking for male stutterers than for other males The isolant habits of both males and females who stutter are such that they are not so liable to be thrown into contacts with eligible members of the opposite sex in such a way as to lead to marriage. Stutterers may have acquired adolescent or postadolescent habits, making marital existence or its prospect less desirable. Finally, those with this handicap who are disposed to conceive of stuttering as the result of heredity may postpone or avoid marriage for fear of perpetuating it in their children.

Other Forms of Social Participation

Of the political and religious participation of stutterers little is known beyond that which can be culled from case histories. There is nothing to prevent stutterers from voting or joining a political party. However, more active political participation which calls for speeches, discussion, door-to-

[39] Johnson, *Influence of Stuttering on Personality*, p 49 Based upon a study of stutterers attending a university

door canvassing, or circulating petitions obviously will be unattractive or repelling to the stutterer. One speech deviant explained that he never took part in political discussions because of their emotional nature, which was most productive of his speech spasms. Church services require little speech from participants and consequently may be attended by stutterers as well as others. This does not hold true for the more informal educational and recreational group activities sponsored by churches. Occasionally a case is encountered where the stutterer becomes strongly antireligious and breaks off all church contacts, even after childhood indoctrination has taken place. Whether some of the archaic reactions of ministers toward physical handicaps and afflictions function here as they do with the blind is a matter for investigation.

Participation of stutterers in recreational activities, as might be anticipated, varies with the amount of speaking required. Many stutterers prefer athletic games, even excelling in them, chiefly because their status in them is not determined by verbal skill. Musical and literary activities are attractive for much the same reason. Generally, the passive forms of recreation increasingly common to our culture, such as motion pictures, radio listening, sporting contests, and reading, pose no participational problems to stutterers. Stuttering students are found to participate somewhat less than others in such things as parties, banquets, and dances. However, from 30 to 35 per cent of one group of college stutterers indicated affiliations with fraternities and sororities, and furthermore they seemed to achieve a genuine integration into these groups.[40]

The participation of stutterers in the armed services during the Second World War was somewhat varied because of differing policies of draft boards, induction officers, and medical examiners. While the Navy unequivocally pronounced stuttering to be a sufficient reason for rejection, the Army had a less clearly defined policy covering speech defects. It is estimated that a little over one-half of all the stutterers called up for armed service were rejected. However, most were rejected on grounds other than stuttering, with a pronounced tendency in such rejections to regard the stutterer as a psychoneurotic or psychopathic personality. The armed forces were slow to take special cognizance of stutterers as such, and even where treated they were generally handled as psychiatric cases.[41] The stutterers in the armed forces apparently fared rather well in so far as advancement is concerned, if the data in Table 16 can be taken as representative:

[40] *Ibid*, p. 48.

[41] Johnson, W., "The Status of Speech Defectives in Military Service," *Quarterly Journal of Speech*, 23, April, 1943, pp 131–136

TABLE 16. RANGE IN MILITARY STATUS OF STUTTERERS SEEN AT BROOKE AND MCGUIRE GENERAL HOSPITAL*

Rank	Preinduction	Postinduction
Prvt	32	10
Pfc	17	13
Tec 5	2	2
Cpl	4	1
Tec 4.	1	1
Sgt	4	3
S Sgt	5	5
T Sgt	0	1
M Sgt	1	0
Aviation cadet	3	0
2nd Lt	4	1
1st Lt	1	0
Capt	1	0
Major	1	0
Lt Col	1	0
Total	77	37

* Preacher, W G, and W. E Harris, "Speech Disorders in World War II Stuttering,' *Journal of Speech Disorders*, 11, December, 1946, pp 303–308.

No indication is given as to the severity of the symptoms in these cases, other than to mention that the highest officer on the list was a very mild stutterer. This, together with case-history materials, suggests the conclusion that the preinduction stutterers in the armed forces, for the most part, consisted of cases with only mild-to-average severe symptoms.

ADJUSTMENT AND MALADJUSTMENT

Measured by the divergence between societal and self-definitions and degree of self-acceptance, stutterers as a class fall somewhere between normal persons and those conventionally thought of as psychoneurotic Various tests and observations more or less concur that, in contrast to control groups, there is a greater incidence of extreme shyness, timidity, seclusiveness, moodiness, depression, anxiety, and paranoid symptoms in the reactions of stutterers. These can all be designated as part and manifestation of a devaluation of the self and an exaggeration of the social handicaps believed by stutterers to result from their speech disability. It is small wonder that this should be the modal or status personality of the stutterer in our culture, where few groups or social situations do not call for a substantial amount of articulate speech. The stutterer finds himself at a distinct loss in a culture where such a large proportion of adjustments are predominantly verbal and where competitive success in many areas depends upon the ability of the person to manipulate others through verbal controls. The stutterer simply does not possess the effective speech through which the more important roles are implemented.

The stutterer is not only faced with the unpleasant version of himself as an incompetent adult but also with the direct judgments which are made of his person through the social evaluations of his speech. Just as the man with feeble, mouselike tones is put down by others as a weak personality, the ineffectual attempts of the stutterer to make himself understood provoke ideas that he is a ridiculous and weak-willed person. Projected before the audience of self-sufficing members of the community living out the Protestant ethic of middle-class America, he is a person who has "lost control" over the verbal self.

The societal reactions are internalized by the stutterer at an early age when he begins to sense the familial anxieties about his speech. His school experiences strengthen his feelings of inferiority, and his visits to clinics and speech correctionists, or being placed in a special class at school, formally conceptualize his status as a "defective." The failures or temporary successes of treatment, followed by greater speech difficulties, bring on a sense of hopelessness about his handicap. Job failures plus awkwardness and ineptitude with the opposite sex are further confirmation of the by now deep inadequacy the stutterer feels.

The secondary stutterer commonly hates his stuttering and the role it symbolizes for him. This role rejection is obversely demonstrated by the free speech which even severe stutterers achieve when they temporarily adopt foreign accents and drawls or take part in dramatics. This is to say that when the stutterer can identify with a role other than his own, if only through such subterfuge, he can for awhile free himself of his blocks. Otherwise the stutterer overtly manifests the rejection of his hated role through withdrawing from as many speech situations as he can. Withdrawal in some part reduces his tensions and attenuates the pain of social rejections. Procrastination frequently becomes his defense against facing social situations he cannot avoid. Conjoined with social withdrawal and procrastination is the pseudoization of the self, or self-enhancement through fantasies of social success and solitary compensatory behavior. By such means does the stutterer manage to preserve a species of integration in his personality. Stuttering seldom generates psychotic reactions for the reason that in itself it provides a kind of meaning and integration to personality.

The greatest barriers to role and self-acceptance are to be observed in those stutterers who have great intellectual abilities or other talents which elevate their aspirational levels. The knowledge or belief that they are potentially capable of high achievement makes their plight all the harder to bear. Such persons, according to our belief, are much more inclined to neurotic, psychotic, and suicidal tendencies. It is of more significance that stutterers seem, in general, to contemplate suicide more often than non-stutterers; the results of one comparison on this score revealed that 28 per cent of a group of 50 stutterers had had suicidal fantasies, while only 15 per cent of a group adjudged as psychologically normal displayed this symptom of ultimate self-rejection.[42]

As we have already mentioned, some stutterers successfully counterfeit roles by the expedient of not talking, by skillfully disguising their blocks, and by conveying the impression of taciturnity. The sense of guilt and anxiety created by social acceptance obtained through these subterfuges are bound to be great and to occasion much conflict and internal pain.

Marginality is less readily discovered among stutterers than among the blind. From the author's limited observations it would seem that marginal stutterers are not so likely to be those with mild symptoms as they are to be those with sharp contrasts between their stuttering speech and their free speech, or perhaps those who have relatively long periods of free speech followed by periods of severe stuttering. The ex-stutterer may also betray signs of marginality – especially if he remains in an environment where he was formerly known as a speech defective. Often marginal stutterers are clinical failures, especially where the therapy employed demands self-conscious avowals of a stuttering role.

There are well-adjusted stutterers in the sense in which we have used the term. However, there are few professional stutterers, because of the absence of opportunities to commercially or otherwise profit from the defect. Our culture has not institutionalized a role of this sort for the speech defective. One exception is the occasional comedian who stutters to entertain others. Some of the outstanding speech pathologists in the country have been or are stutterers at the present time. The fact of their stuttering undeniably has a function in building up rapport with clients and considerably enhances the rewards of their roles. It is significant in this connection that after receiving clinical help many stutterers cherish ambitions to become speech correctionists.

Unsymbolized, primary stutterers may adjust easily to adult roles and even turn minor defects in their speech to good advantage. The picture of how integration of primary symptoms of stuttering into various social roles might be a matter of course if the modal symbolic environment of the child in our culture were a different sort is depicted in the following case history.

42 Johnson, *Influence of Stuttering on Personality*, p. 98.

Y . . . was born in Chicago in 1915. He was adopted in early infancy, and nothing is known of his biological parents. His foster parents had previously adopted another boy, six years older than Y . . . . There were no other children. Y . . .'s foster parents were about forty-five years old at the time of his adoption. Mr. R . . . was a retired broker who had a full-time, but unpaid job, in Masonry. He was a rather severe man, not much interested in his sons. They did not know him very well. Mrs. R . . . was a semi-invalid whose chief interest was in raising her sons to be good Christian men. Both parents were devout Methodists.

By the time he was nine years old, Y . . . was a well-developed stutterer. There was no noticeable change in the type or degree of his stuttering in the next thirty years. His stuttering often occurs at the beginning of a sentence It consists of the rapid repetition of the first syllable of the sentence, or troublesome word, and is usually of short duration. There are no facial contortions and no apparent anxiety.

Y . . . 's foster mother died when he was twelve. This was a severe loss, as he had little affection for his foster father and was not particularly fond of his brother. His father employed a series of housekeepers, and Y . . . lived at home until he finished high school.

Y . . . was large and well developed for his age, and enjoyed considerable prestige in grammar school and high school due to his ability as a baseball player, runner, and seducer. He had his first sex experience when he was thirteen. His partner was an eighteen-year-old waitress at a summer camp. She thought his stuttering was cute. So have a good many subsequent women.

After leaving high school, he attended a small liberal-arts college in the Middle West.

In 1926 he went to work for the sales service department of a motor-car company as a driver at the Milford Proving Ground. He got along well with his employers and the men he worked with, and in three years had been promoted to sales-contact work. This involved calling on dealers and instructing their servicemen in the latest methods and equipment.

Stuttering has been no liability in his work. He speaks very rapidly, and the stutter seems to add a certain intensity to his speech. It is not severe enough to cause sympathetic anxiety in the listener, but gives his speech a sort of rapid-fire quality that requires attention.

After several years with the motor-car company he resigned to go into the real-estate business, in which he has done very well He married in his middle thirties and has two children

Selected Readings

Johnson, Wendell *Because I Stutter*, 1930

——— "The Indians Have No Word for It, Stuttering in Children," *Quarterly Journal of Speech*, 30, October, 1944, pp. 330–337.

———. *The Influence of Stuttering on Personality*, University of Iowa Studies in Child Welfare, 5, No. 5, 1932

LEMERT, EDWIN, and CHARLES VAN RIPER: "The Use of Psychodrama in the Treatment of Speech Defects," *Sociometry*, 7, May, 1944, pp. 190–195.

VAN RIPER, CHARLES "The Growth of the Stuttering Spasm," *Quarterly Journal of Speech*, 23, September, 1937 pp. 70–73

——— *Speech Correction*, 1947, rev ed., Chaps. 10–11.

CHAPTER 7

RADICALISM AND RADICALS

Wherever men and women have been gathered and integrated into communities and societies, there have been some who have become differentiated from others by their critical attitudes toward the cherished norms of the group. Those who persistently challenged the more compulsive norms of their group in articulate terms came to be known as dissenters, agitators, free thinkers, infidels, heretics, rebels, reformers, renegades, Bohemians, and radicals. In some instances these ideational deviants have stood alone against the overwhelming disapproval of their fellows; in other instances they have made common cause with like-minded protestants and organized themselves into subversive agencies of social change. In either case we see many of these deviants appearing in some of the cruelest pages of the history of man's treatment of man. It is for the reason of the frenzied punitive quality of the societal reaction and the frequent disillusionment and isolation of the individual deviant that the subject of radicalism recommends itself for inclusion in this treatise.

The Nature of the Deviation

Radicalism generally has been held to be the advocacy of ideas and beliefs at variance with those of the majority of the group, community, or a society. It consists of deviations in the overt, verbal-symbolic behavior of individuals and groups. It extends beyond the mere verbalization of beliefs to include such behavior as voting, demonstrating in parades, holding meetings, wearing special insignia, and conforming to provocative rituals. The behavior associated with radical verbalizations is a means of further symbolizing and underscoring the unsanctioned and unpopular beliefs of those who express them. Radicalism must be distinguished from beliefs which are merely bizarre, such as those found in the expressions of many psychotic persons. Radical beliefs possess a discernible consistency and rationality and can be related in a contradictory way to the basic ideology of the group in which they are voiced. They can be located on the same polarized continuum of expressive behavior with that of the modal group from which they deviate. Ordinarily it is a practice to speak of ideas and attitudes on the left extreme of continua of beliefs as "radical," those at the other extreme as "reactionary," and those falling close to either side of a central value as "liberal" and "conservative." For practical analysis radical and reactionary behavior can be taken as being of the same generic order of phenomena.

Radicalism may be specialized, in which case it may be called "reform," or it may be a more generalized revolutionary belief system. Writers have customarily marked substantive divisions between economic, religious, and political radicalism, with occasional recognition of a separate type of sexual and familial radicalism. Revolutionary radicalism embraces a broad gamut of beliefs which touch upon most of the institutional life of a whole society, which is another way of saying that it challenges the fundamental compulsive norms underlying an entire culture. Whereas pacifism is simply a systematic proposal to adopt a policy of nonviolence in social relations and a denial of patriotic values, communism contains oral and written specifications to change property concepts, alter the entire political structure, to a greater or lesser extent restrict the activities of organized religion, and to introduce sweeping changes in marital and family relations.

Extent of the Deviation

There is no exact enumeration of the total radical population in our society and probably there never can be. Much radicalism, such as religious and moral radicalism, does not make itself apparent in a way which permits measuring it or the numbers professing the beliefs involved. Furthermore, estimates of the extent of radicalism and the incidence of radicals are not likely to agree from one person to the next, because the definition of radicalism for purposes of measurement has to be arbitrary. Finally, the evanescent and ephemeral quality of radicalism itself creates a serious obstacle to accurate measurement or reliable estimate of the dimensions of the phenomenon. It is, however, possible to secure some notion of the numbers of political, economic, religious, moral, and nationalistic radicals in our population by inspection of national, state, and local election returns. In Table 17 can be seen the contrasting strengths of the majority political parties and those dedicated to variant programs of reform and revolutionary change.

It is clear from these figures that, in so far as national elections are concerned, the American electorate historically has not manifested any great degree of radicalism. Since 1900, with the exception of three presidential elections, those of 1912, 1924, and 1948, the vote of left-wing and minor reform parties has never run as high as 8 per cent of the total. The large Progressive votes of 1912 and 1924 grew out of splits in the Republican party, and while they did reflect a real shift of political opinion, it was largely in the direction of reform rather than radicalism. At times the national vote has failed to reflect fully the radical sentiment in the electorate, while at other times the votes in favor of left-wing programs have been specious, springing from the habit of many American voters of "punishing" the major parties by a protest vote. In some elections, notably the 1928 election, the issues were such that little opportunity existed to express deviant political and economic opinions. It should also be remembered that some groups like the International Workers of the World, which was composed of migratory workers and alien radicals, have been politically

TABLE 17 VOTE FOR PRESIDENTIAL ELECTORS BY MAJOR POLITICAL PARTIES, 1908–1948*

Year	Total	Republican	Democratic	Socialist Labor and Socialist	Miscellaneous independent	Communist	Prohibition
1908	14,887,133	7,679,006	6,409,106	434,645	111,692		252,683
1912	15,031,169	3,483,922	6,286,214	926,090	4,126,020		208,923
1916	18,528,743	8,538,221	9,129,606	598,516	41,894		220,506
1920	26,705,346	16,152,200	9,147,353	950,974	205,411		189,408
1924	29,058,647	15,725,003	8,385,586	27,650	4,826,471	36,386	57,551
1928	36,811,717	21,391,381	15,016,443	289,023	45,994	48,770	20,106
1932	39,751,438	15,761,841	22,821,857	918,057	64,823	102,991	81,869
1936	45,647,117	16,679,583	27,436,673	196,832	1,176,788	80,159	37,082
1940	49,820,312	22,304,400	26,826,742	110,428	472,431	48,579	57,732
1944	47,976,263	22,006,285	24,776,864	106,442	1,011,918		74,754
1948	47,338,337	21,896,927	24,045,052	120,561	2,356,255		95,075

* Compiled from United States Census, 1940, and *World Almanac, 1949*.

disenfranchised. Hence groups of this sort have had to symbolize their radical viewpoints by means other than voting.

Generally American congressional elections have told much the same story; in contrast with European national legislative bodies, radical and reform groups have been conspicuously absent in our Congress. The picture changes somewhat when state and local elective bodies are brought under scrutiny. In 1912, for example, Socialists had 1,141 officeholders in 36 states and 324 municipalities, most of whom, however, were county and minor local officials.[1]

The size of the vote for various radical and reform programs is by no means a measure of the numbers of persons in the population formally identifiable as radicals. Thus, for example, while the Communist party marshaled over 100,000 votes for its candidates in the 1932 presidential election, its average dues-paying membership at this time was only 14,000[2]

[1] Haynes, Fred E., *Social Politics in the United States*, 1924, p 213

[2] Browder, Earl, *What Is Communism?* 1936, p 209

The relationship between voting strength and membership of the Socialist party is given in Table 18.

TABLE 18 SOCIALIST PRESIDENTIAL VOTE AND PARTY MEMBERSHIP, 1900–1920*

Year	Vote	Membership
1900	87,814	10,000
1904	402,283	20,763
1908	420,713	41,751
1912	897,011	118,045
1916	590,294	83,284
1920	915,302	26,766

* Oneal, James, and G. A. Werner, *American Communism*, 1947, p 34 By permission of E P. Dutton & Co , Inc., New York.

In 1948 according to an estimate of the Federal Bureau of Investigation there was one Communist for every 1,814 persons in the United States, which gives a total of 80,800.[3] The membership of the Socialist party at this time probably amounted to 5,000. The combined membership of other radical groups, such as the Socialist Labor party, the American Labor party, IWW, and splinter groups of the Communist party, can have equaled no more than 25,000. Consequently a figure of 150,000 most likely represents a generous estimate of the number of avowed and practicing political and economic radicals in our population at the time this book is written.

Outside of the area of politics and economics the only other well-defined and fairly extensive radicalism lies in certain aspects of the behavior of sectarian religious groups. A few of these sects in the past have advocated and followed sex and marital philosophies at considerable variance with those in the rest of American society. The Mormons stand as the only such Zionistic group of any great size which systematically contravened the sex mores of the larger society. Otherwise, apart from sex and marital customs, radical religious groups have come into ideological conflict with the rest of society over the relationship of the individual to the state in such matters as taking oaths, nudeness, sending children to public school, civil registration of marriages, compliance with health laws, and bearing arms in defense of the nation in time of war or submitting to conscription and military training in peacetime.

There are any number of religious sects which might be classified as "deviant." However, militant religious sectarianism is less common. At the present time the only religious group of any size which can be counted as radical in this sense is the Jehovah's Witnesses. This sect has become distinguished and stigmatized in the public mind for its obtrusive prosely-

[3] *Committee on Un-American Activities*, United States House of Representatives, 1948, p. 2.

tizing, its attacks upon other organized religions, and its militant pacifism, which at times has bordered upon treasonable utterance, as well as simple conscientious objection. In 1941 at the St. Louis convention of this religious group, there were 115,000 persons present.[4]

The most characteristically deviant behavior of the otherworldly religious sect appears in conscientious objection to military service. During the First World War 64,693 persons claimed the right to a noncombatant classification in the draft, the majority of whom were religious objectors. A smaller number must be added to this to account for those who refused to even register for the draft. Of the first figure, 56,830 claims were recognized by local draft boards, of whom 29,679 were placed in class number one which made them liable to induction. The number actually drafted was 20,873, of whom 4,000 remained adamant conscientious objectors after being sent to training camp.[5]

In the Second World War the number of selective service registrants who refused to bear arms or serve in any military capacity rose as high as 10,000 at times. About two-thirds of these were work assignees, and one-third were violators of the selective service laws, ostensibly conscientious objectors. Actually, there were in the aggregate throughout the period of selective service more than 10,000 conscientious objectors, because, like soldiers, they were being discharged as well as called up to service. In addition to these there was a large aggregate of less recalcitrant conscientious objectors classified as 1A-0 who entered the armed forces to work in noncombatant capacities.[6] The number following this modified line of resistance to war probably amounted to about 100,000.[7] In the Second World War the proportions of nonreligious (political and philosophical) objectors to military service increased over the First World War, but the majority still were motivated by religious considerations.

Not all persons in pacifist sects who possess scruples against war are called for service. This means that the numbers so classified by draft boards fall short of the total number of conscientious objectors in the sects from which they come. On the other hand, the size of the populations of the religious groups themselves cannot serve as an index to determine the total number of pacifists because there is not unanimity in the sects on this issue. According to estimate, about 20 per cent of sect members, such as Quakers, Mennonites, and others, carried through the sectarian principles to the point of registering as noncombatants or refus-

[4] Stroup, H, *The Jehovah's Witnesses*, 1945, p 27

[5] Thomas, Norman, *The Conscientious Objector in America*, 1923, p. 81

[6] "Selective Service As the Tide of the War Turns 1943–44," *Third Report of the Director of Selective Service*, 1945, pp 178, 190

[7] Oxnam, G, "Freedom of Conscience in the U S.A.," *Survey Graphic*, 35, 1946, p 309.

ing to register.[8] In England, where conscription in the Second World War included a far larger segment of the population than in the United States, 1.5 per cent of conscripts claimed exemption by reason of conscientious objection.[9] Had drafting reached farther into the ranks of deferred men in this country, the numbers of known objectors to military service undoubtedly would have been much larger.

Differentiation of Radicals

Some effort has been made to assign special inherent qualities to radicals, the most systematic of which was that of Lombroso, who considered radicals in a class with hereditary criminals.[10] Needless to say, there are few who would seriously entertain such ideas today. Apart from improbable genetic differentiation, some few biological differences have been found among radicals, which may or may not be statistically significant. Other studies, by psychologists, have brought out some differences in the physiological reactivity of persons with radical opinions in contrast with those holding more conservative views.[11]

Youth has long been considered the age of liberalism and radicalism, while advanced years have been taken as *ipso facto* evidence of attitudinal rigidity and conservatism. Yet the age differential of radicals and conservatives might better be taken as a subject for study rather than as axiomatic. For example, as the result of a survey of attitude and opinion research, one writer has concluded that while radical-conservative differentials between attitudes of old and young persons do exist, they are not significant and that where majorities of the old take a stand against a change so do majorities of the young.[12]

There seems to be a substantial agreement, based upon observation and partial statistical data, that *active participants* in radical movements and organizations tend to be quite young. Revolutionary movements in different countries have frequently been heavily supported and spearheaded by youth groups or youth movements. The weakening and splitting of the Socialist party in the United States in 1936 appears to have been largely the outgrowth of restiveness of younger socialists in search of a more aggressively radical program. In a study of the characteristics of 163 com-

[8] Freeman, Ruth, *Quakers and Peace*, 1947, p 53

[9] *Ibid.*, p. 54

[10] Lombroso, C, *Les Anarchistes*, 1894, also Allport, Gordon, "The Composition of Political Attitudes," *American Journal of Sociology*, 35, September, 1929, pp 220–238.

[11] Howells, T. H, "A Test of Persistence," *Ninth International Congress of Psychology*, 1930, pp. 229–230.

[12] Pollack, Otto, "Conservatism in Later Maturity and Old Age," *American Sociological Review*, 8, April, 1943, pp. 175–179.

munist leaders in Russia, it came to light that 82 per cent of them were less than twenty-five years of age at the time of joining some revolutionary party.[13] While this is impressive, at the same time it must be recalled that Russian population has long had an extremely youthful age composition, hence this age differential is not so striking as it might appear at first glance. Two other bodies of data descriptive of European anarchists in the latter part of the nineteenth century show 55 per cent of one group and 47 per cent of the other falling within an age range of twenty-two to thirty-three years. Extremely young and extremely old persons had very limited representation in both groups.[14]

A study of the Jacobine clubs, which in many respects were the seedbeds of the French Revolution, presents conclusions which clearly contradict the idea that revolutionists will always be recruited from the youth of a society. For 10 of these clubs the average age of the rank-and-file members varied from 38.3 years to 45.4 years, with an average for all groups of 41.8 years.[15]

In the United States the early strength of the Communist party resided in the membership of foreign-language federations, which suggests a much older age make-up than may have been present at a later date. The probabilities are that, even where a radical party has a majority of youthful members, the inner core of tempered, more systematic radicals are considerably older than the average. A considered judgment brings us to conclude that young adulthood and early maturity are the age of active radicalism, if such an age does in reality exist.

If the radical world is that of young adults, it is also pretty much a man's world. In support of this a number of studies have emphasized the general conservatism of women's attitudes in comparison with men's.[16] Female participants can be found in radical movements but they remain well in the minority. Most women who have entered into radical groups have probably done so for reasons other than deep and sincere identifications with the group objectives. A few hardy females have elected to hew out radical careers for themselves, but in the main the demands of such a life clash with the modal external and internal limits of woman's role in Western and many other cultures. An exception to be noted was the presence of quite a few women in the ranks of European anarchists in the

[13] Davis, Jerome, "A Study of One Hundred and Sixty-three Outstanding Communist Leaders," *Publications of the American Sociological Society*, 24, February, 1930, p. 47

[14] Johns, Patricke Anne, *The Anarchist Movement in the Nineteenth Century*, Ph D. dissertation, University of Wisconsin, 1946, Table II, p. 159

[15] Brinton, Crane, *The Anatomy of Revolution*, 1938, p 119.

[16] Kerr, W. A., "Correlates of Politico-Economic Liberalism-Conservatism," *Journal of Social Psychology*, 20, August, p. 67

1880's and 1890's. In fact, in France and Spain some of the anarchist circles consisted entirely of women who energetically sought recruits and carried on education for the movement. But even here their participation closely touched their sexual role, for the sexual emancipation advocated in the anarchist philosophy did much to attract them to the movement.[17] It is also true that women have been both numerous and active in radical religious groups, for example, in the Jehovah's Witnesses. However, even here they have not held positions of leadership.

Ethnic Differences of Radicals

The ethnic composition of radical organizations varies widely from country to country, both from the standpoint of differentiation from the general population and with regard to the internal homogeneity of their membership. In countries like France, Germany, and Italy Socialists and Communists were and remain pretty much the nationals of their respective countries. In Russia, however, the Bolshevik party even before the 1917 revolution had a much more heterogeneous make-up than parties in other European nations. It was likewise true that nineteenth-century anarchists in most European countries were a notably heterogeneous lot, large numbers of them being recruited from immigrant workers. French, German, and Italian workers in Switzerland; Andalusian migrants in Barcelona, Spain; and migratory journeymen workers in the larger cities of Western Europe were the mainstays of the movement.[18]

While we hesitate to speak of American political and economic radicalism as alien, nevertheless the great ethnic differentiation and heterogeneity of its sponsors and followers, especially since the Civil War, has been very marked. After 1907 the American Socialist party admitted 14 foreign-language federations, mostly in blocs, which became the militant left wing of the organization, and most of which later left the Socialist party to become the formative nucleus of the Communist party. A large number of these blocs were of Slavic origins; their distribution by specific linguistic identity is given in Table 19.

In the twenty years which have passed since these data were first made available, it is hard to say what changes have occurred in the ethnic character of political and economic radical groups in the United States. It may be guessed, however, that the proportion of native-born Americans and second-generation descendants of immigrants has been greatly augmented by the aging of first-generation immigrants and the sharp decrease of immigration after 1921 and 1924.

One ethnic group whose members have been drawn to radicalism pos-

[17] Johns, *op. cit.*, p. 162

[18] *Ibid.*, pp. 70, 242.

sibly more than others is the Jewish. A large number of questionnaire studies all more or less agree in according a larger measure of radical opinions to Jewish than to other student groups.[19] In the study of Russian Communist leaders previously cited, leaders of Jewish descent made up 17 per cent of the total and supplied over three times their expected quota.[20] Whether the ratio of rank-and-file Jewish to non-Jewish members was similar is not stated. In Central Europe, Austria, and Poland, as well as in Russia, Jewish men and women have played outstanding roles in revolutionary movements of the past, probably supplying more than their share

TABLE 19. NUMBER AND PERCENTAGE DISTRIBUTION OF ENGLISH AND FOREIGN-LANGUAGE MEMBERSHIP OF THE COMMUNIST PARTY, UNITED STATES, 1919*

Nationality	Number	Per cent
English	1,900	7.1
Non-Federation foreign-language members	1,100	4.1
Estonian	280	1.0
German	850	3.1
Hungarian	1,000	3.7
Jewish	1,000	3.7
Lettish	1,200	4.5
Lithuanian	4,400	16.4
Polish	1,750	6.6
Russian	7,000	26.2
South Slavic	2,200	8.2
Ukrainian	4,000	15.0
Total	26,680	99.6

* Oneal, James, and G. A. Werner, *American Communism*, 1947, p. 88. By permission of E. P. Dutton & Co., Inc., New York.

of money, ideas, and martyrs in the name of "social justice." But in contrast to this, Jews were conspicuously absent from the nineteenth-century revolutionary movements in France and England.[21]

If Jews have done yeoman duty in extremist political groups of many countries, they have been hard to find in the ranks of conscientious objectors, at least in identifiable terms as Jews. Most of these latter in the United States have come from various sects of German Baptists and Swiss Mennonites. In Canada, also, persons of German descent, Mennonites, and Dukhobors supplied the main group of objectors to military service in the Second World War.

[19] Shuey, Audrey M., "Personality Traits of Jewish and Non-Jewish Students," *Archives of Psychology*, March, 1944, p. 15.

[20] Davis, *op cit.*, p. 45.

[21] Beer, M., *Fifty Years of International Socialism*, 1935, p. 104.

Class Differences of Radicals

From one point of view it is reasonable to expect that radical groups will consist chiefly of persons who would have the most to gain from an overturn and reconstitution of the economic and political system, namely, persons with lower economic or social status. This has held true in a number of instances – as with the IWW in the United States, which depended for its membership upon badly exploited migratory casual workers. As against this, however, Russian revolutionaries of the nineteenth and early twentieth centuries consisted mostly of intelligentsia and members of the *bourgeoisie*, an indication of which is seen in Table 20.

Table 20. Occupational Status of Fathers of 137 Communist Party Leaders in Russia*

Occupation	Number	Per cent
Laborers	30	21 8
Peasants	26	19
Professions	23	16 8
Government officials	19	13.8
"Very wealthy"	11	8
Proprietors of estates or factories	11	8
Nobles	8	5.8
Businessmen	6	4.4
Other (including one general)	3	2.2
Total	137	99 8

*Davis, Jerome, "A Study of One Hundred and Sixty-three Outstanding Communist Leaders," *Publications of the American Sociological Society*, 24, February, 1930, p 48

The occupational make-up of European anarchist organizations at the peak of their power was almost entirely that of skilled, nonfactory workers and professional persons, if such information as we have can be trusted. Three sets of data give percentages of the former as 49, 48, and 75, with the professions supplying 23, 24, and 9 per cent, respectively.[22]

In China the Communist party has had as its main support soldiers and administrative officials of local soviets from areas where the party has been in power. In Germany in 1927 the largest segment of Communist party membership consisted of the "aristocracy" of the working class, being in the main the more highly skilled workers enjoying larger incomes – from construction trades and metallurgical industries. In many ways the status of German Communists at this time paralleled the status of workers in the American Federation of Labor in this country. Table 21 clearly shows the dominance of skilled labor in the German party.

[22] Johns, *op. cit.*, Table I, p. 141.

TABLE 21. PERCENTAGE DISTRIBUTION OF MEMBERS OF THE GERMAN COMMUNIST PARTY BY OCCUPATIONAL CLASS, 1927*

Occupation	Per Cent
Skilled workers	39.92
Unskilled workers	28.18
Agricultural	2.21
Independent craftsmen	9.57
Commercial employees	1.73
Other	17.39

*Borkenau, F., *World Communism*, 1939, p. 365 Reprinted by permission of W. W. Norton & Company, New York.

The socioeconomic status of religious radicals is more difficult to determine than that of politico-economic radicals. Some sketchy impressions make it appear that those who have deviated from conventional religious ideologies in America have had lower class status. This seems to have been true of "freethinkers" or "infidels," whose anticlerical, antireligious movement flourished in the United States from 1825 to 1850.[23] It also is probable that converts to Jehovah's Witnesses have largely been laborers, mechanics, factory workers, and farmers, with the occasional semiskilled or skilled worker.[24] However, leaders of these two movements in either case have usually been drawn from middle and upper socioeconomic strata.

The fluctuations of the occupational composition of radical parties have been almost as impressive as their ethnic diversity. The American Socialist party started out as a working-class party, but by the time it reached the zenith of its power shortly before the First World War, it was ceasing to be a party of wage earners and was appealing to farmers, middlemen, and small capitalists.[25] The German Communist party, which in the 1920's represented skilled workers, had changed within a relatively few years to become a party of the unemployed.[26] The fluctuations in the general socioeconomic make-up of radical aggregates and organizations most likely are a function of the attraction and defection of situational radicals in the ranks. On the whole it seems sound to insist that those who become systematic radicals, both political and religious, originate from the middle classes, and that professional radicalism most often has been a mutation of middle-class behavior.[27] Additional corroboration on this point comes

[23] Post, A., *Popular Freethought in America, 1825–1850*, pp. 32, 87, 187.

[24] Czatt, M. S., *The International Bible Students*, Yale Studies in Religion, Nov. 4, 1933.

[25] Haynes, *op. cit.*, p. 205.

[26] Borkenau, F , *World Communism*, 1939, p. 365

[27] Others reaching this conclusion include Kimball Young, *Social Psychology*, 1945, rev. ed , pp. 334*f.*; Crane Brinton, *op cit.*, p. 118, John Spargo, *The Psychology of Socialism*, 1925, pp. 22–24.

from the studies indicating that more informed and highly educated persons incline more than others toward liberal and radical opinions.[28] It is also worth noting that 62 per cent of the Russian Communist leaders previously alluded to had partial or complete university training.[29] A final item is the finding that while the majority of conscientious objectors of the Second World War had farm backgrounds, nevertheless considerable numbers were professional people. It is also true that the group in the aggregate possessed higher-than-average education.[30]

Rural-Urban Differences of Radicals

Ordinarily it is thought that cities are centers of radical opinion and activity, while rural areas are supposedly strongholds of conservatism and reaction. In some part this can be demonstrated by the voting behavior of our population. However, there are important qualifications and exceptions to this conclusion. One opinion study has shown that students most favorably disposed toward communism lived in towns of 2,500 or less and in cities of over 500,000.[31] An older comparison of voting in two groups of counties revealed a more pronounced liberal-radical sentiment in the group of counties with the higher percentage of rural population. These counties at the same time had higher percentages of foreign-born population, chiefly from Scandinavian countries.[32] In 1912 the greatest strength of the American Socialist party seemed to lie in smaller towns, and the states where its candidates received the heaviest votes were primarily agricultural states: Kansas, Minnesota, Texas, and Florida; and newer Western states: Oklahoma, Nevada, Montana, Arizona, Washington, California, and Idaho.[33] The 1924 Progressive party which aligned Labor, Socialists, and others with farmers in an effort to break the domination of old-line parties, attracted most of its followers from agricultural states west of the Mississippi.[34] As late as 1948, with radical voting predominant in urban areas, there was still a fairly heavy following of the Socialist party in agricultural states. Although the Communist party must be set down as largely urban in the United States, nevertheless militant representatives of this group carry on in rural areas, such as the Finnish Communists in northern Michigan and other Great Lakes areas. Added evidence that the rural population

28 Kerr, *op. cit.*, pp. 63–64.

29 Davis, *op. cit.*, p 49.

30 Gory, A E, and D C. McClelland, "Characteristics of the C O in World War II," *Journal of Consulting Psychology*, 11, September, 1947, pp 245–257.

31 Fay, Paul J., and Warren C. Middleton, "Certain Factors Related to Liberal and Conservative Attitudes of College Students," *Journal of Social Psychology*, February, 1940, pp 107–119.

32 Lundberg, George A., "The Demographic and Economic Basis of Liberalism," *American Journal of Sociology*, 32, May, 1927, pp. 719, 732

33 Haynes, *op. cit.*, p. 206.

34 Cousens, Theodore, *Politics and Political Organizations in America*, 1942, p 258

may furnish a significant number of radicals comes from the fact that the Mennonites and German Baptists, who are most numerous in the ranks of conscientious objectors, are largely rural peoples. Furthermore, strong contingents of nineteenth-century European anarchists could be found in the rural populaces of Spain, northern Italy, and to some extent of Russia. Yet while it can be shown that rural people often have participated in radical movements, it remains debatable whether, in a sociological sense, rural radicals are differentiated in ways comparable to urban radicals. Certainly it would be hard to show that rural communities supply any great number of professional radicals.

The Contexts of Radicalism

Assertions that radicalism is a symptomatic expression of emotional conflicts recur with frequency in literature on the topic. One of the more elegant theoretical contentions of this kind enlists the Freudian concept of the Oedipus complex as the explanation for radical behavior. This attributes radicalism to arrested, neurotic, psychosexual development in the individual.[35] Some partial corroboration has been adduced for this view in opinion and case-history studies. Without committing ourselves to this explanation, let us simply concede that radical behavior may be and is often seized upon by individuals to discharge tensions, and that often it affords opportunities to indulge guilt-ridden impulses and even compulsions arising from difficulties with socially acceptable roles. Persons with ingrained conflicts over their sexual roles, for example, may at least temporarily find some surcease in the atmosphere of a Bohemian colony or a revolutionary group incorporating sex equality or sex freedom among its principles.

Persons with paranoid strivings for power or with more socialized needs to rebel and aggress against symbols of authority may found or enter radical religious sects. Certainly in instances where persons claiming to be conscientious objectors have a long and checkered history of persistent conflict with others serious symbolic disturbances underlying the behavior may be suspected. The behavior of the more intransigent conscientious objectors in prisons and camps has often hinted at some sort of suicidal tendencies, particularly where the persons have not been indoctrinated with a pacifist ideology in a sect or established church. The percentage of persons whose radicalism has symptomatic meaning undoubtedly will be much greater in the early history of a given social movement than later when the movement has given rise to mature organization and leadership. To quote the leader of an American Trotskyite group:[36]

[35] Lasswell, Harold D., *Psychopathology and Politics*, 1930.

[36] Cannon, James, *The History of American Trotskyism*, 1944, p. 92. Quoted by permission of the Pioneer Publishing Co., New York.

Then, as is always the case with new political movements, we begin to recruit from sources none too healthy. If you are ever reduced again to a small handful, as well the Marxists may be in mutations of the class struggle; if things go badly and you have to begin over again, then I can tell you in advance some of the headaches you are going to have. Every new movement attracts certain elements which might properly be called the lunatic fringe. Freaks always looking for the most extreme expression of radicalism, misfits, windbags, chronic oppositionists who had been thrown out of a dozen organizations—such people come to us in our isolation, shouting "Hello, Comrades."

There is room to believe that the anarchist movement in Europe did, in fact, act as a loadstone for many unbalanced persons superficially indoctrinated with its tenets, who used the philosophy as a sanction for their criminal aggressions against society. This may have been one of the factors which led to the ultimate decline of this organization.

Situational Radicalism

A cross-sectional role analysis of the radicals in a given society will reveal not only a number of symbolically disordered persons but also a large number – perhaps the majority – of persons who profess the extremist beliefs because of general or special situational pressures. Several types of data led us to this conclusion. First of all, examination of both the membership and voting strength of radical parties discloses wide oscillations. From 1928 to 1932 (see Table 17, page 177), the Socialist and Socialist Labor vote in the United States more than tripled and at the same time the Communist vote more than doubled itself. The membership figures of radical organizations in other countries tell much the same story. This is made apparent in Table 22.

Table 22. Communist Party Membership in Great Britain, 1925–1929*

Year	Membership
1925	5,000
April, 1926	6,000
October, 1926	10,730
January, 1927	9,000
March, 1928	5,556
1929	3,500

*Borkenau, F., *World Communism*, 1939, p 367. Reprinted by permission of W. W Norton & Company, New York.

Moreover these figures do not bring out the total amount of change in radical-party membership, for even when the yearly figure remains constant, it covers up a very high turnover. So, for example, in Germany in 1929 while the Communist party gained 50,000 new members, in the same year it lost 39,000. For 1930 the respective figures were 143,056 and 95,399.[37] Of course, some of this instability represents shifting from one

[37] Borkenau. *op. cit.*, p. 368.

radical party to another, but at the same time it also speaks of a mutual interchange of persons between radical and conservative beliefs and affiliations. Major strategic or tactical setbacks seem to be one of the more important factors reducing radical-party membership. Economic and other crises also appear to have great effect in augmenting or decreasing the numbers of radicals in a population.

One study of two groups of engineers matched in most respects save employment has shown that unemployed did produce a significant increase in the expression of radical political and economic beliefs in a certain number of cases.[38] This is not an argument that unemployment "causes" radicalism; other research generally concurs that crises, such as unemployment or economic dislocation, magnify discontent but that radicalism is but one of many ways individuals may react to crisis.[39] Within the broader situation which is conducive to a shift of belief to the radical pole, other congeries of circumstances make radicalism much more of an implicit reaction. Thus many wives and sweethearts of radicals undoubtedly reflect their views or follow them into a revolutionary organization simply to be near them and share their lives. A person may be bound to a group by ties other than shared political beliefs but nevertheless feel compelled to endorse a radical program in order to protect his status within this group. We suspect that the radicalism of many Slavic immigrants is of this order. Likewise the member of a small, rural religious community may feel more comfortable with his sectarian fellows by registering as a pacifist in time of war, even though his private views may motivate him to enlist.

In some situations where there is widespread social unrest a radical organization may provide the only means of directly attacking the sources of discontent; hence, dissident elements follow the radical leadership even though the formal program diverges widely from many conceptions of the followers. Some workers have responded to radical leadership simply because no other groups have taken an interest in their problems and because of their inability to organize themselves effectively for action. In some ways the IWW presents an illustration of this; one analyst has rightly given us to understand that few of the migratory workers in this organization had any but the remotest grasp of the syndicalist philosophy and practice with which they were identified in public print.[40] The IWW was simply the only social break they had ever had to counteract the low wages, job insecurity, political disenfranchisement, and police persecution which made up their lives. Quite often the American Communists have

[38] Hall, Milton, "Attitudes and Unemployment," *Archives of Psychology*, March, 1944.

[39] Rundquist, E. A. and R. F. Sletto, *Personality in the Depression*, 1936; Zawadski, B., and P. Lazarsfeld, "The Psychological Consequences of Unemployment," *Journal of Social Psychology*, 6, May, 1935, pp. 224–251.

[40] Parker, Carleton, *The Casual Laborer and Other Essays*, 1920, p. 100.

been the only ones in certain areas to agitate for amelioration of the conditions of workers who have no political or economic power. In earlier times anarchists performed much the same function for the landless proletariat in Spain and Italy.

During the 1930's in the United States, particularly after 1934, large numbers of middle-class professional persons, artists, students, and other "intellectuals" turned toward communism either as "fellow travelers" or as actual Communist party members. The movement was so pronounced that one writer has dubbed this period of American history the "red decade." [41] The trend may be explained by reference to the shattering blows dealt our society by the economic Depression of the time, the ideological poverty of indigenous American radicalism, and the slowness of the traditional political parties to appreciate the mounting threat of a European war. The situational nature of the allegiance to the Communist program stood out in sharp relief with the wholesale desertion of the Communist cause by "fellow travelers" when the pact between Russia and Nazi Germany was announced.

While the proportions of symptomatic, situational, and systematic radicals shift in time within the same group and from one radical group to another, from what we know, it is largely the situational deviants who are the shifting sands from which social protest and reform organization must be formed. The number of dependable professionals in a movement remains only a tiny fraction of the whole. As Lenin trenchantly observed: "Among one hundred so-called Bolsheviki there is one real Bolshevik, thirty-nine criminals, and sixty fools." [42]

It is of some interest here to take notice of the formalized divisions which the Jehovah's Witnesses have introduced to classify their membership. The two terms, "publishers" and "pioneers," are used to distinguish part-time and full-time sectarian workers. In 1943 the former numbered about 65,000 out of a total membership of 85,000 to 100,000 in the United States. The highly dedicated "publishers," presumably the stable and dependable soldiery of the sect, numbered 4,204.[43]

Some evidence inclines to the conclusion that the more drastically deviant are the beliefs fostered by a radical organization the more likely that its members will have had a long radical experience, hence will be more professionalized.[44] This is also deducible from the fact that radical skills are demanded for survival in the face of greater police and other societal aggressions against more revolutionary groups. The importance of such skills and the radical behavior system merits detailed discussion.

[41] Lyons, Eugene, *The Red Decade*, 1939.

[42] Spargo, John, *The Psychology of Bolshevism*, 1919, p. 34.

[43] Stroup, *op. cit*, p. 60.

[44] Lasswell, Harold D., and Dorothy Blumenstock, *World Revolutionary Propaganda*, 1939, p. 278.

Systematic Radicalism

In contrast with the situational radical who retains a basic nonradical role orientation, the systematic radical makes agitational pursuits his central concern and subordinates all other life considerations to the furtherance of his ideological objectives, or those of the organization to which he belongs. Such radicals must be thought of as participating in a definite behavior system, so that their behavior is far better understood from the description of an objective pattern of behavior than from the life history of the individual participant. It is perhaps more correct to speak of radical behavior *systems* than to talk of a single archetype, chiefly because of important differentiations which exist between the mores and folkways of various radical groups. Differences in objectives from one group to another beget differentiation of subculture and organization. Thus a gradualist socialism which subjects its adherents to little or no segregation or persecution will scarcely force them into conspiratorial behavior appropriate to the violent overthrow of governmental forms. For purposes of greater clarity we shall confine ourselves here to the description of the more sectarian and revolutionary radical behavior systems, recognizable in communism, syndicalism, anarchism, and to some extent in the aggressive evangelism of present-day Jehovah's Witnesses.

The verbalized portion of the radical behavior system consists of a dynamic myth, with negative and positive aspects, the former being the systematic critique of the contemporary social system, the latter being a projection of the society of the future to be brought into existence by the promulgation of the myth itself. From one point of view the entire function of the radical behavior system can be thought of as the reinforcement, prepetuation, and dissemination of this myth. The special vocabulary, clichés, and stereotyped phraseology employed to communicate the myth at the same time serve as the argot of the radical. Implicit and explicit in the myth lie the assumptions by which the indoctrinated radical continually interprets the world of facts outside of the intimate interactional circles determined by his radical role.

The techniques of the radical are those of oratory, face-to-face persuasiveness, propaganda finesse, and writing and editing abilities. In addition to these, the professional radical ordinarily possesses the knowledge and art of group and mass manipulation, regardless of whether he and his followers aspire to the overthrow of the government. Beyond these few elements in common, behavior systems of radicals proliferate and differentiate in directions dictated by the nature of the radical myth and the means held best for its realization.

Some radical behavior systems incorporate much of the missionary's behavior and that of the wandering pedagogue, with emphasis upon teaching skills and methods of conversion. Techniques of nonviolent coercion and passive resistance have been popular with some deviant religious sects of the past and have been increasingly favored by American religious and political radicals. Under passive resistance, we find such devices as symbolic "marches," nude parades, hunger strikes, and suicide. During the Civil War Mennonites effectively resisted combat service by obeying every order of their officers, except to shoot straight in target practice. It may be assumed that the more informal ties of radicals loosely knit into a mystic brotherhood, such as is seen in much religious radicalism, will produce less standardization of their behavior systems than is true for more highly organized radicals.

Radicals who seek to overthrow governments by force and intrigue necessarily implement their roles by relevant means of military skills, street fighting, and guerrilla tactics. They also become adept at conspiratorial arts and adopt many of the methods of the criminal, for in revolutionary extremist groups a willingness and capacity to commit sabotage, forgery, robbery, and murder at various times have been requisites of success. In common with the spy, the opportunistic revolutionary must be able to infiltrate organizations in one guise or another and he must be sufficiently adaptable to survive under conditions of high mobility. This last means that he must be able to satisfy his needs for food, clothing, shelter, and sex in strange and hostile environments with only the most limited resources at his disposal.

While the normative prescriptions by which the systematic radical lives stem in some part from the particular ideology which claims his loyalty, they are more directly the outgrowth of the day-by-day technical necessity in promotion of the ideology. The special technology evolved by the radical group, and the elements of the populations it seeks to influence, as well as its insecure status, do much to set the limits of behavior regarded as acceptable in a member. An isolated otherworldly sect not dedicated to converting others to its way of believing is free to differentiate its morality in manifold ways. On the other hand a radical group bidding for the support of the working classes must necessarily mirror working-class morality in rules of conduct for its own members. This comes out in the statement of a radical leader's experience:[45]

> I waged a bitter fight in the New York branch of the Communist League against admitting a man to membership, on the sole ground of his appearance and dress.
>
> They asked, "What have you against him?"
>
> I said, "He wears a corduroy suit up and down Greenwich Village, with a trick mustache and long hair. There is something wrong with this guy."

[45] Cannon, *op. cit.*, p 92.

I wasn't making a joke either. I said, "People of this type are not going to be suitable for approaching the ordinary American worker. They are going to mark our organization as something freakish, abnormal, exotic; something that has nothing to do with the normal life of the American worker."

In order to keep alive, radical groups, unless they become isolated Utopian colonies, must seize upon and exploit all possible issues. This means that their techniques and methods are continually undergoing modification and adaptation to a fluid cultural front. As methods change, norms of professional radical conduct must likewise change to conform with them. Those closest to changing issues, the leaders and members who have professional status and a stake in perpetuating the radical organization, tend to temporize and develop an expediential morality, whereas rank-and-file members and new recruits often take the revolutionary creed as a literal guide for personal and group conduct. Thus there is often a conflict of moralities within radical groups. This stood out very clearly in a rebel offshoot of the IWW, called the EP or Emergency Program. Beginning in 1924 a growing distrust of the leadership was captioned by convention votes of this group to decentralize the organization structure, to expel members who refused to stand trial for their revolutionary beliefs or their consequences, and to expel those who after imprisonment accepted parole or individual clemency. Subsequent conventions also voted that the organization should not acquire or hold property, pay taxes, or in other ways compromise with "bourgeois" morality.[46]

The cleavage between the morality of the professional radicals and rank-and-file membership probably stands as the main reason for the high turnover in the membership of such groups and also for the splitting and fissioning which periodically appear. Among American Communists the cleavage along these moral lines has probably been strengthened by sectional conflict. It has also been aggravated by conflict between the foreign-born members and second-generation and native-born, who, because of their greater familiarity with English and greater acculturation are more likely to hold leadership posts.[47] The International Communist party has striven to avoid and minimize this conflict by the inculcation of its entire membership with a professional revolutionary morality. In order to fully comprehend this morality, it is necessary to probe into nineteenth-century revolutionary philosophy in Russia.

The moral patterns of Russian revolutionism seem to have originated in the religious zeal of certain fanatical Islamic sects and were given their nineteenth-century meaning by nihilists, anarchists, and certain Russian leaders, for example, Nechaev, and Lenin after him. In brief, the morality

[46] Gambs, John S, *The Decline of the I W W*, 1932, Chap. IV.

[47] Lasswell and Blumenstock, *op cit.*, Table IV, p 280

lays greatest emphasis upon complete and unswerving devotion to a cause Going with it is the conviction that in the service of revolution absolutely anything is permissible. killing one's adversaries; killing innocent persons to link revolutionaries in an indissoluble nexus of common guilt; stealing, forgery, counterfeiting, lying, cheating, and misleading; and even doing away with one's own followers. Fundamentally this is a pure morality of power comparable to that of the early Jesuits, in which absolute obedience to authority and selfless devotion to revolution or counterrevolution for its own sake are ascendant values. Disobedience, betrayal, and desertion are the cardinal sins of this Communist decalogue.[48]

The success of the Communist revolution in Russia in 1917 gave the Communists of that country a commanding position in the world revolutionary organization, the Comintern, particularly after 1929. Through the channels of this organization was diffused the peculiarly Eurasian morality which we have described. While this alien code has produced deviations, nonconformity, and internal party conflicts, the presence of large Slavic groups in the party plus the prestige and financial support of Russia generally have been overwhelming factors in its diffusion and dominance It has been the fantastic permutations of policy and behavior of Communists in the spell of this political morality which have been so inexplicable to most Americans. It is in this systematic opportunism that Communists deviate most significantly from American ideals, rather than in the specific economic and social objectives which they have advocated from time to time. In many ways the history of communism in Western countries has been a history of culture conflict, a conflict between a morality of power and a morality of procedural law.

Patterns of Radical Organization

The structure of radical groups has assumed many different forms, ranging from isolant Zionistic colonies with a local base to world-wide, function-oriented organizations like the Comintern. Within the limits of the culture radical groups tend to be importantly structured by (1) the extremeness of their program and militancy of its members; (2) the aggressiveness of police action and severity of judicial treatment, both of which are, in part, a response to this extremeness and militancy; (3) the high turnover in membership, which seems to characterize most, if not all, such groups; (4) the great heterogeneity of membership; and (5) numerical smallness.

Moderate reform groups in the United States have frequently patterned their organization after that of the major political parties, particularly, as in the case of the Socialist party, where constitutional methods of achiev-

[48] Borkenau, *op. cit.*, pp. 22–26.

ing the group aims have been followed. In contrast to this, nineteenth-century European anarchists, who incurred mass hostility and harsh police reprisals by their *attentats*, or spectacular propagandistic crimes capitalized by assassinations, perforce turned to small, attenuated, clandestine organizational forms. The anarchist unit was a "circle," a small group of persons known intimately to one another. Keeping the group small, and intimacy high, was the one sure protection against the known reliance of police upon spies and *agent provocateurs*. While the anarchists worked out types of organization to afford themselves protection from the police, their faith in evangelistic sect organization as a means of spreading their doctrine was clearly misplaced in the face of growing urbanization and industrialization of European society in the late nineteenth century.

The situation of the revolutionary organizations in Russia under Csardom duplicated that of the anarchist groups in most important aspects. However, the ruthless persecution they endured was caused more by their aspirations to power or to their destructive attacks upon government per se than to any great deviation in the substance of their program. It was in Russia that the professional revolutionary sect evolved, composed of young men of many classes who broke all connections with their social backgrounds and lived in hiding in a closed community not dissimilar from that of the early Christian sects. To the extent that diffusion has occurred, this has been the basic cast of Communist parties wherever they appeared in other countries. In Russia itself after 1917 the Bolshevik party disappeared as a radical, subversive organization and became the administrative and police organ of the Soviet state. At the same time it retained a nominal revolutionary status by reason of its being a section in the Comintern – the International Congress of the Communist Parties of the World.

Outside of Russia up until 1929, Communist parties enjoyed a measure of autonomy and to some extent followed democratic procedures in reaching decisions. Thereafter decisions increasingly stemmed from Moscow, and the party control became more and more centralized. At the present time in the United States the party is controlled at the top by a secretariat and a national board. Below this are state or regional district and county units, including special sections, subsections, and shop and neighborhood organizations. Organization rests upon a dual geographic and functional basis, with really important party missions and activities being assigned to specially created functional units.

Native Patterns of Radical Organization

As we look back through American history at groups whose doctrines might be thought of as native or indigenous radicalism, a sharp contrast to this Communist organizational pattern is seen. A maximum looseness, informality, and spatial decentralization is apparent in their structures, all responses to the great heterogeneity of the population from which they have had to recruit members. For example, the leaders of the American Revolution worked largely through correspondence committees. Later the same loose organizational bonds could be seen among the proponents of popular free thought of the second quarter of the nineteenth century. Groupings of freethinkers were usually ephemeral integrations around a few gifted intellectual or inspirational leaders, each highly individualistic and each with his special partisans. Local societies were frequently formed on the basis of a common general opposition to established religion, but all efforts to weld them into a national society failed as a result of dissension, inadequate financial support, and inertia of its members.[49]

The same informality, decentralization, and dependence upon a few inspirational leaders characterized the abolitionist societies prior to the Civil War. Likewise at a much later date we find the IWW revolving around a collection of colorful, bombastic, individualistic personalities who acted as its leadership. While the IWW possessed the external forms of a centralized organization, in actuality power remained diffused throughout the rank and file, which functioned more than anything else like roving guerrilla bands distrustful of all unified authority. They were held together only by a shared hatred for the capitalism they saw personified in the straw boss or the gang foreman.[50]

The contemporary pacifist movement in America seems to be held together largely through informal association. Pacifists and conscientious objectors have tended to work through the familiar American committee system, in which there is power to facilitate exchange of information and propaganda between interested persons and groups, but little power to compel.

The closest approach to radical organization with native antecedents which has been built upon an authoritarian model resembling the Communist party has been the Jehovah's Witnesses. Not only have these religious sectarians constructed a hierarchical pyramid of power within their organization, but they have also formulated a concept of heresy and have developed a spy system to report ideological deviations to the central leadership.[51]

The Jehovah's Witnesses probably have been able to effect the simalcrum of a hierarchy because controls have been set up to arbitrarily standardize only such things as Biblical interpretation, procedures for conducting their meetings, and degree of participation in the group activities. According to the official ideology of the sect their beliefs need not be

[49] Post, *op. cit.*, p. 163.
[50] Harris, H., *Labor's Civil War*, 1940, pp. 86*ff*.
[51] Stroup, *op. cit.*, p. 125.

verified by their experiences. In those cases where practical secular issues have arisen over such things as divorce, sex practices, and drinking alcoholic beverages, the leadership has been vacillating and conciliatory toward local customs.[52]

The real power of American radical organizations, where it has existed, undeniably has come from federations and affiliating and cooperating groups. In other words, where radical groups have realistically adapted their organization to the fractionalized power distributions in our society and worked informally to achieve their aims, they have been most successful. Yet a federated form of social organization where there is great heterogeneity of membership easily conduces to factionalism and ruinous dissensions. It was this reason, together with the Russian influence in decision making, which led to the effort to impose the pattern of centralization upon the mélange of groups composing the American Communist party. The success of this centralization rested upon the adequate establishment of the foundation units, the street or shop nuclei. Yet these nuclei, designed to transect ethnic and other differences in order to give unified expression to party policies, were slow to materialize. In fact we may seriously question whether the problem of integrating the heterogeneous elements of the "American Babel" has ever been solved by the American Communist party, except in so far as consensus is reached at a verbal "party-line" level.

Leadership and Controls within Radical Groups

The high turnover in membership of radical groups poses a real problem of maintaining a continuity of organization. In part such a problem can be solved by preserving a hardened core of professional revolutionaries and disregarding the turnover on the peripheries of the organization. Beyond that is the adoption of mercenary leadership or the use of leadership acquired by the prestige and power which the group confers upon them, leadership responsive to specific and detailed direction from a central point.

Numerical smallness may not be a handicap to a radical group bent upon the overthrow of ruling groups, as was shown by the rise to power of a small number of well-disciplined Communists in Russia in 1917. In fact, some Communist leaders have insisted that the over-all size of a revolutionary group should be kept small. Furthermore, it should be allowed to undergo turnover and splitting of its membership in order to select an incorruptible, tried-and-true body of actionists who will carry the cause to victory. In order to compensate for the lack of numbers and to "exercise power all out of proportion to their numbers," Communists have devised various techniques of "fractional control." Through such methods large non-Communist groups, labor unions especially, are infiltrated by a

[52] *Ibid*, pp 117*ff*.

few or a small number of professional party members who seek salient positions of power from which to manipulate the policies and action of the groups. In other instances "front" organizations are formed for such purposes as labor defense or the protection of civil and minority rights. These are designed to draw the support of liberal and reform interests. Where this is done, care is usually taken to reserve positions of real power for Communist adherents within the groups. Another variety of organizational artifice which has been used by American Communists is the "innocents' club." This is a type of group to which Communists managed to attract respected middle-class – even wealthy – members. These people are induced to contribute financial support to causes which ostensibly are liberal, but which in actuality are closely tied in with, if not identical with, Communist party objectives.

Status in radical organizations is conferred upon members for oratorical and political abilities, long service, and imprisonment for the principles of the movement. The marks of high status in a radical organization are membership on committees, editorships, special assignments of great importance, and being entrusted with party secrets and party funds. Most sought after by the professional revolutionaries are the paying jobs, the so-called "piecards," which permit the worker to devote all his time and energies to organization duties.

Morale of radical groups rises and falls precipitantly with the fortunes of the movement and with risks and dangers to which followers are exposed. Heterogeneity of the membership, factionalism, and ubiquitous spies often undermine group morale as well as do the personal problems of individual supporters. Nevertheless, evidences of high morale often materialize, bolstered by fanaticism of adherents or by the coinciding of cultural backgrounds with radical views. For example, the anarchists (mostly German) executed in 1866 for complicity in the Haymarket bombings in Chicago went to their deaths by hanging without the slightest show of fear, even striving to expound their philosophy at the very moment of death.[53] The morale of the IWW (in a way the transmuted morale of the migratory work crew) rose and remained at a high peak for an extended period during which civil-rights and free-speech were carried on in the early part of our century.

Revolutionary groups have at their disposal certain powerful controls to compel followers to conform. Expulsion or its threat is a very potent control over the professional who has grown old in service of the group and knows no other life. Anonymous exposure of errant followers is no empty threat on the part of determined revolutionists hard pressed by the police. Character defamation or even death at the hands of fellow conspirators may be in store for the renegade – especially if he happens

[53] Schaack, Michael J., *Anarchy and Anarchists*, 1889, pp. 642–647.

to possess too much dangerous information. Social ostracism by former friends may be an effective control for those less highly professionalized. In less revolutionary radical groups, of course, many of these controls are not and cannot be used.

The Social Visibility of Radicals

In one respect it is to the advantage of a radical group for its members and followers to be highly visible, for this helps publicize its aims. Anarchists at one time deliberately chose to commit incomprehensible crimes for the purpose of exciting speculation as to their motives, which in turn was supposed to lead the masses into an inquiry about the anarchist philosophy itself. Parades with black-and-red flags, riots, street fighting, and spectacular funerals have served the same end. Other radical groups have designedly or inadvertently made themselves conspicuous by their mode of dress. For example, it was the habit of Russian nihilists to let their hair grow long, wear Scotch plaids, high boots, and to adorn themselves with dark spectacles.[54] American Communists at one time discarded neckties and affected leather jackets in order to symbolize their working-class identifications. More Bohemian radicals have been indifferent in their personal sanitation, have chosen to live on strange foods and to dwell in perpetually disordered rooms or in houses with exotic decorations.

The necessity for reducing their social visibility increases as radicals become the object of more aggressive and punitive treatment at the hands of the police and courts. This has led some radical sects to "go underground" or to "bore from within." Flamboyant dress and peculiar mannerisms are abandoned and condemned by leaders in such crises. Aliases are assumed, and in extreme cases the radicals may work together without ever identifying one another. American Communists and Socialist groups have been hampered by the high visibility of their foreign-born and minority-group membership, which has given them the stamp of alien undesirables. Undoubtedly this was important among the reasons which were behind the choice of Earl Browder, a former minister from Kansas, to serve as titular head of the Communist party during the 1930's. Other measures which had the effect of decreasing Communist visibility were the use of nationalistic symbols, such as the American flag and large pictures of Washington and Lincoln, at party rallies and the injection of nationalistic propaganda into party publications.

The Jehovah's Witnesses have brought themselves into prominence by their tactics of door-to-door convassing for converts, parading and singing in the streets, and their spectacular conventions. It has been these more visible types of behavior which have directly irritated the residents of the community and have resulted in so many arrests and occasional violent

[54] Footman, D., *Red Prelude*, 1945, p. 61.

reactions against the Jehovah's Witnesses. Their pacifism has also been more vociferous than that of other conscientious objectors. Many other conscientious objectors are seldom known as such to the community, save, perhaps, where it is part of the differentiated culture of such sects as Mennonites and others who follow otherworldly customs in their dress.

The Societal Reaction

The stereotyped ideas about radicals which lurk in the consciousness of the masses of people are easily provoked in experimental free-association reactions to the term, embracing such associations as "red," "alien," "dirty," "soapbox agitation," "Godless," "free lover," "bewhiskered," "bombs," and "sabotage." Stereotypes such as these, circulated in newspapers, fiction, and artistic representations, have been highly colored by the beliefs which grew up around anarchism in the nineteenth century and the IWW in the twentieth. Reports of assassinations by Russian revolutionaries and by anarchists in European countries, the assassination of President Garfield by an anarchist, along with the Haymarket riots in Chicago and IWW violence at Homestead, Pennsylvania, and elsewhere, did much to shape the American fixed notions of the radical. Not only has this older anarchistic stereotype remained alive but it tends to be applied indiscriminately to socialists, Communists, pacifists, and other radicals, as well as to progressives or moderate reformers.[55] While this is in part the consequences of the special conservatism of those who attack radicals, it is also caused by a genuine confusing of different types of radicals in the minds of the uninformed, related to the fact that radical movements frequently have been offshoots of one another and thus are apt to be mistaken for each other.

The mediation of the societal reaction by stereotypes takes on great significance in the light of research upon radical and conservative attitudes. These findings indicate that people react in entirely different ways — often diametrically opposed ways — to issues when they are presented out of context and when they are presented as the components of a radical-party platform. For example, statements advocating such things as public ownership of natural resources are endorsed by many persons when they appear as unlabeled items of a questionnaire. These same persons reverse their positive reactions when the statements are labeled as "Communist," "socialist," or "radical."[56] This same dichotomy between private and public attitudes toward radicals materialized in samples of public opinion

[55] Hapgood, Norman, *Professional Patriots*, 1927, p. 13.

[56] Hartman, G. W., "The Contradictions between Feeling-tone of Political Party Names and Public Response to Their Platforms," *Journal of Social Psychology*, 7, March, 1936; Menefee, S. C., "The Effect of Stereotyped Words on Political Judgments," *American Sociological Review*, 1, August, 1936, 614–621.

toward conscientious objectors in the Second World War, in which it was shown that most individuals generally were not hostile to this group but nevertheless believed others to be quite intolerant.[57] In effect, what happens is that many persons disqualify themselves to make direct judgments of radicals and pass on to authorities or more conservative groups in the community and the state the responsibility for direct dealings with radicals and radical groups.

Such facts as these, along with their Russian cultural ties, make plain why American Communists have turned to "front" organizations and other means of "beating the devil around the stump." They also explain why the person stereotyped as "radical" often loses his value for the radical organization and how, like the highly publicized criminal, he may become a definite liability to the group he affiliates with. These peculiarities of stereotyped response by the masses have been a temptation to more conservative and reactionary groups to manipulate in order to attack moderate reformers and "liberals." The stereotype in this way has been worn thin, and the excesses of reactionary propaganda have led at times to sudden reversals and instability of the public reaction toward radicals.

Private-group Reactions

Antiradical groups under private auspices in the United States have been too many to enumerate here. Generally, however, they have consisted of organizations of war veterans, most notable of which has been the American Legion, reserve-officer groups, vigilantes, various patriotic societies, and vaguely named organizations like constitutional associations and "Better America" leagues. Organizations like these possess little real appeal to the broad public, receiving their support almost entirely from corporate business and industrial interests.[58] Their leaders tend to be Army officers, paid executives, the odd fanatical volunteer worker, and retired corporate businessmen. Their activities run largely to press releases, circulating printed material, and efforts to censor public education. They prefer to attack persons rather than to discuss issues and they mix fantasy with fact in generous proportions. The American Legion has gone farthest in the fight against radicalism, at times administering beatings to radicals and breaking up their meetings by force and violence. They have aggressed against a wide variety of groups, including the Jehovah's Witnesses as well as the Communists and the IWW. Generally organizations such as these have in time discredited themselves by their obvious falsehoods, by their ties with special industrial interests, and by their indiscriminate at-

[57] Crespi, Leo P., "Public Opinion towards Conscientious Objectors," *Journal of Psychology*, 19, April, 1945, pp. 209–250.

[58] Hapgood, *op. cit.*, Chap. IV.

tacks upon moderate reformers, "progressives," and all others working for changes which clash with vested interests. However, in times of stress, organizations like these through their influence upon public officials may canalize and give a special aggressive form to the societal reaction to radicals.

Police and Radicals

The drive of revolutionaries to weaken or overthrow established power, and the need of other radical groups to advance their causes through

"Fellow-comrades and undercover agents of the F B I. "

Fig. 7

parades and public meetings, bring them almost always into conflict with the police. This conflict was particularly great at one time between anarchists and police as the consequence of the former's philosophy of the propaganda crime. Communists, too, have deliberately sought to provoke police into breaking up their parades and meetings as a means of obtaining evidence of the "police persecution of the working class." Members of the IWW in their famous free-speech rights deliberately courted arrest in order to fill local jails and overburden the law-protection agencies of the community. It should be remembered that to have been arrested and jailed is an honorary distinction for the professional revolutionary radical.

The disregard police have shown for civil rights of radicals is a function of the more general illegality of police behavior in the United States. In certain areas, such as the Pacific Coast states, these constitutional violations have been much more flagrant than in others. Here it has been brought out that sheriff departments in some areas have literally worked under orders of corporate agricultural, mining, and lumbering interests, invoking the power of their offices to break strikes and incidentally deny rights of free speech, assembly, and a swift trial to labor organizers and radicals alike.[59] In the minds of the police the stereotype of the radical means something different than it does to the general public. The police see radicals as a class of people who disrespect them and who challenge the very power delegated to them by the community to maintain order. Being reviled, bested in verbal exchanges, humiliated, baffled, and occasionally injured or killed by radical dissenters, the police have little reason to use discretion in arresting and handling radicals who violate the law.

The Courts

If the police have been harsh in their dealing with radicals, the courts have been no less so. Radicals in many countries have been denied fair trials, convicted upon circumstantial, inadmissable, or false evidence and given sentences all out of proportion to the seriousness of their crimes However, any complete assessment of the extent to which factors outside of those which are legally allowable enter into the trial and sentencing of radicals is almost impossible to make. In contrast to straight criminal cases the differential mortality of cases of law violation by radicals appears to be quite low. In 1917 and 1918 approximately 300 members of the IWW were arrested by Federal agents; of this number 160 were convicted.[60] In California at the same time 530 IWW followers were arrested and charged under criminal syndicalism laws; one-half of this number were tried and 164 convicted.[61] It is also true that murders, for which it is ordinarily very difficult to obtain convictions, when committed by radicals eventuate in convictions and death penalties much more frequently than would be expected.

That radicals are very often punished for the political implications of their offenses will scarcely be denied by informed writers on the subject This was illustrated clearly by the old case of a French cab driver who shot at a public official in a moment of anger and then for some incomprehensible reasons claimed in court to be an anarchist. Ordinarily he would have received a light sentence for assault; instead he received six years at hard labor.[62] Data which more generally clinch the point and perhaps provide a measure of the extent to which power-conflict values bias judicial decisions come from the sentences given to selective-service violators during the Second World War. The average sentence for all such

[59] La Follette, Robert, *Violations of Free Speech and Rights of Labor,* United States Congressional Committee on Education and Labor, 1942.

[60] Gambs, *op. cit*, p 27

[61] *Ibid*, p. 29

[62] Vizetally, Ernest A., *The Anarchists,* 1911, p. 154.

violators, of whom two-thirds were conscientious objectors, was 30.6 months. By way of comparison, the average sentence for violators of the narcotics laws was 20.8 months; of liquor laws, 10.7; of postal laws, 27.3; of "white-slave" laws, 28.3. The difference which especially interests us here, however, is between the average sentence of conscientious objectors and other selective-service violators. In 1945 for the former it was 37 months and for the latter 28 months. In line with these more severe sentences dispensed to conscientious objectors was the small percentage placed on probation. For the entire period of 1940 to 1945 only a little over 4 per cent of the cases were granted probation.[63] This is well below the national average of 33 per cent for convicted criminals in 25 states and below the lowest state average of 15.9. Only those guilty of murder showed a lower figure.[64]

The attitudes of radicals in court undoubtedly work to their disadvantage. Many radicals are belligerent, disdainful of the judge or of the authority of the court, and generally behave in a way to excite antipathy toward themselves. In other cases trials are converted into propaganda demonstrations as part of the revolutionary tactics of the radical group involved. There is abundant evidence that radicals and other defendants, such as members of minority groups, have been deliberately exploited and their freedom more or less sacrificed in the interests of revolutionary aims.[65] Again radicals have fared poorly in the courts by refusing to make a defense, or by refusing to agree not to commit the criminal act again, thus excluding themselves from consideration for probation.

Legislative and Administrative Groups

Legislatures have reacted to the rise of radical movements by passage of special legislation, by investigations carried on through special committees, and by publication of the resultant findings. Laws directed to the control of radicalism have undertaken to forbid the display of flags and symbols of certain colors such as red, black, and green, all of which have been regarded as inciteful at various times and places. Other laws have strictly regulated the possession and use of explosives. Perhaps most significant have been special statutes to forbid revolutionary utterances, which in effect have been attempts to abridge freedom of speech and assembly. In some societies such regulations have been established by administrative decree rather than through a legislative process. Generally such measures have been more culturally consistent and capable of enforcement in socie-

[63] Sibley, Mulford, and Ada Wardlaw, *Conscientious Objectors in Prison, 1940–1945*, October, 1945, pp 8–10

[64] *Judicial Criminal Statistics*, U. S. Bureau of the Census, 1945, pp 5–7.

[65] See Waldman, Louis. *Labor Lawyer*, 1944, chapter on "Murder in the Bible Belt."

ties with autocratic political organization, in so-called "police states" where a single-party system operates without constitutional restrictions.

The incongruity and impracticality of laws of this sort in democratic societies with constitutional governments are plain. While it is clear that democratic societies must protect themselves from crime committed or directly inspired by radicals as well as others and take action against threats to their national defenses, in such societies there are adequate safeguards against these things in the common law, which forbids inciting others to commit crimes. There is also protection in the law of treason. Legislation which has gone beyond the common law and law of treason has usually ended up in the form of regulations lacking sufficient precision to meet the requirements of enforceable law. Thus in Massachusetts a law against displaying red flags had to be repealed because it defined the Harvard school colors as illegal.[66] The vague terminology of such laws makes them potential threats to an infinite number of groups and persons who have little or no connection with radical groups. The same generalizations apply to legislation which is aimed at outlawing organizations and their members for being subversive. Unless a society is prepared to carry through with the implications of legislation of this sort and execute its radicals, it had better not use it at all. Imprisonment of radicals in a liberal-democratic society strengthens radical groups by giving them issues and importance, and at the same time swings to their side many groups which otherwise would have nothing at all in common with them.[67]

Many state legislatures as well as the national Congress have empowered committees to conduct investigations into radical activities. Their searches have led them into colleges and universities, into labor unions, the arts, professions, publishing industry, and into the organizations of the foreign-born and foreign-language groups. Perhaps the most famous of such committees were the Lusk Committee, created by the New York legislature in 1919, and the Dies Committee, brought into being in 1938 by the national Congress. Some of the committees, the Lusk Committee among others, have gathered large bodies of data, the quality of which is much higher than ordinarily credited to them by hostile critics. However, in nearly all cases the interpretations and conclusions drawn from the evidence have been unrestrained overgeneralization, or completely unwarranted.

Legislative investigative committees have followed due process of law to the point of insisting upon "yes" and "no" answers to questions put to persons whom they have called before them. There the resemblance to legal process ceases, with the effect that what is in reality a thinly disguised criminal proceedings operates without observance of traditional protec-

[66] Chaffee, Zachariah, Jr., *Freedom of Speech*, 1920, pp. 18*ff*.

[67] *Ibid*., pp 219*ff*

tions of the "accused" person. The result is a contemporary analogue of star-chamber hearings in which the person is presumed guilty of an undefined crime until proven otherwise. Sensational newspapers have been quick to report such hearings with all the stereotypes and clichés designed to discredit radicals, or perhaps just to sell more newspapers.

Many Americans who bother to inform themselves about the work of such committees no doubt dismiss much of their reports as the effusions of publicity-seeking politicians who are playing "politics" or seeking to embarrass the administration or opposition party. Many groups were offended by the illegal searches and seizures by such committees in 1919 and more recently by the irresponsible allegations of subversive radicalism made under the mantle of congressional immunity. Yet the impression exists that many people want such committees to go on with their work, for appropriations continue to be forthcoming. Furthermore, the inquisitorial function of legislatures seems to be firmly established by judicial decision. But in the final analysis legislative committees remain inferior to other governmental agencies, such as grand juries, in fulfilling inquisitorial functions.[68] By procedural changes and clarification of their function they might become efficient research agencies implementing the democratic process through scientifically founded publicity of the doings of radical organizations, but this seems a remote possibility.

Administrative reactions to radicals, as might be expected, have tended to embody the attitudes of more conservative segments of society. Some of this can be laid to the social composition of the bureaucratic personnel itself; much more is secondary response to pressure from private groups and from the legislative branch of the government which holds the strong threat of curtailing appropriations or abolishing administrative positions. Action against radicals by administrative agencies has been in the shape of deportations, prosecution for falsification of passports, and loyalty checks of employees, leading to discharge for belonging to organizations arbitrarily classed as subversive. The Department of Labor working hand-in-hand with the Department of Justice was responsible for the deportation of large numbers of aliens in 1919. The Federal departments mentioned proceeded by first defining certain radical groups as subversive – in the sense of advocating the use of violence as a political weapon – chiefly the Communist and Communist Labor parties of the time, and then made membership in these *ipso facto* grounds for deportation. This introduced the European concept of "guilt by association" into American administrative justice.

In retrospect the deportations of alien radicals have been viewed cri-

[68] Dessions, G. H., and I. H. Cohen, "The Inquisitorial Functions of Grand Juries," *Yale Law Journal*, 41, March, 1932, pp. 687–712

tically as having worked great hardships upon the persons deported and being out of keeping with our democratic values. Furthermore, it has been shown that personal grudges and the desire of industry to break up labor unions or other organizations often became snarled into the web of factors leading to deportation.[69] Yet the Secretary of Labor actually violated no law; we must remember that almost absolute power has been vested in this agency to pass upon the qualifications for entry and residence of aliens in the United States.

More recently we have seen a revival of the concept of "guilt by association" in "loyalty checks" and subsequent discharges of employees for their associations with radical groups. Lists of subversive organizations have been prepared, and membership in any of them has been made the basis for administrative decisions to hire and fire personnel. The inherent weakness in these segregative procedures lies in the practical impossibility of determining what the policy or aims of a given organization are, and also in the assumption that the beliefs and behavior of individual members are determined by the tenuous formulations imputed to the group as its program.

It has been suggested that collective guilt may be imputed to members of the Communist party because of the unique disciplinary characteristics of the organization. From this view, no Communist could be assumed to be under illusions about the meaning of his affiliation or free to make choices as to whether he would or would not conform to party policy. Mere membership *ipso facto* becomes the proof of conformity. Yet even if such facts were conceded, they still do not necessarily demand that we depart from our traditional Anglo-Saxon judicial procedure in order to protect ourselves from conspiratorial crimes.

A society in which nationalism is one of the integrating norms will of necessity make sure that overt sabotage and treasonable behavior will be kept at a minimum in administrative agencies carrying the burden of national defense or offense. It will also eliminate untrustworthy workers from those parts of its technological organization directly related to waging of war. Clear-cut cases of sabotage, conspiracy, and treason can be detected and prosecuted, but the borderline cases pose a special problem. Punitive forays against workers in government or industry for written and spoken utterances which sounded as if "they might" act contrary to national interest or for mere membership in organizations in which there are, or have been, known espionage agents can be tremendously damaging to morale of such workers. This is true whether it takes place in industrial Russia or industrial United States. It may be presumed that in the long run this will come to be recognized.

69 Chaffee, *op. cit.*, pp. 239, 255, 263.

In Russia in the past and today political deviants have been stigmatized, segregated, and bound by formal limits to their social participation. In our society only the adumbrations of such a pattern, mostly at the level of informal social organization, can be seen. In so far as the societal conceptions of the radical are translated into patterns of formal or public segregation, the life choices of the persons so categorized are narrowed. It is in this way that the definitions are given painful meaning for the individual and in this way that the social world created in radical organizations may actually become more attractive, depending, of course, upon their compensating satisfactions.

The Tolerance for Radicalism

The tolerance quotient for radicalism will be sensitive to such factors as the age-sex composition of a population, its class structure, ethnic composition, and various socioeconomic characteristics, as well as to the magnitude of the radical deviation and the organized power of the advocating groups. It may be judged that, for the United States, at least, ethnic and socioeconomic factors are strongly operative in local tolerances for radicalism. The protection afforded radical demonstrations by the police in New York City under Fiorello La Guardia's administration can be related in some measure to the numerous ethnic minorities located there and to the dimensions of their organized power. The ingrouping and power of the ethnic minorities may well act as a protective screen thrown around deviant members of the ethnic community, bestowing a certain immunity upon them, even though the persons in leadership posts may be far from radical themselves. Something of the same holds true for labor unions in which radicals have infiltrated.

Small businessmen, shopkeepers, professional persons, and those more highly educated seem to harbor less hostility toward radicals than others, with the result that their dominance in the local social structure where radicalism exists will buffer and mediate the societal reaction. A recent public-opinion survey disclosed that in answer to the question, "Should the Socialist party be allowed to publish a newspaper in this country?" the greatest differentials in the percentages replying in the affirmative were between those with college education and those with grade-school education. The difference ran more than five times the differences determined by age, by political affiliations, and by voting and nonvoting.[70] Further evidence in this direction is provided in an opinion survey of measures favored to restrict the operations of Communists in our society (see Table 23).

[70] *National Opinion Research Center*, June, 1946.

TABLE 23. PERCENTAGE DISTRIBUTION OF OPINIONS ABOUT COMMUNISM BY OCCUPATIONAL CLASS AND UNION AFFILIATION*

Measures favored	Occupational class or union			
	Semiprofessional	Railroad workers	AFL members	CIO members
Drastic	34 4	56 2	52.1	40.6
Regulatory	15 8	10 0	7 5	5 3
Curative	10.5	5 9	3 1	4 2
Let them alone	23.0	7.5	13 3	15.4
Other	1.0	4.2	2 8	4 4
Don't know	20.1	20 2	24.2	31.4

**Fortune Magazine*, June, 1940, pp. 162–163. The percentages total more than 100 because of the inclusion of multiple answers

It will be noticed from the table that the semiprofessional workers had the lowest percentage favorable to drastic measures toward Communists, and the highest percentages responsive to the ideas of regulation, political rehabilitation, and permissive tolerance. It is of more than passing interest that the workers in the newer industrial unions were much more frequently indecisive on the question. This suggests, without proving, that unskilled workers have less crystallized reactions toward radicalism and may be the more malleable portion of the community responsible for the major changes and reversals in the societal reaction.

If it is true that members of the so-called "middle classes" do indeed follow a moderating course in reacting to radicals, we may have an explanation of the rough treatment of radicals in regions of the South and the Far West. In line with such reasoning is the record of the enforcement of criminal syndicalism laws, the most vigorous application of which occurred in California, Washington, and Idaho,[71] all newer states with social structures organized around large-scale, agricultural interests and extractive and processing industries, where the family farm and the small business of the Middle West have been conspicuously absent. A similar middle-class void is observable in the social organization of single-crop, quasi-feudalistic states of the South, where the history of disregard for the civil rights of radicals and labor organizers is too well known to necessitate documentation. The violence and extremeness of revolutionary action and official reaction in such countries as Russia and Spain, together with the flabbiness of radical movements and their haphazard repression in England and the United States, give further reality to this general interpretation.

[71] Gambs *op cit.*, p. 29

Sequences in Reactions to Radicalism

When our perspective is shifted from spatial to temporal aspects of radicalism and the reaction to it, we meet with cyclical manifestations much like those associated with crime and prostitution, but with special features absent from these. Radical movements undergo periods of growth, efflorescence, and decline. American socialism arose in 1900, reached a peak of influence around 1912, and then declined precipitantly, to be dealt more or less of a death blow by the Roosevelt reform administration of 1932. The IWW went through a somewhat shorter span of growth and deterioration from 1904 to the early 1920's, until by 1930 it counted only a few scattered adherents. Communism in the United States got its start in 1919, rose to a crest of power in the 1930's, and since that time has waned in prestige and influence. To counteract any idea that neat organic cycles function in the history of radicalism, it must be recalled that the revolutionary movement in Russia passed through more than one period of expansion and decline. Furthermore, radical movements proliferate, split, combine, and recombine in ways which as yet have not been reduced to predictable sequences.

Historical data suggest that radical movements tend to merge into one another as cultural change empties current issues of meaning and creates entirely new ones. Thus after the Civil War many abolitionists shifted their interests and activities to the "problems" of the emergent industrial urban community. Collective disillusionment with both the ends and means of radical action become the concomitant symbolic dynamic of cultural change which powers the rise of new radical sects and movements. At the present time American communism has probably outlived its "age," and survives largely through outside support from Russia. Many discerning radicals rightly perceive the complete futility of trying to overturn the powerful modern state by means of direct force. It may be that passive resistance, organized on an informal inspirational basis to attain radical goals, is the emergent pattern of American radicalism.

As a radical movement gathers momentum, it sets off a somewhat proportional societal reaction prompted by accumulating fears aroused among the more conservative groups in the society. At some critical point legal restraints are imposed, stereotypes invented, and special legal and extralegal defensive agencies make their appearance. Once such a reactionary control culture has been erected to cope with disruptive radical elements it becomes viable in its own right, being invoked to repress and manipulate subsequent radical movements or to block changes in the culture of a more diffuse evolutionary nature. That it should become intertwined with a variety of extraneous factors not germane to its original function and that it should generate spurious societal reactions, creating "fears of distant dangers," "red scares," or collective fears of "the enemy in our midst" is a matter for little surprise.

The specious character of the societal reaction to radicalism has been especially obtrusive in the history of American culture. A number of writers have pertinently commented upon the hysteria of fear which sweeps over our populace from time to time, a fear of things alien, insidious, and subversive. The years immediately succeeding the two world wars were noteworthy in this country for extravaganzas of counter-espionage and press campaigns of vilification and harassment directed at radicals and their organizations. The basic irrationality of the societal reaction at these times was attested to by the radicals themselves who asked rhetorically: "Why do they fear us so much when we are so few?" Further testimony to the attenuated allegiance that the societal reaction bears to the facts of radical deviation comes to light in the writings of liberal thinkers who voice the retrospective disbelief of the masses that the radical "threat" ever did exist. Operational demonstration of the thin substance composing the societal reaction is seen in the administrative clemency leading to reduction and commutation of sentences of imprisoned radicals after the crisis has vanished and the society slowly resumes its previous stability.[72]

It is at the crucial stages of the societal reaction that radical organizations are put to test and individual members perceive the segregative implications of the radical role, which in the quiescent interims have been only vaguely felt. The radical myth which is nurtured by ingroup interaction in the absence of disruption from the outside may be rudely demolished, cutting the individual radical adrift from the collective fantasy which has been the chief prop of the self. The pendulumlike swings in public mood must be considered as one of the more dynamic factors conditioning the radicalizing process.

Radicalization

As with many other forms of sociopathic behavior there are numerous and varied ways in which primary radicalism invades and becomes part of the individual's belief system. However, there can be little genuine doubt but that childhood associations with parents function importantly in the acquisition of radical beliefs by the individual. The general tendency of children to follow the political convictions of parents whether they are conservative or radical is well known and demonstrable in statistics on voting behavior. More specifically touching upon this question are data

[72] See Wright, Edward W., *Conscientious Objectors in the Civil War*, 1931, pp. 240f; also Chaplin, Ralph, *Wobbly*, 1948, Chap 27.

revealing significant parent-child correlations in attitudes toward radicalism, shown in Table 24.

TABLE 24. PARENT-CHILD CORRELATIONS IN ATTITUDES TOWARD COMMUNISM*

Relationship	Zero correlation	Partial correlation
Mother-sons ..	.580	.502
Mothers-daughters	.493	.238
Fathers-sons .	.542	.080
Fathers-daughters	.621	.467
All siblings .	.475	
Mothers-fathers	.578	

*Newcomb, Theodore, and George Svehla. "Intra-family Relationships in Attitude," *Sociometry*, 1, July–October, 1937, Tables I–III, p. 182.

All possible pairs of the main sample of 548 families are included in the zero order correlations. The total number of cases for the partial correlations, in which the influence of one parent was held constant, amounted to 190 families.

The partial correlations carry the interesting implications that certain relationships, or perhaps mutual identifications within the family such as father-daughter and mother-son, may be much more significant channels than others for the transmission of attitudes toward radicalism. They also lend some sanction to the general proposition that conflict and antagonisms in parent-child relationships condition the growth of radical ideas. These figures may conceal the tendency for children to seize upon radicalism as a convenient vehicle for the expression of the "adolescent revolt" we have previously alluded to as a feature of American culture. Protest radicalism, if the concept has any meaning, probably has a selective incidence, appearing more frequently at certain ages and in families of certain socio-economic status. A breakdown of findings on parent-child attitude correlations by age and occupational rank of the father is congenial to such an interpretation (see Table 25).

TABLE 25. PARENT-CHILD CORRELATIONS IN ATTITUDES TOWARD COMMUNISM BY AGE AND OCCUPATIONAL LEVEL OF PARENT*

Age	Occupational level		
	I–II†	III	IV–V–VI
19 and under	.710(68)§	.578(210)	.553(158)
20–23	.167(60)	.509(111)	.574(82)
24 and over	253(57)	.378(74)	.768(52)

*Newcomb, Theodore, and George Svehla, "Intra-family Relationships in Attitude," *Sociometry*, July–October, Tables I–III, p. 185.

†Occupational level: I, highest; VI, lowest.

§Number of families in sample is in parentheses.

It may be reasoned from Table 25 that for families at lower socioeconomic levels radicalism is more apt to be the result of transmission of radical attitudes from parents to children; whereas at high status levels, it is entirely possible that radicalism arises out of or is associated with conflict with parents. In so far as foreign-born and Jewish families (both included in the above study) fall into a lower socioeconomic class, it might be said that several forms of radicalism represent a continuity of either a definite revolutionary tradition or of incomplete acculturation. In the latter case the immigrant heritage itself, which was not necessarily radical in an old-world setting, might predispose the children of the immigrants to favorable reactions toward Communist programs and propaganda.

Other cultural components of radicalism which are more indigenous in nature include the special traditions of "Old American" families embodying religious dissent, freethinking, pacifism, and some sort of sense of frontier justice. These in many cases become sources of behavior closely akin to or convertible into radical ways. Where radicalism has a middle-class origin, it seems to be connected with sensitivity to the culture conflicts which follow in the wake of technological and social change, especially as they have occurred in Western societies. More specifically it is the reaction of well-educated persons of the middle class – perhaps some sort of "second-generation middle class" – children of socially upgraded parents who perceive the fallacies of institutional ideologies accepted without question by the parental generation.

Indications are strong that radicalization overlaps or is coterminous with a special educational process. Over one-third of 149 Russian Communist leaders who were studied mentioned varieties of educational experiences as the main contributory influence leading to their becoming radicals.[73] A fair number of autobiographical documents reveal that where active radicalism arises in persons of lower social status it tends to go hand in hand with a type of informal educational process, manifested by avid reading interests and an impelling curiosity about the social system in which they live This seems to hold true for religious as well as politico-economic radicalization. So, for example, the "discovery of truth" in the literature of the Jehovah's Witnesses often has been the first step in the conversions of persons of very limited education to this sect.

Many better educated persons undoubtedly go through a stage early in their lives when they search for "answers" to the inconsistencies and contradictions of the culture in which they participate. Their ideological explorations and meanderings frequently list an interlude of radical behavior in adolescence or early adulthood. Eventually, if the social system of which they are a part does not frustrate their development or is not on

[73] Davis, *op. cit.*, Table 12, p. 54.

the verge of disintegration, these people "settle down" and accept the conventional philosophical or theological resolutions of their conflicts. Failing this, many become more comfortable with their conflicts by compromising their ideals or by contenting themselves with the more generalized satisfactions of family life, the knowledge of a job well done even though its importance may be quite small. Still others seek outlets in forms of sociopathic behavior such as drinking, gambling, carousing, or compulsive indulgence in hobbies and sports. Some few people of the class mentioned may be so fortunately situated that they are protected from culture conflicts and hence never generate sufficient tension to dispatch them on the "quest for certainty."

Among those who become primary radicals are some who, because of absorbing cultural traditions emphasizing social justice, as with many Jews, or because of identification with a critical, rebellious parent, or because of special social trauma breeding a deep and painful disillusionment (often religious), develop compulsive habits of thought and rigid symbolic reactions. They become less responsive to suggestion and to group opinions, more unyielding and uncompromising. At the level of ideas there is a narrowing of internal limits of choice. It must be said that in this connection there is much likeness between the radical and extreme conservative or reactionary person. Such persons may be candidates for membership in religious sects with highly integrated dogma as well as in radical political and economic organizations. It is not happenstance that religious leaders have sometimes turned to radicalism and that a number of radicals have, on disillusionment, turned to the solace of religion. The explanation for the choice of a system of ideas socially defined as "radical" over an equally rigid philosophic or religious ideology thought of as "conservative" has to be found in the general relevancy of the specific ideas involved to the internal limits of the person and the satisfactions associated with the contemplated role and status in terms of these limits.

Secondary Radicalism

We may ask at this point what is responsible for the symbolizing of primary radicalism as "radical" and the assumption of a systematic radical role. Our answer must be looked for in differences of symbolic milieus in which the preliminary radical behavior arises. Some societies not only have clear definitions of the radical but they also have extensive methods for segregating them. These are the autocratic societies with a well-developed concept of political crime covering a multitude of specific activities apart from treason or espionage. In such societies the symbolic environment is such that the individual is not likely to entertain illusions as to the consequences of participating in interdicted activities, so far as his role and status are concerned. The early radical activities of Russian Communist leaders, according to the study we have cited, were nearly all those unequivocally declared illegal by the czarist government, the bulk having to do with assisting a workers' circle or a students' circle. Since almost nine-tenths of these leaders had been arrested, with 69 per cent having been arrested from two to eight times, it would seem that the punitive symbolic reaction was consistent and more or less inevitable. The median age for initial radical behavior was eighteen years, while the median age for joining some revolutionary party fell at twenty years, leaving a short two-year period of maturation before becoming a practicing and probably a systematic radical.[74]

In democratic societies such as the United States and England a person does not necessarily have to join a radical party in order to voice his criticisms and express antagonisms to established institutions. One may become a lone professional agitator – as in England[75] – or a labor organizer, a labor lawyer, or join a group fighting for civil liberties, or in politics become a "fighting liberal." The individualistic ethos of our culture, indeed, ideologically imposes a responsibility upon the citizen to participate in a critical decision-making process. Furthermore, a person may join a radical organization or become the ally of radicals without necessarily identifying himself as a radical. The symbolic environment of radicalism in American culture is blurred and contains numerous alternative definitions for what would be absolutely defined as radicalism in a society like Russia. For this reason the telescoping of choices in progression from primary to secondary radicalism does not proceed to the same extreme.

The oscillating nature of the American reaction to radicalism generally makes for fallacious estimates on the part of radicals of the social reception and the societal definition of their behavior. Thus persons may have been radical party workers for years and then suddenly during a critical period they may be arrested and confronted with prison. If case-history and autobiographical materials are indicative, this frequently comes as a great shock to the American radical. His reaction is likely to be an outcry against the unjustness of his conviction, in contrast with the acceptance of such penal facts by the professional criminal or the professional European revolutionary. Often this is a breaking point at which disillusionment begins for the radical in our culture.

Besides arrest and imprisonment, such things as the loss of a job because of organization work, a divorce in which the conflict between the radical role and family role is sharply verbalized, or a choice between occupational advancement and a low-paying party position may serve as critical points at which secondary radicalism appears. Otherwise the person progressively commits himself or is gradually assigned more and more re-

[74] Davis, *op. cit.*, Tables VI, IX–XI, pp. 47, 50–51.
[75] See Thompson, B., *Hyde Park Orator*, 1943.

sponsibility in the form of appointments to committees or "missions" until he is assimilated into the nucleus of the radical organization where are found those whose entire lives have been given over to the cause or movement.

The symbolic cues to professionalization of the radical lie in his verbal behavior more than anything else. However, the professional also can be discerned by his growing preoccupation with techniques of organizing, agitation, and propagandizing, with perhaps less interest in the abstract merits of ideological controversy with nonradicals. At the same time a sectarian discrimination between types of radical doctrine plus a patronizing or hostile attitude toward other radicals and special disdain for renegades further differentiate the systematic radical. Finally, a changing attitude toward law-enforcement agencies is apparent in the more highly professionalized radical.

Prisonization of the Radical

The probabilities run high that the professional radical will go to jail or prison sometime during his life — even in a society like our own. Consequently part of the parcel of factors molding his role and status is shared with the criminal. Often his sentence is a long one, which provides one of the main symbolic requisites for prisonization. But the very length of his
sectarian discrimination between types of radical doctrine plus a patron-
prisoners know he is not a criminal in a strict sense and they may sympathize with him over his long sentence or "bum rap." At the same time they may regard the radical as foolish for not surreptitiously evading the law rather than openly defying it. Pacifists in jail and prison have occasionally met hostility and even violence from other inmates, but often, too, they have won their respect by consideration and kindness. This seemed to have been the case with conscientious objectors imprisoned during the Second World War. Prison staff members likewise have often been rather considerate of the imprisoned radical.[76] This may be genuine sympathy or simply the consequences of the perplexing administrative problem he presents.

Where groups of radicals have been quartered in the same prison — and this often happens — the individual radical is sustained by the presence of comrades. More than this, prisons may become breeding grounds for revolutionaries, as was true in the latter part of the nineteenth century in Russia, where the process of radicalization was facilitated by the very agencies set up to prevent it.[77] The morale of imprisoned radicals may also be reinforced by the knowledge that friends and organizations outside of the prison are working for their release. The amount of such reinforce-

[76] Sibley and Wardlaw, *op. cit.*, pp. 32, 34*ff*.

[77] Footman, *op. cit.*, p. 54.

ment, of course, will be conditioned by the ups and downs of the larger radical movement.

The morale of the prison groups of radicals may be little more than a fiction where there is great heterogeneity among them. For example, groups of conscientious objectors in work camps as well as in prisons during the Second World War were often fractured by dissensions and conflicts arising from cleavage between men of different religious faiths, between absolutists and less rigid objectors, and between religious and nonreligious pacifists.[78] Among members of the IWW sent to prison in 1917, it was observed by one of their leaders that morale held up well for about one year, after which it began to deteriorate. Disagreement over the acceptance of individual clemency as opposed to clemency for the group was one of the main sources of conflict.[79] However, in the long run, it is most likely that it is the social isolation of the prison environment rather than other factors which has the greatest demoralizing effect upon the incarcerated radical. In general, as we have stated earlier, the period of isolation from society is soon cut short by the swing of public mood. Notwithstanding this, a prison stay probably is a vastly sobering experience for many radicals, and it is a plausible hypothesis that much of the stuff of disillusionment comes from the very real hardships and sacrifices it entails. The long imprisonment of the celebrated anarchist, Alexander Berkman, culminated in symptoms after discharge which strongly resembled a serious psychosis.[80]

If arrest and imprisonment do not destroy the new personal integration of the ideological deviant, they may confirm his adherence to the behavior system of the radical. After release his status is frequently enhanced in radical circles; he is sought after as a speaker and receives more tangible recognition in financial support from associates. His criminal record is now a symbol of formal segregation from society. If he has the required skills and education, it may be the springboard by which he ascends quickly into the higher ranks of his organization.

Social Participation of the Radical

The full-time paid or unpaid sectarian radical finds his entire life pattern altered. The demands of the "movement" are great, and responsibilities will be imposed in proportion to the person's energies and abilities. Conflicts arise within the individual over ideological aims and organizational expedients and must be successfully rationalized or otherwise solved. With full emotional commitment to the ideals and values of a radical way

[78] Dalke, Otto, "Values and Group Behavior in Two Camps for Conscientious Objectors," *American Journal of Sociology*, 51, July, 1945, pp. 22*ff*.

[79] Chaplin, *op. cit.*, pp. 323*ff*.

[80] Berkman, Alexander, *Prison Memoirs of an Anarchist*, 1912, Part IV.

of life, intercourse with those who do not share his views grows more disturbing and difficult for the professional radical – hence, the waxing tendency to shut out extraneous and disturbing social contacts by withdrawal entirely into the radical group. Where the deviant sect places taboos upon contacts with those not of the faith, centripetal social forces reinforce the constriction of social participation of the individual. In societies where conflict with police and the danger of arrest are great, isolation and withdrawal are indispensable safeguards of survival.

The contrast between the intensity of the social participation of the highly professionalized leader and the nominal member of a radical group is most pronounced. A study of time devoted by Communists to propaganda promotion in Chicago during the early 1930's disclosed an average of 20 hours per week for paid party functionaries, 12 hours for unpaid functionaries, and 3 hours for ordinary members.[81] Since propagandizing was only one phase of party work and since the figures given are averages, it may be concluded that the more zealous members were indeed giving over practically all of their time to the program of the Communist organization. Among the Jehovah's Witnesses, which, as a sect, bears many similarities to the Communist party, the apportionment of the members' time has been highly formalized. Thus "Pioneers" pledge from 30 to 60 hours per month to sectarian business. "Publishers" are full-time devotees. In times of special conversion drives these hours may be increased.[82]

The small numbers of professionalized radicals plus the undependability of the great mass of the partially indoctrinated peripheral adherents mean that the former must carry the main burden of radical action. It is pertinent to note the high ratio of party officers to members in the Chicago Communist organization, which ranged from 1.13 in 1930 to 0.8 in 1934, never falling below 0.69 in intervening years. The consequence of this was plural officeholding on the part of party functionaries. In the Chicago Communist party the average number of offices occupied by members during a five-year period ending in 1934 ran from 1.9 to 2.9.[83] This may be somewhat exceptional, owing to the methods employed by Communists to ensure complete control of party structure, but at the same time it reflects the general tendency of sectarian radicals to dedicate the whole of their lives to their organization.

Economic Participation

Public identification as a radical undeniably works a mild to serious economic disadvantage for the person thus made visible. Some businesses and industries in our society have questions concerning radical affiliation

[81] Lasswell and Blumenstock, *op. cit*, p 277.
[82] Stroup, *op cit.*, p. 60.
[83] *Ibid.*, pp. 222–223.

on application blanks to be filled out for employment. Furthermore, some employers refuse to hire known radicals and have arbitrarily discharged others known or suspected of so-called "subversive views." However, there is much variation in the attitudes of employers on this question, and the impulse to discharge a radical employee is tempered by the fact that sometimes he is among the more efficient and productive workers. It is interesting that motion-picture producers in the United States, even those more rabidly anti-Communist, were inclined to resist the efforts of a congressional committee to have them set up a black list for communistic script writers.[84]

Persons in public employment run greater risk of the loss of position and of economic deprivation as the result of radical associations than other workers. Public-school teachers and faculty members of colleges and universities frequently must run the gauntlet of public investigation and occasionally have been discharged because of membership in radical organizations. Ministers who have expressed favor for socialist and communist ideas have at times lost pastorates. The only profession in which dedicated radicals seem to survive in any numbers is law. Here radical views and membership in radical groups tend to limit the type of practice the attorney may build up. However, he may go into the field of labor law or criminal law and, if he does not receive large retainers like the corporation lawyer, at least he can make a satisfactory living within the limits of a highly competitive profession.

Probably the most important economic restrictions upon the participation of the sectarian radical derive from his own conception of his role, which strongly motivates him to achieve the status of a full-time functionary. A few persons of independent economic means are in a position to do this without penalty. Paradoxically enough, during the economic Depression of the 1930's it was also possible for radicals who had gone on relief to spend most of their time in the work of parties to which they belonged. However, most aspirants to the status of full-time worker must demonstrate their loyalty and integrity through apprenticeship until they are selected to join the few paid functionaries of a radical organization. Even then, economic difficulties remain. The pay of the radical seldom is more than enough to cover mere subsistence needs, and he is expected to sacrifice even this if the need arises. The radical thus often lives a hand-to-mouth existence, depending upon the proceeds of the sale of newspapers or pamphlets, or upon the charity of comrades. He must live in the cheapest of quarters, dress poorly, and eat in a most irregular fashion.

The professional radical is everlastingly at the beck and call of his group; as problems come up and plans are changed, he must cease what he is doing and join in conference to discuss strategy and tactics. There is nearly

[84] See Kahn, Gordon, *Hollywood on Trial*, 1948, Chap 3

always something to be done. Demonstrations must be conducted, public meetings held, and literature written, printed and distributed. Meetings frequently come at night and last long and late, often followed by caucuses or more intimate early-morning conferences. These facts, along with the mobility demanded of the professional radical, introduce extreme irregularity into his life, which in concert with his economic impoverishment have far-reaching implications for other forms of social participation.

Sex and Marital Participation

A recognition of the conflict between family life and dedication of one's life to the dissemination of revolutionary philosophy appeared quite early in attitudes of religious prophets. Biblical statements attributed to Christ reflect the conviction that, for apostles and missionaries of Christianity, marriage should be put aside, and that in case of conflict between religious pursuits and family demands, the former should come first. The barriers to reconciling the role of the professional radical with the roles of husband and father are implicitly the same. The all-consuming interest of the radical in his cause, the inordinate exactions in time and energy levied by his membership in a revolutionary group, his precarious financial status, and his relatively high mobility mean that marital and family obligations will be indifferently met.

There is no way of knowing whether professional radicals are single to a greater degree than comparable age groups of the general population, although there is reason to suspect this may be the case. Again there are at hand no quantitative data to tell us what percentage are separated or divorced. However, certain other data make it fairly certain that the percentage runs higher than for the general population. Autobiographies of radicals frequently mention marital problems and divorce. Furthermore, the American Communist party has officially taken note of this problem. To quote from the statement of one of its leaders:[85]

> Within the revolutionary movement we often face this [family] problem in different form. We often receive complaints from the wives and families of men who are active in the revolutionary labor movement, that demands made by the movement take them away from their families so much as to endanger the family's stability. This is a serious problem with which the movement is struggling to find a practical solution. We cannot pretend to have entirely solved it as yet.

One of the surest proofs of true dedication to the faith of the Jehovah's Witnesses, according to the sect members themselves, is family strife. This may come out of lack of faith on the part of one spouse or from excessive

[85] Browder, *op. cit.*, p 202.

amounts of time spent in Witness work by the husband or wife, or it may reflect the drawing apart of husband and wife through special duties assigned to them within the sect.[86]

Wives of participating radicals often feel most keenly the enforced isolation of their status. One wife of an active Communist complained, for example, that she saw her husband only twelve hours per week. In order to remedy this, many wives join the husband's organization, which probably explains the presence of many if not most women members in such groups. However, the wife may discover that companions and acquaintances acquired in this way are not to her liking. If there are children, her ability to attend meetings or follow her husband's movements will be seriously limited. Choice of friends outside the radical circle may draw the censure of her husband or that of his comrades. Additional strain may come from the necessity to go to work to supplement or replace the husband's uncertain income — especially if there are children. The husband's using of the home to supply bed and board to wayfaring brothers in revolt and for conferences lasting out the morning hours are scarcely conducive to equanimity of the household. Perhaps most onerous of all for the wife is the gradual alienation of the husband's interests and the resultant feeling that she and the children rate a poor second in his affections and loyalties.

The extramarital sex behavior of radicals varies a great deal with their status and the degree of systematization of their behavior and also with many personal background factors. A number of persons make their way into radical groups in search of solutions for sexual conflicts, often impelled by the promise of sexual freedom supposed to exist therein. Specific rationalizations for sexual freedom can be excerpted from the writings of many radical thinkers, especially those of Karl Marx and Friedrich Engels. These reasons, along with definite statements by the odd radical renunciate[87] and case-history data, dispose the writer to believe that newly converted and less indoctrinated radicals do quite often participate in a Bohemian type of sexual behavior. Persons who enter radical movements to fulfill deep religious convictions, such as Christian Socialists, or lone radicals, like conscientious objectors, must be counted as exceptions to this. However, that sexual freeness has occurred among some of the Jehovah's Witnesses seems probable.[88]

As radicals pass on to systematize their behavior, they tend to develop a more functional sex morality, which may even have all the external manifestations of Puritanism. Thus they come to look askance at any preoccupation with sex which diverts the participant from the serious business of

[86] Stroup, *op. cit.*, p 116.
[87] Gitlow, Benjamin, *The Whole of Their Lives*, 1948, pp 290–295.
[88] Stroup, *op. cit.*, p. 118.

revolution. Official disapproval of sexual indiscretion may spring from the unfavorable publicity it brings to the organization. Thus beginning around 1935 the American Communist party began to take a definite stand against what was termed "pseudo-Bohemianism." [89]

Recreation

The ingroup solidarity of radicals gives their interaction an intimate quality which often makes their mutual work an intrinsically enjoyable experience. Meetings and conferences often dissolve into recreational communions. Sharing meals, drinking together, and gossip about associates as well as their philosophical discussions fill what limited recreational needs they have. Their meager incomes necessarily curtail participation in commercialized recreation. However, for the newer members of a radical party something more than the excitement of discussion and political intrigue is required to hold interest. Consequently, just as many conventional organizations rely upon the social hour and "refreshments" following the business meeting, so American radical organizations have balanced their serious meetings with "social" meetings in order to attract and hold new members. Noteworthy in this connection is the relatively high attendance at the "social" meetings as compared with other types of meetings held under radical auspices. In the Chicago Communist party from 1930 to 1934 attendance at "socials" was highest in two years, second only to parades for two other years, and exceeded by parades and outdoor demonstrations in the remaining year. Indoor meetings proved least attractive, as measured by attendance figures, for all five years.[90]

The obviously important recreational and generally socializing function of radical social organization brings us to a significant point, namely, that while sectarian affiliation effects an isolation of the person from the larger society, for many people it greatly expands the scope of their social participation. Persons who previously have been socially isolated, with few friends and little contact with the opposite sex, often on joining a political sect have enjoyed more social activity and felt more security than at any other time in their lives. They have grown in social maturity, acquiring ability to express themselves in social situations and to become more at ease with themselves and others.[91] In other words, their participation in radical groups has served a transitional function of establishing them as adults. This interpretation is well in conformity with the facts of high turnover in radical membership. However, it leaves us with the question as to why

[89] Browder, *op. cit.*, p. 201.

[90] Lasswell and Blumenstock, *op. cit.*, p. 232.

[91] See the case histories in Solomon Diamond, "A Study of the Influence of Political Radicalism on Personality Development," *Archives of Psychology*, 203, June, 1936.

so many persons desert radical associations after a period of intensive, apparently satisfying, participation.

The Denouement of Radicalism

For most people radical experience is short-lived and is but a casual incident of their life histories. Many persons are attracted by the programs of radical parties and then upon discovering that they are not what they seem give them no further support. A great many sincere and honest Americans undoubtedly were drawn by the democratic pretenses and liberal tenets of the Communist party during the 1930's. However, after attending enough meetings to come to appreciate the real nature of communism, most of them broke all contacts with the movement.[92] Persons whose radicalism has been a phase of "growing up" usually are "cured" of their deviant ideological tendencies by a satisfying job, a successful marriage, increasing political sophistication, or a general mellowing brought on by age. Others whose stringent protest and sense of social injustice generates from perpetual neurotic conflict have continued trouble in making peace with any organized expression of social life. These people seem to run through brief cycles of inspired radical participation, disillusionment, and then repudiation.[93] They are the chronic joiners, whose histories record dozens of enthusiasms and entrees and exits from deviating cults and sects. Their participational vagaries are captioned in Professor Seagull's poetic avowal of his own sectarian instability [94]

In the Winter I am a Buddhist
In the Summer I am a Nudist.

Deviants whose radicalism is of this symptomatic sort may survive the initial period of sectarian growth in a radical association, but their often disruptive behavior soon gets them into trouble as the group matures. They are seldom candidates for prestigeful roles in a radical group and they may be ejected or made so uncomfortable that they depart of their own volition. However distorted may be the symbolic process in these people, they do nevertheless give it a species of social reality in its external aspects by their overt radical behavior. A few undergo the transformation of their primary deviation into a more systematic radical role. On the whole, however, the organizational instability of sectarian movements themselves is not favorable to this development. Age treats such persons unkindly, and many find their way into mental hospitals.

92 See Franklin, J H , "Why I Broke with the Communists," *Harper's*, May, 1947, pp 412–418.

93 Rice, S., "Motives in Radicalism and Reform," *American Journal of Sociology*, 28, January, 1923, pp 577–585

94 Mitchell, Joseph, "Profile," *The New Yorker*, Dec 12, 1942.

The passage of time has the effect of binding the systematic radical or extreme sectarian more closely to his group. The "all-or-none" quality of the party or sect life alienates him from persons and groups falling beyond the sharp lines of the ingroup. Thus he becomes more and more dependent upon the basic and auxiliary radical roles for a wide variety of life satisfactions. The constant reinforcing interaction with others whose ideas are perforce cut from the same pattern strengthens the reification of the ideology, so that all opposing ideas become self-evidently wrong, immoral, or stupid and incomprehensible. After a person has spent a number of years in the service of a revolutionary sect or organization and has passed beyond his young adult years, he feels more or less committed to his role despite the doubts and qualms which frequently disturb him.

Yet despite these facts, disillusionment and frustrated hopes seem to be the frequent culmination of the radical career. As one writer has put it: "... the apostles of yesterday become apostates, the tribunes turn traitor, and the rebels – renegades." [95] There are numerous reasons behind the defection of the radical, some discoverable in subtle cumulative changes in the covert symbolic process, some found in the kaleidoscopically changing social situation of which the radical ideology and organization are a part The rapid rise and fall of sects and social movements means that the immediate social context in which the radical has a role and status may be precipitantly destroyed. Many radicals in periods shorter than their own lifetimes have witnessed the withering and decay of a movement to which they have given the bulk of their life energies. The high turnover of membership in radical groups can so modify their composition and official policy that earlier recruits find themselves with deviant status within the group, and likely to be shunted aside. They become the "old guard," without power, subject to scorn and ridicule. In more militant revolutionary groups they may be ruthlessly ejected and declared renegades, with whom further social contact is tabooed. If fission takes place, the outmoded radicals may be left in possession of the nominal organization which they may carry on temporarily. Otherwise they have the choice of forming a splinter group and at an advanced age seeking to recapture support of liberal and left groups. Needless to say, there are few with the stamina to thus "begin again."

Where revolutions provide the opportunity for radicals to ride into power, it might be expected that personal fufillment for the individual deviant would accompany the assumption of power by his group. But success of this sort is deceptive, for revolutions often devour their own children. After the interregnum chaos of the revolutionary epoch has been

[95] Nomad, Max, *Rebels and Renegades,* vii, pp 19–21.

succeeded by more stable social conditions, a different type of leadership is called for. The militant, conspiratorial revolutionary is discarded for the administrator with abilities more suited to routine day-to-day governing. Very few of the so-called "old bolsheviks" who rose to power in Russia in 1917 survived in positions of power and prestige twenty years later. The great majority had been executed, exiled, or otherwise eliminated in a much shorter period.

There are a few radicals who manage to salvage some sort of satisfying role despite aging or disappearance of the movement with which they have been identified. These are men whose careers have been fused with the radical myth itself, heroes of the radical world, who have become so well known that it is not easy to discredit them. Their sanction must be sought by revolutionary groups despite disagreement with their views. In other cases a man has perfected his power of leadership and oratorical skill to the point where he can continue to attract large audiences wherever he appears, regardless of the enfeebled support or complete absence of a sponsoring organization. Such persons often turn into professional lecturers.

A quaint and intriguing phenomenon is seen in the handful of ancient veterans of once important radical sects, such as the anarchists and the IWW, still proclaiming the coming revolution, spending their little cash on pamphlets, sallying forth to do verbal battle with class enemies and misguided brother radicals on street corners and in the public parks. Here there are always a few to listen, if only with bored amusement.[96] In contrast to these few unreconstructed radicals many of the aged deviants in this class take on an abiding bitterness and cynicism intensifying the crotchetiness and querulousness characterizing the temperament of many aged persons in our society.

Adjustment and Maladjustment

In the estimation of nonradicals with whom the radical participant comes into contact, he is either a worthless or dangerous member of society. He is stigmatized as a variety of criminal, troublemaker, coward, fool, "crackpot," and insane. In terms of the middle-class values of our society, values stressing occupational stability, working toward advancement, and family responsibility, he is a failure; his behavior is misguided and his life misspent. Consequently the radical must draw heavily if not exclusively upon a definition of the self reflected in the group or sect of which he is a part, or he must react to a societal conception broadened

[96] See Holbrook, Stewart, "Last of the Wobblies," *The American Mercury*, 62, April, 1946, pp. 462–468.

and extended in space and time. His sacrifices become meaningful in the eyes of a universal "mankind" or in the eyes of persons who will populate a future society – the world in the making. The imminence of such an appreciative society of the future is heralded by the myth constructed in the ideological interaction of the radical organization.

So long as a radical group or movement makes headway in tangible and demonstrable ways, its mythology is supported and the self of the participating radical is validated. However, over a long period of time the setbacks received by the movement place greater and greater strains upon the credulity of the followers of the new faith. The time for the coming revolution gets revised again and again; leaders must struggle heroically to define such failures as necessary stages of the revolution or as experiences from which "lessons" for the future are learned. The diminished size of the radical sect is made palatable by reemphasizing the fact that it is the "vanguard" of the revolution or the "little band of determined men" who will precipitate and give form to the revolt at a critical phase. The longer the person remains a member of revolutionary organization and the older he is, the greater is likely to be the trauma suffered from collapse of the movement. Something of the impact of the debacle of the revolutionary movement in Russia after 1905 can be gained from the following excerpt:[97]

> Revolutionists who but yesterday had stood at the head of millions saw the bonds which have linked them to the masses dissolve without a trace. Driven to impotent fury by each day's increment of evil they fell to quarreling among themselves, meanly, bitterly, denouncing error in each other, apportioning blame for defeat. The isolation which seemed more silent for the tumult that had just been stilled, they filled with the sound of their own quarrels. No secret admiration sustained them, no generous contributions, nor general sympathy, nor public expectation followed them as they returned to alien places.

Individuals, of course, differ in their responses to the disintegration of the social movement to which they have permanently attached themselves, depending upon such things as age, financial condition, and personal morale. However, even the tough-willed Lenin was cast into melancholy brooding, became irritable, restless, and, significantly, was unable to eat after he entered exile in Finland following the failure of the 1905 revolution in Russia. Apparently he regarded suicide as the only alternative to not being able to continue his life work with the revolutionary movement, being much impressed by the double suicide of Karl Marx's daughter and son-in-law after the failure of the 1905 revolution.[98] Suicides and in-

[97] Reprinted from *Three Who Made a Revolution*, by Bertram Wolfe, p. 475. Published by Dial Press, Inc Copyright, 1948, by Bertram D. Wolfe.

[98] *Ibid.*, p. 486.

sanity apparently were common in colonies of revolutionary refugees both after the upheavals of 1848 in Europe and that of 1905 in Russia.[99]

Among groups of defeated revolutionaries the revolutionary myth may appear in a form so grotesque and dissociated from reality as to lead to wild impractical ventures and so make the organization repellent to the more hardheaded professionals in it. Marx, Engels, and Lenin all spoke of this phenomenon as the "romantic left," and in the case of the former two it was the reason for retiring from active participation in the radical movement in favor of theoretical research and writing. It is interesting to note that a number of renegade revolutionaries have turned to writing, which suggests that for a few radicals equipped with auctorial skills transition to a reasonably satisfactory social role is possible. Some such writers have grown critical and condemnatory of their previous radical associates and have attacked the radical organizations to which they once belonged, although it must not be assumed that this is always done easily, for they have previously learned to hate the informer's role.

The writings of such ex-radicals tend to be chronicles of conspiracy and books of exposures, and from them we gather that the authors conceive their roles as self-appointed protectors of society against the threat of the radical movement. In this way, by pointing up the negative importance of subversive organizations, they also lend importance to their past lives, for they now become the means by which intimate knowledge of the radical dangers are brought before the public at large. This is made plain in the following direct quotation from an informant of the author

> It took me a long time before I could be frank and admit to myself and to others that I had once been a CP member. But as I look back now I am grateful for what I learned while in the party. My understanding of Communist trickery has helped me do the job of fighting it now when it is obviously the most serious threat we have against our democratic freedoms

The external limits of choice open to the renegade radical are somewhat broader in a democratically organized society than in an autocratic one. Such contingencies as imprisonment, exile, and economic disenfranchisement are less inevitably the consequences of his role, and verbal protest behavior can more easily be recast into forms and roles compatible with the culture. However, within a democratic society social acceptance of the renegade is likely to be greater among conservative and reactionary groups than among other radical groups.[100] It is precisely here that the internal limits in the form of guilt may enter into the symbolic process to make the

99 *Ibid.*

100 In the late nineteenth and twentieth centuries in Russia, renegade radicals were sometimes offered the fairly attractive and remunerative role of the police stool or *agent provocateur*.

renovated self less satisfying. Consequently we may ask most pertinently here whether the ex systematic radical may not, in many instances, find himself in situations conducive to marginality.

The Independent Radical's Adjustment

Most of our discussion of radicalization has concerned the participant in highly organized and sectarian activity in which the deviant ideology is a revolutionary kind. There are, of course, important differences between the sectarian revolutionary and the more individualized, independent or "free-lance" radical whose associations with other radicals are informal, loose alliances. Likewise, the radical whose deviant ideas are segmental and confined to one area of the culture will differ from one dedicated to revolutionary overturn of a whole society. The conscientious objector often has come under both of these two headings. His type of radicalism is expressible mainly during periods of war, although it may come out in fights against peacetime conscription. During a war the conscientious objector meets with discrimination and penalties, but these usually dissolve with the coming of peace. His problems of personal integration tend to be episodical.

The conscientious objector in our culture during times of war must necessarily deal with the unpleasant idea that his behavior reflects cowardice and evasion of civic duty. The frontier values and concepts of masculinity, virility, and willingness to fight for one's rights are not easily dissociated in the role of the pacifist. This does much to explain the dissatisfaction felt by many conscientious objectors with the type of jobs they were given in service camps during the Second World War. Perhaps it also accounted for the striving of many of these pacifists for the opportunity to become "guinea pigs" in scientific experiments. Those who served as fire fighters in forested areas seemed to display much more satisfaction with their roles, largely because the shadow of cowardice was banished from their roles and also because the local communities seemed to appreciate them more for the dangerous work they did.

The Christian ethic of nonviolence generally is a weak rationalization for conscientious objection in our culture unless it is continually reinforced by sectarian isolation. For this reason quite a number of pacifists who started out with religious rationalizations shifted to political conceptions of their roles during and after the Second World War. In service camps this was facilitated by the bad impression given to religious objection by more fanatical and unsophisticated sectarian objectors, the "Bible thumpers," so-called. Quite a few conscientious objectors fortuitously or by design were given deferred status during the war. Their plight was made difficult because of the knowledge that their work was part of the war effort. Furthermore, it was not only difficult but dangerous to carry on propaganda against the war in these roles.

Marginality

Striking cases of dual identifications between radical and nonradical roles arose out of the revolutionary developments in pre-1917 Russia, involving persons who were employed by the secret police to enter and spy upon the organizations striving to overturn the Czarist government. These individuals were not *agents provocateurs* in the ordinary sense of the word, for they rose high enough in revolutionary circles to occupy prestigeful roles of leadership. One such figure was Roman Malinovsky, a labor-union leader with a criminal record who was persuaded by the police to become a spy in their employment. His abilities enabled him to move into the inner circle of Bolshevik leaders and thus he became invaluable to the police. Eventually he was selected to run for election to the Duma itself, witnessing the odd spectacle of both the secret police and his revolutionary comrades working for his election. In the Duma he delivered fiery revolutionary speeches against the government while at the same time he was carrying on his exposures and secret denunciations of Bolshevik leaders. It was by no means clear where his loyalties lay; his behavior was genuinely ambivalent, and his self was badly fractured. For awhile he enjoyed tremendously the rewards of two conflicting roles, but ultimately the tension and guilt grew unbearable and he resigned suddenly from his position. Ultimately he was exposed by the Bolsheviks and shot.[101]

The Intellectual

There are numerous indications and explicit agreement among writers on radicalism that the role of the intellectual in the radical movement is only tenuously anchored in group acceptance, and that the critical, inquiring, factually based reactions of the intellectual cause him trouble in fully and unqualifiedly taking on the radical role and self. The intellectual by reason of his analytical habits of thought is quick to see the weaknesses of the social system in which he lives, and if his rewards are meager – as they are in many industrial societies – he is likely to make tentative or outright moves into the orbit of radical movements. But there he encounters rigidity of ideas and logical closure which are foreign to his nature. Moreover, he is often confronted with the distrust untutored workers hold for the educated person and the ill-disguised contempt of the professional actionists for what they regard as vacillation and indecision on his part. So strong

[101] Wolfe, *op. cit.*, pp. 535–557. Another famous case of dual identifications with the Russian secret police and with a terrorist organization was that of a Russian Jew named Aseff. See Bokolojewsky, Boris, *Aseff*, 1934.

is the reaction against intellectuals at times that some writers have spoken of the anti-intellectualism of radical movements.[102]

The educative process tends to beget ideological disillusionment, whether it is formal and academic or simply a process of self-education. We may grasp an understanding of the plight of a disenchanted intellectual in the following paragraphs recounting his decision to leave the Communist party and also see some of the consequences of his resignation:[103]

It was then that I began vaguely to comprehend that there was no such thing as freedom of thought inside the official Communist movement. These men were telling me that I had no right to select my own reading matter. They were directing me to close my mind to the utterances of persons whom they described as "political adventurers and dangerous renegades." . . . Mentally shocked into a daze by the impact of this blow against my belief that the party stood for decency and freedom, I could do nothing but nod in agreement to all that was said to me during the balance of the meeting. . . .

Breaking faith with a political movement that one has believed in devoutly as the salvation of the human race is an experience full of emotional strain. When I realized that the Communist party insisted on chaining my intellect to the "line" as the price of staying in the fold, I knew that I could not and would not stay. . . .

When the deadline came for me to hand in the polemic against Lovestone which the party bosses had instructed me to write, I sent them instead a polite announcement that I was severing all my past political connections. From that day on I have—so far as the party is concerned—lived in that hobgoblin world inhabited by the "Lovestoneites, Trotskyites, Lewisites, Coughlinites and underminers of big-three unity." These epithets, in CP jargon, connote darkness and evil, a world where all the party's enemies hatch plots to hamper the work of the faithful comrades. . . .

The first few weeks after my walkout of the Communist party into the role of a renegade were full of discomfort and loneliness. Most of my ex-comrades in Local 235 and in the entire CIO movement in Detroit, following the party orders, turned against me and chopped away at my status in the union at every opportunity. . . . For a time I flirted with the notion of skipping the whole works and sliding back into my previous way of life—back to a routine of work, ball games, beer gardens, and hang-overs. . . .

I was out in the cold at Cleveland so far as the CP was concerned. Politically I was a maverick in that convention. The Comies wanted none of me, and the anti-Communists, gathered mostly in the Reuther caucus, still suspected me of being too close to the Communists. As for the Thomas crowd, I was leery of them because I felt that they were too newly divorced from Homer

[102] See Maurer, J., *It Can Be Done*, 1938, for an example of anti-intellectual bias of an early socialist leader

[103] Fountain, Clayton W., *Union Guy*, 1949, pp 92–103 *passim*. Quoted by permission of The Viking Press, Inc , New York

Martin to be trusted much. For this reason I was pretty much of a lone wolf for eleven days of the convention.

Intellectual values must be considered as part of the larger culture complex we think of as "democratic liberalism." They become intertwined with other personal and social values and are given a special individualistic meaning in American culture which makes personal integration on the basis of a role in an authoritarian radical organization exceedingly difficult. Our concluding autobiographical-case material is valuable for illustration of the ramified conflicts distressing an acculturated and literate American girl who was bound to the Communist party by the emotional fulfillment it afforded her and the rescue it provided from her previous social isolation. A significant fact is that her loyalty to the local Communist organization was never entirely broken and that she never felt the compulsion to discredit the party. She wrote the case history only with reluctance, half seriously accusing the present writer of being an FBI agent. Her use of an assumed name and the third person in composing the document also have some meaning in terms of her role conflicts.

Louise B. did not become a member of the Communist party until the age of twenty-one; however the groundwork for her eventual membership had been laid in childhood. Louise had been the product of an unhappy home where there was absolutely no overt display of affection and a tone of emotional insecurity always present. Being orphaned at a very early age, she defined herself as a deviant from the very moment she entered school, seeing between herself and other children a sharp differentiation. She did not have parents, they did. They appeared self-confident, she was completely uncertain. They belonged to a gang, she was unpopular and had only herself and books for companionship. As a means of compensation, and being endowed with an above-average I.Q., she developed a knowledge of books far beyond her years. By the time Louise was twelve she had an understanding of current events that would have surpassed many a person in their twenties. Her favorite periodicals were the *Nation*, the *New Masses*, *Time*, etc., which she found in the home she made with a brother. Since the atmosphere at home was somewhat left of center, it was easy for her to accept and subscribe to much of what she read.

Then, at twelve, she was sent to a summer camp run by the Garment Workers' Union. While the ILGWU leadership was predominantly socialistic, the particular group running the camp had many Communists among them. In the evenings discussion meetings were held to acquaint the children with problems they would have to cope with in adult life. They discussed labor problems, read and criticized Marx and Engels, and were also given sex education. The result was a highly sophisticated group of adolescents. Most of them were like Louise, precocious, over-educated, the products of broken homes, and insecure among their more average contemporaries. They met in the city on Friday nights, as a kind of recreational group, but spent their time in discussions and doing "good works"—which consisted of raising money for Loyalist Spain, marching in May Day parades, boycotting Japan, etc. These friends and activities became the nucleus of Louise's social life for the succeeding three years.

When she went to college, it was with preconceived prejudices against fraternity life—and a natural predisposition to become active in political activities that would campaign against "labor exploitation," "imperialism," and "capitalism." Although she was approached by members of the Young Communist League on many occasions, she always refused to join. She felt that while she subscribed to many of the same ideas, she was too much of an individualist to submit to any organizational discipline. There was something in her "bourgeois" background that made her cling to a vague concept of "freedom of opinion" that she believed would be inhibited by membership in an organization. She always maintained that she was an effective worker, and could continue to be one outside of the party as well as in. There was a feeling she had about the party that she could never quite overcome—perhaps it was based on a kind of snobbery, but somehow she felt they were not quite so civilized, so tolerant, as they might be

A few years passed, during which time Louise left school, tried working, had a few unsuccessful flings at romance. We find her at twenty-one in Hollywood. She has been alone a good deal, 3,000 miles away from her family, and feeling a little bitter about her failure to get a job in the motion-picture industry, which had been a lifetime goal. Without taking the time to go into a complete history of Louise, I hope it will suffice the reader to accept the following as her predominant interests in life—first was the desire to find the affection she had missed during her life, preferably through marriage. Perhaps because of her very eagerness, she found it difficult to acquire. The second desire was to compensate for her imagined inadequacies by becoming famous. The movie industry was to be the means to that end. She would become a famous writer-director and "show them."

Seeing an advertisement about a course in short-story writing to be given by a writer whom she admired, Louise enrolled. Gradually, the school began to offer a happy substitute for loneliness. There were people with common interests whom she met—social affairs which she could attend, and classes at which her talent and precocity were praised. She became good friends with a girl who was, in fact, the first person who had showed her any warmth during her year in Los Angeles. The girl was an admitted Communist—an active worker, and an ardent disciple of the Cause. Louise, who had not been in contact with left wingers for a few years, was happy to be back in what she considered an intellectually stimulating environment—and subscribed to many of the ideas of her new-found friend, but when finally approached on the matter of joining the party demurred—for the old reason—some blockage that made it seem not "quite right." There was no immediate pressure put on her; but a few months later, the instructor of the class invited her to join a group that was to meet at his house. He told her that he had asked only the most promising members of the class to join in this "seminar" which would be concerned about writers' problems—and be mutually beneficial. Flattered, Louise accepted. It developed however, to be actually a class in dialectical materialism. As the group continued to meet, more and more were asked to join the party, until finally Louise was the only nonmember present. Being the last holdout made her feel guilty. These were all older, brilliant people who had been kind to her, and she felt somehow, that her refusal was a sign of ingratitude. The pressure was put on, and finally, at a party at which her friends and several writers who had a good deal of prestige appeal for her were present, a recruiting plea was made. At last her instructor turned to her, in the quiet room, and said "Louise B. is the only person present who is not a member." She felt as if all eyes were upon her—and the implied disappointment was too much for her, she signed up.

Later, she felt even more guilty, because she knew she had not joined because she really believed in Marxism, but because she had felt she owed it to them—because she had been afraid to say "no."

Soon she was assigned to a party group, meetings being held at the home of Mary; and many prominent Hollywood people were present. Although at all the meetings, Louise felt extremely uncomfortable, and did not dare to voice any disagreement for fear of the disapproval of other members, she remained a member. Soon, a job she had been trying to get in a studio for a year opened up miraculously for her. The boss was also a member of the party, as was his assistant. Though nothing was said, Louise felt, in a subtle way, further indebted and obligated. Gradually, her friends became party members, and there was no turning back. All departments of her life were now intimately related to the party. Yet she could never feel any real enthusiasm for it. However, though never an active worker, she dutifully read the literature and subscribed wholeheartedly to the "line." Her inner conflict came into focus a year later when the party announced its new program of no-strike pledges to the government. The painters' and carpenters' union of the studio had gone on strike, yet the party had instructed her to cross the picket line—an act which went against years of left-wing indoctrination. Louise told her boss that rather than do that, she would stay home and take a loss in wages. He became quite angry and chastised her for having poor Marxist discipline, and suggested he might report her to the party. Louise crossed the picket line daily, thereafter, but was deeply troubled at the contradiction to her philosophy which she could not swallow. Then a few weeks later a dear friend of hers resigned from the party. He explained to Louise that he just couldn't stomach the revivalist fanaticism within, and that he was afraid to ever express himself at meetings. She told him she was sorry he felt that way, but while verbally defending the party, agreed with him inwardly. She continued to keep up her friendship with him, and found it a little unbelievable when, a short time later, a committee came to visit her to advise her that she must no longer see this "Trotskyite" this "Enemy of Marxism." When she protested that he had no ill wishes against the party, and that she certainly intended to continue seeing him, she was warned that she, too, would be expelled if she did not obey. Shortly after this, owing to a revision in party tactics, the no-strike pledge was reversed, and Louise's union voted to strike. She felt inward disgust that a strike that only a few weeks before had been termed "unpatriotic" and "undisciplined" by the People's World, was now taken up as a holy cause. Like the other members of her union, Louise was out of work for eight months – yet, with a neat twist of party logic, prominent writers, directors, and actors who were party members along with Louise were permitted to cross the lines with immunity. It was perfectly obvious that the strike was a lost cause unless the actors and writers went out and joined the lesser-fry unions, and yet they refused to support the strike. It made Louise more than a little bitter to stand on the picket line and watch her comrades go through to pick up salary checks every week. Finally at the end of the year, a friend who was head of a department at a studio asked her to do some work. At first she refused, because it would be scabbing – but he argued that her one job would hardly affect the course of the strike. Not only because she needed the money – but more because of her own disgust with the whole situation, she accepted. She was tired of being a martyr for the cause – if it was O.K. for Mr. X., well-known movie star, to cross the lines, and the party did not call him a scab, then neither was she. The logic of the situation appeared just too phony for her to figure out. She worked for one week and promptly forgot about it. Still another change of line occurred within the party, and Louise, disillusioned, stopped attending meetings. Some months later, on being snubbed by a few former friends, she inquired as to why. She was informed that she was a Trotskyite and a scab. Realizing what this could do to her reputation in the small town of Hollywood, she called the party to deny the charges. She was abruptly informed that a "trial" would be held on such and such a date, with her as the defendant.

Feeling something like a victim of the French Revolution, she went – explained her case to a group that was about as receptive as a nest of cobras. At the end of her hearing, a verdict was handed down of "not guilty," and she asked if, in view of her doubts and conflicts, she would be permitted to resign from the party. She was told that, in view of her youth and emotional instability, this request would be granted, that word would be passed from group to group that she was not an enemy of the party, but in return for this leniency, she was to promise never to reveal the names of fellow members. She agreed. Louise left, feeling impressed with the party's largess, and determined to be ever loyal, though no longer a member.

Within a year she was to find out that nobody resigned from the party.

Everywhere she went, she was cut dead socially. A theater group to which she belonged asked her to resign and told her her presence was not welcome. Her friends were forbidden to see or talk to her. When the strike was settled, she found she was black-listed and could not get a job. She got a job working for a theater and was fired in one day – the grapevine had gotten to the boss. Her fiancé came to her and broke off their engagement –"party orders." Everywhere she went she faced complete ostracization. After a year of such treatment, she went to the party to ask why – had they not declared her not guilty? They shook their heads, said it was "unfortunate" and they knew nothing about her. Yet through one friend in the party, she knew that at each meeting her name was among those listed to "beware" of. She was either described as an FBI agent, a Trotskyite, or a Tenney Committee spy. To understand the full implications of the situation, one must realize that the whole life of this person was connected with the party – and that this label completely cut off her life. She pleaded with the party to "let her alone" and asked them what did they expect of her. "Leave town" they advised "and start over again"– if you can, knowing that wherever she went her history would follow. Louise began to suffer from acute depressions and anxiety attacks, and eventually underwent psychotherapy. After a year of treatment, she finally became convinced that she was not "worthless"– and perhaps the party was in the wrong – she was encouraged to find a new life – and gradually formed an adjustment and made friends elsewhere.

The matter of Communist-party membership did not affect Louise's family life, as being tolerant people, they did not care whether or not she was a member. But, as described previously, it affected her sex and social participation. Being cut off from friends and social life, it took her quite some time, almost two years, before she built up even the barest circle of contacts – always with the fear that some new friend might be a party member and "find out" about her. Her occupational status was affected, and necessitated her training to take up an entirely new career in order to make a livelihood. However, having passed through the worst period, she eventually formed an adjustment to life far more satisfactory than the previous one so dependent on a deviant role.

She had, of course, defined herself as a Communist ever since signing up, and could not but be affected by the negative societal definition of the role, no matter how much she attempted to rationalize it as propaganda. She did not, however, accept the definition of herself as a "Trotskyite," and refused to play the role of the disgruntled member who devotes his time to destroying the party. She still feels a kind of loyalty to the party, and will never permit it to be criticized, nor will she ever speak against it – however little value she may hold for individual members.

Selected Readings

Borkenau, F. *World Communism*, 1939

Dalke, Otto "Values and Group Behavior in Two Camps for Conscientious Objectors," *American Journal of Sociology*, 51, July, 1945, pp 22–33

Footman, David *Red Prelude*, 1945

Gambs, John *The Decline of the I.W.W*, 1932

Lasswell, Harold, and Dorothy Blumenstock *World Revolutionary Propaganda*, 1939

Oneal, James, and G. Werner *American Communism*, 1947

Stroup, Herbert *The Jehovah's Witnesses*, 1945.

CHAPTER 8

PROSTITUTION AND THE PROSTITUTE

The scientific study of sexual deviation in our culture imposes more problems than the study of any other form of sociopathic behavior. This is not so much the consequences of any dearth of treatises on the subject as it is the result of the heavily laden emotional content of the materials, the absence of any sure knowledge of what constitutes normal sex conduct, and the culture pattern of concealment associated with it. A large amount of the writing on this topic, particularly as it touches upon such things as perversions, extra-marital sex relations, and prostitution, is polemical or propagandistic to the extent that its value for scientific purposes is seriously compromised. Even the careful studies by social scientists of this area of sociopathic behavior must be accepted cautiously in a culture with strong puritanical antecedents which make dissimulation and dissociation usual concomitants of sexual deviation.

The Nature of Sexual Deviation

In a very general way deviant sex behavior may be classified in terms of its incidence, its visibility, and the degree of stigma and social rejection it provokes. Among the forms of sexual deviation most commonly encountered in our society are masturbation, heterosexual intercourse outside of marriage, homosexuality, and prostitution – probably in that order of frequency. Other unsanctioned sexual behavior is less usual and less well known, tending to be clinically and legally recognized under the ambiguous heading of "psychopathic." This embraces such diversified sexual expressions as exhibitionism, unprovoked erotic contacts in crowded public places (called "bustle-bumping" by some police), voyeurism (peeping), frigidity, impotence, fetishism, necrophilia (intercourse with dead persons), bestiality (intercourse with animals), incest, rape, anal eroticism, oral eroticism, sadism, and masochism. Of this second group, exhibitionism, unprovoked erotic contacts in public places, window peeping, and the oral and anal eroticism practiced by many homosexuals have the highest incidence. The others can be considered as comparatively rare.

The great preponderance of the sociopathic sexual behavior in our society has an extremely low visibility. It is either deliberately hidden or is given the appearance of other forms of behavior which are socially sanctioned. Prostitution in certain forms stands out as an exception to the secretive character of most of our sexual deviation. However, this is not true for all prostitution, especially that carried on by the so-called "higher class" prostitutes.

The most stringent social penalties are reserved for some of the more unusual sexual aberrancies such as incest, forcible rape, sodomy, and pederasty, which are subsumed under homosexuality, as well as for homosexuality in general. Prostitution probably can be placed after this group in so far as public stigma and censure are concerned, followed in turn by nonmarital heterosexuality. This last category, it should be noted, covers several types of sexual indulgence which are not all equally condemned. Sexual promiscuity comes close to prostitution with respect to the stigma it imparts, while adultery not complicated by promiscuity is somewhat less the basis for social rejections. Premarital sex relations arouse a minimum of effective social disapproval in our present-day society. Masturbation, once looked upon as the "solitary vice," stirs a strongly critical reaction in few instances and then usually where it assumes a special compulsive quality.

If we were to select the sexual pathology which is both highly stigmatized and at the same time has a relatively large number of practitioners, our choice undoubtedly would have to be homosexuality rather than the more frequently discussed prostitution. The number of prostitutes in contrast to the 3 or 4 million [1] persons estimated to be homosexuals is very small. Likewise, the penalties of homosexuality, as stated above, far exceed those for prostitution. A further inducement to devote our discussion to homosexuality lies in the well-defined subculture, special argot, and distinctive social organization which has evolved in conjunction with this behavior.

Despite the obvious need for systematic study of homosexuality, there remain good, sufficient reasons for making prostitution the subject of this chapter. The disproportionate significance which has been attached to prostitution in many cultures is in itself a challenging fact. The special nature of the societal reaction, in our estimation, has yet to be studied as primary sociological datum. Despite the many treatises on the subject, prostitution has not yet been adequately analyzed as a dynamic response to the mythology, societal definitions, and manipulations in the name of reform which compose the societal reaction.

Closer examination reveals that the significance of prostitution cannot be gauged by the mere numbers of prostitutes. Prostitution, as we shall try

[1] The lower limit of estimates of the numbers of homosexuals, which has been placed at from 2 to 3 per cent of our population See Ellis, H., *Studies in the Psychology of Sex*, 1936, J. McPartland, *Sex in Our Changing World*, 1947, Kinsey, A., *et al.*, *Sexual Behavior in the Human Male*, 1948.

to show, in many ways is a formal extension of more generalized sexual pathology in our culture, of which sexual promiscuity and thinly disguised commercial exploitation of sex in informal contexts play a large and important part. Prostitution also subsumes many forms of sex pathology, such as oral and anal eroticism, sadism, masochism, exhibitionism, and generalized lewdness which obviously are something more than simple commercialized heterosexuality outside of marriage. In a more general way prostitution must be understood as the organized patterns through which unintegrated sexual impulses of the members of many societies of the world have obtained expression. Its history in countless ways is the history of efforts by various societies to deal with unanticipated and unwanted anomalies of sexual behavior.

The Nature of Prostitution

An older definition of "prostitution" still remains the most tenable formulation. According to this, prostitution is sexual intercourse characterized by barter, promiscuity, and emotional indifference.[2] There must be some exchange of sexual favors for material return, a more or less indiscriminate indulgence in the sex act with many persons, and a dissociation of deeper feeling from the physical sex act in order to have true prostitution. While this conception permits the distinguishing of prostitution as a kind of behavior, it does not generally serve strictly to identify those who are prostitutes. The reason for this lies in the broad gamut of female behavior in our culture containing elements of prostitution. Thus shopgirls who have sex relations in return for a dinner and a show from their dates obviously are employing sex as a means to certain material goals. Wives who associate with other men when their husbands are away often are temporarily playing the prostitute's game. One writer has listed 11 different classes of women who can be defined broadly as "prostitutes," among which can be found juvenile delinquents, "free" girls, kept women, "loose" married women, and "gold-diggers." [3]

The definition of prostitution thus can only be a matter of stress and emphasis, with the most sharply demarcated prostitution apparent in the behavior system of the self-admitted professional prostitute, in which the three requisites of barter, promiscuity, and indifference are completely met. Adjacent to the role of the professional prostitute are a number of other roles implemented by commercialization of sex behavior, each with its differentiated systematic behavior and special symbolism. For example, the "B girl" is one who works at a bar or tavern, inducing men to drink

[2] May, G., "Prostitution," *Encyclopedia of the Social Sciences*, 12, 1933, p. 553.

[3] Reitman, B., *The Second Oldest Profession*, 1931, pp. 6–8.

and receiving a return from the management for this service. Selling her sexual favors may be a part of the role she plays, but both the societal and self-regarding attitudes differ in her case from those of a professional prostitute in a parlor house, where the ideal of a fair exchange for services rendered governs the relationship of the girl and the customer.

The Extent of Prostitution

Estimates of the number of prostitutes in our society are questionable because of the confusion and carelessness in the use of the term "prostitute," which more often than not is applied to any woman whose conduct is reprehensible or results in arrest. Estimates have ranged from 200,000 for the nation as a whole to 100,000 for one city alone.[4] The tendency born of the controversial attitudes toward the subject has been to exaggerate the number of prostitutes. The probabilities favor a conservative estimate, so that the number of women who live by prostitution most likely does not exceed 275,000. This conviction finds support from the fact that a very large number of men can be serviced by a single prostitute in a short period of time. This figure may run anywhere from 25 to as high as 150 in a single night or twenty-four-hour interval. Obviously not many prostitutes are needed to satisfy the sexual demands of the most profligate community. Memphis, Tennessee, with a 1940 population of 292,942 was estimated to have from 500 to 700 prostitutes in 1939. Calculating from this (using a figure of 600), the total number of prostitutes for the entire population of the United States would come to around 270,000.[5] Cincinnati, Ohio, whose population in 1940 amounted to 455,000, had 550 prostitutes known to its police.[6] An estimation based upon this ratio gives a lower figure of approximately 159,000 as the total number of American prostitutes. In 1947, in Los Angeles, arrests of females for prostitution and commercialized vice totaled 1,849 (exclusive of arrests in the county outside of the city). Estimating on the basis of this number, we reach a figure of somewhere near 140,000 prostitutes for the nation.[7] Inasmuch as prostitutes mainly inhabit urban areas, these computations probably are overestimates, although the degree of error is impossible to determine. Other than to indicate that they exist there is no way we know of to take into account the additional numbers of prostitutes who do not become known to the police or health authorities.

[4] See Elliott, M., and F. Merill, *Social Disorganization,* 1941, pp. 244*ff*.

[5] McGines, A. F., and H. Packer, "Prostitution Abatement in a Venereal Disease Program," *Journal of Social Hygiene,* 27, October, 1941, p. 360.

[6] Weatherly, E., "Local Control of Prostitution," *Journal of Social Hygiene,* 28, October, 1942, p. 386

[7] *Report of the Los Angeles City Police Department,* 1947, p. 117.

The Differentiation of Prostitutes

Prostitutes in the aggregate are primarily a one-sex, female group. However, it should not be overlooked that male prostitutes have existed in other cultures at other times, and furthermore that there is a small number of homosexual male prostitutes in our society today, plus a few men alleged to serve women in houses of assignation. Female prostitutes of necessity are young, since youth and physical attractiveness are the chief assets through which they obtain and hold their customers. Research carried on by the League of Nations based upon samples from 26 European and 2 American nations has disclosed that 73.8 per cent of prostitutes were below the age of 31. The modal age fell between 21 and 25 years in nearly all of the samples despite the fact that the samples were far from homogeneous.[8] Los Angeles data corroborate the age characteristics of prostitutes found in other studies. The age composition of women arrested for vice there from 1945 to 1948 is presented in Table 26.

Table 26. Age Composition of 8,991 Women Arrested for Prostitution and Commercialized Vice in Los Angeles, 1945–1948 *

Age	Number	Per cent
19 and under	345	3.8
20–24	3,223	35.8
25–29	2,116	23 5
30–34	1,357	15 1
35–39	1,033	11 4
40–44	490	5 4
45–49	237	2.6
50 and over	190	2.1
Total	8,991	99 7

*Compiled from *Reports of Los Angeles Police Department*, 1945–1948

The racial and nativity characteristics of American prostitutes have undergone pronounced changes in the past several decades. Apparently at one time large numbers of prostitutes in some of our cities were foreign-born. Old data for New York City in the mid-nineteenth century record 1,238 out of its 2,000 prostitutes at the time as having been foreign-born [9] The sample from the United States and Canada in the League of Nations' study to which we have referred showed a disproportionate number of Indian women, Negro women, and those of foreign parentage among the prostitutes. While other studies tend to confirm the disproportions of racial minorities among prostitutes, they refute the idea that the foreign-born

[8] *Prostitutes: Their Early Lives*, League of Nations Advisory Committee on Social Questions, 1938, Part 1, p. 12.

[9] Sanger, W , *The History of Prostitution*, 1927, rev. ed., p. 460

are overrepresented among prostitutes. For example, a survey of sexually delinquent girls found that only 7.8 per cent of the total were of foreign birth.[10] Still other evidence from New York penal institutions demonstrated that the number of the foreign-born inmates was smaller than was expected, and that of the foreign-born delinquents fewer were sex offenders. Also, within the sex-offender category the percentage of foreign-born prisoners who had been prostitutes fell below those of the white and Negro native-born women.[11] In Los Angeles in 1947 only 4.9 per cent of the women arrested for prostitution and similar violations were foreign-born. Only 6 out of 276 "B girls" were foreign-born. However, 44.1 per cent of all women arrested for vice were Negro, and approximately 12 per cent were Mexican.[12] Both figures are out of keeping with the relative sizes of these minority groups in the local community, that for Negroes far more so than for Mexicans. While prostitutes of foreign birth may have once existed out of proportion to their population numbers, it is clear that this is no longer true except perhaps in special ethnic situations. The aging of the immigrant population and restrictive quotas in effect since 1920 have greatly reduced the probability that any large number of foreign-born women will be prostitutes. The apparently high rate of prostitution among Negroes is a special phenomenon connected with their recent urbanization. It is also associated with the social facts of mobility.

Prostitutes in the aggregate display a characteristic of high mobility, a function of their role, which more or less requires that they move from one city to another. The weight of logic and evidence also favors the idea that they are drawn from a class of women who for one reason or another have become detached from their home communities. In a study of sex offenders in San Antonio, Texas, it was brought out that only 11 out of 50 in the group were residents of the community where they were arrested; 15 had come to San Antonio from elsewhere within the state, and 24 were residents of other states.[13] Although we do not have conclusive evidence at hand to clinch the point, there is room to believe that prostitutes have been made up largely of rural migrants to urban areas, or perhaps even more, of migrants from small towns. That migration and mobility are the significant differentiae of prostitutes rather than specific racial or ethnic background receives support from the history of groups predominating among New York City prostitutes. In the middle of the nineteenth cen-

[10] Elliott, M., *Correctional Education and the Delinquent Girl*, 1929, pp. 23–24.

[11] Fernald, M., *et al.*, *A Study of Women Delinquents in New York State*, 1920, pp. 388–389.

[12] *Report of Los Angeles Police Department*, 1945, pp. 126, 128, 135

[13] Waggoner, L., "Girls and Women Apprehended by Police in San Antonio, Texas, for Prostitution and Allied Offenses," *Journal of Social Hygiene*, 28, October, 1942, p. 390.

tury women from the British Isles figured quite large in the prostitute population, these in turn giving way at the end of the century to women from Eastern Europe. From 1920 on, large numbers of Negro migrants from the Southern states swelled the ranks of New York harlotry. In other words, to generalize, a historical sequence obtained in which the most recent migratory population contributed most heavily to the numbers of prostitutes.[14] The demographic qualities of migrant groups which are conducive to prostitution will be touched upon in discussing the patrons of prostitutes.

The findings of a number of researches concur in placing the origins of prostitutes in the lower social and economic strata of our population. However, this is not to say that prostitutes come from a pauper class or to imply that their behavior is an effect of grinding poverty. They have come for the most part from poor but not extremely poor homes, where fathers have been unskilled and skilled laborers. Further evidence of low status prior to prostitution derives from the occupations in which the girls have been most heavily represented. Waiting on tables in restaurants, domestic service, and factory work account for the work experience of most prostitutes. Other early lines of work followed by prostitutes include stenography, nursing, clerking in stores, work in laundries and cheap entertainment.

In Table 27 we see the occupations which were given by women arrested on vice charges in Los Angeles in 1948. Waitresses stand at the top of the list along with housewives, those in domestic service, maids, and factory workers. Taken together this group accounted for 71 per cent of all the arrests. The large number of those giving "domestic service" and "maid" as employment which they have followed is a direct indication of the heavy representation of Negro women in the sample. It is possible that a goodly percentage of the women who have designated themselves as housewives are professional prostitutes living with pimps. Such nominal or pseudomarital arrangements afford a certain amount of concealment of their real vocation.[15]

There is no reliable evidence that prostitutes are generally defective in intelligence, although widespread credence has been given to the idea that a large and significant percentage of prostitutes are feeble-minded. The comparative data on prostitutes from various European and American countries listed two-thirds of all those studied as being normal in intelligence, 4 per cent mentally deficient, and the rest falling into a marginal or borderline category. However, a wide variation existed in the ratios of

[14] Waterman, W., *Prostitution and Its Repression in New York City, 1900–1931*, 1932, pp. 129f.

[15] For occupations of prostitutes, see *Prostitutes, Their Early Lives*, pp. 38–42, and Fernald *et al.*, *op. cit.*, Chap. 11.

the different samples in regard to the percentages of those with normal and abnormal intelligence. Those who assembled the data specifically commented upon their unsatisfactory character on this point.[16] Other research material on this question leads to a conclusion that while mean intelligence for women delinquents in general, sex delinquents and prostitutes, falls somewhat below that of the general population and that of selected samples of working girls, nevertheless the range of intelligence is about the same for delinquent and nondelinquent females. The majority of

TABLE 27. OCCUPATIONS GIVEN BY 1,825 FEMALES ARRESTED FOR PROSTITUTION AND COMMERCIALIZED VICE IN LOS ANGELES, 1948 *

Occupation	*Number*
Waitress	470
Housewife	377
Domestic service.	208
Maid	129
Factory worker	120
Nurse	43
Laundry worker	40
Cook	34
Unemployed	33
Stenographer.	28
Clerk	25
Model.	23
Beauty parlor	21
Saleswoman	20
Others	254
Total	1,825

*Data supplied by Statistician's Office, Los Angeles Police Department, 1949.

sexual delinquents fall under the same portion of a curve representing their intelligence scores as nondelinquents or as nonsexual delinquents.[17] Until it can be shown that a group of nondelinquent women equated for social and economic status with a group of prostitutes have significantly greater average intelligence, then the traditional conviction that the prostitute is a mental defective must be rejected.

The educational attainments of prostitutes throw further light upon this question. In the past, the number of years of education completed seems to have been lower for prostitutes than for the general population. It is very questionable if this is true any longer. Table 28 gives the clear impression that prostitutes are drawn from women with all degrees of education and that a goodly representation of college-trained girls follow the trade. Ideally the percentages in the table would be compared with

[16] *Prostitutes, Their Early Lives,* pp 22–27

[17] Fernald *et al*, *op cit*, pp. 433, 512–516.

percentages of the general female population with different degrees of schooling. Unfortunately the age characteristics of prostitutes make this comparison impossible. In any event the figures stand as a refutation of the popular idea that prostitutes are to any significant extent feeble-minded or illiterate or poorly educated.

In terminating this discussion of the differentiating characteristics of prostitutes, it must be said that much of what is imputed as their differentiae may prove to be in final analysis a function of the societal reaction. Most if not all studies of prostitutes rely for cases upon those who have

TABLE 28. NUMBER AND PER CENT OF FEMALE ARRESTS FOR PROSTITUTION AND COMMERCIALIZED VICE BY YEARS OF EDUCATION, LOS ANGELES, 1947*

Amount of education	Number	Per cent
Not reported	15	0.81
None .	29	1.57
1-8 grades	540	29.20
1-4 years of high school	1,091	59.00
1-4 years of college	174	9.41
Total	1,849	100.00

Report of Los Angeles Police Department, 1947, pp. 150–151.

been arrested or upon cases in social welfare agencies. Many of the more "successful" prostitutes and those who have protection from arrest obviously seldom or never appear in statistical compilations.[18] Until we have studies of these prostitutes with low social visibility, the possibility that we may be dealing with a distorted picture of this sociopathic group will always be present.

THE PATRONS OF PROSTITUTES

The fact that patrons of prostitutes have not been held equally guilty of immoral conduct and thus treated as deviants means that little effort has been made to study them. However, we can set down with reasonable certainty some facts about them. On the whole, patrons of prostitutes tend to be older, middle-aged men who are single, divorced, or separated. These men generally occupy a low socioeconomic position and have limited amounts of formal education.[19] Within the socioeconomic strata from which they come, the customers of prostitutes are more often identified with mobile occupations; migratory casual workers, salesmen who travel, soldiers, sailors, and truck drivers are the classes of employees in which we expect to find prostitute-frequenting men.

Certain types of deviants are more or less compelled to make use of

[18] Landesco, J., *Illinois Crime Survey*, 1929, p. 1,156.

[19] Kinsey *et al.*, *op. cit.*, Chap. 20.

prostitutes for sexual satisfactions because of the rejections they receive from the other women in their communities. Gross ugliness, physical handicaps, lack of social skills necessary to get to know sexually accessible women, and aberrant sexual drives themselves all tend to disqualify men for other heterosexual opportunities and leave them the sole choice of prostitutes for their outlets. It often happens that members of ethnic minorities must turn to prostitutes for sexual gratification because of the unbalanced, very high sex ratios in their own populations. For example, the sex ratio of the Chinese in some American communities in the past ran as high as 10 to 1. Filipinos, Japanese, and other Asiatic immigrants in early days, and even in the more recent past, to some degree have had comparably high sex ratios.

In addition to the classes of men who provide more regular patronage for prostitutes, there must be included the dissatisfied husband, the wealthy playboy (in the old days known as the "sporting man"), the sexually curious adolescent, and criminals of many sorts. The aggregate differentiation of prostitutes must be viewed at least in part as an adaptation to the qualities of the customer population. Likewise, the modal tendencies in the organization and behavior systems of prostitution must be interpreted in the light of the sexual requirements of the patrons as a class. Thus, for instance, the swift consummation of coitus by the prostitute and her lack of inclination for accessory sex play may be class-determined phenomena as well as being the consequences of the impersonal and pecuniary nature of her relationship with her customers. Variations in the patterns of prostitution can be related to the variability in the sociocultural characteristics of the clientele. We shall pay more detailed attention to this in our subsequent discussion of prostitution among minority groups.

The Contexts of Prostitution

The meaning of the act of prostitution for the girl who participates is far from being constant, but on the other hand is not so diversified as to prevent classification. The prostituting behavior may be associated in several general ways with the central or preferred role of the female principals. A substantial amount of disapproved sexual activity, including prostitution, can be laid to unique personal needs which underly the sex indulgence. A girl with a strong sense of inferiority may have a compulsive need to be sexually promiscuous, and some such girls may eventually find an adjustment as prostitutes. Urgent need to rebel against authority may be expressed by a woman through flagrant violations of the community's sexual taboos. Case histories of psychotic women often bring to light interludes of loitering, soliciting, and prostitution in the picture of their symptoms.

A far greater proportion of sexual aberrancy is situational, *i.e.*, a product of the numerous stresses, strains, and conflicts in our culture which surround the sex act and which lead to segmental integration of normal and sociopathic sex behavior. In fact, a strong case may be made that our culture normally disposes women to utilize sex for many purposes outside of the marriage relationship. It provides a widespread impetus to quasi prostitution as well as informal and formal commercialization of the sex act. As one writer has cogently and realistically put it, there are elements of prostitution in the behavior of most women in our culture.[20] Being in an inferior position from the standpoint of power and control over material rewards in our culture, it is not unnatural that women should resort to sex as a means of redressing the status differential. This is perceived in the gamut of reactions from the salesgirl who "charms" a male customer into purchasing goods, through the sale of war bonds with kisses by actresses, to the sexual submission of a secretary to her boss in order to hold her job.

Our laissez-faire economy and its integration through a price system allows the relatively free operation of supply and demand whether it be commerce in grain futures or sex service. The persistent demand for prostitution has been created by many cultural factors; generally in our culture there is a ubiquitous and strong sexual stimulation in the guise of women's dress, advertising, news, literature, art, and the motion pictures. At the same time, as a consequence of our traditional puritanical taboos, there is comparatively little opportunity to indulge in sex intercourse outside of marriage. The postponement of marriage beyond biological maturity in response to our high standard of living feeds the demand for sex outside marriage. Likewise the large number of men in occupations rendering them highly mobile and less likely to marry reinforces the demand for bartered sex. The disorganization of family life in our culture continually supports the need for prostitution, through divorce and unsolved marital tensions. The statement has been made that our traditional Euro-American culture prevents the integrated expression of love feelings in the male in marriage because of the contrary expectations of what the sex act should be for the husband and wife.[21] The presence of a fair number of married men among customers of prostitutes would seem to corroborate this conclusion. Closely related to the contradictory definitions of the sex act within marriage are those pervading premarital courtship and sex relations wherever they occur. Many men enter into sex intercourse with a strong predatory urge which converts the act into one of honorific conquest and makes fulfillment a symbol of prowess in competition. The frustration and sense of being used left in women subjected to rough love affairs of

[20] Davis, Kingsley, "The Sociology of Prostitution," *American Sociological Review*, 2, October, 1937, pp 744–755.

[21] Becker, H., and R. Hill, *Marriage and the Family*, p. 161.

this sort unquestionably provoke a counter-tendency on the part of many of them to structure the sex act in terms of tangible gain.

The press of situational factors making for prostitution falls more heavily upon some women than upon others. It has already been indicated that prostitutes tend to come from families with low socioeconomic status. Their general education and their occupational resources may have been more restricted than is true of women in higher social classes. Nevertheless, they tend to develop the same standards of material aspiration as other women, through a common exposure to mass advertising and other sources of commercial propaganda. Within this general situational impasse and frustration, there are those girls who are more affected than others. For example, girls who come from crowded homes and areas where they have witnessed early in life gross sexual behavior by parents and others may find it much easier to use the prostitute's alternative to reach the cultural-induced goals.

Prostitution may be implicit in occupational situations and roles. Many lower class women find employment in occupations where their superiors and others have preconceptions that low status and sexual laxity go together. Many female pursuits, those of waitresses, domestic servants, show girls, manicurists, masseuses, models, and stenographers, are occupational analogues of prostitution. It is not fortuitous that many prostitutes have been waitresses, taking the next logical step from an occupation in which the female worker is dependent for her livelihood upon masculine largess in the form of tips. In recapitulation, the wonder is not that so many women become prostitutes but rather that so many do not.[22]

A well-defined instance of the way in which even professional prostitution rests upon a recurrent situational basis can be noted in the presence of a sizable number of female drug adicts and chronic alcoholics among prostitutes. Long held to be examples of demoralized prostitutes, in reality these women have resorted to prostitution as a means of securing the money necessary to purchase drugs or liquor. In these cases the prostitute's role is clearly a subordinate one, and were these women supplied with drugs or liquor from some other source, it can be assumed that their prostitution would cease.

Systematic Prostitution

Prostitution is a venerable behavior system with antecedents reaching far back into historic times. Prostitutes were known among the early Hebrews, and their profession flourished among the ancient Greeks and the Romans. While it often has been practiced simply and on an informal basis, the tendency has been for it to be organized, particularly in more

[22] Davis, *op. cit.*

recent times. There are three well-defined patterns of organized prostitution distinguishable in present-day society: that carried on in parlor houses, that operated on a call-house basis, and finally, operation through tenuous connections with nominally respectable business enterprise.

The parlor house presents the most spectacular organization of prostitution. This may be conducted by a female entrepreneur, a madam working on her own, or it may be an integral unit in some sort of vice combine or "syndicate." Houses of this sort are usually in segregated areas, in red-light districts in the so-called "disorganized areas" of the city or on its outskirts. In the past, some parlor houses have been sumptuously decorated and furnished, the most famous of which was run by the Everleigh sisters in Chicago, Illinois, between 1900 and 1911. More often the houses have garish furnishings with an inevitable juke-box to provide a cheap musical setting. In days past, houses retained large numbers of girls, but present-day houses have fewer, often no more than three or four.

In the past, efforts were made to secure girls consisting of a wide variety of physical types, of different races and nationalities, in order to satisfy the exotic tastes of customers. Trading on these known tastes, girls often masqueraded as French or Spanish in order to increase their patronage. There is less of this today, but some effort is made to meet the demand for variety by a rapid change of the house inmates. A house is usually organized with a madam in charge who maintains order and discipline in the house and keeps financial accounts. There is a standard division of the fees collected by the girls, with deductions for the house, for linen, medical examinations, legal protection, and miscellaneous items. In better houses there may be rules governing such things as stealing from customers, protection of their identity, and dating customers outside. Better houses have been known to place great emphasis upon the wardrobe of the girls and to make efforts at instructing them in etiquette and decorum Others, probably the majority, make little pretense at respectability.

Relationships between girls in houses are highly competitive, with status determined by the amount of money earned and the number of customers. Understandings of a monopolistic nature sometimes grow up between the girls to prevent the taking of one another's steady customers. Generally ingroup morale and solidarity is missing in the house, except in relation to raids or arrests by legal authorities. Solidarity is precluded by the keen competition, the social and cultural heterogeneity of the girls, and their rapid turnover. This means that the house organization is implemented by external controls, such as fines and threats of expulsion. The difficulty of working alone in a community with segregation may make this latter threat a powerful control. The girls in the protected parlor house can, and sometimes do, report the independent operator, or "chippie," to the police.

The prostitute's skills are not monopolizable; they do call for a learning period but they can be acquired by almost any woman in a month or two under the tutelage of the other house workers. The girls become specialized as to the type of sex act they will engage in; some are known as "one-way" girls, while others will practice perversions, and still others double in obscene "shows" or dances. The girls not only acquire the art of "pleasing" their customers so that they will return but also become fairly adept at handling unruly or drunken customers. Superficial methods of detecting venereal disease are part of the repertoire of the prostitute's skills.

The morality of the professional prostitute generally overlaps that of the community area and social class from whence she comes in all respects save her commercialism of sexual intercourse and sexual promiscuity. While professional prostitutes often live in the same area with criminals, and may even be in contact with them, they are not given to serious criminal behavior.[23] Certain forms of petty larceny, such as "rolling" drunken customers, apparently falls into the category of permissive norms, "if you can get away with it." On the other hand, among house madams this is likely to be a negative compulsive because of the risk of police action it incurs. For the same reason, the prostitute working alone in hotels may disapprove of robbing customers. Taking drugs tends to be a permissive rather than a compulsive for prostitutes. Prostitutes are just as likely to censure drunkenness as other persons, particularly in a parlor house.

Compared with criminal groups, prostitutes develop only a rudimentary argot, estimated to contain at best no more than fifty words, many of which are secondhand criminal terms.[24] The speech of prostitutes shares many attributes of that of shop and factory girls, being cheap and tawdry and well larded with trite slang from popular songs and pulp magazines. However, the prostitute can make claim to a facile and pungent mastery of profanity, which is freely applied when the occasion demands. The prostitute lacks an argot mainly because secret communication with others is not necessary for her trade. Also, the same factors making for low group morale among prostitutes militate against the growth of a special language.

The institution of the call house has been a response to recent urban trends and the changed societal reaction to segregated prostitution. The call house gives greater concealment to the prostitute and more anonymity to the customer. It reduces the visibility of prostitution and eliminates the troublesome necessity of having to maintain the more elaborate organization of the parlor house, which in many cities must move at short intervals

23 *Prostitutes, Their Early Lives*, p. 59.

24 Maurer, David, "Prostitutes and Criminal Argots," *American Journal of Sociology*, 44, January, 1939, pp. 546–550.

in order to survive. It further permits the utilization of part-time or occasional prostitutes as well as professionals, together with profit making from clandestine sex relations not ordinarily considered prostitution. One modern arrangement makes use of respectable female clerks or shopgirls and others who wish to supplement their earnings. The madam keeps a list of their names and telephones them to go on "dates" with out-of-town men or other men in search of a good time. Control is retained over these contacts by the ever-present threat to turn the girl over to the police if she perchance tries to exploit the contact without paying the madam's price.

Concealment required for successful prostitution in a community where a policy of repression is in force is also made possible by working behind front organizations. On the surface these are legitimate business or professional enterprises but in reality are functioning vice organizations. Cheap hotels, rooming houses, tenements, night clubs, massage parlors, bars, auto courts, and occasionally a chiropractor's office come under this classification. Prostitutes often live in a cheap hotel to which they repair with the men they pick up in the course of an evening, with the ready collusion of the proprietor. The proprietor or desk clerk obtains his share of the proceeds from charging the girls for occupancy of the room, or may take a fixed amount for each "trick." The control over the girls may be vested in a vice ring which places the girls in various hotels, shifting them from one to another as the need arises and reaching appropriate understandings with the proprietor, desk clerk, and house detective.

Some prostitutes carry on as independent functionaries by tacit understandings with landlords and proprietors. They sometimes set themselves up in hotels, flats, or even in apartments in better residential areas and rely upon go-betweens such as bell-hops, taxi drivers, and others to drum up customers for them. Recently in some cities where police aggressively enforce the laws against prostitution, there has been less reliance upon these intermediaries, especially bellhops. In one area familiar to the writer, girls made contacts in a drugstore at a busy intersection where they discreetly passed out cards tokening their wares to likely prospects. The druggist and clerks were fully apprised of the traffic, but since the girls were inconspicuous and because they made generous purchases they were not molested. The clients of the girls made their ways alone to the address on the card after the girls had departed, so it was the most casual and superficially innocent type of solicitation. Although independent operation by the prostitute is fraught with many hazards, above all if the girl is exposed as a prostitute, the trend in the patterning of prostitution seems to be in this direction.[25] This would suggest in some respects greater

[25] Thomas, W. I., *The Unadjusted Girl*, 1925, p 150.

individualization and professionalization which makes business reciprocity the bond between prostitutes and accessories rather than fear, intimidation, or indentured servitude associated with the house pattern of organization.

There are some ecological features of prostitution to be noted; first of all, while prostitution has long been thought of as one of the more scarlet sins of the "wicked city," more recent evidence is to the effect that flagrant prostitution is less characteristic of metropolitan centers than it is of smaller cities and towns.[26] The regions in which prostitution flourishes, at least in more open form, are the South Atlantic, East South Central, West South Central, Mountain, and Pacific states. The New England and Middle Atlantic states in the recent past seem to have had the fewest vice resorts, with the East and West North Central states occupying an intermediate position.[27] All of these data merge to give weight to the idea that open prostitution waxes more in newly industrialized areas into which urban influences are extending and that older urban areas either have less prostitution or that they have considerably transmuted the forms prostitution takes. However, specific local conditions are often more outstanding in the spatial patern than the regional distribution. Thus prostitution thrives in communities or areas with high sex ratios, such as mining and lumbering communities. Towns near army camps and naval bases attract prostitutes more than others, as do seaport towns and border communities, and as do political capitals, including the capital of the United States.

Within urban communities large enough to show ecological patterning, the areas of prostitution tend to be the location of deteriorated housing, high mobility, homeless men, and first-generation immigrant settlement. Spotted here and there in the settlement areas of immigrants are nationality groups among whom no prostitution can be found, at least not within the neighborhoods where they live. In Chicago the Italian area and the first-generation Jewish settlement several decades ago seemed to be free of prostitution in the findings of one survey.[28] In years before the second decade of this century prostitution in the United States was pretty well confined to police-designated areas, but following the reform movements at this time it apparently became decentralized and scattered, not randomly into all areas, however. It tended to invade neighborhoods of declining housing.[29] Commercialized vice now tends to be distributed according to

[26] Kinsie, Paul M., "The Prostitution Racket Today," *Journal of Social Hygiene*, 27, October, 1941, p 333

[27] *Ibid*

[28] Reckless, Walter, "Indices of Commercialized Vice Areas," *Journal of Applied Sociology*, January–February, 1926, pp 249–258.

[29] Reckless, Walter, *Vice in Chicago*, 1933, p 140

mobility, transportation arteries, and the anonymous qualities of the area. While it has long been held that strict repression of prostitution tends to scatter it throughout urban areas, in Los Angeles the recent drive against organized commercialized vice has driven prostitution into the deteriorated areas in the center of the city, with practically no vice found in outlying communities.[30] Efforts to accurately determine the spatial distribution of prostitution within urban communities is complicated by the differential visibility of the behavior, which may be quite high in one area and almost undetectable in others.

Patterns of Prostitution in Ethnic Groups

Prostitution in ethnic groups is often a function of their sex and age characteristics, especially the former. The connection between uneven sex distributions and prostitution in a segregated group seems to be closest where the men of the group are cut off from contacts with the majority-group females. In some part this condition has prevailed among some groups of the foreign-born in which the earliest immigrants consisted largely of males in the young adult years. In so far as barriers of language and culture kept the more differentiated immigrant males from sexual contacts with native females, the tendency was strong for them to rely upon prostitutes for sexual purposes.

The foreign-born female in a masculinized minority group, being much sought after, holds a very advantageous position in so far as profiting from sexual relationships goes. Where she chooses to commercialize her erotic connections, she may enjoy what is practically a monopoly. Exploitation of the men of her group by native harlots augments the call for her services, which are enhanced by a community of language and culture. This type of situation existed in striking form among the Chinese in San Francisco in the first decades after their immigration. In the 1880's one journalist estimated that there were 2600 prostitutes for a Chinese population at the time of 30,000.[31] Both white and Chinese prostitutes earned very handsome incomes from their contacts, which made a Chinese clientele actually more attractive to many white prostitutes than men of their own race. Because many Chinese were laundrymen, who worked long hours, it became a custom of some of the white girls to make the rounds of the laundries to solicit trade. They came to be known as "street pullers." However, a great deal of blackmail arose out of this practice, which partly explains why girls began to be imported from China for special use as prostitutes. This was generally done by the tongs, but was also done by groups of merchants, who usually retained exclusive

[30] *Undercover Survey*, American Association of Social Hygiene, 1947.

[31] Gor Yun, L., *Chinatown Inside Out*, 1936, p. 223.

sexual rights to the girl.[32] This last pattern is occasionally met with among Filipinos in Los Angeles at the present time.

The situation of prostitutes in the Negro group differs in several important ways from that for prostitutes in general. Commercialized vice is a relatively new thing among Negroes, being a product of their recent urbanization. Sex ratios of urban Negroes are much more balanced than in other minority groups and are not too different from that of the white population. Negro women of rural, Southern origin have taken to prostitution in comparatively large numbers, probably because of the freer sex practices followed by this class of Negroes[33] and because less stigma is attached to prostitution than is true among white persons. The economic opportunity which prostitution affords Negro women, who can aspire to little beyond low-paying, menial work, is a strong inducement for many. There is some evidence that prostitution among Negroes is less systematized and more apt to be associated with petty criminal practices. Where white men are involved – and a sizable share of the patronage is from whites – the exploitation of the customer may have certain symbolic value tied up with the dominance-submission relationships between the two racial groups.

Social Visibility of Prostitution

In ancient cultures and in cultures of recent times, including our own in the nineteenth century, prostitutes have been a class set apart, with special locale and formally demarcated status symbolized in dress, manner, and speech. In Japan, special beautified quarters of its cities were designated as sites for prostitution. In Tokyo this quarter was one of the show places of the city. Japanese courtesans often were prominently displayed in cages on the streets; in genteel establishments they had their names and emoluments advertised on the equivalent of a marquee at the entrance. Special costumes and hair-dresses often have been symbols of the prostitute, for example, in ancient Rome prostitutes usually dyed their hair red or yellow. In some cultures these appurtenances were guarded and perpetuated by sumptuary laws. In the nineteenth and very early twentieth centuries in the United States when prostitutes were quartered in red-light districts, they could be told apart from the respectable middle-class women of the community by their flamboyant clothes, abbreviated dresses, bobbed hair, rouged faces and lips, their use of tobacco, liquor, and profanity and general bold mien in public. In other words, the social cleavage between the "good" and "bad" women was not only sharp but could be quickly determined by cultural insignia. Today much of the behavior and morality

32 *Ibid.*, pp 229*f*

33 Frazier, E. F., *The Negro in the United States*, 1949, pp. 318*f*.

of the prostitute has made its way upward and has been appropriated by the middle-class woman in her revolt against her traditional role. The external differentiae of the prostitute have vanished, so that to separate her from the society matron, the debutante, or college girl in a hotel lobby is an almost impossible task.

In addition to all this, the freer circulation of women throughout the community, bringing them into casual public contacts with men makes soliciting far less conspicuous than it once was. Furthermore, urban prostitutes have learned ways and means of deliberately reducing their visibility. Detection of prostitution among Negroes is an especially frustrating job, being made extraordinarily difficult by their crowded housing conditions, the general instability of the marital alliances in the class from which they come, and a collective unwillingness of Negroes to give information to investigators. A partial measure of the ratio between visible and invisible prostitution is brought to light by the comparative success of various vice investigators in Harlem in New York City. In a three-month period one Negro investigator who knew the section reported a total number of sex violations which exceeded the combined reports of four white investigators, even though he worked fewer days per week.[34]

The Societal Reaction

Perhaps no other form of sociopathic behavior, unless it be drug addiction, has accumulated about it such a fund of myths and folklore as prostitution. The folklore of prostitution largely concerns the manner in which women become prostitutes, the type of life they lead, and the inevitable culmination of their lives in demoralization, disease, and early death. This viable mythology has a long-time foundation in ancient Hebraic attitudes toward sex, given Catholic sanction in the writings of the early Christian Fathers, and revived and refurbished in the so-called "Protestant ethic" born with emergent capitalism in the sixteenth century. In general, sex has long been regarded in our culture and its antecedents as sinful, dirty, and debilitating. Woman, as the purveyor of sex, has been held to be mysterious, unclean, a temptress and spokesman of the devil himself.

The most consistent and systematized stereotyped ideas about prostitution arose and gained widespread acceptance about the first decade of the present century. While clearly an extension of archaic sex attitudes, their immediate and special expression was a phenomenon of the change in attitudes toward prostitution associated with the larger processes of urbanization. About this time the white-slave myth began to make its appearance in newspaper and magazine stories, moral tracts, exposés, and "penny-dreadful" novels. It even crept into the writings of more careful

[34] Waterman, *op. cit.*, p. 127.

students and is more than palely reflected in the research conducted by the League of Nations and the propaganda circulated by the American Association of Social Hygiene. In brief, the white-slave myth explains prostitution as the consequence of the machinations of a special class of procurers who obtain innocent, unsophisticated girls, under age or of foreign extraction, by false pretense, drugs, and coercion. These girls are purportedly lured or seduced by the procurers and then held captive in houses of prostitution, beaten and intimidated by cruel madams or pimps, and shunted from one city – even country – to another in what was called the "traffic in young girls." The tenor of the folklore is best communicated by General Booth's plea, "For God's Sake Do Something!" in connection with what was designated as the "greatest crime in history."[35]

The prostitute was the more-than-willing collaborator in the fabrication of the white-slave myth by reformers, churchmen, and others. The inevitable curiosity of the reformers and customers as to how she entered her profession came to be met with a stereotyped story calculated to inspire sympathy and discount her own responsibility.[36] It was easy and even profitable for her to take a page from the white-slave myth and tell the sad story of how she was betrayed by a man in her teens and thus embarked upon her life of shame. Sometimes she even increased her earnings by stereotyped memoirs.

Actually there is only the most fragmentary evidence adducible that any considerable number of girls have been forced into prostitution against their wills. A small number of instances of something like white slavery have been recorded; but, on the whole, force and deceit are not now, and probably never have been, important in obtaining a supply of prostitutes. Men and women engaged in so-called "white-slave" traffic are rarely organized, and gangs of panderers and clearinghouses for prostitutes have been uncovered very infrequently. The average case concerns one man and one woman or two men and two women.[37] The strict enforcement of the laws which govern contributing to the delinquency of minors has generated a careful respect for them among sexual entrepreneurs, and they take no chances of violating them. The appetite that men are alleged to have for sexual intercourse with virgins can usually be satisfied by young professional prostitutes with a flare for dramatic pretense.[38]

The fallacies of the white-slave myth in no way interfered with its function in the societal reaction. It became one of the dynamic rationales for

[35] Bell, E. A., *Fighting the Traffic in Young Girls*, 1910.

[36] *Prostitutes, Their Early Lives*, p 10.

[37] Reckless, Walter, *Criminal Behavior*, 1940, p. 137, Hoover, J. E, "Organized Predatory Crimes: V. White Slave Traffic," *Journal of Criminal Law and Criminology*, 24, July–August, 1933, p. 480.

[38] *Madeleine*, 1919, Chap. X.

"DANGER"

Meeting young girls at Railway Depots is one of the methods of the white slave trader They promise to take the strangers to their friends, in fact, anything to get them to accompany them Once in a closed carriage, they are lost

THE FIRST STEP

Ice cream parlors of the city and fruit stores combined, largely run by foreigners, are the places where scores of girls have taken their first step downward Does her mother know the character of the place and the man she is with?

THE LURE OF THE STAGE—ANSWERING A WANT AD

Disreputable Theatrical Agents sometimes act as white slave traders, alluring positions on the stage being the net used to catch young girls

"MY GOD! IF ONLY I COULD GET OUT OF HERE"

The midnight shriek of a young girl in the vice district of a large city, heard by two worthy men, started a crusade which resulted in closing up the dens of shame in that city

Fig. 8. The folklore of prostitution – white slavery. (Taken from an old propaganda tract on the subject.)

the aggressive reform movements sweeping urban politics in the first part of the twentieth century. Recently the public has grown more sophisticated about white slavery, despite the occasional lurid story that is still written on the subject. In its place has come a group of fallacies about the supposed extent of venereal-disease infection which can be blamed upon prostitution. The viable aggressions against prostitution and prostitutes and the necessity for their repressive control are increasingly rationalized on the grounds of public-health protection and the battle against venereal disease.

The Tolerance for Prostitution

Prostitution has not always been condemned nor is it uniformly tabooed in various cultures where it has appeared. The early Hebrews, according to facts known, did not disapprove of prostitution strongly, except where it involved a non-Jew. In the Near East, prostitution once served as a compulsory religious rite in which all women were expected to indulge at least once in their lifetimes. In Greece in early times, prostitution was a state monopoly and waxed vigorously, especially in the maritime regions. In pre-Chrisitan Rome, while the prostitute had an attenuated social status, prostitution never became the object of strong repressive action. In later times the passage of certain laws further degraded prostitutes. However, these laws appeared to be designs to strengthen the class structure by preventing women of certain social classes from becoming prostitutes rather than being aimed at prostitution itself. Under the early Christian influences regulation of prostitution became more stringent, and strong antipathies grew toward those who traded in prostitution as distinct from the prostitutes. Nevertheless, in the writing of the so-called Christian Fathers, Saint Augustine and Saint Jerome, prostitution is not uniformly proscribed; Saint Augustine, for example, expressed the belief that prostitution was a necessary outlet for the "capricious lusts of society."[39] In medieval Europe we find the church through its councils formalizing the status of prostitutes, prescribing dress and place of residence, and even deriving revenue from the *lupanars*, as the medieval houses in which prostitution was carried on were known. The advent of epidemic syphilis in an acute form at the end of the fifteenth century, working together with the Protestant Reformation, did much to alter attitudes toward sex and prostitution. The Protestants, reacting to the degeneracy of the Catholic clergy and laity, and being sternly dedicated to the religious virtues of hard work and commerce, provided a new rationale for the old Hebraic sex concepts. To them sex was a disruptive factor in the orderly pursuit of business and capital accumulation, and from this conviction there

[39] Sanger, *op. cit.*, p. 91.

developed the puritanical strictures upon sexual thought and practice which have pervaded middle-class morality of the past. Oddly enough, and this point has frequently been ignored, the sex compulsives of the puritanical middle class have centered around the disapproval of overt and indiscreet sex behavior rather than the fact of sex indulgence outside of marriage or prostitution per se. This is borne out by the fact that many states and communities have had no laws against prostitution itself but, rather, have legislated against such things as disorderly conduct, vagrancy, soliciting, and pandering in conjunction with sex indulgence and prostitution.

The policies of repression of prostitution have been followed most consistently in the Protestant countries of the world, with toleration and formal segregation being more common in Catholic countries. This is not necessarily caused directly by the Catholic influence in these countries, since there is a good possibility that those cultures generally more receptive to the institutions of commercialized sex may also have been more congenial to the diffusion and perpetuation of Catholicism. In the United States the Puritan influences have been strongest in New England and those areas of other states first settled by New Englanders and to some extent in localities settled by the Dutch and otherworldly religious sects. A partial indication of the variety and distribution of formal reactions to prostitution may be seen in the accompanying map showing the number of aspects of prostitution covered by state laws.[40]

It will be noted that the earliest, most complete legislation on prostitution is to be found in the New England, Middle Atlantic, part of the East North Central states, and isolated states in other areas. The greatest changes have come about in states of the "New South" and certain border states between the South and the North.

Apart from these more formal variations in the societal reaction to prostitution, the vicissitudes of local policing and administration of the laws account for even greater variation in the tolerance for prostitution. The discrepancies between local community attitudes toward prostitution are far more impressive than regional or state differences. Communities within a few miles of one another often have diametrically opposed reactions to prostitution. Furthermore, in the same community bewildering shifts occur in policing and enforcement of the laws regulating sex behavior, so that there is a significant temporal inconstancy in the tolerance quotient. The variability in the tolerance quotient must be explained by reference to the large number of factors affecting it: the number and visibility of prostitutes, the dimensions of the venereal-disease problem, generalized sex norms – in particular as they permit a greater latitude in

[40] "Social Hygiene Laws in Action," *Journal of Social Hygiene*, 82, No. 8, November, 1946, p 360.

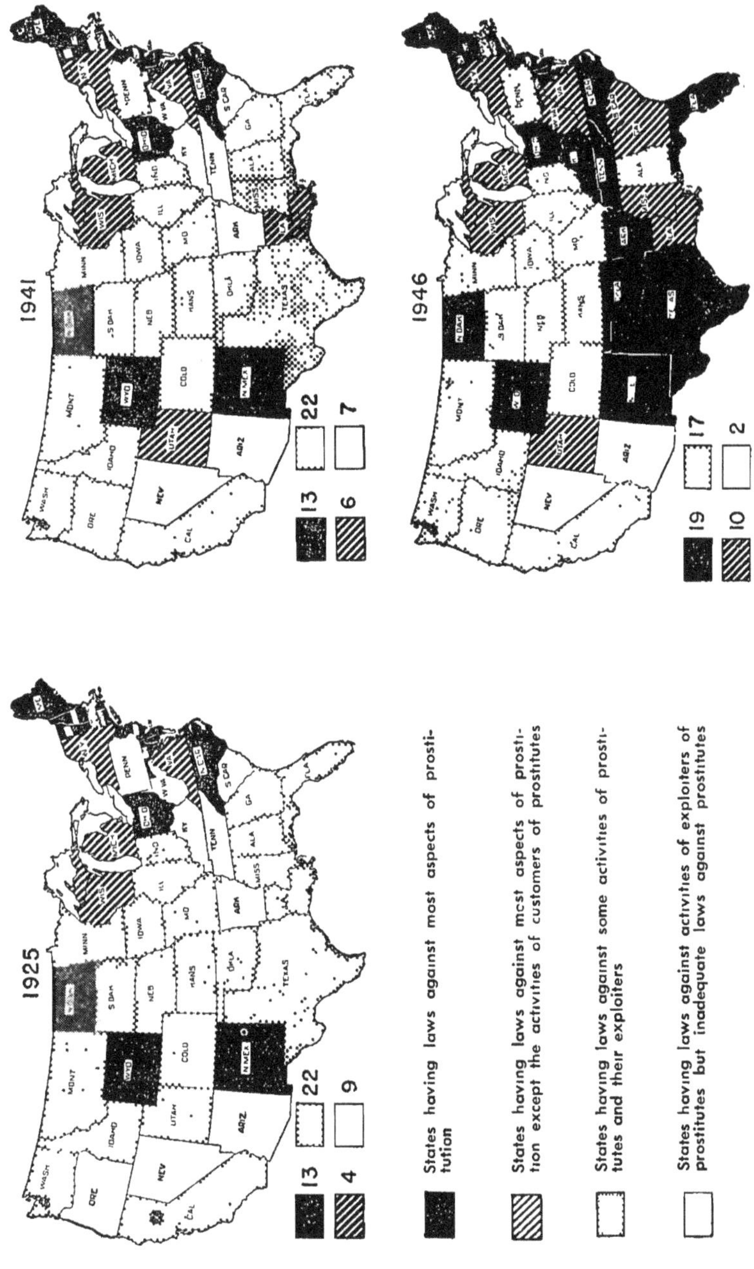

FIG 9 Change in state laws regulating prostitution.

noncommercialized sex indulgence – sex ratios of the population, the number and organization of the police, the policies of judges, the degree of extraneous tensions in the community created by rapid growth or war, and the institutionalized power struggles being waged within the community

The peculiar qualities of the general sex standards in a given locality have much to do with the collective sex-outlet patterns. It may not be correct to say that prostitution protects the family and chaste females in the community, nevertheless the tolerance for other sexual outlets does seem to condition a community's tolerance for prostitution. In 1858 Stockholm, Sweden, had a very high rate of illegitimacy generally assignable to the sexual laxity of domestic servants and shopgirls. During this same year an attempt to set up two houses of prostitution was frustrated, not by police action, but by a mob which actually destroyed the dwellings in question.[41] Soviet Russia's success in repressing prostitution may well be a consequence of the great sex freedom which seems to be tolerated there. In certain smaller cities of western Michigan, prostitution, in so far as can be determined, has been effectively repressed save for that carried on by a few Negro women and one-night transient prostitutes. While the police of these communities are responsible to some degree for this success, it is also true that the culture patterns of large numbers of first- and second-generation Dutch immigrants making up the local population are involved. These settlers carry in their mores a tolerance for premarital sex relations, and at the same time they seem to show a reciprocal intolerance for prostitution at all class levels.

The Power Struggle in the Tolerance for Prostitution

In the early histories of many communities in the United States at a time when the frontier influences were strong, sex ratios high, and police organization wanting or weak, prostitution in close alliance with crime and gambling was carried on with little restraint or concealment.[42] Later, as more balanced population pyramids materialized along with stable family life and better police organization, prostitutes found themselves more or less segregated socially and spatially. Their behavior at this period developed more pronounced institutional form. Then in 1910 came a wave of reform movements with heavy clerical support which culminated in the unstable pattern of accommodation between vice organization and other groups in the community, which holds even today in many areas. The activation of church federations and civic committees with strong church representation to goad the police and courts into the repression of vice is an intriguing phase of our history, which unfortunately has been

[41] Sanger, *op. cit*, p 280.

[42] See Asbury, H, *Chicago*, 1940, Chap. IV.

too little studied. Two reasons suggest themselves in explanation of the clerical interest and zealous participation in these social movements. One is that the great influx of immigrants of Catholic faith so enlarged the Catholic Church as to call out efforts of the Protestant churches to strengthen their own organization by dramatizing the threat made by vice groups to community institutions. The other possibility is that the general decline in the functions of the church led it to seek out new activities and justifications for its existence in the civic sphere.

The aggressive tactics of antivice committees tended to place the police in direct opposition to them, chiefly because the police were being attacked as a group and also because they were as often as not directly profiting from vice organization. It was also true that the police, being in direct contact with vice conditions, were aware of the almost insuperable difficulties in the way of permanently repressing prostitution, and consequently they often found the ideas and programs of the reformers naive. Nevertheless the police could not ignore the storm of public opinion whipped up by the fanatical reform groups in many communities. They were compelled to shut down vice resorts and make wholesale arrests. It was shown that police action could, and did at least temporarily, repress prostitution. But the federated form of organization of the vice committees and their organization for specific objectives meant that they could only be an ephemeral force in law enforcement. In one study of 105 movements for vice reform, only a dozen were found to have resulted in permanent organizations. The outstanding exception in these civic movements developed in New York City, where a civic group of this sort functioned for thirty years.[43] The common result of movements for vice reform has been a cyclic pattern, with alternating epochs of repression and relaxation of control, the duration of the repressive phase being dependent upon the demand of an insistent organized public opinion.[44]

Our rising health standards, caused by medical advances, and the experiences of two world wars have brought a union of health and medical groups with the civic organizations concerned with the elimination of vice. Today attacks on vice are more and more sanctioned in the name of venereal-disease control, with only a rear-guard action being fought on moral grounds. Great publicity has been given to the idea that the prostitute is the chief source of veneral disease, an idea based upon the fact that a high percentage of arrested prostitutes are discovered to be diseased. But it is by no means conclusive that prostitutes can be blamed for any great percentage of the total number of cases of infection from year to

[43] Waterman, *op. cit.*, p. 99.

[44] Woolston, H., *Prostitution in the United States*, 1925, p 217, see also W. Reckless, *Vice in Chicago*, 1933.

year. The figures on the sources of venereal infection of soldiers in the Third Service Command during the Second World War give an entirely different picture (see Table 29).

TABLE 29. VENEREAL INFECTIONS OF SOLDIERS IN THIRD SERVICE COMMAND (MARYLAND, PENNSYLVANIA, VIRGINIA) BY TYPE OF CONTACT (WHITE), 1942*

Contact	Number	Per cent
Wife	109	6 3
"Friend"	248	14 4
Pick-up—no fee	1,107	64 1
Street walker	133	7.7
Brothel.	106	6.1
Call girl	21	1 2
Other	3	0.2
Total	1,727	100 0

*Norris, E. W., *et al.*, "Venereal Disease Epidemology in the Army Third Service Command . . ." "*Venereal Disease Information*, October, 1943, adapted from Table 2, p. 285.

This table shows that wives and "friends," accounting for 20.7 per cent of the venereal infections of this soldier group, were far more dangerous than prostitutes, who infected only 15 per cent of the cases. The real problem obviously rested with the casual sex indulgee, the "pick-up," who transmitted disease to 64.1 per cent of all of this group who were infected.

The very dubious idea that prostitution is the crux of the venereal-disease problem has sprung from a confusing of moral ideas with scientific facts. This confusion is both a cause and an effect of the instability in the societal reaction to prostitution. The joining of forces between clerical and health groups probably has weakened the power of both groups in so far as aligning other groups against prostitution and venereal disease as separate problems is concerned. Nowhere is this plainer than in the ambiguous content of "sex education" and in the ineffectiveness of the propaganda appeals to the individual to avoid nonmarital sex indulgence. In the armed forces during the Second World War the sex propaganda line usually started out as an exhortation to remain continent and ended up with instructions on the use of prophylaxis, thus confusing an issue already muddied by contradictory sex attitudes in our culture. Prophylaxis is efficient, but responsibility for its proper use is not taken by the individual because a sense of guilt makes his extramarital sex indulgence an impulsive act, more frequently than not accompanied by drunkenness and insouciant abandonment.

The militancy of vice-reform groups has often worked against their own best interests. Some recognition of the shortcomings of their aggressive campaigns is seen in a growing tendency to work in cooperation with police departments rather than leading attacks upon them through the newspapers. The impetus to reform has been increasingly leavened by an appreciation that in order to eliminate prostitution drastic alterations in some of our salient institutional patterns will be necessary. Some notion of how great the changes will have to be may be drawn from a cursory examination of the number of groups who directly or indirectly benefit from prostitution.

Exploitation of Prostitutes

In the past the prostitute has been exploited and preyed upon from all sides. While there is less exploitation of vice today, still it supports or adds to the income of many persons and groups besides the direct participants. The madam in the house usually takes anywhere from one-third to one-half of the prostitute's earnings. If she works on her own, the cab driver or the bellhop have to be paid. The disreputable medical examiner and the abortionist take a portion of the prostitute's income, as do the attorneys who obtain her release when she is arrested. Apart from the attorney's fees, money has to go to the "fixer" who sees to it that she escapes prosecution or conviction. This might be a prosecutor, judge, or county chairman. The bail bondsman levies his toll, and often the policeman on the beat is not loath to practice crude extortion on the prostitute either in trade or money. However, there is far less of this than there once was. Customers are not above cheating the prostitute, and some take pleasure in inflicting physical cruelties upon her. If the woman is a drug addict and has turned to prostitution in order to earn sufficient money to purchase her costly opiates, she may be subject to the unscrupulous manipulations of the peddler from whom she obtains the drugs. Of course, not all these relationships are intrinsically exploitative; in many cases tangible services are rendered by those dealing with the prostitute. However, owing to her extralegal status and her lack of organization at the rank-and-file level, the temptation to mulct from the girl as much as possible is always present.

Real-estate owners and managers are able to earn far more on the investments and properties by renting to prostitutes or vice-resort operators than to other tenants. Better class hotels, along with the cheaper ones, owe part of their revenue to the prostitute, as well as taxicab companies, laundries, amusement parks, vacation resorts, and contraceptive manufacturers and distributors. The sale of liquor has always been intimately connected with prostitution, brought out by the large number of contacts between prostitutes and customers made in taverns and bars. The famous Raines law in New York, passed to ensure that liquor served on Sundays would be confined to hotels, actually produced a number of prostitution agencies by necessitating a minimum number of rooms in hotels, whose costs were met by their use for assignation purposes.[45] In other words, prostitution has been, and remains, integrated into many functions oı organizations which are sanctioned enterprises in the community and important in our economy.

Police and Judiciary Control of Prostitution

Three alternative policies may be the choice of police in their control of prostitution: (1) complete repression, (2) formal and open segregatıon, and (3) nominal repression accompanied by tacit segregation and regulation. Formal and open segregation of prostitution has rarely been a popular idea and rarely adopted, although a house of prostitution for students was advocated by Thomas Jefferson as one of his specifications for the University of Virgina. During the Civil War, Nashville, Tennessee, experimented with formal regulation – as did St. Louis, Missouri, from 1870 to 1874,[46] but these are exceptions.

Repression is the rule in some areas, but the most commonly encountered arrangement is that of ınformal regulation. Police periodically arrest prostitutes and charge them from a variety of municipal violations so that they are held pendıng a medical examination. If found diseased, the prostitute is gıven an indeterminate sentence or its equivalent and held until sufficıently treated to become noninfectious. If the girl is free of disease, her case may be dismissed or she may be gıven a "floater" so that she must leave town in order to escape a jail term. There are variations of this procedure in different areas, but the same effect is usually achıeved.

Previously the arrest of prostitutes was the function of the neighborhood patrolman, but the scandals which were aired over the exploitation of prostitutes by corrupt officers along with the disappearance of the "beat" policeman has altered this completely. Most municipal police and sheriff departments now have special vice squads or details organized on a city-wide basis and specially trained in vice detection. Making arrests and obtaining evidence which will stand up in court is not always an easy thing to do in vice cases. The central problem is how to have the officer solicited and have an exchange of money without his being compelled to commit an illegal act himself. Detectives soon become known by the prostitutes and lose their value for provocative purposes. Furthermore, objections have arisen from the community over the "entrapment" of girls by unfair methods. More modern police techniques utilize powdered money, motıon pictures, and dictaphones to gather evidence. However, here, as with crime, as soon as new methods are contrived by police, the prostitutes

[45] Woolston, *op. cit.*, p. 141.
[46] Barnes, H. E., *Society in Transitıon*, 1939, p. 777.

devise ways of evading them. The morale of vice squads is not always the highest; police on such duty are also often less efficient than those in other departments. Reasons for this are the lack of real public support, lack of belief of the officers in the laws they are enforcing, and the unpleasant job of arresting women who are more often than not the scapegoat of the community's unsolved culture conflicts. Perhaps an even greater cause for the cynicism and boredom of the police with their task of vice control is the treatment by the courts of those whom they arrest. For the most part no serious effort is made by courts to work in any realistic way toward the abatement of prostitution.

In the lower courts cases of commercialized vice have been handled in the most perfunctory manner by judges with no special aptitude or training for their jobs. It has been the custom to hand down convictions simply upon the arresting officer's statement, so that the judicial process becomes in effect a taxation process, which has been symbolized in some communities by special days, "ladies' days," on which vice cases are tried. Efforts at severity in the municipal courts lead the girls and men to ask for jury trials, which mean delays and far less possibility of conviction. Where special morals courts have been instituted, judges have generally been more stringent in holding vice operators responsible, but the girls soon learn to ask for a jury trial and thus avoid the more severe penalties in these courts.

Table 30 shows the disposition of persons, male and female, arrested in Los Angeles for vice violations in 1947. Those who received some sort of

TABLE 30 DISPOSITION OF 3,085 MALE AND FEMALE ARRESTS FOR PROSTITUTION AND COMMERCIALIZED VICE IN LOS ANGELES, CALIFORNIA, 1947*

Disposition	*Number*
Jail sentence	484
Jail sentence plus fine	1,273
Fine	5
Suspended sentence or probation plus a fine or short jail sentence	639
Suspended sentence	409
Probation	3
Dismissed or released	159
Other in which no penalties occurred	40
No complaint filed	73
Total	3,085

**Report of Los Angeles Police Department*, 1947, compiled from data on pp. 156–157.

mitigated punishment, such as suspended sentences, probation, or these along with brief jail terms, made up 43.3 per cent of the total. Generally males who profit from prostitution in the roles of panderer or procurer are shown less leniency than the prostitutes themselves. However, in diametric contrast to this, the male customers of prostitutes have not only gone without arrest in a great percentage of cases but have been discharged with proportionately greater frequency by the courts than the girls participating in the prostitution. Sentences are also lighter for the men. From 1920 to 1929 in New York City, 1,743 women were sent to reformatories as compared with a negligible 14 such commitments of men.[47] In Iowa the courts have held that a man cannot be guilty of prostitution on the legal grounds that he does not receive pay for the act in which he takes part.

Abatement proceedings against property owners permitting the use of property for immoral purposes could only be instituted through equity proceedings in days past. Statutory provisions changed this in some states, but in others no laws of this nature have been passed, or if they have been the teeth have been drawn. Ordinances requiring owners to post name plates upon tenements showing the uses to which they are being put have in some instances been successfully challenged in the courts. The familiar legal sanction of no government regulation without "due process of law" have been invoked by criminal and unethical property owners as well as business corporations operating in legitimate spheres. Property owners, whatever their relation to vice organizations, are likely to make common front when legislative and judicial threats to their constitutional protections are made.

Reform Agencies

In New York from 1920 to 1929, 1,743 of the 15,650 women convicted for commercialized vice were sent to reformatories, something over 11 per cent.[48] The imprisonment of prostitutes or their incarceration in reformatories seldom has the avowed effect of reform rehabilitation. The staffs of women's prisons and reformatories contain large numbers of political appointees and many who have sought the employment as a retreat from social and economic failure. Among them not a few unbalanced persons are found. The situation in the institutions is highly conducive to manipulation of the female prisoners by the matrons to work out tensions and conflicts of their own. The symbolic environment sharpens the cleavages existing in outside society between the "good" and the "bad" girls, as a consequence of which many girls redefine their sex misbehavior in the prostitute's terms. Lack of segregation, bringing hardened professional prostitutes into contact with the individual or situational offender, has the same effect. Even under ideal conditions, women in institutions are very difficult to supervise and discipline, let alone rehabilitate, so that

[47] Waterman, *op. cit.*, p. 75.

[48] *Ibid.*

the bulk of the energies of the institution staffs often goes for the simple maintenance of order.

Assistance of a social-welfare kind is made available to prostitutes through a wide variety of private organizations predominately sponsored by religious or quasi-religious groups. Offers of social-work assistance were extended to 366 out of 600 convicted prostitutes studied by the League of Nations Advisory Committee. Presumably such offers also come to prostitutes who are not in the toils of the law. These offers are quite often refused; in a group of convicted British prostitutes one-third chose to ignore the proffered welfare service.[49] The fervent religious atmosphere of homes for prostitutes or sexually delinquent girls often adds to the cynicism of the prostitute, and the accent upon spiritual salvation diverts attention and energy from tangible material rehabilitation. The suspicion is a strong one that many girls cooperate with religious and welfare organizations mainly when they are destitute. Professional prostitutes tend to look upon reformers as a nuisance. On the other hand, the old-time madams became adept in handling vice crusaders who assailed the parlor house intent upon moral rescue. This was often done with extreme care so that unnecessary antagonisms would not be built up in the community. Many a reformer has come away from such encounters with his banners limp.

Individuation of the Prostitute

Prostitution is a further step and formal elaboration of generalized premarital or extramarital sex experiences. The paths leading to the commercialization of sex are numerous and diverse. Generalizations as to why women engage in primary sex deviation become so broad as to be practically without value. It has already been pointed out that formal religious compulsives produced a universal participation in prostitution in one Near Eastern culture area. In some provinces in India, there have been families in which succeeding generations of women upon reaching adolescence have assumed the role of prostitute as a result of long-standing tradition. In Western industrialized cultures poverty has been monotonously called a "cause" of prostitution; however, studies show that candidates for the profession, in the past at least, have come from poor, but not extremely poor, families. Crowded housing and the witnessing of sexual behavior of parents or others in early life have also been played up as contributory factors in the development of the prostitute. Lack of occupational skills or defects and illness which make employment impossible have held prominent places in lists of factors predisposing girls to become prostitutes. Differential association with other prostitutes and the

[49] *Prostitutes, Their Early Lives*, pp. 59*ff*.

cajolery of procurers have been stressed by many writers as precipitating or determining influences in prostitution.

Primary sex deviation, by definition, must be individual or situational; most of it in our culture is situational, although admittedly there is interaction of the two. Previous reference has been made to the general situational impulsions to prostitutional sex behavior in our culture. Other situational pressures can be uncovered in the culture, to which sexual delinquency and prostitution are more implicit responses. Here all the various factors inventoried in the above paragraph can be recalled. Why some girls confronted with these situations turn to sex deviation and others do not must be explained by reference to more subtle cultural and individual differentiations. The girl with a normal material standard of living and limited by lack of work skills and attitudes, assuming no introjected deterents of special strength, may find the prostitute's role one among a very few acceptable alternatives. On the contrary, the girl with low material aspirations may be sexually loose, yet never commercialize her aberrant sex acts. This is seen in some of the female migrants from Appalachian Mountain communities who come to cities in southern Michigan. They remain sexually promiscuous but do not always follow the expected course to prostitution. A still other possibility is the girl with higher-than-average desires for clothes, good times, and money. She may find an occupational role of secretary or shop clerk, in which financial returns are several cuts above those of the waitress or domestic servant. But her situation may be as frustrating as that of either the waitress or the housemaid, and as a result she may elect the prostitute's role.

Girls of lower economic status living in areas of deteriorated housing may more frequently have premarital sex experiences, but such indulgence is nowise confined to this class. Girls of middle and upper class residential areas meet situations conductive to sexual deviations as well, although they are less well known. At least one-fourth of college girls have had premarital sex experiences. Girls placed in special schools and more carefully guarded may not so often have sex relations prior to marriage, but in a certain percentage of cases the debutante of the old New England family is likely to have had her "fling" in a summer-colony romance or on a trip to Europe before marriage. The obvious conclusion from these facts is that premarital sex experiences in themselves are not logical antecedents to prostitution, for many of them remain at the symbolic level of "romances," premature enjoyment of the marital bed, "good times," or youthful peccadilloes, with corresponding self and role definitions. The search for the interactive factor from which professional prostitution culminates leads to an examination and comparison of the symbolic environments in which primary sex deviation takes place.

SYMBOLIZING SEX DEVIATION AS PROSTITUTION

The symbolic environment may compel verbalization and structuring of sex experiences in terms of clearly delineated roles, or it may have the opposite effect of inhibition and dissociation of the intellectual aspects of the actions. For example, in days when immigrants were arriving in large numbers in this country, some of the young, unmarried alien females, when set down into slum environments of the cities, eventually were involved in sexual misconduct. In some of the ethnic groups, such as the Italian, a rigid dichotomy was culturally drawn between "good" girls and "bad" girls. Parents customarily refused to forgive a single misstep, even assuming that if a girl stayed away from home overnight she was guilty of illicit sex behavior. The behavior consequently was unequivocally reflected in the parental reaction as that of the "bad" girl or the folk equivalent of the prostitute. A hypothesis for testing is that girls in certain broader spatial-cultural contexts more quickly and precisely have their sex reactions defined in this way. Families with fewer resources, neighbors, teachers, and social workers in certain areas where prostitutes and sex delinquents already exist are more likely to interpret sex behavior of girls and women as delinquency and prostitution. The formal agencies of the courts and welfare organizations more quickly extend their jurisdiction and legal definitions to embrace these cases than those of females in other areas.

In other spatial-cultural contexts, which for want of better terminology may be called "middle class," the parental and societal reaction is a strain toward concealment of the sexual errancy of female members of the family and a tendency toward minimization and rationalization of the behavior. The beliefs are verbalized that the girl is "really good" and that her present trouble is a temporary slip which fortunately will not happen again. These families through their superior economic and other resources are in a position to interrupt potential sequences in sex delinquency. Consequently, even if the girl arrives at some definition of her behavior as being immoral, subsequent translation of the definition into overt behavior of the symbolically projected role does not follow. This can be done in various ways, but usually it is accomplished by some manipulation of the environment, sending the girl on a trip, or to live elsewhere, or placing her in a different school.

The critical situations in which girls define their roles as prostitutes are reciprocals of different types of societal reactions, some dramatic, some prosaic. Those with more dramatic qualities include arrest and conviction on a formal charge of commercialized vice, infection with a venereal disease and segregated treatment in a hospital or clinic along with loose women and professional prostitutes, role-defining interpretations received from contacts with prostitutes and procurers, and contacts with profane, drunken men. In other instances a girl more or less comes to a conclusion on her own that she is a prostitute, growing out of a long series of quasi-prostituting sex experiences, the implications of which become inescapable. A waitress who has been taken on dates by customers of the restaurant where she works and given entertainment or gifts in return for sexual favors may suddenly perceive the bargaining features of the relationships and decide to formalize them through a prostitute's role in order to improve what frequently is a bad bargain from her point of view. The new role materializes from the sexual exploitation implicit in her former role. Retrospective insight is sometimes verbalized thus: "I suddenly realized I had been giving thousands of dollars worth of it away for free." Once a girl has entered into definite commercialization of the sex act, she becomes subject in varying degrees to the exploitative culture already described. It is here that the functional value of the prostitute's role is perceived and secondary deviation appears in crystallized form. The sex act is bereft of ambiguous feelings; male-female relationships undergo a rigid structuring to prevent the energy-exhausting interaction of an informal date or courtship event and the frustration following brief "love" affairs. The girl becomes "hardened" in manner and speech and betrays the cues of professionalization.

The Professional Prostitute

The symbolic indicators of professional status in the prostitute at one time were easily detected in her dress and postural attributes, but today in many communities the need for concealment and subterfuge has changed this. The residual professional symbols of her role are manifested in her speech and sexual technique. Conspicuous among the symbolic cues are familiarity with the limited argot of the profession, verbal parodies of romantic love, use of diminutives to designate the sexual parts, concealment of origins, adoption of fanciful and sometimes exotic first names with no surname, self-dramatization in synthetic autobiographies, very rapid and gross provocations to sexual consummation, and sudden lapses into profanity where anxieties over exploitation or possible betrayal to police are brought to the surface.

The time lapse between first sex experiences of girls who later become prostitutes and the age of entry into the trade is short. The age of primary sex contacts falls somewhere between 14 and 18, in all probability not too different from the age at which most girls who indulge in premarital relations first know the physical meaning of sex. The age of entry into prostitution varies from 17 to 24, with a peak around 20 or 21 years. Evidence from one study showed that 40 per cent of the women in three different Western Hemisphere countries assumed their roles as harlots less than 2 years after initial sex experiences, 40 per cent did so within 2 to 8 years, and for 20 per cent it was more than 8 years.[50] Some distributions of prostitutes by age of entry into the calling tend to be bimodal, with a fair number turning to prostitution after age 25. The most plausible interpretation of this is that the women who become prostitutes at older ages are situational deviants – drug addicts who turn to the trade to finance their costly habit. Specific information as to how long prostitutes actively

TABLE 31 SUBSEQUENT ACTIVITIES OF 256 WOMEN WHO LEFT OPEN PROSTITUTION, BALTIMORE, MARYLAND*

Activity	*Number*
Returned to prostitution	43
Probably clandestine prostitution	15
Living with men	20
Left town	43
Married	26
In business	15
Working regularly	16
Dead	7
With relatives	5
Unknown	66
Total	256

*Woolston, H., *Prostitution in the United States*, 1925, p. 76. By permission of Appleton-Century-Crofts, Inc., New York.

pursue their trade is absent. However, it can be interpolated from the general age composition of prostitutes and the age composition of girls at the time of entry into the calling. The largest numbers of prostitutes are somewhere between 21 and 25 years of age, dropping off gradually until 35 years of age is reached, beyond which few cases are found. Since the peak age of entrance into prostitution is 20 or 21 years, this suggests a short average professional life of 5 to 6 years, with, however, an average potential life of 12 years.

What happens to prostitutes on the termination of their professional life has never been the subject for careful study. In ancient Rome the prostitute could retire to a midwife's role, amplified by concoction and sale of love potions and probably the performance of abortions. Stories have been told of prostitutes who marry successfully and take over the role of housewife, but nothing is known as to how many manage to do so. While still in the profession, as her physical attractiveness begins to fade, the prostitute drifts from better to poorer professional roles, from callgirl to a low-priced house inmate, and in some cases to cheap bars as B girls,

[50] *Ibid.*, p. 45.

or to being occupants of cribs. When the time comes that her earnings and acceptance are no longer favorable in comparison to other work, she probably turns to other employment, sometimes doing what she did before. Although there is no way of demonstrating this, our impression is that the aging prostitute once again becomes a waitress, domestic servant, store clerk, cheap entertainer, or charwoman. Occasionally the associations built up during her career as a harlot may lead her into work not done previously. A few may become madams of houses of prostitution, or otherwise retain an entrepreneurial relationship to her old trade. A few follow petty criminal pursuits. An older report (see Table 31) on a group of women who left open prostitution is partially suggestive in the answer to this problem.

Social Participation

Unlike blindness or stuttering, the role of prostitute does not carry a high degree of primacy. This means that her role can be temporarily discarded and assumed again; it can be pursued on a part-time basis and integrated with a fairly wide number of occupational roles and with that of the housewife. Of 1,849 women arrested in Los Angeles in 1947 for prostitution or commercialized vice, 827, or 44.7 per cent, were employed in some legitimate occupation.[51] Some professional prostitutes may retain jobs nominally for purposes of concealment of their real role. On the whole, however, professionalization carries with it a strong aversion to work, hence in most of these 827 cases in which employment figured, the prostitution probably occupied a subsidiary role position. A professional house prostitute not only scorns work but finds it difficult or impossible to maintain a job while meeting her customers' demands. She usually works at night so that she must sleep during the day when most jobs would require her services. Her working hours generally make heavy drains upon her energy, which is another reason for her lack of interest in additional employment. A shopgirl can supplement her role through casual prostitution, but it does not work the other way; the professional prostitute cannot easily earn additional money in outside occupations.

It was noted that 53.3 per cent of the Los Angeles arrestees for vice violations listed themselves as without employment. This certainly does not mean that all of these were professional prostitutes, because many undoubtedly were living at home with relatives or as wives of working husbands. The number of highly professionalized prostitutes in a community varies widely, being directly affected by the tolerance quotient and opportunities for formally organized prostitution to develop. Perhaps 10 to 30 per cent of prostitutes are self-designated professionals, leaving anywhere

[51] *Report of the Los Angeles Police Department*, 1947, p 150

from 25 to 40 per cent falling into the category of unemployed casual offenders.[52] Of the differential social participation of the women without employment who casually prostitute themselves, little is known. Many unquestionably are able to dissociate their sexual activities from the rest of their life, so that their social participation is not too noticeably different from that of other women with comparable status.

Sex and Marital Participation

Examination of the marital condition of prostitutes reveals that a very large percentage of them are divorced, separated, or single. From Table 32 it can be seen that only 34.1 per cent of women apprehended on commercialized-vice charges in Los Angeles in 1948 were married at the time.

Table 32. Number and Percentage of 1,825 Females Arrested for Prostitution and Commercialized Vice by Marital Status, Los Angeles, 1948*

Marital status	Number	Per cent
Married	623	34.1
Divorced or separated	670	36 7
Widow	117	6 4
Single	399	21 8
Not given	16	0 8
Total	1,825	99 8

*Data supplied by Statistican's Office, Los Angeles Police Department, 1949

However, as we have stated earlier, this is probably a misleading figure because many prostitutes claim that their pimps are husbands, when in actuality they are not. Nevertheless, it is true that marriage need not deter women from becoming prostitutes. One body of data has disclosed that 22.4 per cent of a group of harlots were carrying on their occupation with the knowledge and even encouragement of their husbands.[53] Despite this fact, we are convinced that, on the whole, women who elect prostitution as a way of life are less marriageable than other women. Thus if we could cull out of Table 32 those women who as a result of the crisis of divorce have prostituted themselves in a casual manner, it is probable that the percentages of single women would increase. Other studies have discovered among prostitutes a large percentage of women who have never married or who have had a brief unsuccessful marriage at an early age.[54]

The more professionalized the prostitute, the lower are the probabilities of her marrying. One house madam of the old days tells how she refused to hire inexperienced girls and widows for her parlor houses because they

[52] Based upon data from Waggoner, *op. cit.*, pp. 391, 398, 400.
[53] Woolston, *op. cit.*, p. 50.
[54] *Prostitutes, Their Early Lives*, pp. 14–15.

were more apt to leave in order to marry.[55] Professional prostitutes are less inclined to marry and have limited chances to do so. The reasons why men do not marry known prostitutes are fairly obvious. The status of the husband of the ex-prostitute is far from enviable in a community where his wife's former life is known. The status of the husband of a practicing prostitute is low, comparable to if not actually that of a pimp in the eyes of others. Furthermore, the whole idea of marriage and prostitution clashes with the concept of romantic love and the idea of sexual monopoly in our culture.

In the case of the so-called "high-class" prostitute there may be a greater probability of marriage. The sexual deviation of these women is less visible, and they are not apt to have a police record. They are probably less promiscuous, and their contacts with men are not so crudely commercialized, being more in the nature of all-night dates. They are often functioning in something like a mistress role for several men at one time. It can be assumed as a fair possibility that such relationships are more frequently the antecedents of marriage than the purely mercenary sex acts of the self-symbolized prostitute.

The incompatibilities between motherhood and the courtesan's life are even more fundamental and inescapable than in the case of marriage alone. The conflicts do not appear very often because prostitutes are more sterile than other women. Venereal disease or its aftereffects makes them less apt to conceive and more apt to abort spontaneously after conception. Many of the prostitutes who do become pregnant – usually earlier in their careers – obtain induced abortions. Without having the facts to prove it, we suspect that the death rate of the offspring of prostitutes is exceptionally high. Once in awhile a prostitute tries to care for her child by maintaining a servant, but the extreme difficulty of providing it with care usually results in the child's being placed with relatives, in a boarding home, or in a charitable institution.

It strikes an odd note to speak of the love life of the prostitute, but none the less it calls for comment. With most customers sexual intercourse is rapid, mechanical, and singularly empty of affection. Many prostitutes eventually become incapable of reaching an orgasm in the sex act. This is given substantiation by an ingenious piece of interviewing done by a female graduate student who passed herself off as an ex-prostitute to the inmates of a house of prostitution in a small Middle Western town. All of those questioned on the subject claimed without exception that they had lost the capacity for a climax in the sex act.

The prostitute soon learns that whenever she compromises the formality of her sexual relations the possibility of exploitation by the customer arises.

[55] *Madeleine*, p. 141.

Hence to the extent that this hazard is recognized, she is cut off from him as a source of affection. Likewise, the prostitute typically has abandoned the family as a means of sexual and affectional gratification. Both facts do much to explain the close, dependent ties of the prostitute with her pimp and her occasional homosexuality. At one time pimps served to protect their girls or "stables" in disorderly houses. Today the pimp still provides tangible services through seeing that she is cared for when she is ill or through fixing arrests and supplying bail when it is needed. But above all other things the pimp showers the prostitute with gifts, special attentions, and tender affection that she gets nowhere else. His price is high, for he frequently takes most or all of her earnings. However, she is willing to pay in return for the security he gives her. Many white prostitutes, perhaps an increasing number, prefer Negro to white pimps for the reason that they can more easily dominate the relationship Also, they need give them less of their earnings or none at all, and they receive all-around better treatment at their hands.

Religious and Other Forms of Participation

Nineteenth-century New York prostitutes, according to the pioneer study we have cited before, while trained in formal religion, did not attend church for the most part.[56] In one or two autobiographies, mention is made of a superstition against attending church, but the writer has been unable to verify its existence through interviews with a group of jailed prostitutes. Indeed, one writer has insisted that prostitutes maintain their religion intact to the same exent that other women do. Devout Catholic girls refuse to work on Good Friday, and Jewish girls if they have been religious previously will honor their sacred days as well.[57] If there is any difference in the effects of prostitution upon religious participation, it will probably make itself felt with girls of Protestant faith. While the present-day American Catholic Church does not sanction prostitution, at the same time it does not bar the prostitute from participation in church ritual. It is doubtful whether formal acceptance of a known prostitute in church membership will be found in many Protestant churches. Negro churches are sometimes an exception to this. The relatively high economic status of the Negro prostitute considerably mitigates the disapproval of her behavior in the Negro community, and the church reflects this. Her ability to make large financial contributions to the struggling Negro churches gains her entree there, even though the minister may repeatedly inveigh in his sermons against the vice she represents.

The high mobility of the prostitute lessens the probability of her

[56] Sanger, *op. cit.*, p 547.
[57] Reitman, *op. cit.*, p. 170.

taking enough interest in political affairs to vote or be a party worker. However, in Japan at one time, prostitutes were supposed to have been represented by a pressure group in the Diet, and quite recently prostitutes in Mexico City were reported to have a politically active union. The pimp may be an energetic political worker, along with madams and others who take large profits from organized vice. On occasion, when an election or some administrative decision has been in doubt, prostitutes in houses have been urged or compelled to vote or have been mobilized for political purposes, as in the case of the famous invasion of prostitutes from the Chicago levee into residential districts when their houses were closed in 1912.[58]

Recreational interests of the prostitute are colored by those of the class from which she comes. Shopping, seeing motion pictures, and reading are common leisure-time occupations. Visiting night clubs with her pimp, casual drinking, witnessing prize fights and similar athletic events, with attendance at horse races, may take up part of her spare time. The professional prostitute is very sensitive about her physical appearance, from whence comes the notion of her being an extremely vain creature. This explains her compulsive shopping habits and much time spent fixing her hair, applying cosmetics, and making clothes. The prostitute likes to give the impression of financial success by "putting on a show," preferably where her finery can be publicly paraded to the best advantage. Two older and rather faded professionals once interviewed by the author told of Sunday morning horseback rides at a riding academy frequented by wealthy members of the upper classes.

Adjustment and Maladjustment

The folk notion, buttressed and reinforced by careless and dubious research studies, is that the prostitute generally is either feeble-minded, psychopathic, or demoralized. A popular conviction is to the effect that no "normal" woman could lead such a life. The public stereotype unquestionably has been based upon mid-nineteenth-century experiences, when in our large cities generalized social pathology and personal demoralization were much more conspicuous among prostitutes. The studies coming to the conclusion that the prostitute is a sociopsychological deviant have limited value because they rest upon cases which have come in contact with the welfare or law-enforcement agencies. The more intelligent, shrewder, and enterprising prostitutes often live out their professional lives without ever being the subject of psychiatric examinations. An additional reason for the limited value of extant psychiatric observations upon the mental characteristics of prostitutes is the tendency for examiners to regard the

58 Asbury, *op. cit.*, p. 301.

socially disapproved traits – functionally necessary in their professions – as symptoms of mental instability. Her professional mobility becomes "psychopathic" wanderlust, her deliberate refusal to take jobs is noted down as abnormal laziness, or her blasé indifference to police and reformers is mistaken for schizophrenia or "olgophrenia," as one writer has somewhere elaborately termed it.

A markedly high percentage of women arrested or otherwise treated as prostitutes are addicted to drugs or alcohol. When studied, 14 per cent of a group of British prostitutes showed a record of numerous arrests for drunkenness, and one-fourth of an American sample took drugs and a third of them drank regularly.[59] Yet many, if not most, of these cases are not symbolically oriented to the prostitute's role but, instead, are primarily employing vice to implement their roles as drug addicts or they are alcoholic women whose associations more or less inevitably conduce to vice as incidents of drinking. If a girl is going to earn much money in a house or on her own and avoid arrest or venereal disease, she cannot afford to drink heavily. While taking drugs does not necessarily interfere with professional prostitution, indications point to a decline in the association between the two. This probably is an incident of the increasing individualizaton of the prostitute.[60]

A common attitude projected upon the prostitute is that she is conscience-stricken and ashamed of her profession. This may be true in the first sex experiences of the prostitute-initiate, but once having participated in the overt act of prostitution, dissociation and rationalization soon allay any moral conflicts which might bother her. An excerpt from autobiographical case material speaks of the ease with which the self-enhancing processes reassert themselves in the newcomer to prostitution

It didn't take me ten minutes to find out what kind of a house I was in. At first I couldn't believe it. After I realized it was true, I got madder than hell. Old Ma Martin just sat there and told me that there wasn't any use of getting mad, 'cause it wouldn't do me any good. She told me that I didn't know a soul in Chicago and that I didn't have a place to go – and that Chicago was an awful big and cold city. She said that she would take care of me and that I could make more money than I had ever seen before. I was still mad, though. Probably I was more scared than mad. I had never been in such a big city, and the whole idea of the thing was so new to me that it just scared me plenty. Anyway I went up to my room and put my things away.

That was strictly a two-dollar house out on the south side. I was there for about three months. That was the "breaking" place. They taught me the ropes there – and I really learned them, too. I learned to be as rough and tough as

[59] *Prostitutes, Their Early Lives*, p. 26

[60] *Prevention of Prostitution*, League of Nations Advisory Committee on Social Questions, 1943, 4, No. 2, p. 24.

the next one. After awhile my conscience stopped bothering me, and all I was interested in was getting the money – and more of it than the other girls got. I learned ways of hiding some from Ma Martin, but in most cases she got her share and more too. She had been in the game too long to let us newcomers put anything over on her. After I "graduated," as you might say, from Ma Martin's place, I was promoted to a downtown hotel circuit.

Prostitutes are inclined to counter moral condemnation with such statements as "I prefer to sell it rather than give it away," implying that what they do sexually is not so different from what all women do in one way or another. There is just enough truth in such assertions to make them congenial rationalizations.

Although group morale among prostitutes is almost nonexistent, their personal morale may be quite high. Some of the indexes of high morale in the individual prostitute are personal cleanliness (two baths per day and purchase of new underclothing every week in some houses), pride in physical beauty, precautions against venereal disease, insistence upon an honest bargain and adherence to it, and profane defiance of the police. Some prostitutes the author has talked to carry insurance policies, and a few own property and automobiles.

Adherence to their deviant morality may be stricter with prostitutes than is true for other women. An artist friend of the author, who was in need of a life model for his classes, once canvassed a large number of houses of prostitution in Gallup, New Mexico, offering regular model rates to the inmates to pose in the nude. But not a single girl took up the offer. Their uniform answer was that "they were prostitutes" and that they would not undress in front of a group of students. Even when prostitutes deteriorate physically and present shabby, sorry pictures to the objective observer, they still show drive and enterprise. One case known to the author was a sixty-year-old woman who injected paraffin into her cheeks, donned heavy make-up, and by soliciting intoxicated men on dark streets managed to earn a living for herself. When the suggestion was made that she apply for relief, she contemptuously scorned the idea. If a prostitute is reasonably protected from arrest or imprisonment, if her strength and physical attractions are not sapped by illness which prevents her from working, and if she can solve the problem of affection, there is nothing to seriously interfere with symbolic integration of her personality. If she is beautiful or masters cosmetic arts enough to attract well-dressed, prosperous men and earn generous fees, she has attained goals motivating most other women in our culture. The societal self-definition is not so differentiated or so negatively evaluated as to be modally repugnant. The fact that men of all social classes persistently seek her out gives her a sense of social worth despite the formal rejections she may receive from them in other capacities.

The conflicts and anxieties of the prostitute center around her affectional relations rather than the moral implications of her life. A disorganizing sense of isolation will grow in the absence of some deeper and meaningful love relationship, although this may be minimized by a selective process which draws to prostitution women who are emotionally more self-sufficient than others. The prostitute-pimp bond gives her the needed affection, but it must be remembered that no centripetal legal forces maintain it. Its instability can be a source of anxiety. There have been the cases in which prostitutes commit suicide over a pimp [61] and the author is familiar with several homicides involving the murder of pimps by prostitutes. There is scant knowledge of the amount of mental disease among prostitutes which can be related to their role. Figures from one institutionalized group of cases put the percentage of commitments to mental hospitals at between 3 and 4.[62] However, because these girls were already imprisoned, not too much importance can be assigned to the figures. Also, the incidence of syphilis may have been much higher in the group, which produced organic lesions of the nervous system, not directly attributable to the prostitute's role.

MARGINALITY

Marginal prostitution probably is less likely to occur today in our culture than in the nineteenth century, chiefly because of the blurring which has come about in the societal definitions of female sex roles. Categorical distinctions between prostitutes and others remain in the law but informally they have become soft around the edges; and, consequently, introjected conflicts and ambivalences of the "good girl"-"bad girl" variety are less often reflected or validated in the objective social participation of the errant female.

Marginality in the prostitute, when it does show itself, is apt to appear if and when she marries – particularly into a middle-class status. In one case of a high-priced prostitute whose history became known to the author, the woman became a psychiatric case after her marriage chiefly as the consequence of fears that former patrons would inadvertently or deliberately expose her past life. Certainly continuing prostitution after marriage will create high stresses in the prostitute who tries to conceal it from husband and friends.

Perhaps the contemporary "B girl" or "gold digger" comes closer to

61 Reitman, *op. cit*, p 23.

62 Fernald *et al.*, *op. cit.*, p. 160.

representing marginal prostitution. Such women, who maintain the pretense of sexual availability without sexual consummation in order to gain money, are beyond question much more isolated than the prostitute and at least several cuts below her in public estimation. Prostitutes as well as respectable community members reject this type of woman. The men who are duped by such women complain loudly, the press editorializes in cartoons against "clip joints," and police treat such girls very roughly.

Age and Prostitution

A special concluding comment needs to be made concerning age and prostitution. The aging process in the prostitute tends to be accelerated by irregular habits. She often does not eat properly or sleep at fixed times. The necessity to travel interrupts her physical regimes. Association with rowdy men may cause her to drink more than is good for her. Venereal infection and the aftereffects of abortions tend to produce menstrual disorders and speed physical deterioration. As her looks and energy fail, her earnings and sexual prestige suffer. Somewhere a critical age point is reached, and conflicts between her former and present self-conceptions may disrupt her behavior. More intelligent and enterprising prostitutes probably turn to other occupations at this time – some socially acceptable. Others move downward into lower levels of prostitution to which they may or may not adjust, depending upon their prior aspirations and the rigidity of their self-definitions.

Selected Readings

Davis, Kingsley: "The Sociology of Prostitution," *American Sociological Review*, 2, October, 1937, pp 744–755.

Madeleine, 1919 (anonymous)

Maurer, David. "Prostitutes and Criminal Argots," *American Journal of Sociology*, 44, January, 1939, pp. 546–550.

Prostitutes, Their Early Lives, League of Nations Advisory Committee on Social Questions, Part 1, 1938

Reckless, Walter *Vice in Chicago*, 1933

Waterman, W. *Prostitution and Its Repression in New York City*, 1932.

CHAPTER 9

CRIME AND THE CRIMINAL

There would be little justification for including the present chapter in this treatise if the contents were a synoptic review of the field of criminology. That field is more than adequately represented by numerous textbooks with a variety of approaches and viewpoints. With one or two exceptions they have followed the older "problems" orientation with which general sociology originally was identified. In these texts we usually find the subject matter focused around the "causes" and the "treatment" of crime. The great lacuna in the field, whose exploration becomes our special concern, falls between these two well-trodden areas. We refer here to the study of criminal behavior itself, which in our estimation is destined to become of paramount sociological interest. Modern theoretical versions of sociology seem to foreshadow the emergence of a "sociology of crime," confined to just such an analysis of criminal behavior, with interests tangential to those of older criminology. Some indications of recognition and tentative acceptance of this newer point of view come to light in several textbooks published on the subject of criminology in the last decade.[1]

Certain types of criminal behavior, namely, systematic crimes, seem to lend themselves exceptionally well to analysis by the theoretical means which have been outlined and followed thus far in our discussion of sociopathic behaviors. Whether some of the unsettled problems of criminology can be studied better with these formulations than with others remains to be seen. However, at least one such controversy, that over "white-collar" crime, gives some promise that it can be resolved by the application of such concepts as differential social visibility, differential societal reactions, and varying symbolization of criminal deviation. It is also hoped that some of the confusion as to what crime is can be reduced by our method for defining it as a special variety of sociopathic behavior.

[1] Cavan, R. S., *Criminology*, 1948, Preface and Chap. 1; Sutherland, E. H , *Criminology*, 1947, 4th ed., Preface; Reckless, W., *Criminal Behavior*, 1940, Chap 1, Reimer, Svend, "Theory and Quantitative Analysis in Criminological Research," *American Journal of Sociology*, 47, September, 1942, pp 188–201

The Nature of Criminal Deviation

There is by no means a fine agreement among sociologists, or, for that matter, among students of jurisprudence, as to just what is meant by the term "crime" and as to who is a "criminal." However, a certain polarizing of thought can be detected, on the one hand among those who adhere to a stringently legalistic viewpoint and on the other hand among those who hold to a more generic sociological conception of crime. This difference tends to cut across rather than follow the formal lines of division between the two disciplines of law and sociology; indeed, some of the more sociologized theories of crime have come from legally trained thinkers.

Writers with strong juristic inclinations prefer to define crime as the violation of a law which has been instituted by a political process and which specifies means and conditions of punishment. Under this definition a violation of the law in order to qualify as criminal must be willful, without excuse, and must grow out of culpable intent. Furthermore, the breach of the law and the identification of its violator as criminal must be established through formal procedure in a court of law.

Critics of this more formal and juridical formulation of crime and the criminal person have rightly shown that it takes no cognizance of the commission of crime and the existence of criminals in preliterate, politically unorganized societies. A more or less forced conclusion is that many primitive societies have no crime, no cultural definition of the criminal, and no concept of criminal justice. This patently is not the case, as many writers on primitive law and crime have shown. Another critical charge which has been levied against the legalistic version of crime is that political authority itself does not always make clear distinctions between crimes and civil wrongs. This is seen in states where some acts are defined both as crime and as torts and may become the object of civil, as well as criminal, procedure. The real objective of criminal complaints and procedure, in many instances, is not so much punishment as to create a leverage for monetary redress; the accusation is a familiar one that the criminal courts are used as collection agencies by complainants.

Still another weakness of the juristic idea of crime lies in the failure to recognize the equivalent of the judicial process which takes place in groups without legally recognized authority, in which violations are defined by reference to constituent group norms instead of laws. An example of this is the intragroup justice meted out in Chinese tongs in the United States. It is also true that the ultimate aim of criminal procedure in our criminal courts today can no longer be simply designated as punishment, in the light of extensive application of probation and suspended sentences and the expanded use of the injunction or positive court orders. Finally it is to be noted that guilty intent is no longer an absolute prerequisite for the commission of crime; some legislatures in recent years have introduced the principle of strict criminal liability for such offenses as the obstruction of highways and adulteration of drugs and medicines. In fact, it is becoming more obvious that the concept of criminal negligence must come into increasing play in a technologically oriented society such as ours.

If the concept of criminal deviation is to have sociological meaning, it has to be sought in the attributes of the societal norms which are violated. The problem is to ascertain which particular norms are involved with which particular attributes. From the point of view we have adopted, crime can be taken as all deviations from those societal norms which have a high degree of compulsiveness, specificity, and universality. Any behavior which effectively sets the majority of the community or society against those who engage in it can be regarded as criminal. The high degree of compulsiveness of the norms which are violated in crimes is operationally made apparent in the ingroup-outgroup cleavage which appears and also in the rough, belligerent treatment of the offender.[2] Something akin to, if not identical with, warfare characterizes the relationship between known criminal transgressors and the members of society, whose strongest sanctions have been challenged. Symbols of this can be seen in law-enforcement campaigns, which are typically captioned as "war on crime," and in newspaper designations of criminals as the "enemies of society."

In small, geographically isolated, and homogeneous societies or communities there is a direct and continuous interaction between offenders against fundamental norms and those who adhere to them and seek their enforcement. Consequently violations in these instances tend to become known to all members of the group in all particulars. The members of the community move in informal concert to apply severe sanctions of execution, banishment, and other penalties. Even though a formal procedure may be followed, as in the case of some South African tribes and formerly among some of the American Plains Indians, it closely corresponds to and expresses the informal genotypic hostility of the group toward the wrongdoer.

In large, complex, urban industrial societies the aggressive reaction to criminal deviation is complicated by the necessary delegation of the punitive process to special political and legal authority. The segmental legal reaction to crime may or may not reflect the more inclusive societal reaction. Many times, on account of both fortuitous and directed influences bearing upon the politico-legal process, the formal definition and penaliza-

[2] Sellin, Thorsten, *Culture Conflict and Crime,* 1938, pp. 32–33; Mead, G. H, "The Psychology of Punitive Justice," *American Journal of Sociology,* 23, March, 1918, pp 577–602, Hall, J., "Interrelations of Criminal Law and Torts," *University of Pennsylvania Law Review,* 43, March, 1941, pp 549–580

tion of criminal acts is dissociated in various ways from the societal antagonisms they originally generate. A specific example of this would be the passage of criminal laws grossly contrary to the normative conceptions of the great majority of the people, as in the case of national prohibition. The failure to convict criminals not because of any lack of evidence but because of a disregard of technical legal procedures by the prosecution is also a case in point. We note, as a last illustration, the lack of legal action against criminals in the presence of a widespread and articulate desire of many persons to have them brought to trial.

The vagaries and inconsistencies of formalized justice in our society have engendered a cynicism among some, who go so far as to claim that really serious misconduct in our society has been only partially codified as "crime" and also that those persons who are actually convicted and punished for these offenses tend to be petty criminals or those who do not have the available political and economic power to avoid arrest and punishment. This has led to a theoretical extension of the concept of crime to cover such things as general socially harmful conduct and violations of the "spirit of the law," particularly in the realm of business activity, phrased as "white-collar" crime.[3]

Deviation Is Criminal Only If Effectively Reacted to and Symbolized as Such

From the standpoint of strict scientific description and analysis it is a fallacy to designate forms of behavior as criminal if in effect they are not symbolized and treated as such by members of the society in which they occur. These behaviors admittedly may have a serious disorganizing effect upon the society, but if there is no informal or formal reaction to them as wrongs, it would be profitless to study the behaviors, concomitant organization, and associated roles and statuses as interactive functions of a segregating and punitive reaction. This holds true even when the behavior is nominally criminal. There are important social reasons over and above any political corruption why activities of businessmen and corporations which are namable violations of the law go unprosecuted. The most general reason is that the social and economic consequences of enforcing many laws are collectively perceived as more injurious than letting the violation go unpunished. For example, a literal enforcement of tax laws undoubtedly would ruin thousands of businessmen or destroy many corporations every year.[4] Hence the Bureau of Internal Revenue makes "deals" with business

[3] See the following by Sutherland, E. H: "Crime and Business," *Annals of the American Academy of Political and Social Science*, 217, September, 1941, pp 112–118, "White Collar Criminality," *American Sociological Review*, 5, February, 1940, pp 1–12, same, *White Collar Crime*, 1949, also his *Criminology*, p. 37.

[4] Herring, E. P., *Public Administration and the Public Welfare*, 1936.

enterprises and individuals, based not upon any corruption of tax officials but upon a realistic appreciation of the inapplicability of punishment as a means of gaining compliance with the law. The same is true of many marriage and divorce laws; their strict enforcement undoubtedly would create more family disorganization than does the extant disregard of their violation.

Such facts as these, however, should not inspire a retreat to the extremely conservative view adopted by a recent critic of the concept of white-collar crime who narrowly holds that behavior is criminal only if legally designated as such, and that "... Only those are criminals who have been selected by a clear substantive and adjective law, such as obtains in our courts," or that, "... Only those are criminals who have been adjudicated as such by the courts." [5] This conception is the partial formulation of a constitutional ideal and is insufficient for purposes of sociological study of crime. For example, it excludes, as noncriminal, cases of confidence men who have carried on for years without being arrested, or, if arrested, without being convicted. In strict legal parlance of this sort they could not be classed as criminals despite the fact that they more or less share the same behavior system and status of confidence men who have been tried and convicted in courts. Yet these unadjudicated confidence men are under no illusions as to the criminal nature of their roles. The obtrusive error in this neojuristic position is the failure to perceive that a society or a community may realistically symbolize behavior and persons as criminal through agencies other than courts of law. In matter of fact it is probably the contact and interaction with the police rather than with the courts in many instances which carry the more indelible social imprimatur of crime for the violators of our laws.

It is to be taken into further consideration that nonlegal groups in society arrogate to themselves a measure of criminal jurisdiction and thereby play a part in the symbolization of crime and segregation of criminals. The very fact that sociologists conceived and applied to some forms of behavior the term "white-collar crime," however misleading it may be, is testimony of this fact. Insurance companies have contacts with thieves within a special symbolic environment outside of the courts. Banks often handle embezzlers without recourse to the courts; department stores, in some cases, have a special nonlegal procedure for dealing with shoplifters without arrest; large insurance companies many times dispose of cases of agents who have criminal shortages in their accounts without legal prosecution. Commercial accountants have concepts of "honest" and "dishonest" corporations which they may use in their reports with special nonlegal implications. The farther removed from the courts these agencies

[5] Tappan, Paul, "Who Is the Criminal?" *American Sociological Review*, 12, February, 1947, p. 100.

with quasi-punitive functions are, the more diffuse become the criminalistic implications of the symbols and actions invoked in their interactions with culprits. For this reason the misbehavior which is recognized and dealt with in social areas peripheral to the court system might better be termed "marginal crime."

The Need to Define and Study Particular Crimes Sociologically

The study in general of crime at best can yield conclusions which will be subject to all sorts of exceptions. Generalizing about a broad range of deviant behavior and roles classified as "criminal" is limited both by the diversification involved and by the variability of the societal reactions to these roles and behaviors by the police, the courts, and the rest of the community. We can see at once that the behavior patterns of sex criminals and professional thieves are grossly different and also that there is a wide difference in the attitudes and the actions of police and court officers toward the two. Consequently if our understanding of criminal deviation is to advance, it is imperative that crimes be grouped into homogeneous sociological classifications.[6] Initial generalization about criminal deviation should be confined to specific criminal behaviors and, wherever possible, to criminal behavior systems.

In order to bring out some of the differences between crimes and criminals, we have chosen to use as the primary substantive data for this chapter the facts we have about a particular form of professional crime. We refer to confidence games and those who play them, the professional confidence men. The reason for this selection is that we know more about professional thieves, among whom con men are classed, than any other kind of professional criminals. By including in detail what we know of them, we are able to particularize our discussion of crime and criminals; in effect, what we shall be doing is to clarify both the generally operating factors which touch all criminals and the special factors which operate within the more immediate context of a particular systematic crime.

The Extent of Criminal Deviation

There is at hand no accurate figure or estimate of the total number of crimes committed in the United States for a selected year, nor of the number of criminals at any given time. Practically all criminologists agree that statistics of known crimes, arrests, prosecutions, convictions, and prison populations are of very limited value as indexes, on account of errors of recording, variable police policy, and vicissitudes of the legal process itself.[7] The situation is well summarized by one writer: "The value

[6] Hall, Jerome, *Theft, Law and Society*, 1935, Introduction.

[7] Sutherland, E. H., and C. C. Van Vechten, "The Reliability of Criminal Statistics," *Proceedings of the American Prison Association*, 1933.

of a crime-rate for index purposes, decreases as the distance from the crime itself in terms of procedure increases." [8] The number of crimes committed outnumbers to an unknown degree crimes known to the police; these, in turn outnumber the crimes cleared by arrest; and these exceed the crimes for which persons are prosecuted, and so on, down the line of the judicial process. It is likewise true that a differential case mortality operates with respect to the likelihood of various types of criminal cases reaching the terminus of the judicial process, so that comparisons of rates for specific crimes drawn from available statistics may be quite misleading.[9]

It is sometimes stated that criminal statistics have value for assessing trends in over-all rates or for determining the relative increase or decrease of various kinds of crime. But even this claim is a questionable one, because changes of police policy or shifts in political power alignments within an area under study may considerably add to or subtract from the body of spurious criminal deviation which overburdens the real criminal deviation. It would be necessary to demonstrate a constancy in the societal reaction, both at the informal and formal level, before trends in crime rates computed from public records could be held to be meaningful. Criminal statistics are a measure of a whole complex of facts, perhaps being best used as a measure of the tolerance quotient. Methods for separating out the amount of real criminal deviation from the complex of other factors involved have not yet been developed.

The Differentiae of Criminals

In setting down those attributes which distinguish the criminal population from the general population, the reservations which have already been made concerning criminal statistics must always be kept in mind. Whether the differentiae of apprehended and convicted criminals are representative of the universe of criminals is a moot point and must remain so until further research has settled it. Meantime, however, it is more or less obligatory to rely upon the much-maligned statistical data, supplementing and correcting them to the best of our ability by information from other sources and by their critical manipulation.

One characteristic of criminals upon which practically all studies concur is extreme youthfulness. The age of maximum criminality is reached in the late teen ages and early adulthood, with a steady decline in crime rates for older population groups. The peak age for crime varies somewhat from country to country and also from one year to the next within the same country. Still, despite these fluctuations, the modal age for criminals tends

[8] Sellin, Thorsten, "The Basis of a Crime Index," *Journal of Criminal Law and Criminology*, 22, September, 1931, pp. 335–356.

[9] Van Vechten, C. C., "Differential Criminal Case Mortality, in Selected Jurisdictions," *American Sociological Review*, 7, December, 1942, pp 833–839.

to fall between 19 and 24 years. However, when attention is turned to persons convicted of different types of offenses, a great deal of dispersion in representative age values is disclosed. Median ages for criminals by type of offense reveal differences running as high as twelve years. This can be seen from an inspection of Table 33.

TABLE 33. MEDIAN AGES OF MALE FELONY PRISONERS RECEIVED FROM COURTS IN STATE AND FEDERAL REFORMATORIES AND PRISONS, BY TYPE OF OFFENSE, UNITED STATES, 1946*

Offense	Median Age
Murder	26 6
Manslaughter	30.5
Robbery.	24
Aggravated assault	28.7
Burglary	23 9
Larceny, except auto theft	25.5
Auto theft	22.7
Embezzlement and fraud	33.8
Stolen property	30 1
Forgery	29 3
Rape	26.6
Commercialized vice	33
Other sex offenses	37
Violating drug laws	34.5
Carrying and possessing weapons	26.4
Nonsupport or neglect	33.8
Violating liquor laws	36.4
Violating traffic laws	29.8
Violating national-defense laws	27.5
Other offenses	30

**Prisoners in State and Federal Prisons and Reformatories*, U.S. Bureau of the Census, 1946, Table 33, p 46.

It is to be noted that the median age for persons convicted of embezzlement and fraud stands comparatively high in the table, being exceeded only by that for three other crimes. Since persons convicted of bunco and confidence-game crimes are included under this classification, it may be presumed that they are typically much older than other kinds of criminals. Chances are good that the age of confidence men is very similar to that of the business and professional men and women who are their victims. This is to be expected if they are to gain the confidence of their victims by posing as business operators themselves. It must also be remembered that the intuitive skills of the confidence man are those which come only with a long learning period and the maturity of years.

In addition to being on the average a deviation of youth, crime is a predominantly male activity, particularly among Caucasoid members of our society. The sex ratio ranges from 10 to 1 for arrests to 20 to 1 for inmates of Federal and state prisons and reformatories. Compared to their age characteristics the sex ratios of criminals seem to be much more variable, even for the same type of crime, from country to country, from one size of community to another, and from one race to another. In some foreign countries and among Negroes in our own society the crime rates of females come very close to those of males. As might be anticipated, women are most commonly arrested and convicted for sex offenses, with disorderly conduct, drunkenness, and homicide ranking high, although still considerably below the sex crimes.

The racial, nativity, and ethnic attributes of criminals are among the most difficult to properly determine, chiefly because it is in the administration of justice to minority groups that bias and prejudice are most likely to intrude. Studies uniformly show that the greatest differential in crime rates appear between American Indian and white and between Negro and white populations. Table 34 presents felony conviction rates for white and minority groups in Los Angeles County.

TABLE 34. FELONY RATES, GROSS AND CORRECTED FOR AGE AND SEX OF WHITE AND MINORITY POPULATIONS,* LOS ANGELES COUNTY, 1938†

Population group	Rate per 100,000 population	Rate per 100,000 male population	Rate per 100,000 males aged 18–39
White	124	248	716
Mexican	174	356	843
Negro	403	835	2,305
Jewish	128	256	
Chinese	181	201	
Japanese	57	101	
Filipino	500	483	
Indian	1,492	2,540	

*Populations estimated from U.S. Bureau of the Census reports, 1920 and 1930; also Hanson, Earl, *Los Angeles, Its People and Its Homes*, Haynes Foundation, 1944.

†Lemert, Edwin M., and Judy Rosberg, *The Administration of Justice to Minority Groups in Los Angeles County*, 1948, Table 2, p. 4.

Certain writers have disallowed completely the differential crime rates between Negroes and whites on the grounds of the greater visibility of Negro crime and the greater likelihood of arrest and prosecution for their crimes.[10] However, more exacting study of the administration of justice to minority racial groups leaves one less convinced that this is true. Probabilities are strong that there is a real, although as yet not accurately measured, difference between the objective criminal deviation of Negroes and whites and between that of American Indians and whites.[11]

[10] Sellin, Thorsten, "The Negro Criminal, A Statistical Note," *Annals of the American Academy of Political and Social Science*, 217, September, 1940, pp. 421*ff*.

[11] Lemert, Edwin M., and Judy Rosberg, *The Administration of Justice to Minority Groups in Los Angeles County*, 1948, pp. 3*ff*.

A convention of criminological literature has been the conclusion that persons of foreign birth have a lower crime rate than native-born population, and that the children of foreign-born parents exceed native-born persons in the rate of crime commission. Unfortunately rigorous controls have not always been maintained in making comparisons of the crime rates of these nativity groups. One important oversight has been of the fact that, for the most part, immigrants have been from the rural areas of Europe and that, to be meaningful, comparisons of their crime rates should be with native-born rural groups of equated age and sex composition who have migrated to urban areas. It may be conceded freely that the crime rates of second-generation immigrants have frequently far surpassed those of the native-born of native parents. At the same time it is also to be observed that the rates show great variation in different parts of the nation and from one area to another within the same community.

Racial and ethnic groups vary as much or more among themselves with reference to general arrest and commitment rates as collectively they differ from the native white population. They also vary greatly as to the specific crimes for which they have relatively high rates. A specimen of this variation for racial groups in a given area is given in Table 35.

Among the foreign-nativity groups, Italians and Irish seem to have characteristically higher crime rates than other nationalities, with Italians more frequently than the Irish being convicted of crimes punishable by imprisonment. There is some evidence to demonstrate that first- and second-generation Americans with Italian, Irish, and, to a small extent, Jewish antecedents have participated in some forms of organized crime more than other groups. According to one informal estimate the ethnic make-up of gangsters and racketeers during the prohibition era in Chicago was 85 per cent Italian or Sicilian, 10 per cent Jewish, and 5 per cent Irish.[12]

Thus far there has been little demographic characterization of professional criminals as opposed to nonprofessional, or of professional criminals by the type of their specialties. For example, the absence of a separate category for confidence-game crimes in statistical records prevents any exact statement of the ethnic composition of those who follow this illegal calling. Apparently there are con men of many different races, but generally those who play the "big con" are Caucasoid. Negroes, Filipinos and other minority racial groups tend to concentrate upon members of their own racial groups for victims and also specialize in forms of con games especially adapted to their sociopsychological peculiarities. Negroes, for example, nearly always play the "pigeon drop," a variety of "short con" exploiting modal status strivings of their group. It has been claimed that white con men tend to be predominantly Anglo-Saxon, with a sprinkling

[12] Asbury, Herbert, Chicago, 1942, pp 325–326, also see Wood, A. E, and J B. Waite, *Crime and Its Treatment*, 1941, pp. 240–244.

of Jews among them.[13] However, out of 115 native-born white persons arrested for embezzlement and fraud in Los Angeles in 1947, 57.3 per cent were descendants of inhabitants of the British Isles; 5 per cent were

TABLE 35. PERCENTAGE DISTRIBUTION OF FELONIES BY POPULATION GROUPS, LOS ANGELES COUNTY, 1938*

Felony	Negro	Mexican	Jewish	Japanese	Chinese	Filipino	Indian	White
Burglary 1st degree	2.4	2.8				12		3.5
Burglary 2d degree	19.6	15.8	6.8	4.7	11.1	12	35.2	14.0
Robbery 1st degree	2.4	2.5	2.3	4.7		8		4.9
Robbery 2nd degree	5.9	2.8				4		1.7
Narcotics Act violation	8.3	5.3	6.0		44.4			1.7
Grand theft plus 503	10.0	26.0	3.4				11.7	12.6
Receiving stolen property	3.8	2.5	4.3				5.9	1.7
Forgery	5.9	4.0	12.8	19.0		12		14.9
Not sufficient funds	0.3		6.0				5.9	7.5
Petty theft plus prior	9.3	4.3	1.7			8		1.7
Grand theft	3.8	2.3	6.0	4.7		8		4.2
Rape, incest, 288a (perversions)	7.2	12.6	1.7			4	17.2	7.0
337a (bookmaking).	0.03	0.8	43.6	28.5	11.1			10.0
Assault with deadly weapon	8.0	7.0	1.7	9.5	11.1	20	5.9	3.4
Deadly Weapon Act violation	2.8	1.8			11.1	8		1.8
Assault	1.3	2.8						1.8
Bigamy .	0.7							
Vehicle Code violation	1.7	5.5		19.0		4	17.6	3.9
Murder .	0.3	0.5		4.7				1.0
Manslaughter	3.1							
Perjury	1.7	0.3	0.8					
Alcoholic Beverages Act violation		0.8		4.7	11.1			0.2
False claims		0.3						
Bribery . .			1.7					
375 (throwing stinkbombs)			1.7					

*Lemert, Edwin M., and Judy Rosberg, *The Administration of Justice to Minority Groups in Los Angeles County*, 1948, p. 7, Table 5.

Jewish.[14] By very rough estimate this would make the proportions of the two groups about the same as for the general community population.

Studies of the economic traits of criminals are, for reasons already made clear, not too reliable. A disproportionate number of criminals have been unemployed prior to their institutional commitments. It is also true that unskilled and semiskilled workers are overnumerous among convicted criminals when projected against an occupational profile of the general population. But the wages of persons in legitimate work previous to committing their crimes do not seem to differ in any important way from the

[13] Landesco, John, *Illinois Crime Survey*, 1929, pp. 1,083*ff*.

[14] *Annual Report of Los Angeles Police Department*, 1947, p. 142.

wages of the general population. Persons convicted of fraud and embezzlement reveal a much lower-than-expected rate of prior unemployment and much higher-than-average earnings at their last legitimate employment.[15]

Persistent attempts have been made in the past to prove that criminals harbor more than a normal quota of feeble-minded persons and those with defective intelligence among them. However, in recent years criminologists have grown increasingly skeptical of claims such as these, with the result that few of them now would be willing to grant that low intelligence is an over-all trait of criminals. It may be that certain types of criminals are deficient in abstract verbal intelligence, but even this is debatable. Educational attainment and criminality seem to be inversely correlated, with a greater percentage of criminals being drawn from illiterate classes and from those with only grade schooling. However, Federal offenders, who may be presumed to be the object of more skillful and energetic police work, are an exceptional note, for they closely resemble the general population in educational attainment. Illiterate persons are practically nonexistent among those arrested and convicted for fraud and embezzlement. Furthermore, the ratio of college-trained persons to those with less education among those imprisoned for fraud has, at times, actually exceeded that of the noncriminal population.[16] Most evidence suggests or indicates that con men are a highly educated group, probably above the average.

A quality possessed by criminals which has been widely recognized and commented upon is their high mobility. Sufficient reason for believing that this is a real differential of criminals is found in figures in which the percentage of persons arrested outside the state of their birth is almost twice that of the general population residing outside of their state of birth.[17] How representative this is of persons convicted of different types of offenses is not known for certain. However, it is probably safe to state that professional criminals are more highly mobile than others. Most assuredly this is true of con men. In Los Angeles in 1947, of all the persons arrested for fraud and embezzlement 22 per cent had been in the city for less than six months, a figure surpassed only by those held on vagrancy and those taken on Federal offenses.[18] For a host of nonsystematic crimes, such as petty theft, assault, and battery, many sex offenses and those against the liquor laws seem to be pretty much those of the fixed residents of the community.

While there is much need to know about the differences in the degree of mobility between criminals and the general population and between the

[15] Lunden, Walter, *Statistics on Crime and Criminals*, 1942, pp 84–87.

[16] *Ibid*, p 43.

[17] *Ibid.*, pp. 134*ff*.

[18] *Annual Report of Los Angeles Police Department*, 1947, p. 145. Most of these Federal offenses are illegal transportation of stolen automobiles across a state line, and by definition they involve mobility.

criminals themselves, there is also a need to learn more about the patterns of movement among criminals, especially those connected with systematic crime. We are inclined to believe that the mobility of criminals, even when they are professionalized tends to be of a delimited kind. Criminals are most likely to confine their activities to regions and to follow itineraries when they move about the country. Con men are supposed to move continually in order to avoid the possibility of recognition by their victims. Yet several sources indicate that theirs is a seasonal movement between certain well-defined types of communities. The biography of the famous con man, "Yellow Kid" Weil, makes it clear that, while on occasion he traveled abroad and into distant states, nevertheless most of his operations were confined to Chicago and the Great Lakes area.[19]

Community Background of Criminals

The relatively high rate of spatial movement of many criminals seriously handicaps any effort to tell with accuracy from which areas the greater number of criminals originate or to tell what their differential origins have been in terms of their criminal specializations. There is, of course, a pronounced differential in rural-urban crime rates in favor of the rural population, but it is not known with any surety what percentage of criminals are persons with rural backgrounds who have migrated to city environments. The figures usually cited on rural-urban crime differentials disclose three to four times as much crime per population unit in large urban communities. From area to area, however, the same size communities may vary widely in their crime rates. The percentage distribution of different types of crimes varies from rural to urban communities, with property crimes and those involving pecuniary manipulations being relatively more urban, and personal crimes being relatively more rural.

Admittedly sketchy data on con men suggest an interesting possible exception to the general rural-urban differential in the origin of criminal populations. Statements of con men themselves run to the effect that large numbers of their recruits have come from Indiana, which below its northern industrial rim has been, and remains today, fundamentally a rural state. More particularly con men have remarked on the sophistication of Indiana farmers on matters pertaining to short-con games.[20] Explanations of this may lie in the fact of circuses having made Indiana their winter quarters for many years. Circuses and carnivals have always carried grifters of many kinds, con men as well as others. It is quite possible that a study of the origins of circus populations might shed much light upon the community origin of professional thieves.

Some broad regional differences come to light in general crime rates.

[19] Brannon, W. T., *Yellow Kid Weil*, 1948.

[20] Maurer, David, *The Big Con*, 1940, pp. 174–175.

However, the rate concentrations for specific crimes are far more impressive. For example, the center of concentration for homicide rates is in the Southeastern states, while for robbery it falls in the Middle Central states.[21] Nevertheless, within regions such as these, variations occur which have often far exceeded the differences between the regions. The average homicide rate in so-called "bloody Breathit" County in the state of Kentucky during the year 1925 and between 1930 to 1934 ran forty-three times as high as the rate in Washington County.[22] Chances are that regional differentiation of crime rates frequently result from fortuitous factors. Certainly space is a relatively unimportant factor in con games. At one time certain cities were notorious locales for con-game operations, and to some extent today con games are more apt to be played in resort towns, but any large city and often small towns will do. Whether or not a "fix" exists in the town is far more important than its general location, and it would be hard to show that the fix is affected by geographic factors. Con men prefer to work on out-of-town victims and often deliberately take them away from their home environments in order to better work their schemes. They think nothing of sending victims thousands of miles to obtain their money, and in one case a victim was sent to Europe and back for his money.

Ecological studies of delinquency, especially in Chicago, Illinois, have found not only heavy concentrations of youthful crime in certain sections of the city but also a spatial patterning of sorts which could be expressed in quantitative terms, gradients. These studies, verified by research in several other cities, have been challenged by some writers as measuring a variety of other factors besides the objective criminality in the areas. These criticisms seem well taken, because it is obvious that differential social visibility of the delinquencies and variant neighborhood and community reactions may be implicit in these gradients. Whether over and beyond these factors the gradients actually measure real differences in the sociological nature of the youthful law violations will be reserved for discussion somewhat later in this same chapter.

The most outstanding conclusion from this cursory survey of the demographic characteristics of criminal populations seems to be that dispersion and variation in crime rates, when broken down according to specific types of crime, are far more significant than central tendencies in crime rates as a whole. The urgent need to work out truly sociological categories and classifications of criminal behavior and to amass or remanipulate data with such tools increasingly makes itself felt. Nothing is clearer than that

21 Lottier, Stuart, "Distribution of Criminal Offenses in Sectional Regions," *Journal of Criminal Law and Criminology*, 29, September, 1938, pp 329–344

22 Wood and Waite, *op. cit.*, p 138

the demographic features of a criminal population cannot be taken *ipso facto* as its sociological attributes. At best such demographic materials can serve for inferential and exploratory purposes to provide cues for research in a sociological frame of reference. An obvious necessity is the careful study of crime by sociological types and, within such a classification as systematic crime, to carefully describe and analyze separate criminal behaviors.

The Social and Personal Contexts of Crime

That similar overt criminal behavior can and does have a wide gamut of meanings and symbolic associations in roles, groups, and in social situations will be easily granted by most sociologists. A certain percentage of crimes are symptomatic of unintegrated impulses and tensions within the person. They are incidents of what is commonly thought of as psychotic, neurotic, or eccentric behavior. It has been shown that in some cases psychotic conditions referred to as schizophrenia and paranoia lead to violence against others.[23] Some of the more unusual sex crimes seem to be a function of dissociated and irrational compulsions, which leave the offenders themselves as well as officers of the law baffled as to their source and motivation. This is not to say that such criminal behavior is meaningless, but rather that the meaning is very complex and highly disguised. It is difficult to relate it in any logical way to the social situation in which it occurs and impossible to construe it as the expression of systematic criminal activity.

Many writers outside the field of sociology are disposed to regard a large number, if not the majority, of criminals as psychiatric problems in the sense of the above paragraph. At the present time, in contrast to this, sociologists are inclined to discount such claims, preferring to emphasize the "psychological" normality of criminals. This is traceable to the scarcity of empirically valid demonstrations that the incidence of neurotic and psychotic cases is any greater in the criminal than in the general population.[24]

From one type of crime to another the proportions of persons whose participation in the crime must be studied in a personal context will be variable. Perhaps some crimes are more likely to be perpetrated by unstable or mentally disordered persons. However, some of the easy assumptions which have been made by psychiatrically oriented writers on the subject, in equating crime with psychiatric categories, need careful examination. We think immediately of such diagnoses as "kleptomania" and "pyromania" in which it is assumed that persons steal or set fires because they are "obsessive compulsive" neurotics, in the same class with com-

[23] Dunham, H. W., "The Schizophrene and Criminal Behavior," *American Sociological Review*, 4, June, 1939, pp. 352–356

[24] Sutherland, *Criminology*, Chap. VII.

pulsive hand washers. Especially dubious are concepts like that of the "psychopathic criminal" whose diagnosis is based upon the fact that he or she has no "moral sense," which is simply a way of saying that such persons show no remorse over their crimes. The fallacy of the assumption that no person can commit crime without guilt or fear feelings unless he is mentally distorted comes out most clearly in available studies of professional criminals.

All facts considered, we believe that the exploration of crime in situational contexts and in the context of learned responses of a behavior system will prove far more revealing to the scientist than the search for a "personality" of the criminal.

Situational Crime

Situational crime is that committed by the ordinarily law-abiding citizen with a relatively well-integrated set of roles or that committed by a noncriminal sociopath. In either case, external stresses and strains temporarily disrupt a personal equilibrium and induce tensions which are expressed in criminal behavior. The unmarried college girl under extreme fear of exposure or the economically hard-pressed slum mother may murder their newly born infants because no legitimate alternatives to their dilemmas are present. These are uncommon crimes and consequently likely to be the result of more fortuitous situations. Other criminogenic situations are more commonplace, resulting from major social or economic transformations such as war, inflation, and unemployment coupled with lowered police efficiency and conditions of increased anonymity. During the bombing raids in England in the midst of the Second World War a great deal of looting went on. Significantly neither professional criminals nor recidivists were primarily responsible; of those arrested for the crime 90 per cent had never before come against the law in any way.[25] In the years 1922 and 1923 Germany saw an increase of 120,000 larceny and burglary offenses, which was a gain of 30 per cent over the previous year.[26] Such a sudden change in the number of property offenses throughout the nation could scarcely be explained as caused by sudden increment of criminaloid psychotic persons or of professional criminals in the population. More correctly they tell of the many deviant reactions made by a segment of the noncriminal population to postwar socioeconomic dislocations in Germany.

The surcharging of large numbers of social situations in our culture with competitive stress has struck many observers as a generally operating variable in American crime. No other culture in the world – perhaps in all history – has elevated its emulative ideals of material success so far

[25] Barnes, H., and N. Teeters, *New Horizons in Criminology*, 1946, p. 20.
[26] Von Hentig, H., *Crime, Causes and Conditions*, 1947, p 11

beyond the level of mass fulfillment and at the same time has applied pressures to secure mass achievement of these ideals. It is a matter of small surprise that so many persons conforming to the demands of the hypermotivated struggle for status overstep the limits of legally acceptable behavior in the direction of crime. As in the case of prostitution there are elements of crime in the behavior of most people; most people "cheat a little" in filling out income-tax returns and some "cheat a lot." A competitive society can avoid criminal excesses only if it is sufficiently homogeneous to foster self-restraint for a common good. The alternative rests in a strong, positivist-oriented government. But American ideology and social organization is uncongenial to this, even when formal developments in such a direction take place through the accretion of laws. The masses of people, at one time or another, clamor for more laws, but the modal distrust of government sabotages the enforcement of the laws they have demanded.[27]

Some social situations in the culture appear more stress-laden than others, and by the same token some crimes are more likely to be situational deviations. Only 5 per cent of cases of embezzlement can be traced to organized criminal endeavors.[28] The bulk of cases of this sort come to light where an individual under financial strain resulting from gambling, playing the stock market, or from expensive tastes in goods or women, "borrows" a little money at a time with the best intentions of repayment, until at last he is enmeshed in a large shortage which cannot be concealed. While shoplifting occasionally may be symptomatic compulsive behavior or bear the imprint of professional grifting, much of it is situational, related to low wages coupled with high prices and to the exposure of an abundance of coveted goods in a mass situation where policing is difficult to maintain efficiently.

The social situation in which other sociopathic deviants find themselves often compels them to turn to crime. The impoverished drug addict, whose expenditures for a supply of narcotics is outstripping his wages, finds crime the only way to avoid the horrible specter of withdrawal symptoms and so begins to forge checks or have a go at shoplifting, or of peddling the drugs themselves. Economically deteriorated alcoholics frequently have behind their petty thieving the need to obtain liquor they can get in no other way.

The appearance and growth of many criminal behavior systems can

[27] Anderson, Henry W., *National Committee on Law Observance and Enforcement*. 1931, Vol. I, "Report on Causes of Crime", Bain, Read, "Cultural Integration and Social Conflict," *American Journal of Sociology*, 44, January, 1939, pp 504*f*. Ploscowe. Morris, "Crime in a Competitive Society," *Annals of the American Academy of Political and Social Science*, 217, September, 1941, pp. 105–111.

[28] Lottier, *op. cit.*

be related to criminogenic situations within the culture. Sutherland, for instance, has trenchantly described and depicted in excellent detail the way in which grifting or theft and fraud grow up and function in conjunction with circus life.[29] Con games bear an obvious kinship to gambling, which has been an informal and formal appurtenance of American culture as long as it has had a separate existence. The short con remained in criminal vogue for many years until the appearance of widespread horse-race betting and the stock exchange made feasible and attractive the large-scale financial manipulations of the big con. Perhaps even more important than these external cultural forms for the fruition of the big con was the speculative mania, the drive to make a "killing" by manipulating money, stocks, and bonds, which had spread through the population. It is this endemic pecuniary fever which con men in our culture trade upon and turn to rich account. These polished professionals uniformly agree that they succeed only where the victim has "larceny in his soul" and that "you can't cheat an honest man." The "victim" of con men, in most cases, is indictable, for he has conspired to violate the law to cheat some third party.

Systematic Criminals

Our knowledge of the patterns of criminal behavior and organization is as yet incomplete, and what is at hand does not come from entirely unimpeachable sources. Journalistic accounts by crime reporters, reports of political investigations, and the autobiographies of criminals themselves cannot be credited as scientific, unbiased documents. There seems to have been a striving in writings such as these to equate criminal organization to business organization, without a critical awareness of the dissimilarities between the two forms of social organization. A readiness to find universal solidarity and a well-defined criminal "society within a society," ineptly termed the "underworld," runs through the more journalistic descriptions of organized crime.

The belief that a criminal code operates for all criminals, enforced by ubiquitous controls of the "underworld" at best is no more than a dubious hypothesis. There may be a common tendency among professional criminals to insist upon an equitable division of the spoils and to interdict informing or "stooling." Criminal individuals and groups will undoubtedly shun a known stool pigeon or criminal who has turned state's witness and even kill him on occasion. However, it is yet a matter for proof that a given criminal group will go out of its way to kill a man who has informed on another criminal organization to which it has no obligations. More exceptional would be the use of murder by certain types of criminals, such as confidence men, even when their own safety is at stake. Confidence men seldom carry guns and regard their use as crude. The nature of their

[29] Sutherland, *Criminology*, pp. 226–229.

behavior system inclines them to seek protection from exposure in other ways. Criminals of all classes are a heterogeneous lot, composed of self-interested individuals, not likely to murder in the name of a putative general code, which, in their jargon, probably would be deemed "sucker morality." Under certain circumstances criminals feel free to consider informing police along with other expedients for their protection. Professional criminal behavior tends to be highly rationalized, not unlike that of the counting house. Criminal "codes," if the term must be employed, are highly specialized and their enforcement local and expediential.

The repeated references to criminal organization as "big business" or as "crime incorporated" are colorful and suggestive but often very misleading. The racketeering gang, even though it may invade legitimate business and labor unions, keep books, and observe other business forms, can scarcely be compared to the staff and line organization of a corporation, partnership, or proprietorship, without stretching the analogy very thin. The racketeering gang or the criminal "mob" is much better described as a retinue of mercenaries held together by the need for protection and the expectation of profits.[30] Only in rare instances do other factors help to integrate a criminal group. Most notable of these would be ethnic homogeneity, which, for example, partially furthered the solidarity of the Al Capone gang in Chicago at one time. Criminal "syndicates," upon rigorous analysis, frequently turn out to be loose alliances of mutually suspicious, specialized criminal groups or rival district gangs which have temporarily worked out jurisdictions and methods for dividing spoils. The agreements behind such working arrangements lack stability, and authority in such organizations has only the most tenuous and shifting bases, constantly being challenged by obstreperous and unruly constituents.

Crimes differ from one to another in the degree to which they can be systematized or professionalized. The specific qualities of the crime also set limits to the size and nature of the social organization connected with it. Thus, while racketeering is highly organizable, a crime like rape is not.[31] The following scheme has been suggested as a classification of organized crime:

1. Thieving, involving either
   a. Violence or the threat of violence
   b. Stealth and dexterity.

[30] See, for example, the "mobbing up" methods used by bank robbers in Everett, De Baun, "The Heist — The Theory and Practice of Armed Robbery," *Harper's*, February, 1950, p. 71.

[31] There is, of course, the "gang shag," and we have run across a type of role referred to as "rapist" among some of the Mexican-American gangs of Los Angeles, but on the whole we would contend that this form of behavior excites too much public hostility to become elaborately organized.

2. Swindling rackets, such as con games, short con games (sometimes called "bunco" games), and blackmail of various types, involving the threat of adverse publicity or exposure.
3. Illicit business and racketeering or gangsterism, involving the organization of legitimate (industrial rackets), quasi-legitimate, or illegitimate business, such as those involved in prostitution, bootleg liquor, drugs, gambling, amusement, slot machines, race-track betting, and allied (*sic*) functions.

The degree of organization decreases from (1) to (3), the number of amateurs decreases from (1) to (3), and the size of the groups increases from (1) to (3).[32]

Aside from the intrinsic organizability of crimes, the norms they violate and the peculiarities of police action give form to criminal behavior patterns. Forgery, for instance, has become systematized to an appreciable degree but it has never been elaborately organized in space and time because the crime strikes directly at the basic technology of business intercourse. Business has organized itself strongly against the forger, and whatever laxness or corruption on the part of police is tolerated by business associations, it does not embrace fixing forgers' crimes. The forger works alone, or with one or two coworkers and may at times prefer arrest and imprisonment for a time to reduce his visibility.[33]

Confidence Games

Confidence games, as the term implies, are crimes of fraud and misrepresentation based upon gaining the confidence of persons with money and taking it from them under false pretenses. There are two general classes of confidence games: (1) big con, and (2) short con. The short con can be played on brief notice and usually it is for small sums. The three-shell game is one of the older and better known short cons. The older big-con games are known as the "rag," the "wire," and the "payoff," and require more time to play, involving sums of money which run from a few thousands to hundreds of thousands of dollars. They consist of complicated procedures by which a victim in the process of supposedly cheating a horse-race betting establishment or a stock exchange puts up cash to ensure getting his money and through a contrived error or mistake loses the entire amount.

The steps in the big con, followed in more abbreviated form in the short con, are as follows [34]

[32] Lindesmith, A., "Organized Crime," *Annals of The American Academy of Political and Social Sciences*, 27, September, 1941, pp 119–127.

[33] Maurer, David, "The Argot of Forgery," *American Speech*, 16, December, 1941, pp 243–250.

[34] Maurer, *The Big Con*, pp 12–13. By permission of Bobbs-Merrill Company, Indianapolis.

1. Locating and investigating a well-to-do victim (putting the mark up).
2. Gaining the victim's confidence (playing the con for him).
3. Steering him to meet the inside man (roping the mark).
4. Permitting the inside man to show him he can make a large amount of money dishonestly (telling him the tale).
5. Allowing the victim to make a substantial profit (giving him the convincer).
6. Determining how much he will invest (giving him the breakdown).
7. Sending him home for this amount of money (putting him on the send).
8. Playing him against the big store and taking his money (taking off the touch).
9. Getting him out of the way as quietly as possible (blowing him off).
10. Forestalling action by the law (putting in the fix).

Big-con games call for finished acting ability, versatility, keen insights into human behavior, judgment, and sense of timing, all skills which are not easily acquired. The paraphernalia includes such things as fake newspaper clippings, photographs, references, a sizable amount of real cash (the boodle), and accouterments for the "store" – a fake stock exchange or bookmaking agency. Con men take great pride in their craftsmanship, especially in the fact that the victim or "mark" freely turns over his money to them. They make sharp distinctions between their profession and criminal occupations calling for less skill – above all, the "heavy rackets" which rely upon force and violence. The con mob is composed of ropers, an inside man, and shills. The ropers, sometimes called "steerers," have the job of singling out likely prospects and must possess the ability to determine whether a man has money and whether he can be played. He must possess social skills, an easy approach to strangers, and an indirect persuasiveness. The inside man is usually an older man who is a master of persuasion and acting. The shills play minor roles, such as clerks or customers of the stock exchange, and may not be regular members of the mob. Con men usually prefer to operate in communities where protection can be arranged through a fixer, a policeman, detective, clerk, judge, or member of the district attorney's office, who sees to it that no arrest or prosecution or conviction occurs. In Denver at one time the fixer, a man named Lou Blonger, was the director of thirty or forty con men who worked the community during the summer tourist season. He had brought a number of policemen and the most important members of the detective bureau under his control, in addition to which deputies in the prosecuting attorney's office functioned for him as informers.[35] The fixer must be regarded as an integral part of the con mob, although at times the mob may risk working in a community without protection.

[35] Van Cise, Phillip, *Fighting the Underworld*, 1936.

The morality of confidence men deviates from that of noncriminal groups chiefly with respect to the grossness of breach of trust they practice. The fraud they carry out differs in degree from old-time horse trading, the sharp deals sometimes put over by farmers, and many contemporary business practices. However, while less ethical businessmen are careful to keep misrepresentation within the letter of the law, confidence men are bound by no such considerations. Confidence men also deviate in their complete willingness to employ bribery and to "frame" their enemies. Con men are usually careful to honor their financial obligations to one another, and in this way their morality closely parallels that of the financial loyalties of businessmen who turn deals simply on one another's words. This pecuniary rectitude is imperative because the con man never knows when he may suddenly need money for bail, bribes, or other purposes.

The sexual norms of confidence men are in a class with those of other criminals, *i.e.*, much of what is tabooed for noncriminals falls into a category of permissives for con men. The con man may be somewhat more careful about unconventional sex behavior where it may lead to publicity or notoriety, but the difference here from other criminals is not great. A con man when he is in poor financial straits may exploit a wife or mistress as a prostitute, but to do so reflects upon his reputation as a successful member of his profession. He is not above using a wife or mistress to embarrass a public official who does not respond to bribes. Con men probably are much closer to businessmen in their attitudes toward alcoholic and narcotic indulgence than they are to many other criminals.

Con men share the more general argot of criminals, especially thieves, to which they have added a more specialized vocabulary of their own. The argot is supposedly the richest and most colorful of all criminal argots. This is related to the generalized inventiveness and creativity of con men. The argot symbolizes their greatly developed professionalization and is necessary to communicate ideas which can only be expressed more awkwardly in conventional language. The argot is seldom if ever employed to communicate in public or in the presence of a victim.[36]

Con men are said to stand at the very top of criminal professions, sometimes being termed "aristocrats" of the criminal world. They are well aware of their exalted status and have a haughty disdain for other forms of crime and other criminals. Their skills are hard to come by and they are monopolizable skills, so that their status pretenses are confirmed by failures of other criminals who have tried to make the grade as con men. Within the profession, ranking rests upon proven ability to rope a mark or upon the smoothness and persuasiveness of the inside man's oratory.

[36] Maurer, *The Big Con*, Chap. IX, according to our investigation, the argot of the "carnie" (carnival concessionaire), which closely resembles the con man's, is used for secret communication in the presence of customers.

The size of the "score," or money taken from the victim, also acts as a measure of professional achievement as well as the ability to obtain protection at a reasonable cost from police.

Social Visibility of Crime

Visibility of crime is far from uniform; some crimes nearly always come to public notice, others seldom, if ever. Robbery, burglary, forgery, and assault generally are high-visibility crimes, whereas insurance and other business fraud, counterfeiting, shortchanging, dishonest gambling, rape, and professional theft are less readily detectable. With the exception of some sex offenses, crimes of low visibility are easier to professionalize than others. All three forms of professional theft, pocket picking, shoplifting, and con games, are crimes of intrinsically low visibility. The skill with which the thefts are consummated renders them even more inconspicuous. Con men make a practice of working resorts and selecting out-of-town marks to play, or they rope a mark in one town and play him in another. Lou Blonger's mob in Denver had a fast rule that Colorado residents under no condition were to be made the object of their swindles.

Con games are played with such skill at times that the victim never knows he has been swindled and attributes his loss to poor business judgment. If the victim is a businessman, he is not anxious to have it printed in the papers that he has been duped, thus becoming a laughingstock or being known as a "sucker." Furthermore, fear of exposing his malefactors is generated by the fact that the victim himself has been party to an illegal conspiracy. The con men cleverly play upon this fear. They also apply an elaborate "cooling-out" technique to the victim, often in collaboration with police so that his desire to expose the crime is diffused or eliminated. In instances of extreme doggedness in attempts to apprehend and prosecute, the victim may receive his money back in whole or part. In addition to these measures taken to guard against exposure, con men move around the country at a great rate, assume a series of aliases, and utilize a host of tricks to avoid identification upon arrest.

The Societal Reaction

Lay beliefs concerning the nature of crime have already been touched upon to some extent. They take the form of exaggerations of the degree and effectiveness of criminal organization, of its power, and of its insidious infiltration into legitimate social organization. A facet of the stereotype inconsistent with this is the conviction harbored in many minds that criminals by and large are mentally deficient or that they are psychopathic. A variation of this stereotype, made popular in fiction and motion pictures, depicts the criminal as fundamentally cowardly, needing narcotics to bolster up his courage, and willing to fight only when cornered "like a rat." Sadistic cruelty is frequently assigned as a personality trait of the putative criminal, shown in the maltreatment of women or "molls" whom he cuffs or kicks unmercifully in his frenzies. Like the prostitute, the criminal is portrayed as inevitably coming to a bad end, remorseful and repentant. The more rigid public ideas of criminals have revolved around murderers and gangsters for the most part, only rarely concerning the professional thief.

In decided contrast to the darker side of the fixed public image of the criminal, a more romantic picture is sometimes drawn. Thus there is the "Robin Hood" variety of thief or robber who steals from the rich and gives to the poor, and makes a business of righting wrongs in a forthright, if illegal, manner. Closely related to this is the glamor with which professional thieves are invested in fiction, illustrated by such novels as *Arsene Lupin* and stories of the Raffles or Jimmy Valentine sort, in which the criminal protagonist continually baffles the minions of the law by his masterful skill and intelligence. Such fiction dramatizes the competitive struggle of American society and at the same time provides a channel for the symbolic expression of traditional antagonism to law and government deep in our culture.

It is scarcely a contradiction that many persons reared in American culture should remain passive when confronted with the necessity to actively collaborate with a government they distrust, in enforcing the criminal laws. Great outcries may go up from the citizenry over criminal acts, but in their individual capacities the community members are reluctant to assist the police and courts perform their functions. This shows itself in the evasion of jury duty (not entirely due to distrust of government, of course) and an unwillingness to serve as witnesses for the prosecution. Individualism asserts itself in the withdrawal of complaints when restitution of losses is proffered. Insurance companies customarily make deals with criminals to recover stolen property when such a procedure is cheaper than paying claims. Bankers have been known to drop criminal proceedings against embezzlers in order to recover part of their losses. Many confidence men have escaped imprisonment simply by returning to their victims part or all of the money they have taken. The flourishing private-detective business in our society bespeaks the individualized reaction of many to crime and the criminal. When these facts are added to the low visibility of most crime, we begin to understand why so few criminals are apprehended and punished in our society.

The Tolerance Quotient

Societal reactions to crime vary broadly from one culture to another, from one place to another within the same culture, and also in time within the same cultural continuum. The number, seriousness, and visibility of crimes committed in a given space-time cultural nexus interact with fixed and variable tolerances to produce a tolerance quotient expressed in aggregate criminal complaints, arrest and conviction rates, and in the severity of sentences meted out to those convicted. There are some data to indicate that the amount of crime is a far more constant factor in the tolerance quotient than the attitudes of the community toward crime, and also, perhaps, that on the whole fixed tolerances for crime are quite high. This was brought out in a comparative study of the adolescent behavior of a group of college students and of a group of juvenile court cases. In this research it was established that aside from small differences the college-student group had participated in the same delinquencies as the court cases. Their delinquencies were equally serious, albeit they did not recur so often as those of the legally defined offenders. Yet only a negligible percentage of the college students had been arrested and remanded to the custody of the juvenile court.[37]

These facts lead us to conclude that in certain contexts, areal or otherwise, there is a proneness to perceive and report youthful crimes which in other contexts pass unnoticed or ignored. Apparently some persons and groups are quicker to invoke the formal agencies of the law against youthful misdemeanants, being more peevish, irrascible, or litigatious. Parents in some of the juvenile-court cases in this study actually registered complaints against their own children, sometimes requesting that they be held in jail as a disciplinary tactic. Stores in certain neighborhoods were found to furnish an unusually large percentage of the complaints against the court cases.[38] This is easily understandable because some stores, ten-cent stores for instance, are much more tempting theft situations for certain classes of children, and at the same time, perhaps on account of smaller markups on merchandise, must pay closer heed to costs and losses such as might come from shoplifting. Employees may be more alert to this type of theft and may especially scrutinize the more poorly dressed children. Some stores handle shoplifting losses by actuarial methods, simply adding a small amount to prices to cover losses rather than depending upon policing of the store. The youngsters caught shoplifting in these more expensive stores may come from families better able to make restitution and thus avoid arrest.

An important, if as yet unmeasured, degree of criminal deviation is almost purely putative. Thus it was found in New York City that many girls were referred to the custody of the court for wayward girls who had never committed a sexual offense. In 1938 out of a sample of 150 cases no

[37] Porterfield, Austin, "Delinquency and Its Outcome in Court and in College," *American Journal of Sociology*, 49, November, 1943, pp. 199–208.

[38] *Ibid.*

sex offense was alleged to have occurred on the part of the girls in 60 cases, and in 1942 only 104 out of a sample of 150 were alleged to have been sexually delinquent. Nevertheless all these girls were remanded to the custody of this court.[39] The same element of putative criminal deviation can be seen in adult cases in the "make sheets" of police departments. These are records of persons who have been arrested or booked or convicted. Some sheets list only arrests on "suspicion." Legally no violation of the law can be proved in these cases, yet police usually treat them in a category with persons who have a record of convictions. These "suspicion" arrests also influence judicial decisions by appearing in the record of the case made up by probation officers and have sometimes been cited as reasons for not recommending probation.[40]

Changing Tolerances for Crime

Viewed from the standpoint of change and time, variations in community tolerances for crime appear as phases of fluctuating personal and collective tensions which arise from culture conflict and become diverted into the legal process. In more organized form they appear as struggles between power groups in the community. A wide variety of personal aggressions and fears may be thrust more or less capriciously into the societal reaction. Through the press and other media of communication these become canalized and resymbolized, often in the shape of "crime waves." During the Second World War very questionable complaints about delinquency at times poured into police and sheriff departments in some areas. Investigations often proved that these were figments of restless minds of neighbors and others. In one Middle Western town a man telephoned the sheriff and demanded that legal action be taken against a three-year-old neighbor boy who left toys in the man's driveway. In another instance a woman telephoned excitedly to the sheriff that a group of boys were setting fire to her fence. The investigator who visited the woman eventually found that: "No, the boys hadn't actually lighted the fire; no, the boys weren't near her fence, *yet*." However, the woman had *heard* several boys say that they would *like* to do it. Furthermore, the woman was unable to say where she had heard this, but she *knew* some boys in the neighborhood who were *probably* the ones planning to do it!

Grand juries in Los Angeles County have long been hampered in their investigations by the necessity of separating actionable complaints from others. One jury listed the following types of complaints: (1) persons with no criminal cases, (2) persons civilly *(sic)* not criminally wronged, (3) persons harboring a personal grudge, (4) chronic complainers, (5)

[39] Tappan, Paul, *Delinquent Girls in Court*, 1947, pp. 154*ff*.

[40] Lemert and Rosberg, *op. cit.*, p. 21.

neurotics and psychotics, (6) political wranglers, (7) meritorious cases outlawed, (8) meritorious cases.[41] While the juries made efforts to discriminate between complaints justifying investigation and the spurious ones, nevertheless they confessed in reports to a sense of inadequacy in doing so.

These same Los Angeles County juries at times became storm centers of controversy when their inquisitional function was expanded by the growth of political conflict and dissatisfaction in the community. In many ways during the 1930's the grand juries in the Los Angeles area became the equivalents of specially constituted committees formed to combat vice and crime in other cities. Ordinarily the alignments of groups in support of the local grand juries, like those in support of vice committees elsewhere, have been weak and unstable. Furthermore, when tentative investigations revealed the triadic alliance between crime, politics, and business, powerful resistances were exerted through the prosecuting attorney's office and even arose within the jury itself to block further action.[42] It required a major economic depression to marshal sufficient community tension and support for a really militant Los Angeles grand jury to appear (in 1934) and bring about long-sought changes.[43]

The outstanding characteristic of the history of crime and the reaction to it, especially in American cities, has been a cyclic patterning of action and reaction, objectively apparent in political reform movements. Thus, as real or putative crime or its visibility has increased within urban communities, more and more groups have been adversely excited; tensions have mounted to critical proportions, leading to the overturn of local administrations. However, few reforms born in this way have struck at the organizational patterns underlying crime, so that following initial periods of good conduct in office "reform," administrations often have become corrupt and gone the way of their predecessors. It has also happened that honest reform governments have lost public support by a rigid, impartial enforcement of the law.[44] Failures of this sort are related to the difficulties in the way of devising a program of law enforcement which will efficiently discriminate between individual, situational, and professional criminals.[45] They suggest that cycles of "reform" are deeply rooted in the nature of our urban social organization.

[41] *Report, Los Angeles County Grand Jury*, 1931, mimeographed

[42] Lemert, Edwin M , "The Grand Jury as an Agency of Social Control," *American Sociological Review*, 10, December, 1945, pp. 751–758

[43] *Ibid.*, p 756

[44] Something like this happened to the police department in New York City under Commissioner Lewis J. Valentine's and Mayor Fiorello La Guardia's administration after 1934. See Limpus, Lowell M , *Honest Cop*, 1939

[45] Smith, Bruce, "Enforcement of the Criminal Law," *Annals of the American Academy of Political and Social Science*, 217, September, 1941, pp. 16*ff*.

The forms of crime and societal reactions to them continually undergo technological and organizational change. Specific patterns of crime tend to arise, flourish, and then disappear as the culture changes or as more adequate police methods are invented. Train robberies are largely phenomena of the past, as well as cattle rustling. Big-con games such as the "rag," "wire," and "payoff" apparently are played less today than they once were. Our changing sex mores and urban sophistication have outmoded the badger game in favor of systematic extortion of money from homosexuals and other sex perverts. As our technology has evolved, the concept of larceny has been progressively redefined to cover a wider variety of property crimes. Larceny "by trick," or fraud and embezzlement, did not become a legal concept until the very end of the eighteenth century, in response to public hostility over stock losses and collapse of speculative booms.[46]

It is possible that certain classes of crimes and the societal reaction to them have some sort of recurrent histories, with ephemeral to long-time life spans. However, as yet, we are devoid of studies on the subject; needed research here might well follow the course of industrialization in different cultures to determine the limits of variability in the forms of crime which rise and fall with successive phases of urbanization.

There are scattered indications that highly organized crime has passed through some sort of cycle in our own culture. After having reached a grand magnitude during the decade of the 1920's, it has gradually lost ground. National prohibition, by enlisting the lay public in a general conspiracy to defeat the law, provided a fallow ground for the proliferation of organized crime and at the same time created the reaction which eventuated in its repeal. The very dimensions to which gang enterprise rose militated against its survival, for it soon threatened the basic power distributions in many urban communities. Vice and crime were more and more projected into the political arena, with all the hazards to power which this entailed. The vast expansion of the functions of the Federal government, especially in direct-relief and work-relief programs during the 1930's, undermined the strength of many urban political machines and weakened the protective screen around organized crime.

At the present time it would appear that most organized crime is integrated into the generalized gambling culture complex in American society, and possibly to a lesser extent it is tied up with traffic in narcotics. The laws covering gambling and narcotic drugs closely resemble national prohibition in so far as opening up interstices in our social structure for the entrance of organized crime is concerned. The Harrison Narcotics Act of 1914 stands out as a particularly criminogenic piece of legislation in this

[46] Hall, *op. cit.*, pp. 6–7.

respect.[47] Whether we are moving to replace prohibition with sanction and regulation in connection with the use of narcotics remains conjectural.

The considerable expansion of organized gambling in the past decade or two has been in part the result of closing off other areas of organized criminal activity and in part the result of the discovery or invention of techniques for setting up monopolistic controls over petty, local gambling. Illegal traffic in liquor was brought to a close with the death of national prohibition; it is also the case that dealings in prostitution and vice, for reasons mentioned in Chap. 8, are no longer so profitable as they once were; finally, governmental legislation has made business and labor racketeering more difficult than it once was. Consequently we have seen these older forms of organized crime replaced by expanded criminal control over gambling. This has involved such things as slot machines, pinball machines, punchboards, numbers writing, and, above all, bookmaking. Controls over the former seem to originate from business organizations which manufacture mechanical amusement devices. They necessitate bribery of local law-enforcement officers as well as manipulation of state legislators.

In the case of bookmaking there is evidence of regional and perhaps nationwide monopolies by criminal agencies. These are made possible and maintained only through a monopoly of the swift transmission of post times, betting odds, and results of horse races throughout the country Without these prompt reports bookmaking can be organized only on a small scale locally. Various attempts have been made to deny the use of telegraph and telephone facilities to the "press services" through which the bookmaking monopoly functions. However, at the present writing, decisions on these matters by the courts remain somewhat inconsistent and inconclusive.[48]

A large number of honest citizens believe that legalized gambling is the way to eliminate the organized crime that is now associated with it in its present illegal form. Claims have been made that this is an easy way of raising money to support state relief and welfare services. Proponents of the idea sometimes point to Nevada communities as examples of how legalization of gambling keeps organized crime at a minimum. Yet government-

[47] Barnes, H. E., *Society in Transition*, 1939, pp 814*ff*

[48] Federal Communications Commission, "Staff Report on the Extent of Communication Facilities Used in Dissemination of Racing Information," 1945, *Second Progress Report of the Special Crime Study Commission on Organized Crime*, State of California, 1949, *Third Progress Report of the Special Crime Study Commission on Organized Crime*, State of California, 1950. For the situation in Chicago, see Paterson, V., "Chicago's Crime Problem," *Journal of Criminal Law and Criminology*, 35, May–June, 1944, pp. 3–15. For the situation in Florida see Frank, P., and L. Voltz, "Florida's Struggle with the Hoodlums," *Collier's*, Mar. 25, 1950, and "Gambler's Siege," *ibid.* Apr. 1, 1950.

regulated gambling in the past has not had a record of unqualified success, especially where it has been in the form of lotteries. Nor does a second look at the Nevada communities show them to be so free of criminal elements as some would have us believe.[49] The only meager proof that legalized gambling is feasible comes from a short period in the history of New Orleans. It seems that there in the nineteenth century a fairly successful system of regulated gambling, called the "Shakespeare plan," was conducted for a number of years. However, its success was ephemeral at best.[50]

Exploitation of Crime and Criminals

Apart from the civic apathy of our citizens when positive aid to law-enforcement agencies is called for, there is, as we noted in our early chapter on the societal reaction, a socioeconomic symbiosis between criminal and noncriminal groups in many communities, which blurs and blunts the societal reaction to crime. Many persons and enterprises profit directly or indirectly from criminal activities. Bankers, criminal lawyers, private detectives, bail bondsmen, fences, pawnbrokers, stool pigeons, and other criminals cut themselves into the profits of criminals, frequently taking all that the traffic will bear. Big-con men in the past, and even today, have found bankers frequently their willing collaborators. In some cases these bankers have not been above applying pressure to the con men to enlarge the "commissions" they received.

In the past, corrupt police and law-enforcement officers levied heavy illegal tolls and requisitions upon criminals. These practices grew to peculiarly flagrant proportions during the days of national prohibition, when a poor-but-honest prohibition agent was the exception rather than the rule. Police on the beat and detectives were accustomed to extorting large sums of money from con men in many cities in days past. The mere sight of a con man on the street was enough to cause some detectives to confront him with the threat of arrest unless a sizable cash sum was forthcoming. The economic bonds between police, judicial officers, politicians, and criminals have been institutionalized in the fix, which according to evidence from criminals themselves functions to a greater or lesser degree in all communities. The Federal government has generally stayed clear of these illegal involvements, but it nevertheless raises revenue by taxation of incomes coming from illegal sources. Furthermore, the Treasury Department has often foregone prosecution of criminals who pay tax arrears and penalties in full, despite having gathered evidence that could result in con-

[49] *Second Progress Report of the Special Crime Study Commission on Organized Crime*, pp. 64–67; Paterson, V., *Gambling – Should It Be Legalized?* Chicago Crime Commission, 1945, pp. 1–2.

[50] Asbury, H., *The French Quarter*, 1938, pp. 335*ff*.

victions.[51] In an indirect way, then, even our national government profits from crime.

Penal Agencies

The more formal expression of public attitudes toward crime and criminals in American penal philosophy and criminal law sharply polarizes into two diametrically opposed points of view. On one hand lies the older, classical conception of punishment and community security as prime functions of law enforcement, while on the other can be found the insistence that reform and rehabilitation, generally by psychiatric therapy, are the necessary and ascendant orientations in dealing with criminals. This latter goes under the heading of "positivist" or "neopositivist" penology. Both conceptions have been translated into contradictory police policy, judicial practice, and prison administration.[52] They are implicit and explicit in conflict between law-enforcement agencies and in inconsistencies of theory and administration of the law within the same agency.

Police

The American police system is best understood as an agency held directly responsible for protection of the community and which becomes the target for general dissatisfaction with law enforcement. The courts often act as obstacles in the fulfillment of the security function of the police by rigid adherence to rules of evidence and by dismissing cases of professional or dangerous criminals apprehended by the police with much labor and danger. When manipulations by unethical or dishonest lawyers, political corruption, and bias of judges are added to these, in conjunction with the constant hate or distrust of the lay public toward the police, the result can be very demoralizing to the best police force. Honest and more aggressive police officials often react to the situation by insulating themselves and their departments from public opinion as much as possible. Driven to some kind of effective policing, they preempt the penal function of the court in many ways, laying down the rule that patrolmen should "carry the law in their night sticks." From this fact has come the allegations that American police are lawless, which indeed they are and must be in some situations. The extralegal measures of the police are directed in the main toward groups from which the fewest repercussions will come. Members of minority groups, migrants, and persons with limited economic means are often the salient objectives, if not scapegoats, of the frustrated police in our local communities. Other police react to their unenviable

[51] Firey, Elmer, and William Slocum, *The Tax Dodgers*, 1949, pp. 28*ff*.

[52] Elliot, Mabel, *Conflicting Penal Theories in Statutory Criminal Law*, 1931, Chap II.

social position with slackness, inefficiency, and outright corruption. When this becomes known, it tends to reinforce or increase the public hostility toward the police as a whole, who must run the risk of wholesale "transfers" or discharges when mounting public dissatisfaction leads to an overthrow of the party in power. This looming danger heightens the sense of internal insecurity and makes for the demoralization of police departments. It makes individual policemen more accessible to corrupt politicians and to criminals and their allies.

THE RELATIONSHIPS OF POLICE WITH CRIMINALS

The attitudes and behavior of the police toward criminals varies according to the type of crime they have committed and according to their personal and social characteristics. It has not been uncommon for police to administer beatings to sexual perverts and then release them, relying upon public indignation at the type of offense to justify their reactions. Likewise, political radicals who have disturbed the peace may suffer indignities and brutalities at the hands of the police. It is also well known that the murder of a policeman has a far different effect upon fellow officers' attitudes toward suspects than is the case where the victim has been a lay citizen or another criminal. In this case the police reaction is to a symbolic attack upon the power and ingroup solidarity of the police group itself.

It must not be assumed that the traditional enmity supposed to exist between the police and criminals actually holds for all criminals. It is seldom that hostility of the police extends to cover their relationships to professional thieves. Honest police and detectives know that the victims of con men have usually been trying to profit by a dishonest deal, and their complaints after being fleeced stir little beyond contempt in many officers. This type of officer customarily does his duty in a perfunctory manner toward the con man. Dishonest police and professional con men rarely hate one another, for they are frequently involved in illegal transactions of mutual benefit and mutual protection. Frequently this is in the form of the fix.

The fix is worked in different ways by different classes of criminals. We shall comment on the fix as it works for confidence men. In some communities established channels and intermediaries must be gone through by con men, with standardized bribes being paid. In other communities the inside man of the con mob deals directly with corrupt detectives. In the past, virtual monopolies were granted con mobs in some towns, so that con men from the outside could not operate without danger of arrests. Some towns, usually smaller ones, have no fix, and con men make their play there at considerable risk. Federal agents and detectives of several large private agencies, the Pinkerton and Burns, according to one account, are relatively incorruptible.[53]

It is hard to say what changes have taken place in the pattern of the fix in the past decade or two. It may be guessed that a highly stabilized pattern of corruption such as permitted con mobs to function with immunity in Denver, Colorado, at one time is no longer possible. It may be that fixing today is much more random and diffused than it once was, being much more difficult to get away with.

The Courts

The elements of the behavior systems of criminals calculated to avoid police annoyance and arrest are extended and supplemented by others which are outgrowths of the stress upon "due process" of law in American courts and of the compromises with its penal function through probation and suspended sentences. In the event of the arrest of a con man, for example, it does not follow that he is destined for prison, even with an accumulation of evidence against him. As with larcenous crimes in general, con-game crimes have a high differential case mortality. Table 36 is very enlightening as to the legal fate of persons arrested for so-called "bunco" crimes in a large metropolitan community.[54]

TABLE 36 DISPOSITION OF 235 BOOKINGS FOR FRAUD (GRAND THEFT AND PETTY THEFT), LOS ANGELES, 1947

Disposition	Number	Per cent
Convicted .	9	3 8
Released to other jurisdictions	9	3 8
Victims refused to prosecute	5	2.1
Dismissed or discharged	3	1 2
Complaint refused	22	9 3
Released and rebooked on another charge	49	20 8
Released .	137	58.3
Other .	1	0 4
Total	235	99.7

Con men make a point of having large sums of money on their persons, so that if bail is not set too high, they may have the choice of jumping bail. Bribing complaining witnesses by offering the return of part or all of the money they have lost is another way of forestalling the course of the law. Continuances over long periods of time may be obtained for the accused con man by his lawyer, on the chance that the victim may die,

[53] Maurer, *The Big Con*, Chap. 7.

[54] Compiled from the *Annual Report of the Los Angeles Police Department*, 1947, pp 154–155.

which is more than a good possibility considering the advanced ages of many of them.

When a trial is inevitable, efforts may be made in behalf of the con man to buy off the judge. This failing, the con man and his attorney may agree to plead guilty to a lesser charge, usually petty larceny, and then apply for probation. If the man is not too well known as a professional, his acting virtuosity may convince the judge that he is a good risk for suspended sentence. However, where large sums of money have been taken or where the marks of the professional "touch" are indelibly written into the evidence, manipulating an honest judge is out of the question – hence the tendency of professional con men to choose jury trials. In the old days much bribery of jurors went on and probably does to some degree even yet. Otherwise the defendant relies upon his air of injured innocence in the courtroom, looking for all purposes like a staid and sober businessman being unfairly used by the prosecution. The dubious position of the complaining witness in court plus the naiveté of juries and their general unpredictability give the accused more than a fair chance of acquittal. This is especially true if the trial can be kept short.

The Prison Community

The formal organization and administration of a goodly number of jails, reformatories, and prisons are mediated and supplemented by informal and unanticipated organization, all of which may be taken as variant expressions of what has been called the "prison community." The prison community includes a more or less indigenous and separate culture, complete with special norms of its own, technicways and argot, differentiation and stratification of groups, social conflict, integration and social control.[55] The organization and culture of the prison community are dynamic responses of inmates to the security function and standardized mass procedures incorporated into the formal prison social structure by the demands of the larger society. Prisons to most people are places for "hardened" criminals, and their administrations are held accountable for the task of isolating dangerous deviants from society and preventing any further damage by them. There are few aspects of the formal and material prison environment which do not symbolize the security tensions of the administrative surrogates of society present in the situation.

The political insecurity of the prison administration motivates officials to shield the prison from publicity as much as possible and by other means to prevent inquisitorial expeditions into its precincts. This functions to increase the isolated and encysted qualities of the prison social organization. Not only is the high-security prison socially and often spatially iso-

[55] Clemmer, Donald, *The Prison Community*, 1940.

lated but it also symbolizes this isolation in prison garb, rules against open communication, and its ultimate in punishment – solitary confinement. Its guards and matrons, as well as the rest of the staff, tend to be social isolants as well as the prisoners.

Formal controls within the prison are authoritative, with practically all conflict repressed. This means that social distance between the staff and the inmates is at a maximum; formal communication has little in common with the dynamic interaction in the prison society. Seldom does the formal organization infiltrate and utilize the informal organization of the inmates for any but security reasons – as when a "fink," or informer, is exploited in order to gain information about the identity of those who violate rules or plan escapes. If anything, the infiltration and flow of power runs from the informal to the formal organization, with prisoners carrying the burden of bureaucratic control of the prison. Many prisons are in fact administered by the prisoners.

The symbolic environment of the prison converts the more general societal definition of the criminal into variations on a common theme. The undertone of the warden's attitude is likely to be a cynical variety of "once a crook always a crook." The chaplain reacts to the prisoners as sinners; many social workers patronize their prison clients as inferiors; and the prison psychiatrist has been quick to apply the label of "psychopathic personality" or "constitutional inferior" from his diagnostic repertoire to large numbers of those whom he interviews. It comes as no surprise that prisoners so often hate or fear the psychiatrist. Therapies based upon such role definitions are usually roughly rejected by the tough-fibered prisoners; or on the other hand if they are accepted, they may become the conscious aspect of a process of demoralization in which independence and self-resolution of the prisoner decay. It has been argued that constructive clinical work can be carried on within such an authoritative environment,[56] but empirical evidence of the truth of such contentions has yet to be furnished. No matter how social workers or clinicians in the prison may construe their rehabilitative efforts, they must always be pursued within a framework of oppressive security regulations. Social communication is blocked by the tendency of the prisoners to symbolize clinical efforts or research either as espionage or as disciplinary measures at work behind a façade of humanitarianism or of little-understood science.

The isolation of the individual in prison cuts across practically every area of his social participation. It produces withdrawal stresses which are initially traumatic for most new inmates. Furthermore, the stresses tend to grow with passing time. These stresses are part of a profound personal disruption, which under controlled conditions might be used to train the

[56] Fink, A E, *The Field of Social Work*, 1949, rev ed., p. 402

prisoner in rehabilitant roles, were it not for the absence of opportunities in the formal prison organization to make these roles meaningful. To use one example: no official recognition whatsoever is taken in American prisons of the abrupt break in the sex and affectional relationships which incarceration brings to the inmate. As a result many of the more heterosexual prisoners turn to homosexuality. This entangles them in a whole web of behavior which makes up the separate prison culture and which, in turn, makes their compliance with formal prison programs external and cynical.

Continuity of control between the formal organization of the prison and the socially sanctioned organization outside of the prison is almost nonexistent, while that between the informal organization of the prison and criminal groups on the outside is relatively high. The arrangements for parole in many states can only be called "systems" by the most charitable use of the words. Parole "systems" are understaffed, lack resources and rational programs, often they mesh more closely with outside politico-criminal organization than with any other groups. A final pertinent consideration is that parole tends to be denied to those prisoners who have been the more recidivistic criminals. Thus extramural legal controls are relinquished over those most inclined to resume criminal roles.

Individuation of the Criminal

Since large numbers of persons committing crimes have records of juvenile crime and since about one-half of the population leaving our prisons become recidivists, role-oriented, habitual, and systematic criminal behavior presents one of our more challenging research problems. The study of these problems requires that the data be thrown into some sort of chronological order with the object of discovering repetitive sequences, or career patterns, leading to professional criminal roles. To the extent that this has been done, it has given us such concepts as "summation," "sophistication," "maturation," and "natural history" to describe the process by which the noncriminal is changed into a criminal social type. Of these, the last seems least applicable to the process; human development, as we see it, is much too dynamic to be compressed into mechanical sequences. The data on the subject are much more congenial to the idea that the developing person is confronted with expanding and contracting areas of choice, the boundaries of which are set by the internal limits of personality and external limits of his situation. These areas of choice include noncriminal as well as criminal alternatives, so that quasi-criminal behavior need not necessarily immediately precede criminal behavior. Thus, specific forms of business and professional behavior may not only incorporate criminal acts but also be the antecedents of a criminal role. It has happened, for example, that victims of confidence men suddenly turned con men themselves.[57]

PRIMARY CRIMINAL BEHAVIOR

In its primary phase all criminal behavior is by definition "symptomatic" or "situational." The situations from which come criminal acts are so numerous in our culture that few if any persons live out their lives without violation of some law or another. Most people violate many laws in their adult as well as childhood lifetimes. In fact, it has been estimated that the "average" law-abiding citizen in one day unwittingly commits enough crimes to call for five years of imprisonment and fines running close to three thousand dollars.[58] Presumably, however, few of these crimes have sufficient visibility to result in apprehension and punitive reaction, and consequently are never symbolized as criminal by either society or by the adult who is guilty of them. Where vague, or even clear and vivid, awareness of the criminal character of the acts is present in the individual, it is soon dissimulated or rationalized in the absence of formal inscription and reinforcement of his ephemeral guilt by an organized response of society.

The demographic characteristics of criminals tell us that the criminogenic pressures of our culture rest more heavily upon urban male adolescents than upon other groups. This fact plus the known relationship of juvenile misdemeanors to subsequent crime has disposed some to insist that the immediate family situation is the dynamic complex out of which primary criminal deviation springs. In essence this is to say that early crime is largely symptomatic of unsolved conflicts over a family role. This may well hold true for a small number of cases, especially at preadolescent ages, but serious doubt remains that the largest portion of adolescent crime can be simply attributed to "delinquent parents." A much better scientific brief can be made that it is the absence of institutions and organization in the local community to effect a continuous transition from childhood to adult roles which constitutes the criminogenic situation.

The stress or *sturm und drang* of adolescence have been cogently described and demonstrated as a phenomenon of American culture conflict.[59] Within the context of our culture it is an average expectancy for adolescents not only to become "maladjusted" but also, as we have seen, to engage in behavior definable as "crime." This general culture conflict finds emphasis in the somewhat higher rates of juvenile crime among children of

[57] Maurer, *The Big Con*, pp. 164*ff*.

[58] Hussey, L. M., "Twenty Four Hours of a Lawbreaker," *Harper's*, 160, March, 1930, pp. 436–439.

[59] Mead, Margaret, *From the South Seas*, 1939

many immigrants, especially in certain city areas, and among the children of rural Negro migrants living in sections of New York and other cities. This general explanation has further corroboration in the comparatively low rates of juvenile crime in rural areas, where social organization provides smoother continuity between childhood and adult roles.

In the absence of directive institutions comparable to *rites de passage* in other cultures the adolescent ordinarily establishes himself in spontaneously generated and self-perpetuating neighborhood gangs or other peer age groups which are integrated very often through conflict with legal authority. A preponderance of juvenile crimes, stealing more than others, are collective crimes and not the illegal acts of isolant adolescents.[60] Consequently it is the socially responsive, normally maturing boy who is most likely to turn to criminal pastimes in striving to establish himself in an adult role.

Secondary Criminal Deviation

The question to be considered at this point is how primary criminal deviation is symbolized as criminal and how the societal definition is introjected and made the reciprocal basis of a criminal role. Since not all persons symbolized as criminal by society adopt criminal roles, it is plain that the internal limits of personality selectively condition the acceptance of such roles. In all probability the receptivity of the primary criminal deviant to an imputed criminal role is greater where the preexisting self-conception of the individual closely conforms to a more generalized societal definition of the person's status or "class" as sociopathic. This, we believe, can be seen in the restrictive effects of family status upon the individual. The close identification between children and parents in our culture means that the status and self-conceptions of family members are readily transferred to the former. Thus if the family contains members, especially parents, who are or have been socially disenfranchised, chances are greater that societal definitions of "criminal" applied to the young deviant will be incorporated as the fulcrum of the self. In support of this are data to show that delinquents come in greater percentage from homes where other sociopathic behavior (chiefly arrests for drunkenness) has been present. Furthermore, the more serious is the juvenile crime, the greater is the pobability of its origin in a family containing a criminal member.[61] Other studies have pointed to a relationship between a child's status as illegitimate, as an institutional child (with the social implication of illegitimacy), and as a foster child, and the probabilities of his being criminally delinquent. While the latter data are

[60] Shaw, Clifford, and Henry McKay, *Juvenile Delinquency and Urban Areas*, 1942, pp 193–196.

[61] *Crime and the Community*, Crime Commission of New York State, 1930, p. 163, also Glueck, Sheldon, and Eleanor Glueck, *Criminal Careers in Retrospect*, 1943, p. 120.

not entirely conclusive, they nevertheless suggest a line of further necessary research in more carefully conceptualized form to more fully test our hypothesis.

It is of symbolic importance that persons of low social status living in deteriorated areas of the community are less mobile than others and that their areas of effective social participation are spatially more circumscribed.[62] From this it may be reasoned that symbolic evaluations of the delinquent youngster's behavior coming from the immediate area are less apt to be corrected or modified by alternative evaluations which might be gained from contacts with the wider community. In line with this are data which tentatively indicate a greater naiveté and credulity among persons with lower status interacting in narrow participational circles.[63]

The incipient generalized self-definitions of the individual as a pariah type may well be reciprocally tied to a certain form of parental reaction to primary criminal deviation. In families of criminal deviants, assumption of a criminal role may be simply a matter of training and inculcation by the parents. In other cases, probably most often among declassed parents who are disturbed by conflicts over their own roles, some sort of mirror symbolism may take place, with parents making a child the objectification of the disowned sociopathic aspects of their own roles. Families in certain contexts, as previously noted, seem quicker to symbolize the misconduct of their children with such terms as "bad," "worthless," "no-account," and with the profane expletives applied to sociopathic deviants in our society. Moreover they display a proneness to reject their offspring by more readily turning to the formal punitive agencies in the community, such as the police and juvenile court, for aid in discipline.[64] Also they are frequently more passive and less resistant in the face of communal action to deal with their children as criminal offenders. Outside the family, complainants against juvenile offenders frequently occupy dubious status in the community, and often it is the marginal or quasi-legitimate organization or group which registers criminal complaints against youngsters.[65] Hence youngsters living in areas close to these persons and groups are more apt to be the object of a societal reaction similar to and reinforcing rejecting family reactions.

Symbolic Impact of the Court

While juvenile and youth courts are theoretically set up to protect children and help them develop normally, it is becoming more clear with

62 Knupfer, G., "Portrait of the Underdog," *Public Opinion Quarterly*, 11, Spring, 1947, p 107.

63 *Ibid*, p. 109.

64 Porterfield, Austin, "The Complainant in Juvenile Court," *Sociology and Social Research*, 28, January–February, 1944, pp 171–181

65 *Ibid.*

passing time that court contacts of this sort are instrumental in formally stigmatizing a child as a young criminal. Regardless of the striving to conceive juvenile and youth courts in positivistic terms, their prime and precluding function is punitive and correctional. To quote the critical analysis of one writer:[66]

> ... the court system is not designed to deal with problems which are not directly associated with law violation. The philosophies of courts, commitment institutions, and probation bureaus are preponderately correctional and punitive. Their roles have been clearly assigned in the mind and reactions of the defendant by the stereotypes of the cop, the criminal court, the reform school, and the probation officer. Similarly the public attitude toward these institutions and the adolescents subjected to them renders it wholly unrealistic for the courts to attempt to operate as general social agencies: they bear the indelible stamp of public stigma and ostracism. *Thus the frame of reference within which the court may legitimately and effectively operate is narrowly limited by public and institutional definition.* Attempts therefore at comprehensive social work are sheer folly; the problems of domestic relations, psychological pathology, occupational maladjustments, etc., are not within the sphere of appropriate function. This is the more obviously true when no offense has been shown—haphazard manipulation by the unskilled or partially trained probation officer in areas of specialized therapy adds misapplied treatment to the injustice of court and institutional contact. Even when an offense has been proven, far greater success in treatment could be achieved by the referral of problems requiring trained and noncorrectional specialized assistance to proper public and private agencies. (Yet, the adolescent courts are far from attaining a nice integration with the varied social agencies of the city, though the fault is not wholly their own.) In addition to the inappropriateness of crimino-legal handling of general social problems, the absurdity of this trend is enhanced by the insufficiency of personnel in the courts. Where, for optimum results, they should work experimentally and intensively on a carefully selected sample of favorable probation risks to ensure creative individualization and reformation, the expansive drive in some courts toward problem solving for all comers has resulted in attenuated, inexact, and ineffectual service. The proper sphere of social agencies and behavior clinics should not be usurped by the courts, however benevolent the motivation. It appears clear that the work of crime prevention must be performed, if at all, *before* court contact and by noncourt agencies. *The personnel of correctional court and institution is not equipped to do a noncorrectional job.*

There are neighborhoods in Los Angeles, and undoubtedly in many other cities, where to have a juvenile court record is a mark of distinction providing entree into local gangs at high status levels. The real function of the court process for many of its charges is to formally fix such status

[66] Tappan, Paul, "Treatment without Trial," *Social Forces,* 24, March, 1946, pp 306–311.

symbols and to confirm the isolation and segregation of the child from the larger community. The self-definition as "delinquent" proliferates into more and more aspects of the child's role by his contacts in jail, detention home, and with the security-minded probation officer. Juvenile and youth courts ostensibly are not courts of records, but facts belie this claim. Police and adult probation officers have access to their records, as well as social-welfare agencies, through the social-service exchange. It is significant to note the invidious distinction observed between "good bad" girls and "bad bad" girls in the intake policies of certain New York welfare agencies, which refuse assistance to girls who have been processed by the courts.[67] School authorities, and even individual teachers, become aware of the court records of their students. During the Second World War the court stigma was carried into the armed services through preinduction investigations for psychiatric purposes. Business and industrial concerns have been known to demand and obtain information on the juvenile-crime records of job applicants.

The specialization of the courts to deal with offenders of different ages, sex, and degrees of recidivism might for research purposes be thought of as a continuum of the varying societal conceptions of the status of the offender. Paralleling the courts are the various types of institutional services used to correct or "treat" the offender, which might also be scaled on the basis of implicit crimino-symbolic features. At one end of such a continuum might be placed the foster home where the mother expresses society's attitudes of restraints to the extent that she is alert to the possibility of the child's running away. At the other extreme would be placed the maximum security prison, such as Alcatraz, symbolizing physically as well as all other ways the complete rejection and isolation of the criminal from society.

Anglo-Saxon justice has traditionally carried the idea of making the "punishment fit the crime." However, research conducted on the Los Angeles County courts gives weight to the contrary idea that, within the formal requirements set down in statutes, judges make categorical groupings of criminals rather than continuous gradations. These judicial stereotypes are clearly expressed in the length of sentences dispensed to felons. For 914 cases in 1938 there appeared to be no continuous distribution in the length of the sentences; instead, the sentences concentrated around a zero point (probation), jail terms of six and twelve months, and finally around five to six years in prison. The distribution is shown in Fig. 10. Although the symbolic differences implicit in varying jail sentences shown here may not be great, those between straight probation and a jail sentence patently are. Even more drastic status implications lie in a prison sentence,

[67] Tappan, *Delinquent Girls in Court*, p. 28.

for this means complete abrogation of civil rights and relatively long isolation from society.

The errant individual's behavior may be symbolized as criminal by identification with a group of self-defined criminals, without arrest or court contacts ever entering into the symbolic process in a direct way. In this way a race-track tout working on the fringe of the law might take an assignment as a shill for a con mob and thereby make the slight transi-

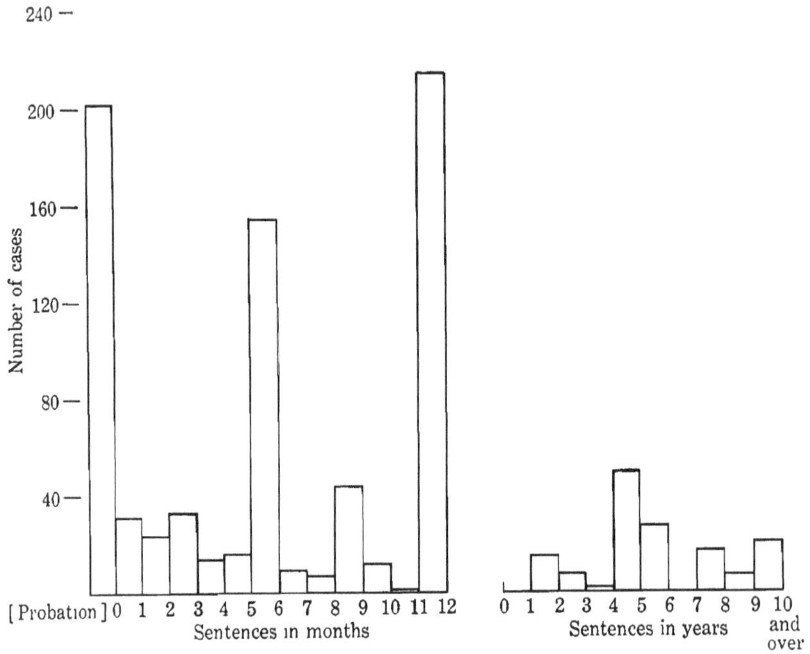

FIG 10. Distribution of 914 sentences for five leading felonies in Los Angeles County. native white, Negro, and Mexican populations, 1938

tion of self-definition required to think of himself as a criminal. The social visibility of the crime and the intensity of the societal reaction together explain whether the criminal self-conception will result from intergroup conflict with legal agencies, whether it will arise in intragroup interaction with criminals, or whether it will be the product of both.

PROFESSIONALIZATION

The cues to extreme systematization or professionalization of criminals will be found in such things as the use of an argot, adoption of aliases, allegiance to a non-"sucker morality," and stylized hostility toward officers of the law. The critical points at which criminal self-realization intrudes in the life history of law violators have not been systematically studied. If the age curve for apprehended criminals in general is followed, an age around twenty-two or twenty-three years suggests itself as an average critical self-defining point. However, this may vary widely for specific types of crimes.

Studies of the age curve of criminals reveal a peak in the young adult years with a steady decline thereafter. Thirty-five years of age is the terminus for most criminal careers, according to one set of findings, with persons persisting in crime thereafter tending to be lone functionaries or abnormal in a psychological sense.[68] These data may be misleading, for active crimes have an earlier maturity than crimes like counterfeiting, forgery and embezzlement, and fraud.[69] With aging and increasing criminal sophistication many criminals probably graduate to crimes with lower social visibility or perhaps acquire greater skills in evading arrests or conviction. If this is true, the rapid drop in the age curve may be more apparent than real.

Vertical social mobility functions for criminal persons as well as for noncriminal, with criminals being "on the make" in their status framework as well as others. Young thieves may begin their careers stealing automobile tires, pass from that to, say, jack-rolling drunks, and from there they may move into "heavy rackets." Professional skill, large earnings, and ability to escape imprisonment serve as the criteria for advancement and acceptability into the higher ranking criminal occupations. Many aspirants never get beyond the lower rungs of the criminal-status ladder. Others get as far as the heavy rackets but never rise to elite status of grifters or to that of the criminal's criminal, the con man.

Con men, as we have stated previously, supposedly represent the aristocracy of criminal groups. While many criminals strive for this select status, few acquire the polished skills to qualify. Big-con men are recruited largely from the ranks of lesser thieves, such as short-con men, pickpockets, or shoplifters. Many have a history of professional gambling behind them, with the odd race-track tout included. Pitchmen, patent-medicine salesmen, concessionaires, and others who travel with carnivals and circuses and work amusement resorts present a reservoir from which talent for the big con is drawn. As stated earlier, a few men have stepped directly from the business world into the big con.

The con man begins his special career at a much older age than other criminals, or perhaps it is better said that he continues his criminal career at a time when others may be relinquishing theirs. Unemployment occasioned by old age does not seem to be a problem of con men; age ripens

[68] Glueck, Sheldon, and Eleanor Glueck, *Later Criminal Careers*, 1937, pp. 105–106, 108–123.

[69] Reckless, *op. cit*, p 152

their skills, insights, and wit and it also increases the confidence they inspire in their victims. With age the con man may give up the position of the roper and shift to being an inside man, but even this may not be absolutely necessary. It is possible that cultural changes outmode the particular con games older men have been accustomed to playing and thereby decrease their earnings somewhat, but this seems unlikely. We know of one con man who is seventy years of age and has a bad heart, but he is still as effective as he ever was.

It would be wrong to assume that many criminals fare as well as some con men apparently do in their old age. From what has been said about the age curves of criminal careers, it would appear that the "average" criminal loses his capacity to carry on in a criminal role about the time when most men are reaching the peak of their occupational effectiveness. The need to reestablish themselves in another role at this time may be hard to meet. This together with their probable failure to accumulate any savings in any great number of cases often leads to demoralization – especially if a prison experience has been involved. Maladjustments commencing at this time may well carry over into advanced ages.

Prisonization

The general individuation of the criminal as well as the genesis of his special self-conception will be greatly affected by whether or not he is convicted and imprisoned for his crimes. If he is incarcerated, he is further affected by the length of his sentence and by the nature of the institution to which he is sent. The generic term which describes what happens to the individual under incarceration in jails, reformatories, and prisons is "prisonization." Prisonization can be most clearly detected in maximum security prisons where there is an informal community culture within the institution. It refers to the slow acculturation of the prisoner and to his growing participation in the special informal organization around him. All inmates of penitentiaries and prisons are prisonized to some degree; but some, probably more than not, go farther than others in taking over the prison folkways and mores. This has reference to learning and using the prison jargon, indulgence in homosexuality, gambling, petty graft, and conniving. Those who become more prisonized tend to be gregarious persons and previously habituated to gambling and regular heterosexual activity. For these obvious reasons they more readily fall into the prison primary groups through which powerful direct and personal controls over behavior are at work to transmit the special prison culture. Apart from these subjective limits, long sentences, being "blasted" by the judge or sentencing board, and prior experience in crime seem to be the dynamic differentials in identifying the inmate with the prison group and promoting his full prisonization.[70]

Being imprisoned or having a record of imprisonment exposes a criminal to somewhat different stereotypic reactions both in legitimate groups and criminal groups. In the noncriminal world the ex-convict is looked upon as a person who can never be fully trusted again, a "jailbird" or "ex-con," the popular attitude in the latter case being formalized in personnel policy and practices which deny him reponsible employment. The attitudes of other criminals toward the man who has served a lengthy prison term are never quite the same as before his imprisonment. In one important measure of the successful criminal – obtaining and maintaining "protection" – he has failed. This probably weighs very heavily for leaders or key figures in criminal organizations. When released after a prison sojourn, it is hard for such leaders to convince other criminals that they will have security working under their direction. It may be that the high status of con men has for its support the fact, among other things, that few of them ever go to prison.

A long sentence is usually feared by the professional criminal because he realizes how difficult it will be to take up his criminal life after discharge from prison. He will be much older and have grown rusty at his former pursuits. He knows too that his contacts will diminish with time and chances are that his mob may no longer be operating when he steps back into free existence.

Social Participation of Criminals

Some few common features of all criminal occupations can be related to the common tendencies in the social participation of criminals. For example, many criminals are highly mobile and all must order their lives with the grim prospect of arrest and imprisonment in the background. Beyond these the more specific function of their behavior system becomes the central limiting factor in the social participation of criminals. For example, some burglars work entirely at night, which means that their social activities in time will resemble somewhat those of actors or workers on night shifts. Some criminal occupations have a higher degree of primacy than others, but in no case does their primacy approximate that of the blind, the alcoholic, or the sectarian radical. This means that the participational patterns of the same type of criminals may be quite varied. The con man is distinguished somewhat more with respect to the primacy of his calling than many other criminals; his mobility is probably higher than that of most criminals, and he must be continually on guard against recognition in

[70] Clemmer, *op. cit.*, p. 301

public by his victims. It is of great interest to note that the functional demands of the con man's role intensify his social participation in the values and activities of the dominant groups of our society, *i.e.*, those of business and professional persons. Con men, like salesmen, must be shrewd judges of personality and possessed of insights into the culture and social psychology of the groups from whom they select "marks" to victimize. This holds equally true for Negro or Filipino con men and others who confine their operations to their own ethnic group.

Economic Participation

The philosophy of the professional or systematic criminal is a formal repudiation of the work values and work morality of our culture. The person who has accepted the values of a criminal behavior system ideally will strive to emancipate himself from the burden of a legitimate occupation. However, few criminals ever achieve complete economic self-sufficiency, hence they must combine legitimate and illegitimate occupations or alternate between them. Some criminals may retain an occupational affiliation for "front" purposes, and occasionally, as with confidence men, they may by choice take a flier at business. Criminals in the "heavy rackets," such as bank robbery, may have many dealings with legitimate business organizations, but on the whole their participation in the business world is attenuated by the need for secrecy and by the risks involved in leaving traceable records of their transactions.

No study has ever been made of the earnings of criminals as a class, and the validity of any such study would be compromised by the habitual fabrication of criminals about the rewards of their calling. Yet there can be no doubt that certain forms of crime have been at times very lucrative. In three years, in 1925, 1926, and 1927, Frank Nitti of the Al Capone organization was alleged by a grand jury to have accumulated $742,887, while from 1924 to 1929 Al Capone himself was charged with having "earned" $1,038,654.[71] In a fifteen-year period in 1948 David Schiffer, specializing in insurance frauds, is alleged to have secured a million dollars.[72] The notorious con mob which centered its activities in Denver, Colorado, from 1919 to 1922 was believed to have taken from 1 to 3 million dollars from a total of 190 victims.[73] In 1934 a case of fraud by con men, tried in New York City, involved a figure of $1,500,000.[74] "Touches" of $200,000 or $300,000 have not been unusual among con men of the past. It is revealing that big-con men seldom make plays where the mark has less

[71] Firey and Slocum, *op. cit.*, pp. 46, 56.

[72] Schiffer, David, "I Stole a Million," *Collier's*, Feb. 5, 12, 1949.

[73] Van Cise, *op. cit.*, Preface

[74] *Ibid.*, p. 12.

than \$5,000 to "invest." Of course, the large figures named here have been for gross income and necessarily were divided between members of criminal organizations and also scaled down by bribes paid for protection, fees to lawyers, bondsmen, and others. Just what the "take-home" pay of these and other criminals is must be left to conjecture. However, a considered opinion would be that professional criminals, at least, do not suffer any great restrictions upon their social participation for financial reasons.

The large earnings and political power of some criminals have at times given them an exalted recognition and status in noncriminal as well as criminal groups. They have bought homes in wealthy residential districts, lived at exclusive resort hotels, and generally in their expenditure habits observed the canons of conspicuous consumption and conspicuous leisure demarcating our upper classes. They have consorted with "café society" and motion-picture celebrities and have been the object of attention and envy by many people. This was most notable in the cases of Al Capone and other prohibition-era gangsters. To quote a report on the status of Arnold Rothstein, a New York gangster of the 1920's:[75]

> Rothstein was a Broadway personage. People pointed him out to their companions at shows, fights, and the race track. They stared at him and told each other stray bits of shocking gossip about him, unsavory scraps which none of them knew to be factual and yet all of them believed somehow to be true. For no one but Rothstein ever knew the full truth about Rothstein.
>
> Successful men in business and in the theatrical, political, and newspaper fields sought his company because they felt they could profit from his tips on races, fights, ball games, and elections. They knew him for what he was — a sure-thing better.

Such facts as these strike one as paradoxical, but in reality they are consistent with the strong tendency in our culture to make social success enviable and desirable, regardless of the means, legal or illegal, which are employed to attain it.

Sex and Marital Participation

There are very definite incompatibilities between criminal activities and the fulfillment of family responsibilities. This is inferable from what we know generally about criminals and demonstrable in statistical data on their marital status. In Table 37 it will be seen that the male prison populations of the country have about twice the percentages of single and divorced persons as those which are found in the general male population. The lower marriage rate of criminals can be related to several factors. Probably the habits built up prior to becoming a criminal as well as the

[75] Thompson, C., and A. Raymond, *Gang Rule in New York*, 1940, p. 54, by permission of the Dial Press, Inc., New York.

criminal pursuits themselves reduce the opportunities for marriage by this class of deviants. A record of delinquency is often sufficient to isolate a youth from marriageable females in his area. Furthermore, the youths who are attracted to crime frequently have an orientation against the impedimenta of marriage and family life. Where the criminal role requires a high mobility, the person who assumes it will necessarily tend to give up marriage and the family as a means of sex gratification and affection.

The higher divorce rate of criminals is understandable as a response to the insecurity of their wives and children. Economic uncertainty, stigma, and periods of separation caused by imprisonment all take their toll of the

TABLE 37 PER CENT OF MALE FELONY PRISONERS IN FEDERAL AND STATE INSTITUTIONS 35 YEARS OF AGE AND OVER, BY MARITAL STATUS AND BY SELECTED CRIMES, 1946*

	Single	Married	Widowed or divorced
U S population, male	11.8	78 6	9 6
Prison population, male	24.7	56.5	18.9
Robbery	29.8	56.9	13.4
Burglary	35.5	45.7	18.9
Embezzlement and fraud	16.8	65.6	17.6
Forgery	21.3	49.3	29.5
Sex offenses (not rape)	32	45 6	22.4
Violating liquor laws	12 8	73.6	13.6

*Compiled from *Prisoners in State Prisons and Reformatories*, U.S Bureau of the Census, 1946; and *Statistical Abstract of the United States, 1947*, Table 42, p. 42.

marriages of criminals. The more mobile criminals must leave their wives alone and are thrown into associations conducive to infidelity.

It can be seen in Table 37 that felons imprisoned for embezzlement and fraud, although married to a lesser degree and divorced to a greater degree than the general population, nevertheless, more closely resembled it in these respects than did those for other selected crimes. The one exception we note is for those imprisoned for violations of liquor laws. This suggests a higher marriage rate for con men than for other criminals. Apparently many con men live with women in common-law relationships, with the studied purpose of avoiding the publicity of marriage; for this same reason they may avoid divorce. Con men and perhaps some other professional criminals may have or perceive a greater need for a wife or a loyal mistress to act as a liaison agent in the event of arrest. The women of the Denver con mob alluded to previously performed important functions of this general kind for their consorts.[76]

Single criminals and those who are divorced, like other unattached men of their class, seek sexual outlets with prostitutes and loose women. Varia-

[76] Van Cise, *op. cit.*, Chap. 34, "Wives."

tions in the sexual behavior of the single criminal may occur with differences in his criminal specialty. For example, single con men and con men away from their wives are not above casual bouts with Eros, but they are likely to be more careful of the women they pick up for such purposes for fear of complicating the delicate interaction in their dealings with victims. Fear of inadvertent encounters with the police or detectives is also a source of caution.

Recreation

The recreational behavior of criminals runs pretty much to commercialized amusements and gambling. Motion pictures, wrestling and boxing contests, night clubs, burlesque shows, and pool and bowling figure large in their recreational tastes. Many criminals gamble continually and heavily at horse races or in games among themselves. Con men, who might be expected to avoid dishonest gambling games often lose their money on the "other man's game." Con men also seem to take idle pleasure from practicing their techniques, which they do continually, conning one another or playing practical jokes among themselves and their female associates.

There is some reason to believe that a fairly close connection exists between the recreational interests of criminals and their deviant behavior. It has been shown repeatedly that there is an intimate tie between delinquent behavior and the leisure-time activities of youth. It is possible that public and supervised recreation comes to symbolize values in direct opposition to those of the habitual or professional criminal. It is both amusing and significant that inmates of prisons often cheer the opposing athletic teams when they come to play in the prison yard.

Political Participation

The interlocking nature of crime and politics in many communities necessitates that certain types of criminals, those in organized rackets especially, take an active interest in politics at the local and state levels. In some cities criminals have been hired to vote illegally, to intimidate regular voters, and to tamper with election returns. Apart from this, criminal organizations have helped to get out the vote at election time and have contributed heavily to the campaign funds of various politicians. Direct corruption of judges and other public officials has been laid to criminal groups. Apparently it has happened that some con men, and probably other criminals, have graduated from straight crime to being fixers and high-ranking members in political parties. However, their status is such that their political power must be exercised "behind the scenes" rather than in political office itself.

Adjustment and Maladjustment

Acceptance of the criminally defined self presents no salient difficulties to the systematic criminal. The many schisms of our culture, its innumerable conflicts and inconsistencies simplify the job of rationalizing and justifying criminal behavior. The blurring between crime and legal business methods diminishes the professional criminal's sense of real difference between himself and others. The con man perhaps more than other criminals is free to repudiate the moral attacks upon his role by reason of the very vulnerable position of his victims – the complainants. In general, professional criminals feel little shame or remorse over their transgressions against legitimate society.[77] The so-called reform of professional criminals, when it occurs, is more like a retirement or a change of jobs based upon calculation of differential risks and rewards than it is an overturn of the moral and philosophic values of the individual.

Certain criminal occupations modally generate tensions and anxieties which may be very exhausting and painful at the time, but they are situational precipitants and thus well oriented to objective reality. Gangsters must live in fear of sudden death at the hands of quick-triggered police or other gangsters. The con man must always be alert to the possibility of being recognized by former victims. Also, at a certain point in the play for the mark's cash, the con man's tensions and anxiety mount to terrific proportions. John Norfleet tells of wild sleep disturbances on the part of con men who slept in the same room with him during a play for his money.[78] Some con men find the occupational stresses too great and give up the game.

Whatever the occupational stresses of criminals, they are probably no greater than those of medical doctors, of utilities linemen, or of professional soldiers at war. We may safely guess that criminals come to deal with such stresses with about the same measure of success as persons in stressful legitimate occupations. Tensions of disorganizing magnitude sufficient to distort the symbolic process of the criminal may have their genesis in gross discrepancies between aspirational roles and achieved roles. However, there is little or no proof that frustration in criminal competition is any more extensive than it is in socially sanctioned competition. A hypothesis which cannot be tested at this time, which nevertheless suggests itself, is that among unconvicted professional criminals or those imprisoned only for a short time, symbolic maladjustment (psychoses-neuroses) is no more or less common than in the general population.

Imprisonment undoubtedly complicates the self and role acceptance of

[77] Sutherland, E. H., *The Professional Thief*, 1937, pp. 176–180.

[78] Norfleet, J. Frank, *Norfleet*, 1924, p. 294.

all who must experience it for any length of time. The prison environment conduces to self-disintegration and psychotic enhancement of the ego. Prison psychosis, or going "stir crazy," is well known to prison administrators and inmates alike. Furthermore, there are English data to show that mental disease rates of prison populations correlate positively with the length of time spent in prison.[79] The self-disorganizing aspects of imprisonment fall unevenly upon the inhabitants of the prison. A deducible hypothesis is that individual and situational criminal deviants are more likely than professional criminals to break under the social isolation of the prison, and the unprisonized more than the prisonized. The individual and situational criminal deviants are symbolically less prepared for their sudden assignment to the role and status of convicted criminals than are the professionals. Presumably they more frequently reject the prison-reflected self, and perhaps from the start they are more likely to be isolated from the prison community as well as from outside society.

Marginality

The most clear-cut examples of marginal criminals are those of persons who have turned state's witness in order to avoid the consequences of criminal acts, "finks," or prison informers, and stool pigeons who directly or indirectly support themselves by divulging information about criminals to the police, prosecutors, or prison administrators. Such persons are hated, rejected, and sometimes painfully scarred or killed by other criminals and at the same time they are looked upon with contempt by the lay public and as necessary evils by police and others who use them. No sociological studies of stool pigeons can be referred to here, but some notion of their unenviable status and subjective conflicts is to be found in fictional treatments of the subject. The impressions of professional criminals are to the effect that suicides among stool pigeons are fairly common.[80]

The status and role of the ex-convict are implicitly marginal, particularly for the nonprofessional criminal. In theory the ex-convict has atoned socially for his crime and has renewed his opportunity to participate in social life on a basis of equality with others. Facts deny this, for discrimination meets the ex-convict at every turn. His greatest barrier is economic; establishing himself in a job with no other references than those supplied by his prison usually becomes a heartbreaking business. He is offered unskilled, low-paying jobs other men refuse and sometimes receives lower wages than others doing the same work. Occasionally he is offered the dubious opportunity to work as a strikebreaker or as a scab. If the ex-convict advances economically to the point where better positions

[79] Hobhouse, Stephen, and A. F. Brockway, *English Prisons Today*, 1922.
[80] Sutherland, *The Professional Thief*, p. 131.

become open to him, he may be rejected because of inability to obtain a bond or because his past criminal record comes to light. If the man's aspirational roles are low, he may adjust successfully as, say, a laborer or casual worker; otherwise, he nearly always shows the marks of his difficult struggle. Harassment by the police often conspires with occupational failure to undermine whatever morale prison existence may have left him. More resilient ex-convicts may return to crime; but while this can be an adjustment for professional criminals, it is not for others coming from the prison, as they may not have the requisite criminal skills, or the criminal status to gain acceptance by a criminal organization. The change in the character of recidivistic crime found among ex-reformatory inmates from property offenses to petty offenses, such as drunkenness, vagrancy, and begging, spells out the process of demoralization through which many ex-convicts go with passing years.[81]

Marginality may be directly related to the nature of the criminal activity itself, being in some part an implicit consequence of a role. The borderline criminal nature of certain pursuits can be demonstrated both by the low earnings from them and the dubious status of those following them, both among criminals and noncriminals. The curtailed earnings from these occupations necessitate some other job, usually a legitimate one, being held, with corresponding contradictory demands being made upon the individual's time, interests, and loyalties. Such a person seldom has sufficient money to make a "show" of prosperity. He is not highly regarded by professional criminals; and when discovered for what he is by noncriminals, he tends to be scorned and despised. The following case history most appropriately illustrates the type of marginality we have described

THE POOLROOM HUSTLER

Speedy Rapp was born in Chicago in 1900. Nothing is known of his early life except that he came from a lower class Polish family, and that he attended public school through the tenth grade.

He got his first job when he was fifteen years old, setting pins in a bowling alley. There was a poolroom in connection with the bowling establishment, and when his alleys were not in use, Speedy practiced on the pool tables, paying for their use by helping the houseman rack balls, clean up, get soft drinks for customers, and so on.

Speedy soon acquired considerable skill as a pool player, and the houseman let him play for the house when a customer could not find another opponent. The only stake involved in these games was rental of the table, which Speedy did not have to pay if he lost. He had an attractive personality and a sense of humor, and the customers liked to play with him. The houseman noticed this, and he soon had a full-time job in the poolroom.

[81] Glueck and Glueck, *Later Criminal Careers*, pp. 121, 350.

He was in a position to observe the operations of pool hustlers and soon began to play for money himself. When he was about sixteen, an older hustler who worked small towns took him on a couple of short tours. Speedy's youth was an asset in getting games with the small-town experts, and the trips were profitable. It was probably at this point, when he first won what he considered important money, a couple of hundred dollars, that he first defined himself as a pool hustler. He left home and rented a cheap room in a small hotel.

It was about this time that he learned what houses of prostitution were for, and became one of their steadiest and most enthusiastic patrons. When one of the girls took a liking to him, and he started "getting it for free," he was sure he had reached full manhood.

Speedy became well-known to the south Chicago poolroom society as a smart kid and made contacts that led to more profitable operations than pool hustling. He was, at one time or another, employed as bookie's runner, steerer for a bordello, bootlegger's delivery boy, and petty con man.

A favorite confidence game in those days was the old "telephone telepathy" caper. This maneuver was started by inordinate praise of the fantastic psychic powers of an acquaintance of the con man. After building up the incredulity of the victim to the point where it became antagonistic, a case of put up or shut up, the sucker was invited to draw any card from a deck, and told that if he called a certain person on the telephone he would be told the card he drew. After drawing, he was given a telephone number and told to ask for a Mr. Smith, or Mr. Jones, or Mr. Something-else, the name of the person he asked for, of course, being the clue to the card he drew. All that was necessary was a list of 52 names, matched with 52 cards in the deck, and a confederate to answer the telephone.

Another favorite was the spelling game. The players took turns adding letters to a series, the first one who completed a word being the loser. Hustlers spent weeks thumbing through dictionaries to find unusual combinations of letters that would trap opponents.

Betting who could name, in a limited time, the most makes of automobiles no longer manufactured was another popular game. Hustlers would spend days in the library, flipping through the ads in old magazines, compiling lists, and memorizing them. This game was varied by substituting cities in the United States with more than a hundred thousand population, names of railroads, brands of cigarettes or cigars. The idea was to have a category to tempt every potential sucker.

Speedy bought a gambler's diamond – a hot stone, of course – not only to make a flash, but as a hock piece, something to be pawned when ready cash was needed quickly. He dressed – or overdressed rather – carefully, wore patent-leather shoes, greased his hair, and cleaned his fingernails.

A Chicago druggist – who, by the way, later became a well-known screen writer – helped Speedy start on a foolproof racket, good for a million dollars, and with no risks. It operated on the theory that there is a little larceny in everybody, and every man who owned a car was a prospect.

It worked like this. The owner parked his car at a prearranged location and left the keys in it. The gang picked it up, drove it to a garage, where radio heater, spotlight, wheels, tires, tools – all detachable and salable parts, in fact – were removed and sold, and the profits split with the car owner. The police were then tipped off as to where the car could be recovered, and the owner was reimbursed by his insurance company. Business was good. It seems that a large number of people must think it is no crime to beat an insurance company.

All went well until the gang decided that paying the owner a cut was a waste of money. How could he squawk? He was as guilty as they were. But they overlooked the possibility of a disgruntled victim giving the police an anonymous tip. This put Speedy in jail for ten months and convinced him that more legitimate rackets were safer.

He got a job with a traveling carnival, running the wheel of fortune. This job lasted four or five years, during which time he traveled all over the country with the show. He also acquired a wife, marrying one of the burlesque dancers in the company, and regarded himself as a more or less established citizen.

Early in the Depression, the carnival went broke in San Francisco and disbanded, leaving Speedy and his wife Mildred without money, and no way to get back to the familiar territory of Chicago.

Carnival jobs were unobtainable, but Mildred managed to get a job in the chorus of a burlesque show. They lived in one room in a cheap hotel, taking their meals in one-arm restaurants, eating more coffee and doughnuts than meat and potatoes.

Mildred's salary of $35 a week did not pay expenses. Speedy's diamond went to the pawnshop, and a little later he sold the pawn ticket. This was rock bottom to Speedy. To admit to himself that he would not get that break in a few days that would solve all their financial problems, and redeem his ring, was a major defeat.

Mildred was an attractive girl, and in her work she met men who were willing and anxious to make a substantial payment for a little of her time. Her rough carnival experience had more or less prepared her for the idea, and Speedy finally agreed that "just once" would not be too important. Just once became just once in awhile, and in a few weeks Mildred had quit her job at the burlesque show and was a full-time prostitute. Speedy did a little pimping.

At first, Speedy would not admit that his wife was in the racket, but in a few months he told prospective clients that it was his wife he was sending them to. He thought it gave her class, something a little special and different that helped keep the price up. "Sure my wife works," Speedy said.

Without the protection of an organization, it was inevitable that Mildred would sooner or later be arrested. It was sooner, and she served thirty days. While in jail, she made contacts with other women that enabled her to get into a regular house of prostitution when she was released. Being still young and good-looking, she worked in one of the more expensive establishments and made more money and did less work than she had as a free lance. Customers were solicited by the organization that ran the house, so Speedy's services were no longer required. He was out of a job again. He and Mildred, with a larger and more regular income, moved to a better hotel, and Speedy had a little spending money.

He tried pool hustling again, but had been away from the game so long that he had lost the old touch and did not win so regularly as he once had. So he started playing pastime pool, games without stakes, to get in practice. This took up his evenings. During the day he worked as a pitchman, selling razor blades and small notions, including a miniature penknife containing an unserviceable nail file and a little cuticle pusher. This was hawked as the smallest manicure set in the world. Occasionally he disposed of a few stolen fountain pens or watches for a fence. His most profitable item was a stem-wind, stem-set, 18-karat white-gold-colored wrist watch. It was stem-wind, stem-set all right, but had no works. This landed Speedy in the pokey for a sixty-day stretch.

When he got out of jail, he went back to his old stand-by, pool hustling. One afternoon a man came into the poolroom carrying a new and expensive electric clock he had just purchased. He took a cue and began to play in an open game, leaving the clock on a bench. Speedy walked over and sat down by it. The price tag was on the box and Speedy examined it. The clock would bring $10 or $15 at any pawnshop or fence in town. The owner of the clock walked toward the men's toilet. Speedy picked up the box and started for the door. He almost made it before the clock's owner and the houseman grabbed him.

This caper got Speedy six months. When he was released from jail, he was rearrested immediately on a vagrancy charge and given a floater – twenty-four hours to get out of town. He got what money Mildred had saved while he was in jail and left for Los Angeles. He was going to get a job, something legitimate, and send for her.

In Los Angeles he hustled pool again, with some success, worked in a dairy lunch, and got a little extra work in motion pictures. While working as an extra, he met a chorus girl and married her without troubling to get a divorce from his wife in San Francisco.

Some of his poolroom associates, who had heard him speak of his wife in San Francisco, guessed his little venture into bigamy; and one of them, who disliked him because of a gambling deal in which the profits were all Speedy's got word of the latest marriage to Mildred.

Mildred was sore over being discarded after what she called her "sacrifices," and had Speedy arrested. Although she regretted her haste in having him pinched, the law operated as usual, and Speedy landed in jail again, this time for a year. His second marriage was annulled, and after completing his term he was given another floater.

He was discharged in 1936; and, although Mildred wanted him back, he headed for Las Vegas, where he hoped to get a job in a gambling house.

In 1939 he was back in Los Angeles, where he spent several weeks visiting a friend he had met in jail, by now a succesful bookie. The Nevada venture had been a failure. He had worked at everything – bus boy, janitor, elevator operator, panhandler – except the kind of job he wanted.

In Los Angeles he tried pool hustling again, but was picked up by the police, given ten days, and sent on his way with another floater out of town.

When last observed, Speedy was hitchhiking his way to San Francisco, where he hoped to find Mildred and a good break.

The life choices of the person in this history clearly were limited in so far as both legitimate and criminal skills were concerned. This meant that the range of roles he could satisfactorily fill was small and, for the most part, they consisted of roles which could be regarded as means of advancement to those of higher status. It will be noted that at least two of his ventures into straight crime ended unsuccessfully because he lacked criminal acumen. Apparently his associations and jail experiences did not provide him with skills and knowledge that would have permitted him to graduate from his marginal status as a poolroom hustler to a more lucrative, ranking criminal occupation. This fact might not have been particularly disturbing to him in his younger years except that he was defined as a "smart kid" by criminal and quasi-criminal associates and more was expected of him than others of comparable status with whom he was classed. His brief experience as an auto thief was a step upward in the scale of criminal roles. However, the organizational skill of the gang carrying out the automobile thefts was limited and its collective judgment defective. In any event it was unable to prevent its being destroyed and its members sent to jail.

After the jail experience it is to be noted that Speedy returned to a quasi-legitimate variant of his central role as a petty gambler in a carnival. It is possible that he might have advanced within the social organization of the carnival had not the Depression intervened to destroy this area of choices. Just as the Depression undercut the organizational basis for many strictly legitimate social roles, so it affected the occupational opportunities of marginal criminals. The forced sale of his gambler's "hock piece" undoubtedly was a critical point of transition or demoralization for Speedy. It should be noted that this occurred when he was about thirty years old, a point when most persons expect to have achieved some higher measure of occupational status and income. At this time, the situation compelled his turning to the role of a pimp. He shared the professional criminal's attitude toward this role to the extent that it could only be an extreme resort, undertaken with reluctance, and never fully accepted. Soon he returned to pool hustling, but found that he had lost the necessary skill to perform the role successfully. It is also true that by this time poolrooms were tending to decrease in number and opportunities for hustling were fewer because of changing recreational habits.

Working as a pitchman was not sufficiently rewarding in terms of prestige and income to Speedy, which gives the reason for his tentative experimenting with the fence's role. His bigamous marriage, something few professional criminals would risk, further revealed his lack of preparation for a criminal role. The long series of legitimate jobs Speedy held and discarded while in Nevada betrayed his continuing dissatisfaction with the type of roles he could fill satisfactorily.

In summary, we see the picture of a man with role aspirations beyond his capacity to play, interacting on the periphery of professional crime, with brief forays as an active criminal which culminated in jail sentences. These built up both fear and a sense of failure, which drove him back to his original role, to that of a pimp, and to various socially acceptable menial roles. While the conflict over the self is not brought out in the case history, nonetheless we believe it is implicit in the fluctuations from legitimate to illegitimate behavior, in the compulsive quality of his theft of the clock, and in the apparent hostility of his poolroom cronies, one of whom was responsible for his last jail sentence.

Selected Readings

HALL, JEROME *Theft, Law and Society*, 1935, Chap 1.

LINDESMITH, A · "Organized Crime," *Annals of the American Academy of Political and Social Sciences*, 217, September, 1941, pp. 119–127

SELLIN, THORSTEN· *Culture Conflict and Crime*, 1938.

SUTHERLAND, E H.. *The Professional Thief*, 1937

——— "White Collar Criminality," *American Sociological Review*, 5, February, 1940, pp. 1–12.

TAPPAN, PAUL: "Who Is the Criminal?" *American Sociological Review*, 12, February, 1947, pp. 96–102.

———: "Treatment without Trial," *Social Forces*, 24, March, 1946, pp. 306–311.

CHAPTER 10

DRUNKENNESS AND THE CHRONIC ALCOHOLIC

The consumption of alcoholic beverages is an integrated feature of many cultures including our own. It fulfills important ritual and symbolic functions for many of our institutions, is widely employed as a condiment, as a medicine, and as a culturally sanctioned means of achieving relaxation and freedom from tensions for the individual. Drinking alcoholic beverages serves to symbolize solidarity, unity, and fellowship at births, weddings, religious communion, and even death itself. In differentiated and highly stratified societies drinking behavior as well as the character of the beverages consumed signify status cleavages and mark off the ingroup from the outgroup. An important segment of our national economy is geared to the production, distribution, and sale of alcoholic drinks, upon which hundreds of thousands of workers depend directly or indirectly for their livelihood. Along with this can be perceived a separate, well-defined, and more or less ritualized drinking culture consisting of techniques for the preparation of drinks, special ways of imbibing them, drinking songs, stories, humorous anecdotes, and legends. It is because of these facts that the task of fixing the limits of normal and abnormal drinking becomes a troublesome one.

As a step in determining what abnormal alcoholic drinking and what the abnormal drinker are, it is helpful, first of all, to summarize the physiological effects of taking alcohol into the body. Consumption of small amounts of alcohol undoubtedly has beneficial physiological effects, improving such things as digestion and muscle tonus. This would apply to alcoholic concentrations of less than 0.05 per cent of the content of the blood. In more prosaic terms, the average tolerance for alcohol runs to about two highballs or one quart of beer. Anything beyond this induces symptoms of intoxication, with a definite intoxicated state appearing as alcoholic concentrations of 0.15 per cent or more are attained. A lethal point is reached somewhere around 0.2 per cent. The immediate effects of alcohol consumption cannot be strictly measured by the quantities of liquor involved, because other physiological variables also operate, namely, the size of the person doing the drinking, the condition of the stomach, the nutritional balance in body cells, and the rapidity with which the liquor is downed.

Generally liquor in intoxicating quantities acts as a depressant, which is to say that the body reactions are slowed down. Ample experimental evidence attests to the decrease brought about by large quantities of liquor, in auditory, visual, tactual, and kinesthetic acuity. Gross and especially the finer neuromuscular coordinations are impaired; hand-eye coordinations suffer, demonstrated by decreases of as high as 50 per cent in target-shooting scores. Errors in estimating time intervals have been shown to increase by 600 per cent as the result of intoxicating doses of alcohol, and the ability to recognize similarities and opposites declines significantly. The higher cortical processes are ordinarily believed to show the effects of liquor in a superficiality of thought, poor judgment, and exaggeration of dissociative mechanisms resulting in lowered inhibitions. Speech is slowed down, thickened, or blurred.[1]

While there is much agreement upon the immediate effects of alcohol upon the body behavior, no such consensus can be discovered in the literature on the long-run effects of heavy drinking. Some of the organic pathologies attributed to alcoholism are cirrhosis and fatty infiltration of the liver, stomach disorders, sterility, anemia, polyneuritis, beriberi, pellagra, sexual impotence, and cellular changes resulting in such things as coarsening of the features, plethoric complexion, watery eyes, and the classic bulbous red nose seen on chronic inebriates. Unhappily it cannot be told for sure in just how many such cases and to what extent these disorders are the direct consequence of alcohol introduced into the body. Most pathological drinkers do not eat properly, which may be responsible in whole or in part for the deficiency diseases from which they suffer. Some support for such a view comes from the staff of a mental hospital in the Upper Peninsula of Michigan where it has been observed by psychiatrists that the old-time lumberjack who ate heavily and did spree drinking deteriorated less rapidly than the heavy drinkers among lumberjacks of today who, due to less stable employment, drink more continuously and eat less regularly. In some degree the lessened appetite of the pathological drinker derives from the partial food value of the alcohol which he literally lives on for long periods. Unfortunately, alcohol lacks vitamins, especially B_1, minerals, and protein. Consequently long alcoholic bouts, with decreased food intake, usually result in avitaminosis and deficiency disease, according to present medical opinion.[2]

THE SOCIAL AND CULTURAL NATURE OF THE DEVIATION

Generally speaking, prolonged alcoholic indulgence tends to undermine the constitution of the individual and thus weaken the organic basis for

[1] For a summary of such studies see Hampton, Peter, "A Descriptive Portrait of the Drinker: I. The Normal Drinker," *Journal of Social Psychology*, 25, February, 1947, pp. 70–72.

[2] See Jervis, G. A., "Experimental Studies in Alcoholism and Avitaminosis," *Quarterly Journal of Studies on Alcohol*, 3, March, 1943, pp. 533–540.

behavior. However, the really significant effects of inebriation do not lie in physiology but rather in social behavior. Thus excessive drinking is conjoined with other forms of behavior which run counter to the normal expectations of the sober community: traffic accidents, sexual immorality, obscenity, brawling and disturbing the peace, destruction of property, disregard of family and occupational responsibilities, misuse of money and credit, and petty crime. In some instances alcoholism brings on, or is associated with, psychotic disturbances making the person uncontrollable and necessitating forcible constraint and incarceration.

Drunkenness and alcoholism have no uniform effect upon social behavior, for they are always interacting with preexisting personality structure and situational factors. The pattern of excessive drinking itself is highly variable from person to person; in one it may take the form of steady, day-by-day indulgence, while in another it may show itself in heavy week-end drinking, or in sporadic spree drinking lasting for days or several weeks at a time. Some heavy drinkers are addicted to hard liquors, while others obtain their desired intoxication from beer or wines. Heavy drinkers under no economic handicaps are more apt to consume beverages of high alcoholic content because the effects come sooner; but the drinker of modest means must drink what he can afford, while the poor drinker takes what he can get, which may mean canned heat, vanilla extract, hair tonic, perfume, or industrial alcohols. Some people prefer to do their heavy drinking in the company of others, while others confine their drinking to periods when they are alone and safe from interruption. A social compromise is struck by some alcoholics, who begin their libations in groups, then leave to be alone for their more intensive drinking. Table 38 gives a summary of the drinking habits of 100 chronic alcoholics.

Mood, temperament, and trait changes brought on by alcoholic indulg-

TABLE 38 DRINKING HABITS OF 100 CHRONIC ALCOHOLICS ADMITTED TO VETERANS HOSPITAL, KNOXVILLE, IOWA, 1937–1942*

Periodicity		Nature of beverage		Sociality	
Regular drinkers	23	Hard liquors	48	Group drinking	50
Spree drinkers	54	Hard liquor and beer or other	32	Solitary drinking	29
Unstated	23	Beer only	3	Group and solitary drinking	18
		Unusual beverages	6	Unstated	3
		Unstated	11		
Total	100		100		100

*Taken from Barrett, T. H., "Chronic Alcoholism in Veterans," *Quarterly Journal of Studies in Alcohol*, 4, June, 1943, pp. 73–75.

ence show no great similarity from one person to another, apart from that which can be related to a similarity of cultural background. We are accustomed to think of the drunken person as growing belligerent, obscene, and profane, but contrary to this, there are many who become mellow, agreeable, and generous when they have imbibed too freely. Even in the process of deterioration of chronic alcoholics, great variations are to be noted; likewise, the symptoms of the so-called "alcoholic psychoses" vary tremendously. The complexity and diversity of our culture as well as personal individuation does much to explain the polymorphous nature of the alcoholic behavior of members of our society.

At this point it is necessary to interject a note of caution with reference to various physiological and psychological studies on the effects of alcohol consumption. We should not let ourselves forget that the subjects for these investigations have been drawn from our own culture and that there are very few cross-cultural studies of the physiology and "psychology" of alcohol ingestion. Such comparative studies as have been made raise more than fleeting doubts that what often passes for constant "physiological effects" of alcohol in American research in reality may be manifestations of a variable cultural overlay. Thus, for example, in one study of the function of alcohol in a primitive Mexican culture located in the mountains of Chiapas few of the more extreme types of behavior which arise in connection with intoxication in our culture were found to occur. There, in the stage of "feeling high," native men could play guitars or handle a machete with perfect safety. In extreme intoxication there seemed to be less interference with speech than that observable in inebriation in our culture, and even in stuporous states the natives carried through with familiar routines and transacted complicated business of which later they had no memory. There seemed to be very little vomiting after overindulgence, and there was little evidence of "hang-overs" beyond mild tremors and shakiness. Little fighting arose in drinking parties, and there was no evidence of lowered inhibition in erotic behavior. These people typically drank for the sense of warmth it induced and as a prelude to sleep.[3]

Returning to the question of the definition of sociopathic drinking, we may say that it is drinking associated with socially disapproved modifications in the drinker's behavior. It is a quantitative problem in the sense that a person "drinks too much" when he is guilty of mild to serious misconduct, when his behavior is unfavorably affected in a large number of social settings, and when there is an accumulation of social failures and transgressions related to drinking over long periods of time. The chronic alcoholic or drunkard is socially recognized by the compulsive or uncontrolled

[3] Bunzel, Ruth, "The Role of Alcoholism in Two Central American Cultures," *Psychiatry*, 3, August, 1940, pp. 361–387.

quality of his drinking, which persists in the face of severe social penalties and countless resolutions of his own to refrain from drinking. In this respect chronic alcoholism resembles drug addiction and stuttering in which inner compulsions more or less irrationally drive the person so afflicted to consume liquor in a manner seldom understandable to a non-alcoholic. In chronic alcoholism there is added to gross physical deterioration a total involvement of behavior, with deviation taking place in all of its aspects: overt bodily reactions, object manipulation, verbal response, and in the covert symbolic process.

Extent of the Deviation

There is no one index which can serve as a measure of the total number of intemperate users of alcohol. The methods which have been employed to throw light upon the quantitative aspect of the alcoholic "problem" include surveys of insurance policyholders, absenteeism records in factories, arrests for drunkenness, death rates caused by alcoholism, and admissions to mental hospitals of alcoholics with and without psychoses. All these methods individually suffer from one defect or another so that they cannot be relied upon alone as measures of alcoholism. Together, however, they have been valuable in arriving at usable estimates of the dimensions of alcoholic deviation in our population. A careful sifting of the available data has led two writers to set the total number of users of alcohol in one form or another and to a greater or lesser degree at 40,000,000 in 1940. Out of this number some 37,600,000 persons were estimated to drink in moderation, leaving 2,400,000 who at the time were drinking to excess. Close to 600,000 persons drank continuously enough and had deteriorated to the point where they could be justifiably designated as chronic alcoholics.[4] From 1940 to 1945 there was a decided increase in the consumption of alcohol, but this was caused by a 35 per cent increase in the number of consumers rather than the result of increased individual consumption. At the present writing there may be 65,000,000 drinkers, with 4,000,000 excessive drinkers and close to a million advanced cases of alcoholism in our population.[5]

The Differentiation of Alcoholics

Writers of an earlier day were convinced that chronic alcoholics were genetically differentiated from the general population in having inherited weaknesses or abnormal cravings for alcoholic drinks. Such convictions

[4] Haggard, H. W., and E M. Jellinek, *Alcohol Explored*, 1947, pp. 16–27.

[5] Jellinek, E. M., *Recent Trends in Alcoholism and in Alcohol Consumption*, 1947. Also statements by Mrs Marty Mann to Town Hall Meeting in Los Angeles, Nov. 9, 1948.

were supported by genealogical records listing disproportionately larger numbers of excessive drinkers in family lines from which chronic alcoholics came. The error in this research lay in the inclusion of psychotic, mentally deficient, and epileptic persons who drank heavily along with mentally normal alcoholics. When a careful study was made of 572 children of normal alcoholics, the number who were defective came to only 4 per cent of the total, no greater than might be expected for the general population.[6] It is also true that children of alcoholics placed in foster homes show no greater percentage of adult sociopathy than children of nonalcoholic parents who have been so placed.[7]

More recently a case has been made for the presence of lower alcoholic tolerances or allergies among alcoholics as a class. In fact, one well-known rehabilitating agency for alcoholics has built its program and organization around the theory that alcoholics are biologically specialized people with allergies which prevent them from ever being normal social drinkers. Such ideas are extremely difficult to prove, chiefly because they come from studies of alcoholics after the fact of their becoming alcoholics. There is the very real possibility that such allergies or low tolerances for alcohol stem from the alcoholism itself, or perhaps from concomitant physiological changes. Until better proof of their existence apart from the alcoholic behavior itself is obtained, allergies and special tolerances for alcohol cannot be seriously considered as differentiating attributes of alcoholics.[8]

Alcoholism falls unevenly into different age groups; chronic alcoholics, like many other sociopathic deviants, have a very high proportion of males among them. Chronic alcoholics are also much older than the general population, chiefly because the deterioration they show ordinarily comes only after many years of drinking. Seldom, if ever, is a full-blown chronic alcoholic found to be under 15 years of age, and only a small percentage fall below 30 years of age. Rates tend to ascend by age from 20 years to a peak somewhere between 45 and 55 years of age, where they level off on a plateau and eventually fall after age 64. The peak age is reached somewhat earlier by females.[9] In the United States there are about 7 male alcoholics for every female alcoholic. Outside the United States this ratio varies widely from country to country. In Norway, for example, the ratio is 23

[6] Haggard and Jellinek, *op cit*, p 214

[7] Roe, Ann, "The Adult Adjustment of Children of Alcoholic Parents Raised in Foster Homes," *Quarterly Journal of Studies on Alcohol*, 5, December, 1944, pp. 378–393.

[8] Haggard, H. W, "Critique of the Allergic Nature of Alcoholism," *Quarterly Journal of Studies on Alcoholism*, 5, September, 1944, pp. 233–241.

[9] Dayton, Neil A., *New Facts on Mental Disorders*, 1940, p. 310.

to 1, in Switzerland, 12 to 1. In sharp contrast to these, the English female rate comes much closer to the male, the sex ratio there being 2 to 1.[10]

For many years the nativity and ethnic characteristics of alcoholics committed to mental hospitals have been recognized as among their more impressive differentiae. Alcoholism both without and with mental disorder occurs with much greater frequency among the foreign-born than among the native-born white population, with second-generation immigrants, *i.e.*, native-born of foreign-born or mixed parentage, holding a middle position between the two.[11] The specific ethnic groups displaying the highest rates among the foreign-born are the Irish, Scandinavians, Italians, English, and Germans. The greatest contrast appears between the rate ratios of the Irish and those of other nationalities, which in some areas runs as high as 5 to 1.[12]

Catholics have higher rates of alcoholic mental disease than Protestants, but this may be a spurious relationship; there is the possibility that it reflects the high rates for alcoholism among first- and second-generation Irish, who are predominantly Catholic in religious affiliation. Research along this same line has shown alcoholic mental disorders to be three times as frequent among Catholic priests as in the general population.[13] However, there is some question as to whether these data were sufficiently refined, especially by age, to permit conclusive generalization on this point. A well-corroborated fact is the low rate of alcoholism in Jewish groups, both for the foreign-born and native-born.

Negroes usually rank higher than whites with respect to both alcoholism and alcoholic mental disorders. Excessive drinking is common in American Indian groups, but there is no accurate estimate of how many Indians are chronic alcoholics. A sizable portion of West Coast Mexicans are intemperate drinkers, if their arrest rates for drunkenness in the region can serve as an index. Presumably Japanese and Chinese contribute only insignificantly to the alcoholic population.

The economic attributes of alcoholics have not been uncontrovertibly established. Numerous data point to a much lower economic status for the alcoholic, but these have been largely drawn from public mental-hospital records. An investigation of mental disorders in the Chicago areas in which claim is made to having balanced data from public and private hospitals reveals a significant economic differential for alcoholics as indicated by a

[10] Bowman, K. M., and Jellinek, E. M., "Alcoholic Addiction and Its Treatment," *Quarterly Journal of Studies on Alcohol*, 2, June, 1941, p 142

[11] Dayton, *op. cit.*, Chap. 3.

[12] Malzberg, B., "Race and Mental Disease in New York," *Psychiatric Quarterly* 5, No. 9, October, 1935, pp. 538–569

[13] Moore, T. V., "Insanity in Priests and the Religious," *Ecclesiastical Review*, 95, 1936.

positive correlation between relief rates and alcoholic-psychosis rates and a negative correlation between these latter rates and median monthly rentals.[14] While it is probably true that chronic alcoholics are more impoverished than other persons, for reasons to be made clear later, it does not follow with certainty that they *originate* in any greater proportions from population groups in lower economic strata.

The same objections made to the studies of the economic differences of alcoholics apply with equal relevance to statistical data on their educational status. There have been several studies which do indeed show alcoholics to have less formal education than the general population, but in nearly every one of these studies the sample has been a selected one. Groups studied have been of persons arrested for drunkenness or of patients with alcoholic psychoses in mental hospitals. There is good reason to believe that both groups come from social and economic strata where one normally finds less education. When alcoholics in private mental institutions are thrown in with those from public institutions, the total groups of alcoholics tends to closely resemble the rest of the population in education.[15]

Some writers have accepted rather uncritically the idea that alcoholics are more likely to be feeble-minded than other people. For example, one author has estimated that around one-tenth of all alcoholics are feeble-minded and another 10 per cent are in borderline categories.[16] We must remain very dubious of estimates such as these. Diagnoses of feeble-mindedness predicated upon mental tests of deteriorated alcoholics must be treated with the greatest caution. Equating intemperate drinking in definitely diagnosable feeble-minded cases with the compulsive drinking in normal alcoholics likewise seems a very debatable procedure.

A good deal of loose – even sloppy – thinking has been done on the subject of the criminality of alcoholics. A note of caution recently has come into the literature on the subject, but the fallacy persists that the alcoholic has criminaloid tendencies. This comes out in a recent concept of the "stupid drinker," who, in the opinion of one writer, "develops into a

[14] Faris, R. E. L., and H. W. Dunham, *Mental Disorders in Urban Areas*, 1939, p 118.

[15] Haggard and Jellinek, *op. cit*, p 257, For an extensive study which purports to prove that alcoholics are less educated than nonalcoholics see Manson, M., "Educational Characteristics of Alcoholics," *Quarterly Journal of Studies on Alcohol*, 11, March, 1950, pp. 31–50. In this study the mean number of years of education for alcoholic males was found to be 10.6 years and for the control group, 13 6 years According to the 1940 census this control group was 3 3 years above the median years of education completed by the general population of California. Also the alcoholic group was 0.3 years above this median!

[16] Hampton, P., "A Descriptive Portrait of the Drinker IV. The Stupid Drinker," *Journal of Social Psychology*, 25, February, 1947, pp. 83–99

dangerous and criminal drinker, because in him the dormant primitive drives are whipped up by drink...."[17] Granted, a great deal of unrestrained drinking accompanies the commission of many serious crimes, but then it also accompanies marriage ceremonies, connubial sex relations which maintain the birth rate, military exploits, and Irish funerals. There is no reason for believing that drunkenness is more of a "cause" of unacceptable behavior – even in mentally deficient persons – than it is a "cause" of socially desirable actions. In so far as crime is concerned, studies show that the crimes of the alcoholic are almost exclusively petty ones.[18]

An examination of the first admissions to mental hospitals throughout the United States discloses that there are pronounced regional differences in the rates of alcoholic psychoses. We can see from Table 39 that the highest rates are found in the New England, Pacific, Middle Atlantic, and East North Central states.

TABLE 39. FIRST ADMISSIONS FOR ALCOHOLIC PSYCHOSES IN ALL HOSPITALS IN THE UNITED STATES, BY REGION, 1935

Region	Number	Rate
New England	497	11.8
Pacific.	528	11.4
Middle Atlantic	1,467	10.9
East North Central	1,178	9.3
South Atlantic	441	6 6
East South Central	214	4.9
Mountain.	67	4 0
West North Central	247	3.8
West South Central	209	3.8
Total United States	4,879	8.1

*"Regional Differences in the Hospitalization and Care of Patients with Mental Diseases," 1940, Federal Security Agency *Bulletin*, Table H, p 80

To an unknown degree this regional pattern is a function of varying hospital facilities and hospitalization customs in the areas. It also very plainly mirrors the generally operating rural-urban rate differential, since the regions with the highest rates at the same time are the most industrialized and most urbanized. Urban rates for alcoholic psychoses run about three times the rural rates. However, state differences may outweigh both regional and rural-urban differences. For example, the state of Nevada has had rates for alcoholic mental disorders which run five to seven times those of other states. California in 1947 led all other states, apart from Nevada, in such things as per capita consumption of alcoholic beverages, arrests for

[17] *Ibid.*, p. 120.

[18] See Brown, L Guy, *Social Pathology*, 1942, p. 157, Sutherland, E H., *Criminology*, 1947, 4th ed, pp. 113*f*.

drunkenness, and admissions of nonpsychotic alcoholics to its mental hospitals.[19]

Spatial concentrations of cases of alcoholic mental disorders are also to be found in local-community areas. In larger urban communities clusters of high rates occur near the center of the city, in areas of high mobility, high sex ratios, and of first-generation immigrant settlements. The alcoholics tend to concentrate in areas where cheap rooming houses, inexpensive restaurants and bars, burlesque houses, and vice resorts abound. These areas are not necessarily points of origin for alcoholics; they are commonly spatial terminals in the deterioration process of the chronic heavy drinker.

THE CONTEXTS OF ALCOHOLISM

Information introduced earlier in this chapter indicate that about one-fourth of all excessive drinkers present pictures of well-defined chronic alcoholism, leaving some 2 to 3 million persons on way stations to this stage, who are currently classifiable as individual or situational alcoholic deviants. The first of these latter, the individual deviants, are those whose intoxicated episodes spring from more or less fixed conflicts over role, status, and self. Their unrestrained indulgence in liquor is symptomatic of conflicts which have acquired relative autonomy from external stimuli. Under this classification must be included the large numbers of psychoneurotic, psychotic, and epileptic persons who drink to reduce intolerable cryptic fears and tensions. The functions of drunkenness in such cases can vary greatly. A mentally disturbed person who is driven by strange and awesome compulsions may find in strong drink the means to avoid their translation into serious overt misbehavior. Drinking may also be an escape from hallucinations during a psychotic episode. It may reduce painful self-doubts by eliciting more self- and socially acceptable traits which are neurotically inhibited in everyday life. Thus a male with homosexual fears may become more heterosexual under the influence of alcohol and gain some temporary reassurance of his essential masculinity. It is a well-known fact that heavy drinking often punctuates critical phases in the lives of schizophrenics, and drunken sprees coincide with the periodicity of the disturbances in manic-depressive mental disorders.

A recent careful study showed that 26 per cent of a group of persons suffering from epilepsy drank moderately, with 6 per cent of the group diagnosed as intemperate drinkers.[20] The latter statistic may be an underestimate; an average of the percentage of chronic alcoholics among epi-

[19] Paper by Alexander Simon, *Third Institute for Alcoholic Studies*, University of California at Los Angeles, February, 1949.

[20] Lennox, William, "Alcohol and Epilepsy," *Quarterly Journal of Studies on Alcohol*, 2, June, 1941, p 11.

leptic patients brought out in five other studies made in different years from 1927 to 1941 came to 14.5 per cent. In addition, it is known that the number of persons who are admitted to hospitals and diagnosed as chronic alcoholics conceals a considerable number of cases of epilepsy.[21] While there is not proof that alcoholism causes epilepsy, there is sound reason for interpreting habitual drunkenness as the product of internal conflicts of epileptics. More specifically it can be held that their heavy drinking frequently is brought on by anticipation (not the aura) and fears of seizures or by the sense of guilt about their affliction. Support for some sort of sociopsychological interrelationship of the two behaviors is drawn from the fact that in 57 per cent of cases in one group, epileptic seizures followed or coincided with drinking.[22]

Situational Alcoholism

An inescapable conclusion from the various data on the differentiation of alcoholics is that the general and specific sociocultural situations confronting the individual have much to do with drinking to intoxicating excess. The high sex ratio of chronic alcoholics and its variability from one culture to another, the high rates of alcoholism among the foreign-born and their great variability from one nationality to another, and the very high rates among the Irish and almost complete absence of alcoholism among Jews provide ample support for this general culture-conflict explanation. The fact that single and married women have a low incidence of alcoholism while divorced women have a much higher incidence is noteworthy along this line. Case-history documents make it explicit and clear that inebriation becomes a reaction to intolerable social situations for many persons who are otherwise normal.

In order to have excessive drinking in a given society, the cultural setting must make alcoholic beverages accessible and reasonably cheap. It is perhaps only because many preliterate societies are without brewing techniques or are at a stage of technological development not permitting expenditures of time, energy, and materials for production of a nonnecessary economic item such as liquor that they are free of alcoholism as we know it. In other instances primitive drinking is, or has been, sacred and ritualistic, so that alcoholic drinks are guarded by chiefs or priests and carefully dispensed on set occasions. A second requirement for culturally endemic alcoholism is that drinking behavior be permissive, sanctioned, or a universal compulsive integrating the culture. Third, the impact of the cultural setting must generate disruptive anxieties, tensions, and aggres-

[21] Bowman, K. M., and E. M. Jellinek, "Alcoholic Mental Disorders," *Quarterly Journal of Studies on Alcohol*, 2, September, 1941, Table 9, p. 380.

[22] Lennox, *op. cit.*

sions. Finally, in order for chronic alcoholic addiction or compulsive drinking to develop, there must be strong disapproval of the consequences of drinking or of drinking itself beyond a certain point of intoxication, so that the culture induces guilt and depression over drinking and extreme drunkenness per se.

Social organization implements the cultural setting of alcoholic drinking and activates attendant culture conflicts in different ways, so that persons are never equally exposed to the forces making for excessive drinking and alcoholic addiction. Children seldom become excessive drinkers, even though in the odd culture such as the Chamula, for example, strong drink is offered to them by parents,[23] because of cushioning devices which protect them from the stresses of the culture. Similarly, women in our culture tend to be shielded from competitive and other cultural strains. Added to this is the special condemnation of intoxication in women which is particularly severe in our culture. The low Jewish alcoholic rates lend themselves to the same sort of explanation. Drinking in traditional Jewish culture was largely sacred, and secular drinking was urgently tabooed. Drunkenness, like sexual promiscuity, by the group member drew intragroup hostility and censure because of the precarious position of Jews as an oppressed minority. Censurable behavior by any person identified as a Jew threw the whole group into an unfavorable light and supplied rationalizations for persecution. Besides these facts there is a very real possibility that the strength of Jewish welfare organization and the internal community solidarity born of their long urban existence may function as buffers to the conflicts of the larger culture within which they operate.

Our insights into the cultural background of drinking behavior would be sharpened by a careful study of alcoholism in old-world and new-world Irish culture. Lacking this, we must fall back upon informal observations. It is known that drinking hard liquors, particularly on the part of men, was one of the informal integrating mechanisms of old-world Irish culture and that it also held a place as a tension-reducing device in the long history of poverty, famine, and oppression which have been the lot of Ireland under English rule. The Irish migrants to America thus carried in their folkways a well-developed culture complex of heavy drinking. Along with this they brought sex and family patterns at considerable variance from American sex patterns. Fundamentally a peasant-folk people, the Irish migrated later than the English and Scotch-Irish and largely settled in urban areas at a time when industrialization was beginning to alter fundamentally the American social structure. The Irish migrants entered this structure at its lowest levels, were exploited as common laborers, and became the object of active prejudice in many areas. Their close identification with the

[23] See Bunzel, *op. cit.*, p. 379.

Catholic Church in a Protestant society and their association with unsavory, corrupt politics made them the target of much hostility and gave them many qualities of a persecuted minority. Unlike the Jews, they lacked an urban-oriented social organization to provide controls over individual behavior in these cultural pinches. While the early hostility toward the Irish has given way to a more humorous tolerance, they are far from being acculturated. The belligerence traditionally conjoined with Irish drinking habits continues to appear in the second generation and probably complicates the community reactions to them, even though they are no longer identifiable as Irish nationals. Significantly enough, 30,000 out of 90,000 arrests for drunkenness by Los Angeles police in 1947 involved persons of Irish descent.[24]

Other ways in which the schisms of American culture make themselves felt through the organizational aspects of the situation and expressed in drunkenness are almost too many to exhaustively catalogue. Research on this subject remains cursory and scant, which rules out systematic statement. However, some facts are known, and others are inferred. For example, alcoholics seem to come from certain occupations more than others, from among waiters, brewery workers, and bartenders in greater proportions than from workers not in direct contact with alcoholic beverages and those who drink them. At one time drinking was an occupational adjustment of printers rationalized as necessary because of their long and arduous hours; it was even believed to be specifically necessary to counteract industrial poisons absorbed from materials which had to be handled continually. In nineteenth-century England, dock workers were also notorious for their high rates of acute and chronic alcoholism. Foremen of work gangs often leased public houses for their workers and gave preference in hiring to those who were drinking men.[25] Any industrial pursuit in which hours are long, the work hard and hazardous, coupled with hostile attitudes toward the job or the employer may be a situation from which chronic drunkenness can arise. The situation becomes more implicitly drink inducing when heavy social drinking is common among employees or persons with whom the employees are likely to be thrown into contact with outside the job.

The situation of the professional worker may be culturally equitable with that of the common laborer. The medical doctor's long hours, disturbed family life, together with the heavy-drinking habits built up in student days and continued in recreational gatherings of the profession mean that the situation potential for alcoholism is high in his case. Added

[24] *Annual Report of Los Angeles Police Department*, 1947, p. 57. These figures probably are distorted in some degree owing to the observed tendency of arrested persons to give Irish as their ancestry.

[25] Samuelson, James, *The History of Drink*, 1878, p. 174.

to this is the special societal condemnation attached to drunkenness in a medical practitioner. Likewise the architect, who must bow to public tastes and design structures in conflict with what he believes to be esthetically and architecturally sound, may dissolve his tensions in alcoholic beverages, especially if others of the profession have followed this custom. The Hollywood writer who must stifle his creativity in writing scripts for "money-making" motion pictures may relieve his situational neurosis through stepping up his cocktail quota before meals or at professional gatherings where heavy drinking is often the symbol of the ingroup.

Migration and mobility, social and spatial, often throw persons into situations where adjustment creates tensions, anxieties, frustrations, and sense of isolation, for which drink may be the sociopsychological reagent. Drinking among migrants to a Connecticut city during the early part of the Second World War increased more on the part of those who had fewer friends and less social life as a consequence of their migration than on the part of migrants better situated for companionship. It was also true that separation from their families brought about more drinking among lone migrants than among those who migrated as part of a family unit. Heavier drinking was also found related to having dates, which suggests sexual irregularities of which drinking was a part, or perhaps is an indicator of the drinking activities "having dates" involved.[26]

Systematic and Organized Drunkenness

No special culture, behavior system, or social organization of chronic alcoholics is discoverable, mainly because there is no need for them in a culture where patterns and institutions for limited, "normal" consumption of intoxicants already exist. The inebriate has merely to express his abnormal drinking through media set up for casual drinking in the nearby bar or night club. When the inebriate reaches a stage of uncontrollable indulgence, as will be brought out later, he has already begun to socially withdraw in his drinking. Often he carefully avoids former drinking companions at this time; hence, chronic inebriates are not likely to be socially organized. It is true that chronic alcoholics possess special techniques for the concealment of their liquor and drinking from friends and relatives. Also they often have a wide knowledge of how to "mooch" drinks and how to secure and process substitutes for commercial alcoholic beverages when they are unable to purchase a supply. To what degree the acquisition of such skills and knowledge comes through interlearning between chronic alcoholics is not known. There is no evidence of an alco-

[26] Dollard, John, "Some Casual Data on Drinking Habits among Two Strata of Civilian War Workers," *Quarterly Journal of Studies on Alcoholism*, 3, September, 1942, pp. 236–569.

holic argot apart from that which serves for communication between persons participating in socially sanctioned drinking behavior.

Our society contains a few odd groups which are integrated around excessive drinking, college drinking fraternities serve as the best illustration of such groups. Their rationale derives from medieval European society in which aristocratic classes symbolized their status by drinking bouts along with other extravagant dissipations. However, the objective of the conspicuous tippling of feudal aristocrats was not merely to get drunk but to get drunk like gentlemen, which meant that one did not brawl, become obscene, insult the opposite sex, or become maudlin in one's cups. This old medieval drinking ethic, which persisted in German universities until modern times, was here and there wedded to the American competitive spirit in the college drinking fraternity and the officer's club. The mark of success of the emulative drinker is to consume larger quantities of liquor than anyone else without showing the effects, in other words, to be able to "hold his liquor." Obviously the compulsive drinker would soon become isolated in this type of group as well as in other social drinking groups.

The situation during national prohibition, of course, differed greatly from that of today. At that time a special illegal culture integrated around the manufacture and consumption of spirituous liquor and other alcoholic beverages did exist. However, this was primarily a perpetuation of a pre-existing drinking culture, modified and supplemented by new techniques of manufacture, distribution, and consumption of liquor, made necessary by legal repression. The chronic alcoholic necessarily participated in this extralegal culture, but then so did excessive drinkers as well as moderate drinkers drawn from a cross section of the entire population.

Social Visibility of Drunkenness and Alcoholism

The symptoms of drunkenness immediately single out the person so effected, particularly if the drinking has occurred in a group situation. The unsteady gait, clumsiness, thickened speech, flushed face, dilated pupils, and alcoholic fumes on the breath all point out the person's condition to others. These signs are more or less common to all intoxication. The behavior manifestations appearing with these symptoms are more variable, depending upon cultural background and individual peculiarities of the drinker. Some persons become noisy, quarrelsome, inclined to laugh at feeble humor, and are socially intrusive. Others become quiet or grow depressed under alcoholic influence. In extreme drunken states the person may smell of sour vomit, have soiled and disordered clothing, and be disfigured by bruises, cuts, and bloodstains from fighting and falls. In some sections of larger cities men can be seen at certain times sprawled in doorways or on the streets sleeping off their stupors.

Drunkenness in a woman has a much higher visibility than that in a man, which can be traced to the symbolic qualities of drinking and drunkenness in women in the past, when drinking customarily symbolized the bawd and the harlot. The lack of a long experience with drinking on the part of women in America may explain the greater loss of control they show in their tippling. Another possibility to be counted is that women are more likely to be badly maladjusted when they first turn to excessive drinking, and as a result their overt behavior becomes more flagrantly disorganized. The high-pitched and shrill laughter of the drunken woman often brands her behavior more quickly for what it is than in a man. Women are supposed to be neater, cleaner, and more fastidious about their dress than the opposite sex, so that disarray brought by drunkenness also demarcates their condition more sharply.

The visibility of the chronic alcoholic consists of his reddened nose and face, his bleary eyes, emaciation, tremors and other vasomotor disturbances, and general "seedy" or run-down appearance shown by unpressed, threadbare clothes and soiled linen. At a time when the compulsive drinker is still interacting more fully within groups of friends, relatives, and occupational associates, he often believes that his drinking is being successfully concealed despite the fact that it has become painfully apparent to all who know him. Various compensatory behaviors may be coupled with his drinking at this time which direct attention to the chronic inebriate. He may grow suspicious, boastful, and grandiose as the sense of guilt and vague realizations of his deterioration multiply. Extravagant spending reactions may also call more attention to the drinker in the early stages of his alcoholism. In time he progressively withdraws from groups, which has the effect of reducing his visibility. Moving his residence to the rooming-house areas of the city also has the same effect, for these are areas of anonymity in social relations. If the chronic alcoholic does not offend against the public order and thus come to the attention of the police and courts, he may quietly drink himself to death here with few people knowing or caring. Being near death, unhappily, does not raise the visibility of the alcoholic.

The Societal Reaction

The folklore of alcoholism encompasses a host of exaggerations and misconceptions, many of which revolve around the deleterious consequences of excessive drinking. Commonest of these, perhaps, consist of beliefs that alcoholism or a pathological craving for intoxicants is inherited, seen in the foreboding rationalizations of relatives of the inebriate who trace his present alcoholic drives to a parent or grandparent or uncle who died the drunkard's death. Another variant of the hereditary fallacy lays before the alcoholic a dismal prophecy that sins of the fathers shall be visited on their children in the form of congenital defects, stillbirths, disease, and assorted sociopathic inclinations. Especially dire predictions in the past were reserved for the children who were conceived by fathers and mothers during a drunken interlude. Other misconceptions still held in various degrees relate to alcoholism as a "cause" of crime, divorce, physical and mental disease, including epilepsy and sexual immorality. Epitomes of these various beliefs are the putative histories, the contemporary equivalents of Hogarth's *Rake's Progress*, of drinkers as doomed to inevitable deterioration into demoralized bums with ultimate ignominy of burial in a pauper's grave. The depressing stereotype of the effects of alcoholism upon the individual and the family has been drawn in older fiction and drama such as *John Barleycorn*, *The Drunkard*, and *Ten Nights in a Bar Room*. Perhaps the greatest distortion in the fixed notions about the alcoholic has been the imputation of gross physical cruelty in his treatment of his wife and children, probably based upon the higher visibility of drunkenness in immigrant families of rural origin in which harsh family discipline is the rule.

Along with the darker and more morbid picture painted of alcoholism and the drinker, our culture contains its polarized opposite in a poetic romanticization of liquor and drinking. Thus, while liquor is looked upon as the insidious perverter of morals, at the same time it has been glorified as a magical potion, a key to good fellowship, and the juice of literary and artistic creation. Liquor in various forms has long been held to possess great medicinal powers, being seriously as well as humorously recommended as an antidote for poison and snake bites, to ward off colds and other infections, and to combat the numerous ailments and discomforts of old age. Stories are sometimes circulated of surgeons who can perform complex operations only when intoxicated, of musicians who perform best when drunk, and of writers whose inspirations for stories and plays come only after having freely imbibed of liquor.

This polarized stereotype of alcohol is an expression of a pervasive ambivalence of attitudes toward drinking in a culture (perhaps the ambivalence is universal) which has never devised adequate definitions and controls to prevent transition from convivial drinking to drunkenness.[27] This ambivalence can be followed back through the European antecedents of

[27] Myerson, Abraham, "Alcohol: A Study in Social Ambivalence," *Quarterly Journal of Studies on Alcohol*, 1, 1940, p. 16.

American culture to comparatively early historic eras. In Hebrew, Greek, and Roman culture of early times the drinking of liquors and especially wines was considered not only desirable but the beverages themselves were deemed god-given gifts. The ideal of moderation and temperate use of fermented drinks tied in directly with the ethical notion of wise employment of the gifts of God to man. The concomitant disapproval of drunkenness has generally operated in the historical continuum from which American culture sprang but in differing contexts at different times. The hostility of the Christian Fathers toward drunkenness clearly arose from their ascetic orientation and adherence to the ideals of virginity and chastity. To them drunkenness was synonymous with vice, and seldom were the two discussed separately. The great sin which followed drunkenness was sexual immorality, so widely believed in Christian Rome as to be the subject of humorous as well as pious writing. A poet of the times comically put it: "Venus shivers unless Ceres and Bacchus be with her." [28]

Protestant attitudes toward drunkenness took their substance from the general Calvinistic condemnation of frivolity and the extollation of frugality, thrift, and industry as religious virtues. Drunkenness among the American Puritans was abhorred along with the sexual shenanigans it precipitated, chiefly because it diverted human beings from the earnest task of making a living and capital accumulation, and also because it interfered with parental instruction of children in lessons of work and religion. The Puritan dismay at idleness shows itself in seventeenth-century legislation in Massachusetts which limited the time persons might spend in taverns to half an hour and the amount of wine consumed to half a pint.[29] At the same time the Puritan traders were not entirely averse to selling liquor to Indians or the practice of intoxicating them in order to drive sharper bargains in trading with them.

While no longer couched in strictly religious terms, the older Puritan attitudes toward drunkenness prevail in the middle-class moral censure of intoxication as leading to the loss of employment and unemployability. Businessmen may drink themselves, often excessively, but take pride in their ability to show up on the job the next day. Failures to do so on the part of their associates or employees arouse suspicions of loss of self-control and the implication of moral inferiority. The nature of contemporary urban industrial society both strengthens the need for drinking as a form of releasing tensions and etches in sharper perspective the extremely high costs of drunkenness, assessed in lowered industrial productivity,

[28] See Raymond, I. W., *The Teaching of the Early Church on the Use of Wine and Strong Drink*, 1927, Chap V.

[29] Thomann, G , *Colonial Liquor Laws*, 1887, p 10.

traffic accidents, and taxation for policing, relief, and hospitals. Consequently the traditional religious attitudes toward drunkenness and the chronic alcoholic tend to be renewed in the context of our modern culture in the face of efforts at their redefinition.

A cross section of the opinion toward the chronic alcoholic in our contemporary society can be seen in a collection of quotations of remarks made to inebriates by the sober public:[30]

> Why don't you be like me, take a couple of drinks and stop?
> Can't you see what it is doing to you?
> If your mother could see you in this condition, it would break her heart.
> Do you love liquor more than you do me? [Substitute "job," "daughter," "wife," etc., for "me."]
> If it affected me the way it does you, I'd never touch the stuff.
> The next time you take a drink, I'm through with you.
> You're as weak as a jellyfish!
> I don't understand it – your mother and father are such fine people.
> I've thrown away every drop of liquor, and you'll not get another cent to buy any.
> You don't think of anybody but yourself!
> I wish they'd close every bar in the country.
> If you keep on, it will kill you.
> Give me your word of honor you'll never drink again.
> How you can drink in the morning is beyond me.
> Is it the taste you are so crazy about?
> Why don't you eat something?
> If you could only see yourself when you're drunk!

While the statements contain explicit and implicit threats, blame, and bafflement, the general theme underlying most of them has to do with lack of self-control on the part of the drinker. This societal symbolization of the deviation as a sign of character weakness is one of the most vivid and isolating distinctions which can be made in a culture which attributes morality, success, and respectability to the power of a disciplined will.

Societal Tolerances for Drunkenness and Alcoholism

The societal reaction to drunkenness is by no means universally one of disapprobation and condemnation. The Chamula, to whom reference has already been made, according to the ethnographer's report, in no way condemned drinking, even in cases of extreme drunkenness. They did indeed deplore the waste, quarrels, and disruptions of life for which alco-

[30] Quoted in Anderson, Dwight, "Alcohol and Public Opinions," *Quarterly Journal of Studies on Alcohol*, 3, December, 1942, p. 383.

hol was responsible, but this was never manifest as moral censure of the drunken individual, hence there were no sociopsychological reciprocals of guilt and shame over a previous night's drunkenness. In the observer's own words:[31]

> Toward a drunken man everyone assumes a protective and conciliatory attitude. He is not considered responsible. If he is belligerent, no one tries to cross him or argue with him. No one, unless he too were drunk, would assume a belligerent or condemnatory attitude. Therefore the man whose head is cracked knows that he himself is to blame. If he tried to air his grievance, he would get no support. "He was drunk, why did you fight with him? . . .

This culture is a decided contrast to the attitudes toward drunkenness in Aztec society and its treatment of the illegal drinker. Consumption of ardent liquors there was stictly taboo for all save priests on ritual occasions and for those who had reached advanced ages. All others were enjoined from spirituous enjoyments upon the penalty of death.

In our own society the most energetic efforts to control drinking habits and suppress drunkenness were made by New England communities of the early seventeenth century. The record of these efforts is left in the legislative enactments, amendments, and repeals in the Massachusetts colony, covering individual drinking habits, methods of manufacture, distribution and sale of intoxicants. Intimations of the force of public disapproval can be gathered from the type of penalties inflicted upon violators of the liquor laws heavy fines, confinement in stocks with stigmatic labels, the drunkard's D, and disenfranchisement. Unhappily for the Puritan magistrates and abstinent elders, their taxation programs worked at cross purposes with their other measures aimed at control of drinking, tending to handicap brewers of beer and ale and inadvertently favor the rum traffic. The shift in drinking from malt drinks to rum, along with the growth of the rum and molasses trade soon extended the liquor problem to a point beyond control. The disorganization and militarization of a portion of the male population in the middle of the eighteenth century further added to the "problem." With the decline in power of the Puritan hierarchy, never more than a small minority in most New England communities, the struggle to contain the drinking habits of the secular community within the bounds of Puritan propriety was finally renounced.

The populating of early America with a basically Anglo-Saxon stock during a period when heavy drinking and drunkenness ran rampant in the British Isles meant that a heritage of wanton drinking was a part of the more general old-world culture diffused into the American environment. However, the rural and frontier nature of this environment acted as a

[31] Bunzel, *op. cit.*, p 378.

leavening agent upon these coarse drinking tendencies. Frontier drunkenness occurred in a rural context where it was more usually convivial and in the form of periodic sprees. In the interims the people who had been drunk ate plentiful food and worked hard, of economic necessity reinforced by social compulsion. The aftereffects of drunkenness quickly passed off. As the lumberjacks in the camps of northern Michigan say of this kind of drinking, "After a few hours of working in the bush, a man's beer is on his underwear."

The urbanization of American culture following the Civil War radically altered the milieu in which drunkenness took place, giving it both changed form and meaning. The ground swell of immigration from Southern and Eastern Europe and from South Ireland grew to a wave of engulfing proportions toward the end of the century. These new immigrants settled in urban communities rather than rural. Drunkenness in the public stereotype became connected with things alien, and with the political corruption, vice, crime, poverty, and family disorganization of the city. The visibility of urban drunkenness was heightened by the spread of the saloon, which for immigrants was the American equivalent of their old-world public house or tavern, through which they tried to achieve a species of social integration in the new environment. Finally, the waxing fears of Catholicism in the Protestant population came to be symbolized in the hostility and alarm aroused by urban drinking behavior.

The Anti-Saloon League of America

By 1914 the mounting reaction against alcoholic drinking was converted into a well-organized social movement, at first in scattered temperance organizations and ultimately in the militant, powerful Anti-Saloon League of America whose activities culminated in national prohibition. Some writers have written off the Eighteenth Amendment to our Constitution as the consequence of political intrigue, "putting over a fast one," by a minority of the population, as it were. A study of the movement contradicts such assertions, for it experienced a steady growth in real political power throughout the first two decades of the twentieth century, shown in its progressive domination of local and state elections. Between 1904 and 1917 the situation with respect to the proportion of "wet" and "dry" counties in the various states almost completely reversed itself. This can be seen very plainly in Fig. 11.[32]

There is more than adequate evidence that the amplified societal reaction against drinking alcoholic beverages in the United States in the initial decades of the twentieth century bore little direct relation to an objective

[32] See Odegard, Peter, *Pressure Politics*, 1928, pp. 164–165.

increase or aggravation of the "problem." In other words, or in terms of the theory of this treatise, the deviation became more and more of an imputed social evil, the aspects of which have to be understood as incidents of conflict and struggle for power between various aspirant groups in the social system. During the period when the power of the Anti-Saloon League was consolidated, the per capita consumption of distilled spirits actually had been declining, while that for beer had been rising steadily. This is significant because beer is a beverage favored by moderate users of alcohol rather than by inebriates.[33] Furthermore, if admission rates for alcoholic psychoses can be used as an index, there was no rise, and probably there was a decline, in rates of alcoholism in the population at this time.[34]

The Anti-Saloon League as a social movement drew its great power from nativist, antiurban, anti-industrial, anti-Catholic, and anti-Negro forces in American society. Its early and perhaps greatest strength came from the rural, Protestant regions of the nation. The Methodist, Baptist, Presbyterian, and Congregational churches gave the League its real force and most widespread support, with no formal backing at all coming from the Jewish churches and only a peripheral kind from the Catholic churches. This latter fact did not go unnoticed or unchallenged by the prohibitionists. Extremists in the movement at different times raised the old cry that the Catholic Church was the vehicle of "Rum, Romanism, and Rebellion," but the movement itself was wisely kept by its leaders from ever becoming openly anti-Catholic.[35]

Besides the generalized support for the prohibition movement which came from rural areas, there was a special sectional reinforcement of the "drys' " program in the Southern states. Here the urbanization of the Negroes raised the visibility of their drunkenness, which became associated with crime and "getting out of place" on their part. Prohibition became a way of setting up new controls over the Negro group by white groups of the South.

The many-sided character of the sentiment favorable to prohibition was additionally apparent in the opposition of business interests to employee drinking. Drinking by workingmen came to symbolize lowered productivity and also was tied up in the minds of management with the saloon which they looked upon as a hotbed of union and radical agitation.[36]

Although not quite so apparent, the function of the League as a social

[33] Haggard and Jellinek, *op. cit.*, p 75.

[34] *Ibid.*, p. 261

[35] See Odegard, *op. cit.*, Chap. I,

[36] McClung, Lee Alfred, "Techniques of Social Reform: An Analysis of the New Prohibition Drive," *American Sociological Review*, 9, February, 1944, pp. 67*ff*.

FIG 11. Growth of the prohibition movement.

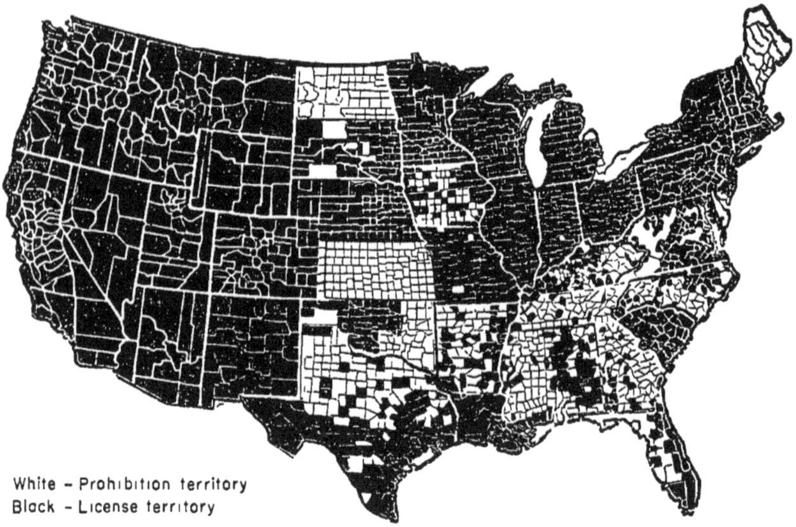

FIG. 11*A*. "Wet" and "dry" county map of the United States, Jan. 1, 1904

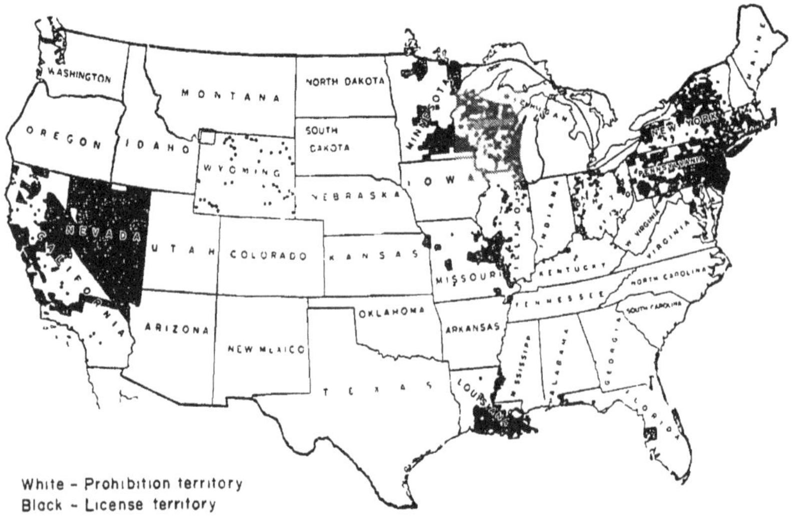

FIG 11*B* "Wet" and "dry" map of the United States, Mar 1, 1917

mechanism through which farmers could channel their long-standing aggressions against railroads, banks, and industrial interests undoubtedly was involved. Finally, prohibitionist groups were able to identify the saloon and convivial drinking groups among immigrants not only with corrupt politics but also, after 1917, with subversive and unpatriotic activities of brewing interests. Exhaustive Senate investigations were carried on to show that German brewing interests were implicated in making hyphenated German-Americans through the institutions of the sängerfest and sangerbund, and that they had conspired to buy up American and foreign-language newspapers and spread pro-German, anti-British, anti-American propaganda.[37]

Since national prohibition, per capita consumption of liquors and alcoholic beverages has climbed somewhat, without, however, approximating 1910 consumption rates. Inebriation is probably less common. Moderate drinking finds wider and wider acceptance. However, the costs of alcoholism and drunkenness in a technologically oriented society such as obtains today are more clearly recognized and may even be more greatly deplored. The societal reaction more and more tends to rest upon a functional or medical rationale in place of the archaic Christian sin-guilt complex. However, this latter development is very uneven, so that marked cleavages in attitudes on the subject and toward the inebriate are discoverable from one class to another, from one locality to another, and between various nationality and racial groups.

The Family Reaction to the Inebriate

Relatives of the chronic alcoholic in a vast majority of cases must be listed as his worst enemies, an understandable fact since they stand to suffer more from his derelictions. Their reaction begins with worry, soon turns into frustration, and ends as a deep and abiding disgust and intolerance. The wife soon develops habitual reproach as the result of her interpretation of her husband's drunken sprees as personal attacks upon herself and the children, if any. Parents and more remote relatives react to the alcoholic as a sore reflection upon the integrity of the family name and reputation. This leads to bitter criticism, or to monotonous inspirational advice, such as injunctions to "buck up and be a man," "show yourself you can lick this!" In many cases the parental family washes their hands completely of the alcoholic. The modal effect of the family reaction intensifies the compulsions to drink in most alcoholics by stressing the fact of his lack of self-control, in effect, his invidious differentiation from normal persons.

Religious Agencies

To the extent that the inebriate has contacts with the church or its representatives, he is likely to meet the same inspirational injunctions as in his family, only now formalized and colored by connotations of sin and wickedness. The church has traditionally sought to reform alcoholics rather than to aid them or to cure them. Methods have been the signing of

[37] *Brewing and Liquor Interests and the German and Bolshevik Propaganda,* Report and Hearings of the Subcommittee on the Judiciary of the United States Senate, 1919.

a pledge not to drink on the part of the alcoholic, conversion to formal religious belief, and casual pastoral counseling. Such devices succeed in isolated cases, but more typically accelerate the growth of fear and guilt in the drinker.

Police and Law-enforcement Agencies

At one time in England drunken persons were taken into custody by police and later released without having to appear before a magistrate. In

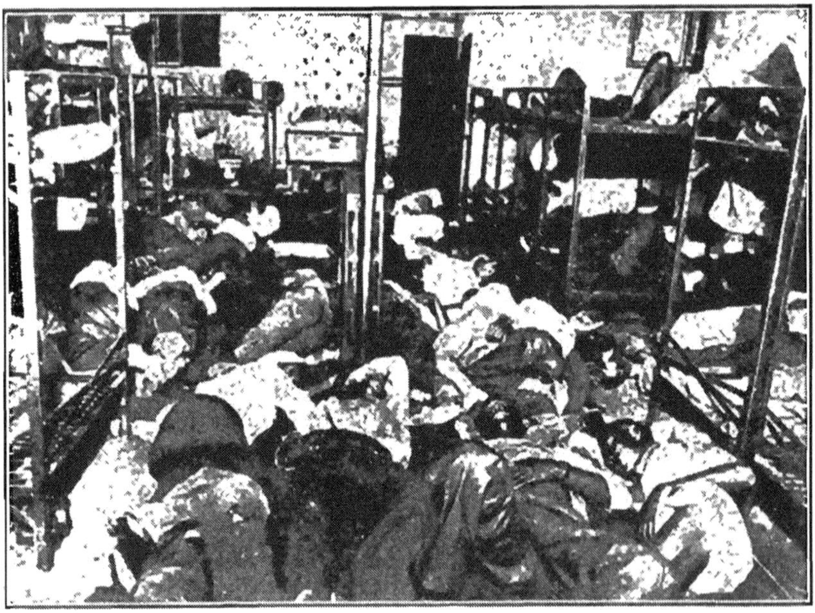

Fig. 12 A drunk tank.

small, especially rural, communities intoxicated persons, if they are local residents, are seldom if ever arrested. Indeed they may be escorted home and even put to bed by the constable. In one or two large cities today the "golden rule" treatment is observed for persons apprehended for drunkenness, which is more or less a protective custody type of arrest followed by release without charges being preferred. The same effect is obtained in other cities by a system of waivers, in which no booking occurs unless other misdemeanors are associated with the drunkenness. Unfortunately in few urban communities today does the drunken individual receive formalized considerate treatment. Common practice dictates that he be arrested, booked, and held for a hearing just like any other criminal. It is customary in many cities to cast the inebriate into a special section of the jail called the "drunk tank," where he often lies in a drunken stupor, soiled and besmirched with dirt and vomit, until he sobers up enough for his hearing. Routine medical examinations seldom are given, so that alcoholics may be dangerously near death yet receive no medical care. The psychic shock for most alcoholics who awaken in such a place for the first time is very great indeed.

Judges ordinarily dismiss cases of drunkenness with a lecture and a warning. If there has been a previous offense, a fine or a two- or three-day jail sentence is imposed; persistent offenders may have to spend thirty to ninety days in jail. The shorter sentences are scarcely long enough to allow a full physical recovery, which may be entirely deferred by a supply of liquor made available through bribery of jailers. Chronic alcoholics are almost never segregated from other misdemeanants for purposes of psychiatric or other treatment, unless the obvious seriousness of their condition warrants taking them to a hospital. Several states, notably Massachusetts and Indiana, have state farms to which alcoholics may be sent. In Massachusetts, however, this farm also receives drug addicts, vagrants, and sex delinquents. The Indiana farm has a better system of classification but no real program of treatment for alcoholics.[38] The police and judicial reactions to the alcoholics are almost entirely punitive, perfunctory, and indiscriminate. They symbolize the deviation involved as criminal and defective and permit confirmation of these imputations in the forced interaction of the alcoholic with a general class of defectives in the jail populations. Small wonder that many chronic alcoholics have no desire other than to get drunk at the end of their sentences. Evidence of this and the manifest failure of the punitive objectives of the legal treatment of alcoholics are found in the high rates of recidivism among them. An investigation of chronic alcoholics on relief in Los Angeles disclosed that 62 per cent of them had been arrested one or more times and that the average number of arrests among those arrested for drunkenness was seven per case.[39]

Treatment Agencies

Most, if not all, chronic alcoholics at some time or another, often many times, come under the care of general medical practitioners. Their reception is a qualified one at best. The physician proves effective time and again in restoring the alcoholic physically but is frustrated and irritated to see the results of his work ruined by what he deems lack of will power and weakness of character. He comes to resent time spent in caring for alcoholics when it might be used on people who, in his mind, are *really*

[38] McCormick, Austin, "Penal and Correctional Aspects of the Alcohol Problem," *Quarterly Journal of Studies on Alcohol*, 2, September, 1941, p. 252.

[39] *Report of Alcoholics*, Los Angeles County Grand Jury, Indigent Relief Committee, Sept. 25, 1940, pp 37–38

sick. The physician is also quick to resent the sin of lese majesty of which the alcoholic is guilty when he takes further drinks in direct defiance of his orders. The lack of success which medical men have in treating inebriation has led to a widespread belief in the profession that alcoholics are hopeless cases.

One might expect a complete receptivity of the alcoholic on the part of the psychiatrist, who is professionally trained to recognize functional as well as organic pathologies of behavior. Yet unexpressed attitudes of condemnation frequently permeate the manner and mien of the psychiatrist where contacts with the alcoholic take place. The psychiatrist's sense of professional frustration as a consequence of cumulative failures in therapy with alcoholics may be even greater than that of the general practitioner. His corresponding trade conviction that "nothing can be done" for the pathological drinkers may also be much more fixed. At the door of psychiatry also must be laid responsibility in large part for formulating and conveying the stereotype of the inevitability of insanity in chronic alcoholism.[40]

The treatment of alcoholism ranges from advertised home remedies to month- or year-long hospitalization in private and public institutions. Most cities of any size have privately operated "institutes" which lay claim with varying extravagance to "curing" alcoholism. Like institutions of a similar nature which deal with speech defectives, they rely upon alarming letters to the alcoholic or his family to secure patronage. The operation of these agencies is perhaps the closest approach to exploitation of inebriates which we have in our society; but it should be emphasized that, despite their exaggerated pretensions and inflated fees, they nevertheless do provide a service for the acutely ill alcoholic. Their true function is aptly described by the alcoholics' own phrase for them: "sobering up stations." In some cases the alcoholic's hostility toward his relatives is built up greatly by the subterfuge employed to get him to enter one of these institutes, so that he protests that he has been tricked and treated like a child by his family. For other alcoholics the experience merely adds to their cynicism and sophistication about "cures" and treatment and symbolizes for them their growing social isolation. The experience is not likely to be too different from this in cases where alcoholics are placed in private mental institutions. Staffs of these hospitals, the attendants in particular, may be less considerate where the alcoholic is concerned than when handling a psychotic patient, chiefly because his symptoms disappear once the sobering-up process has been gone through. The alcoholics are repelled by being grouped in with the insane, which does much to explain their systematic rejection of the hospital environment. Psychiatrists whose theoretical predispositions impel

[40] Anderson, *op. cit.*, pp 386–392.

them to search for hidden homosexuality in the alcoholic's behavior may further alienate the patient and contribute to his feeling of isolation in the hospital. Where special sympathy and extra care is extended to the alcoholic inmate, it may be little more than paternalistic and maternalistic solicitude from doctors and nurses which, in the final analysis, captions the character weakness which has already been ascribed to him.

In contrast with the numerous control agencies our society has formally instituted for, say, the blind, or for dependent children, there is an almost complete absence of specialized public agencies for helping the inebriate to solve his drinking "problem." Although a few nonpsychotic alcoholics can be admitted to state mental hospitals under special conditions, and a few are treated where outpatient departments exist, for the most part they receive no public-sponsored treatment until they are very badly deteriorated. It is largely in response to the lack of facilities for treating alcoholics and the changing sense of responsibility for this deviant group that moves are afoot in different states to establish special institutions for alcoholics and to make clinical services available to them on a local basis. For those alcoholics who are admitted to private mental institutions, the sociopsychological implications of the situation closely resemble those of the public mental hospital. Perhaps his status is somewhat less dependent in the private institution, for here he or his family must pay for the hospitalization. On the other hand, for this very reason, the patronizing attitudes of the staff may be greater. In concluding these comments about hospital or institutional treatment of alcoholics, it is safe to say that, on the whole, it has only a limited success. However, it should be added that hospitalization will remain a necessary preparatory adjunct to treatment no matter what form future therapeutic procedures and organization may take.

The Limited Success of Current Therapies

Estimates of the success of various types of psychotherapeutic treatment of alcoholics range from 13 per cent for hypnosis to 64 per cent for "conditioned-reflex" methods, with an average somewhere around 25 per cent.[41] Countless reasons could be listed why our conventional medical and psychiatric treatment of chronic alcoholics ends in frustrating failure so many times. Four reasons seem to stand out more than others in the light of the theoretical conceptions laid down earlier in this volume. The first of these consists of the formidable barriers to identification and communication between inebriates and clinicians. The keynote of the mental process of the alcoholic is deception, connivery, and complicated rationalization. No one who has not undergone the harrowing experiences of the compulsive drinker can appreciate the deeper, torturously involved meaning of

[41] Jellinek, E. M., *Alcohol Addiction and Chronic Alcoholism*, 1942, p. 76.

those experiences. For example, one alcoholic related how, in trying to convey to a skeptical wife the strength of the obsession for a drink, he pressed lighted cigarettes into his hand one after another, burning the flesh to the bone. The effect, of course, was horror and dread, rather than the understanding he had hoped for.[42]

Aside from the strictures on social communication between the inebriate and the rest of society, which limit effectual treatment, there is poor or little coordination in time of therapeutic services with the needs of the pathological drinker. By this is meant that the psychiatrist or clinician often is not available at times when he is most needed by the alcoholic, unless, of course, he happens to be in a hospital. The alcoholic needs specific assistance at the time his guilt, depressions, or whatever urges him to start drinking reach a critical point. After the drunken spree is underway, little can be done to change the course of the behavior until after sobriety returns. Each such episode crystallizes the inebriate's role and to that extent leaves the drinker less amenable to therapy.

Another complicating factor in current therapeutic procedures comes from the framework of authoritative relationships within which they are applied. The compulsions to drink, as we shall try to show in subsequent discussion, are direct manifestations of the alcoholic's role as a person without power of will and self-resolution. The therapeutic situation formalizes the invidious distinctions the community has already drawn between itself and the alcoholic on this score, despite the efforts of clinicians to preserve medical and scientific detachment. Psychiatric terms, such as "neurotic," "psychopathic," "constitutional inferior," "mother fixant," take on moral connotations, and the clinician often unwittingly becomes the surrogate of a punitive society. A very tenable hypothesis is that the therapeutic experience, as now constituted in many hospitals, intensifies the compulsion of the inebriate to drink. The fact that many alcoholics set out upon colossal drunken sprees within a few hours of leaving the institution where they have been sober for months points to the validity of this contention.

A final limitation of existing clinical procedures aimed at the alcoholic's rehabilitation is the underestimation made of the intensity of the withdrawal symptoms provoked by divorcing the inebriate from liquor. This is related to the apparent normality of the alcoholic after he has been restored physically and also to his special powers of masking his emotions. It is assumed often that the alcoholic needs only some change in his emotive rational processes to fully recover, which assumption nullifies or precludes the effort to provide a type of environment or set of overt activities from which such changes might naturally evolve. Within the protected hospital

[42] Maine, Harold, *If a Man Be Mad,* 1947, p. 189.

environment the alcoholic's life, in some instances, may be temporarily filled up with new activities, and a new role may be successfully defined for him. However, the break in continuity between the hospital and community experiences plus the lack of a realistic correspondence between the two environments commonly negates or truncates the initiation of such potentially workable recovery programs in individual cases.

Alcoholics Anonymous

The rise of the Alcoholics Anonymous organization can be best understood as a spontaneous movement adapted to meet the specific needs disregarded or unfulfilled by the societal agencies striving to restore the alcoholic to usefulness. The organization began in the early 1930's from the efforts of a small number of alcoholics to solve their own drinking problems by assisting other alcoholics in their dismal struggles with the bottle. It grew at an accelerating rate, so that by 1944 10,000 ex-drinkers were enrolled in 300 American and Canadian communities.[43] By 1947 claims were made that over 2,000 chapters of the organization had been formed and that they were taking in new members at a rate of 1,000 per month.[44] The principles guiding the organization have been formalized in a series of so-called "twelve steps," most of which enjoin an affirmation of general religious belief and active measures of character reformation to be achieved through constructive work with other alcoholics.

Viewed objectively by the sociologist, the Alcoholics Anonymous organization is a sect integrated through missionizing activity. It redefines the self and role of the alcoholic as that of an ex-alcoholic, or as that of a special kind of biological person who can under no circumstances drink alcoholic liquors without wanting to drink himself into intoxication. Open confession of past alcoholic and other transgressions or "wrongs" is relied upon as a technique to bring about the unemotional acceptance of the socially castigated self. The attitude of the group is highly permissive in the sense that most of the other members of the group have known experiences just as degrading and probably more so than those confessed by the novitiate. The group permissiveness is made greater in larger communities where the spontaneous growth of the organization has differentiated the chapters on an ecological basis and lent social and cultural homogeneity to each group that could not be matched in any intramural group of alcoholics. A special organizational device designed to further the permissive character of the group is a sponsor-baby relationship, in which an

[43] *A. A.*, pamphlet published by the Alcoholic Foundation, 1944, p. 1

[44] Riley, Frank, *Alcoholics Anonymous*, 1948, p 5 More recently the organization is estimated to have 90,000 members in 3,000 chapters, including many in the British Isles, Norway, New Zealand, and Australia. Alexander, J., "The Drunkard's Best Friend," *The Saturday Evening Post*, Apr. 1, 1950.

older AA member serves as intermediary between the group and alcoholics who are too withdrawn to accept this patently uncritical and sympathetic comradeship. The easy atmosphere in the meetings comes as a surprise and shock to many new members, who find themselves able for the first time in perhaps years to communicate freely with a group. Therapy comes out of the interaction with a peer group in which arrogating and one-sided direction have no part.

The therapy of Alcoholics Anonymous, arrived at empirically and rationalized on religious grounds, constitutes an inverted test of the hypothesis we have enunciated – that changed self-definition must be incorporated promptly in overt behavior as the prelude to effective role changes. As soon as possible after a new member has made his confession of faith, he is assigned a round of duties which consume much of his waking time and energies not spent at work. Participation in activities auxiliary and peripheral to the central function of his AA role soon fills his entire life. It is interesting to note the presence of bars complete with rails and sawdust at some of the recreational meetings of the local chapters. While only soft drinks are served, many if not all of the features of the bar-drinking culture complex are there. In some of these gatherings extensive gambling has been observed. Thus the problem of stress coming in the wake of withdrawal from alcohol has been met by a whole host of socially tolerable substitutes.

Another highly important feature of the organization of these ex-alcoholics comes to grips with the peculiar temporal fluctuations in the alcoholic's urge to indulge. This refers to the staggered meeting times of various chapters in larger communities, so arranged that some place in the city any evening of the week a group of AA members will be in session. During late hours a member may call a central office and receive psychological or moral assistance from other members in his general neighborhood to whom the call has been relayed. The more articulate and informed members of the organization regard this service of utmost importance because the critical point for the alcoholic, they claim, is just before he takes his first drink.

The working philosophy of the AA members takes a broad step away from the medical concept of a "cure" held by general medical practitioners and psychiatrists. They make no claim to being cured, simply pointing with satisfaction to a period of so many sober months or years lived far more fully than was possible as alcoholics. The therapeutic value of such an attitude rests in its prophylaxis against relapses. Anxieties about future failures are discharged by the expedient of realistic acceptance of their possibility, hence they do not become cumulative material for further compulsions to drink. A relapse thus does not lead to rejection of the Alcoholics Anonymous program because it can not be regarded as the "cure which didn't work."

The movement has gained widespread favorable publicity and is recommended by judges, psychiatrists, and social workers. Undoubtedly it has been romanticized, and distorted claims of its success have been made. Officials of the organization give it credit for maintaining sobriety in 75 per cent of those who come into its fold and "really try" the methods.[45] Whether their records are, or can be, accurate is debatable, but of the general superiority of its methods over others in use there can be no doubt. Members freely admit that many persons in the grip of alcoholic compulsions cannot be helped by them. It works best for those who have deteriorated sufficiently and come close enough to social and physical death to generate a motivation for seeking help. Those who cannot accept the generalized religious aspects of the program must be included among those who do not respond well to this new type of group psychotherapy. Women likewise have proved more resistant and complicated cases to unravel through its special methods. The excerpt included here sheds partial light upon the reasoning of a more sophisticated alcoholic's reaction to the program of the Alcoholics Anonymous. Speaking of the meetings, he says:[46]

> I'll never go back to another one of those ... I'd rather be back in C.I.I. milking cows and subordinating myself to idiots. I know some of those people at AA. I like them. I can't stand to see them debase themselves, mewling and puking in public. Every one who slips back into drink will weaken me and every one who stays sober that way will make me lose faith in myself. I'll take some of their principles home with me, and maybe use them, but I won't discuss them with anyone.

Individuation of the Alcoholic

Etiological research and theory on alcoholism have been concerned primarily and almost exclusively with the prealcoholic history of persons so addicted, seeking to clarify the psychodynamics or sociocultural factors leading up to or precipitating grosser forms of inebriation. Factors which have been adduced as "causes" of excessive drinking include such things as misery, occupational exhaustion, early childhood experiences, repressed homosexuality, life crises, inferiority feelings, desire to escape reality, conviviality, and many, many others. Not a few contradictions lurk in this morass of explanations; thus people drink in excess because they are poor and also because they are too rich, because they are depressed and because they are euphoric and elated, because they are psychopathic and because they are normally convivial. The *ad hoc* quality of these many theories is

[45] Ritchie, Oscar, "A Sociohistorical Survey of Alcoholics Anonymous," *Quarterly Journal of Studies on Alcohol*, 7, June, 1948, p. 149.

[46] Maine, *op. cit.*, p. 201. Quoted by permission of Doubleday & Company, Inc., New York.

conspicuously present. Yet there is no overriding necessity to disprove or discard this conglomerate of theories. Let it simply be said that they are good and valid explanations of why certain classes of people become immoderate in their use of alcohol. However, few, if any, of them supply the vital details of the process by which a compulsive drinker develops.

Primary Alcoholic Deviation

The social and sociopsychological routes by which human beings arrive at a point in their drinking which in their situation is considered abnormal are many. Such things as lower tolerances for alcohol, physiologically or sociopsychologically induced, may figure in a small number of cases as interactive factors leading to excess. Sociopsychological characteristics identifiable as neurotic or psychotic can also function to this end. However, it is important to remember that among the unique structural attributes of personality, socially desirable qualities can also interact to bring on excesses. Thus the socially responsive person may yield to group pressures to drink beyond his sober capacity more readily than the socially resistant person. The culture or subculture may sanction drunkenness as an adjustment to certain situations, which is introjected in the structural limits of the individual's personality as freedom to indulge. In brief, a person can come to drink to excess because he feels insecure, as a reaction to life crises, or because he participates in group activity in which heavy drinking is a social expectancy. However it may originate, inebriation remains primary deviation so long as it is satisfactorily rationalized, dissociated, or otherwise dealt with as part of a socially acceptable role, or even as an aspect of another sociopathic role.

The success which the person has in coping with the sociopsychological sequelae of drunkenness will be conditioned by the differential societal reaction he encounters. Obviously the minister or the schoolteacher in a given rural area or in a small town who drinks to excess is more severely condemned than would be, say, an urban factory worker. Some persons, on account of the structural limits of their personality, are more sensitive to the societal reaction than others. Others in the throes of some more or less fixed conflict or struggling with conflicts stemming from critical situations may find the guilt arising in the wake of drunkenness an additional intolerable strain upon their integrating capacities. Three hypothetical interactional sequences suggest themselves as the antecedents of secondary alcoholic deviation:

1. Fixed personal conflicts – excessive drinking – average societal reaction.
2. "Normal" person in crisis – excessive drinking – average societal reaction.
3. "Normal" person – moderate drinking – unusually severe societal reaction

Secondary Alcoholic Deviation

Secondary alcoholic deviation may be taken as one with compulsive drinking or chronic alcoholism. It refers to drinking which is motivated by the conception the drinker has of the self as that of a drunkard, a sot, an inebriate, an alcoholic, or a drunken bum. The exact point at which this occurs in the history of the drinker is not easy to establish, mainly because of the elaborate rationalizing processes characteristic of the alcoholic. If a person drinks excessively over a sufficiently long period and his behavior and social relations are seriously disrupted, the resultant guilt accumulates and becomes the added tensional basis for the drinking. The heightened tensional state of the drinker most likely lowers his tolerance for liquor, intensifies his drunken sysmptoms, and aggravates the withdrawal stress of the hang-over. At some point, a symbolic connection is made between the drinker's tensions and their reduction by means of intoxication. The weight of present evidence and opinion places this point at the time when the person begins to rely upon the "morning drink" as a means of getting himself sufficiently organized to assume his daily responsibilities. The "morning drink" was reported as an early feature of the drinking of 91 per cent of one group of alcoholics whose histories were recorded by questionnaires.[47] The tissue of rationalization woven around a person's drinking and associated social failures concurs in time with the "morning drink" and is the exposed reciprocal of the dissociated self-definition of the person as one dependent upon liquor, as one who qualifies for the cultural stereotype of a weak-willed individual who has lost the power of direction of his own behavior.

Phases in the Drinking History of the Alcoholic

The most systematic investigation of the "natural-history" aspects of alcoholism has arisen out of the interest of the Alcoholics Anonymous organization. A questionnaire designed by ex-alcoholics themselves was printed in a chapter organ called the *Grapevine*, with requests that it be filled out and returned. The returns were submitted to a professional analyst with the hope that some sort of sequence or phaseology might be discovered. Of 158 questionnaires returned, only 98 were used. The sample clearly was selective, being composed of males, members of Alcoholics Anonymous, and probably of less deteriorated alcoholics. Despite shortcomings of the method and data collected by it, freely admitted and pointed out by the analyst, some very enlightening generalizations and hypotheses were formulated from the study.[48]

[47] Jellinek, E M., "Phases in the Drinking History of Alcoholics," *Memoirs of the Section on Alcohol Studies, Yale University*, No 5, 1947, p. 47

[48] *Ibid.*, pp. 70–77.

The method of analysis was to seek correlations between different behaviors recognized by ex-alcoholics as common integral parts of the syndrome of alcoholism and make these the basis for constructing an average sequence of the behaviors and indicating their average age of occurrence. The sequence which materialized from this procedure must be regarded purely as a statistical construction and cannot be taken as a predictive instrument for the individual case. While deviations from the representative sequence were observable for specific behaviors in many individuals, certain classes of alcoholics showed far more discrepancies than others. These consisted of persons, possibly neurotic, who manifested abnormal reactions (black-outs) to alcoholic excesses at very young ages, and those who became addicted at older ages. The general effect of addiction at older ages was to foreshorten the whole process and to reverse the order of some of the behavior. The average age of occurrence of certain of the alcoholic behaviors and age span from earliest symptoms of alcoholism to age of "lowest point" according to age of first symptoms is seen in Table 40:

TABLE 40. PREDICTED MEAN AGES AT ONSETS OF SELECTED SIGNIFICANT BEHAVIORS IN THE DRINKING HISTORIES OF MEN WHO HAD LOST CONTROL OF THE DRINKING SITUATION*

Behavior	Ages at which control was lost			
	20	25	30	35
Blackouts	20	24	28	32
Rationalizing excessive drinking	23	27	31	35
Morning drink	24	28	32	36
Solitary drinking	27	30	33	36
Antisocial acts	24	28	32	36
Benders	25	30	34	39
Remorse	28	31	33	36
Protecting supply	28	31	35	38
Fears	28	31	35	38
Resentments	29	32	35	39
Admit to self	35	37	39	42
Lowest point	38	40	42	44

* Jellinek, E. M., "Phases in the Drinking History of Alcoholics," *Memoirs of the Section on Alcohol Studies, Yale University*, No. 5, 1947, p. 76.

Three phases of drinking history came to light in the investigation of this group of alcoholics, not too descriptively termed "basic phase," "intermediate phase," and "terminal phase." The first and last phases seemed more clearly demarcated than the intermediate development of alcoholism. The time required for completion of the phases varied on an average of from twelve to eighteen years, depending upon the age at which prodromal symptoms first appeared.

About 10 per cent of the group began their alcoholic careers with solitary drinking, the remainder having acquired their excessive habits in social settings such as "liquor parties," taverns, or, most commonly, on "week-end drunks" in the company of others. "Getting drunk" was a pattern of behavior in 71.4 per cent of the cases by the time they were nineteen years of age. At the time most of the men had reached twenty-five years of age, they were drinking excessively, and they showed strong effects of their indulgence in the form of "black-outs," or alcoholic amnesias for events during their drinking episodes. Expansive and extravagant behavior in the shape of overgenerous treating, tipping, and expensive purchases while under the influence of liquor also showed up in this early stage of the alcoholism in a high percentage of cases. "Sneaking drinks" followed close upon the black-outs and related behaviors of this initiatory period. Within two years of the occurrence of black-outs on the average, these alcoholics found that they were nearly always drinking more than they intended, *i.e.*, first drinks nearly always imparted an irresistible momentum carrying the person through to complete intoxication. This development was conceptualized as "loss of control" of drinking. As might be expected, rationalizing reactions soon followed uncontrolled drinking, on the average approximately within two years, at around thirty years of age for the majority of the cases. The captional "morning drink" was begun shortly thereafter, within one year. This, as has been stated earlier, serves as a critical self-defining point in the average history of the alcoholic and marks off the two different types of deviation. The possibility is a good one that many heavy drinkers pass through this beginning phase of alcoholism but stop short of this critical juncture; these become "automatic" remissions. Additional research is badly needed on this subject in order to set down the extent to which normal deviation overlaps into this area of preliminary pathological drinking.

Within one to three years subsequent to acquiring the "morning-drink" habit, the alcoholics manifested true addictive behavior by going on "benders" during which they stayed drunk for days at a time, with no thought for their responsibilities as husbands, parents, workers, or as members of the community. These are clearly the earmarks of acute compulsive drinking. The consequent remorse and traumatic perceptions of the social, chiefly family, disapproval bespeak a possible critical point here in the tolerance quotient in the typical case. In any event the intense remorse and guilt felt at this time work a change in the pattern of drinking itself, with the alcoholic striving for control by such unrealistic shrifts as not drinking until certain hours, confining the drinking to beer and wine, or going on the "water wagon." Needless to say, they usually failed. Meantime the system of rationalization grows more fantastic and comes to embrace practically every aspect of conduct. In this way it apparently performs its function with less success and threatens to break down, for it begins to be supplemented with paranoid reactions which appeared in the questionnaire responses as "unreasonable resentments" and a pervasive egocentrism.

A chronic stage of the compulsive phase of alcoholism was recognizable in the onset of tremors and "indefinable fears" and anxieties over a source of supply of liquor. These can be taken as symptoms of acute anxiety which focuses all waking thoughts and energies of the inebriate toward protecting his supply of liquor. Intoxication becomes the goal or central function around which his total life activity revolves, rather than a means to an end. After three years of chronic inebriation serious physical involvements lead, in a large number of cases, to seeking medical assistance and/or hospitalization. The indelible physical stigmas of the alcoholic's role plus the symbolic impact of therapeutic experiences, also in large numbers of cases, further weaken the structure of rationalizations; although, on the average, it required two more years before the fund of rationalizations was completely bankrupt and a "lowest point" reached. The average age at which most of the inebriates in the group arrived at this terminal point was forty-one years. At this ebb a majority of the cases in this sample admitted they were "licked," further admitting their roles as alcoholics to themselves and to others. Shortly thereafter all these particular alcoholics joined some Alcoholics Anonymous chapter.

Certain behaviors, such as solitary drinking and antisocial acts, were not easily assignable to any particular phases of the drinking history of the group of alcoholics. They tended to occur at different times throughout the different phases, suggesting that the isolation of the alcoholic and his aggressions against others resulting from the breakdown of social communication are more directly related to the objective societal reaction than to the drinking pattern per se. Sooner or later, however, the overwhelming majority of the alcoholics withdraw socially to become solitary drinkers.

Precisely whether the average sequence of drinking behavior discovered in this research can be taken as representative of a broad class of inebriates is an unsettled question. Certainly, since no female cases were included, it cannot be applied to women without further research. The fact that the inebriates in this sample had actively sought aid of the Alcoholics Anonymous and were able to subordinate their egos to the group on religious grounds may betray an important selectivity in the cases. As the analyst recognizes, some alcoholics may cling to their unreasonable rationalizations until an end to their travails is put by death or by permanent hospitalization. Others may sink to such low status and undergo such demoralization that the rationalizations no longer are necessary.[49]

[49] *Ibid.*, p. 75.

Social Participation of the Alcoholic

Alcoholism is very similar to stuttering with respect to its high degree of primacy and with respect to the nature of the forces which bring about a progressive social isolation. As in stuttering, there is a growing pervasion of the different areas of social participation by guilt and anxiety generated, in this case, by past excesses and the correlated social failures and inadequacies. All these ultimately are generalized in a definition of the self as weak and without will power. While there can be no doubt but that objective societal barriers operate to restrict the alcoholic's opportunities to participate, especially when he has reached a chronic and badly deteriorated stage, the more dynamic factor in his isolation lies in his withdrawal tendencies. Thus, many alcoholics do not report for work simply because the anticipated strain of going through their daily work routines without drinking is too much to bear. Many of their jobs are lost by default rather than by outright discharge.

It can be shown that the first important and most universal disruption of the inebriate's social life arises in his occupational and economic adjustments. While social ruptures may take place prior to this, the loss of jobs, with lowered efficiency and earnings, sets in movement a chain of interactions not easily controlled, reversed, or subjectively discounted. A converse hypothesis for testing is that so long as a person can perform in his economic role, no amount of alcoholic excess will lead to addictive intoxication. Some types of work make it far more difficult to carry on under the influence of alcohol than others. A dentist can scarcely work as he does in the close physical proximity of patients if his breath smells of alcohol. Also if he begins to cancel appointments in order to drink during the day, his income quickly suffers. There are numerous statutes which specifically prohibit practicing certain professions while intoxicated, and 15 states make it a misdemeanor for employees in charge of trains to be intoxicated while on duty. About the same number penalize public officers for drunkenness on duty.[50] For legal reasons chronic alcoholics cannot be truck drivers, taxi drivers, or operators of dangerous machinery.

Generally the jobs which remain open to the chronic alcoholic are the unskilled, dirty, and disagreeable ones for which there is less competition. These, too, are the low-paying jobs. If alcoholics have begun pathological drinking at early ages, they may be blocked from upward occupational mobility; and if they have held high positions in the beginning, their movement has most often been downward in the occupational scale. The extent to which job mobility is a characteristic of alcoholism has been touched upon in a study of arrested inebriates in a Connecticut community. Table

[50] Hall, Jerome, "Drunkenness as a Criminal Offense," *Journal of Criminal Law and Criminology*, 32, September–October, 1941, pp 297–309.

41 compares the number of jobs held by arrested inebriates, "other" offenders, and traffic offenders during a one-year period.

TABLE 41. PERCENTAGE OF 1,121 INEBRIATES, 485 "OTHER OFFENDERS," AND 176 TRAFFIC VIOLATORS ACCORDING TO NUMBER OF JOBS HELD DURING THE PAST YEAR*

Number of jobs	Inebriates	"Others"	Traffic
One	35 9	46 6	66 5
Two	26 0	28 3	24 4
Three	13 7	12 2	2.3
Four and more	16 3	10 6	5.7
Odd jobs	7 5	2 3	0.5
Separate contracting	0 6		0.6
Total	100 0	100 0	100 0

* Bacon, Selden, "Inebriety, Social Integration and Marriage," *Memoirs of the Section on Alcohol Studies, Yale University*, No. 2, 1945, Table 18, p. 24

That the job mobility of alcoholics has been downward into jobs with low status may be inferred from the data in Table 42.

TABLE 42. OCCUPATIONAL STATUS OF 799 INEBRIATES, 379 "OTHER OFFENDERS," 164 TRAFFIC VIOLATORS, AND ALL URBAN CONNECTICUT MALES (DESIGNATED AS GENERAL POPULATION); PERCENTAGES OF EACH BY STATUS CATEGORIES*

Occupational category	Inebriates	"Others"	Traffic	General population
Professional, proprietary, managerial	2.4	10 8	12 8	16.3
White collar	3.1	5.3	6.7	15 5
Skilled labor	33.6	40.9	45.7	50.4
Unskilled labor	57.1	39 6	29.3	16.9
Ordinary labor	(31.7)	(28 8)	(24 4)	(8 4)
Farm labor	(5 6)	(0 8)	(1 2)	(0 5)
Service, nondomestic	(13 8)	(6 1)	(0 6)	(7 7)
Service, domestic	(0 6)	(3 9)	(3.0)	(0 3)
Other	3.8	3.4	5 5	0.9
Total	100.0	100.0	100.0	100.0

* Bacon, Selden, "Inebriety, Social Integration and Marriage," *Memoirs of the Section on Alcohol Studies, Yale University*, No. 2, 1945, Table 20, p 26.

There is no comparison of the percentage unemployed for the three categories in the table. However, 28 per cent of the arrestees for intoxication were found to be unemployed. This was during a time of boom and full employment during which no more than 5 to 10 per cent of the general population could have been unemployed.[51] It is probably not a valid procedure to take the differences in status of the arrested inebriates and that of the general population as a crude measure of the stultifying or down-

[51] Bacon, Selden, "Inebriety, Social Integration and Marriage," *Memoirs of the Section on Alcohol Studies, Yale University*, No. 2, 1945, p 22.

grading influence of alcoholism upon occupation for the reason that alcoholics who are arrested may be drawn originally from lower economic strata. However, the comparison of the inebriate group with the "others" group may well provide a usable measure of the degree to which the alcoholism affects occupational status.

A direct consequence of sinking to lower ranking jobs is a decrease of earnings. The picture of the earnings of arrested inebriates in comparison with what must serve as control groups is submitted in Table 43:

TABLE 43. PERCENTAGE OF 886 INEBRIATES, 392 "OTHER OFFENDERS," AND 172 TRAFFIC VIOLATORS, ALL EMPLOYED, IN CATEGORIES ACCORDING TO WEEKLY EARNINGS*

Wage bracket	Inebriates	"Others"	Traffic
Less than $15	11.8	8.7	5.2
$15–$25.	29 6	19.1	11 6
25– 35	25 1	32.9	29.7
35– 45	16 6	25.0	22.0
45– 55	9.7	9.4	17.4
$55 and over	7.2	4.9	13.4
Total	100.0	100.0	100.0

* Bacon, Selden, "Inebriety, Social Integration and Marriage," *Memoirs of the Section on Alcohol Studies, Yale University*, No. 2, 1945, Table 22, p. 28.

It is interesting to notice that the arrested inebriates had a higher percentage of cases in the category of "55 dollars and over" than the "others" class, but not higher than the percentage of traffic offenders earning more than this weekly sum. This may mean that some of the higher paid alcoholics are in jobs which they can continue to hold despite excessive drinking, or it may mean that a certain number of excessive drinkers begin to come into contact with law-enforcement agencies before a decline in their economic fortunes comes about. Obviously more research is needed on this item. While occupational downgrading, unemployment, and curtailed earning power have obvious implications for the self-regarding attitudes of the pathological drinker, their interactional effects extend to abridge and modify practically all other group participation. For example, the chronic inebriate who has lost his job and spent his last money often is driven to "borrowing" or begging money from friends, or to passing bad checks at their expense. Each one whom he leaves with a bad debt or defrauds becomes one less contact with social reality as his guilt prevents his seeking them out or responding to their calls.

SEX AND MARITAL PARTICIPATION

Certain aspects of the relationship between alcoholism and sexual-marital behavior have yet to be made clear. There is no trouble in perceiving that basic incompatibilities between undisciplined drinking and the demands of married existence exist. The high divorce rate of alcoholics convincingly testifies to this fact. The unsettled question, as with mentally ill persons, is whether some sort of third factor operates through the personality structure to induce both the alcoholic behavior and disruption of sex and marital life, and if so, to what extent. The observed and expected marital status of a group of arrested inebriates can be seen in Table 44.

TABLE 44. NORMAL EXPECTANCY OF MARITAL STATUS AND OBSERVED MARITAL STATUS OF 1,196 ARRESTED INEBRIATES*

Marital status	Numbers		Percentages	
	Observed	Expectancy	Observed	Expectancy
Single	649	234	53 1	19 6
Married	280	860	22.9	71.9
Separated	141	42	11.5	3.5
Widowed	61	46	5.0	3.8
Divorced	92	14	7.5	1.2
Total	1,223	1,196†	100 0	100 0

* Bacon, Selden, "Inebriety, Social Integration and Marriage," *Memoirs of the Section on Alcohol Studies, Yale University*, No. 2, 1945, Table 6, p. 9.

† Difference is caused by 27 men being of unknown age.

Over twice as many of these arrestees were single, more than three times as many were separated, and six times as many divorced as would be expected from contrast with the general population in the state where the study was made. The disproportionately large percentage of single alcoholics may well be attributed to the youthful beginnings of alcoholism in a substantial percentage of cases. In the study cited earlier, for example, it was found that loss of control over drinking had occurred before age twenty-five in 39 per cent of the cases and before age twenty in 20 per cent of the cases.[52] Since the mean age of urban males at marriage falls somewhere between 24 and 26 years of age, it follows that many alcoholics have begun to be socially isolated, undergo behavior changes, and perhaps have job difficulties during what is normally the courtship period. Consequently these alcoholics may have less interest in marriage, or their drinking habits may throw them into contact with a class of women whom they would find unacceptable as wives. More respectable women who have known the pathological drinker earlier may be alienated or intuitively sense the dangers in the way of marriage to him. Case-history evidence suggests a much more rapid deterioration of the single alcoholic than of the alcoholic who has married.

[52] *Ibid*, p. 12

The early sex life of the single alcoholic has not been systematically studied, so it can only be inferred that a certain measure of promiscuity is experienced. As the conflicts of the individual focus more and more into a pattern of compulsive drinking, a diminution in his erotic fulfillment results. Generally, while liquor stimulates the sexual impulse, it makes fulfillment more difficult, so that the sex act may be less satisfying to many alcoholics. In the more acute and chronic stages of alcoholism, genuine impotence may develop. The general conclusion, if one can be made, is that alcoholism ultimately diminishes rather than increases the sex activity of single and married persons alike.

If the alcoholic is married, serious disturbances in his relationship with his spouse are inevitable. The wife nearly always becomes the surrogate of a disapproving society, whose reactions are intensified by the social and economic jeopardy in which her spouse's irresponsible behavior places her and her children, if any. Her economic anxieties soon grow large, especially after a job or two has been lost through the husband's drinking excesses. Hostility toward her husband compounds out of experiences with him and his drunken companions, with angry taxi drivers, bill collectors, and the sheriff or police calling from jail to inform her of her drunken husband's whereabouts. Sexual infidelity sometimes numbers among the husband's misdeeds, with the odd crowning humiliation of his bringing his female acquaintances home with him. The wife suffers a mounting isolation as a consequence of her husband's failure to appear for social engagements. If the couple does visit friends for the evening, she can never be sure that her mate will not get drunk and embarrass her and the company. On the other hand, the strain of keeping sober on such occasions may make him a surly and otherwise unpleasant companion. For much the same reasons, the wife seldom dares to invite friends into their home.

The alcoholic comes in time to think of his wife as a "kill-joy" or "wet blanket," and in many instances his drunken excursions must be interpreted as retaliations against her. She, in turn, strikes back at him in different ways; if there is a sexual misstep, for example, she may counter with a retaliatory love affair of her own. In sympathetic interims, she may work courageously with her husband to help him overcome his dependence upon liquor. A common experiment consists of drinking with him in the hope of stopping him somewhere short of gross inebriation. This device seldom succeeds and may be the overture to the wife's alcohol addiction. Disillusionment of the wife proceeds in an uneven fashion with fluctuating hopes and despair, culminating, as we have seen, in separation and divorce in a large percentage of cases. The wife not always feels free to seek such a solution, even when her better judgment tells her it is the thing to do. In-laws may believe she has been responsible in whole or in part for her husband's drinking and may be quick to accuse her of disloyalty to a sick man. For this reason and perhaps because of guilt from other sources, the alcoholic's wife probably remains by his side too long and as a result suffers considerable personality distortion, which, in many ways, is very similar to that of the husband.[53] Few persons can live for long in an intimate, interdependent relationship with an alcoholic and escape neurosis.

There seems to be no significant difference between the percentage of alcoholic women who have been married and that of the general population. However, the percentage who have been married and divorced or separated is extraordinarily large. For example, whereas roughly twelve times as many male alcoholics have been divorced as nonalcoholic men, the ratio for female inebriates runs as high as 32 to 1.[54] The impression is thus created that alcoholism among females quite often is originally a reaction to unsuccessful marriage, divorce, and separation. Further support for this interpretation comes from the much higher-than-expected rates of alcoholism among widows.[55] Alcoholism of women incurs a much more censorious reaction than that of men, and it is possible that men feel fewer restraints in divorcing alcoholic wives than is true of wives of alcoholic men. Alcoholism in women is apt to be much more complicated and much less responsive to treatment. Following divorce or separation, the inebriate woman is probably less able to deal with economic problems unless there is substantial alimony. It may be hazarded as a guess that a certain percentage of them turn to prostitution as a means of solving the problem of gaining a livelihood and purchasing liquor.

Divorce and separation often are a final break with social reality for the alcoholic. When the home is broken up, he or she must find other housing, often in rooming houses. Residential mobility of divorced and separated alcoholics runs much higher than for those who maintain their marital unions intact.[56] Social isolation is magnified by the fact of changing residences and also by location in areas of high mobility, anonymity, and isolation within the city environment.

Other Aspects of the Participation of Inebriates

It may be presumed that the chronic alcoholic has no more interest in religion than other persons. If anything, his desire for good times and being "one of the boys" would suggest he had very early lost interest in church attendance if he had any religious affiliation. The Christian sin-guilt complex may actually make religious persons repellent to him.

[53] See Price, Gladys, "A Study of the Wives of 20 Alcoholics," *Quarterly Journal of Studies on Alcoholism*, 5, March, 1945, pp. 620–627.

[54] Bacon, *op cit.*, pp. 10–11.

[55] *Ibid*, Table 10, p. 11.

[56] *Ibid.*, Table 14, p. 20.

Further, if his drinking is a week-end variety, it will clearly rule out the possibility of church attendance. However, at a certain late stage in his alcoholic history, a certain type of inebriate in desperation turns to religion in hope of mitigating his painful conflicts.[57] Disillusionment ensues in large numbers of cases, with a resultant deepening of the sense of isolation.

TABLE 45 PERCENTAGE OF INEBRIATES, "OTHER OFFENDERS," AND TRAFFIC VIOLATORS IN CATEGORIES ACCORDING TO FREQUENCY OF PARTICIPATION IN FOUR SOCIAL ACTIVITIES*

Frequency of participation	Nature of activity†			
	Visiting	Clubs	Dancing	Motion pictures
Never.				
Inebriates	26.0	86.6	81.0	22.1
"Others"	14.4	79.4	61.8	11.4
Traffic	3.5	66.3	45.8	5.9
Occasionally				
Inebriates	58.1	10.6	16.7	54.2
"Others"	63.7	16.4	31.8	61.9
Traffic	65.9	24.6	42.7	60.4
Frequently				
Inebriates	13.6	1.5	2.0	17.2
"Others"	16.6	3.2	4.7	16.8
Traffic	24.1	3.4	9.4	21.4
Regularly				
Inebriates	2.3	1.3	0.3	6.5
"Others"	5.3	1.0	1.7	9.9
Traffic	6.5	5.7	2.1	12.3

* Bacon, Selden, "Inebriety, Social Integration and Marriage," *Memoirs of the Section on Alcohol Studies, Yale University*, No. 5, 1945, Table 24, p. 30.

† The different questions were answered by the following numbers. visiting—1,077 inebriates, 493 "Others," 170 traffic violators, clubs—1,136 inebriates, 499 "others," 175 traffic violators; dancing—1,167 inebriates, 531 "others," 192 traffic violators; motion pictures—1,269 inebriates, 546 "others," 187 traffic violators

At the terminal stages of alcoholic deterioration, the inebriate may exploit the charity of the religious-sponsored rescue missions or the Salvation Army.

Political interests and civic participation soon disappear from the inebriate's life. His residential mobility most likely disenfranchises him fairly often, even if he retained any sense of civic responsibility.

A further reflection of the isolant status of the inebriate is cast by the paucity of his recreational participation. This is clearly apparent in Table 45. The inebriates in this sample showed less participation in pastime activities than the control groups in all but one instance. Inebriates were

[57] Jellinek, "Phases in the Drinking History of Alcoholics," p 66

slightly more regularly active in "clubs" than the "others" group. However, the percentage of the total inebriates who retained this social contact was very small.

Adjustment and Maladjustment

Alcoholism comes closest of all pathologies to exemplifying a direct relationship between the fact of deviation and sociopsychological maladjustment. From what has been discovered, it can be said that disturbances of the symbolic processes are inevitable accompaniments of acute compulsive drinking, at least in our culture. The fact that pathological drinking moves through stages of increasing compulsiveness tokens a symbolic struggle in which the self becomes less and less acceptable to the drinker. The great premium which our ethos places upon self-control means that behaviors indicative of loss of self-control convergently place the stamp of "pariah" or "weakling" upon the individual in whom it occurs. The number of situational contexts in which social acceptable alternative definitions of the alcoholic behavior can be applied is very limited. The absence of social organization of chronic alcoholics rules out the possibility of drawing self-sustaining rationalizations from a deviant behavior system This suggests certain implicit limits upon the range of possible societal definitions of drunkenness, set by universal attributes of human social organization. The resistance which many people show to present-day efforts at redefining the alcoholic as a "sick man" may also reflect some such limits. The absence of any self-satisfying alternative definitions of continued excessive drinking (at least in our culture) probably explains why the alcoholic begins to build a tissue of rationalizations quite early, even before reaching the "true" compulsive-drinking stage. The continued amplification of the rationalizations in absurd and specious ways suggests the rudiments of delusional escape from the vilified self.

The various social failures of the alcoholic, as a worker, husband, parent, and citizen, become the spreading corroboration of an intolerable basic self, which grows out of a segment of the self reflected from what was originally socially uncomplicated drunken behavior. The spread of this role corroboration into the province of sex delinquency, real or imputed, in the alcoholic woman may explain the more complex nature of her inebriation. These developments for both the male and female alcoholic make more desperate and delusional the search for ways of symbolically translating their drunken behaviors into adjuncts of nonalcoholic roles. At this point it can be asked whether the black-outs, or alcoholic amnesias, of the inebriate are not simply devices whereby unpalatable evidences of the alcoholic role are banished from the conscious symbolic process. Their return as vague fears, anxiety, and tremors speaks of the failure of selective amnesias to work satisfactory enhancements of the self. Most of the so-called "personality modifications" of the chronic inebriate – egocentrism, unreasonable resentments, sudden rages, and suspiciousness – can be cited as incidents in the contest between the "I" and the repugnant "me's."

While there are no data showing mental disease to be greater than expected among such deviants as the blind or speech defectives, this is not the situation with alcoholics. Allowing for exaggeration of the rates of alcoholic mental disease because of failures to properly distinguish symptomatic drunkenness from genuine alcoholism, there still seems to be a higher-than-expected incidence of mental disorder among alcoholics. Thus, it is estimated that about 10 per cent of alcoholics are psychotic.[58]

TABLE 46. PERCENTAGE DISTRIBUTION OF THE ALCOHOLIC PSYCHOSES IN FIRST ADMISSIONS

Diagnosis	Per Cent of Alcoholic Psychoses
Pathological intoxication	2.0
Delirium tremens	37.0
Korsakoff's syndrome	11.0
Alcoholic hallucinosis	20.0
Chronic alcoholic deterioration with psychosis	15.0
Alcoholic paranoid states	10.0
Others	5.0
Total	100.0

* Haggard, H. W., and Jellinek, E. M., *Alcohol Explored*, 1942, p. 222. By permission of Doubleday & Company, New York.

By most generous estimates there can be no more than 1 per cent of our population who are psychotic. While the argument can always be advanced that this greater incidence of psychosis among alcoholics may be caused by the inclusion of a certain percentage of "prepsychotic" persons who become alcoholics early in life, it is still hard to dismiss the mental-disease potential implicit in the sociopsychological consequences of alcoholism. If the sociological theory that mental disease is brought on by social isolation has validity, then alcoholism as a pathology which inevitably narrows choices and progressively constricts social participation must qualify as a variant of the psychotic process.

There is, of course, nothing about the ingestion of alcohol per se which can lead to psychosis. Even where organic disease underlies psychosis with alcoholism, it is the secondary effects of heavy drinking expressed as vitamin deficiencies which are involved. Pellagra may give rise to comparable symptoms. In general terms, psychoses in alcoholics are terminal phases of social isolation, with special differentiating symptoms arising from the peculiar role of the alcoholic in our culture. The formal diagnostic classes of psychoses "caused by" alcoholism, together with their percentage distributions, are given in Table 46.

The general proposition that alcoholic psychoses are not special entities

[58] Bacon, *op. cit.*, p. 5.

or products of a process generically differing from that culminating in psychoses among nonalcoholics can be shown by the ease of equating the alcoholic psychoses with other diagnostic types. Chronic alcoholic deterioration has many features in common with schizophrenia; Korsakoff's syndrome describes symptoms which may occur in arteriosclerosis, pregnancy, influenza, and beriberi. In the case of alcoholic hallucinosis and alcoholic paranoid states, the close similarity of symptoms to those of schizophrenia has occasioned controversy among psychiatrists themselves as to whether they belong in the general class of alcoholic psychoses. Delirium tremens is the commonest single alcoholic mental disorder and by far the most spectacular. It tends to occur among healthier drinkers who temporarily experience disease or injury. Its dramatic visual and auditory hallucinations are of short duration, and they suggest an abortive psychotic seizure precipitated by organic disorders, which bankrupt the alcoholic of energy to deal with the conflicts of his role.

To the question, can a compulsive drinker be adjusted to his role and accept his self, there is no good answer at this writing. This much can be said, however; there appear to be certain persons who adopt pseudo-alcoholic roles, presumably because they find the penalties of the alcoholic status preferable to those of another sociopathic status. Epileptics are a case in point. Many psychotic persons may fall into this category. The author has encountered the concept of "dry alcoholic" in conversations with members of Alcoholics Anonymous. The term is usually invoked to designate persons who have all the "personality characteristics" of alcoholics except the excessive drinking. One such member actually, somewhat pridefully, referred to herself in such terms to the author in an interview.

It may well be that a social class differential operates to instill greater conflicts over self-acceptance in middle-class alcoholics than among those who have lower status and who do not depart so far from the social expectancies of their original roles as a consequence of excessive drinking. The migratory casual worker may confine his drunken sprees or "benders" to periods when he is unemployed and consequently have no sense of not fulfilling his economic role. The casual worker who loses a job through drinking may be better able to rationalize in terms of some special philosophy toward work itself. There are clear-cut signs of the need for further research on alcoholism among persons in unskilled and low-prestige occupations.

Another possibility is that after alcoholics pass a certain critical point in the deterioration process, they no longer strive to live by their previous moral standards. The self-defining process breaks down completely, giving way to a day-by-day, hedonistic, low-level kind of adjustment. Such persons, save for a species of tenuous contact with reality, may be the equivalents of deteriorated schizophrenics in mental hospitals. There is a final alternative which admits a sort of self-acceptance through alcoholic psychosis. This exists where the alcoholic self is rendered congenial through paranoid or delusional distortions, even though at the same time a wide divergence has grown between the societal and individual self-definitions. More complete discussion of this will be reserved for Chap. 11 on mental disorders.

MARGINAL ALCOHOLICS

No basis for marginality can be found in the behavior of drunkenness or excessive drinking itself. No distinctions such as "partial alcoholism," comparable to that in blindness, can be made. The alcoholic process seems to be a dynamic one which seldom if ever becomes stabilized at some interstitial level. The nearest thing to a marginal alcoholic role which can be adduced probably is that of the ex-alcoholic. This would be the person who has gone through the various stages of drinking to acute alcoholism and either by virtue of spontaneous remission, psychiatric assistance, or membership in Alcoholics Anonymous has given up drinking. While such a person qualifies for social acceptance and may even once again climb to high status, his "past" nevertheless remains to create problems of identification with his rehabilitant role.

A careful study of the status and role of Alcoholics Anonymous members from the standpoint of marginality might enlighten the hypothesis that ex-alcoholics never achieve a relatively well-integrated self. Reasons for believing this lie in the somewhat attenuated and skeptical acceptance of the organization by some groups of the community. Behind this is the tendency of many of AA converts to project their missionizing, reform activities into most of their community contacts. The suspicion that the self-control of these ex-alcoholics is the result of artifice and has to be bolstered by an organization probably exists in the minds of many who come to know the group in more than a stereotyped way. Furthermore, the conviction that alcoholism is traceable to allergies is not scientifically corroborated. It has to be maintained by the group myth somewhat in the same way as the radical myth is preserved.

To the degree that the Alcoholics Anonymous provides an integrated microcosmic social experience for its members and effectively mediates their contacts outside the group, adjustments may be satisfactory. There is some reason to doubt whether such is always the case. One can scarcely read the advice to wives of ex-alcoholics in the Alcoholics Anonymous publication [59] without suspecting that wholehearted participation in the organization is almost as disorganizing to family life as was alcoholism itself. However, if we may grant that the organization does truly stabilize the ex-alcoholic's life, then perhaps the search for the alcoholic marginals

[59] *Alcoholics Anonymous*, New York, 1939, Chaps 8–9.

has to turn to the peripheral affiliates who backslide and relapse. These would be persons who alternate between periods of intensive participation in the organization and withdrawals to alcohol, in whom tensions gradually build up from accretional dissatisfactions with opposed roles both within and outside the organization. This is all very speculative, but it points a direction for research on the function of social organization and social participation associated with marginal roles.

Selected Readings

BUNZEL, RUTH "The Role of Alcoholism in Two Central American Cultures," *Psychiatry,* 3, August, 1940, pp 361–387

BACON, SELDEN: "Inebriety, Social Integration and Marriage," *Memoirs of the Section on Alcohol Studies, Yale University,* No. 2, 1945.

HAGGARD, H. W , and E. M. Jellinek· *Alcohol Explored,* 1947

JELLINEK, E. M : "Phases in the Drinking History of Alcoholics," *Memoirs of the Section on Alcohol Studies, Yale University,* No 5, 1946

MAINE, HAROLD *If a Man Be Mad,* 1947.

MYERSON, ABRAHAM "Alcohol A Study in Social Ambivalence," *Quarterly Journal of Studies on Alcohol,* 1, 1940, pp. 11–18.

CHAPTER 11

MENTAL DISORDERS AND THE INSANE

The salient importance of research into mental disorders is brought home to us by the dearth of systematic knowledge available on this form of deviation. The crude empiricism and custodial expedient which mark the treatment and control of those who are formally classified as "insane" further emphasize research needs in this area. There is a deepening appreciation that social and cultural factors in some as yet undetermined but significant way operate in the genesis of mental aberrations, but sociological research on the question remains limited. While several promising sociological hypotheses have come to light, by and large, research efforts have not crystallized into a body of knowledge or special methodology which can be justifiably called a field or discipline of social psychiatry.[1] It may be asked at this point whether the stumbling block impeding sociological research on mental disorders is not of the same order as that which has handicapped students of criminology, *i.e.*, the failure to work out a system of definitions and classifications which have sufficient sociological relevance. We have in mind here chiefly the reliance of sociologists upon psychiatric classifications for descriptions of the elements of the sociopathic phenomena they seek to study.

While the diagnostic concepts employed by psychiatrists – such as organic and functional psychoses, manic-depressive psychosis, schizophrenia, and involutional melancholia – have some medical and administrative value, their usefulness in depicting socially and culturally meaningful aspects of mental deviancy seems decidedly limited.[2] Research formulations resting upon concepts such as these can only by much indirection and inference pose and seek answers to questions of genuine sociological concern about mental disorders. One of the more important sociological questions here is not what causes human beings to develop such symptoms as hallucinations and delusions but, instead, what is it about their behavior which leads the community to reject them, segregate them, and otherwise

[1] Dunham, H. Warren, "Social Psychiatry," *American Sociological Review*, 13, April, 1948, pp. 183–197.

[2] Young, Kimball, *Personality and Problems of Adjustment*, 1940, p. 721; Jellinek, E. M., "Some Principles of Psychiatric Classification," *Psychiatry*, 2, May, 1939, pp 161–166

treat them as irresponsibles, *i.e.*, as insane. A second important question, corollary to this, revolves about the function of such rejections and concomitant societal definitions in the dynamics of mental deviation itself. The insufficiency of classical and even more modern dynamic psychiatric conceptualizations for purposes of exploring these questions places an urgent responsibility upon sociologists to examine more critically their eclectic borrowings from psychiatry. The need is strong to devise formulations or reformulations in this area which are more easily integrated into the general body of sociological theory.

The Nature of the Deviation

It is customary to draw a distinction between "insanity" and "mental disorders." The former refers to a special legal status assigned to an individual as the consequence of a judicial process, while the latter has to do with the medically recognized symptoms of pathological mental behavior. Mental disorders have been further classified into "amentia" and "dementia," which literally mean "without mind" and "deranged mind." Amentia is used to describe conditions in which normal development of abstract or general intelligence has been arrested, known more familiarly as "feeble-mindedness" or "mental deficiency." Mental disorders of the sort we are interested in here may or may not be present or associated with this condition.

Within the broad classification of dementia a clinical division ordinarily is made between organic and functional disorders, a division whose chief value appears in cases where the structural basis of symbolic communication with other human beings has been largely destroyed by disease, toxins, or injury. Behavior in such cases can no longer be called "social" and is amenable to physiological explanation only. However, the sharp separation of organic and functional mental disorders in cases where only partial damage has been done to the nervous system is seldom possible. One reason for this is that as yet it has been impossible to consistently relate the degree and specific symptoms of mental disorder to the extent and nature of lesions in neural tissue. The diagnosis of organic mental disorders depends in a large measure upon observation of behavior of the patient himself, and since the same behavior can occur in the absence of any organic pathology, the establishing of a causal nexus between the two with any surety is fraught with hazards. More cautious clinicians protect themselves from overgeneralization by classifying such cases as organic disease "with psychosis." More recently the term "psychosomatic medicine" has acquired popularity as a way of conceiving the relationship between physical and mental disorders in interactional rather than directly causal terms.

The functional mental disorders are ordinarily classed as psychoses and neuroses, with subclassifications for each of these two major classes. The psychoses are looked upon as being more serious disorders which incapacitate the persons suffering from them to the point where special custodial care is necessary. In contrast, the neuroses are thought of as less serious or relatively benign disorders, which permit the persons showing such symptoms to carry on with their social and economic roles. Some psychiatrists have insisted that psychoses and neuroses are two entirely different orders of phenomena, and that neurotics do not become psychotic. Others have less sanguine views and simply put down neuroses as arrested or abortive psychoses, or even insist that there can be "no psychosis without neurosis." Some have also challenged the idea that neuroses are "less serious" than psychoses, pointing out that in some obsessional neuroses the pain and conflict suffered by the patient may well exceed that of a psychosis.

The subclassifications of the functional psychoses and further breakdowns of these need not detain us here other than to indicate that the commonest and perhaps best distinguished of these disorders are schizophrenia and manic-depressive psychosis. The differences between these seem to center around such things as delusions and hallucinations and the presence or absence of affective disturbance and the tempo of social activity associated with the disturbances. However, even here there is much overlapping in the symptoms, and differentiating the manic-depressed condition from catatonic and involutional states is often impossible without referring to a case history of the patient. In fact the dependence of psychiatrists upon case histories in order to come to definite conclusions about the diagnosis of mental disorders leads us to believe that nearly always they are reacting to something besides the apparent behavior of the patients they examine.

That which needs to be done is to search for attributes which are common to all mental disorders and to discover the continuities between "normal" and psychotic behavior.[3] Fortified with this knowledge, we may then construct serialized classifications in which the basis for inclusion and exclusion of cases in various categories is made explicit. In the course of this procedure existing psychiatric concepts may be fitted into a more general schema, and may be redefined and supplemented with other concepts.

A Sociological Formulation of Mental Disorders

Returning momentarily to the earlier chapter in which the aspects of deviations were distinguished, we may state that our interest here focuses upon the disordering of the individual symbolic process, taken broadly to

[3] Brown, L. Guy, *Social Pathology*, p 260

mean the emotive and cognitive as well as strictly ideational processes which express the self attitudes. This symbolic distortion may take a number of forms, but all may be held to be manifestations of an extreme divergence between the self and "others" attitudes. This divergence signifies the breakdown of social communication in such a way that the individual's conception of the self does not reflect or resemble the societal definition of the person. The "me" of the self no longer approximates within normal limits the socially objective estimates and designations of the person's role and status. This differentiation of the symbolic process of the person is accompanied by a rejection of the self and also of "others" who are the reciprocal points of reference for the intolerable subjective definitions of the self.

The operational or observable aspects of the disordering of the symbolic process and the rejection of the self lie in the expressive behavior of the deviant. The symbolic deviant is differentiated by the relative amount of his behavior which is loaded with meaning for self and others or by the degree of "ego involvement." The enlargement of the expressive portion of the individual's behavior can be seen in the displacement of affect. By this is meant that he either overreacts or underreacts to the self and "others" in a larger number of situations than do other peoples. Affect, or, more commonly, emotion is displaced upon the inner responses or upon the outer responses toward the environment or toward other people. In extreme cases the deviant may spend days in motionless fantasy or pass through a series of episodes in which his hyperactivity makes him a nuisance or a threat to all with whom he interacts.

It will be our contention here that practically all of what is called "neurotic" and "psychotic" behavior can be considered as abnormal variation in the amount and form of self-expression.[4] It would be somewhat premature to undertake an exhaustive systematic classification of mental disorders as varieties of self-expressive behavior. It is of special interest, however, to scan some of the theoretical developments running in this direction. One very insightful theory of schizophrenia is organized exclusively around the conception that schizophrenics are persons in deep conflict over "an intolerable loss of self-respect." Schizophrenic behavior is factored into three general reactions, all of which are ways by which the person seeks to cope with his deep and lasting self-deprecations. These are the continuous equivalents of the formal psychiatric subclassifications of the disorder, simple, paranoid, catatonic, and hebephrenic schizophrenia. The first of these reactions is *drifting*, in which the person more or less

[4] For those who have attempted to formulate mental disorders in terms of the self see Sherif, M , and H Cantril, *The Psychology of Ego-involvements*, 1947, Chap XII, Kisker, G. W , and G W. Knox, "The Psychopathology of the Ego System," *Journal of Nervous and Mental Diseases*, 96, July, 1942, pp. 66–71; Boisen, Anton, *The Exploration of the Inner World*, 1936.

renounces his struggle with the self and surrenders to impulse, idleness, apathy, and daydreaming. A somewhat different reaction is observed in persons who fight back against the attacks upon the self through *delusional misinterpretation*, projecting undesirable aspects of the self onto others, enhancing or endurating the self with grandiose and other attributes which have no allegiance with reality. A third reaction is *panic*, which springs from the recognition of the ominous and disastrous implications of the drifting or delusional patterns into which the person has fallen. Fear and shock arise with the perceptions that self-control has been lost or that thought has been warped dangerously. This panic generates the disturbed behavior of the catatonic. Catatonic stupors in the light of this theory become the supreme effort of the deviant to think through his massive conflicts. Hebephrenia, instead of requiring a separate classification, is simply considered as the ultimate outcome of the drifting pattern – complete deterioration.[5]

Another theoretical formulation focused about the notion of self and others has introduced the concept of the "pseudocommunity" to describe many of the general aspects of the symbolic life of mentally deranged persons. The pseudocommunity is a nexus of subjective reactions brought into existence by a delusional process in which the person creates and peoples an imaginary social world. Within this pseudo world or community the self and others are protected, punished, evaded, or otherwise manipulated in accordance with the nature of the unreal assumptions adopted by the deviant. The pseudocommunity grows in clarity and sinister quality, being progressively expanded to include new activities and new personnel until the threat it represents reaches a crucial stage. At this point overt defensive or vindicative behavior bursts forth which antagonizes others and provokes counteraggressions which become the final verification of the deviant's fears and suspicions.[6] While the best organized pseudocommunities are exemplified in the paranoid disorders, they are also a feature of schizophrenia, in which elaborately fantastic and autistic, albeit less well-organized, inner symbolic environments are produced. They frequently develop in manic and depressed persons as well.[7]

Just what form the sociological classifications of mental disorders ultimately will take quite naturally will be influenced by the nature of the problems raised for inquiry. As our concern shifts away from the "causes" of mental disorders to the behavior itself, such things as the manner of onset of symptoms and the relation of the inner and outer life of the psychotic person become relevant bases of classification. The well-known

[5] Boisen, *op. cit.*

[6] Cameron, N., "The Paranoid Pseudocommunity," *American Journal of Sociology*, 49, July, 1943, pp. 32–38.

[7] Cameron, N., *The Psychology of Behavior Disorders*, 1947, p 439.

fact that remissions are more numerous where symptoms have a rapid onset and where they have some understandable reference to critical social situations may be of special interest to us. Such characteristics of remissions suggest a difference in the relative importance of the purely covert symbols and the external socially expressed symbols in precipitating the intolerable self-definitions which underlie psychotic behavior. In other words, even clear-cut cases of mental disorder can be located on a continuum which measures the degrees to which social and cultural realities enter into the deviation. This topic will be given our further attention in subsequent discussion.

Extent of the Deviation

We are dependent for a measure of the number of mentally deranged persons in our population upon the records of those who come to public notice through hospitalization. First admissions to all public and private mental hospitals in 1946 numbered 153,025, giving a rate of 110.6 per 100,000 population.[8] The total number of resident patients in reporting hospitals at the end of 1946 was slightly over 529,000, which meant a rate of 382.4.[9] The ratio of these hospitalized cases to the larger population of mental deviants is as yet not established. However, estimates place the numbers of noninstitutionalized psychotics as at least equal to the numbers under psychiatric care.[10] Assuming the validity or reasonable accuracy of such estimates, we arrive at a figure of 306,000 new cases of mental disorder each year and at least 1 million as the total number of such deviants in the population.

Differentiation of the Mentally Disordered

Most, if not all, demographic descriptions of mental deviants are seriously compromised by our ignorance of the vagaries of the hospitalization process. There is no good way of knowing whether or not the characteristics of mentally disordered persons discovered by studying hospital samples of the universe of neurotics and psychotics reflect a selective bias. If it is assumed that they do, then we are at further loss to know in what direction the bias runs. These unsettled questions must stand in the background of any discussion of the differentiae of the mentally disordered population.

[8] *Patients in Mental Institutions*, 1947, U.S Department of Commerce, Bureau of the Census, Table III, p. 12

[9] *Ibid.*, Table VI, p 16.

[10] Lemkau, R., C Fietz, and M. Cooper, "Report of Progress in Developing a Mental Hygiene Component of a City Health District," *American Journal of Psychiatry*, 97, January, 1941, pp. 805–811, Roth, W. F., and F. H. Luton, "The Mental Health Program in Tennessee," *ibid*, 99, March, 1943, pp. 662–675.

There is a conviction, held for so long as to become practically a tradition, that mentally disordered persons come from a special population class with defective or "bad" heredity. These people are assumed to possess genes for mental disorders or gene combinations which predispose them to mental breakdown. The proof of these assertions is for the most part inferential, being derived from comparisons of families in which mental disorders have occurred with families in which there is an absence of these disorders. Findings indicate that the ratio of mentally disordered persons coming from families in which mental disorder has previously appeared to those coming from families free of mental disorder runs about 2 to 1. However, efforts to show that mental disorders in family genealogies behave as simple Mendelian recessive traits have not been successful.[11] Furthermore, no great homogeneity of symptoms can be uncovered from one family member to another where they have broken mentally. Whether the higher incidence of the disorders in families with positive histories is a real or only an apparent difference is by no means easily settled. There are many questions which can be raised about the test data themselves – as to the sufficiency of samples, the reliability of the methods used to obtain family histories, and the consistency of diagnoses. The samples used as controls are very fractional in size; often one or two hundred cases are taken as representative of our total population. In the bulk of studies of the influence of heredity upon the development of mental disorders, random sampling is an assumption rather than a demonstrated fact. The carefully considered conclusion of one investigator after reviewing a large number of these studies is that *probably* for *some* types of mental disorder a higher incidence exists in some family lines. How much higher the incidence runs is a moot point.[12] Whether this means a differential in genetic constitution of the family members or whether it means a differential continuity of family interactional patterns conducive to mental deviation must also be left open for further investigation.

Aside from the endeavors to discover genetic differentiae among the mentally disordered, some research has been directed to the subject of constitutional types and their connection with not so much the actual presence of the disorders as with the type of symptoms which appear. These investigations have been seriously hampered, if not nullified, by the insuperable difficulties of verifying the constitutional types themselves and by the failure to control the factor of age in the test samples.

Age-sex differentials of mental deviants invite our interest not because of any possible biological variables involved but because of their close ties with role, status, and cultural conflict. The situation is decidedly confused

[11] Pollock, Horatio, *Mental Disease and Social Welfare*, 1941, pp. 118*ff*.

[12] Myerson, Abraham, *et al.*, *Eugenical Sterilization*, 1936, Chap VI.

when it comes to separating the real incidence of mental disorders in the two sexes from their more nominal hospitalized incidence. In 1946 for every 100 females admitted the first time to a mental hospital, there were 136.4 males.[13] But in the same year the sex ratio for resident hospital populations was only 114.[14] Facts of additional significance along this line are the higher ratio of female readmissions to first admissions and their longer average hospital stays. The facts suggest that females who are hospitalized have more flagrant mental disturbances and that their behavior is socially

TABLE 47. RATIOS OF ADMISSION RATES OF THE VARIOUS AGE GROUPS TO THOSE OF THE 10–19 YEAR GROUPS, FIRST ADMISSIONS "WITH MENTAL DISORDERS," BY SEX, 1917–1933 (NEW YORK STATE HOSPITALS)*

Age groups	Males	Females
10–19	1.0	1.0
20–29	3 8	3.1
30–39	4.6	4.2
40–49	4.9	4.6
50–59	5.3	5.0
60–69	7.2	6 0
70–79	12 9	11.2
80–89	19.9	18 8
90 and over	19.8	17 0

* Dayton, Neil A., *New Facts on Mental Disorders*, 1940, Age Table 2, p. 53. By permission of Charles C Thomas, Publishers, Springfield, Ill.

more disruptive. The higher proportion of female hospital cases diagnosed as having manic-depressive psychoses fits into this interpretation. Thus there is a moderate probability that a proportionately greater number of less mentally deranged females are kept at home.[15] If true, such a fact would considerably alter the over-all sex ratio of the mentally disordered population. It is entirely possible that we shall ultimately find the sex differential for this form of deviation to be slight or unimportant.

The picture with reference to the interrelationship of age and mental disorder is less perplexing than in the case of sex, but still it leaves something to be desired in the way of clarity. There are many factors associated with older age – widowhood, physical ailments, and economic impoverishment – which militate in behalf of a greater likelihood of hospitalization of those who become mentally disordered at advanced years. However, the age differential in first-admission rates between old and young age groups is large enough not to be more than partially accounted for by these facts. The extent of these differences is plainly shown in Table 47.

[13] *Patients in Mental Institutions*, 1946, computed from Table I, pp. 51*f*.

[14] *Ibid.*

[15] See Dayton, Neil A., *New Facts on Mental Disorders*, 1940, p. 370.

In general, the results of examinations for military service in the Second World War tend to confirm the relationship between age and hospitalized mental disorders. However, they reveal an exception for the youngest age group to be called, those who were 18 to 20 years old. Mental disorders for youths of these ages exceeded all ages up to 30. The rate differences are presented in Table 48.

TABLE 48 PREVALENCE OF MENTAL DISORDERS PER 1,000 SELECTIVE SERVICE REGISTRANTS EXAMINED FROM NOVEMBER, 1940, TO DECEMBER, 1943, BY AGE GROUPS*

Age Groups	Disorders per 1,000 Registrants
18–20	52.5
21–25	34.5
26–29	48.9
30 and over	87.2

* *Physical Examination of Selective Service Registrants*, Special Monograph 15, III, Appendix F, Selective Service System, 1947, Table 78, p. 39

We are left with strong indications that older age is a real differential of mental deviants and that it does not vanish when weight is given to factors making hospitalization of the aged more likely to follow in the wake of mental aberration.

The ethnic differentiation of the total psychotic population presents certain problems of analysis which are not too easily solved. Negroes, for example, have greater-than-expected first-admission rates to mental hospitals and they make up a larger part of the resident inmates than would be anticipated from their general population numbers. However, this may be a function of their low economic status, which makes it more likely that they will be institutionalized when symbolic disturbances occur. Some reinforcing of this idea comes from the results of examinations of selective-service registrants in which Negroes fell below the whites in the incidence of mental disorder. Negroes had a rate of 48 cases per 1,000 registrants whereas whites ran 57.1.[16]

A conspicuous characteristic of admissions to mental hospitals and of their inmates is the unexpectedly high numbers of foreign-born and native-born of foreign or mixed parentage among them. New York data have shown the foreign-born to have the highest rates of first admissions to mental hospitals, with native-born of foreign or mixed parentage coming next above the native-born of native parents. Refinement of these data by correcting for age differences tends to lower the rates of the foreign-born until they approximate those of the native born. Nevertheless a differential still remains even after adjustments are made in the rates, according to one study, leaving a foreign-born rate about 18 per cent higher than that of

[16] *Physical Examination of Selective Service Registrants*, Special Monograph 15, III, Appendix F, Selective Service System, 1947, Table 78, p. 38.

native-born of native parentage. However there are wide differences between the nativity groups; the Irish, for instance, contribute heavily to the mentally disordered class because of the high incidence of psychoses with alcoholism among them.[17]

The mere facts of foreign birth and alien cultural antecedents in themselves seem not to be significant differentiae of mental deviants so much as they are when taken in conjunction with other differentials. For example, it was found in Massachusetts that immigrants who immigrated to this country at younger ages made poorer showings in so far as first admissions for mental disorders went than did those who migrated at older ages.[18]

There are some grounds for believing that children of immigrants have a greater expectancy of mental disorder than the native-born with native parents and perhaps greater than their parents. An investigation of first admissions to New York mental hospitals for a three-year period has disclosed that native-born population with foreign-born parents had higher first-admission rates than the native-born with native parents. Significantly, however, the native-born with mixed parentage showed rates exceeding not only the native population but also those of the foreign-born population.[19] In the predominantly rural area of the Upper Peninsula of Michigan, research by the author has shown that native-born population of foreign or mixed parentage ran well ahead of the other two nativity groups in first admissions to the regional state hospital. This is apparent in the data given in Table 49.

TABLE 49. FIRST ADMISSION RATES FOR MENTAL DISORDERS PER 100,000 POPULATION, 21 YEARS AND OVER, TO THE NEWBERRY STATE HOSPITAL, 1938–1942, BY NATIVITY AND SEX, 1940 CENSUS*

Nativity	Total	Male	Female
Native-born	40.8	44.9	36.7
Foreign-born	119.2	137.8	100.7
Native-born of foreign or mixed parentage	131.7	149.6	113 9

* Lemert, Edwin M., "An Exploratory Study of Mental Disorders in a Rural Problem Area," *Rural Sociology*, 13, March, 1948, Table III, p. 58

While the various data we have presented permit us to say that foreign birth has some association with mental disorders, they more emphatically suggest that mental deviation occurs with greater-than-anticipated frequency among *partially acculturated persons of immigrant origin.*

Another closely related differentiation of mental deviants is the high mobility they show in comparison with the general population. A study

[17] Malzberg, Benjamin, "Race and Mental Disease in New York State," *Psychiatric Quarterly*, 9, October, 1935, pp. 538–569.

[18] Dayton, *op. cit.*, pp. 109*ff*.

[19] Malzberg, Benjamin, "Mental Disease in New York State According to Nativity and Parentage," *Mental Hygiene*, 19, October, 1945, pp. 635–660.

of an earlier decade brought out the fact that Norwegians in Minnesota were admitted to mental hospitals twice as frequently as their fellow countrymen in Norway.[20] Outstate migrants to California as well as to New York State reveal first-admission rates to mental hospitals so greatly in excess of the rates of the stable residents in these states that the differences cannot be explained away entirely as functions of the vicissitudes of the process of hospitalization.[21]

While the urban rate of hospitalized mental disorders runs considerably higher than the rural, there is good reason to set this down simply as a measure of the variation in hospitalizing preferences and tendencies of the two classes of population.[22] The same reasoning applies to the recorded differences of a regional nature in the incidence of mental disorders. There is good agreement that first-admission rates to mental institutions vary on a geographic basis with the superiority of hospital facilities, their accessibility, and the reputation they have for the quality of treatment provided.[23] The high rates of first admissions in New England and the Pacific Coast states as well as in various smaller areas throughout the nation can well be laid to the numbers, size, and equipment of the hospitals available in these places.

Dependent and marginal economic status together with low-ranking occupational position have been demonstrated by a number of studies to be important differentiae of mental-hospital populations. However, these cannot be taken as entirely reflecting the economic position of the whole population of mental deviants, because of the obvious vulnerability of the impoverished groups to hospital commitment. After making allowance for this factor, there probably remains some tendency for the mentally disordered to concentrate in lower income and less prestigeful occupational groups, particularly those persons in whom the mental symptoms have existed for any length of time. This can be laid to the employment problems created by certain types of psychotic behavior.

The same reservations and conclusions about the economic status of mental deviants apply to their educational differentiation. In addition there is cause to believe that degree of education operates to retard hospitalization by reducing the visibility of mental disorders. Consequently the more highly educated persons of disordered mentality may not be comparable

[20] Odegard, O, "Emigration and Mental Health," *Mental Hygiene*, 20, October, 1936, pp. 546–553

[21] Rosanoff, A. J, L M Handy, and I. R. Plesset, "Some Neglected Phases of Immigration in Relation to Insanity," *American Journal of Psychiatry*, 72, July, 1915, pp 45–58, Malzberg, Benjamin, "Migration and Mental Disease among Negroes in New York State," *American Journal of Physical Anthropology*, 21, January–March, 1936, pp. 107–113.

[22] Landis, C, and J. Page, *Modern Society and Mental Disease*, 1938.

[23] *Patients in Mental Institutions*, 1939, U S. Department of Commerce, Bureau of the Census, p. 5.

to those of less education where the social implications of their psychoses and possibilities of institutionalization are concerned.

According to Massachusetts data, Protestants lead Catholics and Jews out of proportion to their population numbers in contributing to mental-hospital inmate populations. However, 40 per cent of the population upon which the rates in this research were based were not connected with any religious denomination when the religious census was taken. This must be taken as nullification of the religious differences, particularly between Protestants and other faiths, chiefly because the unclassified population in this census most probably contained a high percentage of peoples who were of Protestant origin.[24]

Differentiation of Mental Deviants by Type of Symptoms

At the present time all attempts to describe differential characteristics of the psychotic population by psychoses must be seriously questioned because of the inconsistency in diagnostic practices. Estimates supplied to the author by superintendents of six Middle Western hospitals fixed the proportion of cases in which inconsistent diagnoses would be reached by different hospital staffs at 10 to 15 per cent of all first admissions. In 1933 at Northhampton State Hospital in Massachusetts, 35 per cent of the first admissions to the institution were diagnosed as schizophrenic, while at the Boston State Hospital only 3 per cent fell into this classification.[25] Similar discrepancies can be uncovered in other states. One institutional staff known to the author seldom if ever employs the diagnosis of involutional melancholia, while a hospital not many miles away every year enters this diagnosis for substantial numbers of its patients.

Anyone who has ever sat in a diagnostic staff meeting of a mental hospital will appreciate the disagreements continually arising over the appropriate diagnosis for a patient and also the fortuitous factors often determining what diagnosis is finally chosen. In some hospitals the superintendent more or less arbitrarily settles such controversies; in others, a sort of supreme court procedure rules, with 5-to-4 decisions no less common than in that great tribunal. Such things as the patient's economic status, whether admission has been voluntary or not, whether a pension is at stake as in the case of war veterans – all of these as well as the special biases of staff physicians may give directional prejudice to the cumulative diagnostic picture of hospital mental cases.

Observers probably can agree on such things as the presence or absence of hallucinations, delusions, depressions, hyperactivity, and other specific psychotic symptoms. Disagreement arises chiefly in the process of grouping these symptoms together in categories and in assigning particular cases

[24] Dayton, *op. cit.*, pp 376*ff*.
[25] *Ibid.*, pp. 457*f*.

to these classes. The problem is not too different from that which perplexes physical anthropologists in classifying races. Consequently a much more promising lead may be the differentiating of mentally disordered persons according to specific symptoms. However incomplete and partial this may be, it has the virtue of converting data into forms which allow others besides the original classifier to manipulate them.

One piece of research following this plan has attempted to relate such specific psychotic symptoms as delusions, hallucinations, and paranoid ideas to the social and cultural background factors of the persons in whom they appear. A brief summary of the study, which covered records of approximately 500 adult white patients and 400 Negroes is included here.[26]

Men were more inclined to delusions of grandeur than women.

Negro men and women were similar with respect to the presence of grandiose delusions.

Negro delusions tended to be religious in nature, while those of white persons tended to revolve around financial power.

Religious delusions were more frequent among white females than white males. This difference was not so noticeable among Negroes.

Delusions concerning literary and educational aspiration were third most common among Negroes but comparatively absent among whites.

White women were more prone to paranoid delusions than white men, the reverse was true of Negroes.

Negroes exceed whites in hallucinations; women in both Negro and white groups exceed men in this respect.

Somatic delusions were equally frequent among Negro and white men, but white women exceeded all groups in the presence of this symptom.

About one-half of the Protestants had delusions with religious coloration; however only one-quarter of the delusions of Catholics centered around religious topics and not a single case with religious delusions was found among Jews.

Paranoid ideas were more frequent among the foreign-born than among natives; also grandiose and persecutory ideas occurred more often among Northern than among Southern Negroes.

Hallucinations had a higher incidence among Southern Negroes than Northern Negroes.

Lack of education was related to the presence of paranoid ideas. Where more educated persons had delusions, they were likely to be of the grandiose variety. Somatic delusions came out more in cases of patients with little education.

The Contexts of Mental Disorder

It seems gratuitous to discuss the contexts of mental disorders as we have, for example, in the case of such pathological deviations as crime and

[26] Sherman, M., and I. C. Sharman, "Psychotic Symptoms and Social Backgrounds," in *The Problem of Mental Disorder*, Committee on Psychiatric Investigations, National Research Council, 1934, Chap. XVIII.

prostitution. However, if we bear in mind the distinction between the actual symptoms of mental disorders and the role of the "insane" person as traditionally conceived by members of society, it is still possible to uncover evidence of our threefold division between symptomatic, situational, and systematic deviants. At the outset such a thing as systematic insanity seems a contradiction of terms. However, here and there cases come to attention in which there seems to be real "method in the madness" of certain persons. We have in mind instances from the past when beggars feigned insanity in order to excite sympathy and generosity, also more recent cases in the Second World War when draftees imitated the behavior of the insane, or what they thought was insanity, as a device for avoiding armed service. At one time the author sat in a staff meeting of a mental hospital in which it became increasingly apparent that the patient before the group had more or less deliberately taken on characteristic symptoms of the mental disorder for which he previously had been committed, solely in order to be readmitted to the hospital. By and large, however, such cases are rare, chiefly because of the intolerable social connotations of insanity and the rejection and isolation such a role, real or pseudo, entails in our culture. It may even be argued that to assume the role of an insane person will actually result in the development of the self-disturbances it externally symbolizes.

It is controversial whether the concept of situational mental disorders is sufficient to account for a portion of mental disorders, as is true of certain other forms of sociopathic behavior. Some psychotic symptoms indeed do appear and disappear as transitional responses to critical life situations – as with psychoses associated with pregnancy and bereavement. In many ways the symptoms summarized in the psychiatric diagnosis of "involutional melancholia" resemble a situational psychosis. Psychotic episodes sometimes appear in prisoners without previous history of psychosis. Significantly, these symptoms clear up rapidly after transfer to a mental hospital.[27] Many of the war-time neuroses give every impression of being a response to unendurable situations. Observations in various armies during the First World War concur on the relevance of situational stress to many psychiatric breakdowns. For example, in the British Expeditionary Force psychiatric casualties did not become an acute problem until July, 1916, during the terrific carnage in the Somme battle zone. With regard to the specific situational dynamics in psychiatric disorganization, different writers have independently come to an agreement that the incidence of neuroses and psychoses was relatively greater in (1) fresh troops arriving in the combat zone, (2) in battle-tested troops after prolonged trench

[27] Branon, A. Brooks, "The Social Structure of a Criminal Unit of a Psychiatric Hospital," *Journal of Clinical Psychopathology*, 9, January 1948, pp 128–135.

warfare, (3) in men over forty, especially married men, (4) in rapidly trained volunteers.[28]

Some writers have favored the idea that antecedent mental disorder or a predisposition toward mental disorder must be present where neurosis arises from external stress. Others have been receptive to the alternative hypothesis that mental disorders theoretically can be induced in any and all persons; that each person has his "breaking point." [29] A congenial formulation would be to recognize a continuous variation in mental disorders ranging from those in which the symptoms appear to have a relative autonomy of their own, to those where a dependence of symptoms upon the exigencies of situations is more obviously present. Clear-cut cases of

TABLE 50. DISTRIBUTION OF FIVE TYPES OF PSYCHOGENIC FACTORS AMONG A RECOVERED GROUP, A HIGHLY IMPROVED GROUP, AND A DETERIORATED GROUP OF SCHIZOPHRENIC PATIENTS*

Status	Total N	Strain I	External conflict situation II	Endogenous sex conflict III	Loss of rapport IV	Symbolic events V	Total psychogenic cases VI
Recovered	39	19	8	1	1	0	29
Improved	22	5	2	0	3	1	11
Deteriorated	100	1	0	4	5	6	16
Total	161	25	10	5	9	7	56

* Kant, Otto, "Psychogenic Precipitation in Schizophrenia," *Psychiatric Quarterly*, 16, April, 1942, pp. 341-350.

the latter stand out in the literature of military psychiatry, where soldiers successfully treated for combat neurosis have had a recurrence of symptoms upon discharge from the hospital to their units, the symptoms growing progressively worse as the soldiers approached the fighting lines.[30] Psychoses probably are less frequently situational phenomena than neuroses, and where they do have this appearance, they are more likely to be fleeting and superficially similar to psychoses as recognized in mental hospitals. One study of 56 hospitalized schizophrenics revealed that extraordinary psychogenic (situational) pressures had been present in only three cases.[31] Further demonstration of the point was found in the types of precipitating factors of psychosis in recovered patients in contrast with those who were marked down as "improved" or "deteriorated" (see Table 50).

28 Miller, Emanuel, *The Neuroses in War*, 1942, pp. 8–9.

29 Grinker, R. R., and J. P. Spiegel, *Men under Stress*, 1945, p. 11.

30 Miller, *op. cit.*, pp. 125*f*.

31 Kant, Otto, "Psychogenic Precipitation in Schizophrenia," *Psychiatric Quarterly*, 16, April, 1942, pp. 341–350

From the figures in the table the differences between the two extremes of "recovered" and "deteriorated" patients appear very pronounced in so far as the significance of strain and externally precipitated conflict is concerned. The closest approximation of situationally derived breakdown in which any number of the deteriorated patients played a part in these cases sprang from loss of rapport with single persons who were more or less shielding or protecting the individuals from their unrewarding environments.

Specific neurotic symptoms can be traced more directly to the contradictory demands of situations than is true of specific psychotic symptoms. Thus a student who is failing in school may develop a hysterical blindness which functions to excuse him from the chief responsibility in the situation which is distressing him. Neurotic impotency, vagisimus, and many psychomatic symptoms can also, without too much analytical skill, be perceived and understood as reactions to insupportable role requirements in certain situations. Psychotic symptoms, on the other hand, more usually defy attempts to show their functional relationship to the immediate situation. However, part of the difficulty may be the highly complex nature of the symbolism through which the psychotic person expresses his or her reactions. We usually see psychotic persons at the terminal phases of the psychotic process when the behavior is most difficult to interpret.

Social Visibility of Mental Disorders

It is important to differentiate mental deviation on the basis of the degree to which it is obvious to others. It is from the visible aspects of mental deviation that signs arise to initiate the segregative action of the members of the community and make the deviant a candidate for the status of "insane." The visibility of the mental symptoms will vary not only with their intrinsic features but also with the larger cultural and more immediate social context in which they appear. Generally in our culture an outgoing type of psychotic reaction expressed in agitation, meddling, interfering with, and attacking others more often excites comment than a silent withdrawal from social relations or apathy and fantasy. Perhaps this will be true for any social context.

A social milieu in which relationships are personal, intimate, and direct will unquestionably raise the visibility of peculiarities of the individual, regardless of whether they are made known by attack or withdrawal. From this it also follows that mental aberrancy is more perceptible to the immediate family in which the deviant resides than to the larger community.

Apart from these few generalizations it must be said that the more specific content of neurotic and psychotic symptoms in relation to specific beliefs, feelings, and practices of community residents determine the visibility of the mental deviation. For a Negro woman in an isolated rural area to claim she communicates with spirits may arouse little comment if the local populace believes in the objective reality of such phenomena. Likewise for adult white women to express great fear of mice or snakes provokes little beyond amusement in most people of our society. However, in a community where women customarily hunt and prepare small rodents and reptiles for food, patently the latter form of behavior is unusual and invidiously marks off the deviant.

Undoubtedly a large amount of neurotic and even psychotic deviation becomes hedged and so canalized in our culture as to give it a minimum visibility. It is now more and more widely accepted that much of what passes as socially acceptable physical illness has no verifiable organic foundation and must be attributed to disordered symbolic processes in the sense in which we have employed the term. Obsessional neurotic fears frequently are projected upon aspects of the environment, notable among which are the exaggerated fears some persons have developed of atomic warfare. Compulsions easily find an outlet in many forms of sport, hunting and fishing, and observer participation in baseball. Compulsive cleanliness and orderliness escape general attention when framed within a background of a germ-conscious and technologically mediated culture such as our own.

Efforts to find instances in which psychotic symptoms like hallucinations, maniacal flights of activity, and delusions are compressed into socially tolerable ways are less rewarding. However, in contrast, paranoid delusions of grandeur and persecution, even in extreme forms, are often quite similar to normal symbolic reactions in our competitive culture. Court litigation and politics are areas of our culture in which psychotic symptoms and normal symbolic reactions merge in common overt form. Highly integrated delusions of the sort described by psychiatrists as "true paranoia" seldom are reacted to as insanity in a community setting. In any event very few cases of this type of paranoia find their way into our mental hospitals.

The Societal Reaction

Current popular notions of mental disorders generally cluster about the supposed physical appearance of the mental deviant, the conduct of the personnel of mental hospitals, and the assumed causes of mental disorders. While there are still people who believe that mental patients are chained in dungeons in hospitals, ignorance rather than the primitive myth once widespread best describes the state of public opinion on these subjects today. Most people entertain a stereotype of the mentally disordered as hyperactive persons, unkempt, noisy, wild-eyed, and homicidally impelled, ever on the alert to escape their keepers and do damage to life and property in the surrounding community. The lighter side of the stereotype construes the mental deviant as a pixylike creature who is totally unpredictable but nonetheless charming and interesting. Another conception allied with this pays some inverted deference to the mentally disordered by dwelling upon the connection between genius and mental disorder. Insanity is thus held to have social value, somehow causing some deviants of this sort to make great contributions to their cultures. A common thread joining all these concepts, however, is the belief that these deviants can never be trusted to carry burdens of responsibility in so far as everyday life goes.

Mental hospitals in the minds of naive laymen loom as distant, prisonlike places where cruelty to patients theoretically is not permitted but which "everyone knows" is practiced, where doctors may not be above "railroading" patients and keeping them incarcerated against their wills. As part of this mythology many persons impute insidious or nefarious character traits to psychiatrists, assigning them quasi-mystical powers which enable them to "look at you and know what you are thinking without being told."

When the informed person stops to think about the cause of mental disturbances, he usually falls back upon such explanations as "overwork," shock, injury, or heredity. Implicit in much public thinking about the heredity of mental aberrancy is the familiar idea we have already run across in the public attitudes toward the physically handicapped, namely, that "sins of the father are handed down to the sons." Since about 1910 in this country the conception of mental deviation as a form of disease or ill health has diffused among professional persons directly charged with the treatment of the mentally disordered. There have been large-scale national campaigns to popularize this medical formulation. Despite these efforts at public reeducation, there can be little doubt but that the older connotations of insanity persist and that the various synonyms for mental disorder, scientific and otherwise, continue to be used as invidious terms by the great mass of Americans. The decline of the older moralistic evaluations of deviant human behavior has been more nominal than real. The ethical and moral overtones of concepts such as "constitutional inferior," "psychopathic," and "neurotic" or "psychotic" are ubiquitous.

Tolerances for Mental Disorders

It would probably be the consensus of most trained observers of mental disorders that psychotic deviation as described in formal psychiatric categories is not in itself the reason for collective action to bring mentally disturbed persons under restraint. Rather it is the highly visible deviations of the psychotic person from the norms of his group, placing strain upon other persons, which excite his family or the community and cause them to take formal, legal action against him. Many instances can be uncovered in which the psychotic symptoms of a deviant are socially benign, and he is tolerated in the community as a harmless eccentric providing some amusement and a source of gossip for others. One celebrated case of this sort was the "Emperor" Norton who lived in San Francisco in the middle of the nineteenth century under the delusion that he had been chosen emperor of the United States by the California legislature. The county board of supervisors on one occasion appropriated money for his uniform; he customarily ate without paying in the city's cafés, issued 50-cent bonds, and drew checks on local banks which invariably were honored by bankers and merchants.[32]

It may be that certain forms of psychotic behavior such as the speeded-up, meddlesome, and sometimes suicidal attempts of persons going through maniacal episodes will be penalized to some extent in almost any cultural milieu. Contrariwise, withdrawal and seclusive psychotic reactions may find wider receptivity in cultures of the world. A much more significant fact, however, is that definite recognition, definition, and treatment of psychotic symptoms as abnormal or insane vary in contradictory ways from culture to culture. Many of the behavior manifestations we deem psychotic are regarded as normal in other societies, or even looked upon as the prerequisites of candidacy for roles of prestige and power. For example, the extreme suspiciousness, ideas of reference, and delusions of grandeur and persecution which American psychiatrists define as "paranoia" come well within the limits of normal behavior among the Northwest Pacific Coast Indians.[33]

Hallucinations have at other times and in other societies been held to be the voices of spirits or gods inspiring their mortal communicants, rather than evidence of undesirable abnormality. Among the Indians of the American plains, a young man at the time of entry into a warrior's status normally sought to have a vision by a ritual of self-imposed isolation, starvation and self-torture. It is interesting to note the case of a Winnebago chief whose history of maladjustment seemed to arise out of his *inability* to have such a vision and his subsequent guilt over lying to tribal members to cover up this deficiency.[34]

However, broad generalizations such as these about the relevance of certain psychotic symptoms to the general qualities of a culture are of less value to us than a detailed knowledge of how they relate themselves

[32] Asbury, Herbert, *The Barbary Coast*, 1947, pp 218f

[33] Benedict, Ruth, *Patterns of Culture*, 1946, pp. 235ff

[34] Radin, Paul, *Crashing Thunder, The Autobiography of a Winnebago Chief*, 1920

to role demands and social expectancies based upon age, sex, marital status, occupation, ethnic and locality group affiliations. It is necessary to know the consequences of psychotic symptoms in a given social setting in order to understand the reactions of others to the deviant. For example, extreme apathy and daydreaming in one worker may result in the loss of his job; in another worker the fact that he is under close supervision and performing a mechanical routine may mean that these symptoms do not count so much against him, and he can manage to carry on as a family provider. Collective action on the part of a family, neighborhood, or community to hospitalize a mentally disordered person will always be an interactional product of the degree of stressful deviation and the tolerance of the group for the behavior. The critical point in the tolerance quotient at which institutionalization comes about may reflect limited psychotic variation in relation to limited group tolerance; or, on the other hand, it may be a measure of high group receptivity, where commitment to a mental hospital follows only after long and exhausting provocation by the psychotic individual.

If first-admission rates to mental hospitals are taken as a measure of familial and community tolerance as well as a measure of the incidence of psychotic behavior, then a research problem is presented to discover ways of assigning values to the two general variables involved. This means that some new devices will be needed for computing the incidence of psychotic persons in the community and it also means that indexes will be required to measure the tolerances for psychotic deviation shown by groups in various geographic areas and social strata. One suggestion has been to employ the degree to which direct, face-to-face, and personal interaction characterizes social contexts in which psychotic persons live as an index of the area tolerance.[35] Whether this or some indexes of urbanization will suffice as adequate measures of these tolerance differentials can only be settled by empirical research. We suspect, however, that other significant factors may enter into area tolerances for mental disorders. For example, we have already seen how the mere physical proximity of a mental hospital seems to raise first-admission rates for mental disorders in some areas. The nearness of the hospital becomes an important concern to relatives. They are much more likely to hospitalize their family members if they can visit them regularly, but refrain where they must be sent hundreds of miles away.

Such areal phenomena as the percentage of a given population living in family groups, the type of housing in an area, and physical characteristics of the neighborhood all become conditioners of tolerance differentials.

[35] Owens, M. B., "Alternative Hypotheses for the Explanation of Some of Faris' and Dunham's Results," *American Journal of Sociology*, 47, July, 1941, pp. 49*f*.

Age, sex, and marital status of psychotic deviants, as well as the presence or absence of children in families where they live, are likewise expressed in the hospitalizing tendencies in an area. The social expression of the psychotic impulses, interacting with these factors all are implicit in the hospitalization process.

A study of hospitalization of mental cases in Peiping, China, casts helpful light upon the relation of some of the factors we have mentioned. There a sample study of first admissions to a psychopathic hospital revealed that 40.64 per cent of all cases were committed by police action; 36.5 per cent of the cases were placed in the hospital by families, relatives, or community agencies; and, finally, 22.86 per cent of the patients in the study had been sent to the hospital by families, relatives, and community agencies through their referral to the police. Family cases, on the whole, tended to fall into a younger, narrower age range than police cases. It was also true that women were less frequently dispatched to the hospital by the police than by their families (33.3 per cent versus 66.62 per cent). Finally it came out that police cases had a higher percentage of laborers, soldiers, and police themselves, whereas family cases included relatively more housewives, governmental employees, clerical workers, and students. The comparative frequencies of different classes of symptoms in the family and police cases can be studied in Table 51:

TABLE 51. TYPE OF SYMPTOMS LEADING TO HOSPITALIZATION OF 342 MENTAL PATIENTS BY FAMILIES AND BY POLICE, PEKING, OCT. 1, 1934, TO OCT 31, 1935*

Behavior	Family cases		Police cases	
	Number	Per cent	Number	Per cent
Attacks on others	312	29.40	116	35 91
Delusions	187	18.20	25	7 73
Hallucinations	29	2 70	4	1.23
Confusion	56	5 31	55	17 02
Restlessness	173	16 33	33	10 21
Apathy and negativism	44	4.19	22	6 80
Physical complaints	144	13 60	22	6.80
Spasmophilic tendency	38	4.00	6	1 85
Suicidal attempts	27	2 55	33	10 21
Not classified...	7	0.66		
Total number of symptoms	1,049	100 00	323	100 00

* Hsu, Francis L. K., "Police Cooperation in Connection with Mental Cases in Peiping," in *Neuropsychiatry in China*, edited by R. S. Lyman, V. Maeker, and P. Liang, pp. 203*ff*., 1939, Table 3, p. 209.

It is plain to be seen in this table that delusions, restlessness, and physical complaints were more likely to lead families to place relatives in a hospital, while police were more impressed – as we might expect – with attacks upon others, confusion (wandering), and suicidal attempts, when they took action to hospitalize psychotic persons coming to their attention.

Another factor which often becomes injected into the hospitalizing process – a factor whose weight is exceedingly difficult to determine – is the power differential between family factions and between various community groups. Not infrequently conflicts arise over such matters as divorce, custody of children, wills, control of property, automobile accidents, and crimes in which cleavages of persons and groups increase or diminish the sensitivity and tolerance of family and community to psychotic aberrations of the person involved. In many such cases the psychotic person becomes more or less the symbol of a patterned social conflict. Persons who otherwise would be hospitalized stay at large, or persons who might be carried along without too much trouble by the community or their families are nevertheless hospitalized. However, recognition of these facts is not to say that persons are "railroaded" into mental hospitals; this rarely, if ever, happens.

In the following abridged case history, from the report of a community investigation by the author, we see in time perspective the way in which minor changes in behavior, changing tolerance associated with maturation of the deviant, and the modified structure of the neighborhood and the deviant's family interacted with culture conflict to bring about his hospitalization:[36]

S was a boy of eighteen, a member of an isolated Polish family living in a sparsely populated township in a Middle Western state. Most of his life he was mentally retarded, this being explained by the mother as the result of an accidental head injury at an early age. Neighbors generally thought the boy queer but not particularly dangerous. A nearby nurseryman gave him occasional work, which he was able to carry on under the close supervision of his brother.

A pronounced ingroup-outgroup cleavage existed between a group of the neighbors and the boy's family, hostility being directed at the whole family group instead of any one of its members. Attention of the investigator was called to such things as the father's terriffic temper and beating of the boys and to the mother's refusal to talk to people and her habit of gathering pebbles along the road. Credence was given stories that the family did not eat together at a table in their home, supported in part by the uncouth manners of the boys when they ate in neighbors' homes. Hostility grew out of the feeling of S's brother that they were exploited by farmers for whom they worked; ultimately they refused such work. Many farmers termed them "lazy."

When S reached eighteen, his brother got a job in a nearby town, and the work of S became less dependable. He was rejected for military service as mentally deficient. One day he was in the company of a group of boys in front

[36] Lemert, Edwin M., "Legal Commitment and Social Control," *Sociology and Social Research*, 30, May–June, 1946, pp 375*ff*.

of a ramshackle old house owned by a senile man who lived in a lean-to affixed to the rear. This man was considered by many neighbors to be more peculiar than the boy. He had been something of a nuisance to the Polish family. The boys made joking threats to hurl stones through the sagging, half-broken windows of the house. S went farther and actually threw the stones, making wild threats to "blow the house into the sky with dynamite."

The boy was taken into custody on complaint by the old man. In the course of an examination it was revealed that the boy habitually engaged in autoerotic practices. On this discovery a woman recently moved into the neighborhood became much concerned for the safety of her daughters. The sheriff also was much impressed by this fact. Over strong resistance of the mother and later of the father, the boy was committed to the state hospital for the insane, where a psychiatrist tentatively diagnosed him as schizophrenic. When the father carried his complaint to the governor of the state, there was a tendency for some of the staff to consider him demented.

Changing Reactions to Mental Disorders

The history of mental disorders and their treatment in our society leaves us with no incontestable proof that the present-day incidence of these disorders is much greater than in the past, despite the impression created by rapidly growing hospital populations. If due allowance is made for population expansion, there has been little significant increase in first-admission rates to hospitals for mentally disordered persons since the turn of the century, save for those in the age groups sixty years of age and over. Even for these age groups the rise in first-admission rates is best interpreted as a function of lowered family tolerance for the physical disabilities and dementias of old age rather than as a real increase in their incidence.[37] Generally the urbanization of our society, the constriction of housing facilities, the dangers of public transportation, the financial burdens which dependent family members entail, together with a shift in conceptions of family responsibilities have all merged as influences to make hospitalization of the aged much more common than it once was.

As we glance back beyond 1900 in this country, little in the way of trustworthy statistical records can be consulted to tell us whether mental disorders in early colonial populations and those of the agrarian frontier populations in the early nineteenth century were relatively less common than today. However, evidence that mental deviants did complicate family and community life in these earlier periods is abundant. Until the end of the seventeenth century the colonial folk theory of mental disorders was simply a variety of primitive belief in demoniacal possession. The scourge, the stock, pillory, and burning at the stake were the usual

[37] Landis and Page, *op. cit.*, Chap. XII; Winston, E., "The Assumed Increase of Mental Disease," *American Journal of Sociology*, 41, January, 1935, pp 427–439.

lot of the person who developed symptoms of mental disorder. By the end of the century, the belief in evil spirits and demonology had declined rapidly in favor of naturalistic theories of mental disorder. However, it could hardly be claimed that demented persons were much better off as a consequence.

During the eighteenth century propertied families usually cared for deranged relatives in their own homes, in special strong rooms, cellars, or in attics fitted with chains for demented kin who were prone to violence. As much as possible mentally deviant relatives were hidden away from view so that the family "disgrace" might not be noised abroad. They received such medical care as was available for their special disability, which often was as fantastic as it was crude. Among the poorer classes the plight of the insane was far less enviable. If they were harmless, they might be treated as paupers, being placed in the county poorhouse with the rest of the community dependents. If combative, they were thrown into jails or dungeons with criminals. The roughness of pioneer life on the frontier meant that when lower class families chose to shelter their insane relatives, it was likely to be in a barn, a chicken coop, or outhouse of some kind. Lying behind such treatment was the prevailing and seldom questioned conception of the insane as being like "wild animals," insensitive to heat and cold and to all things human.[38]

While a hospital exclusively for the insane was organized as early as 1769 in Williamsburg, Virginia, no considerable number of mental institutions was built until the period following 1833. At this time crusades led by a middle-aged schoolteacher of a single-purposed idealism, Dorothea Lynd Dix, and others induced legislatures in state after state to appropriate money for the construction of mental hospitals. A powerful factor facilitating this charitable movement was the myth or cult of the curability of the mentally disordered widely diffused at the time. This peculiar expression of American optimism reached such proportions that it was fully believed by various authorities on the subject that 90 per cent of all mental disorders could be completely "cured." The ideal of the early mental hospital consequently came to be entirely that of therapy and rapid turnover so that patients could be promptly returned as functioning citizens to their families and communities. The incurable cases were to be returned to local community hospitals or to custody of their families.

By 1850 the myth of curability had been pretty well punctured and was beginning to be replaced by an alternate myth of the incurability of insanity. However, mental hospitals continued to be swamped with incoming patients, and pressures built up apace for the state to take on full responsibility for the custodial care of chronic mental cases as well as for

[38] Deutsch, Albert, *The Mentally Ill in America*, 1949, rev. ed., pp. 39*ff*.

treatment of the more acutely disordered. In a way this was part of the whole tendency to centralize in state governments the care and responsibility for special sociopathic groups – the deaf, blind, mentally deficient, epileptic, and dependent children, as well as those classed as insane. It is not hard to perceive the relationship between these movements of reform and reorganization and the industrialization and urbanization of our society which began to accelerate in the mid-nineteenth century. In addition to the less stable humanitarian impetus behind these changes of public policies toward the mentally deranged could be detected the growing power of business groups and their hardheaded interest in reducing the costs of government and raising the efficiency of state bureaucracy.[39]

The Mental-hygiene Movement

The early years of the twentieth-century stand in sharp historical relief as an era of protean reform movements spawned by the asymmetrical change and conflicts in American culture. Among the many targets for reformers and their organizations, the antiquated policies and administration of mental hospitals commanded a place no less important than physical illness, political corruption, crime, and prostitution. Sparked by the restless drive of an ex mental patient, Clifford Beers, and dramatized by his book, *The Mind That Found Itself*, an early twentieth-century reform movement was launched in the name of "mental hygiene," designed to fulfill a number of ambitious objectives. To implement these goals, the National Association of Mental Hygiene was formed in 1908, followed subsequently by the organization of state and local associations.

The objectives of the mental-hygiene movement can be listed as follows:

1. The improvement of facilities for custodial care and treatment in mental hospitals.
2. The promotion of research on mental disorders.
3. The dissemination by means of existing education knowledge concerning the causes, treatment, and prevention of the mentally ill.

The chief emphasis of the mental-hygiene movement was laid upon the *prevention* of mental *disease*, by implication and explicit admission, through a process similar to the prevention of physical disease. The assumptions adopted by leaders of the movement were that through a hygiene of the mind, through self-discipline, and training of the thought and emotions of the individual, mental *disease* could be avoided.

It has now been thirty-one years since the inception of the mental-hygiene movement – time sufficient for the birth and maturation of a whole generation of Americans – but we are without clear demonstration

[39] *Ibid.*, Chap. XII

that it has made any appreciable inroads upon the mentally disordered population. The suspicion is a strong one that this movement is a contemporary manifestation of values in our culture which, if not part of the process producing mental disorders, at least conspire to defeat efforts at scientific understanding and complete rehabilitation of mentally deranged persons. Careful analysis of the mental-hygiene movement has disclosed its close kinship to the "Protestant ethic" of our culture – the intensely competitive, individualistic ethos which composes the transcending values of our social life. It has been shown that, behind a façade of scientific terminology and high resolve, the social philosophy of this movement incorporates the middle-class Puritan conviction that, as in the case of alcoholism, drug addiction, and sexual delinquency, some sort of character defect is present in the mental deviant. From this it follows that what is needed by the mentally disordered person is a restoration of initiative and ambition by an intellectual manipulation of the will. The whole approach to the phenomena of mental disorders is psychologistic in that human behavior is assumed to be understandable in terms of individuals abstracted from their society.[40]

We are less interested here in evaluating the effectiveness of the mental-hygiene movement than in estimating and describing the symbolic attributes of its associated propaganda and organized activities. These interests lead us to inquire pointedly whether it has really modified public attitudes toward mental disorders and the stereotypes of the insane, and if so, in what ways. We are disposed to the answer that, in so far as our culture is concerned, this movement represents a pouring of old wine into new bottles, a perpetuating of the invidious distinctions between those who have self-control and those in whom self-control has decayed. While the introduction of the concept of mental *disease* and mental *illness* is an effort to escape the traditional stigma of insanity, it must be recognized that the older evil connotations can and still do attach themselves to the concept of mental disease. Even if we grant gains from the introduction of this idea, it will be apparent from later discussion that the disease conception of what we have preferred to call "symbolic deviation" can create a whole series of conflicts over self and social acceptance.

A very practical consideration here is the rationale chosen for the agencies such as the juvenile court, child-guidance clinics, mental-hygiene clinics, and visiting-teacher programs which in whole or in part owe their creation to the mental-hygiene philosophy. In the early history of several of these agencies it is significant to note that they were set up and organized to *prevent* delinquency or to *prevent* mental disorder. Their pro-

40 Davis, Kingsley, "Mental Hygiene and Class Structure," *Psychiatry*, 1, February, 1938, pp. 55–65.

grams have rested upon the notion that there are recognizable predelinquent and prepsychotic behaviors or personalities. The notion, we believe, is an ill-considered one. Not only is it contradictory to any hypothesis deducible from our theoretical scheme, but, as we shall show later, it is empirically unfounded. Furthermore, this idea, to the extent that it is implemented, may well function in the dynamics of mental disorder itself. The symbolic potentialities of exposing a nondelinquent or nonpsychotic person to "treatment" calculated to forestall what is regarded as emergent sociopathic behavior plainly include the possibility of definition of self and role in terms of this same behavior.

Exploitation

Exploitation of neurotic and psychotic deviants has received small attention, perhaps because of the more newsworthiness of their neglect and maltreatment, real or alleged, in mental hospitals. Systematic exploitation occurs in larger communities at the hands of so-called "quacks," "spiritual advisors," "counselors," self-styled "analysts" and "psychologists." Aside from the pecuniary losses involved, it is difficult to state authoritatively what the effects of contacts with such fraudulent consultants are upon their clients. Qualified practitioners in the field probably exaggerate the damage done by such charlatans. Most of the "harm" probably is the malrepute such persons cast upon bona fide psychiatrists and psychologists. Otherwise they are agents in social experiences in which emotionally distressed persons bare intimate aspects of their lives without receiving tangible help and aid. In our culture each such exposure tends to be a confession of weakness, and the accumulation of such experiences can easily become a history of progressive personal failure and social isolation.

Not a few physicians will give expensive medical treatment to persons who are patently psychoneurotic and in need of psychiatric help. Some of the more candid doctors rationalize this on the grounds that if they do not take the person's fee, some other doctor will. A certain class of physicians, known vaguely as "society doctors," have built up lucrative practices by catering to the symptomatic fears of neurotic female patients. Lawyers may not be too scrupulous about the rights of the mental deviant where large fees are at stake. The stories of Ephraim Tutt, by Alfred Maine, tell us of certain law firms in New York which, with the connivance of psychiatrists, specialized in breaking wills of aged persons by twisting their senile peculiarities into proof of mental incompetence.

Stories and rumors circulate at times about the exploitation of mental patients in private sanatoriums and proprietorial hospitals. However, about all that we can be sure of is that such institutions do frequently charge exorbitant rates and perhaps, in order to keep them longer, the staffs tend to give more favorable prognoses to wealthy patients than is justified. In public mental hospitals it is known that superintendents often are loath to discharge patients who are good workers because of lack of personnel and because of the difficulty of replacing them. Outside of the hospital, discharged patients commonly meet exploitation from employers who hire them for dirty, unpleasant, and poorly paying jobs.

Control Agencies

At one time in our colonial past, commitment of a mentally unbalanced person was a highly informal and socially uneventful process. The desire or acquiescence of relatives or a statement from a physician sufficed in most cases to remove the subject from the community. Then, in the 1860's, the myth grew large that sane persons were frequently incarcerated in mental hospitals or held there against their will by the connivance and conspiracy of relatives or evil superintendents. High-lighted by several sensational novels and exposés of cases of this sort, a move was set afoot to erect legal safeguards for mental patients. Ultimately some states went to the lengths of requiring a jury trial for every person before he could be committed as insane, and at least one state, California, still has such a law. On the whole, psychiatrists oppose such procedures as being traumatic and harmful to patients and their relatives. Many relatives prefer to keep their psychotic relatives at home rather than go through such an ordeal. One observer of the period when jury trials were more widely used contended that more sane persons were committed by juries than by the staffs of mental hospitals.[41]

Today most states have simplified their commitment procedures by requiring a petition signed by one or more qualified medical examiners as the legal requisite for hospitalization, with the proviso that a jury trial must be held if demanded. Liberalization of commitment laws has also come about in the form of voluntary commitment procedures in a number of states. Despite the early and continuing dissatisfaction with many of these laws, in our culture it was inevitable that protection of civil rights of mental patients would be framed into law, considering the fact that very substantial strictures upon the legal status of the mentally deranged person are imposed with his formal designation as insane.

In so far as commitment procedure becomes a public spectacle, it symbolizes for the psychotic person as well as for others the painful fact of his social irresponsibility, the loss of free movement in the environment,

[41] Dewey, Richard, "The Jury Law for Commitment of the Insane in Illinois," *American Journal of Insanity*, 69, January, 1913, pp. 579–584.

and loss of control over the self as represented in the use and management of physical property. In rural jurisdictions in some states the symbols of irresponsibility are strengthened and given criminal implications by the practice of holding mental charges in jail pending the completion of sanity hearings or proceedings. However much the mental deviant may be shielded from traumatic symbolization of his status at this stage of commitment proceedings, his insane status must ultimately be communicated. The symbols of irresponsibility and restraint which may be only adumbrated in some jurisdictions later become inescapable aspects of the hospital environment into which the insane person is projected.

The Social Structure of the Mental Hospital

Our comments on the mental hospital will be directed almost entirely to the state hospital. There are, of course, other types of mental hospitals such as Veterans' Administration hospitals, private or proprietorial sanatoriums, city and county hospitals. These vary considerably from one another, and together they differ from the pattern of the state mental hospital. However, a glance at the size of the resident populations of the different categories of mental hospitals is sufficient to convince us that only a small and insignificant proportion of the mentally disordered population is cared for in nonstate hospitals. In 1946 the percentage of resident mental patients in private hospitals was 2.2; for city and county institutions this percentage was 4.3; and for Veterans' Administration hospitals it was 9.2. The remaining 84.1 per cent of the nation's mental cases resided in state hospitals.[42]

The most significant fact about state mental hospitals is their large size. As far back as 1931 the average size of state mental hospitals was 1,589 patients.[43] Since that time the constantly growing masses of mental patients have been accommodated primarily through expansion of the size of the hospitals in existence. Building new hospitals has not been resorted to where the other expedient could serve. Many of the newer hospitals have been planned for very large patient populations. An average size of 2,000 or 2,500 patients probably would not misrepresent the situation for mental hospitals today. Some states have no hospitals smaller than 2,500 beds. Four out of California's seven mental hospitals house more than 4,000 patients. New York State has jumbo hospital plants running up to 8,000 and 9,000 patients.

Much publicity has been given to the deteriorated quality of the buildings of state mental hospitals and to such things as overcrowding, under-

[42] *Patients in Mental Institutions*, 1946, p. 11.

[43] Grimes, J., *Institutional Care of Mental Patients in the United States*, 1934, p. 17.

staffing, poor food, and lack of sleeping quarters for inmates. While these things are undeniably important, we are here more interested in the sociological characteristics of the hospital environment.[44] The sociocultural prototype of the mental hospital has a history reaching back into medieval times. Originally conceived as a retreat and an asylum for religious purposes, the contemporary mental hospital has perpetuated this ancient separation and isolation from the larger society, albeit on other grounds. In the United States many state hospitals originally were located in rural areas and in small towns in order to be able to purchase large tracts of land and make the institutions partially self-sustaining through agriculture. While the spatial isolation of the mental hospital is no longer so apparent, the social isolation continues, conserved by the stigma and disgrace felt by relatives of mentally disordered persons and by the fact that the state formally segregates mental cases in its commitment procedure in order to protect the community from their threat.

Political factors are also of great importance in preserving the social isolation of the mental institution. The practice of making state, and to some extent Federal, hospitals public "whipping boys" for publicity-hungry politicians and targets for sensational newspaper campaigns, as in the case of prisons, further attenuates the direct contacts the hospital has with the community. Superintendents grow hypersensitive and fearful of political aggressions, which leads them to prefer anonymity and seclusion for themselves, their staff, and their patients. Premiums are placed upon institutional loyalties and routine to the exclusion of flexibility and experimental adaptation.

The failure of our society to achieve balance between flexibility and rigidity in its bureaucratic structures is no less striking in the administration of public mental hospitals than in other governmental agencies. Here, as in other areas of public administration, bureaucratic rigidity begets public dissatisfaction and disruptive investigations, which in turn beget more bureaucratic rigidity. Political forays have taken a heavy toll in the form of demoralization of hospital staffs and sharp rises in the turnover of personnel, which at times has reached as high as 100 per cent

[44] Whether the observations we make here are representative of state hospitals as a whole or whether they picture a theoretically "worst hospital" is a moot point. We have made use of several observational studies by sociologists who have tried to see the mental hospital in terms of social structure and interactional processes. The author has had the opportunity in a professional capacity to become thoroughly familiar with one state mental hospital which probably would be rated as "above average" in so far as its physical plant and equipment are concerned. He has observed several other Middle Western mental hospitals somewhat less intensively. Upon the basis of these observations and the cited studies he has been far more impressed by the homogeneity in the social structure and processes in state mental hospitals than by the variations and dispersions

in some hospitals.[45] Nor has the installation of civil service systems in many states increased the receptiveness of hospital administrators to changing methods and new ideas, nor has it done away with political interference with their administration.[46]

In a climate of political insecurity, with a mediocre-to-poor staff constantly going and coming, with authority-minded, medically trained psychiatrists in charge, the totalitarian pattern of the ancient hospital is conserved despite the more democratic trends beginning to be manifest in the treatment of sociopathic deviants by social workers and clinicians in many welfare agencies. The person adjudged insane and subsequently hospitalized moves from a society of freedom and choice into a more or less self-contained miniature society of constraint, where nearly every area of choice is preempted from above.[47] Withdrawal symptoms are correspondingly great, mitigated only by the preexisting deterioration of the patients at the time of entrance into the hospital world.

At the top of the social hierarchy of the hospital control system are the administrative officers, below whom in their respective order come supervisors of special departments, social workers, educational workers, and occupational therapists, nurses, office workers, maintenance employees, and finally at the lowest echelon, the attendant group. Frequently the protocol of interaction between these status groups is no less strict than that found in a formalized caste system. The various groups have behavior systems of their own and are ingrouped in terms of their own functions, institutionally integrated through formal organization and a defensive morale born of the ubiquitous threat of outside political attack. From the top of the hierarchy down, personnel is differentiated by security-oriented temperament. Below the upper levels the staff population for the most part is further differentiated by being unmarried. Even when staff members at these lower levels are married, their lives are singularly devoid of family life as it is known outside the hospital.[48] Social selection and formative pressures of the immediate environment produce a special class of societal surrogates who are composed primarily of conformity-conscious individuals and at the same time social isolants to whom family life is neither possible nor desirable.

[45] Jaffary, S. K., *The Mentally Ill and Public Provision for Their Care in Illinois*, 1942, p 29.

[46] Deutsch, Albert, *The Shame of States*, 1948, Chap XVII

[47] Rowland, Howard, "Interaction Processes in a State Hospital," *Psychiatry*, 1, August, 1938, pp. 323–338, Rowland, Howard, "Friendship Patterns in the State Mental Hospital," *Psychiatry*, 2, August, 1939, pp. 363–373; Devereaux, George, "The Social Structure of a Schizophrenic Ward," *Journal of Clinical Psychopathology*, 6, October, 1944, pp. 231–265, Sprague, G., "The Role of The Psychiatric Hospital," *Mental Hygiene*, 21, October, 1937, pp. 69–78.

[48] Rowland, "Friendship Patterns in the State Mental Hospital," p. 368.

If we disregard the maintenance employees, it is apparent that the amount of direct, interpersonal, and continuous interaction between staff and patients is in a rough way inversely correlated with the status of the former in the social hierarchy. Significantly enough, the immediate authority in the life of the patients rests with the ward attendants, the lowest paid, least respected group in the hierarchy. These members of the hospital community are recruited from our marginal working class, "floaters," recent immigrants, ex-convicts, ex-alcoholics, ex mental patients, and professional "bughousers" who periodically migrate from one mental hospital to another throughout the country.[49] Supervision of the attendants is very formalized, especially in larger hospitals. Beyond holding them responsible for general equanimity of their wards and visible accidents to patients, the administrative staff leaves them to handle the patients according to the dictates of a coercive behavior system which has evolved autonomously over centuries.

The supervening elements in patient-staff interaction in the mental hospital are restraint and punishment. These are unmistakably present in attendant attitude and behavior. They also are strongly suggested if not fully symbolized by most of the things termed "therapy," no matter how they are formally interpreted. Such measures as continuous baths, wet packs (encasing patients in tightly wrapped wet sheets), sterilizing operations, shock treatment, and prefrontal lobotomies are generally looked upon as punishments and coercive devices within the hospital. Some hospital authorities frankly admit that the roughly induced paroxysms of shock treatment and the surgical incision of the cerebrum are expedients to make intractable patients more responsive to hospital routine. Certainly many patients regard them in this light. Transfers from one ward to another and solitary confinement undoubtedly are interpreted by most patients and staff in the light of an institutional system of rewards-punishment symbols. All of these procedures function in a configuration of the compulsory presence of the patient in a physical environment of locked doors and barred windows, where the possession of keys marks off the coercing class from those held in restraint.

Segregation of patients within the mental hospital tends to be upon the basis of the special custodial problems they present rather than according to their diagnosis. Thus, disturbed patients are placed with other disturbed patients, and those with suicidal tendencies are kept together in wards where a higher standard of custodial vigilance is maintained. Wards in time get to be known informally as "untidy," "runaway," "wetters," or "going-home" wards, each with special implications for the status and aspirations of the patients. Within the wards patients group themselves

[49] *Ibid.*, p. 370

roughly in line with the levels of insight and self-control they possess.[50] The closer patients are to discharge, such as having status in a "parole" ward, the greater is the tendency for groupings on the basis of precommitment interests and prior social background to appear. So-called "institutional cures" and alcoholics rank highest among all patient groups, as tokened by the privileges granted them and the confidence reposed in them by the staff.

At the lower level of deteriorated patients, little in the way of social interaction can be detected. The diagnostic class of catatonics ordinarily display little interest in the social environment except in response to rhythmic suggestion and mass stimulation. Despite this fact, they are recipients of special attention in most hospitals owing to the belief in their curability and the sense of reward which comes to the staff member who succeeds in making them talk. The relatively high rate of recoveries for catatonics, observable even before the days of shock treatment, may be in part a function of the differential stimulation received by them from the nursing and attendant staff.

Treatment of the Mentally Disordered

Because of the high patient-psychiatrist ratios in most of our public mental hospitals, few patients are subjected to intensive therapy. In cases where they are singled out for psychotherapy, the techniques by and large are directive and authoritative – even repressive. Psychiatrists often gauge recoveries by the disappearance of the symptoms they define as "psychotic." Not infrequently this leads patients to disguise or cover up their delusions and hallucinations in everlasting hopes of "going home." The directive therapy applied by many psychiatrists, out of institutions as well as within, generally has the effect of building up a pattern of dependence upon the therapist. In effect, the patient is pressured to renounce his power of self-resolution, which in the institution, as we have already seen, is already hampered and hedged in most areas of his behavior. Psychoanalytic therapy is more characteristically authoritative than the empirical or eclectical techniques of less sectarian or less "school"-conscious psychiatrists. Criticism and resistance to the use of psychoanalytic methods have accumulated in recent years among certain clinicians and social workers who have objected to the cloying dependence of the patient or client upon the therapist and to the long, drawn-out process of therapy, which lasts for years in some cases. These critics have also pointed out that psychoanalytic theorists and practitioners have never solved the problem of reestablishment of independence of the patient and responsibility for the self which inevitably arises at the termination of

[50] *Ibid*, p. 327, Banon, *op cit*, p 355

psychoanalysis. Success in the analytic process frequently is confined to the relationship with the clinician alone and rarely does it carry over into other roles. Empirical demonstration of the effectiveness of psychoanalytic methods has yet to be convincingly made.[51]

Somewhere between 35 and 40 per cent of hospitalized psychotics "recover" sufficiently to be discharged and remain outside of the hospital.[52] Nevertheless, there is no way of knowing whether these remissions are the consequence of hospitalization, whether they occur in spite of hospitalization, or whether they would have come about without hospitalization. Until we have control groups of nonhospitalized psychotics with which to make comparisons, such questions must be left unanswered. Some exception to this general conclusion has to be made in the case of malarial treatment of paretics, which has proven efficacy in ameliorating and permitting discharge of patients who otherwise would languish and die in the hospital. Various convulsive therapies, insulin, metrozol, and electric-shock treatment also give promising results, with improvement and cures ranging from 16 to 65 per cent of cases so treated, with an average running 5 to 10 per cent above remission rates obtained previously. However, there has been a tendency to exaggerate the results secured by shock treatment and to gloss over relapses which come with time.[53] Furthermore, it has been noticed that shock treatment seems to make some patients worse.

Shock treatment is almost purely empirical in the sense that knowledge of the process by which it brings improvement is absent. Some physicians have looked upon this form of treatment as evidence for organic causation of the functional mental disorders, which has led them to prescribe shock treatments as they would medicine or drug specifics. Some military hospitals at one time even standardized a course of treatments. Cases are on record in which two or three hundred such convulsions have been administered to patients. Other psychiatrists perceive the sociopsychological function of such induced trauma and apply the shocks in order to break down the "autistic barrier" in the patient and render him accessible to psychotherapy.

Other forms of treatment in an experimental stage, such as group psychotherapy and psychodrama, are signs of a trend away from interindividual psychotherapy, a trend more in keeping with the practicalities of

[51] Sears, R., "Survey of Objective Studies of Psychoanalytic Concepts," Social Science Research Council, *Bulletin* 51, 1943.

[52] Landis and Page, *op. cit.*, Chap. XI.

[53] See Hinko, Edward, and Louis S. Lipschultz, "Five Years after Shock Therapy," *The American Journal of Psychiatry*, 104, December, 1947, pp. 347–390, also, Feldman, Fred, Samuel Susselman, and S. Eugene Barrera, "Socioeconomic Aspects of the Shock Therapies in Schizophrenia," *ibid.*, pp. 402–409.

physician-patient ratios in hospitals and more congenial (we believe) to the preservation of the integrity of the self of the patient which seems to be so necessary to adult life in our culture. Administrative psychiatry, sometimes called "total push," likewise recommends itself as a way of interweaving a therapeutic plan with the social organization of the hospital. Where this is successfully instituted, every intramural contact with the patient, through doctors, nurses, attendants, and others, becomes an organic part of a therapy specially designed and executed for each patient.[54]

Individuation of the Mentally Disordered Person

No subject has inspired more conjecture and theorizing than the question of how persons become mentally deranged. But despite widespread preoccupation with the problem, we have not come far beyond evil spirits and demoniacal possession as explanations of the phenomena.[55] Many hereditary explanations, for example, deal in reified concepts such as genes or "predispositions" which have obvious metaphysical connotations. Psychological and sociological concepts have also been called upon in the same way as if they were entities or real things having fixed consequences. Theories couched in such a way leave us with little understanding of the process by which two different classes of phenomena are interrelated or *how* one condition in the person leads to the sociopathic reactions from which we infer the existence of psychoses.

The hereditary theory of mental disorders has already been discussed and in some respects disposed of. A deducible hypothesis from our general theory is that *behavior* which can be variably defined as "insane" or "normal" in different sociocultural contexts *cannot be inherited.* Proceeding on to the idea that these are hereditary *predispositions* to mental disorder, we then have to ask, in precise terminology or in operational terms, what is the predisposition? Is it a biological structure or a differential physiological response? How do we get from the predisposition, so defined, to the state of mental disorder?

Granting for purposes of discussion that differential physiological reactions are involved in the production of mental disorders, does empirical research tell us what the significant differentials are? While experiments with animals provide flimsy foundations for generalizing about human behavior, nevertheless some of them are highly suggestive for the purpose of our discussion. It has been possible to breed strains of white rats which differ significantly in emotionality, one strain being more timid, less aggres-

[54] See Myerson, Abraham, "Theory and Principles of 'Total Push' in the Treatment of Chronic Schizophrenia," *American Journal of Psychiatry*, 95, 1939, pp 1,197–1,204.

[55] See Zilborg, G. A., *A History of Medical Psychology*, 1941, pp. 519f.

sive, and slower at maze learning than the other strain. But when the two strains were exposed to traumatic stimuli, such as an air blast, the "non-emotional" rats underwent much more severe conclusive seizures than the more "emotional" rats. The crucial and unanswered question becomes: which strain of rats is better equipped to adapt to its environment?[56]

Converting the analogy, it may be asked whether a person with great inhibitory power is better prepared to avoid psychosis than the one who "blows up" easily and discharges his tensions before they reach a critical point. Obviously the cultural setting of the reactions cannot be ignored in answering the question. Nor can the introjected cultural definitions of the reactions as they bear upon the self-conception of the person be left out of any valid explanation.

Reasoning further, let us grant that there is something like a difference in the genetic or constitutional capacities of human beings to tolerate conflicting social and cultural pressures, expressed as differential tolerance either for the degree of conflict or for its duration.[57] We then must seek the nature of the distribution of this conflict tolerance in the population. Is it normally distributed in graded series or is it a unitary factor? No complete answer for this is at hand. However, all that we know about mental disorders strongly supports the former point of view, namely, that there is no sharp cleavage between normal and psychotic persons. Sane prototypes of insane behavior are everywhere apparent.[58] Since there must be variable amounts of social and cultural conflict to discover the critical point in the conflict tolerances of different individuals, an interactional process behind the development of mental disorder must be postulated. Person A with a low conflict tolerance may never become psychotic if he spends his life in an environment where few conflicting cultural requisitions are made of him. Person B with a high conflict tolerance may nonetheless become a psychiatric charge if he is thrown into a social situation where each choice he makes or each role he plays draws him more deeply into a web of cultural incompatibilities. The agreement of many psychiatrists that each person has his "breaking point" weighs heavily in favor of this general kind of interpretation.

Another fact which cannot be slighted is that a conflict tolerance always makes itself known as behavior, *i.e.*, the capacity to act or refrain from acting with respect to a social situation. This means that the behavior must therefore be the interactional product of genetic factors and the prior sociocultural conditioning of the person subject to the stress situation. This means further that the conflict tolerance may be environment-

[56] Martin, R. F., and C. S. Hall, "Emotional Behavior in the Rat," *Journal of Comparative Psychology*, 32, August, 1941, pp. 191–204.

[57] Rosenzweig, S., "An Outline of Frustration Theory" in J. Hunt (ed.), *Personality and Behavior Disorders*, 1944, Chap. 11.

[58] Brown, *op. cit.*, pp. 259*f*.

ally lowered or amplified, depending upon the socializing process the person has experienced.

At the present time it is not possible to say what type of sociopsychological differentiation contains potentialities for psychotic development. Some writers have made reference to the "prepsychotic personality" and "schizoid personality" as if they were definitely recognizable entities of some sort. Others, following an older notion in psychiatry, contend that the "shy," "timid" children are the ones from whom adult schizophrenics are most likely to be recruited. Our comments upon the hereditary predisposition to mental disorder can be applied with equal pertinence to the concept of the "prepsychotic" personality. Such a concept is incompatible with the nondeterministic position made explicit in our frame of reference; hence, we are led to exclude it on a priori grounds. Furthermore, up to the present time, attempts to verify the existence of prepsychotic personalities by objective research have been unrewarding.[59] Disconcertingly for the advocates of the prepsychotic personality, it is found that the stuff making psychotic behavior may also produce normal or superior deviant behavior. The difficult child may become a hopeless schizophrenic patient but then he also may turn into the exceptional adult.

Generally speaking, sociologists have placed emphasis upon a variety of hypotheses as to how mental disorders develop, among which are listed the social-complexity theory, the culture-conflict and social-isolation theory, and a theory of competitive stress. Of these the first has only a minimal plausibility and only the grossest kind of proof.[60] The other two theoretical positions give much more encouraging leads to solving the riddle of the genesis of mental disorders. They can be treated as generally consistent with our frame of reference and corroborative of the hypotheses derived from it. Of course, care must be taken to avoid reifying the idea of culture conflict by making it an explanatory concept. As we have emphasized repeatedly, it must be shown how culture conflict is transformed into organizational and participational nexuses which progressively restrict the fields of choice and eventuate in total blockage and compulsive behavior. Corollaries covering the growth of an intolerable and unacceptable self must be stated and demonstrated.

The data which can be drawn up to test the culture-conflict and social-

[59] See Klein, D. B., *Mental Hygiene*, 1944, pp. 197*ff*.; Myerson *et al.*, *op. cit.*, p. 110, Faris, R. E. L., and H. W. Dunham, *Mental Disorders in Urban Areas*, 1939, pp. 175–177, Watson, G., "A Critical Note on Two Attitude Studies," *Mental Hygiene*, 17, 1933, pp. 59–64; also, Kemble, Robert P., "Adolescent Prepsychotic Conditions—Criticism of a Concept," *Smith College Studies in Social Work*, 12, December, 1941.

[60] Devereaux, George, "A Sociological Theory of Schizophrenia," *Psychoanalytic Review*, 26, July, 1939, pp. 315–342; Gillin, John, "Personality in Preliterate Culture," *American Sociological Review*, 4, October, 1939, p. 687; Cuber, John, and Robert Harper, *Problems of American Society*, 1948, p. 120; Beaglehole, Ernest, "Cultural Complexity and Psychological Problems," *Psychiatry*, 3, August, 1940, pp. 329–340.

isolation hypotheses as amended above are not scientifically impeccable or unamenable to alternative interpretations. Nevertheless, we deem them serviceable and more responsive to this sociological theory than to alternative explanations. The reasons for making this claim are several. First, careful reading of case histories of mentally disordered persons, in nearly all instances, discloses the presence of serious status problems, self and ego involvements.[61] The fact that the highest rates for mental disorders appear among the aged in our society is of undeniable social and cultural significance. The data documenting the general social isolation and loss of a sense of personal and social worth among the aged are great to the point of being almost overwhelming.[62] The comparative absence of psychotic behavior among children in our culture becomes another facet of the proof of our general theory of mental disorders. The clustering of somewhat homogeneous psychotic symptoms at certain ages, namely, at adolescence and at the time of the climacteric as well as at advanced ages, bolsters the sociological conception of the mental-disease process. When these are cast against the known discontinuities of our culture in so far as "growing up" and "becoming old" are concerned, they press us more and more toward the type of explanation we have set up. Whereas in many other cultures becoming an adult or passing to the status of "old man" are uneventful, in our own culture, despite the folk humor on the subject, there is a desperate seriousness to the first sexual experiments of the adolescent and to passing one's fiftieth birthday – the "old age of youth and the youth of old age."

The implications of the relationship of remissions and "recoveries" to age and specific psychotic symptoms which cut across psychiatric diagnoses are obtrusive and, we believe, recalcitrant to other than a social and cultural interactional analysis of mental aberrancy. The apparent improvement in the mental-disorder rates of the older foreign-born with aging, as they come to accommodate to our culture with protective social organization of their own, seems an important addition to the store of evidence on the side of the culture-conflict hypothesis. If the indications that younger immigrants do less well in escaping mental troubles than older immigrants (at the time of immigration) are borne out by further research, then our case will be strengthened. Likewise, the limited evidence that second-generation immigrants in certain contexts outstrip their parents[63] in contributing to the rates of mentally unbalanced persons in our population is provocative data for our purpose. Findings in the study

[61] Davis, *op. cit.*, p 61, Campbell, C M., *Destiny and Disease in Mental Disorders,* 1935.

[62] Cameron, N., "Neuroses of Later Maturity," in O. Kaplan, *Mental Disorders in Later Life,* 1945.

[63] Lemert, E., "An Exploratory Study of Mental Disorders in a Rural Problem Area," *Rural Sociology,* 13, March, 1948, p 58.

of the distribution of mental disorders in the Chicago area, while open to criticism on several scores, stand out in at least one important respect, *i.e.*, that the rates of mental disorders rose highest among foreign-born persons living in areas not predominantly inhabited by members of their own ethnic group.[64] This correlation of mental disorders with a social-isolation measure has some further indirect backing in a study of mental disorders among the foreign-born populations of the Upper Peninsula of Michigan.[65]

Some writers have been reluctant to couple manic-depressive psychoses with other varieties of mental deviation as products of culture conflict and social isolation. Creating a cleavage of this sort seems entirely uncalled for in light of the obvious overlapping of manic-depressive with other psychotic symptoms. One careful examination of manic-depressive cases has repudiated in large part this older belief that personal and social factors are unrelated to manic and depressive upsets. Fully 80 per cent of these cases revealed seriously disturbing life situations as direct factors in the onset of the conditions.[66] Desperate preoccupation with status and the self are prominently spelled in almost any case history of manic and depressive persons that one might select from the files of mental hospitals.

Some of the most convincing evidence of a direct tie between social isolation and mental disorders has accumulated from the clinical observations of military psychiatrists during the Second World War. The immediate process coterminous with neurotic disablement of combat troops in the majority of cases was one in which the individual soldier became symbolically detached from the group – his combat team or larger units of identification. Generally the things disrupting communion between the individual soldier and his group were the factors making for unmanageable fears, anxieties, and guilt. The ingredients of low morale – poor food, lack of sleep, long, uninterrupted combat duty, ill-considered commands by superiors – all have modal symbolic implications for the soldier as well as lowering his energy reserves. Commonly they mean that the social organization of which he is a part somehow has let him down and that he must carry out his dangerous assignments without the support of his group.[67]

Primary Psychotic Deviation

Most of the symptoms which in certain contexts are declared to be neurotic or psychotic can be encountered among persons who are nowise

[64] Faris and Dunham, *op. cit.*, pp 56–57, 169.

[65] Lemert "An Exploratory Study of Mental Disorders in a Rural Problem Area," pp 56*ff*.

[66] Rennie, T., "Prognosis in Manic-depressive Psychosis," *American Journal of Psychiatry*, 98, May, 1942, pp. 801–814.

[67] Kardiner, Abram, and H. Spiegel, *War Stress and Neurotic Illness*, 1947, Chaps. III–IV.

thought to be abnormal either by society or by themselves. Auditory hallucinations are often reported by normal persons, who hear voices of dead relatives, usually as a nocturnal occurrence. Elaborate fantasy and daydreaming are supportive mechanisms for the sane as well as the insane. Delusions of uxorial infidelity, of approaching economic disaster, that one has been "framed," that the neighbors have poisoned the pet dog of the family, or that other people are insane or "need a psychiatrist" are all commonplace reactions in our society, which do not necessarily brand those holding to them as insane. High-tensional states and pervasive anxiety may also be found to accompany the fulfillment of everyday tasks of nonpathological members of the community. In general these symptoms are episodic and transitory, or they have such low visibility that they do not precipitate secondary psychotic differentiation of the person.

Such symptoms as these may arise in many different ways. The situational conflicts confronting the person, which narrow the external limits of role choice in the face of strong aspiration to an unattainable role, are fertile sources of fantasy, delusion, tension, and disassociation. Likewise the narrowing of the internal limits of choice in such a manner that few or no roles can be satisfying to the person generates many responses of primary neuroses and psychoses.[68] Undoubtedly the constriction of choices takes on its greatest import in connection with the discontinuities of our culture. Nowhere is this more obvious than in the anomalies in socialization of the child in the American family, although we must guard against the notion that converging limits and total blockage does not materialize after reaching adulthood.

Parents, responding to insupportable demands of their own roles in our culture or to unfulfilled aspirations, not uncommonly impede or distort the development of their children. They make them overcritical of their own role-fulfilling behavior and that of others; they overstimulate them to learn behavior beyond their age capacities; they build up a sense of guilt over sexual curiosity and experimentation, as well as over eating and elimination. Thus, the only daughter is made to feel guilty because she was not the boy her father wanted, or the boy is a "sissy" and kept dependent by a mother who secretly hates her husband. As long as the child can be kept within the confines of a carefully controlled family environment, all is well; but gradually as childhood aspirations change or as age of the child necessitates that he assume extrafamilial roles, these various limits become serious sources of inadequacy or tension, and disturbing aspects of the self-image increase.

[68] Muncie, W., "The Rigid Personality as a Factor in Psychoses," *Archives of Neurology and Psychiatry*, 26, August, 1936, pp 359–370.

As was true in the case of "family radicalism," the primary psychotic reactions may be a reaction to intrafamily conflict or they may be acquired through learning. It is not unusual for "vicious cycles" of interaction to complicate parent-child relationships. For example, parents often find that their criticism, punishment, and other methods of "control" over an undesired infantile habit of their child actually fixes and intensifies the habit. The oversensitive mother exerts too much effort to get her child to eat, and the child becomes even more difficult at the table. Parents may punish rivalrous siblings only to find that each interprets the penalties as favoritism toward the other sibling — hence, the rivalry becomes cumulative. Sometimes reciprocating conflicts become "vicious cycles" transcending generations. The woman who has had a dominating mother may resolve to give her children the freedom she never had, and these children as adults decide that the lesson of their own lives teaches them to give "firm guidance" to their offspring.[69]

Many primary psychotic deviations may be learned directly from parents; children are taught to be overaggressive or distrustful of others. Frigid mothers inspire distaste for sexual intercourse or terrific fears of pregnancy and childbirth in their daughters. Dire warnings about the "change of life" may be added by the grandmother full of "old wives' tales." The example of the father who habitually blames others for his own failures and transgressions is not often lost upon the son.

It is not clear that a full-blown neurosis or psychosis can be acquired through a simple learning process, although cases resembling this have been culled from the literature.[70] More likely is the acquisition of the components or behavioral building blocks of a psychosis by imitation and direct learning. Research into the effects of psychotic parents and family members upon the socialization of children has long been indicated as a necessary control in order for any research on the hereditary aspects of mental disorders to have any really scientific value. Beyond this it can add to and strengthen our knowledge of the dynamics of primary psychotic deviation. We have seen already in Chap. 10 on alcoholism that wives of alcoholics tend to respond neurotically to the intimate life they must live with their isolant husbands. The author has yet to interview the child of an alcoholic who does not in some way betray symbolic disturbances. Study of children of psychotic parents has brought to light a much higher incidence of behavior difficulties than found in other families, pretty obviously the results of the neglect in a home disrupted by mental

[69] Bain, Read, "Personality Development and Marriage," in H. Becker and R. Hill, *Marriage and the Family*, 1924, pp 147*f*.

[70] Gralnick, A., "Folie à Deux, The Psychosis of Association," *Psychiatric Quarterly*, 16, July, 1942, pp. 491–520.

[71] Myerson *et al.*, *op. cit.*, p. 87.

disorder.[71] The damage one neurotic person can do in the intimate, closely bound family circle needs little documentary emphasis for the person who has participated in or observed such a group. Before leaving the subject of psychosis and family relationships, it is proper to raise the question of the importance of psychotic relatives or "insanity in the family" in producing identifications and symbolizing primary psychotic deviations as insanity. This brings us to the critical pass at which secondary deviation occurs.

Secondary Psychotic Deviation — Insanity

To speak of symbolizing symbolic responses has a strange tautological sound to it. Nevertheless, this is precisely what we mean when we speak of a process of becoming insane. The onset of insanity coincides with the awareness of one's behavior as being invidiously different from that of all other people's. A progressive investiture of situations, reactions of others, and one's own responses with meaning for self and status where none existed before takes place, with cumulative fears and tensions growing out of the meaning attached to the secondary reactions. To illustrate: a woman may have a long period of trying crises coupled with illnesses, which taken together leave her with a persistent fatigue. The techniques she has used in the past to banish the fatigue fail her, and she is unable to discover new ways of restoring her energies and zest. She now begins to react to the fatigue symptoms as something different and unusual. More and more of her little energies go into the preoccupation with this difference, and she neglects her maternal and domestic duties. Her guilt and anxiety arising from these omissions reinforce her fatigue and intensify the ruminative behavior, which further bankrupts her energy resources. Her feelings become stranger and stranger to her. "Reaction sensitivity" [72] spreads from one role to another, each invasion corroborating the highly verbalized or dimly conscious perception of unwanted and intolerable difference from others.

At each step in the psychotic process there is an interplay between the internal and external limits and the symbolic process, with social failures leading to a distortion of the anticipatory reactions, which attenuate communication and make for more social failures. Because of these failures, subtle or outright rejections and segregational responses of others toward the deviant increase.

The low visibility of early psychotic reactions and the variability of the overt behavior associated with them make it difficult to isolate phases in the process by which primary psychotic symptoms are converted into symbolized psychosis or insanity. However, in wartime, battle-induced neurosis the whole process is sufficiently foreshortened and focused to permit a more concise delineation of developmental phases. It is of consid-

[72] Cameron, *The Psychology of Behavior Disorders*, pp. 68*f*.

erable interest to read of the division of the neurotic process into incipient, acute, and chronic phases in a recent recapitulation on the subject. Significantly in this treatise the incipient stage of the battle neurosis is described as "amorphous and unstructured." In this phase it is exceedingly difficult to draw any sharp lines between normal and abnormal combat fatigue, fear, anxiety, "jumpiness," and sleep disturbances. Importantly, the transition from an incipient to an acute phase in which the soldier "surrendered to his neurosis" *was found to vary closely with the way in which the soldier was handled.* Oversympathetic battle surgeons and evacuation out of the battle zones were discovered to be dynamic factors in converting the amorphous symptoms of the incipient stage into definitive neurotic form. Conversely, the absence of any rear area for evacuation, a "tough" attitude by battle surgeons, and direct discipline on the battlefield often were means by which badly disturbed soldiers bore up with their roles.[73]

While we are hesitant to insist that the growth of a traumatic neurosis of war is entirely comparable to the more insidious development of a psychosis, nevertheless the function of symbolism in the two processes seems essentially the same. In the case of psychosis in civilians the overt aspects of their roles may remain unchanged for a long time, because the persons are reacting primarily to the covert symbolic aspects of their behavior. Also, the overt changes may have such low visibility that public recognition of the deviation does not come until it is well developed. The family of the mental deviant, because of the stigma and disgrace of insanity, tends to reduce the visibility of the deviant by concealment, rationalization, and adaptation of family life to the distorted demands of the deranged member. Explaining the unusual behavior as the result of physical disease is common. Where conflict is present, the deviant's reactions may be symbolized by the family as "laziness," as "delinquency," as the consequence of excessive drinking, or as the accompaniment of a particular habit, such as reading too much or practicing the piano too long. Only reluctantly do most families come to conclude that mental disorder is present, and then only inadvertently and indirectly is this symbolism communicated to the deviant. This type of symbolic reaction in the family may have two effects, depending upon the contacts and interaction of the person outside the family. It may permit the psychotic deviation to grow and become so complicated that the family will fail in efforts to conceal it; secondary deviation becomes inevitable. On the other hand, it may help the deviant define his own reactions in such a way as to weather the changes in his covert behavior without having to deal with the greater deviation that the introjected symbols of insanity would bring on.

Where other members of a family have previously been declared insane

[73] Kardiner and Spiegel, *op. cit*, Chaps. III–IV.

and hospitalized, the factor of identification intrudes in subtle ways to magnify tensions, fears, and other primary stuff of psychosis. An investigation into behavior problems of children of parents who had been hospitalized and diagnosed as psychotic revealed that 25 per cent of the children were troubled by fears of their becoming psychotic.[74] Fear of insanity acts as a dynamic factor in the exaggeration of psychotic behavior in different ways. Identification with a father or mother who has been insane often gives special meaning to what actually may be normal social failure or to common behavioral disturbances such as nightmares, moodiness, or depressions. Parents with fears of insanity may project these onto children and symbolize entirely normal deviation as antecedents of mental breakdown.[75] Perhaps such persons more readily hospitalize their mentally upset relatives. It would be interesting to have data on this question. On the other hand, the knowledge that a near or remote ancestor suffered delusions or hallucinations but kept out of mental hospitals and made valuable social contributions may be a source of great strength to a mental deviant struggling to assign some acceptable meaning to his strange feelings and compulsions. The concept of the social value of insanity may be invoked as symbolic insulation of the primary psychosis.

No matter how the family may react to primary psychotic symptoms, the outside community is not deterred from candid appraisals of psychotic behavior. Thus, prior to hospitalization of the deviant, neighbors and community members may come to symbolize him with terms like "queer," "sick," "tetched," "loony," "cracked," and with other folk-term variants of insanity. The symbolic reaction of the community is made tangible in its segregative treatment of the deviant. In small towns the person may become the butt of jokes and crude provocations. If the person is delusional and aggressive, he may build up hostilities in others which lead to his being arrested many times or engaged in civil litigation. A psychotic woman may turn to drunkenness to conceal her symptoms or have an interim go at sexual promiscuity. Police and local authorities eventually become irritated to the point where they insist upon institutionalization of the deviant. Incarcerations in jail and adverse decisions in civil suits symbolize punishment and rejection by the community for many psychotic persons and add to their own hostilities, aggressions, or guilt and anxiety.[76]

Hospitalization

The full symbolic impression of the societal definition upon the insane is conveyed by legal commitment and forcible hospitalization. Symbolized

[74] Lampron, Edna, "Children of Schizophrenic Parents," *Mental Hygiene*, 17, January, 1933, pp. 82–91.

[75] *Ibid.*

[76] Cameron, "The Paranoid Pseudocommunity," *loc. cit*

as insane, the deviant becomes a ward, unable to sue or be sued, and unable to enter into contracts or otherwise conduct business or professional affairs. His changed status is quickly made plain on entry into the hospital, where his possessions are removed, where nurses and attendants patronize the patient, where his mail is censored and he is forced to do "what is good for him," his own feelings to the contrary notwithstanding. Not all patients react in comparable ways to these initial hospital experiences; some probably welcome the change they offer from an intolerable home situation, while others are too confused and disoriented to absorb the full social meaning of their environment until later. The full impact of this meaning unquestionably fixes and aggravates the symptoms of many patients.

When they arrive at the hospital, a goodly number of mental deviants have behind them a long history of conflict with their families. Their bitterness and hostility, or delusions of persecution where they exist, find much to sustain them in the perfidy which their kinfolk seem to show in having them "put away." Symptoms which have hithertofore been vague and half formed often are crystallized into bold relief following entry into the hospital. Senile persons whose condition has been that of generalized cantankerousness and crochetiness prior to being hospitalized quite frequently develop well-defined persecutory symptoms with reference to their families and the hospital staff. Many alcoholics who are nonpsychotic build up rejections of the hospital environment with paranoidlike ideas. In fact, a very defensible hypothesis is that a parnoid reaction to the mental-hospital situation is "normal" for our culture.

It would be of great value for us to know how much of the patient's combativeness, negativism, mutism, and other resistive behavior is a response to the hospital environment or to the hateful status and self-definition it signifies to the inmate. Here and there bits of evidence come to attention which betray the deep hostilities patients nurture against the hospital situation. The description of the feelings of a female patient after her recovery from a psychosis vividly emphasizes the central fact of hostility in her attitudes toward the hospital staff.[77]

> During the days and nights that followed, the resentment and bitterness of that experience continued. Only when I could get off somewhere by myself and could lose myself in my own fantasy creations did it subside. At other times, everything that was said seemed an insult; every nurse who came near me was an enemy with diabolical intent. I seethed with hatred. What was it these women were after? What was it I had done or not done? As they struggled to get me into a pack, they seemed to me fiends, a sort of human embodiment of all that was hateful. Resistance at such times became a virtue....

[77] Kindwall, Josef A., and Elaine F. Kinder, "Postscript on a Benign Psychosis," *Psychiatry*, 3, November, 1940, pp. 527–534.

As we have tried to show earlier, the central function of the modal state-hospital social organization is to subordinate patients to institutional routines. A special manifestation of this general function is the prompt demonstration to new patients of the power of the ward attendant. In the course of this a dramatic struggle usually is carried on by combative patients with attendants in the early months of hospitalization, pending the final acquiescence of the patient. Some are quickly subdued, others retreat to fight back more obliquely, while a few are never brought to bay. These latter get to be known as "trouble makers" by attendants, and their reputations precede them as they move from ward to ward.

The first few months and the first year of hospitalization give every indication of being a critical period in the life history of the psychotic person. Patients who are going to recover tend to improve within a few months or at most within a year of hospitalization. Otherwise their chances of recovery diminish rapidly. It was found in one study that 72 per cent of patients with a favorable outcome to their disorder were discharged from the hospital within one year.[78] Variations within this general picture occur according to the type of symptoms, sex, and age of the patient. Those in whom the onset of the disorder has been swift and "stormy" typically have a briefer hospital sojourn than others. Men with favorable outcomes of their disorders improve somewhat sooner than women. It is also true that a higher percentage of women remain in hospitals for long periods.[79] Aged psychotics have a short hospital stay because death soon overtakes them.

About 49 per cent of mental patients remain in the hospital for more than a year. A study alluded to above [80] brought out the fact that the average duration of the hospital stay for those left in the hospital beyond one year was 8 years. Fourteen per cent in this sample were hospitalized for 15 years or more, 19 per cent for 10 or more years, and 27 per cent for 5 or more years. What of these mental deviants who are unresponsive to treatment or custodial care, who eventually are shut away on back wards for a large part of their adult lives? Many of them are converted into what are known familiarly in hospital slang as "institutional cures." Such persons, usually those with grandiose and persecutory delusional symptoms, either slough off or successfully conceal the signs of their disorder so long as they are not removed from the hospital milieu. However, discharges or visits to the outside world soon precipitate their old conflicts, which sound a retreat to the sheltered hospital world. Within this world the institutional adaptees often enjoy high status, with consid-

[78] Fuller, R G, and M. Johnston, "The Duration of Hospital Life for Mental Patients," *Psychiatric Quarterly*, 5, April, 1931, pp. 341–352

[79] Landis and Page, *op cit.*, pp. 132, 126.

[80] Fuller and Johnston, *op cit*, p 661

erable privilege, and with recognition from the attendants and physicians as valuable adjuncts of the staff.

Closely akin to the institutional cures are those patients whose psychosis has "burned out." They are hospital residues who are normal but have been in the hospital so long that relatives have died or forgotten them and they are retained as patients simply because no feasible way of discharging them can be found. A last group of long-time inmates is composed of patients who slowly deteriorate over spans of time until they are pure custodial cases.

Discharged Patients

Prolonged hospitalization with a continuous life of enforced dependency works slowly but surely to remold the behavior, role, and self-conception of the mental deviant. The effects are best observed in the residue cases in which no psychosis is present at the time of discharge, but they may be seen in any case which has been hospitalized for a long period of time. In institutional recoveries the patient has acquired a role in which requirements are neither rigorous nor stress-laden. Hospital personnel are extremely tolerant of the patient's mistakes and minimize their consequences by close and constant supervision. Programs of economic rehabilitation are standard for many hospitals, but the best of intramural occupational therapy is poor preparation for responsible employment in the outside world.[81] The patient has long been exempt from the urgencies of intimate interaction in a family group; sex long since may have been eliminated from his mind and behavior or changed in its expression; eating, sleeping, sanitation, and leisure-time activities have been compressed into fixed habits suited to impersonal mass existence.

Discharge for the patient rudely shatters the cloistered life he has known for so many years. He again is thrust into personal interaction in a small group, with relatives, neighbors, employers, and members of the larger community, all pressing him for independent and purposeful decisions. The oncoming events brook little delay on his part, nor are they simple and unified experiences. Rather, each is baited with alternatives and freighted with conflict – and each decision threatens painful repercussions for his status and self. The withdrawal stress coming with discharge of the mental patient after protracted hospital existence is fully as great as that occurring at the time of commitment, and perhaps greater. Its intensity is at least sufficient to reawaken old conflicts and psychosis in many cases, and perhaps it can create an entirely new psychosis.

The reception of the discharged patient by the community is well

[81] Proehl, Elizabeth, "The Transition from Institutional to Social Adjustment," *American Sociological Review*, 3, August, 1938, pp. 534–540

calculated to set in motion a symbolizing process which can quickly convert what may well be a normal amount of conflict into the signs of recurring insanity:[82]

> The local community, of which the patient was a citizen and in which he has made his home, makes no provision for his return. It has no responsibility for his condition and care; it receives no notice of his impending return, and for the most part it is indifferent to his return and subsequent welfare.

There is, then, an unbridged gap and lack of continuity between the mental-hospital experience and life in the community outside, a gap ignored by the community and, of necessity, only superficially touched by the social-service work of mental hospitals themselves. The apathy of the local community stems from the older concept that a person is either insane or he is sane. Oddly enough this view is abetted by the medical concept of a "cure" for mental disorder. The community tends to expect the "cured" patient to carry on without help or special consideration. But this idea is tempered and compromised by the common belief that "once insane, always insane." The behavior of the paroled (an invidious term itself) mental patient takes on a much higher visibility than it had before his entry into an institution. It is the attitude of doubt and suspicion which constitutes the substance of his stigma in the community and which so greatly complicates the deviant's posthospital adjustment. Such facts as these are doubly meaningful when it is recalled that the overwhelming percentage of discharged mental patients are not recovered at all but are merely "improved." In Illinois in 1936 to 1937 only 16 per cent of all discharged patients were called "recovered" by the hospital staffs. Eighty-four per cent were classed as other than recovered.[83] More comprehensive figures for state mental hospitals show that, after a ten-year period, 21 out of 100 discharged patients have returned to hospitals and another 19 are charges on the community welfare agencies.[84]

Social Participation and Mental Disorder

The interplay between the sense of isolation of the mental deviant and his social participation is an obtrusive fact. Where the disorder has appeared in early youth, patterns of social withdrawal soon become well established and are one of the most significant indications of the deviation. Psychoses of later maturity may be preceded by periods of relatively full social participation – particularly where exogenous, situational pressures have entered in a large way into the onset of symptoms. However, even

[82] Jaffary, *op. cit.*, p. 159.
[83] *Ibid.*, pp. 100*f*.
[84] Landis and Page, *op. cit.*, p. 136.

in cases such as these, careful scrutiny of the deviant's behavior supplies evidence that his participation has been of a tenuous variety, qualitatively distinguished by anxiety and tension. The generic factor operating to reduce and attenuate the social participation of all mental deviants is the high expenditure of energies upon or in the symbolic process itself. This means that the amount of energy left for effective social participation is reduced. Only where persons are extraordinarily healthy and have a high energy output can they power external social adjustments along with an exhausting ruminative process.

The first interference in social participation of mental deviants is often seen in withdrawal from school. For example, 63.1 per cent of a group of college students with psychotic symptoms were found to be unable to follow through with their schooling. In their class work only 36.9 per cent made satisfactory grades (C or better); 12.3 per cent made "fair," and 37.7 per cent had their work graded as "unsatisfactory." A final 13.1 per cent received no grades.[85] A few mentally disturbed students here and there use their scholastic endeavors as a saving compensation for generalized social withdrawal, and where they manage to make excellent grades, they may stave off a more complete psychotic disorder.

Economic Participation

While much interest and research surrounds the question of how economic status is causally related to mental disorder, practically no well-designed study of the consequences of mental disorder for economic status and participation is available. It would be agreed generally, however, that mental disorders delay the economic establishment of the person, disrupt careers, and lower earning capacity. To the extent that schooling is interfered with, difficulties of economic placement are created, especially for better paying positions.

The nature of his symptoms and the requirements of the particular job have a good deal to do with whether or not the mental deviant will be able to adequately perform an occupational role. Some mentally disordered persons, even though badly dissociated and apathetic, may be able to work if they are under close supervision; they may even outdo normal workers in certain routine and monotonous jobs. Persons with strong paranoid tendencies often are hard and skillful workers and may do well if working alone. In general it is probably true that psychotic persons do better in farm employment than in factory work.

Long hospitalization, as we brought out earlier, tends to undermine

[85] Raphael, Theophile, and Leonard Himmler, "Schizophrenia and Paranoid Psychoses among College Students," *American Journal of Psychiatry*, 100, January, 1944, Tables 7, 9

work habits of the psychotic person. Many discharged patients are completely incapacitated for further employment, and many others adjust economically at lower levels than before commitment. In one follow-up study of 98 men one year after discharge from parole in New York, 47 were doing well in their jobs, 27 were partially satisfactory to their employers, and 24 were failures. Those with manic-depressive disorders did better than those who had been diagnosed as schizophrenic. Altogether, 55 per cent were self-supporting, and 20 per cent were entirely dependent upon government subsidy or upon aid from their relatives. Forty of the men operated at about the same level of efficiency as they had prior to hospitalization, 30 at a lower level of efficiency, and 14 displayed greater efficiency than before.[86]

Except for the more wealthy families, psychosis in one or the other member imposes great financial strain. Private psychiatric treatment is very expensive and when administered in a private hospital is even more so. If the husband must be hospitalized, income is lost and the wife often must seek employment, or obtain public assistance, with an attendant lowered plane of living. If the wife is mentally incapacitated, domestic help must be hired, particularly if there are children in the home. Long years in a mental hospital prevent the accumulation of savings, jeopardize the education of children, and in many other ways impoverish the mental deviant and his family.

The knowledge that his wife must work to support herself and the children, or the humilitation of having them become relief clients, plus the downgrading which may come in his occupational status upon leaving the hospital are all powerful blows to the self-esteem of the psychotic deviant in our culture.

Sex and Marital Participation

Since many of the conflicts of neurotic and psychotic persons are of a sexual bent, interference with their overt sex behavior is to be expected. There is, however, no fixed sexual response to these internal conflicts. The histories of some psychotics record a considerable diminution of sex interest and activity, while others give indication of sexual promiscuity and perversions; the former is probably the commoner reaction. In cases where social withdrawal, elaborate fantasy reactions, and extreme disassociation stand out in the symptom picture – usually where the trouble has developed early in life – an infantile or adolescent sexuality is present.[87] Fear of the opposite sex may be strong because of early rejections, and

[86] Fitch, Eda W., *A Study of the Social and Occupational Adjustment of 100 Men Discharged from the Manhattan State Hospital*, 1924.

[87] Landis, C, *Sex in Development*, 1940, pp. 63*f*.

compensatory autoerotic practice may have been substituted for heterosexual contacts. With deterioration in psychotic persons, concern with sex may totally disappear or it may become a compulsive preoccupation. In women who are psychotic, sometimes it is an interlude of sexual promiscuity which magnifies the visibility of their deviation and provokes husbands or relatives sufficiently to have them hospitalized.

Practically all studies we have of the marital status of hospitalized mental patients point to higher percentages of single and divorced persons among the psychotic population than in the general population. One challenging exception to this comes from a study of selective-service rejectees in Washington, D.C., during the Second World War, where married rejectees were proportionately the same or slightly more numerous than single rejectees.[88] However, we may well question the representativeness of such a sample. It is likely that wartime conditions may lead to higher marriage rates of psychotic and neurotic persons. It is also possible that more stable married persons, well established in jobs and professions, may have been deferred in greater numbers in this area. Noteworthy was the fact that when broken down by diagnostic groups the same type of differences in marriage rates appeared in this group as in civilian mental-hospital populations. The comparatively low rates of mental disorders among married persons shown in hospital statistics are partly caused by a lag in the hospitalization of this group. Marriage serves as a buffer for the mentally disordered person in the community. Also the need to keep the husband and father as a means of family support functions to slow down hospitalization in his case. However, after allowing for these factors, we may still have some reason to believe that mental disorders work against chances of marrying.

Female mental deviants do somewhat better than males in so far as marrying goes. Whereas psychotic women were found in one study to run 7 per cent below the general female population with regard to those married, males had 17 per cent fewer married than the general male population. These differences vary a good deal with age groups, being far greater for younger psychotic persons than for those who have been hospitalized at older ages.[89] This would support the idea that not only does mental disorder remove many persons from the marriageable population but also that it delays marriage for many others. The factors behind such postponements most likely are those of general psychosexual immaturity of many psychotic persons and their difficulty in acquiring and holding employ-

[88] Hadley, Ernest E., *et al.*, "Military Psychiatry," *Psychiatry*, No. 7, November, 1944, pp. 393–399.

[89] Malzberg, Benjamin, "Marriage Rates among Patients with Mental Disease," *Mental Hygiene*, 22, October, 1938, pp 634–644.

ment sufficiently rewarding to permit the assumption of marital responsibility.

The conflicts arising between psychotic persons and their spouses in the intimate preemptive dyadic relationship of marriage are reflected in the relatively high divorce rates of the mentally disordered. Marriage levies claims upon participants which the more rigid mental deviant is often poorly prepared to meet. Guilt and conflict over sex relations enter marital interaction to make for unbearable tensions. The isolant tendencies of the psychotic partner also isolate the normal member of the couple. Frequently the normal husband or wife gets drawn into the delusions of the psychotic spouse. Delusions of infidelity, for example, which are common in the paranoid disorders, often make the marital plight of the stable one of the pair intolerable. Quite a few divorces occur after hospitalization of the psychotic spouse. These tend to come in response to the recognition that recovery of the husband or wife may not come for years or perhaps never. Hospitalization is comparable to imprisonment in this respect. Husbands and wives simply lose the common interests which held them together, or the normal spouse concludes that he or she cannot, or will not, sacrifice a large portion of his or her life to lonely years of waiting.

Another cue to the disruption of the sex and marital life of mental deviants comes from the somewhat lower birth rates characterizing their marriages. According to an investigation into the family size of over 15,000 patients consecutively discharged from two mental hospitals in New York State, both native-born and foreign-born parents who became psychotic at ages over ten years had smaller families than found in the general New York State population. Similarly, mothers of psychotic offspring tended to have fewer children than the average for the state. The low reproduction rate of the mental patients was partially a consequence of hospital separation, divorce, and widowhood, but not entirely. This was demonstrated by the higher-than-average sterility rates for married patients in whom the onset of the psychosis came after fifty years of age.[90]

While we have dwelled upon the interaction between psychotic persons and their marriage partners, it is obvious that the presence of such a deviant has an impact upon the entire family unit. In some cases housing problems are created by the paranoid suspicions a psychotic person develops toward the neighbors: evictions may follow. Eating habits may be used to express hostility of the deviant toward his or her family environment. Sleep disturbances are common among psychotic people, causing them to roam about the house or neighborhood late at night. This places additional strain upon other members of the family who lose sleep and

[90] Dayton, Neil A., "Size of Family and Birth Order in Mental Disease," *Publications of the American Sociological Society*, 24, May, 1930, pp. 123–137.

who not infrequently have their health jeopardized by the continual necessity to keep watch over the demented person in their midst. Where a mother has become demented, children are affected not only through her inadequate and inappropriate discipline but also through outright neglect. Such mothers fail to cook properly for the children, are unable to give medication in their illnesses, to dress them, and get them to school in accordance with their maternal responsibilities. There are strong indications that the brunt of family disruption brought about through mental disorders often falls upon adolescent daughters, who are blocked from using their homes and families to reinforce their status in the peer age group.[91]

Participation in Military Service

Mental disorder was one of the main causes for rejection of recruits and selectees for military service during the Second World War. It was also a principal source of discharges and combat casualties. Some persons with less serious disorders were accepted for limited service, but on the whole to be mentally deranged was to qualify one as 4F. Within the armed forces, mass existence in heterogeneous groups, monotony in isolated posts, and impersonal treatment often interacted to produce and precipitate mental breakdowns. Apparently the most significant factor in psychiatric casualties was the inability of the individual soldier to accept the necessity of the war itself and to justify it in his system of values. Viewed in another way, this meant simply that those who could best accept their roles as soldiers with the attendant sacrifices and hardships were most likely to avoid mental disorder.[92]

Certain classes of persons who had minor mental disorders in civilian life were much easier with their roles as soldiers. This seemed to be true of persons with so-called "psychopathic" disorders and those with obsessive-compulsive symptoms. The unruly combativeness of the "psychopath" often was the material from which exceptional combat soldiers were formed. Also it became apparent that civilian experience with anxiety and tension often protected the soldier against severe neurosis or psychosis. In contrast to such soldiers, the boy who had never experienced conscious anxiety oftentimes fell into psychoticlike states when stresses of battle overwhelmed his defenses. The anxious neurotic soldier sometimes was able to diminish his sense of difference from others by projecting his fears upon the dangers of combat and thus identify himself with those having normal combat fears.[93]

[91] Truedley, Mary B., "Mental Illness and Family Routines," *Mental Hygiene*, 30, April, 1946, pp. 235–249.

[92] Snyder, Howard, "Observations of Psychiatry in World War II," *American Journal of Psychiatry*, 104, October, 1947, p. 222.

[93] Grinker and Spiegel, *op. cit.*, p. 17.

Although the concept of psychiatric casualty has gained general acceptance in our armed forces, the role of the psychotic soldier is far from enviable. The term "psycho" still carries unpleasant connotations in many military contexts. The dividing line between malingering and neurosis often cannot be drawn. Company commanders and officers faced with disciplinary and morale problems are not always charitably disposed toward psychiatrists or the soldiers they disqualify for duty. The military police in some areas during the Second World War manifestly disliked and distrusted psychiatrists because of the practice that many enlisted men followed in pleading insanity in court-martial cases.

Mental disorder acquired in military service is sufficient grounds for disability pensions, which means that the psychotic or neurotic war veteran has a somewhat more secure economic status than other psychotic persons. Now and then we meet a case of a psychoneurotic war veteran who gives some evidence of being a professional neurotic in the sense of using his official status as a mentally unbalanced person as an excuse for socially undesirable behavior. Nor is this completely unknown among ex mental patients with civilian status.

Other Aspects of the Social Participation of the Mentally Disordered

The conflicts which distress mental deviants over role and self-esteem unquestionably are instrumental in their greater responsiveness to sectarian appeals of unconventional religious, political, and recreational groups. Indication of their participation in radical movements has already been given. The association of mental aberrancy and religious fanaticism is well enough known to require little comment. Persons with paranoid delusions not infrequently are the founders of unusual sects. Other individuals may pass through a period of intense religious fervor in the course of their psychotic individuation.[94] At one time religious mania was looked upon as a separate form of mental disorder. Food cults, physical culture, and nudist groups attract goodly numbers of psychotic and neurotic persons. Mass athletic spectacles also serve as outlets for aggressions and exhibitionist impulses of unstable members of our population.

The impersonality and anonymity of social relationships in these mutant groups in our society lessen the probabilities of immediate rejection of the mental deviant. They may even give a structuring and form to psychotic impulses and compulsions which temporarily reduce their visibility and make them more congenial to the deviant himself.

We have no way of telling how many or what class of psychotic deviants seek and find some escape or release from the intolerable self by

[94] Clark, Robert A., "Theosophical Occultism and Mental Hygiene," *Psychiatry*, 7, August, 1944, pp. 237–243.

such social participation as we have described. It is most probable that these participants suffer less deterioration, are closer to social reality, and are still struggling with their internal problems. Common among them will be those with paranoid delusions and manic-depressive disturbances. Close observation differentiates them from others by the intense or desperate searching quality of their interaction with others in these groups. They penetrate little beyond the periphery of the group, make undependable members, and are wont to fall out as their attention is shunted elsewhere. They may join many sects and cults which hold forth promise of stilling the turmoil within, each experience being a further source of guilt or failure.

Adjustment and Maladjustment

It is almost tautological or redundant to discuss the adjustment of mental deviants, who, by our definition, are symbolically disordered. However, if we recall the dual classification of primary and secondary psychotic deviation, then it becomes possible to speak of relatively well-adjusted insane persons. The "institutional cures" within mental hospitals give every outward sign of recognizing and accepting their role and self-definitions within the microcosmic social world in which they live. This is equally true for patients with "burned-out" psychoses who have the role and status of insane and are unable to get along outside the hospital. Occasionally in the community persons who are stigmatized and treated as "crazy" seem to be content with their role and status. Some even seem to use their "insanity" to manipulate other people.

Marginality – The Ex Mental Patient

From what has been said previously, the situation of the discharged mental patient makes role integration and self-acceptance hard to achieve. Even though his symptoms have been eliminated and he is restored to full economic and social competence, his welcome back into the community is a qualified and watchful one under the best of conditions. Some persons are strong and flexible enough to dismiss or disassociate the hyphenated social acceptance they encounter. For others the veiled or open suspicion of others in the community is more than enough to reinforce or dramatize normal mistakes, inadequacies, and conflicts as incipient relapse. This person is sometimes socially sentenced to wander between the two opposed conceptions of the self – sane and insane.

"Recovery"

The medical concept of a "cure" or even "recovery" from mental "disease" is, at best, an analogy and cannot be objectively descriptive of the process by which mental disorder is abated. No person who has known an epoch of psychotic behavior and hospitalization will ever be the same as he was before the experience. There can be no restoration of the person as he was previously, in the same way that metabolic norms are reestablished after an illness. Something new and different is created by the interaction of the old role and the hospital or psychotic experiences.

We may ask for purposes of research whether recovery from mental disorders is not fundamentally a matter of recanalizing and resymbolizing primary psychotic deviation, perhaps with a scaling down of aspirational levels. Certainly it presses the facts of mental disorder heavily to insist that the substructure of limits from which mental disorder has been compounded originally are drastically altered when the symptoms are no longer present. A more realistic appraisal leaves us with the idea that the delusions, tensions, fears, and other psychotic elements are converted into new social and cultural forms or they are resymbolized by the deviant in such a way as to be subjectively less painful and damaging to the self. The famous story of Clifford Beers himself is an illustration in point. In the course of his mental hospital stay and after discharge he was able to bring his hostilities and delusions into a focus in which he came to attack, not persons or himself, but the backwardness, decadence, and evils of the state-hospital system. He came to attack persons no longer in a blind way but abstractly in a certain aspect of their behavior and in their attitudes toward the mental deviants in society.

Of course, not all ex mental cases restructure their primary psychoses in such a spectacular manner. Others come to perceive their delusions, hallucinations, fears, and compulsions in a more prosaic fashion and develop methods of reducing their visibility and integrating them into socially acceptable roles. The case of a schoolteacher who periodically felt a compulsion to jump up on his desk and shout obscenities to all his students is enlightening. He found that by taking out his shirttail and cleaning his glasses he could contain the compulsion. Today the compulsions have vanished, but the habit remains, a defense should the compulsion ever return. Such a person might be called neurotic, but the important thing is that he is a functioning, contributing member of society.

When people come to face their psychotic reactions and take them as part of the self without the immediate, panicky need to repudiate them, their tensions slowly die down, and with this their delusions and hallucinations attenuate and often completely disappear. As people become friends with their psychoses, the cycle by which the symbolic disorders were developed and preserved is broken. All this does not mean that the early conflicts which were symbolically amplified into psychoses are gone nor that the conflicting pressures of a dilapidated extramural social world will be any less gentle when they return to it. However, the surplus of symptoms traceable to the societal reaction and its subjective incorporation will be stripped away. In many instances this means that the person is converted from a "happy psychotic to an unhappy neurotic." In time, he may even become a relatively happy neurotic.

Selected Readings

Davis, Kingsley. "Mental Hygiene and Social Structure," *Psychiatry*, 1, February, 1938, pp 55–65.

Deutsch, Albert *The Mentally Ill in America*, rev. ed, 1949

Cameron, N. "The Paranoid Pseudocommunity," *American Journal of Sociology*, 49, July, 1943, pp. 32–38

Lemert, Edwin "Legal Commitment and Social Control," *Sociology and Social Research*, 30, May–June, 1946, pp. 370–378

Proehl, Elizabeth "The Transition from Institutional to Social Adjustment," *American Sociological Review*, 3, August, 1938, pp. 534–540

Rowland, Howard "Interaction Processes in a State Hospital," *Psychiatry*, 1, August, 1938, pp. 323–338

APPENDIX

SUGGESTED OUTLINE TO BE FOLLOWED IN STUDYING AND WRITING THE LIFE HISTORY OF A DEVIANT

I. *The Nature of the Deviation*

A. Describe in detail the ways in which the person or persons deviate from the normal. Attempt to distinguish biological variation from behavior variation if the former is involved. Measure or informally estimate how great the deviation is.

B. Distinguish the deviation in terms of its context. Does it appear to be a symptomatic reaction, situational behavior, or is it systematic behavior?

C. If there is a subculture connected with this deviation (regardless of whether the deviant participates in it), describe the folkways, techniques and skills, and the mores. Under mores distinguish prohibitions, permissives, and compulsives.

D. If it exists, describe the social organization associated with the deviation; describe technical groups (such as the shoplifters' organization), social and auxiliary groups. Describe the various roles within the deviant organization, methods of social control used in the group, leadership, and social ranking. What is the degree of solidarity and morale of group. These data and that in I. C. may be obtained from library sources.

E. What is the situation in your deviant's particular environment? Does a culture and a social organization exist? What are the local variations? Primary sources within the community should be consulted, if possible, for this information.

II. *The Societal Reaction to the Deviant*

A. What is the general reaction to this type of deviation (1) acceptance, (2) rejection, (3) inconsistent.

B. What is the degree of social distance between deviant and community.

C. Describe the societal definitions of the deviant: Attitudes, stereotypes, special folklore, and mythology centering around the deviant.

D. What is the nature of the exploitative culture? Is there exploitation by sanctioned commercial agencies, by other deviants, by illegal agencies?

E. In the public control or manipulative culture, what are the objectives of control: limited services, rehabilitation, and institutional custodial care? In evaluation of the experience with the control culture:

1. What degree of isolation is involved; how much withdrawal stress is there?

2. Are controls paternalistic or democratic; what are the opportunities for personal development or growth within the control jurisdiction?

3. To what degree does experience with agencies of control over this deviation provide the individual with a role suitable for independent life in society?

III. *The Natural History of the Deviant*

A. Describe the childhood and adult development of the deviant. Are there any crisis points in the history at which the self-conception changed?

B. How did the family react to the deviant behavior? Was deviant behavior learned in the family?

C. Describe the special societal reaction to which the deviant was exposed. What are the regional, communal, and class variations of the reaction in the deviant's case? Has the deviant been exploited, institutionalized, or manipulated in the name of community welfare? Describe.

D. If there is a deviant social organization in the community, does the individual participate? If so, how did he begin? What is his or her status in the deviant group?

E. What sort of self-conception does the deviant have? How does this correspond with the societal definition, with the definition in the deviant group, if any?

F. Estimate the adjustment of the deviant. How much emotional conflict, anxiety, neurosis, or psychosis is there, if any? Is the deviant demoralized, parasitic, or dependent?

IV. *Social Participation*

A. How has the deviant's occupational status and income been affected?

B. What has the deviation done to sex and family participation?

C. Describe political, religious, educational, recreational, and other aspects of participation which have been affected by his deviation.

GLOSSARY

Ad hoc. A kind of explanation which can be applied only to a special class of cases. Theory which lacks true generality.

Anomie. A condition of society in which there is a lack of balance in the emphases upon ends and means. As originally used by Durkheim, *l'anomie sociale* was a condition resulting from a sudden shattering of the social equilibrium and moral constitution of society.

Closed participational circles. A series of limits which interlock and reinforce one another, so that exclusion of a deviant from one group leads to his exclusion from many other groups.

Compulsive deviation. Deviation, such as alcoholism, in which the person engages in the behavior in spite of heavy social penalties and in spite of resolutions of his own to discontinue it. Distinguished by ambivalence on the part of the participant.

Compulsive norms. Rules of a group or a community whose violation arouses strong reactions from the members.

Control culture. A general term for the laws, procedures, programs, and organizations which in the name of a collectivity help, rehabilitate, punish, or otherwise manipulate deviants.

Counterfeit role. A deviant role with which a person superficially or formally identifies himself in order to mitigate the penalties of his real role. An example would be the epileptic who prefers to be known as an alcoholic.

Covert deviation. Deviant symbolic responses or abnormal attitudes toward the self.

Cultural discontinuity. Discrepancies between the basic role which a person has and a new role which he is expected to acquire in the course of his life history. The discrepancies appear in the amount of authority, degree of responsibility, and extent of the sexual prerogatives of the two roles.

Deviation. This is a term which simply means "other than normal" in the statistical sense.

Effective cause. The immediate cause in a delimited sequence of events.

Empathic response. The imaginative assumption of the bodily responses or posture of another person or of an object.

External limits. Barriers to social participation arising from the social and cultural environment.

Folk society. A small, isolated, homogeneous, nonliterate community or society integrated through religion and tradition.

Genuine culture. Similar to a folk society. Genuine in the sense of being integrated and providing psychologically satisfying social relationships to the individual.

Imputed biological limits. Stereotyped ideas of the biological capacities associated with age, sex, and physical handicap.

Individual deviation. Deviation which arises in connection with the creative, dynamic, or integrative and disintegrative function of the personality.

Interaction. A very general term meaning dynamic interplay of factors.

Internal limits. Resistances, blocks, sets, or attitudes which restrict choice-making by the individual. These are the structural elements of personality.

J curve. A statistical distribution in which the bulk of the cases fall into the first class interval of a calibrated scale

Maladjustment. A condition or process in which there are deviant attitudes toward the self. The maladjusted individual's self-conception varies greatly from the conceptions which others have of him. *See* Covert deviation.

Marginality. A condition in which the person's life choices are narrowed to two incompatible roles, neither being completely or permanently satisfying to him because of the nature of the external and internal limits involved.

Modalities of behavior. The most frequently occurring behaviors.

Multiple-factor theory. Theory which gives equal stress to many factors.

Natural history of a social problem. The sequence of deviation and societal reaction. Implies the idea that there are recurrent stages or phases in this process.

Normal curve. A statistical distribution in which cases cluster around a central value.

Overt behavior. Readily observable behavior. Behavior which is reacted to in terms of its observable features.

Permissive. A rule of behavior which admits of wide variation

Person field. A configuration of internal forces which play upon the person.

Personal disorganization. A condition or process in which the person has not stabilized his behavior around a major role. There is conflict and confusion over his choice of roles. Such disorganization may be transitional or it may be continuous.

Positivism. A philosophy based upon the idea that only sense-observable facts are data for study. It also embodies the ideal of a society integrated through scientific control.

Postulate. A statement of fact not requiring proof. It differs from an axiom in that it contains an empirical element.

Primacy of a role. The quality of a social role which gives it precedence over other roles and causes it to permeate subsidiary roles enacted by the person

Primary deviation. Deviation which is not invidiously symbolized by the person and which is integrated into the socially acceptable role of this person.

Professional deviant. One who exploits his deviation and gets his living as well as his major ego satisfaction thereby.

Putative deviation. Deviation which has not actually taken place but which is socially attributed to a person or class of persons.

Reserve potentialities. Tendencies, attitudes, or elements of behavior which under appropriate circumstances can be organized into new deviant or normal behavior.

Role. The part played by the person in society. A person has as many roles as he has groups in which he participates. Usually there is one dominant role.

Self. The individual's awareness of how he differs from others, plus evaluations, socially derived, of those differences.

Situational deviation. Deviation which is a direct and immediate response to external factors. It is implicit to the degree that the situation restricts the possible deviant reactions.

Social disorganization. A very general term meaning imbalance, disequilibrium, and extensive conflict between the groups and institutions of a society.

Social distance. Degree of felt intimacy and social contact between persons of different groups or status.

Social field. The configuration of forces playing upon the person from his external environment. Similar to the social situation.

Social norm. Limits of variation in behavior tolerated in the individual by members of his group. Implicit or explicit in the control reactions of members of the group.

Social problem. A term we have used to mean behavior or a situation effectively regarded as dangerous or harmful by a large number or the majority of a community or society.

Societal definition. Stereotype, fixed notion, or public opinion of the role and characteristics of a person or of a class of people.

Societal reaction. The over-all responses of persons and groups of a society to deviation.

Sociopathic behavior. Behavior which is effectively disapproved of in social interaction.

Spurious societal reaction. A group or community reaction which is disproportionate to the extent and seriousness of the deviation provoking it.

Symbolic process. Social communication, which is seen as the process of reflective thought in the person and as a reciprocal process of public opinion in the group or society.

Systematic deviation. Patterned deviation which is socially transmitted and associated with special social organization.

Withdrawal symptoms. Sometimes termed "withdrawal stress." In a generic sense it refers to behavior symptoms which result from the disruption of the socially oriented habit systems of the individual. The symptoms may be either organic or nonorganic. The intensity of the symptoms will depend upon the symbolic value of the habits to the person and the extent of his social participation affected by their interruption.

INDEX

N

O

P

CPSIA information can be obtained
at www.ICGtesting.com
Printed in the USA
BVHW090853150221
600147BV00012B/1177

9 781258 291563